MASS MEDIA
AND THE
INDIVIDUAL

MASS MEDIA AND THE INDIVIDUAL

Donald N. Wood
California State University, Northridge

with contributions by
A. Arvo Leps
California State University, Northridge

Heritage Fund

The purchase of this material was made possible through an Alberta Advanced Education and Manpower Library Development Grant from the Alberta Heritage Savings Trust Fund.

West Publishing Co.
Saint Paul   New York   Los Angeles   San Francisco

To Bridget and Brian

and their millions of peers who must learn to
cope with mass communication in the
twenty-first century

COPYRIGHT © 1983 By **WEST PUBLISHING CO.**
          50 West Kellogg Boulevard
          P.O. Box 3526
          St. Paul, Minnesota 55165

Library of Congress Cataloging in Publication Data

Wood, Donald N., 1934–
    Mass media and the individual.

    Includes index.
    1. Mass media.   I. Leps, A. Arvo.   II. Title.
P90.W6 1983   001.51   82-21812
ISBN 0-314-69687-3

PHOTO RESEARCH: Leslie Andalman
ARTWORK: Karen McBride
PRODUCTION MANAGEMENT: Robert S. Tinnon
COMPOSITION: Publisher's Typography

Credits All photographs not otherwise credited were taken by A. Arvo Leps. **5** The University of Michigan, Paul Jaronski, photographer; **13** *(bottom left)* KNXT/CBS Los Angeles; **25** United Press International; **29** Olive R. Pierce/Stock, Boston; **44** Library of Congress; **56** *(left)* The Mansell Collection, Limited; *(right)* Brown Brothers; **66** *(top left)* Israel Museum, Jerusalem: The Shrine of the Book Collection; **68** The Huntington Library, San Marino, California; **69** St. Regis Paper Company; **79** *(left)* Brown Brothers; *(right)* Brown Brothers; **83** *Chicago Defender;* **98** RCA; **100** RCA; **105** Academy of Motion Picture Arts and Sciences; **107** Academy of Motion Picture Arts and Sciences and RKO General Pictures, Inc.; **108** Academy of Motion Picture Arts and Sciences and United Artists Corporation; **110** De Wan; **111** *(top)* U.S. Department of the Interior, Edison National Historic Site; *(bottom)* Don Wood; **113** RCA; **121** RCA; **140** R. R. Donnelley & Sons, Inc.; **145** Dino De Laurentiis Corporation © 1976; **146** Ellis Sorkin; **148** *(left)* KLCS-TV, Elisa Leonelli, photographer; **197** The Copperman Collection; **207** *Daily News,* Los Angeles; **208** *Daily News,* Los Angeles; **212** KNXT/CBS Los Angeles; **215** *(left)* KNXT/CBS Los Angeles; **219** Jerry Shea; **222** Jesse Seigel; **229** UCLA Instructional Media, Bruce Butterfield, photographer; **243** Don Wood; **269** UPI photo by Leslie H. Sintay; **272** United Press International; **288** United Press International; **291** United Press International; **315** *(top left)* © Academy of Motion Picture Arts and Sciences®, reproduction of this still courtesy of the Margaret Herrick Library, Academy Foundation; **317** Michael Myers; **322** *(top left, top right, bottom left)* Embassy Television; *(bottom right)* © Witt/Thomas/Harris Productions; **329–330** American Society of Newspaper Editors; **340** Field Enterprises Syndicate; **342** Cable Satellite Public Affairs Network; **346** KNXT/CBS Los Angeles; **348** KNXT/CBS Los Angeles; **349** United Press International; **359** United Press International; **376** Sony Corporation of America; **377** James F. Blinn/Jet Propulsion Laboratory; **379** *(left)* RCA; **383** *(top)* Studio Hamburg; *(bottom)* Jet Propulsion Laboratory, Don Davis, artist; **388** Hughes Aircraft Company; **394** JVC; **397** Toshiba Corporation; **400** *(both)* University of Illinois; **407** Sony Corporation of America; **418** Andrew Lippman, Architecture Machine Group, M.I.T.

CONTENTS

LIST OF INSETS

LIST OF INSETS

Mass communication is possibly the most important and involving area of study for the general college student. No intelligent and responsible citizen of a free society can afford not to understand the structures, processes, and effects of modern mass media. The scope of the discipline is vast—encompassing virtually every means you have of interpreting your political and economic environment, defining social reality, shaping your family relationships and your personal lifestyle, providing the bulk of your entertainment experiences, and incorporating every conceivable means of persuasion and propaganda. As we rush toward the twenty-first century—with our emphasis upon increasingly complex media forms, sophisticated electronic delivery systems, and personalized media environments—it is imperative that you learn how to interact with and exert control over these media operations.

This book is written as an introductory text for either the aspiring professional in the mass communication fields (for the beginning student in journalism, broadcasting-film, or speech-communication courses) or for general liberal arts courses in mass communication (offered by departments of English, social sciences, political science, humanities, and so forth). As such, this book is written with the receiver of the mass media message—the consumer of mass communication—firmly in mind. This receiver orientation is necessary not only for the beginning student majoring in mass media (who will devote the rest of his or her academic career studying production, writing, criticism, management, and other specialized areas within the discipline, but it is also a necessity for the mass media consumer who will spend more time attending to the mass media than to any other activity except sleeping and earning money.

There are numerous ways you could begin a study of mass communication. You could examine theories and history of the mass communication process; you could look at the mass media from an economic standpoint; you could investigate the media as social phenomena; or you could speculate on the future of communications technology. In fact, some idea of each of these various perspectives is necessary to understand this complex field. Therefore, in this book we have tried to incorporate these several approaches; each of the four units of the text corresponds to one of the four viewpoints mentioned above.

The book also tries to take an integrated look at all mass media and their interrelated structures and effects. Except for two history chapters (3 and 4), the book avoids devoting separate chapters to individual media industries. All media are viewed in an integrated, interwinding relationship as you look at their corporate frameworks, social and personal effects, and future implications.

At the outset of Chapter One, we set forth a few basic assumptions regarding the pervasiveness of media and the necessity for studying mass communication. Then, at the beginning of each chapter we state a basic theme for that chapter. These essential assumptions and themes form the guiding structure for discussion throughout the book.

The discipline of mass communication—like medicine and space technology—is one which is constantly progressing and shifting directions every day. It is virtually impossible to keep abreast of all the evolving developments in business patterns, current research, government regulation (and deregulation), programming trends, technological breakthroughs, and latest box office receipts for *E.T.* Therefore—even though every effort has been made to make sure that all facts and descriptions are accurate and up-to-date as of early 1982—current developments and actions require continual research and updating on the part of the reader.

An Instructor's Manual with test questions has been prepared to accompany *Mass Media and the Individual*. The instructor should find useful teaching tools in this supplement designed to allow the most advantageous use of the text.

Finally, it must be recognized that no book of this scope can be produced without the support and contributions of dozens of individuals. The authors wish to thank their colleagues, students, and associates for their invaluable assistance in pulling it all together. Many were involved in helping to gather research materials and other resources: Leslie Andalman, Barbara Brittell, Debra Dorso, Vic Grabar, Judith Hastings, Susan Hill, George Ingram, Bill James, Nora King, Kerby Lecka, James Poteat, Brad Powell, Wilbur Schramm, Frida Schubert, Ellis Sorkin, Barry Stagg, Linda Taubenreuther, Alexandria Thompson, Steven Traiman, Harry Waterson, and Mary Wilson.

Several reviewers from around the country helped shape this book by providing comments, criticism, encouragement, and suggestions. We wish to express appreciation to:

Douglas Anderson
Arizona State University

Lillian S. Bell
Northern Illinois University

Beverly M. Bethune
University of Georgia

Shirley Biagi
*California State University
Sacramento*

Joseph M. Foley
Ohio State University

Daniel Garvey
Long Beach State University

Barbara Hartung
San Diego State University

Don Jacobs
*Orange Coast College
California*

Edward M. Kimbrell
Middle Tennessee State University

Frederic A. Leigh
Arizona State University

James Martin
Scottsdale Community College
Arizona

Haluk Sahin
Cleveland State University

Diane Turner
Tarrant County Jr. College, South Campus

Raymond G. Wilke
Villanova University
Pennsylvania

Clint C. Wilson II
University of Southern California

Among the many who helped in various stages of production, we thank especially the following: Claire Comiskey, Rena Copperman, Meg Flanders, Carole Grumney, Brian Hamilton, Bill Stryker, and Bob Tinnon. And—above all else—we gratefully appreciate the unflagging support and encouragement from Clyde Perlee, Virve Pold, and Marie Vayo.

DNW
AAL

To understand and interact with the mass media, you should examine them from more than one perspective. Therefore, each of the four units in this book will look at the phenomena of mass media from a different viewpoint. In the first unit, you will consider mass media within a *broad theoretical communication framework*—examining communication theory and functions of mass communication, investigating the political and philosophical underpinning of our media systems, and surveying the technical and historical background of the mass media.

The focus of this book is on the individual—you—and your relationship to the media. In fact, there is one underlying question that will guide our inquiries throughout the book:

How can the individual interact with the mass media in the most effective and positive manner?

In attempting to answer this question, the book will look at the role of the individual from four different perspectives—perspectives which correspond to the four units. In Unit I you will consider the individual as the theoretical *receiver* of messages in a model communication framework. In subsequent units you will consider the individual as a *consumer* (Unit II), as a *regulator/activist* (Unit III), and as a *member of the audience of the future* (Unit IV).

Mass Media in a Communication Framework

1

The Theoretical Foundations of Mass Communication

This book is written with two basic assumptions in mind. The first simply assumes the existence of the media:

• *The mass media are a permanent and pervasive part of our environment. Regardless of our occasional longings for a return to a simpler lifestyle and the pre-electric days of our forefathers, the media are with us to stay and will continue to permeate every aspect of our existence.*

The second assumption concerns your responsibility in relation to the media:

• *The more you know about the media, the better off you will be. Only with increased knowledge can you be a more effective receiver/consumer/regulator/audience member.*

In addition to these two fundamental assumptions, each chapter will develop one major theme. In Chapter 1, the basic theme is:

• *You, the receiver, can have an impact upon the mass communication process.*

Not only can you play an important role in the way you function as the receiver of the communication message, but you can also exert considerable influence at other stages of the communication cycle. This is to be a recurring theme throughout the book.

In this context, it is the aim of this book to make people more intelligent and responsible users of the media. By users we mean not only citizens and receivers, but also media professionals. Many of you reading this book will go on to employment in the mass communication fields. Although the book focuses primarily upon the citizen–receiver, it is intended also for the would-be media practitioner.

1.1   The Significance of Media Study

The typical person in the United States spends more time involved with the mass media than with any other waking activity except working at a job.

1.1.1 PERVASIVENESS OF THE MASS MEDIA

You are encapsulated in the mass media environment. In our contemporary civilization, the media permeate every niche of our existence. Their saturation is total. The average American adult spends three and a half to four hours a day watching television. He or she also takes half an hour or more to read the daily newspaper. The ubiquitous radio follows us wherever we go—from bedroom to automobile to mountaintop.

"Going to the movies" is the universal American social outing. Every household has access to a dozen or more general interest magazines and specialized journals. The book is the symbol of culture and intellectual achievement. And everywhere we are surrounded by other uninvited mass mediums—billboards, display signs, matchbook covers, blimps, political leaflets, telephone pole posters, "junk" mail, and so on.

It is as if we crave constant media companionship. The printed page and electronic voice represent our twentieth-century security blanket. If you are a typical American, you sit down at the breakfast table with the morning paper. You walk into an empty house and click on the TV set in order to listen to a familiar voice. You turn on your car radio as you turn on the ignition. You carry your favorite light literature into the bathroom. You flip on the stereo as soon as you settle down to study. You share your dinner with your favorite newscaster. You grope for a two-year-old magazine as soon as you sit down in the waiting room prior to an appointment. As a people, we seek uninterrupted media intercourse.

INSET 1–1
Media Saturation

The average American home has its television set(s) turned on more than six and three-quarter hours a day. In a typical urban community, the indefatigable viewer will have upwards of one hundred hours a day of programming from which to choose.

There are close to 1,800 daily newspapers in the United States. Another 7,600 weekly and semi-weekly newspapers help to blanket the country. A total of more than 60 million copies of these various papers are delivered every day. And three out of four American adults go through their papers daily.

There are well over 400 million radios in the nation—an average of two for every man, woman, and child. As a constant traveling companion, the radio takes almost as much of our time as does television. If all "background" uses could be tabulated, we would probably find that we spend more time with radio than with any other medium.

In the United States and Canada, more than 62,000 different magazines and professional journals are available. About two-thirds of the population read at least three magazines a month.

More than 40,000 new book titles are published each year in the United States. And, on any given day, about one-third of the population will spend between fifteen minutes and an hour reading a book.

Like radio, the movies and audio recordings appeal primarily to a younger audience. About one billion paid admissions to movie theaters are sold every year. Well over three billion dollars are spent on phonograph records and audio tapes annually.

1.1.2 IMPACT OF THE MASS MEDIA

Virtually all of your news—your perception of reality—is distilled and interpreted for you by the media. Almost all of your entertainment—your leisure pursuits—are packaged by the media. To quote Wilbur Schramm, one of the foremost researchers and writers in the mass communication field, "the modern media are inextricably intertwined with modern life."[1]

Societal Impact of the Media Throughout their history, the mass media have been alternately blamed and praised for most of our social ills and advances. The "dime" novels of the nineteenth century, the "scandalous" Hollywood films of the 1920s, the comic books of the 1940s, and (of course) television today—all in turn have been condemned for glorifying violence, contributing to juvenile delinquency, promoting promiscuous sex, increasing the national crime rate, and generally undermining the moral fabric of our country.

At the same time, the printing press and the wonder of electronic journalism have been praised for spreading enlightenment throughout the land, educating the citizenry so that representative government is possible, exposing tyranny and corruption, facilitating universal education, providing mass entertainment, and disseminating great works of art to all the people.

Undoubtedly, in our pluralistic system, there is some truth in both views. (See Section 8.4.) The media have been involved in every major social, political, intellectual, economic, industrial, and religious revolution in recent centuries.

Economic Impact of the Media In our modern economic system, the mass media play an indispensible part in the manufacture, transportation, advertising, and selling of goods and services.

Advertising contributes not only to the distribution of information regarding *needed* products and services, but it also contributes greatly to the creation of wants for *unnecessary* products, products that had no existing

Wilbur Schramm, noted mass communication writer and researcher.

demand. The issue of creating false needs, as well as questions about the ethics of specific persuasive techniques, is examined in Section 6.5.

The mass media themselves are a vital part of the nation's economy. More than 50 billion dollars are spent every year on advertising, an expenditure that helps to keep the economy moving. And, looking at the mass communication field as a whole, we find that more people are engaged in discovering, processing, and distributing knowledge and information than are employed in all of agriculture and industrial work combined.

Political Impact of the Media The structure of the governmental system of the United States could not exist, as you know it, without the role played by the free press. From early nineteenth-century scandals to Watergate to many more recent revelations of governmental abuses, the press has been expected to play a substantial role as investigative reporter, editorialist, and voice for the opposition (Section 1.5).

We must also be aware, however, that politicians strive to use and abuse the media and that such attempts, when successful, can upset the delicate balance between the government and the press. From campaign strategies to legislative publicity to executive press relations, politicians are constantly trying to manipulate the media for their own purposes (Section 9.2).

Educational Impact of the Media   The media have played an important role in the evolution of our free public education system. It is not altogether coincidental that the movement for universal education developed hand-in-hand with modern printing technologies which could give us the inexpensive textbook. At the same time, the mass media have also served a crucial function in the informal education of the citizenry. Through newspapers, broadcast news and informational programming, news magazines, documentaries, educational films, and the like, U.S. citizens have enjoyed a high degree of continuing adult education.

On the other hand, media excesses are pinpointed as a cause of some of the educational problems of the country. Recent scholastic testing programs tend to indicate a rise in the illiteracy level among our school-age youth, a development which is blamed partially on too much television viewing.

The mass media's role in education also has much broader implications, as the authors Davison, Boylan, and Yu point out:

Finally, the media rank with the educational system as a prime means by which society transmits its culture and values from one generation to another. It is important to consider how well the communication system functions and in whose behalf, for what it transmits will help determine the shape of American society in years to come, as it has in the past.[2]

Entertainment Impact of the Media   Most of us turn to the media primarily for entertainment. Here, too, the popular media have altered our living patterns. The trend has been consistently away from live events toward more home entertainment. The vaudeville circuit was replaced by radio; the weekly outing to the "Grade B" movie was replaced by television; and the phenomenon of the rock concert is giving way to special pay-TV concerts by popular performers.

Personal Impact of the Media   Finally, we must be aware of what may be the most crucial consideration of all: How are the media affecting our personal lives and individual schedules and routines? If we are spending four to six hours a day attending to the different media, where is the time coming from? What is it we are *not* doing? Are we becoming a nation of spectators rather than participants? What happens to our institutions of social interaction (schools, churches, neighborhood forums) if more and more of our needs for information and entertainment are met through our home communications centers? (See Section 12.5.)

If our tastes, standards, and ethics are shaped to some extent by the omnipresent media, how much influence do we have—or even want to have—over our individual preferences and values? Does it matter what we care to preserve as individuals? Does it matter that our likes and dislikes may be subtly altered to conform to the homogeneous profile of the "typical" reader/listener/viewer in order to make us more efficient consumers?

These are just some of the questions we will look at in succeeding chapters as we try to assess the impact of mass communication on our lives—and to determine what the individual can and should be doing.

1.1.3 IMPORTANCE OF COMMUNICATION STUDY

The human animal is, above all else, a communicative being. The act of communication is fundamental to everything we do or attempt to do. When humankind fails in its attempt to promote the goals of a civilized society, more often than not the failure is due to a breakdown of the communication process. As the theorist Melvin DeFleur points out, "such a wide variety of human problems in some way begin with the communication process that its nature urgently needs to be understood more adequately."[3]

Thus, we will be concerned with the study of mass *communication* in this book, not just with mass *media*. Although the media—the means of communication—will often be the focus of our inquiry, we must remember that the media, the channels, form only one part of the total communication act. It is with the control of the media, the messages of the media, the receivers of the media messages, and the reactions to media operations that we must be concerned.

Before we can examine how free citizens may control the communication process with which they are so intimately intertwined, we must understand what the process is. As Schramm wrote in 1973,

During the next half-century man will finally have to come to terms with his extraordinary ability to process and share information. He will have to learn to use it for his own good rather than for his own destruction, and for further humanization and socialization rather than alienation or regression. At this moment in history, therefore, it seems reasonable to take stock of what we know about human communication.[4]

In our attempt to determine the differing roles that you—the individual receiver—can play in the mass media milieu, we must examine several aspects of the total process. First, we must define the *theoretical structure* of the communication model (Sections 1.2, 1.3, and 1.4). Second, we need to understand

---

INSET 1-2
Life Without Mass Media

One way to assess the impact of mass communication upon our personal lives is to ask not, "What are the media doing to me?" but rather, "What would I do without the media? To what extent have I become dependent on the media?" Take a moment to conjure up an image of what your life would be like if there were no mass media.

You would awaken without the assistance of any early morning news. No bright-voiced disc jockey. No morning newspaper to start your day. No car radio. No source of news at all to tell you where we stood in the world, whether you needed your umbrella, what the latest crisis was, and what the traffic conditions were. No background music to ease your way through the day. Nor would there be any news when you arrived home at night. You would be denied all of your favorite magazines. And your evening alternatives would be severely limited: no television; no stereo to listen to; no movies to go to; no books to curl up with.

Furthermore, if such a deprivation were to continue, it would not be long before you began to feel some of the secondary effects. You would be paying higher prices for your goods and services due to the lack of advertising, and your choice of products would be considerably reduced. You would lose whatever control you previously enjoyed over the political system; officeholders would now be functioning without the checks and balances of an inquisitive press. And soon, when hundreds of thousands—possibly millions—of former media professionals were added to the unemployment ranks, you would feel the economic impact even more heavily.

---

the *functions* of mass communication (Section 1.5). And finally, we must look at some of the inherent *characteristics of the media* themselves (Sections 1.6 and 1.7).

1.2 The Communication Process

One profitable method of defining and studying the communication act is to break down the process into its component parts and then to analyze the various components and their relationship to one another.

1.2.1 COMPONENTS OF THE COMMUNICATION ACT

All communication begins with a human source or *sender*. The sender may be a single person, or it may be a group of persons— such as the editorial staff of a newspaper or the production crew of a television station—

who are organized for specific communication tasks. The sender starts with some *referent* or inner event (internal response, meaning); this may be an attitude or feeling, a concept or idea, an emotion or fact.

This inner event or referent must then be translated or *encoded* into a set of signs or *symbols*. These symbols typically are words (either oral or written), but they also may be pictorial representations (photographs, paintings, statues), nonverbal symbols (mathematical or scientific notation, musical notes), actions and gestures, or anything else that can be used to stand for the original referent.

The encoded symbols, arranged by the grammar and rules of the *language*, then form a *message* which—depending upon the nature of the symbols—may take many forms. The message may be a speech, a caress, a musical score, a newspaper editorial, an oil painting, a television script, an angry gesture, a chemical formula, or a raised eyebrow.

The message then must be *transmitted*

Sender. A person or group of people responsible for initiating a given communicative act.

Referent. The original object or event, existing within the mind of the sender, for which a given sign or symbol stands.

Symbol. That which is used to represent something else; specifically, that which stands for a referent. A "significant symbol" is one which carries the same meaning for the receiver as it did for the sender.

Language. A system of symbols used in a pattern understood by both sender and receiver.

Message. The content of the communicative act which is created when the referent is encoded or translated into a language by the sender.

Medium. The intervening substance, means, or environment through which a message is transmitted.

Channel. The specific assigned portion of a medium designated for a particular message or series of messages.

Receiver. A person or group of people to whom a message is transmitted.

Feedback. A message sent from the receiver to the sender to complete the communication cycle.

Noise. Any interference or disturbance which interrupts or distorts the communication process.

INSET 1–3 Common Elements of Communication Models

through a *medium*—any intervening environment or substance that can be used to conduct symbols from one place to another—which serves to connect the sender and the receiver. Depending upon the complexity of the communication situation, the medium may be as simple as sound waves and light energy (ordinary conversation between two people in the same room), or it may be a highly intricate combination of typesetting and printing equipment, electrical energy in wires, magnetic recordings, celluloid film, electromagnetic vibrations in space, laser beams, and similar elements.

The medium may also be divided into specific segments or *channels* which can be designated for particular message assignments. The television portion of the electromagnetic spectrum, for example, is divided into the familiar TV channels. The abstract medium of "air waves" can be thought of as being divided into specific channels associated with actual physical space—like rooms in a house or assigned classrooms, for instance.

Regardless of the complexity of the medium involved, the message—if the communication act is successful—is eventually received by some communication recipient, which may be a single individual or a group of persons. As the receiver *decodes* the message, the communication process undergoes further deterioration because we rarely deal with "significant symbols"—those signs which have identical meaning for both the sender and the receiver.

Feedback The communication is completed when there occurs some sort of *feedback*—the process whereby the receiver of the original message provides a response to the sender. In a simple conversation, this can take the form of a nod of the head, a shrug of the shoulders, a vocalized "Uh huh," or a verbal response. In a classroom setting, feedback would include puzzled expressions,

---

In 1948, Harold Lasswell, a professor of law and a media theorist, set down his cogent communication schema by suggesting that any act of communication could be described and analyzed by answering questions pertaining to five components:

**INSET 1–4
Lasswell's
Communication
Model**

WHO says
WHAT in which
CHANNEL to
WHOM with what
EFFECT?[5]

In essence, he identified the five major elements with which we shall subsequently be concerned: Sender, Message, Medium, Receiver, and Feedback.

Lasswell pointed out that virtually all research in the field can be conducted by focusing on one or another of these five elements: control or source analysis (Who is the sender?); content analysis (What is the message?); media analysis (What channels are used how?); audience analysis (The receiver is whom?); and effects of behavioral analysis (What is the effect or feedback?).

---

raised hands, questions, and snores, as well as the students' written responses in papers and tests. In a mass media situation, feedback would encompass telephoning a station, writing a letter to the editor of a paper, responding to an advertisement, cancelling a subscription, and so on.

In any case, the receiver of the original message becomes the sender of the responding message; the original sender becomes the receiver. In this way, the original sender of the message receives data which he or she can use to modify his or her continued message. Feedback, therefore, contributes to the continuation of the communication process—and it is important to emphasize the two-way nature of the act. Not even in a mass medium context can you think of communication as a one-way avenue. Without feedback, the sender of the message has no idea whether or not any actual contact—any communication—has taken place. Communica-tion is not complete until a feedback message is received.

Noise   Superimposed over the entire communication model we must add the element of "noise"—any kind of disturbance or interference which interrupts or distorts the communication process. Broadly, noise can be though of in two categories: *mechanical noise* and *semantic noise.*

Mechanical noise (also referred to as "channel noise") is any interference which occurs from the time the message is formulated to the time it is received. The most obvious examples of mechanical noise involve actual physical impairment of the message, such as that caused by radio static, broken print type, visual "snow" on a television screen, smeared ink on a newspaper, scratches on a film, and so forth.

INSET 1–5   Comparative Communication Acts

Communication Component	Example A	Example B	Example C
Sender	Wife	Teacher	Advertising agency
Referent	Outrage over a social injustice	Appreciation of Greek art	Need to sell cars
Symbols/ Language	Spoken words	Spoken words Printed words Pictures	Printed words Pictures
Message	"We really must do something"	"These are beautiful classical statues"	"Buy a Zonkmobile 6"
Media/ Channels	Conversation	Classroom Chalkboard Slide projector	Magazines
Receiver(s)	Husband	30 students	Thousands of readers
Feedback/ Response	Decision to join an organization	Ninety-three percent of students pass an exam	Two percent buy a Zonkmobile within six months

---

Other examples of mechanical noise include distractions in the transmission process—a noisy film projector, an unruly audience in a viewing room, your pet cat leaping onto your lap while you are trying to read the paper, or a loud party at your neighbors' house. Note that, in many instances, one set of communication signals interferes with another communication act. In the above examples, the unruly audience, the cat, and your neighbors all are sending out their own messages ("I don't like the movie," "I want to play," "I'm having a good time"), which, in turn, interrupt your primary communicative process.

A related mechanical noise problem is that of channel overload. Sometimes messages become garbled simply because there is too much information being carried on one channel. A large number of people in a small room at a party may produce more conversations than the available channel (the air waves in that particular room) can handle without considerable interference. Due to a peculiarity of an atmospheric layer known as the Heavy-side Layer, which very efficiently reflects radio signals at night, many radio stations have to sign off or reduce power at dusk or else there would be too much information being carried on each available radio channel.

Semantic noise, on the other hand, consists of those distortions in the communication process which occur when the sender and the receiver have problems with symbols and language usage. The message is misunderstood even though it is received exactly as it was transmitted. The sender and receiver are not using significant symbols; that is, they are trying to communicate with signs that have different meanings for the two parties. This may be caused by something as obvious as speaking in two different languages or by something as subtle as using symbols that are not specific enough. For example, when you hear a word like "dog," "tree," "school," "boat," or "police," how many different images might you come up with? Which

image did the sender intend? And, if you have trouble with such simple physical objects, how do you deal with an intangible concept like "love," "liberty," "equality," "patriotism," "soul," "socialism," or "freedom of speech" when they are used by a sender?

Much semantic noise is caused by the differences in perspective of the communication parties. Many factors contribute to such differences in perspective. Among the most common are divergent backgrounds, varying levels of intelligence, contrasting environmental conditions, conflicting attitudes or beliefs, and disruptive emotional states.

1.2.2 BASIC COMMUNICATION MODEL

Having examined the several components of the system, we can now work with a fairly simple generalized model of the communication pattern. This model, which follows Lasswell's framework, has five primary elements—*sender, message, channel, receiver,* and *feedback*. Present in every communication operation, these five elements can normally be separated and studied as distinct factors (see Inset 1–6).

As indicated in the "two-way pattern" version of the model, many communication situations—conversations, small-group discussions—involve all participants equally as constant senders *and* receivers of messages. Therefore, instead of thinking in terms of specific messages serving a feedback function, it is more accurate to think of each message building upon preceding communication steps. In other words, every message is, to some extent, a reaction to a previous message. Thus, each message serves simultaneously as an original message and as a feedback message.

In the next section, we shall see how this basic model also applies to mass communication situations.

1.3 Levels of Communication

Much mass communication is dependent upon interpersonal relationships and, even, upon intrapersonal communication patterns. Thus, we can better understand mass communication by comparing and contrasting it to other levels of communication.

Intrapersonal Communication At the simplest level there is communication that takes place solely within the individual—talking to oneself, decision-making, imagining, problem-solving, day-dreaming, reminiscing, planning. This is the internal communication that Schramm calls

the silent talking all of us do to ourselves, which we sometimes dignify by calling it *thinking* and which uses the same signs [symbols] one would use in talking with someone else. As a matter of fact, this . . . communication activity probably fills more time in our experience than any of the others.[6]

In this basic model, S = sender, M = message, C = channel (or medium), R = receiver, and F = feedback.

**INSET 1–6
Basic
Communication
Model**

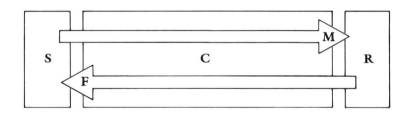

Two-Way Pattern The above model implies that the sender always originates the message and that the receiver functions only as a reactor. In actuality, in many communication situations, both parties function as sender and receiver almost simultaneously. Every message originates as a reaction to the previous message and is, in effect, a form of feedback. Therefore, in the model below, the transmitted communications are designated not as "message" and "feedback" but simply as "message 1" and "message 2."

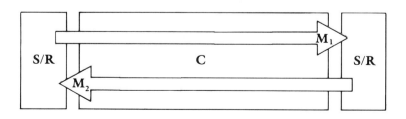

Five levels of communication (clockwise, from top):
Intrapersonal (thinking); conversation; small group
discussion; large group meeting; mass media newscast.

Conversational Communication This communication pattern is characterized by a lack of distinction between sender and receiver. The two or three persons involved are constantly shifting responsibilities, so that both (or all three) are virtually filling both roles simultaneously. Every message is partially a reaction—providing feedback—to the message preceding it.

In a conversation, the message is almost always a combination of spoken words, gestures, and facial expressions, with occasionally a touch (a caress, a slap on the back). The feedback is constant and direct. The two-way flow is uninterrupted. The feedback channels are identical to the sending channels—the spoken word, the gesture, and touch.

Small-Group Communication With any number from four to eight or ten people, conversation gives way to a slightly more structured discussion format. We can pinpoint, at any given moment, the discussion leader or source of messages. However, this position may rotate as one person after another assumes the role of sender.

Feedback is still constant and direct. However, in a small-group discussion (committee meeting, family council, planning task force, after-dinner social conversation) the sender tends to be somewhat selective in his or her attention to feedback. Also, ordinarily, not all receivers or discussion participants are providing feedback at any one moment.

Large-Group Communication When the number of people involved goes beyond ten or twelve, the situation assumes the characteristics of large-group communication. One person is formally recognized as the leader or source of messages. (Depending upon the situation or ceremony, of course, several different persons may assume the role of sender in the course of the gathering.) The messages still will be composed primarily of the spoken word and physical action, although other

signs may be used also. These include the written word (the chalkboard, printed handouts), the picture (slides), and various symbols (flags, religious artifacts). Such signs are definitely part of the overall message. And, in the case of groups with hundreds of receivers in the designated audience, the spoken word may have to be amplified through the electronic medium of the public address system.

In this situation feedback becomes less precise. The input from each receiver is blended with that of everyone else, so that the impact from any single receiver is greatly reduced. There is immediate feedback in the form of applause and yawns, cheers and jeers; but there are often mechanisms for providing later, and more important, feedback—test scores on an academic exam, offerings in the collection plate, votes on election day, and so on.

Mass Communication Having examined the characteristics which distinguish the four levels of *personal* communication (thinking, conversation, small and large groups), you can now understand *mass* communication more easily. In mass communication, the source is often a group of individuals rather than a single sender—a production team, an editorial staff, an advertising agency. One individual or another may assume more responsibility at a given time than others, but the final message is likely to be a committee project (and thus the result of extensive small-group communication within the source itself).

The signs or symbols which can be used to construct the mass communication message are usually somewhat restricted compared to personal or direct communication because the mass media do not have the capability to transmit as many subtle symbols. The sense of touch is eliminated, the slight facial expression may be masked, the grand gesture seems less grand on the small screen, visual cues are lost on the printed page, sound fidelity is reduced in audio systems, and so on.

The main distinction, of course, is the interposition of one or more media machines in the transmission process—the typewriter, the printing press, the camera and microphone, the magnetic recorder, the delivery truck, the broadcast transmitter, the U.S. mails, the film projector, or any of a host of other paraphernalia. Not only do these interposing media cut down on the intensity and fidelity of the original symbols, but they also increase the possibility of mechanical noise at every step.

The nature of the receiver also is changed. The sender has to be concerned with an audience more than with individual receivers. The audience is largely unseen, fragmented, and heterogeneous. In addition to being massive (consisting possibly of millions of individuals), it also is tremendously varied and hard to predict. Despite all the demographic groupings developed through intensive market research, the mass media audience is composed of individuals who vary greatly in their personal likes and dislikes, habits, and response patterns.

Finally, a primary consideration in mass communication is the extent to which feedback is altered. The utilization of a mass-medium device restricts both the nature and the speed of feedback. Two primary factors characterize mass media feedback. First, it is *indirect*. The audience cannot respond directly to any aspect of the mass communication message. Whereas the message may be transmitted through the printing press or broadcast station, the individual receiver responds through telephone calls, surveys, letters, consumer action, and other indirect means. Second, mass communication feedback is usually *delayed*. Except for live television events, "talk-radio" phone-in formats, and some two-way cable TV systems, there is virtually no way for the receiver to provide instantaneous response. Feedback may be delayed anywhere from a few minutes to several weeks.

This is not to say that mass media feedback cannot be effective. Quite the contrary, one of the themes of this book is that mass communication can be greatly influenced by the individual. Audience response, even indirect and delayed, can have a powerful impact on the total communication process. The receiver exerts ultimate control over the mass media operation.

INSET 1–7 Comparison of Communication Levels

Level	Source	Message	Medium	Receiver	Feedback
Intrapersonal	Oneself	Verbal, unspoken	Brainwaves	Oneself	Simultaneous
Conversation	Two persons	Spoken Visual Touch	Conversation	Two persons (same as source)	Constant Personal
Small group	One leader (rotates)	Spoken Visual	Conversation Small room	Various participants	Immediate Direct
Large group	Speaker Teacher Lecturer	Spoken Print Visual Pictorial	Classroom Auditorium Pulpit Union hall	Students Congregation Live audience	Immediate (some delayed) Direct
Mass communication	Editorial staffs Production team Agencies	Spoken Print Sound and moving pictures	Newspapers Television Radio Magazines Books Film	Unseen Large Fragmented Heterogeneous	Indirect Delayed (usually)

1.4 The Role of the Receiver

Historically, it was assumed that sophisticated propaganda stimuli could be designed so that each member of the audience would perceive the message and react to it in the same way as every other receiver. This was known as the "bullet" or "hypodermic needle" theory—once you reached someone with a shot of propaganda, he or she would have no choice but to react to your stimulus in the prescribed manner (Section 8.3.2).

As Schramm explains, this viewpoint has been drastically revised in recent decades:

Indeed, the most dramatic change in general communication theory during the last forty years has been the gradual abandonment of the idea of a passive audience, and its replacement by the concept of a highly active, highly selective audience, manipulating rather than being manipulated by a message—a full partner in the communication process.[7]

1.4.1 IMPORTANCE OF THE RECEIVER FUNCTION

Picture, if you will, the position of the individual in the total communiction environment. He or she is enmeshed in a complex tangle of personal and mass communication circuits which provide connections with family members, friends, business associates, groups (social, professional, charitable, political), institutions (schools, government agencies, church, credit companies), mass media news and information deliverers, mass entertainment opportunities, sellers and persuaders, and so on. The individual, at any given moment, has numerous communication choices to make. Many personal needs, peer-group pressures, and professional priorities may influence the choice, but essentially it is up to the individual to decide which communication experience to plug into at any particular time.

The model we build is one of a very active, very selective media receiver—one who

should have personal power over the media selections that are made. Your choices at any moment—what TV program to watch, what magazine you will buy, which advertisements to believe, and whether to attend to *any medium at all*—will ultimately shape the mass media content that is offered to you.

In addition to making the decision to select or reject any particular medium, the receiver can exercise other forms of control and influence. For example, the receiver can telephone or write media managers, initiate formal protests to governmental bodies and regulatory agencies, join activist groups, and apply pressure directly to the media channels for public access.

1.4.2 LEVELS OF RECEIVER INFLUENCE

In deciding how to provide meaningful media feedback, the receiver should think in terms of three different levels of action—action as an individual, as an influence in an immediate circle of contacts, and as part of a larger group.

Individual Response As an individual, you can have a substantial influence. First of all, you have complete control over your own reading, listening, and viewing patterns. You decide what television programs to watch, whether to read the paper today, when to turn on your radio, which book to buy, whether to go to a movie. Nobody else can make those decisions for you—unless you turn responsibility for control of your life over to others.

Also, you can initiate individual action with a single phone call or letter to an appropriate media manager. Media executives are surprisingly responsive to feedback from individual audience members. If all else fails, the threat of legal action is always a possibility (see Inset 1–8).

Immediate Peer Pressure A second form of personal influence is pressure exerted on one's relatives, friends, and business associates. The "two-step flow" communication model, developed by Paul Lazersfeld in the

1940s (Section 6.2.3), points out that much of the impact of mass communication is filtered through "opinion leaders" who exert pressure on their peers. Assuming the role of an opinion leader, the individual receiver can make his or her views known to acquaintances, suggest avenues of action to friends, and modify the media habits of family members.

Large-Group Action   As a third form of action, the receiver can join an established group that is concerned with the same problems or reforms. Such committees, commissions, and coalitions abound within the American structure. Some are large groups which were formed for other professional or social purposes but which have taken a strong position regarding mass media issues. Two examples are the Parent-Teachers Associ-

ation and the American Medical Association, both of which have become vocal about the effect of violence on young television viewers. Other groups were formed specifically to tackle a particular reform. An example of this type is Action for Children's Television, which is concerned with violence and with excessive advertising. The groups also vary in affiliation. Many are non-sectarian, while others are church-related agencies like the Catholic Church's Legion of Decency, which was concerned primarily with film content. Still others are broad-based citizens' groups concerned with all aspects of a given medium, such as the numerous state press councils, the National News Council, and the National Citizens Committee for Broadcasting. (See Section 10.6.)

As an example of the impact that one person can have on the media, the instance of John Banzhaf is outstanding. In 1966 Banzhaf, citing the Fairness Doctrine of the Federal Communications Commission (Inset 9–11), requested television station WCBS in New York City to provide free broadcast time for anti-smoking announcements. His argument was that—in light of the 1964 report of the Surgeon General pointing out the dangers of cigarette smoking—the use of tobacco was a controversial topic. Therefore, he claimed, he should have air time to respond to cigarette spots.

When the station refused his request, Banzhaf appealed directly to the FCC. In 1967 the Commission granted his request, and the decision was upheld by the U.S. Court of Appeals in Washington. WCBS and, by implication, all other stations were ordered to air public service announcements pointing out the health hazards of smoking.

Under increasing pressure from the public and the regulatory agencies (both the FCC and the Federal Trade Commission), the tobacco industry considered voluntarily suspending all broadcast advertising. The broadcasters, however, balked at the anticipated loss of revenue. Finally Congress was pressured into action; it banned all cigarette advertising on television and radio, the law becoming effective on January 2, 1971.

Banzhaf, by knowing whom to write and what kind of action to request, managed to alter drastically the nation's advertising channels.

**INSET 1–8
John Banzhaf
and Cigarette
Advertising**

The individual mass media receiver has an extremely wide variety of channels to choose from.

1.4.3 TYPES OF RECEIVER FEEDBACK

On the individual-response level, there are six different categories of ways in which the receiver can provide feedback to the mass media.

1. Financial Support The most obvious and unmistakable method of receiver feedback is direct financial support. More than anything else, cash receipts tell the mass media organizations whether or not they are reaching their intended audiences. The most indicative area of support is *single-item purchase*. This refers to all media products that are sold as single items or admissions, such as movies, records, audio tapes, books, and single copies of magazines and newspapers. Versions of pay-TV in which the viewer pays only for the actual selections viewed each month also fall into this category.

A second kind of financial support is *subscription,* in which the receiver contracts for a specified number of purchases. This category includes newspaper and magazine subscriptions, book-of-the-month and videocassette-of-the-month clubs, record clubs, and those

cable TV and pay-TV contracts in which the viewer pays a set rate for the month regardless of how much is viewed. Although subscription support is not quite as direct as single-item purchase, it nevertheless is a strong indication of which media and which features you wish to attend to.

2. Audience Membership In commercial broadcasting the receiver does not pay directly for television or radio programming, and thus there is no direct financial support. However, the number of persons who tune in to specific programs is estimated by the ratings services. This head-counting function is of crucial importance to the success of commercial broadcasting because the size of the audience determines the amount of money that a network or station can charge sponsors for advertising time.

With mass communication the receiver can be more selective than with most forms of personal communication. You can decide when you want to read a book, which TV channel to turn to, whether to read the newspaper. The more personal and direct the communication, the more difficult it is to tune out or control. As Schramm points out, "It is easy to change the television channel,

Letters to the Editor

Most major newspapers offer individual media receivers the opportunity to provide feedback through "Letters to the Editor" columns.

[but] hard to tune out face-to-face communication without being rude. It is easier to doze in a large class than in a small discussion group."[8]

For this reason, the receiver has much more control over the mass media. You decide which newspaper to read, when, and which sections. You decide when to turn on the radio for news and when for background music. You decide when to watch the tube and whether to turn to a game show or a news documentary. You decide whether or not to attend a movie, what book to buy, and which magazine to subscribe to. Unless you surrender control over your media usage to members of your family or peer group, or to opinion leaders or media publicists, you remain in control of your mass communication activities.

3. The Marketplace Another important form of receiver feedback is the marketplace served by commercial media. Consumer action can be an effective means of providing a reaction to the system. The most direct route is simply to let the advertiser know when you are upset about the content of a specific message—or to praise the advertiser for bringing you a particularly outstanding piece of content. Neither a broadcast sponsor nor a newspaper advertiser will ignore a substantial outpouring of consumer comments about a given medium or a particular message carried by that medium. If any kind of concerted consumer action which might hurt the sales of an advertiser's product is seriously threatened, that advertiser will respond to your feedback in a hurry (Section 10.6).

4. Direct Participation Another important avenue of receiver feedback is active, immediate participation in the process. Writing letters to the editor of a newspaper, for example, is a common method of participation. Most large dailies can print only a small fraction of the letters they receive, but if you succeed in getting a letter printed you have reached a sizable number of people with your particular message. On the other hand, many smaller local papers—especially weeklies—have a policy of printing every letter they receive. Many papers also will accept feature articles and guest columns from the public.

In the broadcast media it is more difficult to participate directly, but it is not impossible. "Talk-radio" formats allow listeners to call in and have their few minutes on the air; with enough patience and perserverance, most persons can manage to get on the radio. Individual access to television is more difficult. In 1972, the FCC ruled that large cable-TV systems must set aside a "public-access" channel which would be open to all members of the community on a first-come-first-served basis. Although this ruling was later nullified, many larger cable systems still make such a channel available to their service areas.

In 1977, the Warner Cable Corporation inaugurated a large-scale demonstration project in Columbus, Ohio. Known as QUBE, the system features a two-way interactive cable hookup which enables subscribers to provide instantaneous feedback to various programs and surveys. The system has three components: conventional cable channels for the reception of open-circuit stations; a pay-TV service featuring current movies and other special attractions; and the two-way hookup, which provides receivers with a chance to vote on community issues, participate in local game shows, purchase products, respond to local questionnaires, and interact with other unique programming. The system gained nationwide public attention in 1979, when the QUBE subscribers were polled immediately after one of President Carter's televised addresses, and their responses were integrated into the live NBC magazine program *Prime Time Sunday*.

5. Delayed Response Due to the nature of the mass communication experience, perhaps the most important type of direct receiver feedback is delayed activity. One of the most efficient methods is direct personal contact. To file your reaction as soon and as forcefully as possible, you can telephone the newspaper office or radio station. Most media organiza-

tions are equipped to handle and process such direct appeals. If you want a more permanent impact and a record of your response, you can write a letter. In his book *How to Talk Back to Your Television Set*, former FCC Commissioner Nicholas Johnson makes the point that

it is easy enough to write or phone a local station manager and even to arrange a conference with him. He is not likely to be unresponsive. Similarly, letters to network presidents and to advertisers can be influential. (If one-tenth of one percent of the audience of the average network series show were to request its continuation it probably would not be canceled.)[9]

Another method of direct delayed response is to file formal complaints with the proper governmental and regulatory bodies. (Recall the Banzhaf example, Inset 1–8.) Johnson stresses the fact that when appropriate procedures are followed, effective results can be obtained.

One basic principle, which I will call the law of effective reform, is this: in order to get relief from legal institutions (Congress, courts, agencies) one must assert, first, the factual basis for the grievance and the specific parties involved; second, the legal principle that indicates relief is due (constitutional provision, statute, regulation, court or agency decision); and third, the precise remedy sought (new legislation or regulations, license revocation, fines, or an order changing practices). . . . [By] understanding and using the right strategy the meekest among us can roll back the ocean.[10]

Other types of delayed response and receiver feedback exist. The National News Council and many state and local press councils function to process citizen input regarding the performance of newspapers (Section 10.5). Similarly, many broadcast stations work with various citizens' advisory groups, which can be effective avenues for reaching media management. Some newspapers have also initiated ombudsman services, an ombudsman being an in-house critic whose job it is to process complaints against the paper (Section 10.5).

6. Professional Criticism One final category of feedback is represented by industry self-criticism. The receiver can often become involved in such a quasi-professional capacity. The ombudsman and advisory council mentioned above are two examples of this kind of involvement.

Many of the media outlets are actively concerned with criticism of various facets of the several media. Newspapers and many magazines regularly carry film and television criticism, television news programs often present movie and television reviews, and so on. In these columns and features, there is often room for receiver feedback. In addition to contacting a station and its sponsors and the FCC, you can get in touch with the media critic for your local paper. You might be surprised at how accessible and interested he or she will be.

This section has introduced some of the ways in which an active and concerned mass communication receiver can be heard. As you have seen, there is no need for the receiver of the mass media message to feel overwhelmed and powerless at the hands of the mass communication industries. For the alert and concerned receiver, there are many opportunities to get involved.

1.5 Functions of Mass Communication

After examining the theoretical *structure* of mass communication by looking at various models and schemes, we can inquire into the *functions* of mass communication. What is it that mass media exist to do? What are the purposes of mass communications?

1.5.1 SOCIAL FUNCTIONS OF MASS COMMUNICATION

In his landmark essay, Lasswell held that there are three social functions of mass communication.[11] Other writers have added to his categories, retitled them, and redefined them, but essentially his three functions have held up through the years.

Watchdog Lasswell defined the first function of the mass media as *"the surveillance of the environment."* Others have labeled this the "monitoring" or "watchdog" function—the essential task of keeping an eye on what is going on, specifically as it relates to the political and economic events which shape our lives. We rely almost exclusively on the mass media to inform us about the latest crisis in the Middle East, the scientific breakthroughs in energy, the activity on Capitol Hill, the ups and downs of Wall Street, and the scandal in city hall.

Forum Lasswell defined the second function as *"the correlation of the parts of society in responding to the environment."* By this he was referring to the task of facilitating the decision making that is necessary for the orderly governance of society. The media serve as a forum for public debate, a means for the open management of the decision-making process. The media present the many sides of a given issue, bring us the commentary of leaders concerned with the issue, and then allow the citizenry to come together to make informed decisions about the appropriate response to the issue. Without this "forum" function, democracy as we know it would not exist.

Teacher The last function that Lasswell formulated was *"the transmission of the social heritage from one generation to the next."* This is the "teacher" function, or the job of instruction. In a formal sense the media, of course, play an important role in the instructional system—from textbooks and chalkboards to filmstrips and educational TV. But Lasswell was also referring to the informal task of passing on all aspects of our civilization, maintaining our social norms, and preserving the essential characteristics of our culture.

Entertainer Lasswell was primarily concerned with the political-economic-informational roles of the media. But other writers

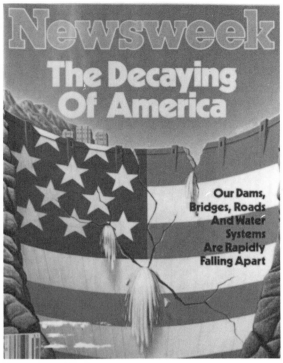

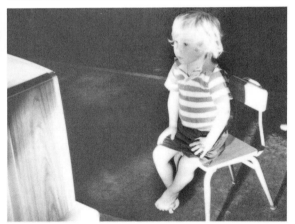

The four social functions of mass communication (clockwise; from top): the "watchdog" (*Newsweek* investigative report); the "forum" (a variety of columnists and commentators); the "teacher" (child watching *Sesame Street*); the "entertainer" (the portable stereo balladeer).

have pointed out that the media also serve an undeniable function as mass entertainers. We turn to the media most of the time for entertainment, diversion, and artistic satisfaction. We cannot ignore this role of the media as court jester, balladeer, magician, poet, gladiator, and storyteller. This, too, is a vital social function handled by all the mass media.

1.5.2 COMMUNICATION FUNCTIONS OF THE MASS MEDIA

Another way to approach the study of the functions of mass media is to look at the traditional functions or purposes of any communicative act. From most analyses of communication and books on public speaking, three basic purposes can be distilled.

Escapism   The first purpose is simply *to entertain*—to keep the audience pleasantly occupied for a period of time. No greater purpose is intended. The entertainment may range from true artistic achievements in opera and fine literature to diversions such as crossword puzzles and video games. This "escapist" function is what draws most people to the media gates. Most media observers and critics would not deny that this is a proper function for the printed page and the electronic media. Controversy arises, however, over the issue of how well and constructively this function is being carried out.

This first function, to entertain, is the underlying foundation of all communication activity. We must successfully entertain an audience—that is, keep its attention—before any loftier goals can be attempted.

Reality   The second potential purpose of any communicative act is *to inform*—to interpret the world of reality to the communication receiver. This function is sometimes divided into two general areas: *news,* including hard news, features, human interest items, commentary, and the like; and *education,* specific courses of instruction which may be offered either as formal schooling or as informal adult education. In both cases, however, the message is concerned with aspects of reality—facts, documentation,

knowledge, issues, and problems. And, of course, the line between news and education is often blurred, as when you are dealing with a science feature in the newspaper or an election analysis in the classroom.

This "reality" function of mass communication is the primary task of the media as envisioned by early theorists. For example, two of the three social functions described by Lasswell ("watchdog" and "teacher") are aspects of this broad category of information and instruction. The third social function—correlation of society's response to the environment ("forum")—involves the category of persuasion and decision making.

Propaganda   A third purpose of communication has long been recognized—*to persuade* or *to influence*—to change the receiver's way of thinking to agree with the sender, to move the receiver to a desired course of action. Indeed, this one of the most pervasive of all communication objectives. Persuasion underlies much of modern mass communication. It is the purpose of editorializing, crusading for social issues, and political campaigning; and, of course, it is the very root of our commercial media system. Without advertising designed to persuade you to buy goods and services, the modern American mass media complex as we know it could not exist.

1.5.3 RECEIVER–SENDER ORIENTATION OF FUNCTIONS

All of the functions listed above can be considered either *receiver-oriented* or *sender-oriented.* That is, either the receiver originates the mass communication process, or the sender initiates the process.

Receiver-Oriented Functions   In light of the importance of the receiver in the mass communication process (Section 1.4), it could be stated that in most mass media situations it is the receiver who initiates the communication act by completing the communication cycle. You, the receiver, decide which newspaper to read and which sections to turn to, when to turn on the radio, which TV channel to flip on, what movies to go see, which magazines to subscribe to, what records and books to buy. Nobody forces you to attend to these messages. In a very real sense, it is up to you to decide when and how mass communication will take place. The sender has no influence (other than publicity and indirect pressure) over your decisions to use the mass media.

The control exercised by the receiver is especially evident in the first two communication functions discussed above, *escapism* and *reality*. The receiver decides when to be entertained, to escape from the realities of the world; and when to be informed, to study the realities of the world. Two of Lasswell's social functions, "watchdog" and "teacher," are controlled by the receiver of the message. Neither of these functions takes place unless the receiver specifically initiates them.

Sender-Oriented Function   When we turn to the *propaganda* function, however, we find that we are confronted with a sender-oriented purpose. It is the sender who decides to initiate the persuasive message. The politician wants to get reelected and initiates his or her campaign. The newspaper publisher wants to call attention to a social evil and starts an editorial series. The manufacturer wants to sell more products and begins a nationwide advertising blitz. In each case the message is initiated by the sender; the receiver has indicated no desire to receive such a message. In fact, when exposed to the propaganda message, the receiver will attend to it only as long as he or she finds it attractively packaged (entertaining) or interesting (informative).

Seldom, if ever, will a receiver deliberately seek out a mass communication message for the expressed purpose of being persuaded. The receiver will turn to the classified advertising section of a newspaper to look for used car ads or will purposefully tune in a television campaign speech in order to find out

---

Communicative Purposes	*Corresponding Social Functions*	INSET 1–9
Receiver-Oriented Functions		Communication Functions
TO ENTERTAIN ("ESCAPISM")	Entertainment	
Diversion	*(Entertainer)*	
Art		
TO INFORM ("REALITY")		
News and Information	Surveillance of the Environment	
	(Watchdog)	
Instruction and	Transmission of Social Heritage	
Education	*(Teacher)*	
Sender-Oriented Function		
TO PERSUADE ("PROPAGANDA")	Correlation of Society's	
Editorializing	Response to the	
Advertising	Environment	
Political Persuasion	*(Forum)*	

more about a particular candidate. But, in each case, the receiver is initiating the communication process for the specific purpose of seeking *information*. The receiver wants to find out the price of used cars or the political platform of the candidate; the receiver is not seeking deliberately to be persuaded into buying a certain car or voting for the candidate. It is in this state of mind that the critical receiver attends to any advertising messages or political propaganda.

In making a distinction between receiver-oriented messages and sender-oriented messages, we are not implying that any communicative act can occur without the full participation of both parties. It is simply that some functions (entertainment and reality) are attuned to the needs of the receiver, while some communicative acts (persuasion) reflect the sender's needs.

In the introduction to this chapter, we stated that it was the aim of this book to make people more intelligent and responsible users of the media. Recognition of the distinction between receiver-oriented messages and sender-oriented messages will help you, as a responsible media user, in your approach to a given communication act. In dealing with receiver-oriented functions (entertainment and reality), you can become more selective and deliberate in your usage patterns. In dealing with the sender-oriented function of persuasion, you can become a more critical and discerning user by analyzing *who* is trying to manipulate *whom, how,* and for *what purpose* (to paraphrase Lasswell's basic model).

1.6   The Media as the Messages

Up to this point you have been examining the mass media as if they were merely empty conduits through which one passed a message from Point A to Point B; the media have been treated as neutral components in the mass communication process. However, as you examine the total communication environment—and as you try to figure out how you, as a receiver, can interact with the media

Marshall McLuhan, controversial mass media theorist and popularizer.

in the most positive and effective manner—you must examine the dynamic nature of the various print and electric media. This is necessary because the essential characteristics of each medium greatly affect the manner in which you can use and relate to that medium.

In undertaking an examination of the media, one cannot ignore the insights and controversies served up by Marshall McLuhan. A Canadian scholar with a background in English literature and sociology, McLuhan achieved a high degree of visibility and notoriety during the 1960s. Alternately acclaimed and denounced, McLuhan did manage to stimulate considerable thought and debate about the nature of the media.

1.6.1   THE MEDIUM IS THE MASSAGE?

McLuhan's most attention-getting statement was, "The medium is the message"—or, as he later elaborated on his own pun, "The medium is the massage." In other words, the very existence of a particular medium is far more important than the content of any messages that may be transmitted through it. The medium itself is actually the significant event.

Societies have always been shaped more by the nature of the media by which men communicate than by the content of the communication. The alphabet, for instance, is a technology that is absorbed by the very young child in a completely unconscious manner, by osmosis so to speak. Words and the meaning of words predispose the child to think and act automatically in certain ways. The alphabet and print technology fostered and encouraged a fragmenting process, a process of specialism and of detachment. Electric technology fosters and encourages unification and involvement. It is impossible to understand social and cultural changes without a knowledge of the workings of media.[12]

Undoubtedly, the course of history has been repeatedly altered by the introduction of new communication breakthroughs—and the significant factor has been the nature of each medium, not the content of the messages. Section 1.7 explores in more detail how the great communication technologies of print and the electric media have fostered societal changes throughout human history.

Examining the impact of media upon our lives (Section 1.1), we might find that the single most important factor is simply that we spend so much time with the media. What we watch on the tube is not nearly as significant as the fact that we spend three or four hours a day watching it!

In your daily experiences you constantly run into examples where the medium is more important than the actual content. The morning newspaper is delivered on your doorstep at dawn, and once more you are assured—regardless of the specific content of the paper—that the world is in place and the system is functioning normally. It is Saturday night, and you decide to go to a movie—almost any movie—because you want to get out of the house or enjoy a date with someone special, or because it is a socially accept-

able activity for your peer group. Many other examples could be drawn—watching TV (regardless of the program), turning on the car radio (to hear whatever music does not matter), curling up with a good book (as a matter of routine before bedtime). In each case it is the medium, not the content of the medium, that is the significant message.

1.6.2   LINEAR MEDIA

According to McLuhan, the significance of print is that its use results in a "linear" pattern of comprehension and thought. This pattern, he contends, has come to characterize Western civilization. To read a printed page requires a one-line-at-a-time sequential experience that necessitates a logical discipline unknown to nonliterate societies. Without the print phenomenon, civilization could not have evolved into the rational, technological culture we have today—not because print is the medium that has transmitted our knowledge, but because print itself has transformed our thinking patterns.

In interpreting McLuhan, Schramm states that McLuhan "contends that communication through print imposes a 'particular logic on the organization of visual experience.' It breaks down reality into discrete units, logically and causally related, perceived linearly across a page, abstracted from the wholeness and disorder and multisensory quality of life."[13]

On the other hand, aural media (media that appeal primarily to the ear) constitute an "all-at-onceness" that puts the receiver in the center of a communication experience, surrounded with a media environment that permeates his or her perception in all directions. This engulfing immediacy is exactly the opposite of the detached, logical perception of a linear print message. And this distinction leads to a difference in media patterns that we shall discuss later.

1.6.3   VISUAL AND AURAL MEDIA

Related to the linear quality of print is the distinction between the physiology of the eye and the ear. The eye is selective, can pick up signals only from one general direction, and can be readily closed to stimuli. The ear, on the other hand, picks up messages from all directions and cannot be closed to stimuli.

Schramm also points out other distinctions: "Among single-sense channels there is reason to suspect differences also, because good evidence exists that the eye can absorb information more rapidly than the ear. . ."[14] This helps to explain why, for example, we can generally comprehend more words per minute through the eye than through the ear.

1.6.4 LOW-EFFORT AND HIGH-EFFORT MEDIA

Any medium which requires substantial symbol manipulation and interpretation requires more effort than a direct aural or pictorial medium. Although speech does employ oral verbal symbols (the spoken word), the symbol manipulation is handled smoothly by most humans by the time they are a few years old. Therefore, all audio (sound) media are considered relatively low-effort media.

Visual media, on the other hand, may be either *pictorial* (involving little or no symbol sophistication) or *print* (involving a high degree of symbol interpretation). Because of the skills required to decode abstract print symbols, reading is considered more of a "high-effort" medium than an audio-pictorial medium like television.

Schramm hypothesizes that, all other factors being equal, people will tend to use a low-effort medium over a high-effort medium. You will look at the pictures in a book before reading the words. You will get your news from television rather than the newspaper. You will watch a movie on TV rather than go out to the theater (which requires more effort). One factor that counterbalances this tendency, however, is the promise of reward. If you know the newspaper contains more detail about an item you are interested in, you will read the paper. Schramm gives another example:

Countless audience studies have shown that people select easily available entertainment from their television tube in preference—other things being equal—to going out for equally promising entertainment. Yet when the reward of peer group company is added in, we see teenagers go to the movies or even the public library.[15]

In addition to peer-group pressure or social prestige, there are several other rewards which lead to the use of the high-effort medium of print. More information can be assimilated in a shorter period of time. Print is a more convenient medium for storage and review. Print is generally less expensive than pictorial media. Also, because it makes more use of symbols, print is better suited for communicating abstract messages whereas audio-pictorial media are more appropriate for concrete communications.

1.6.5 "HOT" AND "COOL" MEDIA

One other concept of McLuhan's should be mentioned in any discussion of the nature of media—the classification of "hot" and "cool" media. Hot media are those which saturate a single sense with much information ("high definition") and therefore require little receiver participation to complete the message. Hot media include high-fidelity audio recordings and radio, motion pictures, and books.

Cool media are those which contain less information ("low definition") and therefore require more receiver participation in order to make the message complete. Cartoons, the telephone (because much of the audio frequency range is filtered out), and television are all cool media. Television is cool partly because of the nature of the electronic composition of the video picture. The hundreds of scanning lines on the face of the tube result in a "mosaic" message, and the individual viewer has to participate in the completion of this low-definition picture by filling in (physiologically) between the scanning lines.

McLuhan goes on to claim that since the cool media involve the receiver more than hot media, the cool channels can be used more effectively for different kinds of purposes:

Any hot medium allows of less participation than a cool one, as a lecture makes for less participation than a seminar, and a book for less than dialogue. With print many earlier forms were excluded from life and art, and many were given strange new intensity. But our own time is crowded with examples of the principle that the hot form excludes, and the cool one includes.[16]

As intriguing as McLuhan's hot and cool explanations appear on the surface, they do not explain away Schramm's observation that television is basically a low-effort medium. Rather than involving the receiver, as McLuhan claims television does, Schramm points out that people turn to the tube as the path of least resistance.

Nevertheless, McLuhan's ideas and "probes" (as he calls them) continue to stimulate controversy and get people thinking about the nature of mass media—the concept of the medium as a message, the idea of the linear impact of print, the difference between visual and aural media and between high-effort and low-effort media, and the questions of hot and cool media.

1.7 The Impact of Media Technologies

Whereas the previous section looked at the distinctions among various media from the standpoint of the individual receiver, we now turn to the impact of media from a broader societal perspective. Historically, the evolution of different mediums has dictated the course of human development.

Writers and scholars have identified three broad periods of media technology which have determined the nature of humankind's societal structure—the *oral tradition*, the *written word*, and the *electric media*.

1.7.1 THE ORAL TRADITION

Before humankind developed written symbols, all communication was on the personal level, through the spoken word and the physical gesture. Although there might be an occasional traveler's report, the average person's knowledge was limited to the immediate environment—the village, the tribe, or perhaps city–state. The world beyond the horizon was largely unknown.

Another recent development which apparently contradicts McLuhan's concept of hot and cool media has been in the area of brain-wave research.[17] Tentative conclusions indicate that viewing television is such a low-effort, noninvolving task that it tends to put the viewer into a semitrance. Several scientists, working independently, have found that while you are watching television your brain-wave activity is dominated by alpha waves. This indicates a state of mind in which the individual is passive and unfocused—not paying attention to anything. This is hardly the kind of participation that McLuhan would describe as being indicative of a person's involvement with a cool medium.

One scientist working with brain-wave research has suggested that television induces a semihypnotic state similar to staring into a campfire. This has prompted Peter Crown to label television the "electronic fireplace." There is increasing interest in the area of brain-wave research, not only by scientists but also by market researchers and commercial network executives. And the results so far tend to uphold the view that television is a very low-effort, sleep-inducing experience.

INSET 1–10
The Electronic Fireplace

Even in modern society, the oral tradition is continued as elder citizens pass on local tales, family traditions, and native folklore to younger generations.

The collected wisdom and heritage of society was held together, from generation to generation, by the elders of the community. Schramm summarizes this period: "Knowledge is power in a traditional village as elsewhere, but in a premedia culture that form of power tends to reside with the old men who can remember the wisdom of the past, the sacred . . . laws, customs, and family histories."[18]

In such oral societies religious institutions were dominant because of the traditions of the spoken and visual religious media—the ceremonial dances, the songs and chants—which preserved and transmitted the collected histories, rules, and taboos of the culture. History was simplified and personally felt by every individual man and woman.

1.7.2 THE WRITTEN WORD

Early geometric designs and animal representations found in cave drawings and rock paintings were refined into various ideographic symbolic systems such as the Egyptian hieroglyphics, Babylonian and Persian cuneiform, and Chinese ideograms. Then, between 2000 B.C. and 1000 B.C., alphabets as we recognize them today were developed. And with this revolutionary technology of the written word, the social fabric of humankind was completely rewoven.

With writing, it was possible to structure social, economic, military, and political institutions on a scale previously unknown. The administration of vast empires was facilitated by consistent and detailed laws and regulations, military instructions to distant commanders, accurate records, and legal contracts. The memory of the elder was replaced by the pen of the scribe. The power of the church was supplanted by the secular authority of governmental civil service. McLuhan colorfully summed up the impact of the written word:

The goose quill put an end to talk. It abolished mystery; it gave architecture and towns; it brought roads and armies, bureaucracy. It was the basic metaphor with which the cycle of civilization began, the step from the dark into the light of the mind. The hand that filled the parchment page built a city.[19]

Writing Media   The first written symbols were chiseled on *stone,* but this medium did little to facilitate long-distance communication. *Clay tablets* were more easily worked than stone but still contributed little to conquering space. However, with the Egyptian contribution of *papyrus*—made from a variety of rush found along the Nile—humankind developed a portable medium. Papyrus documents and manuscripts not only made possible the administration of the vast Roman Empire, but they also facilitated the origin of modern scholarship and academic inquiry.

Closely following upon the invention of papyrus, the Greeks created a method for preparing long-lasting and flexible *parchment* from the skin of sheep and goats. By 800 A.D., the Chinese invention of *paper* had been brought into Turkey through the capture of Chinese papermakers. And within four or five hundred years, the spread of paper had given the Western world its most flexible and plentiful printing medium.

The Printing Press   When the medium of paper was coupled with the technology of the printing press in the mid-fifteenth century, the power of the written word was magnified tremendously and the resulting societal upheavals were unparalleled. The widespread use of vernacular language, the rise of nationalism, the positive values placed on privacy and individualism, the Reformation, and eventually the Enlightenment of the eighteenth century were all made possible by the printing press. The media theorist Neil Postman emphasizes this by stating,

Print, in even more revolutionary ways than writing, changed the very form of civilization. It is not entirely coincidence, for instance, that the Protestant Reformation was contemporaneous with the invention of moveable type. . .

The book, by isolating the reader and his responses, tended to separate him from the powerful oral influences of his family, teacher, and priest. Print thus created a new conception of self

as well as of self-interest. At the same time, the printing press provided the wide circulation necessary to create national literatures and intense pride in one's native language. Print thus promoted individualism on the one hand and nationalism on the other.[20]

Up until this time, books had been copied by hand and thus were the province of a relatively small, elite group of scholars, government functionaries, wealthy aristocrats, and church officials. But by placing mass-produced copies of books in the hands of the common person, the printing press altered the social structure profoundly. From now on, control of the mass communication message would be up to the receiver.

1.7.3   THE ELECTRIC MEDIA

McLuhan popularized the term "the electric media," which refers broadly to the telegraph, telephone, audio recordings, radio, movies, television, cable TV, satellites, and so on. In the late nineteenth century the first of these media appeared, and they foretold the drastic cultural changes which would occur.

Founded by Ptolemy I around 300 B.C., the Great Library in Alexandria was to become the most celebrated library and media operation in antiquity. It was the intellectual center of the Hellenistic Empire. The most famous classical scholars, scientists, poets, philosophers, and artists were associated with the library complex, which was actually a combination of library, museum, research institute, and botanical gardens.

At its peak, the library contained between half a million and a million (estimates vary widely) painstakingly hand-copied papyrus volumes. This academic center heralded the beginnings of scholarship as it is known in the Western world. The vast repository represented (for perhaps the last time on this planet) the collection of almost all of Western civilization's recorded knowledge in one location.

Burned and ravaged alternately by the Romans, civil war, and the Christians, this irreplaceable resource was completely devastated by 400 A.D. The world's greatest intellectual treasury had been wiped off the face of the globe.

**INSET 1–11
Papyrus and the
Great Library
at Alexandria**

The modern web press is one of the wonders of the twentieth-century printing world.

According to McLuhan, the speed of electric media returns us to the "all-at-onceness" environment of the oral/aural media (Section 1.6.2). We are enmeshed once again in the nonprint, nonlinear, nonsymbolic communication characteristic of the oral tradition. Whereas the printed word tended to isolate the individual receiver and remove him or her from the tribal consciousness, McLuhan argues that telecommunications media can reunite the peoples of the planet through a shared electric/oral communication experience that transcends national boundaries—a sort of worldwide tribalization, with everyone living in the same "global village." He states that print is a specialist medium (available only to the literate elite) and that any form of specialist-medium exchange of information will serve to fragment a tribal structure.

Similarly, a very much greater speed-up, such as occurs with electricity, may serve to restore a tribal pattern of intense involvement such as took place with the introduction of radio in Europe, and is now tending to happen as a result of TV in America. Specialist technologies [such as print] detribalize. The nonspecialist electric technology retribalizes.[21]

Schramm succinctly sums up McLuhan's position. Television, argues McLuhan, "will restore the healthful balance of the senses. It will de-privatize, 'retribalize' man, lead him back to the communal experience of an oral culture. It will encourage participation rather than withdrawal, action rather than meditation, peaceful relations rather than nationalism."[22]

SUMMARY

In this opening chapter, we have tried to look at the mass communication process from several theoretical perspectives—always stressing the all-important role of the receiver of the communication message. Looking at various levels of communication, we have seen that the role of the receiver is more critical in mass communication than in any of the four levels of personal communication (intrapersonal, conversational, small-group, and large-group). We have looked at the functions of mass communication from the standpoint of the two receiver-oriented functions (escapism and reality) as well as from the one sender-oriented function (propaganda). We have examined several aspects of the media themselves as messages—the importance of the existence of the media, the impact of linear media, the difference between visual and aural media, between low-effort and high-effort media, and between hot and cool media. And finally, we have glanced at the impact of oral, written, and electric media throughout the history of humankind's evolving societal structure.

In Chapter 2 we will look more specifically at the relationship of a nation's political philosophy and the structure of its mass media system.

Notes to Chapter 1

1. Wilbur Schramm, *Men, Messages, and Media: A Look at Human Communication* (New York: Harper & Row, 1973), p. 15.

2. W. Phillip Davidson, James Boylan, and Frederick T. C. Yu, *Mass Media: Systems and Effects* (New York: Praeger, 1976), p. 3.

3. Melvin DeFleur, *Theories of Mass Communication*, 2nd ed. (New York: David McKay, 1970), p. 77.

4. Schramm, *Men, Messages, and Media*, p. 17.

5. Harold D. Lasswell, "The Structure and Function of Communication in Society," in *The Communication of Ideas*, ed. Lyman Bryson (New York: Harper & Brothers, 1948), p. 37.

6. Schramm, *Men, Messages, and Media*, pp. 97–98.

7. Wilbur Schramm, "The Nature of Communication between Humans," in *The Process and Effects of Mass Communication*, rev. ed., ed. Wilbur Schramm and Donald F. Roberts (Urbana: University of Illinois Press, 1972), p. 8.

8. Schramm, *Men, Messages, and Media*, p. 119.

9. Nicholas Johnson, *How to Talk Back to Your Television Set* (Boston: Little, Brown, 1967), p. 212.

10. Ibid., p. 202.

11. Lasswell, "Structure and Function," p. 38.

12. Marshall McLuhan and Quentin Fiore, *The Medium Is the Massage: An Inventory of Effects* (New York: Bantam Books, 1967), p. 8.

13. Schramm, *Men, Messages, and Media*, p. 127.

14. Ibid., p. 116.

15. Ibid., p. 108.

16. Marshall McLuhan, *Understanding Media: The Extensions of Man* (New York: New American Library, Signet Books, 1964), p. 37.

17. Some of the pioneers in brain-wave research include Dr. Herbert Krugman of General Electric; Dr. Thomas Mulholland of the Veterans Administration Medical Center in Boston; Prof. Peter Crown of Hampshire College; and Dr. Valentine Appel of Simmons Market Research Bureau.

18. Schramm, *Men, Messages, and Media*, p. 14.

19. McLuhan and Fiore, *Medium Is the Massage*, p. 48.

20. Neil Postman, *Television and the Teaching of English* (New York: Appleton-Century-Crofts, 1961), p. 9.

21. McLuhan, *Understanding Media*, p. 38.

22. Schramm, *Men, Messages, and Media*, p. 129.

A Russian factory worker scans the front page of *Izvestia* to see how the recent crop failure will affect the price of bread for the next year. An African teenager walks down the dusty road to his village with his portable transistor radio pressed to his ear, listening to American rock music. In an isolated village some 150 miles from New Delhi, an Indian mother of five joins a dozen of her neighbors at a government screening of a film on birth control. And a supermarket manager in Denver picks up his copy of *Reader's Digest* to read a scathing attack on big government and bureaucratic inefficiency.

Ask these four persons what they think of when you say "mass media," and you will get four widely divergent views—for a society's political system will determine its mass media structure. The authors Hiebert, Ungurait, and Bohn make the point:

A country's political structure and attitudes influence the development of a media system. The amount and kinds of control over mass communication are determined by the nature and structure of the government in power. Political forces establish the laws under which media institutions must operate. Media regulations may be repressive or permissive depending on the political atmosphere of a particular society.[1]

This relationship of the media system to the political structure leads to the basic theme of Chapter 2. Referring specifically to the United States, our theme is this:

• *A free democratic society is dependent upon a free, open, and pluralistic mass communication system.*

In order to have a free and representative political system, a nation must have a competitive and minimally regulated media structure.

2

The Political Foundations of Mass Communication

THE "FOUR CONCEPTS" THEORY

If a society's media system is based upon its political philosophy, we must also consider that a society's political system is based upon its philosophy of the nature of human beings—and of the relationship of the people to the state. In essence, there are two basic views about the nature of humankind. One set of philosophies contends that people are inherently weak and subject to corruption and are therefore in need of a well-structured, disciplined society. This view of humankind leads to the establishment of a strong *authoritarian* government.

The opposing view of the human condition holds that people are rational, essentially fair and honest, and freedom-seeking. This philosophy leads to a less structured, less dominating *libertarian* governmental system.

Such a clear-cut dichotomy is, of course, somewhat simplistic. Neither human beings nor governments can be so easily pigeonholed into one neat compartment or the other. However, as a starting point for our consideration, it is helpful to think in terms of these two basic approaches to the relationship between the people and the state.

Elaborating upon this division, the authors Siebert, Peterson, and Schramm compiled a landmark work in 1956 which outlined what they termed the "four theories" of the press.[2] As an intensification of the *authoritarian* concept, they added the *Soviet Communist* role of the mass press. And as an adaptation of the *libertarian* approach, the authors defined the *social responsibility* concept of the media. These four "theories" or concepts form as solid a base as any for examining the relationship between the structure of political systems and the nature of mass communication systems.

2.1 The Authoritarian Concept of Mass Media

Any authoritarian system is one in which a leader has complete control of authority over the people. Authoritarianism characterizes many relationships other than governmental. It exists within numerous religious bodies—the Roman Catholic church under the authority of the pope, for example. The family may be an authoritarian system if the father (or the mother in a matriarchal society) exercises complete control. The classroom can be an authoritarian setting in those instances where the teacher retains full domination.

2.1.1 CHARACTERISTICS OF AUTHORITARIANISM

An authoritarian leader may assume power by any one of several means. Heredity, wisdom and experience, and military strength are several of the most obvious ways of gaining authoritarian control.

The Authoritarian State Regardless of how dictatorial leaders are installed in power, authoritarian governments assume certain common characteristics. First and foremost, the *position of the state ranks above everything else*. The government is all-powerful. Preservation of the state is the chief goal of society.

Second, because the perpetuation of the state is society's primary function, *any means used to uphold the state is allowable;* the end justifies the means. Therefore, truth is relative; truth is irrelevant; truth be damned. The truth may be redefined as often as necessary in order to maintain the government in power.

Third, *the individual is insignificant*. The individual can accomplish nothing of merit working alone. Individuals must work together collectively, under the state, in order to accomplish anything of value. This is because the human being is essentially weak and frail, selfish and irrational, subject to corruption and confusion.

As a result of these attitudes, the rulers of an authoritarian nation exhibit a marked distrust of the people. The authors Merrill and Lowenstein describe such a state:

A desire for strong government, a fear of the masses, an inclination to personal arrogance based on a felt superiority, a respect for power, a hatred for anarchy, and a desire to control: these—among others—are the natural proclivities of the elitists and authoritarians. . . .

The basic characteristic of the authoritarian orientation is political and intellectual arrogance by a small elite group having a deep-rooted suspicion of the masses.[3]

The Authoritarian Truth   Authoritarian truth may be founded on any one of several claims: divine revelation, generations of experience, a superior intellect, or the collective wisdom of a ruling elite. But, whatever its basis, authoritarian truth always has several characteristics.

First, authoritarian truth *always flows from the top down*. It is revealed only to the authorities. Individual citizens have no access to the fountains of verity. Truth is interpreted by the leaders and then transmitted to the masses.

Second, authoritarian truth is *subject to revision and reinterpretation* by the top authorities. It is somewhat mercurial, changing form, slipping out of one's grasp, readily altering its shape. History is readily rewritten.

Third, authoritarian truth becomes *the absolute standard for all members of society*. No individual may experience a version of truth which is not sanctioned by the authorities; no deviations from the established truth can be tolerated. These three characteristics, as we shall see below, essentially determine the role that mass media can play in such a society.

2.1.2 AUTHORITARIAN THINKERS

The nature and philosophy of authoritarianism have been shaped by some of the greatest minds in history—thinkers and writers whose observations and arguments have provided fodder for those who would establish totalitarian regimes.

Plato   The most significant and one of the longest of Plato's dialogues, the *Republic*, is often interpreted as the philosopher's ultimate justification for authoritarian rule. In examining the nature of happiness and justice, Plato described in great detail the function of the

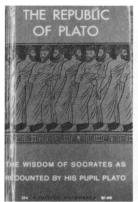

Plato's *Republic* and Machiavelli's *The Prince* represent two differing approaches to authoritarianism.

"philosopher-kings" who would govern the ideal state with wisdom and justice and absolute authority. Although Plato did not necessarily intend his theoretical model (which was designed primarily to probe the psychology of the individual being) to be taken as a literal blueprint for a political state, his *Republic* nevertheless has often been described as "aristocratic communism" and has been interpreted as a defense for benevolent authoritarianism.

Other Political Thinkers   Throughout the centuries many other philosophers and political writers have contributed much, either directly or obliquely, to various concepts of authoritarianism. In many ways *Niccolò Machiavelli* (1469–1527) symbolized the transition from the Middle Ages to the modern world. His most famous political writings, especially *The Prince* (1513), were basically amoral and realistic treatises on the acquisition and exercise of political power.

More than a century later, the English philosopher, scientist, and man of letters *Thomas Hobbes* (1588–1679) was one of the most vocal advocates of a strong authoritarian state. Hobbes' lifetime spanned an era of intense debate and controversy over the

English monarchy, and throughout his writings Hobbes maintained a pessimistic view of human nature. He consistently argued that humankind would be best served by an absolute monarch who could protect individuals from their own destructive tendencies.

Two German philosophers contributed significantly to the authoritarian cause. *Georg Wilhelm Friedrich Hegel* (1770–1831) has sometimes been called the father of communism as well as the father of modern facism. Some interpreters—claiming that he was only indirectly a forerunner of later totalitarians—point out that he endowed the state with an "ethical spirit" and that to him the state was an end in itself. Consequently, the highest duty of the individual was to be a member of the state and to submit to its ultimate control.

Disclaiming Christian love (as being primarily selfish) and belief in life after death (as a compensation for failure in one's mortal existence), *Friedrich Nietzsche* (1844–1900) contended that all human beings desire power and mastery. Therefore, the state represents a discipline and code of behavior that is necessary for an orderly society.

Although many other writers and philosophers contributed to the theory of the totalitarian state, these five typify the kinds of thinking that gave a sense of direction and foundation to authoritarianism: the individual is weak and corrupt, a strong state is necessary for a stable society, the masses are not to be trusted.

2.1.3 AUTHORITARIANISM AND THE MASS MEDIA

During the fifteenth century, the reality of authoritarianism hung heavily over most of Western civilization. The authority of the Roman Catholic church was yet to be seriously challenged. Most of the countries of Western Europe were headed by strong monarchies. Into this milieu was delivered the printing press.

A primary concern of the authoritarian state is self-perpetuation, and to meet this goal the state may employ whatever tools of coercion and persuasion it controls. The printing press was obviously an important tool in this regard. Schramm sums up the significance of mass communication to the authoritarian state:

The concept of public communication which developed in these first 250 years of printing was exactly what would be expected in an authoritarian setting. Printing was simply another tool to promote unity and continuity within the state. It was to carry wisdom and truth as wisdom and truth were identified by the rulers. Access to the medium was to be restricted to those individuals who would operate for "the good of the state" as judged by the rulers. The public at large were considered incapable of understanding political problems, and communication was therefore forbidden to "disturb the masses" or interest them in something they could not "understand."[4]

Authoritarian Controls on the Media

Whether it be authoritarianism of the political right (fascism) or the extreme left (communism), the totalitarian government has several methods which are used in controlling the mass press.

The first step is to limit access to the media by *issuing state licenses* to printers and publishers. Thus, without government permission, no one could operate a printing press. This was the common means of control during the sixteenth and seventeenth centuries. Such a licensing requirement was in effect under the British Crown until Parliament allowed the Licensing Act to expire permanently in 1694. The residual effects of this governmental sanction were spasmodically carried over to the American colonies, however, into the early eighteenth century. When the first continuously published weekly paper was started in the colonies—the *Boston News-Letter* in 1704—it was allowed to print regularly because the editor, John Campbell, submitted to voluntary censorship by having the authorities screen all material before printing.

When licensing did not provide sufficient control, the authoritarian government could institute *prior censorship*. This required that all printed copy had to be approved by an official government censor before the material could be printed and disseminated. This often proved quite cumbersome, however. In the American colonies, for instance, there were simply too many printing presses and too many clever publishers.

In the eighteenth century, then, control by prior censorship was largely replaced by the threat of *punishment after publication*. Using laws of treason (an act with the intention of overthrowing the government) and sedition (an act showing disrespect for the government), the state could prosecute any publisher for printing materials which the government deemed dangerous to the authority of the state. The John Peter Zenger trial of 1735 was one of the most famous blows against the repressive nature of the sedition laws (see Inset 2–2). However, in 1798, the U. S. Congress, with a small Federalist majority, passed the Alien and Sedition Acts. Ostensibly directed against the subversive activities of foreigners in the United States, the acts were more often used to silence anti-Federalist criticism by the Jeffersonian Republicans. Public reaction was so strong, however, that the popular backlash against the repressive acts helped to elect Jefferson in 1800. Very shortly thereafter each of the acts was repealed or allowed to expire, lessening the opportunities for authoritarian control in the new nation.

A fourth form of authoritarian control over the press is *government ownership and operation of media channels*. In its extreme form—where the government owns all media operations—this becomes the Soviet Communist concept of mass media (Section 2.3). In many countries a dual system has evolved whereby government channels and privately owned media systems function side by side. Virtually all free societies have some sort of official press (for example, the U.S. Government Printing Office, the *Congressional Record*); and many countries, like Japan and

---

**INSET 2–1
Benjamin Harris's
*Publick Occurrences***

France, have government-supported television networks which compete with commercially supported systems.

A final form of authoritarian media control occurs through *government subsidization of private channels*. A variation of this takes place when a government supports a public, government-chartered (but not government-operated) nonprofit corporation—such as the British Broadcasting Corporation or the Corporation for Public Broadcasing in the United States. In these instances, however, the government theoretically exerts no direct control over the actual content of the programming. A more insidious form of government subsidization occurred in the United States in the late eighteenth and early nineteenth centuries, when many privately owned papers were supported by political parties. Newspapers in these cases became direct spokesmen for the parties (see Section 3.3.1).

Despite these various avenues for authoritarian control over the media, the free spirit of humankind has consistently led people to chip away at the doctrines of licensing, prior censorship, post-publication punishment, government ownership, and government subsidization. Schramm describes the decline of authoritarianism:

Communication authoritarianism waned notably by the second half of the eighteenth century. By that time a line of liberal thinkers had thrown stones at the theory, and in several Western countries a succession of democratic revolutions had knocked holes in the practice. The tide seemed to have turned away from authoritarianism. The new concept of public communication was that it should serve the individuals, not the state; that it should not offer unity, but rather diversity; that it should contribute to change as well as to continuity; and that it had every right to criticize the government in power.[7]

INSET 2–2
Trial of
John Peter Zenger

John Peter Zenger was an immigrant printer who published a weekly paper, the *New-York Journal*, which frequently carried columns criticizing the colonial governor, William Cosby, for various arbitrary actions. Zenger was arrested and brought to trial in 1735 on a charge of seditious libel. Because it was clearly against the law to criticize the government—regardless of whether or not the accusations were true—the state had only to prove that he had indeed printed the inflammatory columns.

Zenger's remarkable eighty-year-old lawyer, Andrew Hamilton, readily admitted that Zenger printed the material in question; therefore, Zenger was technically guilty of printing seditious material. However, despite explicit instructions from the judge, Hamilton went on to insist that the jury be allowed to decide the merits of the case on the basis of whether or not the materials were *true*—not whether or not they were printed. In a ringing appeal, Hamilton challenged the jury to ignore the technicalities of the law; "The question before the court . . . may in its consequence affect every freeman . . . on the main[land] of America. It is the best cause; it is the cause of Liberty . . . the liberty both of exposing and opposing arbitrary power . . . by speaking and writing Truth."[6]

Responding to Hamilton's oratory and ignoring the law, the jury acquitted Zenger. Although the threat of trial for sedition remained until the end of the century, the Zenger jury made it clear that truth was to be considered a higher good than government authority.

In the Soviet Communist form of authoritarianism, all media channels are owned and operated as part of the state or party government. *Soviet Life* is an example of the state's propaganda efforts designed for an English-speaking audience.

2.2 The Libertarian Concept of Mass Media

In contrast to the authoritarian view of the nature of humankind—which sees human beings as weak, subject to corruption, and in need of a strongly disciplined society—is the libertarian viewpoint. According to libertarians, human beings are intelligent and rational, basically fair and honest, capable of improvement, and freedom-seeking.

2.2.1 LIBERTARIANISM AND THE AGE OF ENLIGHTENMENT

The libertarian movement, Schramm says, "was foreshadowed in the sixteenth century, envisioned in the seventeenth, fought for in the eighteenth, and finally brought into widespread use in the nineteenth."[8] A number of developments in Europe during the fifteenth, sixteenth, and early seventeenth centuries had

the effect of undermining the social, philosophical, and political solidarity of authoritarianism. Explorations and discoveries had begun to shape a new image of the nature of the human being:

• Scientific revelations starting with those of Galileo had broadened people's view of nature and of the universe. As a result, the anthropocentric authoritarianism of the church was severely shaken.
• Exploration and geographical discovery proved conclusively that the world was round and, more importantly, provided an avenue of escape to those who were dissatisfied with aspects of European society.
• The rising merchant class challenged the privileges of the nobility. Capitalism was fostered by the growing middle class.
• The Protestant Reformation freed the individual from the dogmas of the established church and unseated the priesthood as the source of all ecclesiastical truth.
• Political and social revolutions (against the Stuarts in England, for example) undermined the authoritarian concept that the state was superior to the individual.

Every one of these developments resulted in a challenge to traditional authority—to the church, the state, or the economic system. The cumulative impact was a massive challenge to the very concept of authoritarianism —a challenge that was put into philosophic terms by the great thinkers of the Age of Enlightenment.

Stretching roughly from the late seventeenth century to the end of the eighteenth century, the period known as the Enlightenment was one of the greatest periods of humankind's intellectual expansion. Peter Gay characterizes the Enlightenment by referring to Immanuel Kant's exhortation, "Dare to know! Have the courage to use your own intelligence!":

Kant's words summed up the most cherished convictions and ambitious designs of radical eighteenth-century scholars and intellectuals. His

INSET 2–3   Key Figures of the Age of Enlightenment

The men listed below are the primary shapers of the libertarian philosopy. Their key writings are indicated (with dates of publication in parentheses).

1600   1700   1800   1900

1608 ├──── **John Milton** ────┤1674
Areopagitica (1644)

1632 ├──── **John Locke** ────┤1704
Second Treatise of Civil Government (1690)

1642 ├──── **Isaac Newton** ────┤1727
Mathematical Principles of Natural Philosophy (1687)

1694 ├──── **Voltaire** ────┤1778

1706 ├──── **Benjamin Franklin** ────┤1790

1712 ├──── **Jean Jacques Rousseau** ────┤1778

1723 ├──── **Adam Smith** ────┤1790
The Wealth of Nations (1776)

1724 ├──── **Immanuel Kant** ────┤1804
Critique of Pure Reason (1781)

1743 ├──── **Thomas Jefferson** ────┤1826
Declaration of Independence (1776)

1806 ├──── **John Stuart Mill** ────┤1873
On Liberty (1859)

words implied that man was mature enough to find his own way without paternal authority; they urged man to understand his own nature and the natural world by the methods of science. In short, they were a declaration of freedom. Kant and his fellow thinkers wanted men to shake off the hand of authority in politics and religion, and think for themselves.[9]

2.2.2 LIBERTARIAN THINKERS

Many philosophers, writers, and practitioners during the Age of Enlightenment contributed to the formation of the libertarian concept. Those mentioned below are but some of the more outstanding thinkers who were instrumental in contributing philosophies and theories which shaped the concept of a free press as we recognize it today.

John Milton (1608–1674)   In any discussion of the shapers of libertarian thought, the name of the English poet John Milton must receive early consideration. He was one of the first and most eloquent defenders of the concept of a free press.

In 1643, when the Parliament passed a new press licensing act reinstating the licensing arrangements that had been abolished in 1641, the renewed attempt to control the press incensed Milton. In 1644 he published his famous treatise on the evils of press licensing, the *Areopagitica*, the title of which alludes to the classic Greek *Areopagitic Discourse* of Isocrates (about 355 B.C.).

In the *Areopagitica*, Milton offered three basic arguments against licensing. First, *licensing was the evil offspring of a repressive church.* Initiated centuries earlier by the Roman Catholic church, licensing had long been identified with authoritarian attempts to stifle free opinion.

Second, Milton argued that *licensing was impractical.* It would take too many government censors—all of whom must be possessed of infallible judgment and unimpeachable character—to do the job right. Not only would all contemporary writings have to be thoroughly scrutinized, but historical works

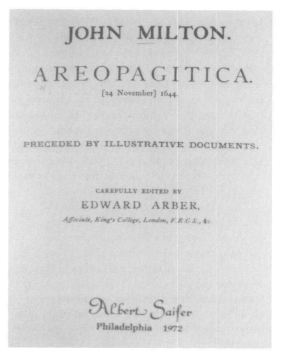

John Milton's *Areopagitica* was one of the most influential seventeenth-century treatises attacking government licensing.

would have to be expurgated of all tainted material.

Third—and this was the main point that would ring throughout the centuries—*licensing frustrates the search for truth.* Milton championed the position that if all persons are allowed to express themselves freely, truth will ultimately triumph over falsehood. Let all opinions clash and vie for acceptance; eventually the true position will prevail over the erroneous. Milton stated his argument eloquently in the *Areopagitica:*

And though all the winds of doctrine were let loose to play upon the earth, so Truth be in the field, we do injuriously by licensing and prohibiting to misdoubt her strength. Let her and Falsehood grapple; who ever knew Truth put to the worse in a free and open encounter?

John Locke (1632–1704) Whereas Milton was concerned specifically with the evils of state licensing, Locke was a philosopher who was concerned with the nature of human beings and with their relationship to the state. Following Hobbes (Section 2.1.1) by roughly half a century, Locke agreed with Hobbes that the state was a necessary creation, but he went far beyond Hobbes in arguing that the state was created by a free people—out of their own free will—in order to serve the interests of the people.

This view of government formed the basic premise of many of Locke's writings, such as his *Second Treatise on Civil Government* (1690), and it led him to a number of important corollaries: the natural rights and freedoms of the individual are paramount; government exists only to guarantee these rights and freedoms; the individual is more important than the state; the people have the right to abolish the state if it does not protect their rights. Schramm sums up Locke's position:

The people—each individual among them—has certain natural rights which cannot justifiably be abridged. In a rational act man has surrendered some of his personal rights to the state, but only in order that his natural rights may better be maintained and defended. The state, Locke argued, must be centered on the will and well-being of the people.[10]

From a review of Locke's contributions to the libertarian theory of a free press, three momentous concepts emerge. First, *humankind is essentially rational and just*. This principle follows upon the third point that Milton used in his argument against licensing. If human beings are allowed free and open discourse, truth will eventually emerge. This is the "self-righting" process of libertarianism; all unjust acts, all falsehoods, all governmen-

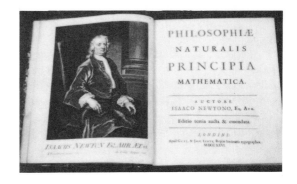

Isaac Newton's *Principia Mathematica* has often been hailed as a cornerstone of the Age of Enlightenment and the symbol of the libertarian quest for Truth—as a rational understanding of the physical universe.

tal abuses will ultimately be discovered and corrected if men and women can openly and freely argue, challenge, and investigate.

Second, *freedom of expression is one of the natural rights of every individual*. Along with the rights to life, to freedom, and to earn and hold property, the right of free speech and printing cannot be denied any citizen.

Third, *government exists only at the pleasure of the people who created it*. This tenet of Locke's is the cornerstone of every free democratic society.

Isaac Newton (1642–1727) The shapers of libertarianism came from many fields. Sir Isaac Newton represents the foremost scientific mind of the period. In fact, if a single date can be pinpointed as the beginning of the Age of Enlightenment, it may very well be 1687, the date of publication of Newton's monumental *Mathematical Principles of Natural Philosophy*. Following upon his pioneering theories and discoveries in calculus, optics, and gravitation, this landmark work in essence set down the laws of the universe.

Newton's great contribution to libertarian development was two-fold. On the one hand, his overwhelming genius was a testimony to Locke's faith in the rationality of the human intellect. Second, Newton made a direct contribution to the libertarian movement by presenting the natural laws of the cosmos as immutable and as comprehensible by human beings. Newton gave us "a new picture of the universe as an orderly machine, timeless, unchanging, running on according to certain discoverable laws of nature."[11] This reinforced the concept of truth as an attainable goal, a set of principles and ideals which can be grasped as long as people are free to experiment, to search, and to debate.

Adam Smith (1723–1790) Building upon the French idea of *laissez-faire,* the economist Adam Smith defined modern capitalism. His classic work, *An Inquiry into the Nature and Causes of the Wealth of Nations* (1776), has long been regarded as one of the most important documents of political economy. His theories, simply and optimistically, stated that the role of government should be kept to a minimum, allowing the free marketplace—the laws of supply and demand—to guide the economic structure. Schramm describes Smith's approach:

Leave the market alone, he said, and it will regulate itself. Thus to Adam Smith, as to Jefferson, the best government is the one that governs least. In the eighteenth century, the central ethic was already coming to be the work-success ethic,

in which man found his own level by the skill and hard work with which he seized opportunities in the free market.[12]

Smith's contributions to the theory of the libertarian press are based, then, upon free enterprise and the profit motive. Let anyone start a press for his or her own economic gain. Let people print whatever they wish. The more presses we have, the better off society will be because there will be more attempts to define truth.

Benjamin Franklin (1706–1790) The seeds of the Enlightenment may have been planted in Europe, but nowhere was the harvest more bountiful than in the American colonies. Philosopher, scientist, printer, diplomat, educator, inventor, author, statesman—Franklin was all of these. And yet, for all of his intellectual prowess, he was also a *doer,* a practical man of action. Apprenticed as a printer at an early age to his older brother, James, Ben soon mastered the newspaper business. Together they wrote and published the *New-England Courant* in Boston, "the first readable and exciting American newspaper." [13]

INSET 2–4 Basic Authoritarian and Libertarian Tenets

	Authoritarianism	*Libertarianism*
Nature of human beings	Dependent, weak, needs guidance	Rational, just, capable of finding truth
Nature of truth	Handed down by authority	Discernable by reason and discourse
Individual/state relationship	State is dominant	State exists only to serve the individual
Leadership selection	Divine selection, heredity, wealth, strength, or wisdom and experience	Decided by the people
Human rights	Granted by the state	Inalienable, natural and undeniable

Benjamin Franklin was a practical printer-scientist-philosopher who typified the colonial libertarian.

At the seasoned age of twenty-three Ben Franklin bought the Philadelphia *Pennsylvania Gazette* and carried on as a crusading publisher. Combining feature stories, well-written news articles, personality sketches, and political essays (modeled after the essays of Joseph Addison and Richard Steele in England), the paper maintained high literary standards and, more importantly, helped to define the role of the libertarian press in Colonial America.

Thomas Jefferson (1743–1826) Whereas the middle-class Franklin was the pragmatic embodiment of the libertarian press, the aristocratic, slave-holding Jefferson was to become perhaps the greatest idealistic defender of the free press. Jefferson stated:

No experiment can be more interesting than what we are now trying, and which we trust will end in establishing the fact, that man may be governed by reason and truth. Our first object should therefore be, to leave open to him all the avenues of truth. The most effectual hitherto found, is the freedom of the press. . . . I hold, therefore, to be certain, that to open the doors of truth, and so fortify the habit of testing everything by reason, are the most effectual manacles we can rivet on the hands of our successors to prevent their manacling the people with their own consent.[14]

And in 1787 he declared: "The basis of our government being the opinion of the people, the very first object should be to keep that right; and were it left to me to decide whether we should have a government without newspapers, or newspapers without a government, I should not hesitate a moment to prefer the latter."[15]

In Jefferson's steadfast defense of the freedom of the press, two libertarian propositions stand out. First, *a free press is needed for the enlightenment of individual citizens in a democracy.* This is the basis for the underlying theme of this chapter. In order for a people to be self-governing—to make responsible decisions and intelligently elect public officials—the people must be well informed. And a free press is the best assurance that people will have access to facts and ideas, that they can hear all sides of every debate, that they

This was a period, you will recall, between the expiration of the Licensing Act (1694) and the John Peter Zenger trial (1735). And, following upon the influential works of Milton and Locke (among many other early libertarians), both printers and government officials were groping for guidelines. No one was sure how much censorship authority was retained by the government or how much freedom of the press could be enjoyed by the newspaper publishers. It was an exciting time, and young Ben Franklin enjoyed being in the thick of it. For example, while his brother James was in jail for an article criticizing the Massachusetts government—and while government harassment continued—sixteen-year-old Ben reprinted some of "Cato's Letters" (see Inset 2–5) in the *Courant*.

can have the opportunity to determine truth and falsehood. In essence, this is Lasswell's "forum" function of the media, "the correlation of the parts of society in responding to the environment" (Section 1.5.1).

The second proposition we can draw from the writings of Jefferson (and many others) is that *the press must serve as a check on the activities of public officialdom*. This corresponds to Lasswell's "watchdog" function, "the surveillance of the environment." In order to guarantee that the government does not overstep its delegated authority, does not get mired down in corruption, does not endanger the personal and natural liberties of the individual citizen, the press must maintain a constant watch on the elected authorities—ready to sound the alarm and arouse the citizenry as necessary.

John Stuart Mill (1806–1873) Writing some two hundred years after Milton, the English economist and political reformer John Stuart Mill argued for freedom of speech on the grounds of utility, not on the grounds of natural rights. According to Mill, the goal of all human conduct is happiness, which he defined as intellectual satisfaction. And the role of government—indeed, the end of all human effort—should be directed toward obtaining the greatest happiness for the greatest number of persons.

This does not mean, however, that the rights of a single individual must be sacrificed to obtain that greater good. On the contrary, Mill eloquently defended the right of every single person *not* to be silenced. In his famous essay *On Liberty* (1859), he wrote, "If all mankind minus one were of one opinion, and only one person were of the contrary opinion, mankind would be no more justified in silencing that one person, than he, if he had the power, would be justified in silencing mankind."[16]

Many other great thinkers of the eighteenth century contributed to the formulation of the libertarian theory of the free press. Philosophers such as *Voltaire (François Marie Arouet)* (1694–1778) and *Jean Jacques Rousseau* (1712–1778) were deists like Franklin and Jefferson who emphasized the natural order and human rationality. *Immanuel Kant* (1724–1804), in his famous *Critique of Pure Reason*, also helped define the limits of science and logic.

John Trenchard (1662–1723) and *Thomas Gordon* (1685?–1750) were two English political writers who, using as a pseudonym the name of the Roman statesman Cato, wrote a series of "Cato's Letters" which provided the American colonies with some of the most popular and readable essays defending freedom of expression.

English jurists such as *William Murray, Lord Mansfield* (1705–1793), and *Sir William Blackstone* (1723–1780) helped to assure freedom of press without prior restraint—although they provided that printers would be subject to post-publication penalties for abusing this freedom by printing material that offended Parliament. *Charles Pratt, Lord Camden* (1714–1794) and *Thomas, Lord Erskine* (1750–1823) argued for a purer libertarian position and applied Locke's philosophy by arguing that the government should not restrict printing either before or after printing.

**INSET 2–5
Other
Libertarian
Thinkers**

2.2.3 CHARACTERISTICS OF LIBERTARIANISM

Summing up the contributions of all the libertarian thinkers, we can divide these broad ideals into six basic elements or concepts.

1. *The world is governed by truth, by certain immutable laws of nature.* Truth is absolute and unchanging. It is not a substance that can be shaped or altered by human manipulation; truth is not to be created or destroyed by a voice of authority. In many instances it may be difficult to ascertain—in which cases we must keep looking, using observation, experimentation, and reason. And the media must be free to assist in this search.

2. *The individual human being is guided by reason.* The philosophies of Locke, Voltaire, Rousseau, and many others all contend that men and women will make rational decisions when they are presented with sufficient data, exposed to all ideas and viewpoints. The human being will rely upon reason to distinguish between fact and falsehood. And eventually, as we use our ability to reason, truth will emerge.

If people are rational beings, then we are also capable—rationally—of improving ourselves. Perfectibility and morality are human traits. The individual, as a matter of natural inclination and rational choice, will try to improve himself or herself. Democracy assumes that we are moral, as well as rational, beings.

3. *A free marketplace of ideas is essential.* Flowing from the first two tenets comes this third concept: If in the pursuit of *truth* we are to use our *reason*, then we must have access to the full range of ideas and opinions of humankind—an open marketplace of ideas. This is the essence of Milton's main point: "Let [Truth] and Falsehood grapple; who ever knew Truth put to the worse in a free and open encounter?" Schramm sums up this basic aspect of libertarianism:

The task of society, then, is to provide a free market place of ideas, so that men may exercise this God-given gift of reason and choice. That is the essence of libertarian theory. The less control by government, the better. In place of more formal controls, libertarianism chose to trust the self-righting process of truth. That implies, of course, a truly free market place. Everyone must have access to the channels of communication. No viewpoints or opinions must be silenced, unless they are truly dangerous to the welfare of the whole group, and even that is hard to prove.[17]

4. *Every individual has certain inalienable rights.* A fourth libertarian concept is that people in a natural (nongoverned) state are completely free and equal and have basic inviolable rights by virtue of their status as human beings. These absolute rights include life, liberty or freedom, and the right to earn and hold property.

By extension, these rights include the right to express oneself—freedom of speech. From Locke to Jefferson, and in the Declaration of Independence and the First Amendment of the Constitution, this right has been considered vital to a free society. It is the essential guarantee that can keep a society open and free.

5. *The government exists solely to serve the interests of the individual.* This fundamental precept, voiced by Locke and supported by every libertarian through Mill, defines the relationship of the citizen and the state. Individual citizens come together voluntarily to form a government to do certain things collectively that they cannot do separately—for example, to provide for a common defense, to establish a system of currency, or to establish mosquito abatement programs. One of the functions of government under this concept is to protect the inalienable rights of each individual. Under this philosophy of a democratic government, the media play a crucial role. Without a free press, there would be no effective check on the powers of the state.

6. *The press under a libertarian system should be a free, competitive enterprise.* An integral part of the libertarian construct is Adam Smith's theory of capitalism, which is built upon a *laissez-faire*, free-enterprise approach.

WHEN in the Course of human events, it becomes necessary for one people to dissolve the political b. with another, and to assume among the powers of the earth, the separate and equal station to which the Laws of Nature and of Nature's G. to the opinions of mankind requires that they should declare the causes which impel them to the separation. We hold these truth: are created equal, that they are endowed by their Creator with certain unalienable Rights, that among these are Life, Liberty and the purs: these rights, Governments are instituted among Men, deriving their just powers from the consent of the governed. That whenever any Form of of these ends, it is the Right of the People to alter or to abolish it, and to institute new Government, laying its foundation on such prin. in such form, as to them shall seem most likely to effect their Safety and Happiness. Prudence, indeed, will dictate that Governments changed for light and transient causes; and accordingly all experience hath shewn, that mankind are more disposed to suffer, while evils a

The Declaration of Independence and the U.S. Constitution with its Bill of Rights define humankind's "unalienable rights" to include freedom of speech.

Let the free marketplace and the laws of supply and demand determine the flow of goods and services.

This economic principle applies directly to mass communication. Media outlets must be owned and operated by individual entrepreneurs competing with one another for the largest possible audience. Thus, the greater the number of printers trying to make a profit, the greater will be the number of voices proclaiming separate versions of truth. The more competition there is among profit-making publishers, the more diversity there will be among media messages. If the press is to be a strong independent voice, it must be a profit-making financial success.

Much of the discussion about freedom of the press in America is based upon the First Amendment to the Constitution of the United States. However, the first ten amendments, which comprise the Bill of Rights, were by no means unanimously welcomed by the framers of the Constitution. The Bill of Rights represents a compromise between the Federalists, such as Alexander Hamilton, who wanted a strong centralized federal government, and the anti-Federalist or Democratic–Republican party headed by Thomas Jefferson. The anti-Federalists, fearful that a strong federal government would undermine the traditional states' authorities and individual rights, insisted on the first ten amendments before ratifying the Constitution.

The First Amendment, which went into effect in 1791, is as follows:

Congress shall make no law respecting an establishment of religion, or prohibiting the free exercise thereof; or abridging the freedom of speech, or of the press; or the right of the people peaceably to assemble, and to petition the Government for a redress of grievances.

INSET 2–6
The First
Amendment to
the Constitution

These six concepts form the underlying tenets of all libertarian thinking—the world is governed by truth, humankind is guided by reason, we must have a free marketplace of ideas, every individual has certain inalienable rights, the government exists solely to serve the individual, and the media are part of a free-enterprise competitive system. They form the basis for our system of mass media in the United States.

2.2.4 THREE "RIGHTS" OF THE PRESS

The story of media development in the United States is, to some extent, the history of increasing freedom of the press, although there have been many setbacks and continual threats along the way. The libertarian cause can be traced through three "rights" that the press has won, at least partially.

The Right to Print William Caxton brought the printing press to England in 1476. However, for more than two centuries printers were prohibited from publishing anything without obtaining approval beforehand—initially from the church and later from the government. For the first half-century or so, such prior restraint could be handled relatively informally as there were few presses operating in the country, and most of them were subsidized by the ruling class.

An increase in the number of presses complicated the picture, however, and in 1534 Henry VIII—in his attempt to grab absolute power—issued an edict ordering all printers to obtain permission from the Crown before setting up their presses. For the next 150 years or so, the struggle for printing freedom is the story of individual printers, in increasing numbers, defying the licensing laws. Despite severe punishment—arrests, smashing of presses—defiant printers continued to publish clandestinely.

The Licensing Act was laid permanently to rest in 1694. Although the practice continued for another two or three decades in the

American colonies, under the authorities of various colonial governors, it could be said that around 1700 publishers had generally won the right to print without prior approval.

However, no right is ever won in perpetuity without constant vigilance. In 1971, for the first time in the history of the United States, an American president succeeded in obtaining a prior restraint order in the "Pentagon Papers" case (Inset 9–2). And in 1979, in an even stronger instance of prior censorship, the government succeeded in obtaining a preliminary injunction in the *Progressive* "H-bomb" case (Inset 9–7). These two cases—both of which involved national security—tend to underscore the point that the rights granted under the First Amendment are not absolute.

The Right to Criticize Winning the right to publish without prior restraint in the early eighteenth century was only part of the libertarian battle. The heavy hand of authority was still active and had ability to prosecute a printer after publication.

In 1690, Benjamin Harris was silenced after one issue of *Publick Occurrences* because he failed to obtain prior permission (Inset 2–1). In 1704, John Campbell was allowed to print the first continuously published weekly paper in the colonies, the *Boston News-Letter*, because he promised never to offend the authorities. But by 1721, James Franklin was publishing his *New-England Courant* in defiance of colonial authority—and going to jail for doing so.

From the 1720s on, the main weapon used by the authorities was prosecution for treason or sedition. The most popular charge was *seditious libel*, which "consisted of scandalizing the government, by reflecting on those who were entrusted with the administration of public affairs, by publishing material tending to breed in the people a dislike of their governors, or by alienating the affections of the people from the government in any way."[18]

This was a favorite indictment because all the government had to do was prove that the printer had, indeed, published something of a critical nature. To the authorities, the mere act of criticizing a government figure was in itself a crime. Indeed, if the criticism was based on factual data, the crime was even more serious because it caused more damage to the authority of the government. The fact that the printer was telling the truth was no defense; it only made the situation worse.

In 1735, however, the jury in the Zenger trial (Inset 2–2) told the authorities that they would consider truth an adequate defense and would not find the defendant guilty of any crime merely for reporting honest facts. Although the threat of prosecution for seditious libel remained on the books, no colonial authority tried to enforce the law after the Zenger decision.

Government harassment continued in various forms, however. Even after the Revolution, the early American government held a tight rein on the press. The Federalist majority in the new Congress managed to pass the repressive Alien and Sedition Acts in 1798 (Section 2.1.3). However, with Jefferson's election in 1800, the acts were allowed to lapse. From the beginning of the nineteenth century on, newspapers and other media have enjoyed the freedom to criticize the government, although they are subject to laws protecting the rights of individuals and the national security (Sections 9.2 and 9.4). Precisely where these rights intrude on the freedom of the press, however, is a continuing regulatory problem.

The Right of Access A third "right" that the press has been fighting to win is the right of access to information, or, as it is sometimes called, the right to report. This is still very much an ongoing battle. Interestingly, although the Constitution and the Bill of Rights provide us with the right of expression (freedom of speech), nowhere is there a constitutional guarantee of the "right to find out."

Shortly after the Republic was founded, several basic avenues of access were opened up. The House of Representatives allowed reporters to cover its sessions in 1789, two days after it formally convened. And the Senate opened its doors to the press in 1795.

Access to many governmental sessions is still severely limited. The press may obtain access to committee meetings only with permission of the committee members (about forty percent of congressional committee sessions are closed to the news media). Reporters are allowed in courtroom proceedings only due to tradition. Although citizens are guaranteed a "speedy and public" trial under the Sixth Amendment, there is no stated right of media access to courtroom proceedings.

Press photographers and broadcast media have encountered special problems in trying to gain access to legislative and judicial proceedings with cameras and recording equipment. Canon 35 (replaced in 1972 with Canon 3A7) of the American Bar Association has long excluded cameras and microphones from the courtroom, although several states have recently been experimenting with recording equipment in court proceedings, generally without any negative results. And in 1979, the House of Representatives initiated routine television coverage of its daily sessions—with the cameras and microphones operated by House staffers—for transmission by the Cable Satellite Public Affairs Network to subscribing cable TV systems throughout the country.

Perhaps the most significant progress in recent years was the passage in 1966 of the Freedom of Information Act. Strengthened in 1974, the act opens to public scrutiny the records of the executive branch of the federal government and its many regulatory agencies. Numerous exemptions, however, tend to weaken the effectiveness of the act (Section 9.1.2). Nevertheless, the act is a major step in gaining access to information.

A companion to the Freedom of Information Act is the "Government in the Sunshine Act," which took effect in 1977. This law requires most major federal boards and agencies to schedule open meetings for the conduct of routine business. All meetings are to be scheduled and announced in advance, and the public must be allowed access to the sessions. (There are special exemptions for justifiable reasons—personnel matters, national security—when meetings can be closed to the public.) Both the Freedom of Information Act and the Sunshine Act represent significant progress in the struggle to guarantee a flow of information. But the libertarian purist would argue that there still is a long way to go.

2.2.5 MEDIA FUNCTIONS OF LIBERTARIANISM

It would be interesting to speculate what would happen if we could bring together the greatest minds of the libertarian doctrine—Milton, Locke, Newton, Smith, Kant, Jefferson, Mill—as in the PBS series *Meeting of the Minds*.[19] One of the most interesting discussions would undoubtedly center on the roles or functions that should be assumed by the mass media in the twentieth century. Drawing upon their various writings, we could probably come up with about six major functions that the media should play in a libertarian society.

1. Dissemination of Information in a Search for Truth The first libertarian function of the mass media would probably be defined generally as public enlightenment. The media provide broad and informal channels of mass education and information distribution, assisting every individual in his or her search for knowledge, truth, specific facts, and general guidelines.

It is no accident that a free press and free public education developed concurrently; they are interdependent, each feeding upon the other. The growth of newspapers in the nineteenth century, as Schramm points out, "was intertwined with the growth of schools and cities and people's governments. . . . [E]arly newspapers in this country tended to appear where there were post offices and to grow as school population grew."[20] Mass circulation of newspapers was fostered by the rise in literacy due to public schooling.

Outside the formal educational systems, the mass press also played a significant role in the general enlightenment of the adult citizen, especially the newly arrived American immigrant. Between 1820 and 1930 about 38 million immigrants, largely non-English speaking, entered the United States. And yet—partly due to the mass media—illiteracy had dropped to eleven percent by 1900, and by 1910 it had been reduced to less than eight percent.

2. Facilitating Self-Government A more specific role of the mass media is to assist in self-government. Democracy demands an enlightened citizenry, which is dependent in turn upon both a widespread educational system and a free press.

Any form of self-government requires that the individual citizen-voters must elect representatives, communicate with those public officials, vote directly on certain issues, participate in public forums, and so on. And the mass media have the crucial responsibility of providing the citizens with the information they need in order to make those decisions. Expanding upon Jefferson's ideals, Brown et al. write,

Democracy places a heavy burden on individual citizens. They must be enlightened in order to govern themselves wisely. The press is an important auxiliary of government as the means of giving citizens the facts and ideas they need for intelligent self-government. . . . [They] must be aware of the problems and issues confronting the state and of their possible solutions and consequences. In a government resting on public opinion, then, the press furnishes the people with the information and ideas they need for making sound decisions.[21]

3. Surveillance of the Government A corollary to the above function is that the media must also assume the "watchdog" role of monitoring the government in order to safeguard our civil liberties. The media should uncover and disclose attempts by dishonest officials to mislead the public as well as inept or misguided governmental actions. An even larger potential danger comes from the natural tendency towards ever-increasing governmental authority—the insidious encroachment upon individual rights caused by the normal empire-building of public officials, the growing bureaucratization and extension of redtape, and the inherent inclination of people to "let George do it."

If the media remain free and independently strong, then there will be that many more competitive voices clamoring for the public attention—that many more voices proclaiming their version of truth. Even if the established press completely ignores any obligation to seek out the truth, the free, competitive marketplace of ideas will assure a balance of facts and opinions.

4. Supporting the Economic System The media provide a vital function in Adam Smith's capitalistic libertarianism by servicing

---

In the text, we discuss the six media functions of libertarianism in a more-or-less descending order from the most utopian (searching for truth and facilitating self-government) to the most mundane (making a profit and providing entertainment). In the model below we have used a different perspective. We have presented the same six functions in a realistic hierarchy, starting with the most basic as a foundation and building up to the more idealistic.

INSET 2–7
Six Libertarian
Media Functions

Gov't
Watchdog

Facilitating
Self-government

Advertising Channels,
Supporting the Economy

Widespread Search for Truth,
Dissemination of Information

Providing Popular Entertainment,
Escapism for the Mass Population

Economic Self-sufficiency, Making a Profit,
Establishing a Financial Base for Operation

the free-enterprise structure through advertising—by bringing together the manufacturer, the seller, and the consumer. By providing advertising channels, the mass media help to maintain a high level of consumption, encourage product variety, and generally keep prices lower through competition.

The media also support the economic system directly by the distribution of business and economic news. One of the earliest functions of the media was that fulfilled by the mercantile press of the seventeenth century, which carried news about commercial ventures, business announcements, trade columns, and the latest merchant shipping information (Section 3.3.1). This important business function continues in contemporary media. Examples include the financial columns in general-interest newspapers and magazines; specialized technical, business, and trade publications and journals; and popular business organs within generalized formats, such as the *Wall Street Journal* and the long-running PBS series *Wall Street Week*.

5. Economic Self-Sufficiency A fifth function of the libertarian media is simply to stay in business—to make a profit. Only if the media channels can remain economically healthy as successful business ventures can they remain independent of outside pressures and thus contribute to the libertarian concept of a free society. The first four functions listed above cannot be carried out unless the media can operate as viable, unfettered voices.

6. Providing Entertainment This function can be seen as a segment of the libertarian construct in at least two ways. First, in a completely free society, each individual should be allowed to seek out whatever diversions and amusements he or she may want. There should be no official censor or arbitrator of taste to tell us what we can and cannot, should and should not, enjoy.

Second, because people turn to the mass media primarily to be entertained, the entertainment function is necessary to guarantee enough of an audience so that the other

functions may be carried out. Even the newspapers draw a substantial portion of their readership from those who turn first to the comics, the sports section, the astrology feature, the gossip column, the crossword puzzle, and other entertainment features. The formats of virtually all media provide for all three communicative purposes—entertainment (escapism), information (reality), and advertising (propaganda). (See Section 1.5.2.) But if the need for entertainment is not met, many popular media would not reach enough receivers to accomplish the other functions. Thus, the fifth role mentioned above (economic self-sufficiency) is dependent upon the sixth function (entertainment); and the first four functions are dependent upon the fifth!

In summary, one could look at the three social functions of Lasswell and find a corresponding role among the libertarian divisions. Lasswell's "teacher" function corresponds to the first libertarian mission, *dissemination of information*; Lasswell's "forum" function certainly corresponds to the second libertarian role, *facilitating self-government*; and Lasswell's "watchdog" function is equivalent to the third libertarian job, *surveillance of the government*. The two remaining libertarian functions, *supporting the economic system* and *economic self-sufficiency*, are facilitating roles beyond those Lasswell had conceived. And the final function, *entertainment*, is added to the others to provide a firm communicative base.

2.3 The Soviet Communist Concept of Mass Media

As stated at the outset of this chapter, both the authoritarian and libertarian philosophies have spawned at least one major variation each that needs to be examined in studying the political Foundations of Mass Communication. The authoritarian offshoot that bears investigation is the Soviet Communist concept.

2.3.1 NATURE OF THE SOVIET COMMUNIST THEORY

Drawing upon some of the ideas of Hegel, Karl Marx (1818–1883) laid the basic foundations for modern "scientific socialism." In collaboration with Friedrich Engels (1820–1895), Marx essentially defined communism both as an historical theory and as a blueprint for the revolution of the working class against the capitalistic state—a revolution that he saw as inevitable. After the workers threw off the yoke of the capitalistic exploiters, Marx believed, they would establish the utopian system of a socialistic classless society.

In theory, Marx saw any state government as a form of oppression and prophesied the dissolution of all state controls. In actuality, the characteristic pattern of all Marxist countries has been a totalitarian bureaucratic dictatorship.

Soviet Truth   In the Soviet communist system, "truth" is of two varieties. The basic Marxist doctrine is immutable and unchallengeable; such concepts as the inevitable class struggle are the authoritarian Word that cannot be questioned. On the other hand, many of Marx's ideas as to implementation of the ideal state are open to interpretation; this accounts, for example, for the differences in governmental structure and ideals among various communist states. This second variety of truth can therefore be changed from nation to nation and from leader to leader. For instance, in both Russia and China there was considerable revision of the offical party version of truth after the deaths of Stalin and Mao. Communist truth—like that in all authoritarian states—is handed down from on high and is subject to redefinition at any time by the authority in control.

2.3.2 MEDIA THEORY IN SOVIET COMMUNISM

Under the Soviet communist concept, all media are owned by the state and operated as part of the state. They are an integral component of the state and party bureaucracy. Schramm sums up this approach:

Soviet mass communication is an *instrument* of the government. All the media are conceived of instrumentally. They are tools to do the work of

Pravda, the official newspaper of the Soviet party, is literally translated as "truth."

the state. Private ownership of the media was therefore no more thinkable than private ownership of heavy industry, which also was a tool to do the work of the state.[22]

Whereas the press in a libertarian state is deliberately encouraged to foster diversity and embrace opposing viewpoints, in the Soviet system the press is designed solely to foster unity—to promote the party line. Without the unifying channels of the press, the communist government could not easily instruct and mold the people. The concepts of press and propaganda become as one. Kenneth E. Olson describes this function of the Soviet media:

The Soviet press . . . has developed a form of journalism totally different from anything in the Western world. News is incidental, for the chief function of papers is to serve as a collective propagandizer, agitator, and organizer for the Communist cause. Stalin spoke of the press as "the transmission belt between the party and the masses," and Khrushchev said, "Just as an army cannot fight without arms so the party cannot carry on its ideologic missions without the efficient and powerful weapon, the press."[23]

The Russian Press This function of serving as a "collective propagandizer" underlies all organs of the Russian press: *Tass,* the official U.S.S.R. news service; *Pravda* ("Truth"), the Soviet party newspaper which serves as the official record of party policies and governmental actions; and *Izvestia,* a newspaper published by the Kremlin with a more popular and less theoretical approach than *Pravda.* In addition to these primary national organs, many ministries of government publish their own newspapers, and each of the fifteen republics throughout the U.S.S.R. has its own regional and local press. Throughout all levels of the Russian media, the function is the same—to interpret the "truth," the party line, for the masses; to provide proper propaganda for the proletariat.

Soviet Communist Theory Contrasted with Authoritarianism One of the clearest ways of understanding the Soviet communist concept of mass media is to contrast it with the authoritarian system. (See Inset 2–8.) The first and most obvious point of difference is *ownership* of the media channels. Under the Soviet communist concept, media are owned and operated directly by the state (or the party); no further regulation is needed. In the authoritarian system, however, the media may be owned by private interests; and the state will rely upon patents and licensing, prior censorship, post-publication prosecution, government subsidization, and government pressure to control the media.

The difference in ownership policy also dictates the basic rationale for the existence of the media. Under the communist system, the media exist purely to help the party control of the masses—they represent "collective propaganda." It is a *planned* system; all media efforts are geared toward the objective of

directing and instructing the people. The media exist *only* to do the state's work. In the authoritarian system, on the other hand, privately owned media channels exist in order *to earn a profit.* Although heavily regulated, the media still are business enterprises. Whereas the Soviet approach results in a planned system, the authoritarian-based press may be called a *controlled* system; it exists not necessarily to do the work of the state, but it is controlled to make sure that it does not work against the state.

This distinction in rationale also results in a difference in outlook or tone. Media in an authoritarian system are controlled with essentially a *negative* approach; they are told what they *cannot* do. The media under a communist regime, on the other hand, are directed with a *positive* viewpoint; they know what they *must* do. Censorship is negative; propaganda is positive.

One final contrast should be noted—the difference in content. The work of the state is serious business. Therefore, under the Soviet system, the business of mass communication is serious. Content is concerned with *reality* (news) and *propaganda.* There is little room for frivolity and entertainment. In the authoritarian state, however, the media— being operated on a profit basis—must attract an audience. Therefore, *entertainment* can be a mainstay of the media system as long as the content of the entertainment does not harm the state in any way.

2.4 The Social Responsibility Concept of Mass Media

Just as the Soviet communist concept was an adaptation of the authoritarian viewpoint, so has the "social responsibility" theory evolved from the libertarian philosophy. It is not so much a distinct concept that has become separate from libertarianism as it is a pragmatic modification of libertarianism, a modification that takes into account some of the realities of the nature of human beings and of democracies today.

2.4.1 DECLINE OF LIBERTARIANISM

During the mid-nineteenth century—even while John Stuart Mill was refining the definition of libertarianism—some of the framework of the concept was beginning to weaken. The idealism of libertarianism was progressively shaken as humankind gained more insights into the laws of the nature, the realities of human behavior, the scope of government, and—especially—the evolution of the free press.

The Laws of Nature Charles Darwin in the late nineteenth century and Albert Einstein in the early 1900s both shook the foundations of Newton's view of the universe as an "orderly machine, timeless, unchanging." The theory of evolution and the theory of relativity both strained the abilities of science to find neatly packaged answers to questions about natural law and the principles which regulate the universe. The laws of nature are not so clearly organized; and the notion of truth may be relative.

The Realities of Human Behavior Just as Darwin and Einstein changed our view of the nature of the universe, so Sigmund Freud changed our view of the nature of men and women. The philosophical, simplistic view of the human animal as a rational being was modified by new theories about our subconscious selves and the strength of our irrational drives and emotions. We have come to question the assumption that every individual is essentially a moral being and that each of us is perfectible. Libertarian faith in human morality and rationality has been severely shaken.

INSET 2–8   Comparison of Four Concepts of the Media

	Authoritarian	*Libertarian*	*Soviet Communist*	*Social Responsibility*
Media ownership	Essentially private Possibly some state	Private	State/Party	Private Some supplemental state-owned
Media control and regulation	Licensing Prior censorship Post-publication prosecution	None	Direct operation	Self-regulation Public pressure Minimal government regulation
Social/Political influence of the media	None, neutral Controlled Media generally defend the status quo	Neutral to negative Not planned Media serve as a check on the government	Positive Media facilitate planned change	Neutral to positive Media are responsible for some controlled change
Basic functions of the media	Profit motive Education News and information Some entertainment	Profit motive Entertainment Education News and information Facilitates self-government Watchdog on government	State education Controlled news Propaganda (Little or no entertainment)	Profit motive Entertainment Education News and information Facilitates self-government Watchdog on government
Responsibility of the individual	Minimal	Extensive	None (Follow instructions)	Moderate

Charles Darwin, with his interpretation of the theory of evolution, and Sigmund Freud, with his insights into the irrational nature of the human subconscious, both contributed to the decline of libertarianism.

Government and Society Early libertarian thinkers could not possibly have foreseen the effects of modern urbanization, techno-logical complexities, and social problems—all of which fostered the need for increasing governmental tinkering with the system in order to prevent economic chaos, widespread inequities, social anarchy, and military inse-curities. And, as society became more com-plex, the individual could no longer function unfettered—in a "natural" state. The individ-ual has become subservient to larger societal units, including government, big business, and labor unions.

Carl Becker, in 1941, summed up the chal-lenges to libertarian philosophies:

What confuses our purposes and defeats our hopes is that the simple concepts upon which the Age of Enlightenment relied with assurance have lost for us their universal and infallible quality. Natural Law turns out to be more than a convenient and temporary hypothesis. Imprescriptible rights have such validity only as prescriptive law confers upon

them. Liberty, once identified with emancipation of the individual from governmental restraint, is now seen to be inseparable from the complex pat-tern of social regulation. Even the sharp, definitive lines of reason and truth are blurred. Reason, we suspect, is a function of the animal organism, and truth no more than the perception of discordant experience pragmatically adjusted for a particular purpose and for the time being.[24]

The Evolution of the Free Press The heaviest blows to the ideals of libertarianism have probably come, however, from the man-ner in which the free press has evolved. Despite the high goals held up for mass com-munication, the media have fallen somewhat short of idealistic performance. Many differ-ent types of criticism have been leveled at the media over the last century or so. Using the term "press" to refer to all media, Theo-dore Peterson, in 1956, summed up the main areas of media criticism:

1. The press has wielded its enormous power for its own ends. The owners have propagated their own opinions, especially in matters of politics and economics, at the expense of opposing views.

2. The press has been subservient to big business and at times has let advertisers control editorial policies and editorial content.

3. The press has resisted social change.

4. The press has often paid more attention to the superficial and sensational in its coverage of current happenings, and its entertainment has often been lacking in substance.

5. The press has endangered public morals.

6. The press has invaded the privacy of individuals without just cause.

7. The press is controlled by one socio-economic class, loosely the "business class," and access to the industry is difficult for the newcomer; therefore, the free and open market of ideas is endangered.[25]

Most of the serious objections to media development over the past century could probably be summed up in three broad categories.

First, the media have simply become *too big,* too centralized; more and more media outlets are controlled by fewer and fewer owners (Chapter 5). According to Schramm, problems developed as the media grew "big and concentrated, hard to enter, and farther removed from the people, so that the self-righting process was less likely to have a chance to work. Minority opinions were less likely to be heard, and there came to be less and less assurance that idea would clash against idea in a free market place."[26]

Second, the media have become controlled almost entirely by *economic interests*—by profit-oriented organizations which are primarily concerned with advertising revenues, circulation figures, broadcast ratings, and sponsor influences, and which identify generally with the interests of big business.

Third, the media are inclined to distort our pictures of reality. News items, background stories, commentaries, and editorials all are supposed to help us deal with reality, to give us valid insights in our search for truth. However, the press has frequently been quick to lead us in one direction or another—intentionally or unintentionally—with little regard for the search for truth. Charles Beard, in 1938, made the observation that freedom of the press as far back as the mid-nineteenth century meant "the right to be just or unjust, partisan or nonpartisan, true or false, in news columns and editorial columns."[27]

2.4.2 CHARACTERISTICS OF THE SOCIAL RESPONSIBILITY CONCEPT

By the turn of the century, then, there was considerable concern in the United States that the press had grown too big for the ordinary person, that the press reacted primarily to economic pressures, and that the press too frequently was distorting the truth for its own ends. As strongly as Americans wanted to cling to the ideals of a libertarian media system, it was becoming apparent that some modifications would have to be made.

The concept which evolved—the "social responsibility" theory—simply recognizes the fact that freedom and responsibility go hand in hand. The media cannot expect to enjoy unlimited freedom without accepting certain responsibilities. According to Siebert, Peterson, and Schramm,

Freedom carries concomitant obligations; and the press, which enjoys a privileged position under the Constitution, is obliged to be responsible to society for carrying out certain essential functions of mass communication in contemporary society. To the extent that the press recognizes its responsibilities and makes them the basis of its operational policies, the libertarian system will satisfy the needs of society. To the extent that the press does not assume its responsibilities, some other agency must see that the essential functions of mass communication are carried out.[28]

As pure libertarian functioning has been impaired by the technological and bureaucratic institutionalization of society, the media must assume more social responsibility for tinkering with the system in order to keep society functioning. A pure libertarian media structure cannot exist in a less than pure libertarian social and governmental structure. Also, as Agee et al., point out, "Concentration of much of the mass media in the hands of a relatively few owners imposes an obligation on them to be socially responsible, to see that all sides of social and political issues are fairly and fully presented so that the public may decide."[29]

Thus, the social responsibility concept is an extension of the libertarian theory in that it adheres to many of the same principles: it supports the same general functions of the media (Inset 2–7), it esteems the dignity of the individual, and it serves as a check on the government. It differs from orthodox libertarianism in that it recognizes that the self-righting process seldom works in our complex society; it replaces the free marketplace of ideas with the acceptance of an obligation to present all sides of an issue as fairly as possible.

2.4.3 EVOLUTION OF THE SOCIAL RESPONSIBILITY CONCEPT

The idea of the social responsibility of the press began to evolve during the latter half of the nineteenth century, when newspaper editors such as Horace Greeley of the *New York Tribune* and Henry Raymond of the *New York Times* rose above the penny press (Section 3.3.2) to conscientiously promote social good and community welfare.

At the turn of the century, Joseph Pulitzer was probably the strongest voice crying out for a clear sense of social responsibility: "Without high ethical ideals a newspaper not only is stripped of its splendid possibilities for public service, but may become a positive danger to the community."[30]

Shortly after the turn of the century, the first journalism education programs were started—at the University of Illinois and the University of Wisconsin. In 1908, at the University of Missouri, the first separate school of journalism was founded. It was followed in four years by the Columbia University School of Journalism. By that time more than thirty colleges and universities were offering journalism training, stressing high

By THE COMMISSION ON FREEDOM OF THE PRESS

A FREE AND RESPONSIBLE PRESS

A General Report on Mass Communication: Newspapers, Radio, Motion Pictures, Magazines, and Books

"If there is ever to be an amelioration of the condition of mankind, philosophers, theologians, legislators, politicians and moralists will find that the regulation of the press is the most difficult, dangerous and important problem they have to resolve. Mankind cannot now be governed without it, nor at present with it." JOHN ADAMS to JAMES LLOYD, February 11, 1815.

THE UNIVERSITY OF CHICAGO PRESS
CHICAGO · ILLINOIS

Although initially rejected by the press, the 1947 Report of the Commission on Freedom of the Press (Hutchins Report) embraced both libertarian and social responsibility concepts.

ideals and professional standards consistent with the social responsibility concept of media.

Industry self-regulation also reflected the press's acceptance of social responsibilities. The national professional association, the American Society of Newspaper Editors (Section 10.1.1), adopted its Canons of Journalism in 1923. These guidelines reflected both libertarian principles and social-responsibility realities, calling for newspapers to serve the public with truthfulness, impartiality, a sense of fair play, decency, respect for individual privacy, and concern for the general welfare.

Finally, mention should be made of the Commission on Freedom of the Press. Established in 1942 and chaired by Robert M. Hutchins, then chancellor of the University of Chicago, the commission issued a rather strong report in 1947. While embracing many of the libertarian ideals of freedom of the press, the report called for a positive commitment to social responsibility by the press. Although many members of the news media reacted negatively to the report (partially because no journalist had been invited to serve on the prestigious twelve-member commission), the report did serve to codify many aspects of press responsibility. It was the document which, as much as any other modern report, served to define and amplify the concept of the social responsibility of the media.

2.5 The Media, the Government, and the Individual

If the Russian, African, and Indian—whom we met at the beginning of this chapter—were asked how much input they had into their respective countries' media systems, they would probably answer, "Not much." They attend to whatever media are presented to them, with few options available. The American, one hopes, would pause before dismissing his relationship with the media. If he did not care for the conservative slant of his *Reader's Digest*, he could get some contrary opinions from *The New Republic* or *The Progressive*. If he wanted a more in-depth, analytical essay, he might try the *Atlantic Monthly*. For up-to-date accounts he has his daily newspapers as well as his subscription to *Time* or *Newsweek*. If he wanted more specific information, he might even send directly to the U.S. Government Printing Office for the latest report. And he has not even turned to his radio or TV set yet.

With grants from Time, Inc., and Encyclopaedia Britannica, Inc., the Commission on Freedom of the Press was established to investigate the current status and future outlook for freedom of the press in the United States. The 1947 report, although not immediately welcomed by the media, provided a coherent statement of the social responsibility of the press.[31] Its five recommendations were as follows:

1. Provide a truthful and intelligent account of the day's news. The media should give a comprehensive report of the current news events "in a context which gives them meaning." This includes separating news and opinion, and providing interpretation when needed.

2. Serve as a forum for the exchange of comment and criticism. The media should provide a means whereby opposing viewpoints and conflicting ideas can be presented.

3. Present an accurate picture of the constituent groups in American society. The media should project a true portrayal of all ethnic, racial, and religious social groups; they should not perpetuate stereotypes. (Section 10.7 deals specifically with this problem.)

4. Circulate and clarify goals and values of society. As educators, media managers should exercise editorial leadership in "stating and clarifying the ideals toward which the community should strive."

5. Gain full access to information. Media should enjoy as much "access to the day's intelligence" as is consistent with national security and rights of privacy. (The Freedom of Information Act and the "Government in the Sunshine Act" were steps toward this goal.)

INSET 2–9
The Commission on Freedom of the Press

Upon reflection, the American would also agree that he does, indeed, have several channels of feedback to the media. He can write letters, cancel subscriptions, ask questions, call editors, and make visits (Section 1.4). Despite the size and complexity of U.S. mass communication operations, the American has more opportunities for media interaction than the people in most other countries in the world.

Not only do you have more alternative media choices—and more opportunities to interact with the media—but you also have the *responsibility* for exercising those options wisely. You have the obligation to seek out contrary viewpoints, collect as much data as you can, and then formulate your own position after a rational analysis of the alternatives.

Receiver Obligations It should be apparent from our discussion in the first four sections of this chapter that under the authoritarian and Soviet communist systems the individual media receiver has little responsibility. Under most *authoritarian* systems it matters little whether or not the receiver pays much attention to the media; the media are essentially apolitical. Under the *Soviet system* the basic responsibility of the receiver is to pay attention and follow orders; the media are used primarily as one-way instructional systems from the state to the individual.

However, within the *libertarian* state, the individual has considerable responsibility. In fact, there is virtually no control except that exercised by the individual. It is entirely up to the media receiver to decide what media to attend to, what messages to receive, and—in the free marketplace of ideas—which version of "truth" to accept. The communication receiver in a libertarian society must adopt the consumer's watch words, *Caveat emptor* ("Let the buyer beware").

Under the *social responsibility* concept, certain obligations are placed on the media

channels—there must be fairness in reporting all sides of a controversy, honesty in advertising, accuracy in investigative journalism, balance in presenting background analysis, social awareness in exerting editorial leadership, and so on. However, this does not lessen the responsibility of the individual receiver to seek out different opinions, receive messages critically, and analyze issues carefully. As society becomes more complex and as our total environment becomes more institutionalized, the need for responsibility is increased on all fronts. The media must exercise more self-regulation, the government must be involved with more controls, and the individual must become more critical and more discriminating as a receiver. Schramm concludes, "Our viewpoint is that the responsibility is shared by government, media, and public."[32]

Media receivers may be either *passive*, consuming whatever media messages happen to be available in the most convenient "low-effort" channels, or *active*, purposefully seeking out those entertainment and information messages that most appropriately meet their needs. The active media receiver—the one who is deliberately selecting and attending to the most meaningful messages—is the one who is most faithfully carrying out his or her obligations under the social-responsibility framework.

2.5.1 RESPONSIBILITIES OF THE INDIVIDUAL

Under the social responsibility concept of the media, there are three identifiable responsibilities that the individual receiver should fulfill.

1. *The receiver must seek out all viewpoints.* You have the obligation to be a discriminating and discerning consumer of media messages by attending to those channels which can best meet your specific needs. The citizen must assume the burden of becoming a well-informed and critical reader/listener/viewer. This means examining all arguments, sifting through all evidence, discarding the irrelevant and untrue, using the media deliberately to collect all the honest data possible.

2. *The individual must make decisions.* Once you have attended to the media critically, you then have the obligation to reach some intelligent conclusions. You must take a stand on issues and be ready to defend your positions. Just reading about the issues and viewing the latest developments is not enough. The responsible citizen must be willing to commit himself or herself on the important questions of our times.

3. *The citizen must act.* Finally, you must turn decisions and convictions into actions. One can contribute to a participatory democracy only if one participates. It is imperative that all free citizens take an active role in the governance of a free society. Vote. Sign petitions. Attend meetings. Speak out. Contact elected officials. Apply pressure wherever possible. Provide feedback to the system. In a modified libertarian political structure such as the United States, citizen involvement and action is mandatory. No freedoms can be guaranteed if the people are not willing to work to preserve those freedoms. Although you may be a minority of one—even if you suspect your opinion may not be entirely correct—you still have an obligation to voice that opinion.

Most American adults spend four to six hours every day interacting with the various mass media. This, by far, is the most pervasive social activity we engage in. It is a responsibility not to be taken lightly.

SUMMARY

We have seen that in *authoritarian* and *Soviet communistic* countries the individual is considered weak and dependent. Truth is relative, revealed only to the leaders, and the state is considered more important than the individual citizen. Under such a political system—especially under communism—the media are considered merely part of the governing system, "the transmission belt between the party and the masses." It is a political structure in which the individual has virtually no responsibility, except to follow orders dispensed through the media.

Under a *libertarian* political philosophy, the individual is presumed to be rational and just, moral and freedom-seeking. Truth can be discerned by intelligent men and women using their powers of reason; the individual is endowed with certain inalienable rights including life, liberty, property, and—by extension—freedom of expression; and the state exists only to serve the interests of the individual. Media systems within such an idealistic political framework are free and unregulated. They represent an open marketplace of ideas wherein every viewpoint and opinion can be expressed. Media channels are privately owned, profit-oriented, and competitive. The basic functions of a libertarian media system are to disseminate information in the search for truth, to enable the populace to be self-governing, to serve as a check on the activities of government, to service the business enterprises of the nation, to remain independent by being a successful financial operation, and to provide entertainment.

Under the *social responsibility* modification of libertarianism, media operations are expected to assume certain social obligations —balance in news reporting, fairness in analyzing issues, leadership in editorial positions, honesty in advertising, concern for the general welfare, and so on. The individual receiver also assumes certain basic responsibilities—to seek out diverse opinions and become well-informed, to reach intelligent decisions, and to actively participate in the governance of society.

In Chapter 3 we will trace some of the historical and technological highlights of print development in the world and, specifically, in the United States.

Notes to Chapter 2

1. Ray Eldon Hiebert, Donald F. Ungurait, and Thomas W. Bohn, *Mass Media II: An Introduction to Modern Communication*, 2nd ed. (New York: Longman, 1979), pp. 39–40.

2. See Fred S. Siebert, Theodore B. Peterson, and Wilbur Schramm, *Four Theories of the Press* (Urbana: University of Illinois, 1956). This work was compiled from earlier papers written by the three authors.

3. John C. Merrill and Ralph L. Lowenstein, *Media, Message, and Men: New Perspectives in Communication*, 2nd ed. (New York: Longman, 1979), pp. 156–157.

4. Wilbur Schramm, *Responsibility in Mass Communication* (New York: Harper & Row, 1957), p. 65.

5. Charlene J. Brown, Trevor R. Brown, and William L. Rivers, *The Media and the People* (New York: Holt, Rinehart and Winston, 1978), pp. 285–286.

6. Quoted in Warren K. Agee, Phillip H. Ault, and Edwin Emery, *Introduction to Mass Communications*, 6th ed. (New York: Harper & Row, 1979), p. 38.

7. Schramm, *Responsibility in Mass Communication*, p. 66.

8. Ibid., p. 72.

9. Peter Gay, *Age of Enlightenment* (New York: Time, Inc., 1966), p. 11.

10. Schramm, *Responsibility in Mass Communication*, p. 70.

11. Brown et al., *The Media and the People*, p. 153.

12. Schramm, *Responsibility in Mass Communication*, p. 68.

13. Agee et al., *Introduction to Mass Communications*, p. 47.

14. A. A. Lipscomb, ed., *The Writings of Thomas Jefferson* (Washington: Thomas Jefferson Memorial Association, 1904), 2: 32–34.

15. Quoted in Agee et al., *Introduction to Mass Communications*, p. 31.

16. John Stuart Mill, *On Liberty* (1859), reprinted in William Ebenstein, *Great Political Thinkers: Plato to the Present*, 3rd ed. (New York: Holt, Rinehart and Winston, 1963), p. 560.

17. Schramm, *Responsibility in Mass Communication*, p. 73.

18. Leonard Levy, ed., *Freedom of the Press from Zenger to Jefferson: Early American Libertarian Theories* (Indianapolis: Bobbs-Merrill, 1966), p. xxxi.

19. *Meeting of the Minds* was a television series in the late 1970s and early 1980s, created by Steve Allen and broadcast over the Public Broadcasting Service, in which great historical figures were hypothetically brought together in a twentieth-century setting to participate in a fictionalized "talk show."

20. Schramm, *Responsibility in Mass Communication*, p. 19.

21. Brown et al., *The Media and the People*, pp. 159, 167.

22. Schramm, *Responsibility in Mass Communication*, p. 81.

23. Kenneth E. Olson, *The History Makers* (Baton Rouge: Louisiana State University Press, 1966), p. 325.

24. Carl L. Becker, *New Liberties for Old* (New Haven: Yale University, 1941), p. 93.

25. Siebert, Peterson, and Schramm, *Four Theories of the Press*, pp. 78–79.

26. Schramm, *Responsibility in Mass Communication*, p. 86.

27. Charles A. Beard, in *St. Louis Post-Dispatch Symposium on Freedom of the Press* (St. Louis, 1938).

28. Siebert, Peterson, and Schramm, *Four Theories of the Press*, p. 74.

29. Agee et al., *Introduction to Mass Communications*, p. 32.

30. Joseph Pulitzer, "The College of Journalism," *North American Review*, 178 (May 1904):667.

31. Commission on Freedom of the Press, *A Free and Responsible Press* (Chicago: University of Chicago Press, 1947).

32. Schramm, *Responsibility in Mass Communication*, p. 8.

Chapters 3 and 4 are concerned with the backgrounds of the various media that all of us attend to daily. How did they develop? How have technological advances altered each medium? How have patterns of distribution evolved?

Although we will be dealing with questions of history, we shall refrain from unrolling a straightforward chronological canvas. However, as a convenient reference tool, the Unit I Appendix (p. 127) does present an intergrated historical time-line which summarizes all of the major dates mentioned in this book.

3

The Print Foundations of Mass Communication

3.1 Parallel Development of the Media

As we look at the evolution of each medium, we will see that there are certain parallel developments which were common to all of the media. According to Merrill and Lowenstein, all media in a country develop in three specific, identifiable stages—a phenomenon they call the "elitist-popular-specialized curve":

In the elitist stage, the media appeal to and are consumed by opinion leaders, primarily. In the popular stage, media appeal to and are consumed primarily by the masses of a nation's population. In the specialized stage, the media appeal to and are consumed by fragmented, specialized segments of the total population.[1]

This parallel development leads to the basic theme of Chapters 3 and 4:

• *Within a given culture, each medium will develop along similar lines, broadly following an elitist-popular-specialist evolutionary pattern.*

As we explore this theme in these two chapters, we will look separately at each of six different mediums—books, newspapers, magazines, motion pictures, radio and audio recordings, and television—although they obviously share many technical and cultural characteristics in common.

In the **elitist** stage, we will of necessity have to consider some technological developments. And in at least one medium—motion pictures—we find that the so-called "elitist" stage really is concerned with the lowest class in the socioeconomic scale.

The **popular** stage can be divided into several distinct periods for some of the media. There was a period of *initial awareness,* when the medium was first thrust upon the public consciousness; a period of *self-regulation,* when the medium undertook to exercise some internal censorship in order to avoid possible government action (Chapter 10); a critical period of popular erosion due to *media competition* from new and emerging media; a period when *chains or syndicates or networks* developed in order to pool content resources; and, in most cases, a period of increasing *group ownership* during which ownership became concentrated in fewer and fewer hands (Chapter 5).

The **specialist** stage occurs, as Merrill and Lowenstein suggest, only after four factors have coalesced—*higher education, affluence, leisure time,* and *population size.* A country can support a fragmented group of specialized audiences when the potential audiences are highly literate in specialized areas, when the audiences have the wealth to finance parallel specialized media, when the members of the audiences have sufficient leisure time to pursue individual interests, and when the total population is large enough to support a number of smaller homogeneous audiences. To date, the United States is the best example of a society in which these factors have evolved sufficiently to allow specialized media to emerge. And in the United States, some media like books, magazines, motion pictures, radio, and audio recordings have obviously developed more clearly specialized patterns than others like newspapers and, especially, television.

Periods of Print History   Another method of outlining the development of the various media is to divide history into categories that are easy to remember. Grouping events and trends into distinct eras or periods is a convenient approach for both the reader and the writer, and it has been employed in the next two chapters. However, you should be aware that arbitrary chronological labels can be somewhat artificial and simplistic. History is always more complex than it appears to be in books. With the exception of an occasional outstanding invention or innovation (for example, the invention of the printing press or the emergence of the "penny press"), few events have dominated their times to the extent that periodic labels suggest.

3.2   Books: From Clay Tablets to Computers

When you turn to a book, you turn to a permanent record. Although the contents of other media may be preserved for archival purposes and historical research (newspaper and magazine microfilm files, audio and videotape recordings, for example), only the book is designed from its inception to be preserved and passed on from one hand to another.

In this sense, perhaps even the ancient Mesopotamian clay tablets could be considered "books." Devised as insurance against the loss of oral transmissions—religious rituals and prayers, magic incantations, tribal and dynasty records, narrative tales and sagas, laws and traditions, medical formulas, and so on—these earliest written records were clearly intended as permanent records.

3.2.1 ANCIENT AND MEDIEVAL BOOKMAKING

Certainly by the time papyrus scrolls were being extensively used, perhaps by 2000 B.C., the art of bookmaking was firmly established. Throughout the ancient world of Egypt,

Greece, and Rome, these delicate scrolls or volumes (from the Latin *volumen,* "roll") were manufactured in standard sizes, copied, collected, stored, purchased, and read much as modern books are today.

Much of the intellectual grandeur of ancient Greece was captured in written documents. The first public library was established in Athens about 540 B.C. A nephew of Plato, Speusippus, compiled the first known encyclopedia about 370 B.C. Soon after, the cultural center of the ancient world shifted to Alexandria and the Great Library, founded about 300 B.C. (see Inset 1–11).

The classical book trade reached its peak in Rome. Papyrus rolls were produced in standard grades and widths. Hand-copying, from oral dictation or from carefully prepared master copies, was a major occupation. Bookselling became a thriving business, with both retail and secondhand stores being concentrated in definite parts of the city. And the

export trade was extensive. Archaeologists have unearthed ancient scrolls—the longest of which exceed a hundred feet in length—which are inscribed not only in Egyptian, Greek, and Latin, but also in Arabic, Hebrew, and Syrian.

With the disintegration of the Roman Empire, the book trade deteriorated substantially. New publications were few; the buying and selling of manuscripts was brought almost to a standstill. The light of the book was considerably dimmed during the Dark Ages.

The Medieval Codex During the early Middle Ages, the awkward scroll was replaced by the *codex*—a stack of folded leaves that was bound along one side and protected by heavy wooden covers. This forerunner of the modern book was superior to the scroll

---

As simplistic and arbitrary as such divisions may be, the following periods have generally been identified and used in discussing the development of each of the print mediums.

**INSET 3–1
Historical Periods
Common to the
Print Media in
America**

General Characteristics	Books	Newspapers	Magazines
Experimentation	The Colonial Era (1650s–1860s)	Colonial and New Republic (1600s–1833)	Colonial Attempts and Failures (1700s–1820s)
Expansion	The Gilded Age (1865–1900)	The Penny Press (1833–1890s)	Early Successful Magazines (1821–1890s)
Exploitation	Commercialization of Literature (1900–1945)	Yellow Journalism (1890s–1920s)	Popularity and Muckraking (1893–1920s)
Responsibility		Objective Journalism (1920s–1950s)	Modern Magazine Publishing (1920s–1960s)
Competition	Publishing Goes Public (1945–Present)	Advocacy Journalism (1950s–Present)	Reaction and Redirection (1960s–Present)

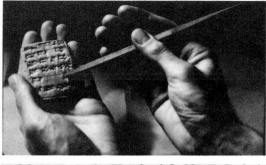

Detail from papyrus scroll, Mediterranean cuneiform, and medieval hand-transcribed page. All were precursors to the modern publishing industry.

because it permitted quick access to information, accurate indexing, and more efficient reference.

At the same time, animal parchment was replacing papyrus as the writing medium. More durable than the brittle papyrus, parchment stood up better to the folding required by the codex. Also, during the first millenium A.D., the Chinese were perfecting and using paper made from tree bark, old rags, hemp waste, and fishnet. The art of papermaking slowly spread through Europe around the twelfth century.

Monasteries and Universities Virtually all of the bookmaking and manuscript-copying activity in the Western world during the Middle Ages was carried on by cloistered clerics in their various monastic orders. Therefore, most of the medieval codex production was centered on works of sacred significance—Bible texts and interpretations, liturgical manuscripts, and the works of philosophers and classical authors whose thoughts contributed to Christian principles.

By about the thirteenth century, however, a secular stirring was felt throughout Europe. There was renewed interest in science and philosophy, a flowering of new languages, the literature of chivalry, and a broadening of popular secular education. The emergence of the new European universities gave rise to an increased book trade reminiscent of that in classical Rome.

During the entire history of bookmaking up to this point—at least three thousand years of laborious handcopying of papyrus, parchment, and paper manuscripts—book production was still in the *elitist* stage. The vast majority of the world's population had no regular contact with the written word.

Codices were reserved for church officials, a handful of scholars and researchers, physicians and lawyers, government bureaucrats, and a few aristocratic noblemen. In fact, it would still be a couple of hundred years before the book would reach the *popular* stage—despite the imminent technological revolution.

3.2.2 THE PRINTING PRESS

From China came the art of papermaking, and probably also the horizontal loom and the spinning wheel. These two devices appeared in Europe during the eleventh and thirteenth centuries, respectively, and made possible the production of large quantities of linen—which, when discarded as worn-out clothing, could be made into high-quality paper. From Western Europe came the wine press, which was eventually converted into the first crude printing press. Block printing—using artistically carved woodcuts—was used in the early fifteenth century for playing cards, textile printing, and religious tracts.[2] Printing inks were originally developed in Egypt, China, and India. The concept of printing with movable type also originated in the Orient.

In the mid-fifteenth century, many Europeans were working on similar approaches for printing multiple copies of a book with movable type. But the credit for pulling it all together usually goes to Johann Gutenberg of Mainz, Germany. He produced a suitable printing ink, improved upon Chinese papermaking, devised a method for casting metal type from a mold, and developed the first practical printing press around 1450. Undoubtedly this achievement was the greatest single technological breakthrough in the history of written communication. Schramm summarizes the impact of the German printer:

Technically what Gutenberg did, and what all the mass media have done since his time, was to put a

Johann Gutenberg is generally credited as being the inventor of the printing press.

machine into the communication process in such a way as to duplicate information and to extend almost indefinitely a person's ability to share it. The communication process was little changed, but because man lives by information this new ability to share it had a profound effect on human life.[3]

The Spread of Printing From Mainz the technology of printing spread rapidly; within thirty years printing presses were at work in almost every country in Europe. Still, printed books remained essentially an elitist means of communication for many decades, being utilized primarily by the clergy, educators, scientists, professionals, and members of the aristocracy. It was during the Reformation that the book first came into popular use. The series of pamphlets written by Martin Luther in the 1520s, for example, awakened many common people to the power of the written word.

3.2.3 DEVELOPMENT OF PRINTING TECHNOLOGY

For about 350 years after Gutenberg's invention, printing technology progressed only slightly. In 1800, paper was still being made by hand, one sheet at a time; type was still set manually; the type forms were slowly inked with leather-covered inking balls; and the actual printing was still accomplished one sheet at a time on a screw-type hand press. The laborious process had improved very little over Gutenberg's ability to print sixty sheets an hour.

Around the beginning of the nineteenth century, however, several developments took place which were to change drastically the tempo and quality of printing in four separate areas: papermaking, printing presses, composing of type, and photoreproduction.

Papermaking Papermakers had long sought to develop a system for producing paper in a continuous roll, instead of painstakingly turning out one sheet at a time. An Englishman, Henry Fourdrinier, perfected the process in 1805. (The name Fourdrinier is still used to

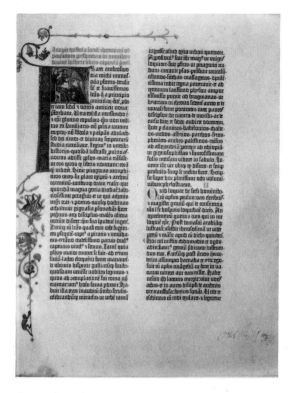

A page from the Gutenberg Bible, printed sometime around 1455.

Johann zum Gensfleisch zur Laden, called "zu Gutenberg," was born about 1397 and died in 1468. By about 1450 he had already demonstrated that printing with movable type was practicable. With substantial financial backing, Gutenberg established what has to be one of the world's first authentic print shops and set about to revolutionize written communication by printing multiple copies of a work with movable metal type set up temporarily in a press.

After several early religious printing jobs, Gutenberg turned out his magnificent Bible—two columns to a page, forty-two lines to a column. Handsomely illustrated and decorated, the Gutenberg Bible was a remarkably sophisticated technical accomplishment. It was completed sometime before 1456.

Forty-seven copies of the Gutenberg Bible are extant in various museums and collections around the world. Of the thirteen copies in the United States, three are printed on a type of fine parchment known as vellum. There is one each in the Library of Congress, the Huntington Library, and the Pierpont Morgan Library.

INSET 3–2
The Gutenberg Bible

The Fourdrinier paperforming machinery of a modern paper mill.

label the paperforming component of the modern paper machine.) With this process, paper could now be formed in rolls to facilitate continuous printing.

But there still was a need to mass produce large quantities of paper inexpensively. Because more and more consumers were purchasing books, newspapers, and magazines in the mid-nineteenth century, the absence of a cheap paper supply threatened to become a bottleneck. The answer was soon found—in the forest. The first patent for manufacturing paper from wood pulp was issued in 1840, and by 1850 chemical processes had been developed to manufacture wood-fiber paper economically.

Printing Presses As books and other printed materials became increasingly popular, there was a drastic need to speed up the printing process. The first major development, in 1798, was the introduction of cast-iron presses to replace the older wooden presses. With improved leverage and precision, these new iron presses were capable of producing 250 to 300 impressions an hour by 1800. Then, in 1827, came the development of the Washington press, which was both lighter and faster. Manufactured by R. Hoe & Company, the major American press builder of the time, the seven different models

of this press became the mainstay of much of the early nineteenth-century printing activity.

The basic design of all these presses dated back to Gutenberg. They were of *platen* construction, wherein a flat bed holding the type is pressed against a flat platen which holds the paper to be imprinted. A faster method of printing was needed, and the answer was found in the *cylinder* press. The cylinder press has a flat printing surface like the platen press, but the paper is continuously fed around a rotating cylinder which rolls the paper into contact with the moving flat bed.

Simultaneously with the introduction of the cylinder press came the application of steam power to the printing process. The first successful steam-driven cylinder press was put into operation in England about 1812 and in America two decades later. This press was capable of turning out approximately 1,100 copies an hour.

Even faster printing speed was achieved with the invention of the *rotary* press. In this system both the impression surface and the printing surface are on cylinders which rotate against each other at fast speeds. The rotary

The iron press replaced the Gutenberg wooden press around 1800.

press is ordinarily used only for high-volume, high-speed printing operations. In 1846, R. Hoe & Company introduced the Hoe Type Revolving Machine, the forerunner of the early rotary press. And in 1865, William Bullock of Philadelphia devised the first rotary press to print with a continuous roll of paper. With further improvements and greater efficiency, these machines were capable of printing tens of thousands of copies per hour by the turn of the century.

Composing of Type The next bottleneck in the printing process was the composing of type—setting the actual type into the printing plates. The first attempt to replace the slow hand-typesetting process was the Chadwick Typesetter of about 1775. This mechanical apparatus could physically assemble precast founders' type, cutting the typesetting operation to about a third of the time it took to do the job by hand.

INSET 3–3   Three Basic Types of Letterpress Printing Operations

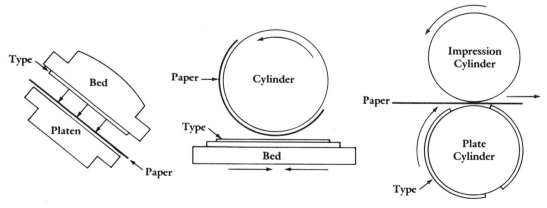

Platen The paper to be printed is held on a flat impression surface or platen. The flat bed holds the inked type which is pressed against the paper.

Cylinder The paper is fed around a moving cylinder and pressed against the inked printing bed, holding the type, which slides back and forth as it comes into contact with the cylinder.

Rotary The paper is fed between the cylindrical impression surface and the inked printing cylinder, which holds the type on a curved surface, as the cylinders rotate against each other.

Variations of this mechanical process were employed until 1884, when Ottmar Mergenthaler unveiled the *Linotype*. This typesetting equipment used molten type metal to cast each line into a new, ready-to-print "slug" (as opposed to the Chadwick Typesetter, which used the original precast pieces of type for the actual printing). Variations and improvements upon the Linotype included the *Monotype* (which uses an automated punched-paper system to cast individual type) in 1897 and the *Intertype* (which was built upon expired Linotype patents) in 1913.

Phototypesetting and "impact" typesetting machines (the Vari-Typer, IBM Electric Executive, and similar units) were developed in the twentieth century to give increased flexibility to the entire typesetting operation (Section 12.1).

Linotype "slugs" of type ready for the printing press.

Several distinct types of printing processes have evolved through the centuries. These can be categorized as follows:

INSET 3—4
Printing Processes

Letterpress   In this "relief" process, the type or image to be printed is raised above the surface of the printing plate. Cast type, line engravings, and halftone etchings may be used in any combination. Letterpress printing has been the basic printing technique, from pre-Gutenberg woodblocks to the bulk of printing today.

Lithography   Also called planography, offset, photo-offset, and photolith, this process was first developed around 1798. The image to be printed was reproduced originally on the lithographic stone or presently on a flexible plate in a greasy medium which will hold the printing ink. The rest of the printing plate is moistened with water. When the printing ink is applied, the ink washes off all areas except those treated to receive it.

Intaglio   This process is the exact opposite of relief letterpress. The type or design to be printed is below the printing surface. The ink is then transferred from these subsurface areas to the paper by capillary action. The primary example of intaglio is rotogravure printing.

Stencil   In this familiar process, the area to be printed is cut out of a master stencil, and ink is then forced through the openings onto the paper. Silk-screening and mimeographing are both stencil processes.

Xerography   Not, strictly speaking, a traditional printing process, "xeroprinting" rivals conventional press printing for inexpensive, rapid reproduction of limited-copy runs. Invented in 1937, it is basically an electrostatic reproduction process which uses electrically charged plates, paper, and fine ink powder to reproduce images photographically.

Modern typesetting is accomplished by an electronic composer or other computer-based system which uses a video-display terminal (VDT) to show the information that is used to control the photocomposition.

Photoreproduction Experiments with reproducing and printing photographs go back to the 1820s. It was not until fifty years later, however, with the development of the halftone screening process, that photoengraving became a practical printing procedure.

About the same time, around 1800, the art of *photogravure* was developed. Whereas photoengraving uses a relief letterpress printing process (with the material to be printed raised above the level of the printing plate), photogravure uses an intaglio or subsurface process (with the design to be printed sunken into the printing plate and the printing ink deposited in these depressions).

Other developments of the late nineteenth century included the mechanization of bookbinding, the introduction of cloth binding, the perfection of stereotyping for making curved type impressions on papier maché matrices for the rotary press, color printing, and improvements in the lithography or offset printing process. The twentieth century would see many more improvements in high-speed printing, computer-based typesetting, and other scientific feats (Section 12.1), but by the end of the 1890s the modern book publishing trade had been firmly established on a solid technological base.

3.2.4 BOOK–PUBLISHING TRENDS IN FICTION AND NONFICTION

Narrative fiction is as old as the story of humankind itself. Ancient literature, including some Egyptian works which date back to 2000 B.C., entertained readers with tales of the fantastic, magicians' wonders, romantic adventures, and epic battles. Although religious and educational works dominated the book business for centuries, narrative fiction has always played a significant role—from the Greek and Roman epics of Homer and Virgil, the medieval romances, and the Renaissance novel to the modern novels of the seventeenth century onward.

Charles Madison divides American book publishing into four eras.[4] The evolution of the medium through its elitist, popular, and specialist stages can be traced in these eras.

The Colonial Era In the first period, from the mid-seventeenth century to about the Civil War, books were still a relatively elitist medium. Publishers were few, and they tended to be aristocratic and well educated. Printing technology was only slowly emerging from its Gutenberg heritage; books were scarce and expensive to obtain, costing up to a dollar a copy—one day's pay at that time. And the populace was just starting to take advantage of free public education by the middle of the nineteenth century.

The Gilded Age The second identifiable period of the American book extended from 1865 to 1900. Modern technology—especially the cylinder and rotary presses and the plentiful supply of wood-pulp paper—opened the way to mass production of the inexpensive novel. The "dime" novel, which had first appeared around 1840, was now plentiful. The book had clearly arrived at its popular stage.

This era was ushered in by mid-century literary accomplishments such as Nathaniel Hawthorne's *The Scarlet Letter* and Herman Melville's *Moby Dick*. And the social impact of Harriet Beecher Stowe's *Uncle Tom's Cabin* helped to establish the novel as a powerful persuasive medium. The post-Civil War period was dominated by such authors as Mark Twain, William Dean Howells, and Henry James. However, perhaps the most commercially successful of all nineteenth-century writers was Horatio Alger. During the last third of the century, he penned some 135 titles—all following a similar rags-to-riches plot built on the success story of the poor but pious, hard-working, and intelligent young boy who makes it to the top by virtue of his virtue.

This era also saw the flowering of the public library. Benjamin Franklin established the first subscription library in Philadelphia in the late eighteenth century, and the first public library was started in 1833 in Peterborough, New Hampshire. However, it was not until the last half of the nineteenth century that public libraries really became widespread. The free public library is a remarkable and unique institution. Without it, popular dissemination of the book never could have been successfully accomplished.

The Commercialization of Literature The third era identified by Madison, from 1900 to 1945, saw the continued rise of the popular book. Upton Sinclair's *The Jungle* (1906), which exposed the intolerable working conditions of the meat-packing industry, and John Steinbeck's *The Grapes of Wrath* (1939), which dramatized the plight of those trying to flee the Depression, were but two examples of the many novels which served to raise the social consciousness of the reading public.

This period also saw the rise of the motion picture as a powerful popular medium. The movies undermined the narrative monopoly enjoyed by the book. No longer was the novel the unchallenged medium for the longer fiction format. From the 1930s on, the printed page would have to share story-telling honors with the silver screen.

Publishing Goes Public Madison's last stage covers the period from 1945 to the present. During this period, the ratio of literary works—fiction, biography, poetry, and drama—slipped drastically compared to nonliterary works—textbooks, professional

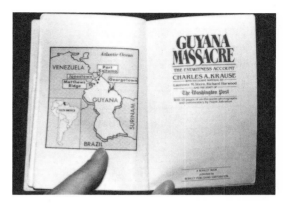

The modern "instant book" often can be printed and rushed to retail outlets within days after an actual event.

books, reference books, "self-help" and "do-it-yourself" guides, cookbooks, and so on. Curtis Benjamin points out,

In the early years of the century, newly published literary works outnumbered nonliterary works by two to one. Then, starting with the 1930s, there came a change in this imbalance; the production of literary works declined, while that of nonliterary works increased in proportion. . . .

Then came the 1960s and the spectacular leap ahead in the production of nonliterary works. . . . [A]nd by 1969 new nonliterary works outnumbered new literary works by more than two to one.[5]

Content has changed in other ways. The advent of the so-called instant book has provided the other news media with more competition. Some official documents and reports have been issued directly as paperback works, such as the Warren Commission Report on the assassination of John F. Kennedy and the 1967 Carnegie Commission Report on public broadcasting. Instant paperbacks also have appeared on dramatic historical events; after the Israeli Army's daring and successful raid on the Entebbe airport in 1976 to free hostages, three books were written and printed and distributed within thirty days. And one book based on the amazing victory of the U.S. hockey team in the 1980 Winter Olympics was compiled and printed within two days.

Books have been used more frequently to present background news and interpretation. Examples include the "new journalism" approach of Truman Capote in *In Cold Blood* (Section 3.3.5) and "muckraking" investigative works like Bob Woodward and Carl Bernstein's *All the President's Men*. Earlier in the century, such works would have appeared in a serialized magazine format.

The concept of the book has also been changed by packaging and marketing techniques. The paperback, introduced more than a century ago, enjoyed a major revival in the 1940s and 1950s and now accounts for about one-sixth of all book sales. Marketing through book clubs makes up another ten percent of all sales.

3.2.5 THE FUTURE OF THE BOOK

As a work of art, the book has always earned considerable respect. The earliest scrolls and codices were richly decorated and illustrated. The elaborate woodblock printing and color engraving of Renaissance works are unmatched for their beauty. Although the less expensive paperbacks (starting with the nineteenth-century dime novels) tended to cheapen the image of the mass book, there have always been those who appreciate good contemporary printing jobs. Improvements in quality printing, color rendition, and photographic reproduction have given the modern "coffee table" picture books a deserved place of honor and permanence.

Although computer tape and microimage storage techniques will undoubtedly fulfill many of our future needs for information handling and processing, the book can never be replaced. Lehmann-Haupt reverently sums up the special qualities that are offered by the medium of the book:

In some quarters the future of the book as a vital and indispensable form of communication has been seriously questioned. Other media, especially computers in their capacity as "information storage and retrieval" devices, are looked upon by some as a future substitute for books. . . . These prophecies fail to take into account that books also transmit spiritual values and ideas, that there is a special magic in the written word of poetry, drama, and fiction, and they ignore the beauty of the book as a work of art in itself.[6]

3.3 Newspapers: The Daily Press of Reality

When you unfold the morning edition of your local newspaper, you are responding to an urge as old as humanity itself—the instinctive urge to find out what is going on. Even Thoreau derisively acknowledges the human quest for news and gossip:

Hardly a man takes a half-hour's nap after dinner, but when he wakes he holds up his head and asks, "What's the news?" As if the rest of mankind had stood his sentinels. . . . After a night's sleep the news is as indispensable as the breakfast. "Pray tell me anything new that has happened to a man anywhere on this globe,"—and he reads it over his coffee and rolls, that a man has had his eyes gouged out this morning on the Wachito River. . . .[7]

Government activities, economic problems, rumors of war, neighborhood gossip—we must have it all. Throughout the ages, people have devised many systems for spreading and transmitting the news—African drums, Indian smoke signals, Alexander the Great's torch beacons, the ballad singers and town criers of the Renaissance, the coffee houses of the sixteenth century, and the Chinese poster wall.

The Written Newsletter The heritage of the written newspaper can be traced back at least to 59 B.C., when the Roman government posted official public news sheets called *Acta Diurna* ("daily acts"). In the early seventeenth century, the first regular weekly "newspapers" appeared in several German cities. Occasionally hand-printed and usually just a one-sided broadsheet, these prototype newsletters gradually spread throughout Europe.

The *London Gazette,* started in 1665 as the *Oxford Gazette,* was published as the official organ of the government and was the first real, regularly scheduled English-language newspaper. The *London Daily Courant* began publishing as the first daily newspaper in the country in 1702, eight years after the Licensing Act permanently expired (Section 2.1.3).

Meanwhile, over in the colonies, the early American printers were not faring so well. Partly because they did not enjoy the full privileges of British citizenship, the colonial printers lagged behind their English counterparts in gaining press freedom. *Publick Occurrences* (1690) failed after one issue, and the *Boston News-Letter* (1704) was allowed to publish only because its owner promised not to offend the governor (Section 2.1.3).

3.3.1 THE COLONIAL AND EARLY REPUBLIC PRESS (1600s–1833)

During this early period the colonial press took two distinct forms, the *mercantile paper* and the *political pamphlet*. The earliest mercantile press was aimed at a very elite audience of merchants, shippers, and bankers. Sold on a subscription basis (there were no newsstands), these papers typically had circulations of less than a thousand each. The content of the mercantile press consisted largely of market information, commercial notices, ships' arrivals and departures, import and export news, and, of course, mercantile advertising.

However, as resentment against the British Crown grew, colonial editor-printers could not help becoming embroiled in the political controversies of the time. Emboldened by the 1735 Zenger decision (Inset 2–2), American publishers became more outspoken in their rebellion against second-class colonial citizenship. It is no coincidence that many of the prominent names of the American Revolution were associated directly or indirectly with the press: John Adams, Samuel Adams, John Dickinson, Benjamin Franklin, Thomas Jefferson, Richard Henry Lee, and Thomas Paine, among others.

Such political writings represented the second type of early American publication, the political pamphlet. Some pamphlets were written to be printed in the newspapers; others were distributed on the streets as separate political tracts. All of these pamphlets—from John Dickinson's moderate "Letters from a Farmer in Pennsylvania" (1767–68) to Thomas Paine's fiery "Common Sense" (1776)—played a crucial role in stirring up the populace for the coming War of Independence.

The Post-Revolutionary Press   After the Revolution, the press continued to play an important political role. As the new republic split into the Federalists (led by Alexander Hamilton) and the Republican Anti-Federalists (led by Thomas Jefferson), the press also lined up on the two sides. Carrying the idea of a partisan press one step further, the Federalists directly subsidized a number of newspapers which became, in effect, party organs: John Fenno's *Gazette of the United States,* William Coleman's *New York Evening Post,* Noah Webster's *American Minerva,* and William Cobbett's *Porcupine's Gazette.* Not to be outdone, Jefferson replied with his own party organs, such as Philip Freneau's *National Gazette,* Samuel Harrison Smith's *National Intelligencer,* and Benjamin Franklin Bache's *Aurora.* It was partly a desire to silence these Anti-Federalists that led the Federalist Congress to pass the short-lived Alien and Sedition Acts in 1798 (Section 2.1.3).

In the early 1800s, then, the new nation's publishers merged the contents of the mercantile commercial newsletter and the political pamphlet to form the prototype of the

American newspaper. But this paper was still aimed primarily at a rather select, elite audience of politically aware citizens and concerned merchants.

3.3.2 THE PENNY PRESS: A TRUE MASS MEDIUM (1833–1890s)

As mentioned earlier, dividing any historical subject into distinct periods is often an arbitrary and imprecise operation; history seldom lends itself to neat compartmentalization. However, occasionally there is an event of such obvious impact that it is possible to say with certainty, "Here we enter a new era."

Benjamin Day and the *New York Sun*
On September 3, 1833, Benjamin H. Day launched a new daily paper, the *New York Sun,* which was totally novel in its approach. Instead of aiming for sophisticated readers who could pay the customary six cents a copy, Day published his paper for the urbanized masses—the industrial workers, the immigrants, the newly literate readers. Pricing his four-page paper at *one cent a copy,* he hired newsboys to go out and hawk the paper on the streets. To appeal to the masses, the *Sun* concentrated on news of local crimes and accidents, human interest, murders, fires, trials, executions, and other sensationalistic items.

Day's formula of combining editorial popularity, mass circulation, and advertising produced a truly popular newspaper—the first actual mass medium. Starting with a hand press that turned out 250 copies an hour, Day was able to achieve a circulation of 10,000 by the end of the *Sun's* first year. Five years later, after Day acquired two Napier double-cylinder presses capable of printing 4,000 sheets an hour, the paper's circulation was exceeding 30,000 daily.

James Gordon Bennett and the *New York Herald*   Success spurs competition, and in 1835 James Gordon Bennett (like Day, a printer) started the *New York Herald.*

Bennett actually could be called more appropriately the man who made news into a readily salable consumer commodity. . . . His was the first paper to "cover" a city, to send reporters to Wall Street, to the churches, to society events, and especially to the courts, which yielded rich returns in human waywardness and wretchedness. Bennett further spiced the paper with stunts and occasional hoaxes. His innovations shocked traditionalists, but his was the most widely read paper in America at that time.[8]

Horace Greeley and the *New York Tribune*   Many other mass-appeal penny newspapers were soon following in the wake of the *Sun* and the *Herald.* One of the most significant was the *New York Tribune,* started by Horace Greeley in 1841. Concentrating on editorial leadership, Greeley hired others to manage the business side of the paper, thus foreshadowing the structure of the modern newspaper. Using his editorial columns to make his influence felt throughout the land, Greeley became one of the most powerful editorial writers of the nineteenth century.

Henry J. Raymond and the *New York Times*   Following Greeley by ten years, Henry J. Raymond founded the *New York Times* in 1851. Inspired by the *Times* of London, Raymond concentrated on news interpretation and background reporting, developing a strong editorial policy. He personally accompanied presidential candidates so that he could write first-hand campaign stories, and he hired European correspondents to cover foreign stories exclusively for the *Times.*

Press Associations and Syndicates   During this era it became apparent to struggling newspaper editors that effort and expense could be avoided if the papers were to pool some resources and settle for joint coverage of certain activities and events. The first such cooperative endeavor occurred in 1848, when six New York papers formed the Harbor News Association to meet large merchant vessels while they were still at sea; it was more efficient to send one boat to gather the incoming news than for the six papers to send out six competing boats. The first press association or wire service, which later became the Associated Press, also pooled telegraph services from Boston and Washington.

Following the Civil War, one other major form of cooperative endeavor was initiated. In 1865 Ansel Nash Kellogg began the earliest independent newspaper syndicate, supply-

ing features to rural papers in the Middle West. Then, in 1884, Samuel S. McClure started the first large-scale newspaper syndicate to furnish non-news features and entertainment material to participating newspapers, concentrating initially on women's features and the serialization of popular novels. Syndicated material today

---

The worlds of politics and the press always have been, and always will be, thoroughly intertwined—especially in a modified libertarian society. From Jefferson and Franklin through the partisan papers of the nineteenth century and into the twentieth century, many of the nation's leading editors and publishers have become directly involved in the politics of the country.

When Horace Greeley launched the *New York Tribune* in 1841, his forceful editorials—logical, eloquent, persuasive, and idealistic—championed educational and social reforms, economic conservatism, and the fortunes of the Whig Party. He later broke with the Whigs, helped to form the Republican Party, worked for Abraham Lincoln's nomination in 1860, and helped to shape the Republican platform. After a decade of political equivocation, he ran for the presidency in 1872 on the ticket of the Liberal Republicans.

Joseph Medill, who owned and edited the *Chicago Tribune* for forty-five years (1855–1899), maintained that paper as the nation's most openly partisan organ for the Republican Party. Claiming credit for engineering Lincoln's nomination in 1860, Medill was always active in national and Illinois politics. He served as the mayor of Chicago during the 1870s.

Joseph Pulitzer immigrated to the United States when he was seventeen years old. Five years later, in 1869, he was elected to the Missouri state legislature. After bringing the *St. Louis Post-Dispatch* into national prominence, he moved to New York, purchased the *New York World,* and in 1885 was elected to the U.S. Congress as a representative from New York. Failing health and poor eyesight forced him to resign, however, and he concentrated his efforts on directing the policies of his newspaper empire.

William Randolph Hearst, however, was probably the most politically ambitious journalist of the last century. Backed by the millions of his family's fortune and by the popularity of his *New York Journal,* Hearst served as a congressman from New York from 1903 to 1907 and fought a spirited battle for the Democratic presidential nomination in 1904. After failing in his attempts to become mayor of New York city in 1905 and governor in 1906, he used his enormous wealth and journalistic influence to exercise his power behind the scenes. He is sometimes credited with securing the Democratic nomination for Franklin Roosevelt in 1932.

**INSET 3–5
Politicians and
Publishers**

includes comics, editorial cartoons, columnists, humor material, puzzles, and the like.

Near the end of the century, newspapers had evolved into quite a massive media enterprise. With rotary presses driven first by steam and later by electricity, a publisher could print close to 100,000 copies of a twelve-page newspaper in one hour. The half-tone photoengraving process was perfected in the 1880s, and newspaper and magazine photos were commonplace soon thereafter. Fast-drying inks and automatic devices for cutting, folding, and bundling papers also increased the output.

3.3.3 YELLOW JOURNALISM (1890s–1920s)

Shortly before the turn of the century, it was obvious that the newspaper had entered another period of its evolution—a curious blend of sensationalism at its worst and crusading journalism at its best.

Joseph Pulitzer The Hungarian immigrant Joseph Pulitzer purchased the *New York World* in 1883. Typical of the competitive times, the *World* maintained a "front page of crime, sex, scandal, and corruption."[9] However, this sensationalistic façade did not hide Pulitzer's strong crusading spirit. His challenging editorials continually called for a fight against injustice. He was particularly concerned with the plight of the hundreds of thousands of his fellow immigrants, who were the victims of discrimination, poverty, ignorance, and crowded slum conditions. Pulitzer maintained that the newspaper should be

an institution that should always fight for progress and reform, never tolerate injustice or corruption, always fight demagogues of all parties, always oppose privileged classes and public plunderers, never lack sympathy with the poor, always remain devoted to the public welfare, never be satisfied with merely printing news, always be drastically

independent, never be afraid to attack wrong, whether by predatory plutocracy or predatory poverty.[10]

Despite his high ideals, Pulitzer allowed himself to be dragged into a degrading circulation battle with the wealthy editor of the *New York Journal,* William Randolph Hearst.

William Randolph Hearst With his family's mining fortune as backing, William Randolph Hearst built up the *San Francisco Examiner* and then, in 1895, purchased the *New York Journal*. At that point Pulitzer's *World* had the largest circulation of any paper in the country, and Hearst was determined to best him. Hearst, however, lacked Pulitzer's sense of idealism. "Hearst did not blink at coloring, stealing, or even faking the news; he did not hesitate to appeal to jingoism and a variety of other cheap emotions; and the tone of discourse in his papers often fell to mere abuse."[11]

In the ensuing circulation battle—during which the two papers sometimes succeeded in selling a million copies a day—both publishers resorted to the heavy excesses which characterized "yellow journalism." These included lurid headlines (occasionally occupying half of the front page), intensive coverage of crime, sex, and violence, sensationalistic photojournalism, and fantastic promotional stunts. Hearst was even accused of fomenting the dissension which led to the Spanish-American War. Pulitzer eventually lost his appetite for this kind of gross competition and withdrew from the contest, leaving Hearst to rule as the lord of "yellow journalism" for another two decades.

In the meantime, Edward Scripps and his brothers were building the first successful chain of newspapers in the country. At one point, they had controlling interest in more than thirty papers. Scripps also founded the Newspaper Enterprise Association (NEA) syndicate in 1902 and the United Press wire service in 1907. Hearst built up a similar empire. The Hearst chain of newspapers included papers in Chicago, Boston, Los Angeles, and many other major cities. By 1915 Hearst also controlled four different

BROWN BROTHERS

BROWN BROTHERS

William Randolph Hearst (left) and Joseph Pulitzer (right) both founded their newspaper empires during the sensationalistic period of Yellow Journalism.

In the early 1890s, continuing cartoon characters had already appeared in several papers. But the modern comic strip had its real beginning in 1895. Richard F. Outcault, already a nationally known cartoonist, created a cartoon strip entitled "Down Hogan's Alley" for Joseph Pulitzer's *New York World*. Dealing with the problems of recent immigrants living in the New York tenements, the comic strip was an instant success. Pulitzer further enhanced the appeal of the strip by using a yellow tint to color the sacklike garment worn by the young ragamuffin who was the central character of the cartoons.

Determined to beat Pulitzer in the circulation battle that he had entered, William Randolph Hearst resorted to the competitive weapon that he understood best—money. In 1896, Hearst lured Outcault to the *Journal,* and Outcault's yellow kid of "Hogan's Alley" became the kingpin of Hearst's expanded colored comics section. Pulitzer fought back by hiring another cartoonist, George B. Luks, to continue the "Yellow Kid" for the *World*.

In the ensuing circulation battle, each newspaper heavily promoted its own version of the "Yellow Kid." The publicity war only served to underscore the demeaning tactics that each paper was using in its attempt to be more sensational than its competitor. Thoughtful critics, in condemning the excesses of the two newspaper giants, used the symbol of the "Yellow Kid" in denouncing the entire phenomenon of sensationalism in the press as "yellow journalism."

syndicates (which were merged in 1931 as the King Features Syndicate); the International News Service (INS) press association; and numerous magazines including *Cosmopolitan, Good Housekeeping,* and *Harper's Bazaar.*

3.3.4 OBJECTIVE JOURNALISM (1920s–1950s)

Not all journalists were swept up in the "yellow journalism" rush to greater circulation. A countertrend of objectivity was kept alive by many responsible journalists. Primary among them was Adolph Ochs. Ochs purchased the *New York Times* in 1896, rescuing the faltering paper from bankruptcy. Determined to build the *Times* into *the* "newspaper of record," he guided it for forty years, gaining the paper worldwide respect for its comprehensive, accurate, and balanced news coverage.

There was also a growing sense of professionalism among newspapermen shortly after the turn of the century. The first schools of journalism were founded around 1910, the Columbia University Graduate School of Journalism being established with a bequest from Joseph Pulitzer. (See Section 2.4.3.) In the 1920s the newly formed American Society of Newspaper Editors stressed the necessity for a balanced and responsible press. This is one of the first instances of any of the mass media being concerned with some degree of self-regulation.

3.3.5 "ADVOCACY" JOURNALISM (1950s TO THE PRESENT)

Finally, during recent decades, several distinct trends have emerged as elements of the press have swing back to a less objective position. These trends might be collectively labeled "advocacy" or "subjective" journalism.

INSET 3–7
Jazz
Journalism

During any designated historical period, countertrends and remnants of previous periods are evident. Thus, during the period of Objective Journalism, strong elements of sensationalism were revitalized under the banner of "jazz journalism"—appropriately labeled for the Jazz Age of the 1920s.

Breaking with family tradition, Joseph Medill Patterson (the grandson of Joseph Medill and co-editor of the *Chicago Tribune* for a period) in 1919 founded the *New York Illustrated Daily News.* Sensing that New York was ready for a sensationalistic alternative to the staid *New York Times,* Patterson stressed the spicy sex, crime, and violence formula which had proved so successful for Hearst twenty-five years earlier. Patterson added two new elements, however. First, he used the *tabloid* format, which is approximately half the page size of the standard paper; this made the paper more convenient to handle, easier to read on the subway, and quicker to sell on the street corner. Second, Patterson made heavy use of *photographs,* often covering most of the front page with one or two pictures.

These elements succeeded in attracting a completely new class of reader, and by 1924 the *Daily News* (having dropped the "Illustrated" from its title) was the best-selling newspaper in the country—a position it still holds. Many other papers adopted the "jazz journalism" format, and today several national papers such as the *National Enquirer* and *The Star* carry on the same sensationalistic style.

Activist Journalism "The journalistic activist believes he has a right (indeed an obligation) to become personally and emotionally involved in the events of the day. He believes he should proclaim his beliefs if he wishes, and that it is not permissible but desirable for him to cover the news from the viewpoint of his own intellectual commitment."[12] The "truth-as-I-see-it" reporter is more concerned with revealing the "essence" of the truth than with accurate reporting of the "facts," which, according to this view, can be misleading.

Muckraking Investigative reporters came into their own around the turn of the century, concurrent with the crusading zeal of Pulitzer and Hearst. Theodore Roosevelt used the term "muckraking" in reference to the man with the rake in *The Pilgrim's Progress* who continued to rake the filth and muck rather than look up and see the celestial glory. Tar-

gets for the muckrakers of 1900 to 1920 included graft and corruption in city governments, monopolistic abuses of the oil and railroad industries, fraud in advertising and manufacturing, and similar topics.

Starting in the 1960s, investigative reporting enjoyed a resurgence. A 1969 *Time* magazine article relates investigative journalism to a need for periodic soul-searching: "For reasons that seem to be rooted in the public mood, muckraking is a cyclic form of journalism. If a society is troubled, it suspects that something is wrong with its system or its leadership; a free press responds by finding out what that is."[13] Among the many recent examples are Bob Woodward and Carl Bernstein's investigation of the Watergate story, Seymour Hersh's revelations about the My Lai massacre, and Jack Anderson's continuing Washington-based column.

The distinction between the objective reporting of "facts" and the interpretive reporting of "truth" is clearly detailed in the case of Senator Joseph McCarthy from Wisconsin. In the early 1950s, Senator McCarthy began his anti-communist crusade from the floor of the Senate by making repeated allegations about communists in government. Although he could seldom offer any evidence to support his charges, his accusations were faithfully and objectively reported by the press as *facts* (it was a fact that he had made the charges).

The rules of objective newswriting dictated that reporters should not interject their personal opinions into the coverage of the Senator's accusations even though most journalists sensed that there was no basis to his allegations. So the *truth* went unreported while the *facts* were objectively relayed to the public without interpretation or modification. Variations of the same phenomenon—accurate reporting of false information—can occur every time the news media faithfully print a press release from a government bureau, objectively interview a prominent newsmaker, or thrust a microphone in front of a terrorist spokesman.

Senator McCarthy's downfall was precipitated partially by the fact that a few news channels went beyond the superficial facts to reveal the truth about his tactics. The most influential of these channels were *New York Times* editorials, columns by Drew Pearson, and Edward R. Murrow's famous *See It Now* television broadcasts.

**INSET 3–8
Objectivity and
Senator Joe
McCarthy**

New Journalism   The term "new journalism" has been used to refer to various periods in American newswriting. Most recently it has been applied to those writers who adapt literary techniques to journalism. The result is a semi-objective, journalistic view of reality written from a subjective, first-person viewpoint. Tom Wolfe, one of the leading practitioners of the form, has described the "new journalism" as the use in nonfiction of techniques "which had been thought of as confined to the novel or the short story, to create in one form both the kind of objective reality of journalism and the subjective reality that people have always gone to the novel for."[15] Other writers who have practiced the form successfully include John McPhee, Jimmy Breslin, Truman Capote, Joan Didion, Norman Mailer, and Gay Talese.

Alternative Journalism   Another major development in specialized journalistic formats during the past couple of decades has been the emergence of the alternative media or "underground press" (see Section 11.5.2). Responding to the need for an alternative to the traditional "establishment press," underground papers began springing up in the 1960s. These papers voiced a definite anti-establishment, nonconventional viewpoint. Responding specifically to American involvement in Vietnam, deterioration of the environment, racial unrest, and unsettled economic and social conditions, the underground press was generally in favor of radical politics, ecological safeguards, free speech (profanity), personal freedom (drugs, sex), youth, racial minorities, and the poor.

There were a number of historical precedents for such an anti-establishment press—the pre-Revolution pamphleteers, the "fugitive press" of the Revolutionary War, and the

---

On September 6, 1969, a routine military press release briefly announced that a Lt. William L. Calley, Jr., had been charged with murder in the deaths "of an unspecified number of civilians in Vietnam." Two remarkable factors were involved in the eventual unfolding of the appalling drama. One was that stories and rumors about the My Lai massacre had been circulating among military personnel for twenty months without word ever leaking to the public.

The second factor was that the country's major newspapers and wire service were very slow—seemingly uninterested—in following up the story. In the two months after the press release, only a few perfunctory and nonrevealing articles were printed. As with most investigative stories, it took the intuition, foresight, and perserverance of one reporter to dig into the real story.

Seymour Hersh, an independent newswriter who eventually released his stories through the Dispatch News Service, took an intensive and in-depth interest in the story. Within a couple of weeks, Hersh traveled thousands of miles to interview witnesses and participants.[14] As a result of his series of syndicated stories and a television interview with one participant, the major media finally revealed the scope of the tragedy. Calley was charged with the murder of 109 Vietnamese civilians; he was found guilty of the murder of 22 individuals.

**INSET 3–9
The Uncovering
of the My Lai
Massacre**

"abolitionist press" of the Civil War. The modern underground press probably started in Greenwich Village with the *Village Voice*, founded by Norman Mailer and Edwin Fancher in 1955. At its peak the *Village Voice* had a circulation greater than ninety-five percent of the daily papers in the United States. During the next two decades, between four hundred and three thousand underground papers were started—estimates vary because the papers do not lend themselves well to definition or convenient census taking. Well-known examples include Los Angeles's *Free Press*, Chicago's *Seed*, Boston's *Avatar*, New York's *East Village Other*, San Francisco's *Rolling Stone*, and campus papers such as the *Berkeley Barb*.

The Minority Press Minority newspapers are based upon ethnic, religious, language, and racial interests. There are many such papers in the United States. For example, more than fifty Chicano newspapers have been started since 1960.

The first black newspaper in the country, *Freedom's Journal*, was started in 1827 in New York. By the mid-1970s there were more than 325 black papers with a total circulation of over seven million. Only two were dailies, the *Chicago Defender* and the *Atlanta Daily Word*. Others were published weekly or twice weekly. Most of the black papers are conservative and represent the middle-of-the-road black establishment position (Section 11.5.1). However, two of them—*Muhammad Speaks* and *Black Panther*, both of which have national circulations—represent a strong militant position.

The Elitist-Popular-Specialized Curve
The history of newspaper development in the United States can be fairly conveniently broken down into the elitist, popular, and specialist stages. The Colonial and Early Republic period, during which newspapers catered to the mercantile class and to the politically active, is distinctly the *elitist* stage. And the *popular* stage clearly began with Benjamin Day's *New York Sun* in 1833. However, the *specialist* stage overlaps considerably with the popular stage. This is true of other media

The *Chicago Defender* is one of the country's leading Black newspapers.

also. While the popularity of a medium is swelling, the conditions which facilitate specialization (education, affluence, leisure time, and population size) are also developing.

3.4 Magazines: Storehouses for Specialized Interests

Over six billion copies of magazines are printed in the United States every year—more than two and a quarter copies each month for every man, woman, and child in the country. Derived from the French word *magasin*, meaning "warehouse" or "storehouse," the modern magazine almost defies explicit description. About the only generalizations one dares to toss out are that the magazine is *usually* bound or stapled (unlike most newspapers) and is *normally* published on a regular schedule (unlike most books).

The one characteristic common to the magazine industry is that, with a few notable exceptions, magazines are aimed at specialized audiences. As magazines evolved from the elitist to the popular stage early in their development, they simultaneously eased into the specialist stage. Don Pember notes, "Think of something that might be interesting to several thousand Americans and you can be fairly certain of finding one or more magazines on that topic."[16] Houseboating, shoe manufacturing, ancient African cultures—find a potential audience, and you will have a potential marketplace for a new magazine.

3.4.1 OVERVIEW OF AMERICAN MAGAZINE PUBLISHING

The history of the American magazine roughly parallels the evolution of the American newspaper (see Inset 3–1). Its earliest roots can be traced back to Great Britain at the beginning of the eighteenth century.

Colonial Attempts and Failures (1700s–1820s)
Early magazine endeavors in the colonies were not financially successful. Benjamin Franklin's *General Magazine and Historical Chronicle, for All the British Plantations in America,* started in 1741, lasted only six issues. Andrew Bradford, in a spirit of competitiveness which has always characterized American mass media development, actually published his *American Magazine, or a Monthly View of the Political State of the British Colonies* three days before Franklin got his magazine printed; but Bradford's pioneering effort lasted only three issues.

During the next sixty years, another dozen or so national magazines were started in the colonies. However, for a variety of reasons, none of them managed to stay in business longer than fourteen months: advertising support was slow to develop; the colonies had yet to establish any literary traditions; and the pioneering temperament of the restless colonists was more suited to the impatient newspaper than to the contemplative magazine.

Early Successful Magazines (1821–1890s)
After the turn of the century, however, magazines became a potent factor in the political, religious, educational, and cultural life of the new country. Probably the most famous of these early successes was the *Saturday Evening Post,* founded in 1821 as part of Benjamin Franklin's printing empire and tracing its heritage back to Franklin's *Pennsylvania Gazette* in 1729. Another early success was the *North American Review,* started in 1815, which was a major literary influence until its demise in 1938.

During the 1850s, the magazine became recognized as a leading literary medium with the founding of magazines such as *Harper's Monthly* and the *Atlantic Monthly.* Virtually every major American author of the late nineteenth century received early recognition through works published in these or similar literary magazines of the period.

Popularity and Muckraking (1893–1920s)
During the heyday of the penny press and the dime novel, it was inevitable that the magazine would launch a low-priced counterpart. When most magazines were selling at twenty-five or thirty cents, Samuel S. McClure founded *McClure's Magazine* in 1893 and sold it for fifteen cents a copy. Frank Munsey countered by lowering the price of *Munsey's Magazine* to ten cents a copy, and the magazine industry entered its period of competition for the popular audience. Hearst's *Cosmopolitan* and other new magazines offered low-cost mass entertainment, featuring popular fiction, lavish illustrations, and abundant human interest stories.

By lowering its literary standards and setting its sights for the larger mass audience, the magazine industry was successful in vastly increasing total circulation figures. At the same time, a number of magazines engaged in questionable practices like those employed in the yellow-journalism newspaper competition between Hearst and Pulitzer. One critic later wrote: "Frank Munsey contributed to the journalism of his day the talent of a meat packer, the morals of a money changer, and the manner of an undertaker."[17]

During this period, however, magazines also contributed significantly to the rise of investigative journalism. Many of the finest writers of the times—Lincoln Steffens, Ida Tarbell, Samuel Hopkins Adams, Ray Stannard Baker, Will Irwin, and others—contributed to the muckraking series featured in many of the leading magazines of this era.

Modern Magazine Publishing (1920s–1960s)

Following World War I, magazine publishing evolved into a pattern that we can recognize today. Muckraking, as a primary political force, declined. Light entertainment features increased, photojournalism flourished, and magazine publication proliferated.

Many of the magazines that shaped the image of the modern industry were founded during this period—*Time, Reader's Digest, The New Yorker, Life,* and their many imitators. In a little over three decades, from 1919 to 1951, the gross annual revenues from magazine advertising increased from $100 million to $500 million annually. In the 1950s several successful new magazines, including *TV Guide, Mad Magazine,* and *Playboy,* indicated the next trend—specialization.

Reaction and Redirection (1960s to the Present)

The sting of television was felt during the 1950s, and by the 1960s it had turned into a deadly bite. As the video tube supplied America with enough light fare to satisfy the need for general-interest mass entertainment, several general-appeal magazines found they could no longer satisfy their advertisers. *Collier's, The Saturday Evening Post, Look,* and *Life* all failed as regularly scheduled weekly general-interest giants (see Inset 3–11), although two of them have since been revived as monthly or special-issue publications.

3.4.2 LITERARY MAGAZINES

One of the earliest functions of the magazine was to provide a literary outlet for both established and aspiring authors and poets. As in the case of books (see Section 3.2.4), the

The *Port Folio* was typical of the many literary magazines launched at the beginning of the nineteenth century.

proportion of fiction in magazines has been constantly decreasing. Today less than a quarter of all magazine content is devoted to fiction and dramatic literature. However, in the nineteenth century the magazine was the primary outlet for literary works.

In the first half of the century, the medium took hold of the imagination of the young writers. Edgar Allan Poe, a magazine editor and writer, wrote in the 1830s, "The whole tendency of the age is Magazineward. The magazine in the end will be the most influential of all departments of letters . . ."[18] The *North American Review,* founded in 1815, was the first major literary magazine which survived into the twentieth century.

In the mid-nineteenth century several other major literary magazines were founded: *Harper's Monthly* (1850); *Atlantic Monthly*

(1857); *Century* (1881); and *Scribner's* (1886). These magazines served as important showcases for American fiction and literary essays, short stories, poetry, and serialized novels. Relatively expensive (thirty-five cents) and sophisticated, they were not aimed at the mass audience.

Other prestigious magazines joined the ranks of these literary models, including the *Saturday Review of Literature* and, later, *Horizons* and *American Heritage.* As the content of these journals expanded to provide essays in philosophy, science, and art and culture, other more specialized periodicals such as *Scientific American* and *Smithsonian* made their debuts. In the fields of political thought, however, another whole genre could be isolated—the news and opinion journals.

3.4.3 NEWS AND OPINION MAGAZINES

Time, Newsweek, and *U.S. News & World Report* have a combined circulation of close to ten million. The forerunners of such news and opinion magazines date back to the *Independent,* founded in 1848; *Harper's Weekly,* the public affairs counterpart of the literary *Harper's Monthly,* founded in 1857; and William Godkin's *Nation,* founded in 1865. Of these early opinion magazines, only the *Nation* is still published today. Like most other politically oriented periodicals (*New Leader, New Republic, Progressive, Ramparts,* and *New Times,* for example), it leans to the left with a definite liberal/progressive tilt. The one outstanding opposing voice is William

---

In 1923 Henry R. Luce began one of the most successful and diversified of the twentieth-century publishing chains when he co-founded, with Briton Hadden, *Time* magazine. With its crisp writing style, varied editorial sections, emphasis on personalities and photos, and balance between background detail and brisk summaries, *Time* established the format for the modern news magazine.

In 1930 Luce started the successful and prestigious *Fortune* magazine, which stood as the premier business publication for decades, and in 1936 he founded *Life.* With a large-page format and a heavy reliance upon high-quality photojournalism, *Life* quickly became the standard for the general-interest weekly magazine. Blending news, human interest features, fiction (including original stories by Hemingway, Mailer, and others), oddities and tragedies, and memoirs of the outstanding people of the period (including Churchill, Truman, de Gaulle, Eisenhower, and Khrushchev), the magazine became the pictorial guide for a generation of Americans which came to comprehend wars, sports, politics, fashions, and celebrities only as interpreted in the pages of *Life.* Although it ceased regular weekly publication in 1972, it was resurrected—after a series of special issues—as a monthly magazine in 1978.

Luce continued to build his publishing empire by buying or creating new entries in the specialized magazine market. He almost always emerged with one of the top magazines in each specialized field: *House and Garden,* a residential spin-off from *Architectural Forum,* which he acquired in 1932; *Sports Illustrated,* started in 1954; *Money,* a consumer-oriented counterpart to *Fortune;* and *People,* launched in 1974 as a smaller, livelier, and more gossip-oriented replacement for *Life.*

**INSET 3–10
Henry Luce and
the Time-Life
Chain**

Buckley's conservative *National Review,* founded in 1955.

Most Americans, however, are more interested in the basic news magazines. *Time* was started in 1923 as the keystone of the impressive Time-Life chain. Ten years later *Newsweek* was begun as a channel of direct competition. And *U.S. News & World Report* emerged in the 1940s as a consolidation of two of David Lawrence's Washington-based publications.

Muckraking has always been effective in building an audience. One of the first major investigative journalism exposés was the 1871 attack on Tammany Hall, the New York City political machine. Both *Harper's Weekly* (featuring the pungent political cartoons of Thomas Nast) and the *New York Times* unmasked the corruption of the city's political bosses in a classic investigative effort. Around the turn of the century many of the popular magazines also jumped on the muckraking bandwagon. In 1903, one issue of *McClure's* featured Ida Tarbell's examination of Standard Oil (which ran for nineteen months), Lincoln Steffens' "Shame of the Cities" series on corruption in local government, and Ray Stannard Baker's investigation of labor practices. Other popular exposés focused on railroad practices, insurance frauds, patent medicines, other business monopolies, and political profligacy.

3.4.4 GENERAL-INTEREST MAGAZINES

Although the magazine is the most specialized of all mass media, there has always been room for a number of general-appeal magazines—until recently. From Franklin's *General Magazine* (1741) on through the nineteenth century, many generalized magazines were launched. Only a few survived.

One of the oldest, the *Saturday Evening Post,* was floundering until it was purchased by Cyrus Curtis in 1897 for $1,000. Curtis built up its circulation from 2,200 to 2,000,-000 within fifteen years. With its popular light content and its Norman Rockwell covers, it represented the virtues of small-town America for most of the twentieth century.

Joining the *Saturday Evening Post* and *Collier's* (which rose to prominence during the turn-of-the-century muckraking boom) were *Life* magazine, founded in 1936, and *Look,* created one year later as an imitation of *Life.* However, by the mid-1970s all four of these mass-circulation, general-content giants had failed. The appeal of the general-interest magazines seemed to have disappeared—with one very notable exception.

DeWitt Wallace and his wife, Lila, founded their magazine business in the basement of a Greenwich Village speakeasy in 1922. With borrowed funds they put out a small, unpretentious digest of interesting articles reprinted from other magazines and journals. Today, the *Reader's Digest* has a monthly U.S. circulation in excess of 18 million and a worldwide readership of 30 million (in fifteen languages).

Today, the circulation of *Reader's Digest* is exceeded in the United States only by *TV Guide* (see Inset 3–12). Some observers classify *TV Guide,* like the *Reader's Digest,* as a general-appeal magazine, pointing out that it attracts a wide readership. However, it may be more accurate to consider *TV Guide* a special-interest magazine which appeals only to people who have an interest in watching television. As such, it undoubtedly is the largest specialized magazine in the world.

3.4.5 SPECIAL-INTEREST MAGAZINES

To a considerable extent, radio stations have adopted specialized formats; many motion pictures aim for a particular audience; and most books are targeted for a specific group of readers. But no other medium has achieved the degree of specialization characteristic of magazines. The magazine-buying public is composed literally of hundreds of separate audiences.

Women's Magazines   Of the top ten best-selling American periodicals, five are women's magazines. One of the first and most successful magazines was *Godey's Lady's Book,* started by Louis Antoine Godey in 1830. Edited for forty years by Sarah Josepha Hale, the magazine was noted for its moral leadership as well as its articles on fashions and home-making. Another early successful women's magazine, *Ladies' Home Journal,* was started in 1883 by Cyrus Curtis as part of his large magazine empire. Like many other women's magazines, the *Journal* was edited by a man—Edward Bok, one of the innovative leaders in magazine publishing.

Most of the women's magazines are primarily concerned with housekeeping chores, sewing, beauty tips, cooking, home decoration, and so forth. In fact, in a typical super-

---

One of the publishing phenomena of the last quarter-century has been the demise of the general-interest mass magazines. The first to fall was *Collier's,* which went under in 1956. The *Saturday Evening Post* managed to survive until 1968; despite valiant attempts to trim its bloated circulation and freshen its small-town appearance, it could not last out the turbulent sixties. *Look* and *Life* finally give up in 1971 and 1972, respectively, and this sealed the fate of the mass-circulation picture magazine. Like the *Post,* both *Life* and *Look* had circulations of close to seven million when they finally went out of business. If the problem was not sagging sales, what then caused the downfall of all four magazines?

Ironically, part of the problem was that the circulation of each of the magazines had grown too large. Rising costs—editorial expenditures, postal rates, printing and paper expenses—made it increasingly difficult to produce a magazine for such a large, dispersed, and heterogeneous readership. Before its last gasp, each magazine made a vain attempt to cut costs by trimming its circulation figures.

Television, also, was a prime culprit. The TV tube simply was more effective at meeting the generalized needs of a mass audience—it provided pictorial reports of news highlights, in-depth analyses of popular news items, and a format for fiction for the masses.

Ultimately, of course, each of the magazines failed as an advertising channel. Advertisers found that they could use specialized magazines and other media to reach the specific segment of the audience they viewed as prospective buyers—for example, urban males, teenagers, middle-aged housewives, sports fans, debutantes, or stamp collectors. For those advertisers who did need to reach a large undifferentiated audience, television was a far more cost-effective medium to use.

Since their demise, two of the magazines have enjoyed a modified revival. Both the *Saturday Evening Post* and *Life* have returned to the newsstand, propelled by a profound sense of nostalgia, with special editions. The *Post* promises to publish nine issues a year, and *Life* has returned on a monthly basis.

INSET 3–11
The Fall of
the Four Generals

Godey's Lady's Book was one of the first successful women's magazines.

market, you might find up to four different magazines devoted solely to needlecraft. Not until Gloria Steinem and Elizabeth Forsling Harris founded *Ms.* in 1971 was there a magazine devoted to the feminist movement. Under the editorship of Helen Gurley Brown, *Cosmopolitan* also represented a departure from the traditional women's magazines with its emphasis on female sexuality and career alternatives.

Men's Magazines   Several categories of magazines have been designed to appeal specifically to men. They range from sophisticated magazines like *Esquire* to outdoor and adventure magazines like *Field and Stream* and *True Detective*. But the success story of the postwar magazine publishing business began in 1953 in a kitchen with a paste pot, some tantalizing nude photographs, $600 in cash, and Hugh Hefner's uncanny sense of timeliness.

Playboy became the magazine sensation of the half-century, spawning many imitators over the past three decades. The timing was perfect for the slick publication that Hefner produced. John Brady assesses Hefner's influence,

It seems safe to conclude . . . that *Playboy* . . . helped bring about a cultural change in our society much more rapidly than would have occurred otherwise. Hefner's magazine became the foremost chronicler of sexual change throughout this period. Thus, following closely on the heels of Dr. Kinsey, and paralleling the development of The Pill, *Playboy* served as midwife while the age of sexual candor was born unto the popular press in America.[19]

City Magazines   Bucking the concept of national circulation, the "city magazines" have provided a valuable civic outlet in many metropolitan centers. The prototype of the modern city magazines is the *New Yorker,* started in 1925 by Harold Ross. Dapper, slick, sophisticated, satirical, and literary, the *New Yorker* has inspired many imitators. Part gadfly, part muckraker, and part civic booster, metropolitan periodicals now flourish in at least seventy-five major urban centers.

Regional Magazines   Seeking a somewhat wider distribution, the regional magazine has emerged as a high-quality publication which can be tailored specifically for the population of an identifiable region of the country. *Southern Living, Sunset* (in the West), and *Yankee* (in New England) are all successful magazines which feature the life-styles, housing, cooking, travel hints, and cultures of their particular areas.

Travel and Exploration Magazines   Travel journals have always been popular with travelers and non-travelers alike. Slick magazines such as *Holiday* and *Travel and Leisure* and less pretentious magazines published by automobile clubs and commercial airlines all serve to introduce the would-be voyager to faraway lands and vacation spots. However, the *National Geographic,* launched in 1888 and currently the third most popular magazine in America, reigns supreme in this field, setting photographic and editorial standards of excellence in the presentation of journeys to the exotic corners of the globe. Brown *et al.* point out the timelessness and enduring quality of the *Geographic:* "It [is] not a publication read on the run and discarded. Bookshelves around the world groan under the weight of back issues of the *Geographic.*"[20]

Minority Magazines Virtually all minority and ethnic groups have turned to the magazine as a vehicle for their particular cultures, causes, and crusades. Many minority periodicals are modeled after successful general magazines. In the black press, for instance, *Ebony* started out in 1945 as an imitator of *Life, Black World* is modeled on the *Reader's Digest,*

Tan copied the format of the "true confession" magazines, and so on. *Essence* was started in 1970 as a fashion and beauty magazine for black women. (See Inset 11–8.) Various ethnic groups have their own magazines—*Identity,* for example, was launched in 1977 for the Italian-American community. Many other groups have initiated their own journals. The gay community has its *Advocate,* and even marijuana supporters have their *High Times.*

Other Specialized Magazines The list of special publications continues as far as people's interests and imaginations can stretch. There are hobby magazines, from *The American Blade,* on the history of knife collecting, to *Pacific Skipper,* "the magazine for western yachtsmen." There are agricultural journals—

The best-selling magazines in the United States are ranked below according to 1980 circulation figures. (The figures have been rounded off to the nearest thousand.)

**INSET 3–12
The Top Twenty
Best-Selling
Magazines**

Rank	Magazine	Circulation
1	*TV Guide*	17,981,000
2	*Reader's Digest*	17,898,000
3	*National Geographic*	10,800,000
4	*Better Homes & Gardens*	8,052,000
5	*Woman's Day*	7,748,000
6	*Family Circle*	7,529,000
7	*McCalls*	6,200,000
8	*Playboy*	5,743,000
9	*Ladies' Home Journal*	5,500,000
10	*Good Housekeeping*	5,290,000
11	*National Enquirer*	5,024,000
12	*Time*	4,364,000
13	*Penthouse*	4,330,000
14	*Redbook*	4,300,000
15	*Star*	3,508,000
16	*Newsweek*	2,952,000
17	*Cosmopolitan*	2,837,000
18	*American Legion Magazine*	2,599,000
19	*People*	2,315,000
20	*Sports Illustrated*	2,250,000

the *Tribune and Farmer* was the beginning of Cyrus Curtis's publishing empire. There are romance and fan magazines like *Modern Screen* and *True Confessions*. There are more than two thousand religious publications in the United States. Electronics and popular science account for three magazines in the most popular forty. Humor and satire magazines include *National Lampoon* and *Mad*, the only large-circulation newsstand magazine which succeeds without advertising. Consumer-protection magazines like *Consumer Reports* also decline advertising support. There are magazines for all sports, including every momentary fad to come along. There are dozens of magazines devoted to automobiles, motorcycles, and recreational vehicles—count them in your local discount drug store. You can read about food and life-styles in publications ranging from *Bon Appetit* to *Wet*,

"the magazine of gourmet bathing." And on and on.

Despite the trouble that general-appeal magazines have had in competing with television for advertising dollars, the future of special-interest magazines appears to be secure. Sandman et al. summarize the position of the special-interest magazine:

There are thus two ways for a specialized magazine to earn a profit. By offering advertisers just the right market for their products and services, it can justify high advertising rates. By offering readers editorial content that is tailored to match their interests, it can justify high subscription rates. Many of the most successful specialized magazines are able to make money from both advertisers and readers.[21]

INSET 3–13
The Comic Book

Although newspaper cartoons and comic strips can be traced back to the 1890s (see Inset 3–6), the "comic book" emerged in 1933 when *Funnies on Parade,* a collection of reruns from various Sunday newspaper comic strips, was bound as a magazine and sold on newsstands. *Detective Comics,* published four years later, was the first comic book to be devoted to a single theme. And in 1938 *Action Comics* made its debut with America's classic superhero, Superman. The popularity of the comic book was instantaneous. More than 60 different comic book titles were marketed in 1940; by 1941 there were 168 titles.

Parental concern with excessive violence and stereotyping led to charges that the comic book was contributing to juvenile delinquency and general moral degeneracy. Under pressure from psychiatrists, legislators, and self-appointed local censorship groups, the Comics Magazine Association of America adopted a forty-one-point code in 1954 as a means of industry self-regulation. The code established standards regarding violence, religious and ethnic references, depiction of monsters, profanity, and general questions of morality.

Today more than 100 comic-book publishers, printing abut 300 separate titles, sell more than 250 million copies each year. At least ninety percent of the comics adhere to the code standards, but the concern—although considerably diminished as attention has shifted to the evils of television—still continues.

3.4.6 SCHOLARLY JOURNALS, PROFESSIONAL MAGAZINES, AND HOUSE ORGANS

In addition to the generally recognized consumer magazines discussed above, there are tens of thousands of other specialized publications. The *Standard Periodical Directory* lists at least 62,000 different journals and magazines in the country: academic publications, college alumni magazines, trade journals, monthly reports from professional associations, industry magazines, free-circulation magazines (like those produced by the airlines), business publications, and so on.

Specialized areas of study produce an incredible array of scholarly journals. For example, in the limited area of film and motion pictures alone, over a hundred magazines are regularly published in the United States.[22] Academic and critical journals within the communication field include—to name but a few—*Columbia Journalism Review, Journal of Broadcasting, Journalism Quarterly, Quarterly Journal of Speech,* and *Communication Review*. Numerous professional magazines such as *Broadcasting, Advertising Age,* and *Editor & Publisher* abound. There are at least twenty major independent publications concerned with communications, media, and advertising.

When you consider all of the varied professional activities and businesses in our contemporary culture, you will not be surprised to learn that there are thousands of specialized magazines and journals. The 1980 *Encyclopedia of Associations* (Gale Research Company, Detroit) lists more than 14,000 active organizations and associations in the United States—and almost all of them have their own newsletters, journals, or other periodicals.

Corporate publications or "house organs" make up another whole category of periodicals. These are the internal newsletters and company magazines put out by major businesses of all descriptions. Distributed to employees, stockholders, and customers,

The modern magazine publisher has to be as concerned with layout, art work, and audiovisuals as it is with writing and editing.

many of these industry magazines are very sophisticated publications—written and edited by large professional staffs, and featuring slick layouts and high-quality photojournalism. Some large corporations publish a variety of such company magazines; International Harvester, for example, publishes about two dozen. And some of the more ambitious corporation publications have circulations in excess of a million.

3.4.7 THE OUTLOOK FOR THE MAGAZINE

The magazine has an ability to specialize and intensify information for a particularized audience that no other mass medium can match. Freed from the daily—and hourly—constraints of newspaper deadlines, the magazine can afford to probe more deeply, interpret more accurately, and report more clearly than the newspaper. And yet the magazine also has the ability to examine current issues and to pursue a topic with more continuity than the book.

Despite the decline of the general-interest magazine, the medium has flourished handsomely since World War II. In a quarter of a century, from 1950 to 1974, advertising revenues for magazines tripled, going from $485.5 million to $1.5 billion. And in the same period per-issue circulation increased forty-four percent.

Further Specialization Using computer-ized editing, printing, and distribution techniques, the magazine industry is perfecting methods of specializing its audience even further. Using zip codes and reader-preference data, a national magazine like *Time* could print many different regional editions in order to attract different regional advertisers and could also print numerous versions of a given issue with specialized—almost personalized—sections for individual subscribers. One subscriber (a teacher, for example) might receive a given issue with an expanded section on education, while a next-door neighbor might receive the same issue—but with an expanded emphasis on science. Such technology already exists. Other magazines use zip codes for "controlled-circulation impact," which refers to the ability to reach homes with a given occupational, racial, income, or age characteristic. Also, as Hiebert et al. point out, the industry is continually turning to innovative ideas in its attempt to compete successfully:

Magazines are also making improvements in the product itself, with experimentation in hard and plastic covers; looseleaf and book bindings; more opaque, smoother, and lighter paper; full-color printing; faster presses; shorter closing times; three-dimensional visual effects; and "scratch-'n'-sniff" for olfactory appeal. These extensions of magazine production will aid in the economic battle for survival in the jungle of mass media.[23]

SUMMARY

As both the print and the electric media have developed, they have followed similar paths of evolution. Starting out with a relatively small audience, each medium began by serving an *elitist* function. As technology progressed, circulation increased and advertising revenues grew; and each medium entered a *popular* stage. With increased education, affluence, leisure time, and total audience size, each medium eventually moved into a *specialist* period, serving a smaller group of readers with a common specialized interest.

Each of the primary print media (books, newspapers, and magazines) also experienced related patterns of growth and development—from early *experimentation* (leading to advances in printing technology), to an age of *expansion* (the Penny Press and the early successful magazines), to a period of *exploitation* (the commercialization of books, yellow journalism, and muckraking), to an awakening of *responsibility* (objective reporting and self-regulation), and on into a period of increasing *competition*.

This latter phenomenon of media competition was especially heightened with the introduction and early successes of the various electric media (film, radio and audio recordings, and television), with which we are concerned in Chapter 4.

Notes to Chapter 3

1. John C. Merrill and Ralph L. Lowenstein, *Media, Messages, and Men: New Perspectives in Communication,* 2nd ed. (New York: Longman, 1979), p. 29.

2. Block printing was highly developed in Asia during the European Dark Ages. The oldest printed work in existence is a Korean scroll ("Sutra"), printed from wooden blocks and dated around 704 A.D.

3. Wilbur Schramm, *Men, Messages, and Media: A Look at Human Communication* (New York: Harper & Row, 1973), p. 13.

4. See Charles A. Madison, *Book Publishing in American Culture* (New York: McGraw-Hill, 1966).

5. Curtis G. Benjamin, "Book Publishing's Hidden Bonanza," in *Readings in Mass Communication: Concepts and Issues in the Mass Media,* eds. Michael C. Emery and Ted Curtis Smythe (Dubuque, Iowa: Wm. C. Brown, 1972), p. 182.

6. Hellmut Lehmann-Haupt, "Book," *Encyclopedia Americana* (1970), 4: p. 231.

7. Henry David Thoreau, *Walden: Or, Life in the Woods* (New York: New American Library, Signet Books, 1963), pp. 67–68.

8. W. Phillips Davison, James Boylan, and Frederick T. C. Yu, *Mass Media: Systems and Effects* (New York: Praeger, 1976), p. 11.

9. Charlene J. Brown, Trevor R. Brown, and William L. Rivers, *The Media and the People* (New York: Holt, Rinehart and Winston, 1978), p. 57.

10. Quoted in Edwin Emery, *The Press and America: An Interpretive History of the Mass Media*, 3rd ed. (Englewood Cliffs, N.J.: Prentice-Hall, 1972), p. 311.

11. Davison et al., *Mass Media,* p. 15.

12. J. K. Hvistendahl, "The Reporter as Activist: Fourth Revolution in Journalism," in Emery and Smythe, *Readings in Mass Communication,* p. 117.

13. Quoted in Carey McWilliams, "Is Muckraking Coming Back?" in ibid., p. 108.

14. For the details of Hersh's own story, see Seymour M. Hersh, "The Story Everyone Ignored," in Emery and Smythe, ibid., pp. 434–439.

15. Brown et al., *The Media and the People,* p. 356.

16. Don R. Pember, *Mass Media in America* (Chicago: Science Research Associates, 1974), p. 339.

17. Quoted in Edward Jay Whetmore, *Mediamerica: Form, Content, and Consequence of Mass Communication* (Belmont, Calif.: Wadsworth, 1979), p. 73.

18. Quoted in Ray Eldon Hiebert, Donald F. Ungurait, and Thomas W. Bohn, *Mass Media II: An Introduction to Modern Communication,* 2nd ed. (New York: Longman, 1979), p. 237.

19. John Brady, "The Nude Journalism," in Whetmore, *Mediamerica,* p. 80.

20. Brown et al., *The Media and the People,* p. 92.

21. Peter M. Sandman, David M. Rubin, and David B. Sachsman, *Media: An Introductory Analysis of American Mass Communications,* 2nd ed. (Englewood Cliffs, N.J.: Prentice-Hall, 1976), p. 286.

22. One publication, *Film Literature: Current,* is devoted entirely to compiling and reprinting the tables of contents of 130 different international journals dealing with film and television.

23. Hiebert et al., *Mass Media II,* p. 245.

Although you may spend considerable time with various print media, the chances are that you allocate most of your mass communication time to the electronic media. Our national preoccupation with television, the omnipresent use of radio as a background companion, and the ever-radiant silver screen of the motion picture all attest to the popularity of the "low-effort" aural/pictorial media (Section 1.6.4).

4

The Electronic Foundations of Mass Communication

4.1 Seven Technical Phenomena of the Electric Media

Our study of radio, television, and motion pictures will follow the theme introduced in the previous chapter, that is, *each medium develops broadly in an elitist-popular-specialist pattern*. We will begin by exploring some of the physical characteristics of the media. There are seven technical principles which you should understand before you investigate some of the economic, regulatory, and social developments of the media.

4.1.1 THE PROJECTION OF IMAGES

Essential to the development of both motion pictures and television are the concepts of optics—the science of lenses that led to the development of the camera and, for moving pictures, the projector.

By the Renaissance, scientists and magicians had begun to experiment with the illusions of the *camera obscura* ("dark room"). By making a pinhole aperture in the wall of a darkened box or small room, one can project an upside-down and reversed image of an external scene on the wall opposite the opening. Leonardo da Vinci systematically set down the principles and characteristics of the camera obscura—which, when reduced in size and outfitted with a lens, became the basis for our modern still camera.

If the camera was one result of the camera obscura, the corollary development was the projector. By substituting artificial light for

The camera obscura (top) first demonstrated the principles of modern photography. The 17th century "magic lantern" (bottom) was the forerunner of today's slide projector.

natural sunlight, passing this light through a transparency (of necessity a picture painted on glass), and projecting the resulting image through a lens onto a screen, early experimenters created the "magic lantern." By the seventeenth century a practical prototype of the modern slide projector had thus been introduced.

4.1.2   CHEMICAL PHOTOGRAPHY

Painted slide transparencies took time to prepare, and—more importantly—they were only artists' impressions of reality, not the actual images of real objects. The next step, therefore, was to devise a way to capture the camera obscura's images permanently on some sort of physical medium. The answer lay in the advancing science of chemistry. It

was known even before the beginning of the nineteenth century that certain chemicals —most notably various salts of silver—were rapidly altered when exposed to light.

In the late 1830s the Frenchman Louis Daguerre perfected a process that enabled him to capture images on a copper plate coated with silver iodide. The popularity of the *daguerreotype* spread rapidly, and by the 1850s more than a thousand commercial photographers in the United States were producing more than three million portraits a year.

By the 1880s, several competing inventors had filed patents for a flexible film base. Prominent among them was George Eastman, whose nitrocellulose film proved to be the most practical. In 1888 Eastman also introduced his "foolproof" Kodak camera, which opened the door to the amateur photographer. With these developments, chemical photography was firmly established.

The next step was to make pictures move.

4.1.3   PERSISTENCE OF VISION AND MOVING PICTURES

The illusion of "moving" pictures is actually produced by projecting a series of still pictures, each one slightly changed from the preceding one, in rapid succession. The illusion results from the fact that the human eye can perceive only up to fifteen individual pictures per second as still images. When images are received at a faster rate, the brain combines these separate, frozen images to re-create the smooth continuity of motion. Also, the eye retains each separate image for a split second; this after-lag is what is termed *the persistence of vision.*

As long as a series of still pictures is projected faster than fifteen images per second, the eye will perceive apparent continuous motion. The standard projection rate for modern motion pictures is twenty-four images or "frames" per second. The television picture is projected at thirty frames per second.

Thus, by the 1890s, the basic theories of the motion picture had been put together: chemical photography, the ability to create an illusion of motion, and the optical camera-and-projection system. But, in order to add sound to the moving picture—or actually to send audio signals through the air—considerable electromagnetic sophistication was needed.

4.1.4 ELECTRICAL TRANSDUCTION OF SOUND WAVES

The term "transduction" merely refers to the transformation or changing of energy from one form to another, for example, the changing of sound waves into electrical energy. This crucial phenomenon had to be understood and applied before the telephone, radio, audio recording, television, or sound motion pictures could be developed.

The first practical use of electricity for communication came in 1844, when Samuel F. B. Morse (a distinguished portrait painter and daguerreotype photographer) demonstrated his long-distance telegraph system. On telegraph lines strung between Washington, D.C., and Baltimore, Morse sent the prophetic message, "What hath God wrought?" Telegraph lines were quickly stretched throughout the country, culminating in the transcontinental line in 1861. However, the telegraph's message was limited to content that could be coded into dots and dashes; telegraphic transmission was little more than a means of interrupting an electric flow. What was needed next was some method of sending actual sounds—voices and music—through electrical wires.

Hundreds of Americans were working simultaneously on this problem of inventing an audio transducer—a device to transform sound waves into electrical energy. This actually required the invention of two

---

INSET 4–1
Edison
and the
Kinetoscope

Many inventors and scientists contributed to the development of the electric media, but none commands more amazement than Thomas Alva Edison. With the help of his disciplined and well-equipped laboratory staff, working in the first industrial research lab to be operated on such a large scale, Edison made contributions that were indeed impressive.

In 1889, one of Edison's assistants, William Kennedy Laurie Dickson, integrated elements of the theory of optics, the phenomenon of the persistence of vision, and Eastman's flexible film base. He added sprocket holes to the film and assembled one of the world's first motion picture cameras and projectors.

Edison introduced his "peep-show" device, which he called the Kinetoscope, in 1894. Within five years, dozens of entrepreneur/inventors had designed rival systems, applied for patents, and secured financial backing; and they were all competing for public attention—some with peep-show (one-viewer-at-a-time) formats and others with large-screen projection systems.

Launched in the environment of the carnival side-show and penny arcade, the Kinetoscope parlors and their competitors initiated the era of the moving picture with sixty-second filmed excerpts of prize fights, vaudeville acts, horseraces, slapstick comedy, and exotic dancers.

devices, a microphone to *encode* sound into electricity and a receiver (headset) to *decode* the electrical signal back into sound waves. Alexander Graham Bell invented the first workable telephone in 1876. By the end of the 1870s, therefore, it was possible to take the human voice and change it into electrical energy which could be carried over wires. But we were still a quarter of a century away from being able to *broadcast* the voice to a mass audience without wires.

4.1.5 ELECTROCHEMICAL TRANSDUCTION OF LIGHT

If sound waves could be transduced into electrical energy, there had to be a way to transduce light waves into electrical signals. The key lay in the electrochemical properties of certain materials. Some substances, such as selenium, are *photoemissive*—that is, they give off electrical current when exposed to light. These substances gave scientists the first step of the sending process. Then, by using phosphors—substances which emit light when bombarded by electrons, just the opposite of photoemissive substances—scientists came closer to today's receiving apparatus. However, a satisfactory television image could not be composed electronically until some way of obtaining detail was devised.

4.1.6 THE PRINCIPLE OF SCANNING

Because it was obviously impractical to use tens of thousands of wires to connect each and every sending point (selenium cell) with its corresponding display point (phosphorous dot), a system had to be developed that would divide a picture into tiny fragments which could then be sent sequentially, dot by dot, over a single wire. The answer lay in perfecting some sort of scanning system that could scan a picture in minute segments, or pinpoints of light information, and send an indi-

Vladimir Zworykin with an early model of his iconoscope tube, the first practical television camera tube.

vidual pulse of electrical information corresponding to every light or dark dot.

What evolved was the iconoscope tube developed in 1923 by Vladimir Zworykin, a Russian immigrant working as part of the Westinghouse research staff. In this system, light reflected from an object passed through a lens into the glass-walled iconoscope tube. There it fell on a plate composed of thousands of selenium-coated silver particles. A magnetically controlled beam from an electron gun, also inside the tube, then scanned the selenium-coated plate pinpoint by pinpoint and line by line in a descending pattern. In the process, corresponding electrical signals were generated sequentially on the reverse side of the plate. These signals could be amplifed and transmitted through a wire to a kinescope, or receiving, tube. The kinescope contained a plate coated with phosphors on which the image could be reproduced by another magnetically controlled electron beam which corresponded to the scanning beam in the pickup or camera tube.

With the development of the iconoscope and kinescope tubes, the principles of electronic television were essentially established. Smaller, simpler pickup tubes like the vidicon would later be developed, but from here on it was a matter of refinement and improvement.

4.1.7 MODULATION OF A CARRIER WAVE

The one major hurdle remaining was the actual broadcasting transmission—sending electronic signals, sound and pictures, through space without wires. The Scottish physicist James Clerk Maxwell developed the theory of the electromagnetic spectrum. In his comprehensive *Treatise on Electricity and Magnetism* (1873), Maxwell predicted that it would be possible to generate electronic signals which could be sent through free space at the speed of light—without the use of wires.

Fifteen years later, the German physicist Heinrich Hertz (whose name we use to designate the frequency of radio waves) experimentally proved Maxwell's theory correct by sending wireless signals from point to point in his laboratory. Guglielmo Marconi, a young Italian inventor-entrepreneur working in England, received his first patent on radio telegraphy transmission equipment in 1896, formed the British Marconi Company in 1897, and continued to experiment with longer and longer transmissions. In 1901,

---

INSET 4–2 Simplified Television Pickup Tube

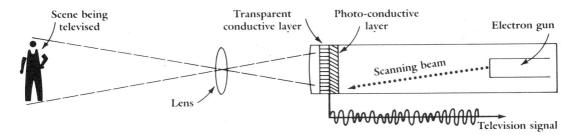

The vidicon pickup or camera tube, developed in the 1960s, was the forerunner of more sophisticated later models. The light waves reflected from the scene being televised are focused by the lens and directed through a transparent conductive layer onto a layer of photoconductive elements. This layer produces an electrical pattern analogous to the pattern of brightness in the light waves reflected from the scene. The scanning beam then causes an electrical discharge from each photoconductive pinpoint corresponding to the amount of light hitting the photoconductive element from the scene. This electrical discharge is carried from the conductive layer as a television signal output.

This process takes place as the scanning beam is pulled horizontally across the pickup tube, line by line, to form a composite picture of 525 scanning lines. Because there are up to 500 pickup points on each scanning line, this means there are potentially a quarter of a million (500 times 525 scanning lines) pieces of electrical data in each complete picture, or frame. And because thirty frames are created every second—producing the illusion of motion—this means that the television signal is capable of sending up to 7.5 million units of information each second!

Guglielmo Marconi posed with his 1901 wireless radiotelegraphy receiving set.

Marconi succeeded in sending the first message (the letter "S" in Morse code) across the Atlantic Ocean. The era of radiotelegraphy had been born.

Still to come, however, was the achievement of sending actual sounds—voices and music—through space without wires. The marriage of the telephone (voice through wires) and radiotelegraphy (electric signals without wires) was on the horizon.

Prominent among American inventor-entrepreneurs working on this problem was Lee De Forest, often called (at least in America) "the father of radio." His biggest contribution was the invention in 1907 of the *audion,* a three-element vacuum tube or "triode" that facilitated greater fidelity, facilitated signal amplification, and resulted in

INSET 4–3   Steps in Transducing Audio Energy

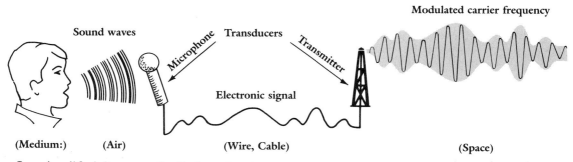

In a simplified diagram of radio broadcasting, the audio message is present in three different forms. The message starts out as *sound pressure waves* traveling through the medium of air. This sound energy is changed (transduced) into electrical energy by a microphone (transducer); the essential audio characteristics of the original sound are maintained in the medium of the electric wire. This *electrical energy* is then amplified and superimposed onto a given electromagnetic carrier frequency assigned to a specific radio station (for example, 640 kiloHertz). The transducer is the radio transmitter, and the resulting energy form is the altered or *modulated carrier frequency,* which also maintains the essential characteristics of the electrical impulses and the original sound waves. The medium of the modulated carrier wave is open space.

A carrier frequency may be modified either by changing the *amplitude* of the carrier wave ("amplitude modulation" or AM broadcasting), as illustrated above, or by changing the *frequency* of the carrier wave ("frequency modulation" or FM broadcasting).

INSET 4—4 Broadcast Portion of the Electromagnetic Spectrum

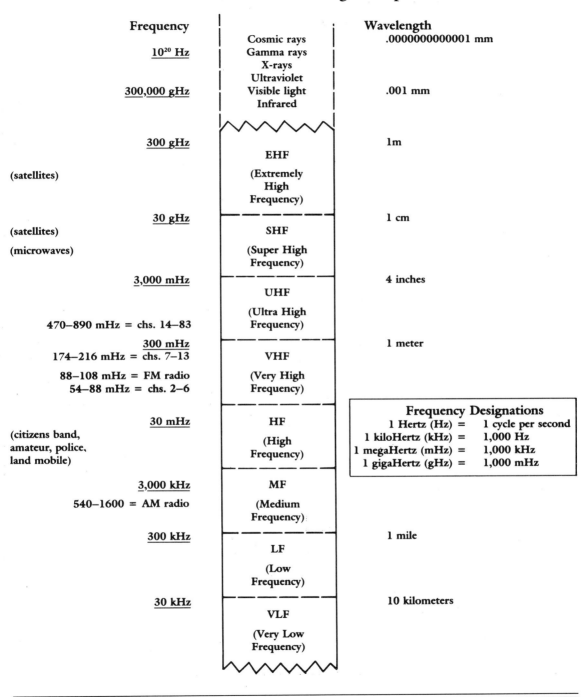

Frequency

10^{20} Hz

300,000 gHz

300 gHz

(satellites)

30 gHz
(satellites)

(microwaves)

3,000 mHz

470–890 mHz = chs. 14–83

300 mHz
174–216 mHz = chs. 7–13

88–108 mHz = FM radio
54–88 mHz = chs. 2–6

30 mHz
(citizens band,
amateur, police,
land mobile)

3,000 kHz
540–1600 = AM radio

300 kHz

30 kHz

Cosmic rays
Gamma rays
X-rays
Ultraviolet
Visible light
Infrared

EHF

(Extremely
High
Frequency)

SHF

(Super High
Frequency)

UHF

(Ultra High
Frequency)

VHF

(Very High
Frequency)

HF

(High
Frequency)

MF

(Medium
Frequency)

LF

(Low
Frequency)

VLF

(Very Low
Frequency)

Wavelength
.0000000000001 mm

.001 mm

1m

1 cm

4 inches

1 meter

1 mile

10 kilometers

Frequency Designations

1 Hertz (Hz) =	1 cycle per second
1 kiloHertz (kHz) =	1,000 Hz
1 megaHertz (mHz) =	1,000 kHz
1 gigaHertz (gHz) =	1,000 mHz

more accurate detection of signals. Used in both transmitting and receiving apparatus, this basic vacuum tube (and its many off-shoots) became the fundamental component in radio and television development until the invention of the transistor in 1947.

Contemporary with De Forest was a former Canadian, Reginald Fessenden, who did some pioneering work with Edison. After several early failures with voice transmission, Fessenden succeeded in sending out a well-publicized voice and musical program on Christmas Eve, 1906. Sterling and Kittross sum up the significance of this and other early broadcasts made by Fessenden:

If one considers the "general public" of the day as those few who owned and used receiving equipment, mainly ships at sea, and the newspapers as representatives of the public, then the 1906 transmissions were the first broadcasts. They were scheduled, they were for the general public, and listening required no special knowledge of code since they consisted of voice and music.[1]

Fessenden, De Forest, and many others had succeeded in taking electromagnetic waves (as theorized by Maxwell, demonstrated by Hertz, and used for telegraphy by Marconi) and use a given frequency as a "carrier wave" to carry an electric signal. The electric message, representing the actual sounds, was superimposed or *modulated* onto the electromagnetic carrier wave.

Most of the radio and television broadcasting that the public is familiar with takes place in four designated portions of the electromagnetic spectrum: the MF (medium frequency) band, where AM radio is located; the HF (high frequency) band, which houses most "short wave," amateur, police, citizens band (CB), and marine broadcasting; the VHF (very high frequency) band, which carries FM radio and TV channels 2–13; and the UHF (ultra high frequency) band, where we have TV channels 14–83, more citizens band (CB), and microwave transmissions.[2]

Actually,, these few "public uses" account only for a small percentage of the total radio spectrum. Most electromagnetic frequencies are devoted to land mobile uses, ship-to-shore, aeronautical, navigation, satellite, meteorological, specialized business uses, and a number of military applications. In fact, there are so many needs for the usable portions of the spectrum that user demands far exceed available channels. It is for this reason—the equitable distribution of available resources—that government regulation of the available electromagnetic space has become a necessity (Section 9.1.3).

Most of the developments outlined above were products of theoretical research or by-products of other, immediately practical inventions. Neither Daguerre, Morse, Bell, Maxwell, Hertz, Marconi nor even Edison initially had much of a concept of his contributions to mass communication. But from these crude nineteenth century beginnings, the age of the electric mass media was to be born.

4.2 Motion Pictures: The Flickering Illusion

The study of motion pictures can be broken into four fairly distinct periods. The first decade of the earliest period, "Experimentation and Exploitation," corresponds to the *elitist* stage—if we may distort the definition of "elitist" to refer to a small, self-selected group of the population (in this case, the lower classes, recent immigrants, and the semi-literate). The eras of "The Silent Feature" and "The Golden Age of Hollywood" certainly were part of the *popular* stage—as was the beginning of the "New Realism." However, by the late 1960s—with the MPAA ratings system, the emergence of youth-oriented films, the proliferation of pornography, art films, foreign-language movies, horror flicks, and other non-mass-audience attractions—the *specialist* stage could be clearly discerned.

4.2.1 EXPERIMENTATION AND EXPLOITATION (1894–1914)

No inventor, artist, or businessman could begin to envision what the moving pictures' future would be when the first Kinetoscope parlor opened on Broadway in 1894.

From Peep Shows to Vaudeville to the Nickelodeon Edison initially felt that the movies' best chance for commercial success was in peep-show apparatus, designed for one viewer at a time, installed in penny arcades. However, the advantages of large-screen projection soon became apparent, and by 1896 various competing movie projection formats were featured in many of the larger vaudeville houses across the country.

Shortly after the turn of the century, Thomas Tally of Los Angeles opened up a storefront "electric" theater and featured an all-movies format. This was perhaps the first actual movie house. Following Tally's lead,

many arcade owners, former circus operators, and medicine showmen bought second-hand projectors, rented empty stores, set up benches or chairs, and they were in the motion picture exhibition business. Melvin De Fleur comments:

Various names were popular, but the name "nickelodeon" caught on as a popular way of referring to these enterprises. The most important thing about them was that they were popular with people at the bottom of the social structure, and they made money. . . . The first decade of the twentieth century, then, saw a new form of communication begin to spread. It was to become a true mass medium.[3]

Content of the Early "Movies" The earliest moving pictures lasted about sixty seconds and made no pretense to any substantial content. There were no stories, no plot lines, no social messages—just flickering images of things that moved. Although variety acts were popular for the first peep shows, when

---

Following the pattern used for print media (Inset 3–1), the following periods have been used in discussing the development of each of the electric mediums.

INSET 4–5
Historical Periods Common to the Electric Media in America

General Characteristics	Motion Pictures	Radio and Recordings	Television
Experimentation	Experimentation and Exploitation (1894–1914)	Radio Telegraphy (1901–1919)	Early Experimentation (1920s–1940s)
Expansion	The Silent Feature (1915–1927)	Chaos on the Airwaves (1920–1927)	
Golden Ages	The Golden Age of Hollywood (1928–1949)	The Golden Age of Radio (1927–1948)	The Golden Age of Television (1948–1957)
Competition	New Realism (1950–Present)	Records and Talk (1949–Present)	Dominance of Network TV (1958–1970s)
			The New Technologies (1980s–Present)

movies moved into the vaudeville houses the audiences wanted something that they could not ordinarily see on the live stage—onrushing locomotives, faraway places, the unusual and exotic.

However, as the vaudeville audiences tired of these non-content films, moviemakers turned—as they have for decades since—to more risqué themes. Around the turn of the century, titles such as *How Bridget Served the Salad Undressed, What the Bootblack Saw,* and *Trapeze Disrobing Act* were popular fare. At the same time, however, some insightful moviemakers began to sense what form the future motion picture would take. The movies, they realized, were theater!

Porter and the Narrative Feature

Working for Edison, Edwin S. Porter had filmed several successful short films before he created *The Great Train Robbery* (1903), which film historian Richard Griffith has called "the first real movie . . . a classic overnight."[4] In producing this eight-minute western milestone, Porter pioneered the cinematic art of storytelling—especially in his editing techniques. According to film critic Arthur Knight, "In short, the technique that Porter had hit upon in assembling this unpretentious little Western provided the key to the whole art of film editing, the joining of bits of film shot in different places and at different times to form a single, unified narrative."[5]

Others followed Porter's lead, and the short feature became the standard nickelodeon attraction of the next ten years. But the improvised storefront movie houses were still looked down upon as low-class entertainment. They were unable to shake off their peep show and vaudeville heritage.

[T]he respectable shuddered away from them and murmured against them. It began to be said that something ought to be done about policing them or maybe banning them altogether. But the city nickelodeons thrived. Even more than in rural

---

INSET 4–6
Edison and the Trust

Instead of trying to fight his film competitors, Edison invited his major rivals to join him in forming a joint company to share their patents. As a result, ten of the largest film concerns created the Motion Picture Patents Company in 1909, establishing a virtual monopoly on motion picture production. The same ten then also formed the General Film Company to control the distribution and exhibition of films. Together, the two companies were referred to as "the Trust."

In an attempt to maintain its stranglehold on the industry, the Trust tried to freeze the state of the art. Ignoring (or unaware of) the desires of the audience, the Trust dictated that no motion picture should be longer than one or two reels (ten to twenty minutes), and it insisted that—despite public curiosity—the names of the actors and actresses in their films would not be known to the public lest they become popular and demand higher salaries. The Trust also extracted a license fee of two dollars a week from all exhibitors.

However, some of the nickelodeon operators and distributors chose not to give in to the Trust. Under the leadership of Carl Laemmle and others, many of the independents fought back by forming their own production companies to compete with the Trust and by taking anti-trust legal action. By 1915 the monopoly of the Trust had been decisively broken.

D.W. Griffith's *Birth of a Nation* (1915), with its innovative pictorial devices and controversial story line, demonstrated the power of the feature film.

America, they were the only entertainment available to the poor. Especially they were the chief entertainment of the hordes of immigrants from southern and eastern Europe who poured into the metropolis in the early 1900s.[6]

Thus, the nickelodeons continued to flourish. By 1911, between five and seven million Americans went daily to the movies in some thirteen thousand theaters.

4.2.2 THE SILENT FEATURE (1915–1927)

As the world perched on the brink of World War I, so the movie industry perched on the edge of a new era. With brand-new plush movie theaters, the promise of new formats and filmic techniques, and a new economic structure, moviemakers were finally beginning to attract a middle-class audience.

The Rise of the Major Studios With Edison's Trust in shambles (Inset 4–6), a new group of film industry leaders emerged—and the major Hollywood studios were born. Most of the studios were founded by theater owners and distributors who wanted to ensure themselves a supply of quality films: Carl Laemmle, who had spearheaded the fight against the Trust (Universal Studios); Adolph Zukor (Paramount); William Fox;

the four Warner brothers (Harry, Jack, Sam, and Albert); and Marcus Loew (M-G-M).

The opposite approach was taken in 1919. Four of the leading artists of Hollywood— three actors (Charlie Chaplin, Douglas Fairbanks, and Mary Pickford) and the top director of the era (D. W. Griffith)—incorporated to form United Artists to provide the machinery for the distribution, promotion, and exhibition of their productions.

Other major studios—Columbia, Goldwyn, RKO—were to follow in the twenties. During this period, the practice of "vertical integration" was firmly established. Vertical integration meant that the same company controlled all three phases of its film involvement: production, distribution, and exhibition. This pattern gave the studios considerable financial security in their operations, but within a couple of decades it also would give them serious legal problems.

D. W. Griffith and the Feature Film
A proud Southerner, David Wark Griffith started out in the film business as an actor for Edwin Porter in 1907, and within a few years he was recognized as one of the top

movie directors. Taking up where Porter had left off, Griffith pioneered or perfected most of the tools of the directing trade—the extreme close-up, the long shot, the moving camera (mounted on a truck), the split screen, and the fade-out. He also refined pacing in editing, camera composition, lighting, and subdued (non-theatrical) acting.

Griffith turned out his masterpiece in 1915—the three-hour epic *Birth of a Nation*. Throughout the decades film scholars and critics have pointed to this film as the real beginning of the modern feature film. Stunning in its visual impact and controversial in its subject matter (it supported the post–Civil War Ku Klux Klan), *Birth of a Nation* remains perhaps the most important film ever produced.

The sensation it created was without precedent and has never been duplicated. People had not known that they could be so moved, so roused, by what is, after all, only a succession of pictures passing across a screen. . . . His picture went on to a success whose dimensions can never be accurately calculated. . . . Its initial earnings rocked Wall Street, evoked a press interest which the movies had never before been able to attract, and brought comment even from governmental figures.[7]

The Star System Hollywood of the 1920s belonged to the movie star. Freed from the restraints of the Trust, studios initiated monumental publicity campaigns to build their respective stars; the public flocked to see a favorite star in his or her latest release; and the stars, of course, were able to demand fantastic salaries. Chaplin's salary went from $150 a week in 1913 to $14,000 weekly by 1917. At the same time Mary Pickford, "America's Sweetheart," was making close to a million dollars a year. Douglas Fairbanks, Theda Bara, Buster Keaton, William S. Hart, Clara Bow, Gloria Swanson, Valentino, Harold Lloyd, Ben Turpin, Laurel and Hardy, Tom Mix: the list of Hollywood's silent stars—romantic, comedic, adventurous, seductive—became the list of the world's best-known names.

4.2.3 THE GOLDEN AGE OF HOLLYWOOD (1928–1949)

The boisterous, glamorous age of the Silent Feature came to a roaring close in October 1927, when Warner Brothers released *The Jazz Singer* with Al Jolson. Basically a silent feature—it had three songs and a small amount of dialogue recorded on a synchronized disc—*The Jazz Singer* ushered in the era of the "Talkies." By the end of 1928 about 1,300 theaters were equipped for sound; by the end of 1929 some 9,000 (close to half of all the movie houses in the country, and virtually all of the larger ones) were equipped. "Overnight the public seemed to have forgotten that the silent film ever existed."[8]

Color arrived in Hollywood about the same time that movies learned to talk. There were some crude attempts at a color system earlier, but Douglas Fairbanks' *The Black Pirate* (1926), which used the Technicolor process developed by Herbert Kalmus, is generally considered to be the first successful color film.

Film Genres and Stars Most of the stars of the Golden Age came in with sound, and many of them became rather consistently identified with a particular genre or style. The *gangster* film was the first new genre of the 1930s, with fifty produced in 1931 alone. Among the stars introduced by this genre were Edward G. Robinson, Humphrey Bogart, and James Cagney. To escape from the Depression, audiences turned to the *musical,* with Fred Astaire and Ginger Rogers, Judy Garland, the operatic duets of Nelson Eddy and Jeanette MacDonald, and the extravagant stage productions of director Busby Berkeley. The audience turned also to the *comedy*—the zany slapstick of the Marx Brothers, the farce of W. C. Fields and Mae West, and the "screwball comedies" of the late 1930s featuring screen idols such as Clark Gable, Cary Grant, Jimmy Stewart, Claudette Colbert, Carole Lombard, and Katharine

Hepburn, among scores of others. There was also the venerable *western,* America's only indigenous dramatic format, which encompassed the heroism of John Wayne, the stoicism of Gary Cooper, and the singing of Roy Rogers.

Other specialized genres included the *horror/fantasy/science fiction* film, the *historical/biographical* film, and the *romance/adventure/spectacle* film. Chronologically, the genre which dominated the latter part of the period was the *war drama.* Hollywood turned its patriotic guns on the Nazis and Japanese in 1940 and was still going strong by the end of the decade.

Many of the outstanding films of the Golden Age, of course, transcended any generic description. The ageless *Wizard of Oz* (1939) combined the fantasy and musical formats to capture the imagination of three generations (so far). Later in the same year, *Gone with the Wind* combined history, romance, and spectacle to revive a sagging Hollywood economy and become the industry's largest moneymaker until the mid-1970s. Orson Welles' *Citizen Kane* (1941) pioneered several new cinematic techniques and remains today the most studied film in cinema departments throughout the country.

The "Paramount" Case Concerned with the practice of vertical integration—the control of production, distribution and exhibition of a given film by the same company—the Justice Department in 1938 launched a vigorous anti-trust suit against eight major studios: Paramount, Loew's–M-G-M, Twentieth Century–Fox, Warner Brothers, RKO, Universal, Columbia, and United Artists. An interim compromise was implemented during the war years, but the Justice Department renewed its case in 1944. After four more years of investigation, litigation, and appeals to the Supreme Court, the final decisions were handed down in 1948 and 1949. The studios were ordered to divest themselves of their theater holdings, a ruling which, in

Powerful camera work and stunning visual imagery in *Citizen Kane* (1941) established Orson Welles as an original Hollywood director.

effect, broke up the monopolies. This proved to be only one of several blows which seriously weakened the power of the major studios. The glow of Hollywood's Golden Era was beginning to fade during the late 1940s.

4.2.4 NEW REALISM (1950 TO THE PRESENT)

The Paramount decision meant that the studios, after losing ownership of their theater outlets, could no longer maintain distribution of their low-budget or "Grade B" films through the block-booking practices by which distribution of every film had been previously guaranteed. That was the first blow.

Second, Hollywood came under heavy attack by the House Un-American Activities Committee (HUAC) during the nation's post-war anti-communist fervor. (See Inset 10–2.)

The period of anti-Communist madness in American life was a time when accusations without proof were immediately granted the status of truth; when guilt was assumed, and innocence had to be documented. . . . A perverse kind of democracy was practiced: all accusations, no matter from whom, were taken equally seriously. A housewife or a grocer, a "nobody," could by simply writing a letter jeopardize the career of a wealthy, glamorous movie star.[9]

The third, and perhaps the heaviest, blow came from Hollywood's embryonic electronic stepchild. Television had as yet made no impact in 1946, when movie attendance was at an all-time high of 90 million viewers per week. But by 1953 almost half of all American families owned television sets, and movie attendance had been cut almost in half. People were staying home to watch the tube; the 21-inch screen had replaced the "B" picture.

Still other factors contributed to the erosion of Hollywood's monolithic structure. Following the war, *foreign moviemakers* were rejuvenated and entered international competition with a freshness and sense of realism that caught the major studios by surprise. As an aftermath of the Paramount decision, many *independent producers* found that they now could gain access to the theaters, and numerous non-studio productions made their impact felt. Finally, the *cost of doing business in Hollywood* had become outrageously high; soaring union costs and huge overhead expenses sent major producers out of the country—to Mexico, Canada, Europe, Asia—where authentic locations could be used on much smaller production budgets. Clearly, the economic picture of 1950 represented a "new realism" for Hollywood's corporate structure.

The "New Realism" and Content of the Movies Largely as a reaction to the factors outlined above, the content of films underwent a change during this same period. The motion picture reflected a more realistic and mature approach. Films around 1946–1949

With his co-star Vivien Leigh, Marlon Brando ushered in a new school of realistic "method" acting in *Streetcar Named Desire* (1951).

began to take a hard look at the American fabric; and the result frequently contradicted the "happy Hollywood ending" of the films of the Golden Age. Racial and religious injustices were explored in *Crossfire* (1947), *Gentlemen's Agreement* (1947), *Home of the Brave* (1949), and *Pinky* (1949). Alcoholism, physical rehabilitation, and mental treatment were tackled in such diverse films as *Lost Weekend* (1945), *The Best Years of Our Lives* (1946), *The Snake Pit* (1948), and *The Men* (1950).

A new type of star was introduced in *The Men*. A brooding, introspective, explosive, mumbling Marlon Brando (who also appeared in *A Streetcar Named Desire* the same year) typifies as well as anyone the age of the New Realism. "Method" actors such as Brando, Paul Newman, James Dean, Rod Steiger, Eli Wallach, George C. Scott, Montgomery Clift, Julie Harris, Kim Hunter, Eva Marie Saint, and many others brought a depth and naturalism to the screen that had never existed prior to the 1950s.

The nature of the leading character of the movie also changed. No longer could we be assured that we were going to the movies to witness a hero, the "good guy," triumph over evil. More often than not we now explored the inner turmoil of the anti-hero.

For examples one only has to look at some of the more popular roles portrayed by Newman, who is "closer to the public's image of the traditional screen superhero than any other contemporary actor."[10] Newman has played a gambler, a villainous son, a convict, an outlaw, a con man, and a Mafia-related liquor dealer in *The Hustler* (1961), *Hud* (1962), *Cool Hand Luke* (1967), *Butch Cassidy and the Sundance Kid* (1969), *The Sting* (1974), and *Absence of Malice* (1981).

Technological Reactions to Television

Hollywood also reacted to the threat of the video tube with several technological changes—devices and gimmicks designed to get people out of their houses by offering something they could not get on the TV set. The *drive-in theater* sprouted after the war, offering parents a chance to leave the house without hiring a babysitter and giving young lovers an opportunity for privacy not found in the theater.

The promise and appeal of *three-dimensional pictures* flourished briefly around 1953. The 3-D process accomplished its depth perception by having movie patrons wear inexpensive cardboard-framed polarized glasses which allowed the eyes to blend two images of a given scene shot from slightly different angles. Because of the combination of uncomfortable glasses and cheap sensationalistic productions, the 3-D craze peaked and died within a year. There have been periodic attempts at resurrection, however.

The one technological improvement which worked was the *large screen*. The Cinerama process, unveiled in 1952, was soon followed

---

INSET 4–7
Movies and the Large-Screen Processes

The first of the big-screen techniques, Cinerama was also the most sensational. Originally accomplished by using three lenses to record three synchronized pictures—and then projecting them on a giant screen higher and more than three times the width of a normal screen—Cinerama gave the audience a sensation of being surrounded by the action, peripherally engulfed in all the details of the acetate environment. Knight describes the sensation:

Because Cinerama parallels our field of vision both in its curve and range, we are no longer on the outside looking in on a scene that has been artificially foreshortened and tricked to give the illusion of depth. Rather, we have passed beyond the boundaries of another realm and are on the inside looking around. It is almost like being projected into the fourth dimension![11]

The effect of Cinerama was magnified by ambitious stereophonic sound systems that used six or seven microphones—and corresponding high-fidelity speakers placed throughout the theater—to reproduce the source of each sound at the same location as its visual origin. The "wrap-around" effect was truly sensational.

Cinerama was followed by other, single-lens systems that eliminated the mechanical and visual problems of the three-projector design. Cinema-Scope, the most successful, used an anamorphic lens to "squeeze" the image onto a 35mm film and a corresponding projection lens to fill the wide screen in the theater. VistaVision recorded on a 70mm negative and then reduced the print to 35mm for distribution. The third system, Todd-AO, used a wide 65mm film both for recording and projection.

In this scene from the original film *This is Cinerama* one can clearly see the lines where the three separately projected Cinerama images meet.

by several other less expensive formats. What they succeeded in producing, with color and stereophonic sound systems, was a sense of scope and grandeur that simply could not be transferred to the twenty-one-inch screen in the living room. Here was one spectacular answer to the television threat.

Relevance and Specialization of the Late Sixties   Sometime around the late 1960s, several trends could be pinpointed which signaled the beginning of the *specialization* phase of the medium, as promulgated by Merrill and Lowenstein (Section 3.1). *Easy Rider* (1969), the odyssey of two cocaine dealers motorcycling across the South looking for meaning in their lives, ushered in a new era of low-budget "youth-oriented" (often anti-establishment) films. In the early 1970s, pornography films also became a potent economic factor; two hard-core sex flicks, *The Devil in Miss Jones* and *Deep Throat*, ranked sixth and eleventh respectively in gross box office receipts in 1973. Other clearly defined formats—art films, black motion pictures, horror/terror exploitation movies, foreign imports—continued to grow and attract significant specialized audiences.

Despite the growing competition from television and other home entertainment media, the movies—even with lower attendance, higher budgets, and fewer motion pictures—remain an established social force in American culture.

4.3   Radio and Recordings: The Background Sounds

All of the communication media development discussed up to this point has been based upon direct receiver support: the receiver *purchases* a copy of a book, *subscribes* to a newspaper or magazine, or *pays* his or her admission to the theater. The concept of broadly casting out a message at no charge to whomever might be listening has not yet been considered.

4.3.1   RADIO TELEGRAPHY (1901–1919)

Initially, radio telegraphy was used primarily for maritime purposes—ship-to-shore and ship-to-ship communication. By the turn of the century, ships were using wireless apparatus for distress transmissions and sea rescues. One of the most famous maritime disasters was the sinking of the "unsinkable" luxury liner *Titanic*. The historian Sydney Head comments on this 1912 catastrophe:

Her passenger list, studded with famous names in the arts, the sciences, the financial world, and diplomacy, made the *Titanic* disaster the most dramatic tragedy of its kind in history. And the fact that for days radio telegraphy maintained the world's only thread of contact with the survivors brought the new medium to public attention as nothing else had done.[12]

The Radio Act of 1912 As a direct result of the *Titanic* catastrophe, Congress passed the Radio Act of 1912. Among other things, it required all ships' wireless equipment to be manned by licensed operators twenty-four hours a day. (One potential rescue ship during the *Titanic* sinking was only a few miles away, but its lone wireless operator had signed off for the night only fifteen minutes before the accident.)

Although the Radio Act of 1912 was primarily concerned with detailed technical requirements and assignment specifications, it firmly established the precedent for government regulation. The secretary of commerce was given jurisdiction over the licensing of all wireless—and, by implication, broadcasting—stations. However, the secretary was given no real powers of enforcement, an omission that would lead to substantial problems a decade later.

The Navy Steps In During this period the technical quality of voice transmission was being constantly improved, and by the beginning of World War I a practical medium of wireless telephony had evolved. One of the miracles of radio's development was that such technical progress could be made while its most prominent inventor-entrepreneurs were locked in legal battles with one another over patent infringements. The problems of litigation were temporarily shelved, however, when the U.S. Navy—in the name of national security—took charge of all radio operations during the war. Following the war, the navy was instrumental in working out a series of corporate compromises and patent pools which resulted in the formation of the Radio Corporation of America (RCA). By 1919–1920 both technical developments and business structures had progressed to the point where it was feasible to begin thinking about the possibility of broadcasting mes-

Thomas Edison with an 1888 version of his wax cylinder phonograph (top). Edison "home phonograph" (gramophone) was first patented in 1896 (bottom).

sages out to the great unseen audience who might have access to wireless receivers.

From Cylinders to Discs When Edison devised his crude wax cylinder recording system in 1877, no one could have foreseen the relationship between the recording industry and radio broadcasting. One decade after Edison's cylinder, Emile Berliner devised the method of disc recording; by 1896 he was pressing copies of his Gramophone records from a negative master disc. Shortly after the turn of the century records were being sold commercially. The Victor Talking Machine Company was featuring Gramophone discs, and the American Graphophone Company began selling lateral discs as well as the Edison-type cylinders.

4.3.2. CHAOS ON THE AIRWAVES (1920–1927)

Much of the early progress in radio telephony was due to the work of thousands of amateur radio operators who kept in constant contact with one another, swapping technical hints and frequently transmitting specific programming material—news, weather, sports results, and recorded music.

Station KDKA, Pittsburgh   One such "ham" operator was Dr. Frank Conrad, an engineer with Westinghouse in Pittsburgh. Encouraged and supported by his employer, Conrad upgraded his transmitting equipment, changed its call letters to KDKA

**INSET 4–8
David Sarnoff
and the
"Radio Music Box"**

The Russian immigrant youngster meant to apply for a job as copyboy on a New York newspaper, but he accidently knocked on the wrong door and wound up as a messenger boy for the Commercial Cable Company. Through that quirk of fate, David Sarnoff got his start in electric telecommunications rather than in the print media. By 1906 the fifteen-year-old Sarnoff was employed by the prestigious American Marconi Company, where he eventually worked his way up to become one of their top telegraph key operators.

Five years later, fate placed Sarnoff at the wireless key when the first news of the *Titanic* sinking came in. "For three days and nights he received and transmitted messages. . . . Sarnoff's wireless became the nation's information link with the disaster of the decade."[13] Promoted to assistant traffic manager, Sarnoff proved to be one of the great oracles who foresaw the potential of radio broadcasting. In a 1916 memorandum to his boss, Sarnoff wrote:

I have in mind a plan of development which would make radio a "household utility" in the same sense as the piano or phonograph. The idea is to bring music into the house by wireless. . . . The receiver can be designed in the form of a simple "Radio Music Box" and arranged for several different wave lengths.[14]

When the assets of American Marconi were transferred to the newly formed RCA, Sarnoff went along as commercial manager. By the time he was thirty, in 1921, Sarnoff was general manager of RCA. One of the first to envision the role of radio networking, Sarnoff was instrumental in setting up the NBC networks. He was president of RCA by 1930 and chairman of the board in 1947. Until his retirement in 1969 (and death in 1971), Sarnoff remained one of the premier forces in American telecommunications—from immigrant telegraph key operator to innovator in the Age of Satellites. Horatio Alger would have loved to have created the Sarnoff story.

In the early 1920s, before radio receivers had speakers, people would listen to their crystal receiving sets with headphones. Sixty years later young radio listeners are still listening to their personal receivers with headsets.

(becoming the first licensed standard broadcast station in the Department of Commerce records), and inaugurated a new type of public service by broadcasting to the public at large the Harding-Cox presidential election results on November 2, 1920.

Many other broadcasting stations began operations at approximately the same time as KDKA. They were supported by electrical equipment companies, department stores, educational institutions, newspapers, and churches—anyone who had a public relations interest in reaching large numbers of listeners. General Electric, Westinghouse, AT&T, and RCA were all early station experimenters. Programming was informal and improvised, often relying heavily upon records borrowed from a local music store. Thus the symbiotic relationship between the radio and recording industries was established early in the development of both media.

Station WEAF and the Commercial   More than two hundred radio stations were operating by mid-1922, but none of them had any means of generating financial revenue. Up to this point, it had been assumed that every radio sponsor would simply operate its own station in the manner of Westinghouse and KDKA. AT&T felt, however, that a station—operated by the telephone company—could function as a common carrier, letting anyone who had a message pay a fee for a few minutes of air time to broadcast the message to the public. Thus, only two weeks after it went on the air in 1923, AT&T's station, WEAF, sold ten minutes of air time to a real estate firm in Long Island for a "toll broadcast" extolling the virtues of living in Hawthorne Courts. The radio commercial was born.

Creation of the Networks In 1924 AT&T built a six-station network around WEAF which carried three hours of shared programming a day; in the same year it put together a twenty-two-station temporary hookup to carry a speech by President Coolidge. Although AT&T tried to stifle competition, in 1925 RCA managed to string together a competing fourteen-station network based upon programming from its New York station, WJZ.

At that point AT&T decided to get out of the radio business. The giant telephone monolith had created serious public relations problems for itself by trying to exercise too much authority over the broadcast industry, and it decided to concentrate on its telephone monopoly. In the ensuing corporate agreements, RCA wound up with two networks—the WEAF-based AT&T network became the NBC Red network, and the WJZ web became the NBC Blue network. The telephone company retained rights to all network relay connections.

One other major network was started in 1927 when a record corporation, the Columbia Phonograph Record Company, teamed up with a talent agency, United Independent Broadcasters, to establish the Columbia Phonograph Broadcasting System. With financial backing from his family's tobacco fortune, William S. Paley bought the floundering network in 1928, shortened the name to CBS, and lined up a sizable number of affiliates. CBS was operating in the black by 1929 and soon began to offer NBC serious competition. And for almost half a century, William Paley shared the spotlight with David Sarnoff as one of the two corporate giants of the broadcasting industry.

Growth and Confusion As the concept of commercial radio caught on, the spread of radio broadcasting was inevitable. By 1927 there were close to seven hundred radio stations on the air. And almost seven million households were equipped to receive radio transmissions. This growth, however, was virtually uncontrolled and unregulated. Because the secretary of commerce was given no actual authority to enforce the Radio Act of 1912, radio stations operated on unauthorized frequencies or used illegal channels, at prohibited times, and in excess of licensed transmitter power. The result was utter chaos. (See Section 9.1.3.)

4.3.3 THE GOLDEN AGE OF RADIO (1927–1948)

Most students of broadcasting concur that radio experienced a "Golden Age" during the Depression and World War II. It was an era marked by technical improvements, strong network development, unparalleled commercial success, universally popular entertainment programming, and maturing news coverage.

Order out of Chaos The spectacular success of radio was facilitated by government action which ended the clutter and anarchy which had characterized the medium in the middle Twenties. The Radio Act of 1927 created a five-person Federal Radio Commission (FRC) with broad powers to straighten out the engineering disarray of the radio industry by assigning channel frequencies, determining transmitter power, and so forth (see Inset 9–3). In 1934 the FRC was replaced by the seven-member Federal Communications Commission (FCC), which was given jurisdiction over all forms of telecommunications—including telephone, cable, and telegraph as well as radio and experimental television activity.

The Dominance of Networking The two NBC chains and Bill Paley's CBS network dominated the commercial and programming structure of the 1930s and early 1940s. However, in 1934 a group of four stations (none of which was affiliated with either NBC or CBS) formed a "mutual" network to interchange programming, starting off with *The Lone Ranger*. Thus the Mutual Broadcasting System (MBS) was created.

In reaction to the strong control exercised by the networks, the FCC initiated a thorough study of radio network practices in the late Thirties which resulted in the "Chain Broadcasting Regulations" of 1941. Among other things, this anti-trust move (which paralleled the "Paramount" case in film, Section 4.2.3) stipulated that no corporation could own more than one chain or network. Consequently, NBC sold its Blue network in 1943 to a candy manufacturer, Edward Noble, who renamed it the American Broadcasting Company.

Programming Series and Formats   What made the Golden Age truly "golden" was primarily the popular entertainment programming, the fun and fantasy which delivered America from the depths of the Depression and the gloom of impending war clouds over Europe. Two of the nation's favorite programs both made their debuts in 1929— the *Amos 'n' Andy* comedy series and Rudy Vallee's *Fleischmann Hour*, which was perhaps radio's first network variety show.

Many of the radio dramatic formats paralleled those popular in the movies at the same time. There were gangsters and police/action series (*Gangbusters, Mr. District Attorney*), westerns (*The Lone Ranger, Tom Mix*), mystery and suspense (*Inner Sanctum, The Shadow*), situation comedies (*Blondie, Henry Aldrich*), and many others. Radio launched its own formats with the anthology dramas (*Lux Radio Theater, Mr. First Nighter*) and the daytime serials (*Ma Perkins, Life Can Be Beautiful*), which were nicknamed "soap operas" because soap manufacturers were prominent among the regular sponsors. And younger listeners had their own afternoon "cereal serials"—fifteen-minute episodes of continuing dramas such as *Captain Midnight* and *Jack Armstrong*.

The morning after Halloween, 1938, the *New York Times* reported:

A wave of mass hysteria seized thousands of radio listeners throughout the nation between 8:15 and 9:30 o'clock last night when a broadcast of a dramatization of H. G. Wells's fantasy, "The War of the Worlds," led thousands to believe that an interplanetary conflict had started with invading Martians spreading wide death and destruction in New Jersey and New York.[15]

The radio drama—one of the most famous broadcasts ever—was produced by Orson Welles for the CBS *Mercury Theatre of the Air*. In the show, a simulated program of dance music was repeatedly interrupted for a series of news bulletins regarding a mysterious landing of alien spacecraft. The tension built throughout the hour as "newscasters" reported the progress of invading Martians who were supposedly terrorizing the East Coast.

Designed innocently as a Halloween offering, the *War of the Worlds* drama included a series of announcements reminding the audience that it was only a play. However, hundreds of thousands of listeners had already panicked. Thousands fled their homes. In one city block in Newark, twenty families rushed from their houses with wet handkerchiefs over their faces to protect them from a gas attack. And there were even several reported suicides. Never before or since has a single dramatic program resulted in such an unanticipated mass reaction.

Radio may be remembered most fondly, however, for the hybrid comedy/variety/talk formats which kept America laughing for a quarter of a century with comedians such as Ed Wynn, Eddie Cantor, Jimmy Durante, Fanny Brice, Bing Crosby, George Burns and Gracie Allen, Jack Benny, Fred Allen, Red Skelton, Bob Hope, Edgar Bergen, and Abbott and Costello.

News Coverage and the War   Radio was born in 1920 with coverage of election news, and by 1930 it had its first regularly scheduled daily newscast (Lowell Thomas over the NBC Blue network). It was with the outbreak of World War II, however, that radio achieved its full maturity as a news medium. Correspondents such as Edward R. Murrow, Eric Sevareid, Howard K. Smith, Winston M. Burdett, Charles Collingwood, and Richard C. Hottelet covered the conflict live, from every corner of the globe, to keep America informed of the daily progress of the war.

4.3.4   RECORDS AND TALK (1949 TO THE PRESENT)

Just as the giant silver screen had to find ways to respond to the challenge of television, so did Sarnoff's little "radio music box." Radio networks phased out their long-standing popular programs (variety shows, comedy, drama, soap operas, and other formats taken over by television) and concentrated on periodic national news and information services—news summaries, commentaries, sports, human interest features, and the like. Radio programming increasingly became the province of the local station, and the stations turned increasingly to inexpensive recorded music and local personalities.

Records and Tapes   Technologically, advances in audio recording evolved even as radio began searching for new formats.

Audio tape recording—based upon German developments during World War II—made a large impact in the late 1940s. Not only did magnetic tape lead eventually to a new revolution in retail distribution of recorded music with the cassettes and eight-track cartridges of the 1960s and 1970s, but tape recording also revolutionized the audio recording/production industry by introducing multi-track recording, better fidelity, echo effects, track superimposition, and other modern techniques. The record industry was also turned around in 1948 when long-playing vinyl "microgroove" records—spinning at either 45 or 33⅓ revolutions per minute (rpm)—replaced the older, heavier, more brittle, and musically inferior 78 rpm shellac discs.

With the technical innovations in recorded audio came musical and marketing innovations—a new sound, a new audience, a new culture. Bill Haley was one of the first record personalities to combine Black-inspired rhythm-and-blues with country-and-western, creating a new musical form with a hard-driving beat which came to be called "rock and roll." His "Rock around the Clock" was the best-selling record of 1955. The next year saw the meteoric rise of "a white boy who can sing colored,"[16] and Elvis Presley was the unchallenged king of rock. In the early 1960s the Beatles invaded America and defined a whole new era.

With new aggressive marketing and promotional campaigns aimed at the younger audience, the recording industry soared during the Sixties and Seventies. Record sales increased thirty-four percent, for example, during the early Beatles period, between 1964 and 1966. By the late 1970s the recording industry was the nation's second largest entertainment business, television being the largest.

The Rise of the Disc Jockey   As local record shows replaced network radio programming, it was inevitable that the persons spinning the discs would become featured personalities. Don Pember summarizes the new format:

The disc jockey emerged in the Fifties as the demigod of modern radio. He was frequently as glamorized and idolized as the stars whose records he played. . . . To the teenagers, the DJ was somebody who dug their music, who understood their problems. . . . To housewives, he was a man around the house after the family had left for the day and the kitchen got quiet and lonely, someone to share that second cup of coffee with. The drive-time jock was a traveling companion to the men, a pal during that long ride to work, somebody who understood the feeling of four-putting the seventeenth hole on Saturday.[17]

The Talk Formats If the disc jockey program is one of the most prevalent forms of radio today, the other staple of the modern airwaves could be loosely labeled "talk radio." After all, talk—like recorded music—is cheap, and easily programmed by local stations. The origins of the various talk formats could probably be traced back to the easygoing banter of earlier radio hosts like Arthur Godfrey, Dave Garroway, and Steve Allen.

At the local level, the talk format has taken many forms. The *all-news* station, one of the most ambitious and expensive types, emerged in the sixties in many of the larger markets. One popular talk-radio format was pioneered in the late 1950s and early 1960s by Joe Pyne in Los Angeles and "Long John" Nebel in New York—the *phone-in* program. "This kind of format adopts two of America's basic rural pastimes as its attractions—listening in on the party line and talking at the town meeting."[18] By inviting listeners to telephone the talk-show host and participate in the on-air discussion, this programming innovation helps to compensate for the one-way nature of broadcast media, allowing the receiver to furnish continuing feedback. Both Mutual and ABC launched nationwide network versions of the phone-in talk show in the early 1980s.

INSET 4–10   Broadcasting Stations, 1922 to 1982

The growth of AM radio, FM commercial radio, FM educational radio, commercial TV, and educational TV ("public TV") is shown below by four-year periods.[19]

Year	AM Radio	FM Commercial	FM Educational	Commercial TV	Educational TV	Total
1922	30					30
1926	528					528
1930	618					618
1934	583					583
1938	689					689
1942	887	36	7	2		934
1946	948	48	9	6		1.011
1950	2,086	733	48	98		2,965
1954	2,521	560	112	354	2	3,549
1958	3,196	537	141	495	28	4,396
1962	3,618	960	194	541	62	5,375
1966	4.065	1,446	268	585	114	6,478
1970	4,292	2,184	413	677	185	7,751
1974	4,407	2,502	652	697	241	8,499
1978	4,513	3,001	926	727	259	9,426
1982	4,634	3,349	1,118	774	271	10,146

FM and Specialization The growth of specialized radio can be attributed to a great extent to technological advances during this period. By 1951, almost every car on the American road had a radio receiver, foretelling the portability and personalization of the medium. This trend was encouraged by the development of the transistor by the Bell System labs in 1947—the first major breakthrough in receiver and amplification technology since De Forest's audion vacuum tube. The transistor radio brought receiver size and price down to where a family of modest means could afford to put a radio in virtually every room, equip their auto(s), and carry a portable to the beach.

After a slow start, FM radio got off the ground in the late 1950s. During the Sixties the number of FM stations just about tripled. FM was given a big boost in 1961 when the FCC approved technical standards for stereophonic transmission. Coupled with other technical advantages in fidelity and clearer reception, stereo broadcasting helped to push the popularity of FM radio.

Both AM and FM services were characterized by the post-television trend of radio specialization. Scarcely a station exists today that cannot be neatly categorized by a recognizable pattern or catchy slogan: top 40, rock (which has several different sub-categories, such as acid rock, hard rock, disco, soft rock, punk, funk, and other current designations), middle-of-the-road, "beautiful music" (or "wallpaper" music designed to blend into the background), classical, jazz, country-and-western, ethnic (many varieties to choose from), all-news, all-talk, and similar labels.

Noncommercial educational or "public radio" stations also follow the general pattern of specialization within the medium. College and school stations have been in existence since the earliest days of radio broadcasting. Funded largely by educational institutions and private foundations, educational radio has provided a valuable service to specific, if small, audiences—farmers, school students,

special-interest groups, and so forth. Educational radio—largely utilizing FM channels—was advanced significantly in 1971 when the Corporation for Public Broadcasting created the National Public Radio (NPR) live network. Today close to three hundred NPR stations provide a variety of specialized music and ethnic, public affairs, and news programming services (both local and national) to diversified audiences.[20]

The Background Media The term "background media" can be applied to both radio and the recording industry. We often turn on the radio or play a stack of recordings not so much for specific content as for the constant background companionship of a particular sound. Demonstrating McLuhan's observation that "the medium is the message," we use radio and recordings to a great extent—more than any other mediums—for their background messages while we pursue other tasks that demand foreground focus.

4.4 Television: Magic Window or Boob Tube?

While the movies and the radio enjoyed their golden years during the 1930s and 1940s, the phosphorescent eye of the television tube glowed on the horizon like a beckoning Cyclops. This gestating giant gave only a slight hint of its impending destiny—that it would soon absorb and dominate the corporate and economic structure of radio, that it would become the consumer and distributor of a new Hollywood industry.

4.4.1 EARLY EXPERIMENTATION (1920s TO 1940s)

Zworykin's iconoscope tube heralded the glories of the coming electronic image. An AT&T research scientist, H. E. Ives, built a prototype electronic system in the Twenties and succeeded in sending a closed-circuit TV picture of Herbert Hoover (then secretary of commerce) from Washington to New York in 1927.

Television Reaches the Public Television's slow technical progress was accompanied by occasional bursts of public excitement and premature expectations. Early TV endeavors suffered from several false starts. America's first large-scale public demonstration took place in 1939 when RCA televised opening ceremonies from the World's Fair in New York City, featuring an address by President Franklin Roosevelt. The same year saw the first sale of TV receivers to the public.

Technical Standards and Interruptions
Television development was continually frustrated by conflicting technical standards and incompatible systems. From the 50- and 60-line scanning systems of the 1920s, television had progressed to the 441-line electronic scanning process demonstrated at the 1939 World's Fair. RCA pushed for adoption of this standard, but most of its competitors held out for a higher-line standard that would provide better resolution. When the FCC adopted the current 525-line system in 1941, manufacturers readily accepted this standard because they were anxious to get on with the business of selling television to the American public. However, many observers point out that if we had taken more time to develop an even higher-line standard (as many of the countries of the world did), we would now be enjoying finer picture quality. (See Section 12.2.3.) The earlier an industry adopts a technical standard, the lower the quality will be at which the state of the art is frozen.

National priorities adopted for World War II decreed that television would have to take a back seat to other military and commercial needs. Only six licensed stations operated through the early 1940s. But, by about 1947, the electronics industries were again focusing on the commercial potential of the glowing tube. This time the public was ready, better cameras had been introduced, and the FCC was encouraging. Following a quarter-century of technical development, false promises, premature commercial anticipation, and wartime delays, television was finally poised on the brink of public consciousness.

4.4.2 THE GOLDEN AGE OF TELEVISION (1948–1957)

Television was to benefit from the experience gained during two decades of radio broadcasting: the corporate structure of commercial broadcasting—stations and networks—was firmly established; the economic base of advertising support was operating efficiently; the concept of broadcast journalism had proved itself; and the programming formats and entertainment stars were eagerly accepted by the American public.

The years of 1946 and 1947 represent the *elitist* period of American television. Only about 14,000 households had television receivers in early 1947. However, at the beginning of the *popular* stage, television drew its audience not so much from the affluent but rather—like the movies—from the working classes. An estimated 3.9 million people watched the 1947 World Series on television—3.5 million of them in neighborhood taverns and bars! "The TV set over the corner bar was a first introduction to the new medium for many people, and it helped sell thousands of sets for the home."[21]

Audience Growth Most critics and observers pinpoint 1948 as the year when the new video medium really started its spectacular climb in popularity. The number of TV stations on the air rose from 16 in early 1948 to 108 by January 1952. At the same time, the percentage of households equipped with TV receivers increased from less than one percent in 1948 to about half of the population by 1953. And by 1957, the end of the "Golden Age" of television, about three-quarters of all American homes had TV sets.

Programs, Formats, and Stars McLuhan observed that the content of any new medium is basically that of the older media revised and transplanted.[22] Certainly this is obvious with television. To create dramatic programs, the new medium simply took the pictorial story-telling format from the movies and put it on the tube. In the same way, and even more directly, television took many other early formats from radio—variety shows, comedy programs, musical revues, quiz shows, documentaries, and news programs.

Comedy and variety programs dominated the new medium. Milton Berle, as "Uncle Milty" in the original *Texaco Star Theater* first captured the imagination of early TV viewers in 1948 with his slapstick antics. Then in 1951 a zany radio comedienne named Lucille Ball made television history with her filmed situation comedy, *I Love Lucy*. The series was America's favorite program for six years,

never slipping below third place in the popularity ratings; it finally went off the air in 1961.

The "Golden Age" Defined   Most critics and scholars of television programming associate the "Golden Age" of TV with that period of network television which was characterized by the live "anthology" dramatic series. These continuing series featured a completely self-contained drama, with a different cast, in each scheduled production (every week or every other week). The preeminence of the dramatic productions of this period lies in the fact that they were produced "live" (as opposed to being recorded on either film or videotape), and thus they

---

The growth of television was delayed in part because of the technical "lock-and-key" nature of the electronic process. Specific technical standards had to be established concerning the number of scanning lines, number of frames per second, and method of controlling the scanning beam. Unlike radio—where any standard radio receiving apparatus (headsets, crystal receivers, tube sets) could pick up any AM radio transmission—TV receivers had to be synchronized with a specific telecasting system. As long as there were competing television transmission systems, it was difficult to promote any significant spread of receivers. "Unless both transmitter and receiver operate on the same line and field frequencies, and unless the receiver is designed to receive and interpret specific synchronizing signals, the key will not fit the lock."[23]

It took the FCC many years of careful maneuvering, public hearings, and industry compromises before technical standards could be established. Some of the highlights of the FCC rulings and decisions are listed below:

INSET 4–11
Technical Standards and FCC Allocations

1937:   The VHF band from 20–300 mHz was designated for experimental TV stations. Nineteen channels were established, each at the present standard band width of 6 megaHertz.

1938:   The first tentative reservations were set aside for educational radio stations. Twenty-five AM channels were designated in the 41–42 mHz band (the lower VHF portion of the spectrum); this was soon changed to five FM channels in the 42–43 mHz range.

1941:   Today's technical TV standards were adopted. These standards called for a 525-scanning-line picture, with 30 frames per second, and FM audio. The FCC then allocated eighteen VHF channels for TV development.

captured intensity, excitement, and enthusiasm that has seldom been matched.

During the peak year of live TV drama, the 1955–56 season, there were eighteen different prime-time anthology series on the air. Some of the memorable series of this period included *Kraft Television Theatre* (1947–1958), *Studio One* (1948–1958), *Philco TV Playhouse* (1948–1955), and the *U.S. Steel Hour* (1953–1963). The most ambitious and widely heralded product of the Golden Age was probably *Playhouse 90* (1956–1960), although it came at the end of the period. The series was live for only one season (1956–57), but it continued to represent the highest standard of anthology drama for the remainder of the decade.

4.4.3 DOMINANCE OF NETWORK TELEVISION (1958–1970s)

The transcontinental coaxial cable and microwave hookup in 1951 made coast-to-coast transmission possible. Even before then,

As soon as it was introduced in the 1940s, the television receiver became the dominant piece of furniture in the nation's living rooms.

1945: The number of TV channels was reduced to thirteen as military and other government uses demanded more spectrum space. FM was moved up to 88–108 mHz (where it is presently located), with twenty FM channels (88–92 mHz) reserved for noncommercial educational use.

1948: Channel 1 was deleted from the allocations, resulting in the current twelve VHF channels. FM was nestled in between channels 6 and 7 (see Inset 4–4).

In September, a "freeze" halted all applications while the FCC wrestled with questions of additional spectrum space (twelve channels were obviously woefully inadequate to serve the country), color technical standards, and reservations for educational (ETV) broadcasters.

1952: The Sixth Report and Order ended the freeze, creating seventy new UHF television channels and allocating a total of 2,053 specific station assignments on a city-by-city basis (about two-thirds of which were UHF). Approximately twelve percent of the assignments (242 stations) were reserved for noncommercial educational use.

1953: After years of intra-industry fighting and backtracking, color technical standards were approved. These standards were based largely upon the RCA compatible electronic system.

however, the commercial networks had dominated the television industry. By the end of the 1950s and on through the 1960s and 1970s, the video picture was clearly characterized by three factors: it was *network-oriented* (despite the importance of the individual station, the industry has been dominated by the networks); it was *commercial* (noncommercial "public" broadcasting notwithstanding, television has been primarily an economic commercial enterprise); and it was *recorded*.

Videotape Technologies   The complicated process of recording a video picture on magnetic tape was mastered in 1956, and by 1957 the industry was switching to the new recorded medium. Sterling and Kittross summarize some of the advantages of videotape:

The arrival of tape led to some changes in television programming and production. It made editing much faster than with film because the tape did not have to be processed. It made special effects possible with the push of a button, and far cheaper than on film. It produced much higher quality than either kinescope recordings [a method of filming a television image directly off the face of a receiver] or film. . . . Using an erase/rerecord (make/remake) system, one could easily remove a mistake in an original production.[24]

But with these advantages came some aesthetic and emotional disadvantages which helped mark the end of the Golden Age. "Some critics claimed . . . that actors rarely gave performances with the same intensity as in the 'live' days, since they knew that a 'fluff' or mistake could be removed, however expensively, before it went on the air."[25] Television programming became more predictable, more easily imitated, smoother, less experimental, and less exciting.

Programming Trends   During the late 1950s the industry was caught rigging quiz shows, and the nation reacted with indignation (see Inset 11–11). From that point on, TV programming appeared to become even more cautious and bland, less controversial and seldom innovative. Cycles became evident as different formats (westerns, variety shows, police dramas) waxed and waned through the TV seasons. But a generally repetitive pattern prevailed as the three networks imitated each other's winning formats and hastily dropped any program which did not immediately rank high in the audience ratings.

One new source of programming was found in 1961 when NBC introduced *Saturday Night at the Movies,* inaugurating the practice of releasing fairly recent major theatrical films in prime time. Five years later, the "made for TV" movie was introduced—a programming concept which was to come as close as any other format to replacing the anthology dramas of the Golden Age. Another new dramatic format, the "TV novel" or mini-series, was introduced to commercial television in a big way with *Roots* in 1976.

Noncommercial "Public Broadcasting"
While commercial television was building larger corporate profits with its repetitive but popular programming formats, the concept of noncommercial, educational public broadcasting was slowly making inroads on the nation's consciousness. Started in the early 1950s, educational TV (or ETV) got off to a shaky financial start. Supported by contributions from individual viewers, local community groups, local schools, state agencies, and private foundations (especially the Ford Foundation), ETV provided a blend of in-school instruction, general adult educational fare, and cultural programming. Then in 1967, with the establishment of the Corporation for Public Broadcasting, ETV (now labeled "public television") and educational/ public radio received a greatly needed federal shot in the arm. The Public Broadcasting Service (PBS) was formed as the live interconnection service for the PTV stations, and programming quality improved significantly. Federal support for public broadcasting has diminished considerably, however, since the beginning of the Reagan administration.

Public television represents a significant step toward the *specialization* of television. Serving a conglomerate of small specialized audiences (school children, the elderly, opera buffs, news analysts, serious drama fans, and so forth), public TV seldom tries to reach a mass audience, and only rarely does it receive more than four or five percent of the audience at any one time. It is truly a specialized medium.

4.4.4 THE NEW TECHNOLOGIES (1980s ON)

Many observers and media critics agree that the age of network dominance of our TV sets is rapidly dwindling. New audio and video technologies will provide increasing competition for the commercial networks, emancipating the viewer from the twin tyrannies of fixed schedules and limited choices. Programming choices will be unlimited; the home video receiver complex will be an interactive center rather than just a passive device; and the consumer-viewer will be in charge. The true age of television *specialization* has begun. These technologies and their potential applications are discussed in detail in Chapter 12.

Cable TV The phenomenon of cable television started out as "community antenna TV," in essence a "super antenna," to pull hard-to-receive TV signals into an otherwise isolated community. As early as 1949 and 1950 some hilly and mountainous towns were building simple systems; a group of individuals or a local business (often the village TV set salesman) would place a powerful antenna on some nearby mountaintop, run cable down into the valley, and attach subscribers' TV sets to the community antenna for a relatively small fee.

By the 1960s cable entrepreneurs were bringing in distant stations and giving subscribers more channels of programming than they could otherwise receive locally. In the early 1970s larger cable-TV systems also started originating their own productions—weather and news services, local high school

events, and so forth. By the end of the Seventies cable-TV systems were offering, for an additional fee, special programming not available over any broadcast station—first-run movies, sporting events, exclusive variety productions, and similar attractions. These "pay-cable" services are generally sent to cable systems by satellite.

Another development was the introduction of *interactive* cable systems, which enabled subscribers to provide instantaneous feedback to the cable service. One of the first major installations of this type was the QUBE project introduced by Warner Communications in Columbus, Ohio, in 1977. This two-way system enables viewers to respond to local politicians, participate in straw votes, predict sports plays, and help to judge amateur talent contests. Video banking, remote-controlled shopping, and burglary surveillance are all feasible applications of interactive cable.

Satellites The use of artificial satellites for telecommunications started in the early 1960s. The first geostationary synchronous satellite—which appears to remain in a stationary spot above the earth's surface—was launched into orbit in 1963 (see Inset 7–10).

Today, special television networks are connected entirely by satellite—foreign language hookups, all-sports programming, religious chains, all-news services, and daily coverage of the U.S. House of Representatives. Most of these services are relayed to the home viewer by means of cable-TV systems. Home Box Office was the first major cable-TV service (in 1975) to make regular use of satellites to transmit its programming to its cable systems. The noncommercial PBS interconnection service became the first regular network (in 1979) to use satellite technology to tie all of its stations together.

Cassettes and Discs Commercial videotape recording became feasible in the late 1950s. By the late 1960s a less expensive system of video recording had been developed and was widely used in educational and industrial applications. By the early 1970s this simpler technology had been put into cassette format.[26] And by the mid-1970s standardized cassette formats (Betamax and VHS) were being marketed for home use. It was now possible to purchase pre-recorded cassettes of special entertainment programs, first-run movies, home instructional lessons, pornography films, and other materials. It was also technically possible, of course, to record programs off the air for later viewing. And, with the addition of an inexpensive video camera, it was possible to make home "movies" on videotape rather than on film.

Roughly analogous to the phonograph record, the videodisc is a playback-only system which cannot be used for home recording. However, it has several substantial advantages: the disc is potentially far less expensive than the video cassette; the *laser* system requires no mechanical contact with the playback stylus so there is virtually no wear of the disc (the competitive RCA *capacitive* discs do use a mechanical stylus-in-groove system); and the user can select and display any one of 54,000 video frames owing to the disc's tremendous still-frame storage capacity (the entire Encyclopedia Britannica, for example, can be stored on one thin disc).

Games and Computers   Even more amazing for its miniaturized storage and retrieval capacity is the microchip. Soon after the development of the transistor, integrated circuits were imprinted upon silicon chips the size of a fingernail, and the microprocessor was created.

The first video contact that many of us had with these amazing mini-computers was the coin-operated "video pong" games introduced in the mid-1970s. By the end of the decade, sophisticated video games and simulation programs had become routine household attractions. The simple introduction of video games had a subtle but profound impact on the relationship that many of us

had with our television sets. No longer were we to be passive consumers of whatever the networks fed us. We could now interact with the video display. A totally new concept of the role of the TV receiver emerged.

The next logical step was the introduction of a home computer which used the TV receiver as the video display component of the system. By 1980, a few hundred dollars would purchase a basic domestic computer system that could process household accounts, manage tax records, play sophisticated simulation games, compose musical scores, provide automatic appliance controls, conduct financial transactions, function as a surveillance system, handle complicated communication situations, and perform dozens of other tasks. Again, the consumer/communicator was placed in even greater control of the communication process. We were removed one more step from the role of the passive receiver.

Other Technological Developments   Still other electronic breakthroughs promise even more revolutionary results, as discussed in Chapter 12. Digital audio recording can reproduce sound with a clarity and fidelity never dreamed of with magnetic analog recording. Laser distribution and fiber-optics promise a plethora of distribution channels that will dwarf the most massive cable systems. Pay-TV (both open-circuit and cable) will offer an even wider diversity of programming choices—for those who want to pay extra.

Many innovations in receiving and display facilities also promise to change the picture in the immediate future: large-screen receivers will become more practical; flat-screen (wall hanging) video display will take the bulk out of the receiver; multi-picture receivers are available, displaying the images from four or more channels in different parts of the screen; improved audio will lead to high-fidelity and stereo TV reception; and a three-dimensional TV system is still a real possibility.

SUMMARY

The focus of Unit I has been the role of the individual as a *receiver* in a mass communication framework. In both a theoretical context and a political context, we examined the importance of the individual receiver. As we looked specifically at the backgrounds of the print media and the electric media, we also tried to focus on the role of the receiver and the importance of the audience.

With the coming increase in specialization of the electric media, we will see even more emphasis placed upon the receiver. UHF networks, public broadcasting, cable systems, satellites, pay-TV channels, cassettes, discs, and computers will all be competing for the receiver's attention. More and more programming will be narrowly designed to attract specific viewers with particular interests and tastes. And the individual audience member will be increasingly in a commanding position to determine the nature of the mass communication process. The communication cycle is not completed until the receiver makes his or her decision and purchases a specific print publication or plugs into a specific electric channel.

The authors Merrill and Lowenstein sum up the importance of the individual audience member in a specialized communication environment:

As a country moves completely into the specialization stage, there is a withering away of the mass media as we know them today. "Mass" media cannot exist without a mass audience. Specialized tastes and abundant channels in every medium must result in an end to the age of the mass audience. Taking its place will be highly fragmented, "specialized" audiences.[27]

Notes to Chapter 4

1. Christopher H. Sterling and John M. Kittross, *Stay Tuned: A Concise History of American Broadcasting* (Belmont, Calif.: Wadsworth, 1978), pp. 28–29.

2. Because all electromagnetic energy travels at the same speed—186,000 miles or 300,000,000 meters per second—the frequency and wavelength are inversely related. The shorter the wavelength, the higher the frequency (cycles or crests per second). And the lower the frequency, the longer the wavelength. This can be expressed as a mathematical formula: *Speed (300,000,000 meters per second) = wavelength × frequency.* For example, a radio station broadcasting on a frequency of 1070 kiloHertz would have a wavelength of 280.4 meters. That is, 1,070,000 Hertz or waves per second (frequency) times 280.4 meters (wavelengths) equals 300,000,000 meters per second (constant speed of all electromagnetic energy).

3. Melvin L. De Fleur, *Theories of Mass Communication,* 2nd. ed. (New York: David McKay, 1970), p. 37.

4. Richard Griffith and Arthur Mayer, *The Movies* (New York: Simon and Schuster, 1957), p. 10.

5. Arthur Knight, *The Liveliest Art: A Panoramic History of the Movies* (New York: New American Library, 1957), p. 25.

6. Griffith and Mayer, *The Movies,* p. 19.

7. Ibid., pp. 36–37.

8. Knight, *The Liveliest Art,* p. 141.

9. Robert Sklar, *Movie-Made America: A Cultural History of American Movies* (New York: Random House, Vintage Books, 1975), p. 266.

10. Charles Champlin, *The Flicks: Or Whatever Became of Andy Hardy?* (Pasadena: Ward Ritchie, 1977), p. 144.

11. Knight, *The Liveliest Art,* p. 291.

12. Sydney W. Head, *Broadcasting in America: A Survey of Television and Radio,* 2nd ed. (Boston: Houghton Mifflin, 1972), p. 121.

13. Edward Jay Whetmore, *Mediamerica: Form, Content, and Consequence of Mass Communication* (Belmont, Calif.: Wadsworth, 1979), p. 98.

14. Quoted in Gleason L. Archer, *History of Radio to 1926* (New York: American Historical Company, 1938), pp. 112–113.

15. *New York Times,* 31, October 1938.

16. The quotation is attributed to Sam Phillips, a record promoter who was one of the first to recognize Presley's potential. See Whetmore, *Mediamerica,* p. 125.

17. Don R. Pember, *Mass Media in America* (Chicago: Science Research Associates, 1974), pp. 140–141.

18. Ibid., p. 147.

19. Figures for AM radio include noncommercial educational stations, currently numbering approximately twenty-five. Data are compiled from Sterling and Kittross, *Stay Tuned,* 510–511, and from FCC summaries tabulated by *Broadcasting* magazine. The figures are as of January 1 each year.

20. For a detailed account of the history of public broadcasting, see Donald N. Wood and Donald G. Wylie, *Educational Telecommunications* (Belmont, Calif.: Wadsworth, 1977), Chaps. 2–4.

21. Tim Brooks and Earle Marsh, *The Complete Directory to Prime Time Network TV Shows: 1946–Present* (New York: Ballantine Books, 1979), p. xi.

22. See Marshall McLuhan, *Understanding Media: The Extensions of Man* (New York: New American Library, Signet Books, 1964), pp. 23–24.

23. Head, *Broadcasting in America,* p. 185.

24. Sterling and 321–322.

25. Ibid., p. 322.

26. The term "cassette" refers to a self-contained unit that has two reels—a feed reel and a take-up reel. This is contrasted with a "cartridge," which is a self-contained single-reel unit that is automatically threaded into a player.

27. John C. Merrill and Ralph L. Lowenstein, *Media, Messages, and Men: New Perspectives in Communication,* 2nd ed. (New York: Longman, 1979), p. 35.

UNIT I APPENDIX
Communication Time Line

A chronological outline of noteworthy media events

c. 20,000 B.C. Cave paintings initiate communication records.

c. 3,500 B.C. Sumerian cuneiform is earliest pictograph writing.

c. 2,500 B.C. Papyrus is developed in Egypt.

c. 1,700 B.C. First "modern" alphabets are devised.

c. 300 B.C. Great Library at Alexandria is founded.

c. 250 B.C. Archimedes demonstrates the basic principles of lens optics.

c. 150 B.C. Parchment is developed in Greece.

59 B.C. Romans post the *Acta Diurna* news sheets, earliest public news medium.

c. 105 A.D. Chinese perfect the making of paper.

c. 150 Parchment is folded into codices, replacing the awkward scroll.

c. 800 Papermaking spreads to the Middle East.

1221 Chinese develop the concept of movable wooden type.

c. 1450 The mechanical printing press is assembled in Mainz, Germany.

1456 The Gutenberg Bible is printed.

1472 Da Vinci notes the phenomenon of persistence of vision.

1476 William Caxton introduces the printing press to England.

c. 1500 Da Vinci sets down the principles of the *camera obscura*.

1534 Henry VIII requires all printers to be licensed by the Crown.

1550 European trading companies circulate handwritten commercial newsletters.

1621 *The Continuation of Our Weekely Newes* is the first paper in England.

1638 Stephen Day establishes the first American printing press—at Harvard College.

1644 John Milton publishes his *Areopagitica*.

c. 1645 First successful demonstration of the "magic lantern," by Athanasius Kircher.

1665 The *London Gazette* starts regular publication.

1666 Sir Isaac Newton develops the prism.

1687 Newton publishes his monumental *Mathematical Principles of Natural Philosophy*.

1690 John Locke writes his *Second Treatise of Civil Government*.

1690 Benjamin Harris prints one edition of *Publick Occurrences* in Boston, the first attempt at a colonial newspaper.

1694 The Licensing Act permanently expires in Great Britain.

1704 John Campbell starts the *Boston News-Letter*, the first regularly published colonial paper.

1722 Sixteen-year-old Ben Franklin continues to print the year-old *New England Courant* while his brother, James, is jailed.

1725 William Bradford starts New York City's first paper, the *Gazette*.

1729 Franklin buys and prints the Philadelphia *Pennsylvania Gazette*.

1733 Franklin starts his *Poor Richard's Almanac*.

1735 John Peter Zenger is acquitted on a charge of seditious libel.

1741 Andrew Bradford's *American Magazine* and Franklin's *General Magazine* are the first regularly scheduled American magazines.

1750 Franklin experiments with wire communications and formulates a theory for the telegraph, identifies positive and negative charges two years later.

1771 First edition of the *Encyclopaedia Britannica* is published.

1772 Samuel Adams is a regular contributor to the radical *Boston Gazette*.

1775 The Chadwick Typesetter is the first mechanical type-assembling machine.

1776 Thomas Paine writes *Common Sense*, gives it wide circulation.
Adam Smith publishes his *The Wealth of Nations*.
Thomas Jefferson is the principal author of the *Declaration of Independence*.

1783 *The Pennsylvania Evening Post and Daily Advertiser* is America's first daily paper.

1787 Alexander Hamilton, John Jay, and James Madison write the *Federalist Papers*.

1791 The First Amendment is ratified.

1798 The iron press is invented; it could turn out 250 impressions per hour.
The Alien and Sedition Acts are passed; they expire two years later.

1805 Henry Fourdrinier perfects continuous-roll papermaking.

1812 The cylinder press is unveiled in England; it uses steam power to print 1,100 copies an hour.

1818 Jons Jakob Berzelius discovers and isolates selenium.

1821 *Saturday Evening Post* is founded, the first magazine to appeal to women as well as to men.

1827 The first Black newspaper, *Freedom's Journal*, is started in New York.

1830 *Godey's Lady's Book* becomes the first successful woman's monthly magazine.

1831 Michael Faraday discovers electromagnetic induction.

1832 R. Hoe & Co. builds the first steam-driven cylinder press in America.

1833 Benjamin Day inaugurates the "penny press" with his *New York Sun*.

1835 James Gordon Bennett starts the *New York Herald*.

1839 Louis Daguerre, in France, perfects a workable still photography process.

1841 Horace Greeley launches the *New York Tribune*, features hard news and strong editorials.
Volney Palmer establishes the first advertising agency.

1844 Samuel Morse invents and demonstrates the telegraph.

1846 The type-revolving press is introduced by R. Hoe & Co.

1848 The forerunner of the Associated Press is founded in New York City.
Karl Marx and Friedrich Engels publish the *Communist Manifesto*.

1850 *Harper's Monthly* is started, with an emphasis on science and travel.

1851 Henry J. Raymond establishes the *New York Times*.

1852 Harriet Beecher Stowe's *Uncle Tom's Cabin* strengthens the abolitionist cause.

1854 John Stuart Mill publishes his *On Liberty*.

1860 The U.S. Government Printing Office is established.

1864 James Clerk Maxwell publishes theories on nature of electromagnetic energy.

1865 E. L. Godkin starts *The Nation*, forerunner of modern news magazines.
First newspaper syndicate started by Ansel Nash Kellogg.

1869 N. W. Ayer & Son introduces the concept of the modern ad agency.

1873 The Scripps family starts the *Detroit News*, the first in their chain.
Anthony Comstock forms the New York Society for the Supression of Vice.

1876 The telephone is invented by Alexander Graham Bell.

1877 Eadweard Muybridge and John Isaacs use a 24-camera sequence to photograph a race horse in motion. Thomas Edison invents the phonograph, using an acoustical wax cylinder.

1878 Joseph Pulitzer starts the *St. Louis Post-Dispatch*.
Sir William Crookes perfects the cathode ray tube.

1883 Pulitzer purchases the *New York World*. Cyrus H. K. Curtis launches the *Ladies Home Journal*.

1885 Ottmar Mergenthaler patents the first Linotype machine.

1887 William Randolph Hearst takes over the *San Francisco Examiner*.

1888 George Eastman starts to market his "Kodak" camera, which uses a flexible celluloid film.

1888 Heinrich Hertz tranmits electromagnetic energy in his lab.

1893 *Munsey's* magazine cuts price to 10 cents, opens up popular market.

1894 Edison unveils the Kinetoscope projector to the public.

1895 Hearst purchases the *New York Journal*.

1896 Both Hearst and Pulitzer publish versions of "the Yellow Kid."

1901 Guglielmo Marconi transmits "wireless" signal across the Atlantic.

1902 E. W. Scripps starts the Newspaper Enterprise Association, the first feature syndicate.
McClure's magazine launches a 19-month attack on Standard Oil, the first major magazine muckraking exposé.

1903 Edwin S. Porter makes *The Great Train Robbery*, the first movie with a plot.

1906 Lee De Forest invents the "audion" tube, making modern radio possible. Reginald Fessenden transmits a Christmas Eve music and voice program.

1907 Scripps establishes the United Press.

1908 The University of Missouri School of Journalism is formed.

1909 Hearst launches the International News Service.

1912 The Radio Act of 1912 requires all wireless stations to be licensed.

1914 The Federal Trade Commission is established.
Hearst begins the King Features syndicate.
The Audit Bureau of Circulations is created.

1915 D. W. Griffith stuns the nation with *The Birth of a Nation*.

1917 The American Association of Advertising Agencies is set up.

1920 KDKA begins broadcasting as America's first regularly licensed station.

1922 The movie industry sets up the Hays Office (MPPDA).
The first radio commercial is broadcast on WEAF.
The American Society of Newspaper Editors is formed.

1923 Vladimir Zworykin invents the iconoscope tube and the kinescope tube.
Henry R. Luce and Briton Hadden publish *Time* magazine.
The radio industry creates the National Association of Broadcasters.

1926 RCA organizes the National Broadcasting Company; AT&T turns its radio network over to NBC—which then operates two networks.
The Book-of-the-Month Club is started.

1927 The Federal Radio Act creates the Federal Radio Commission.
William S. Paley starts up the Columbia Broadcasting System network.
The Jazz Singer is the first major "talkie."

1928 *Amos 'n' Andy* becomes network radio's first mass hit.

1933 Four radio stations inaugurate the Mutual Broadcasting System (MBS) network with *The Lone Ranger*.
The American Newspaper Guild (the first newspaper union) is founded.
Franklin D. Roosevelt begins his radio series of "fireside chats."
Edwin Armstrong announces the invention of FM (frequency modulation) radio.

1934 The Federal Communications Commission replaces the FRC.
The Legion of Decency is formed.

1936 Luce launches *Life* magazine.

1938 Orson Welles' broadcast of *War of the Worlds* panics America.

1939 Open-circuit television is demonstrated at the New York World's Fair.
Paperback books appear on the mass market.

1941 The FCC's "Chain Broadcasting Regulations" reduce network authority.

1943 The American Broadcasting Company is formed from the sale of the NBC Blue Network.

1946 The FCC "Blue Book" encourages public affairs programming.

1947 The Report of the Commission on Freedom of the Press encourages social responsibility.

1948 The FCC announces its "freeze" on all TV station applications.
TV Guide is started, the nation's first major post-war magazine success.
The record industry introduces both 45 and 33⅓ rpm discs.
Milton Berle becomes the first popular TV star.

1949 The Supreme Court's "Paramount" decision breaks up Hollywood's vertical integration; major studios get out of theater ownership.

1950 The "Fotosetter" process makes offset printing of newspapers possible.

1951 Coast-to-coast live television networking is initiated.

1952 The FCC lifts its "freeze," establishes UHF reservations, channels for ETV.
Mad Magazine is launched.

1953 *The Robe* is the first Cinemascope film to be released.
The FCC authorizes NBC's compatible color system.
Hugh Hefner starts *Playboy*.

1955 AT&T's Bell labs announce the invention of the transistor.
General Tire & Rubber buys RKO Pictures, becoming the first of the conglomerates to take over a Hollywood studio.
Bill Haley's "Rock around the Clock" tops the charts, ushers in rock and roll.
The *Village Voice* becomes first modern underground newspaper.
Reader's Digest starts to accept advertising.

1958 INS and UP merge to form United Press International (UPI).
Stereophonic records are introduced.
Quiz show scandals shake up the television industry. "Payola" revelations soon have similar impact on radio.

1961 The FCC approves multiplex stereo broadcasting for FM.

1962 The Telstar satellite makes live international TV possible.

1963 Newspapers start setting type by computer.

1964 The FCC rules that all TV receivers must be equipped for both VHF and UHF.

1966 The FCC assumes authority over cable TV and initially discourages growth of cable to promote UHF.
Three New York City papers merge (the *Herald Tribune, World-Telegram & Sun,* and *Journal-American,*) only to fold a year later.

1967 The Public Broadcasting Act is passed, resulting in the creation of the Corporation for Public Broadcasting.

1968 The FCC authorizes commercial pay TV.

1969 Live television coverage records men landing on the moon.
Saturday Evening Post ceases weekly publication.
Sesame Street debuts on PBS.
Easy Rider symbolizes new era of low-budget, youth-oriented films.

1971 The National Advertising Review Board is established.
The *New York Times* is temporarily restrained from printing the "Pentagon Papers."
Look magazine goes out of business.
Cigarette advertising is banned from broadcast media.
All in the Family launches a new era of adult situation comedy on TV.

1972 "All-news" radio format proves popular in major cities.
Life magazine suspends regular publication; it is resurrected as a monthly magazine six years later.
Deep Throat popularizes pornography for large audiences.
Reporters Woodward and Bernstein pursue the Watergate story.
The FCC reverses its cable position; new rules allow cable growth.

1973 Television provides live coverage of the Watergate hearings.
The Supreme Court, in the Miller decision, rules that states are to set obscenity standards.

1974 *TV Guide* overtakes *Reader's Digest* as the nation's largest-selling magazine.
Richard Nixon resigns on TV.

1975 A "Family Viewing Hour" is voluntarily adopted by the networks.
The FCC's "divestiture" ruling states that no more cross-media ownerships will be approved.

1975 Time, Inc., starts Home Box Office, the first cable TV program supplier.

1976 The FCC authorizes 17 new channels for the increasingly popular "citizen's band" radio.

1977 *Roots* is the most popular TV programming ever; it defines the "mini-series" concept.

1978 MCA-Philips introduces its laser-based videodisc.
The Supreme Court rules in favor of search-warrant explorations of newsrooms in the *Stanford Daily* case.
Videocassette players, in the Beta and VHS formats, make a big impact on the home entertainment market.

1979 The *Chicago Daily News* folds, its failure symptomatic of problems faced by afternoon dailies.
Gannett Newspapers merge with Combined Communications Corporation.

1980 Ted Turner starts the 24-hour-a-day Cable News Network.
The FCC announces it is stripping RKO General (General Tire & Rubber Co.) of all 16 of its radio and TV station licenses.
The Privacy Protection Act makes search-warrant intrusions into news-rooms more difficult.
The FCC announces plans for low-power TV stations to increase TV coverage.
Computer subscription services such as The Source and CompuServe begin to reach the home market.

1981 Sony introduces the MAVICA, a video-based still-photography camera.
The FCC authorizes limited commercials for some public broadcasting stations.
Selected TV stations begin experimenting with various teletext formats.

1982 Anti-trust action against AT&T results in the telecommunications monolith selling its local phone companies.
Personalized mini-stereo and radio players increase the tendency towards individualization and alienation.
The FCC authorizes plans for direct satellite-to-home transmission (DBS).

There are several ways to approach the study of mass communication in the United States. One method is to examine the various factors which have shaped the institutions of American mass media. These include *technological developments* (which we outlined in Unit I), *government regulation and public pressures* (which we will examine in Unit III), and *individual involvements and responsibilities* (which we will consider in Unit IV). One all-important influence in the American modified libertarian/social-responsibility media environment is the *economic factor*; and this is what we will be concerned with in Unit II.

As stated in the introduction to the first unit, our focus in this book is on the individual. In Unit I we were concerned with the individual as the *receiver* of the communication message. In this unit we will be focusing on the individual as the *consumer*, the *purchaser* of the media experience. Where does the individual fit in the economic structure of mass media in America? How extensive is the big business of mass communication? Who owns the mass media? How are the mass media supported? What role does advertising play? How and how much does the individual media consumer pay? What is the scope of the media-related professions involved directly and indirectly in mass communication? These are some of the questions we will be exploring in Chapters 5, 6, and 7.

The theme for this unit underlies all three chapters:

Mass Media are businesses.

Easy reading is damned hard writing

Mass Media
in an
Economic Framework

As you look at the economic structure of mass communication—and the media are, indeed, economic institutions—one of your first concerns must be with the structure and ownership of the media. How, exactly, are the individual media organized? Who owns the channels in each medium? To what extent do individual owners and large corporations have ownership interests in more than one medium? What are the advantages and drawbacks of large corporate media ownership? As we examine these questions, the theme of Chapter 5 will become evident:

• *Under a modified libertarian (social responsibility) free-enterprise economic system, ownership of the media channels will always tend to become concentrated in fewer and fewer hands—unless restrained from doing so by governmental restrictions.*

Before you explore the ways in which ownership of the commercial media tends to become centered in a small number of big business operations, you should note that not all media channels are owned by profit-oriented institutions.

Government Ownership   In totalitarian political states, of course, media systems are under complete government control. And under a Soviet communist system, all media channels are owned directly by the government (see Section 2.3). Except for illegal and covert "underground" media operations, all channels are designed as instruments of the government. The media serve as a "collective propagandizer."

Even in the United States there is considerably more government media ownership than you might at first imagine. The U.S. Government Printing Office is the largest publisher in the country, with an annual printing output of more than 6,000 titles (new and continuing publications). A major form of media distribution in the United States is the library, especially the public (government-owned) library. Of the almost 30,000 libraries in the nation, nearly half are

5

Ownership and Business Patterns

Three Classes of Media Ownership

Government Agencies	Special-interest Organizations	Profit-making Businesses

• Libraries • Government Printing Office • Government Films • Propaganda	• Educators • Religious Groups • Foundations • Political Parties	• Publishers • Broadcasters • Producers • Performers

community libraries. The Library of Congress is an institution of almost incomprehensible proportions. More than 5,000 staff members supervise a collection (as of 1982) of almost 80 million holdings. And this number increases by approximately 1.3 million new items every year—more than 3,500 every day, or about 2.5 new acquisitions to be cataloged and processed every minute, 24 hours a day, 365 days a year.

Government ownership and operation of media channels are also evident in the electric media. The federal government is the largest film producer in the country. Virtually all of the major executive departments (Defense, Health and Human Resources, Education, Commerce, Agriculture, and so forth) turn out large numbers of motion pictures annually.

Special Interest Groups Many of our mass mediums can trace their beginnings back to ownership by *special-interest groups*—particular classes of people who had some vested interest in using a specific medium. Books were started both by merchants and by religious scribes who needed to preserve, respectively, secular and sacred records. Newspapers trace their heritage back to political pamphleteers who had messages they wanted to disseminate. The first radio stations were owned and operated by various institutions (electrical corporations, department stores,

schools, and churches) which wanted to reach the public with their particular messages.

Today there are still many examples of media channels which are owned by special-interest groups desiring to spread their tidings: philanthropic foundations (such as the six Pacifica FM stations), religious sects, political activists, and educators.

The most interesting example of educational media is probably noncommercial broadcasting, which has evolved into "public radio" and "public television."

Colleges and universities were among the pioneer radio station owners and operators back in the 1920s. After the first FM channels were reserved for noncommercial use (see Inset 4–11), public schools began to put stations on the air. With the television channel reservations in 1952, a new category of non-commercial broadcasting enterprise was created—the "community station," owned and operated by a non-profit community board of directors whose sole purpose is the operation of the noncommercial Public TV station. Finally, many PTV stations and state-wide networks are owned and operated by state agencies. Within a given state this may be the state department of education, a state university system, or a specially chartered state PTV commission.

Although government-owned media play a substantial role in America's mass communication matrix, and although special-interest media channels are important for many individuals, the predominant mass media structure in the United States is profit-oriented,

Including university and community libraries, there are some 20,000 public (government owned) libraries in the United States.

free-enterprise, commercial publishing and broadcasting and filmmaking. This approach is consistent with Adam Smith's libertarian definition of the role of the free press in a classic capitalistic system (Section 2.2.2). This perspective—the business of commercial mass media—is the focus of the rest of this chapter.

5.1 The Big Business of Media

Figuring in your share of advertising costs, you probably spend close to $250 a year to pay for the mass media—not including outlays for major appliances (TV sets, stereo systems), repairs and maintenance, and the cost of electricity to operate the electric media. "Without question, the economic dimension of mass communication is overwhelming; Americans are the world's biggest spenders on media activities."[1]

Media Revenues and Profits   Although souces differ in their figures, and data vary according to purposes, it is safe to estimate that the gross revenues of the media covered in this book totaled well over $50 billion in 1980. Newspapers topped the list, bringing in over $19 billion in 1981. Television

was a distant second with over $10 billion in total revenue. And revenues are expected to continue to increase, depending upon the medium, from ten to fifteen percent annually.

5.1.1 BOOK PUBLISHING

The oldest of the mass media, book publishing is also one of the most successful. During 1981 the total gross revenues from book publishing approached $7 billion. And the trend has been constantly upward; the total volume of book sales has more than doubled in the past decade.

The health and vitality of the book publishing business is all the more remarkable for two reasons. First, books—like movies and the record industry—do not rely upon any substantial advertising revenue; they have to depend entirely upon consumer purchases. The fact that the buyer has to bear the entire cost of the medium is reflected in the increase in book prices over the last thirteen years. The average cost of a hardcover book went up from $7.65 in 1965 to more than $21 in 1980. During the same period the cost of the average paperbound trade book increased from $2.50 to more than $8, and the typical mass-market paperback (popular books sold in drugstores and newsstands) jumped from 62 cents to more than $2. Even when inflation is taken into consideration, the increase is real.[3]

Second, the book market is a relatively small audience compared to other mass media. The American Booksellers Association estimates that only five to six percent of the American population are "regular" book buyers. Some specialized textbooks and initial novels by new authors may sell fewer than 1,000 copies; an average hardcover trade book may sell 10,000 copies; a successful mass-market paperback will reach 100,000; and a bestseller will occasionally hit 2 or 3 million. By contrast, the *daily* circulation of the *Wall Street Journal* has attained 2 million; *TV Guide* and *Reader's Digest* both are approaching 18 million per issue; and any respectably popular TV program will pull in between 20 and 30 million viewers. Still, there are approximately half a million differ-ent book titles in print, and about 40,000 new titles (or new editions) are added each year.

The Educational Market   For years the book industry has been broadly divided into two sectors—the general (or "trade") market and the educational market. Although text-books make up most of this latter category, several other educational and academic publi-cations should also be included: university press books (which are usually specialized scholarly and regional works); professional and technical books (which report recent developments in medicine, law, engineering, business, and other technical areas); and reference works (encyclopedias, atlases, and directories).

In the 1960s many educational publishers also began to produce various non-textbook materials—standardized tests, films, records, filmstrips, audio tapes, and video materials. As indicated in Inset 5–2, this area accounted

---

Listed below are the estimated 1980 gross revenues for each of the media included in this book.[2] These figures do not include capital outlays for major equipment and appliances (TV receivers, CB radios, stereo systems, etc.), repair and maintenance costs, or electricity. The figures do encompass all direct purchases, admissions, and subscriptions, as well as indirect costs borne by advertising charges. These costs average out to approximately $246 for every man, woman, and child in the United States.

**INSET 5–1
Media Industry
Revenues, 1980**

Medium	Gross Revenues
Book Publishing	$ 6,350,000,000
Newspapers	17,410,000,000
Magazines	9,051,000,000
Movies	2,750,000,000
Radio	3,530,000,000
Recordings	3,682,000,000
Television	10,300,000,000
Cable TV	2,238,000,000
Total	$55,311,000,000

The following table lists by category the total dollar volume of book sales in the United States for 1980. The designation "trade" books refers to all general-interest books, fiction and non-fiction, aimed at the general public and usually sold in bookstores. The "mass-market paperback" category refers to less expensive fiction and non-fiction works, usually printed on less costly paper in a standard 4¼-by-7-inch format and marketed chiefly through newsstands, drugstores, discount stores, supermarkets, and similar outlets.

Category	Volume of Sales (in millions of dollars)
Academic	**2,207.6**
Elementary and high school texts	940.3
College textbooks	952.7
University press	80.7
Standardized tests	67.2
Audiovisual and multi-media	166.7
Trade (Adult and Juvenile)	**1,271.3**
Hardbound	864.4
Paperbound	406.9
Professional	**999.1**
Business, law and other	424.4
Technical and scientific	334.8
Medical	239.9
Mass-Market Paperback	**653.3**
Religious	**351.4**
Bibles, hymnals, etc.	168.3
Other religious	183.1
Contract Sales	**1,489.9**
Book clubs	538.3
Mail-order publications	566.9
Subscription reference	384.7
Other Sales	**233.5**
Total	**7,206.1**

Note that the total figure does not correspond with that given in Inset 5–1. Different sources often list quite divergent numbers, and even the same source may be inconsistent. *Standard and Poor's Industry Surveys: Communication* (15 April 1982) lists the 1980 book sales total at $6,350,000,000 on page C73 (the source for Inset 5–1; the same article gives the 1980 book total as $7,206,100,000 on page C76 (the source for this inset). Wherever such discrepancies occur, this text will attempt to strike a median between the extreme figures unless it is necessary to print both sets of figures and point out the discrepancy.

The modern web press can produce as many as 28,000 impressions an hour.

for more than $166 million in sales in 1980. Over the years, the educational/academic market has accounted for roughly fifty percent of the total book publishing business, with slightly over half of that amount being strictly textbooks.

Fiction and Literary Works During the earlier periods of American book publishing (see Section 3.2), works of fiction dominated the market—from the post–Civil War dime novels to the romantic and historical novels of the early part of the twentieth century. However, after World War I—partly due to competition from the electric media, which

offered popular vehicles for works of fiction, and partly due to the knowledge explosion and increasing emphasis on education—non-fiction books became dominant. Today, less than eight percent of all books published are fiction.

The Paperback "Explosion" Although inexpensive paperbound books have been a part of the publishing industry for well over a century, it was not until the 1940s that they became popular enough to be recognized as a major part of the field. And even while many prognosticators foresee a future when paperback editions will dominate the industry, the fact remains that today paperbacks account for only about fifteen percent of the total sales volume of all books.

Book Marketing and Retailing   There are more than fifteen thousand bookstores of various descriptions in the United States. In addition, there are approximately ninety thousand "mass-market" outlets—newsstands, supermarkets, drugstores, discount stores, and similar retail establishments.

More than fifteen percent of the total bookselling business takes place through the mail. The Book-of-the-Month Club was started in 1926, and the Literary Guild was founded the next year. Today, there are more than a hundred general and special-interest book clubs, with more than a million members who regularly buy their books via contract sales and subscription services. Many other specialized mail-order books are offered to subscribers. Magazine publishers have led the way, with Time-Life, *National Geographic, Playboy, Reader's Digest, Newsweek,* and others all offering handsome trade books to their readers.

5.1.2   THE NEWSPAPER BUSINESS

In terms of sheer dollar volume, the newspaper business is the most massive of all the mass media. The annual revenues—more than $17 billion in 1980—are more than double the second largest medium (see Inset 5–1). One reason for this volume is, of course, the tremendous scope of the newspaper industry. In 1979, the total circulation of all daily newspapers in the United States was 62,200,000 (up more than 8,000,000 from 1950).

The average daily newspaper is 60 pages long, and the median Sunday paper reaches 196 pages. (Many exceed these averages greatly; the daily *Los Angeles Times* is about 100 pages and the Sunday edition runs close to 500 pages!) This means that close to *33 billion pages of American newspapers are printed every week*—about 150 pages for every man, woman, and child in the country. (Compare this to the number of book pages you purchase each week.)

The cost of publishing a major newspaper today would be incomprehensible to the early newspaper pioneers. Benjamin Day started the *New York Sun* with virtually no capital in 1833; it cost James Gordon Bennet $500 to start the *Herald* two years later; Horace

---

According to Audit Bureau of Circulation figures, these were the twelve largest daily newspapers in September 1981:

Newspaper	Circulation
Wall Street Journal	2,000,000
New York Daily News	1,483,000
Los Angeles Times	1,011,000
New York Times	887,000
New York Post	764,000
Chicago Tribune	754,000
Chicago Sun-Times	649,000
Washington Post	635,000
Detroit News	625,000
Detroit Free Press	622,000
San Francisco Chronicle	510,000
Long Island Newsday	507,000

**INSET 5–3
Largest
Local
Newspapers**

Greeley invested $2,000 to get the *Tribune* started in 1841; and ten years later the *New York Times* was founded by Henry Raymond for $100,000. When Joseph Pulitzer bought the shaky *New York World* in 1883, it cost him $346,000.

The cost of newspaper acquisition continued to escalate, and by the late 1970s some typical transactions included the following: Time, Inc., purchased the *Washington Star* for $20 million (1978); the Australian press mogul Rupert Murdoch picked up the *New York Post* for $30 million (1976); the *Buffalo Evening News* was purchased by Blue Chip Stamps for $33 million (1977); the *Wilmington News-Journal* (Delaware) went to the Gannett chain for $60 million (1978); and Capital Cities Communications, Inc., bought the *Kansas City Star* for $125 million (1977).

5.1.3 THE MAGAZINE INDUSTRY

With total revenues just slightly behind television, the magazine industry ranks as the third largest mass medium. There are about twenty thousand magazines of general circulation published in the United States, with the more popular titles being sold through more than a hundred thousand retail outlets. The author Frederick Whitney underscores the diversity of this specialized medium:

Magazines are published by magazine groups, by individual publishers, by newspapers, by small esoteric societies, by giant corporations, by trade associations and churches, by varying levels of government, and by all political parties. The roster of publishers is almost as varied as the titles themselves. Magazines are issued daily, weekly, semi-monthly, and monthly for the most part, some bimonthly and quarterly, and a few annually.[4]

In terms of gross magazine publishing revenues, the twelve largest U.S. magazine publishers are listed below. Because many of the firms are diversified in different fields, these estimated 1980 data include only income derived from magazine publishing.[5]

**INSET 5—4
Largest Magazine
Publishers**

Company	Magazine Revenues (in millions)	Number of Domestic Magazines
Time, Inc.	895	7
Triangle Communications	650	2
Hearst Publications	391	12
CBS, Inc.	363	10
McGraw-Hill, Inc.	288	17
Washington Post Co.	284	3
Reader's Digest Assn.	261	1
New York Times Co.	253	4
Condé Nast Publications	238	7
Charter Co.	222	3
Playboy Enterprises	204	2
Meredith Corp.	204	4

Companies Small and Large Because of the degree of specialization involved, it is still possible to enter the magazine market with a relatively small capital investment—perhaps only a few thousand dollars. Magazine publishers normally do not own presses and equipment; instead, they contract out their printing.

Indicative of this ease of entry into the magazine field is the fact that between 250 and 300 new magazines are started each year in the United States. (Many, of course, do not last as successes.) The major share of the market, however, continues to be dominated by the large corporate publishers and the long-established circulation leaders (see Inset 3–12).

Up to 1971, the federal government furnished a form of indirect subsidization to the magazine industry through its low-cost second-class mailing rate. However, since its reorganization, the U.S. Postal Service is attempting to reduce its traditional losses by making all postal users pay the full cost of mail deliveries. The mailing costs that magazines have to pay may soon be nearly double the previous amount. This is a substantial increase, totaling millions of dollars for some of the larger magazines. Such an increase could eventually force hundreds of marginal magazines into bankruptcy.

5.1.4 MOVIE MILLIONS

Like the book business, motion picture revenues are generated almost entirely by direct consumer purchases—in this case, admission tickets. Unlike the book business and other print media, however, the movies were big business almost from their start. By 1907, during the era of dingy nickelodeons and low-class patronage, the gross revenues from films had already topped legitimate theater and vaudeville combined.

Robert Stanley points out that the film has to combine communication and artistic aims with financial considerations. "But more than any other art form, the creation of motion pictures is rooted in the realism of dollars and cents. Few artists in other fields have to work under the exacting circumstances which prevail in the movie industry. Indeed, the exigencies of business too often take priority over the principles of cinematic expression."[6]

In the 1920s the average cost of producing a major Hollywood picture with a top star was $100,000. By 1979 the average cost of making a major entertainment feature by one of the MPAA (Motion Picture Association of America) member producers had multiplied to $8.5 million. And blockbusters (like *Superman, Cleopatra, Moonraker, Jaws II, Star Trek, Apocalypse Now,* and *Heaven's Gate*) exceeded $30 million each!

Theaters and Tickets As mentioned above, the revenue to pay for these multi-million dollar movies is generated largely by tickets sold at the 17,000 theaters in the United States. The average American went to the movies five times during the year, paying an average price of $2.50 a ticket in 1979. A total of 1.12 billion movie admissions was sold that year.

Television and Foreign Markets

Although domestic box office receipts are the standard by which the movie industry gauges its annual operations (the $2.8 billion gross revenues listed in Inset 5–1 are solely from U.S. ticket sales), there are other substantial sources of income. International sales and rentals, for example, have become an increasingly important source of revenue. Today, approximately half of the movies' gross income comes from international sales and rentals.

The love-hate relationship between the television medium and the Hollywood industry has been undergoing a constant metamorphosis as the motion picture studios become increasingly dependent upon television as an outlet for their product. By the 1970s television networks were paying between half a million and a million dollars for TV rights to the typical major motion picture. Outstanding box office attractions were bringing much more. *Gone with the Wind* and *Cleopatra* each brought in $5 million·for their initial TV airings, and NBC paid an unprecedented $10 million for the rights to telecast *The Godfather*. CBS later paid $35 million for the exclusive twenty-year rights to *Gone with the Wind*.

Future video technologies cast many more uncertainties upon the theatrical distribution of motion pictures. Nobody can say for sure how the Hollywood industry will ultimately be affected by pay TV, cable TV, videocassettes, videodiscs, and satellite networks. It is likely to be a long transition period for the moviemakers.

5.1.5 RADIO REVENUES

Edging ahead of the movies, radio reported gross revenues of over $3.2 billion during 1980. The use of specialized formats to reach specific audiences maintains radio as a valuable advertising medium.

The FM Boom While the overall radio picture has remained fairly stable, with an annual income growth of about twelve per-

---

One of the greatest frustrations and biggest gambles of the Hollywood film industry is that there is no guaranteed correlation between the cost of a film and the amount of revenue it may bring in at the box office. The fifteen financial winners listed below are the atypical kinds of successes which can carry a studio through several box office flops.

INSET 5–5
The Top Grossing Films

Film	Gross U.S. Revenues through December, 1981
Star Wars (1977)	$185,000,000
The Empire Strikes Back (1980)	134,000,000
Jaws (1975)	133,000,000
Grease (1978)	96,000,000
Raiders of the Lost Ark (1981)	90,000,000
The Exorcist (1973)	89,000,000
The Godfather (1972)	86,000,000
Superman (1978)	83,000,000
The Sound of Music (1965)	80,000,000
The Sting (1973)	79,000,000
Close Encounters of the Third Kind (1977)	77,000,000
Gone with the Wind (1939)	77,000,000
Saturday Night Fever (1977)	74,000,000
National Lampoon's Animal House (1978)	74,000,000
Superman II (1981)	64,000,000

The figures listed above are from *Variety,* January 1982, and represent rentals to distributors. Future re-releases will increase the gross income for each of these films.

There are more than 200,000 people working in various aspects of filmmaking in Hollywood and across the country.

cent a year, the radio success story has been in FM. The revenues and profits of FM stations have been increasing at a far greater rate (over thirty percent a year) than those of AM properties (about eight percent annually). This FM boom reflects the popularity of the medium's greater sound fidelity and, usually, less commercial formats. In 1970, FM accounted for about five percent of all the total revenue of all radio stations; by 1980, the FM percentage had increased to about thirty-five percent. Some industry experts are predicting that FM will account for half of all radio's revenues in the 1980s.

As these figures indicate, FM broadcasting has been increasing much faster than AM radio.[7] Note that these data do not coincide with those used in Inset 5–1; again, this is due to different sources using different numbers to compute their totals. Revenue is given in millions of dollars.

**INSET 5–6
AM and FM
Radio Revenues,
1970 to 1980**

Year	AM Revenues	FM Revenues	Total Revenues	FM Percentage of the Total Radio Market
1970	1,077	60	1,137	5.3%
1972	1,292	115	1,407	8.2%
1974	1,410	193	1,603	12.0%
1976	1,687	332	2,019	16.4%
1978	1,974	570	2,544	22.4%
1980	2,073	1,100	3,173	34.7%

5.1.6 THE RECORDING BUSINESS

Starting with the phenomenal popularity of rock'n'roll records in the late Fifties and early Sixties, the recording industry has soared into preeminence as *the* entertainment medium—outstripping both radio and the movies in gross revenues. As a 1978 *Forbes* article put it,

Outsiders may know little more about the industry than occasional scandals involving payola to radio station disc jockeys, cocaine and instant-millionaire star performers studying Oriental philosophy. But people in the business know that it *is* a business and that, these days at least, intelligence, business sense, marketing and market-sensitive commercial taste are the edge that the gorilla [outstanding large record success] owners have had.[8]

Not only did the record industry gross approximately $3.7 billion in 1980, but its top artists in 1978 alone pulled in another $260 to $265 million in live concerts. The recording industry has mutually profitable, symbiotic relationships with live concerts and radio (Section 4.3) and also with the movie industry. Both the recording business and the movies are assisted immeasurably by the

The free-lance audio engineer is only one of the numerous positions working in the $4 billion a year record business.

release of sound-track albums such as (in 1978 alone) *Grease, The Last Waltz, The Wiz, The Buddy Holly Story, FM, Star Wars, Sgt. Pepper's Lonely Hearts Club Band,* and *Saturday Night Fever*—which became the first

---

As the figures in this table indicate, gross television revenues increased at an annual rate of eight to nine percent during the 1960s and early 1970s. However, after the 1974–75 recession, television revenues jumped up at an annual rate more than fifteen percent. These figures are for U.S. domestic income only.[9]

**INSET 5–7
Television
Revenues,
1960–1980**

Year	Gross U.S. Television Revenues (in thousands)
1960	$ 1,504,000
1965	2,328,000
1970	3,337,000
1975	4,860,000
1980	10,300,000

---

album to sell 15 million copies, grossing approximately $150 million by itself.

5.1.7 TELEVISION INCOME

Broadcast television, with gross receipts of more than $10 billion dollars in 1980, is the second largest of the mass media. And the annual growth rate is one of the highest of all media as advertisers willingly pay higher and higher prices to get their messages on the video tube.

Indicative of the escalation of media costs is the price of producing TV programming. By 1980 it cost the networks an average of $250,000 to $300,000 for one episode of a half-hour dramatic program. A typical hour-long drama cost from $500,000 to $600,000. The three commercial networks were spending collectively just about $40 million for one week of prime-time programming in the spring of 1980.

Foreign Sales Like the movie industry, television earns a considerable portion of its income from foreign sales and rentals. About twenty-five percent of its total revenue comes from overseas. Generally, if a series has run successfully for three or four years on a commercial U.S. network, it has recovered its production costs, and the foreign distribution revenues represent close to clear profit. The United States ranks as the world's most popular television exporter, selling about 150,-000 hours of programming a year on the international market.

5.1.8 CABLE, PAY TV, CASSETTES, AND DISCS

The financial status of non-broadcast video technologies has progressed to the point where they can be examined apart from broadcast television.

Cable TV. By 1982 over twenty-five percent of all American homes were connected to a cable-TV system, paying an average of eight to ten dollars a month for more and clearer channels than they could pick up off the air. Many subscribers also pay considerably more each month for special programming features otherwise unavailable—sporting events, first-run movies, special

---

From its inauspicious beginning in the early 1950s, cable TV had grown into a $2.2-billion enterprise with 24 million subscribers by 1982. The outlook appears even more promising as cable systems offer more and more special programming services and options to their patrons.

**INSET 5–8
Growth
of Cable TV**

Year	Number of Systems	Number of Subscribers
1952	70	14,000
1955	400	150,000
1960	640	650,000
1965	1,325	1,275,000
1970	2,490	4,500,000
1975	3,506	9,800,000
1978	3,997	13,000,000
1982	4,743	23,700,000

The TV studio is the scene of hectic activity and pressures during live and recorded productions.

Four standard videocassette formats are (clockwise, from top left): the ½-inch VHS cassette, the ½-inch Beta format, and ¾-inch U-matic cassette, and the compact mini U-matic cassette for portable ¾-inch recorders.

variety programs, and so forth. The total cable revenues for 1980 were estimated at about $2.2 billion.

The ten largest cable-TV companies control approximately forty-two percent of the nation's cable business, and that percentage is expected to go higher as the major cable operators buy out smaller independent systems. Many of the larger cable companies also furnish programming services to other cable systems. Group W cable (formerly Tele-prompter), runs Showtime Entertainment jointly with Viacom Communications, the nation's ninth largest system. Time, Inc., the second largest cable owner, owns and operates Home Box Office.

Pay TV. Contrasted with "pay cable" as described above, the term "pay TV" is usually used to refer to open-circuit pay television service—wherein a regular over-the-air station scrambles its signals, and the participating viewer has to use a special decoder to unscramble the picture. The viewer then pays, either on a monthly basis or on a per-program basis, for the special programming. Although pay-TV schemes have been tried for at least two decades, truly functional, non-experimental systems have been operational only since the late 1970s. One media prognosticator foresees the combined annual income of cable TV and pay TV hitting $6 billion by the end of the 1980s.[10]

Cassettes and Discs One final television technology that must be considered is the videocassette and videodisc field. Two rival cassette formats, Betamax and VHS, began competing for the home market in the late 1970s. And, although their total revenues are relatively small, they are expected to command an increasingly large portion of the consumer's home entertainment dollar.

On the videodisc front, three different—and incompatible—systems were being introduced in the early 1980s. (See Section 12.4.2.) Each format offers advantages and features that the other systems do not have, and the success of the three competitors will be determined by the consumer marketplace. But, in any case, RCA has predicted a $7.5 billion videodisc market by 1990.

5.2 The Dilemma of Large-Ownership Patterns

The problem with success is that it breeds the need for more success. If an entrepreneur is successful in any business venture—furniture making, fast-food chains, housebuilding, media ownership, or shoe repair—tax laws and other financial incentives encourage reinvestment of the profits back into business.

Thus, the key concept is "growth." Small media systems expand by acquiring more channels. Giant media firms buy small media systems. And conglomerates take over the

Three Types of Big Media Ownership

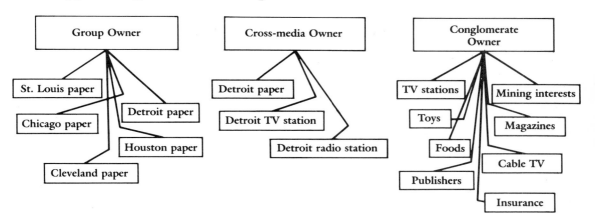

giant media firms. Power becomes concentrated in fewer and fewer offices. This would appear to be an inevitable corollary of the free-enterprise libertarian philosophy. As indicated in the theme for this chapter, unless this tendency is artificially restrained, media operations will always grow into larger units. The noted media critic and observer Ben H. Bagdikian describes the process as it relates specifically to newspapers:

Modern newspaper companies . . . are not supposed merely to pay handsome dividends. They are supposed to be financially "agressive," which means squeezing profits from existing papers in order to buy other papers in other places. It means borrowing on assets for tax purposes and to help speed acquisitions. It means trading in "funny money" instead of cash, swapping unissued stock certificates from the company safe for smaller corporations. By such means are formed the diversified conglomerates favored by Wall Street investors, who then buy up the stock and provide even more money to buy even more papers.[11]

The chief danger of such concentration of media ownership is that the number of voices contributing to the media mix is thereby reduced. The authors Sandman, Rubin, and Sachman express the cause for concern:

The concept of freedom of the press is based on the conviction that truth somehow emerges from the conflict of many voices. But freedom can become a dangerous luxury when the number of voices falls to just two or three. The growth of giant media monopolies—networks, chains, conglomerates, and the like—has drastically reduced the diversity of media voices. This concentration of power in the hands of a few media "barons" represents a major threat to our First Amendment freedoms.[12]

5.2.1 DISTINCTIONS AND DEFINITIONS

In an examination of large-ownership tendencies, three general patterns can be discerned. Although there is considerable overlap among these three varieties of big-media ownership, it is helpful to distinguish among them.

Group ownership or "chain ownership" occurs when one owner (an individual or a corporation) owns and operates many different outlets or channels of a single medium. Usually these channels—newspapers, broadcast stations—are located in different communities. Thus, the owner has a "chain" or group of outlets located throughout the country.

Cross-media ownership, sometimes called "cross-ownership," occurs when an individual or corporation owns properties in two or more media. Specifically, the term is applied when the two or more media channels are located in the same community—for example, when the same owner has both the only newspaper and a radio station in the same town.

Conglomerate ownership is a combination of group ownership and cross-media ownership on a national scale, but the conglomerate also engages in non-media business activities. Although the term "conglomerate" is sometimes used to refer to those firms involved almost entirely with media (such as the Gannett Company, which owns more than eighty newspapers, seven TV stations, twelve radio stations, and a top outdoor advertising concern), the term is more properly used to designate those which are diversified into many fields other than media (such as RCA, which has owned Hertz auto rentals, CIT Financial Corporation, Banquet Foods, and manufacturing firms as well as the NBC television and radio networks, five TV stations, eight radio stations, RCA Victor records, and videocassette and videodisc equipment).

5.2.2 PROFITS AND POLITICS

In examining these practices of groups, cross-media, and conglomerate ownership, you need first to be aware of the underlying motives involved. The basic reasons for concentration of ownership can be summed up in three words: profits, profits, and profits. Quite simply, the larger a corporation is, the easier it is to show big profits.

Although media owners have promoted their particular political ideologies (see Inset 3–5), there is no overall, organized philosophical push behind concentration or ownership. In fact, just the opposite phenomenon occurs—*the larger a media organization becomes, the less likely it is to promote any non-center-of-the-road political or ideological viewpoint*. The more a particular media organ grows the more it has at stake in preserving the stability of the status quo; the less it wants to rock the boat by advocating any position that might alienate any segment of its audience. There appears to be little reason to fear that concentration of media ownership will result in a mass brainwashing designed to indoctrinate the public in some extremist political viewpoint.

Quite the contrary, the greater danger may be that concentration of media ownership will result in editorial viewpoints that are too bland and non-controversial. The threat to our diversified "search for truth" is that too many of the big media are doing their "searching" while traveling together down the ruts in the middle of the road. The larger a media enterprise becomes, the more concerned it becomes with controlling people's wallets rather than with controlling their minds.

Questions and Issues You need to be concerned with the issue of concentration of media control because it may represent a danger to the libertarian ideal of open communication. But then, on the other hand, might it not also help to facilitate a more open search for truth in some ways? In examining these issues, there are several specific questions we will want to consider.

1. *Group Ownership:* To what extent does the consolidation of media ownership in a few hands constitute a threat to the free flow of ideas?
2. *Cross-media ownership:* What are the dangers of a single owner controlling all or most major media in a given locality?
3. *Conglomerate ownership:* What problems are raised when non-media capitalistic conglomerates own and operate media channels?

5.2.3 ADVANTAGES AND DRAWBACKS

Before we turn to a specific discussion of the three categories of large ownership, there are several potential benefits and problems that could be listed.

Advantages of Large-Group Ownership

Due merely to the size of the media operation, there are certain advantages to group, cross-media, and/or conglomerate ownership. Efficient management can be achieved by centralizing staff services (budgeting, payroll, personnel, purchasing) and consolidating offices. Prices of supplies and equipment (for example, newsprint) can be cut by quantity purchasing for all of the outlets in a chain.

Large-group owners often can instill a sense of professionalism and quality in reporting, writing, and production by bringing in top-quality personnel that otherwise might not be available. More experience can usually be brought to bear on local publishing and broadcasting situations. It is also possible to pool resources in order to establish non-local bureaus in major cities and foreign countries. Media outlets often lose their limited, provincial political and geographical perspectives when operated by larger companies.

Larger operations also can bring in financial support that exceeds local resources. It is easier to finance plant modernization, for example, or to withstand the ups and downs of a community economy which may falter when a local industry suffers a major setback.

A final advantage is that big media are better able to resist the pressures of big business and big politics. The veteran media commentator and author Edwin Newman states it this way:

With big business, big labor, big government, and big movements such as the women's movement and the environmental movement, a news organization must be on something like an equal footing if it is to be as independent and enterprising as news organizations ought to be. A willingness to do battle with the president of the United States on issues such as Vietnam or impeachment has to be backed by sizable resources.[13]

Dangers of Large-Group Ownership

There are, obviously, several drawbacks to various forms of big-media ownership. Many of these anxieties are related to journalistic standards. Concern for corporate profits could easily outweigh concern for quality in reporting and writing. Journalistic integrity might be lost on the profit-and-loss sheet.

A major concern about chain ownership is that the vast majority of local outlets could be controlled by a small handful of large companies, with a resulting loss in local diversity and independent voices. John Stuart Mill's fear of the tyranny of the majority—his concern that not one contrary voice should be silenced—could come to pass not because of political tyranny but because of economic tyranny.

A corresponding concern about cross-media ownership is that all of the local community channels could be controlled by one viewpoint. If a town's only newspaper, radio station, and TV station were all owned by the same person, there would be considerable local monopolization of news, ideas, and culture.

Wilbur Schramm also points out how the concentration of mass media control has altered the relationships of media, government, and the people.

The small, numerous media, as we knew them in the eighteenth and nineteenth centuries, were representative of the people in their checking on government; in fact *were* the people. But the larger and more centralized media have to some extent withdrawn from the people and become a separate set of institutions, parallel and comparable with other power centers such as business and government.[14]

5.3 Group Ownership

In discussing group or chain ownership, we will be concerned primarily with those media that are identified with local community outlets—newspapers and broadcast stations.

5.3.1 NEWSPAPER CHAIN OWNERSHIP

The genesis of the newspaper chain can be traced back approximately a century. About that time, Edward W. Scripps and his brothers were laying the foundation for their Midwestern chain, which evolved into the present Scripps-Howard group. In the late 1880s, George Booth and his brother Ralph started their family chain, which was purchased by the Newhouse group in 1976. Pulitzer and Hearst both started their newspaper empires in the 1880s also.

By 1910 the number of daily newspapers circulating in the United States had reached its peak—about 2,400 papers were spread throughout the country. There were 13 chains in existence that year; those chains controlled 62 papers, or about 2.5 percent of the total number. After World War II, the number of daily newspapers stabilized between 1,750 and 1,800. However, the

percentage of newspapers controlled by chains rose from 20 percent in 1945 to almost 62 percent in 1978. The newspapers owned by these 167 groups currently account for more than 70 percent of the daily circulation of U.S. newspapers.

The Largest Newspaper Chains Most of the group ownership is concentrated, as might be expected, in a relatively small number of chains. In fact, by 1978 about half of the daily circulation of all U.S. papers was accounted for by twenty publishing groups. And the concentration of ownership in fewer and fewer hands continues to grow as more of the larger chains buy out the smaller groups. Bagdikian observes, "Among chains, the big are getting bigger. . . . Now that practically all the financially attractive individ-

---

INSET 5–9   Daily Newspapers and Chain Ownership

The total number of daily newspapers for selected years is indicated below in the white columns. The dark columns represent the number of papers (out of the total) that were owned by chains or groups. The numbers in parenthesis are the actual number of chains operating in each year.

Figures were compiled and averaged from several sources, including *Editor & Publisher International Yearbook, Statistical Abstract of the U.S.,* and *Ayer Directory Publications.*

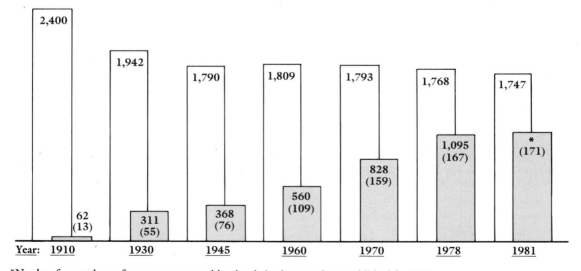

*No data for numbers of newspapers owned by the chains have yet been published for 1981.

---

ual newspapers have been bought by groups, the process of concentration is taking the form of chains buying other chains."[15]

It could be argued that with 170 groups involved in newspaper chain ownership, there still exists a considerable diversity of opinion. After all, 170 voices searching for truth should result in quite a clamor. Also, it should be mentioned that the national directors of most of the larger chains do not necessarily dictate local editorial positions; as pointed out above, these groups are primarily concerned with the profit-and-loss sheet, not with spreading political propaganda.

The danger, however, is still two-fold: First, the number of chains (voices) will continue to decrease as the top ten or twenty groups continue to swallow the smaller chains (see Bagdikian's observation above). Second, the larger the media giants become, the less likely they are to stray from the middle of the road, thus reducing the chances for non-establishment viewpoints to be expressed.

Local Monopolies Of even more concern than chain ownership might be the lack of local competition in most American cities. The number of cities and towns which have competing daily newspapers has decreased alarmingly over the decades. In 1890, for example, New York City had fifteen competing daily newspapers. While no other city boasted that much diversity, most cities which once had competing daily newspapers are now served by only one newspaper. (Cities which have a morning paper and an evening paper published by the same owner are included among those communities which have no effective newspaper competition.) By the end of the 1970s there were fewer than 40 American cities which had competing daily papers; this figure is down from a high of 680 in 1910.

There are several ways of determining "largest" group owners. The table below lists twelve of the leading newspaper publishers by daily circulation and by the number of daily newspapers owned as of January 1981.[16]

Company	Daily Circulation	Number of Dailies
Gannett Co.*	3,563,000	81
Knight-Ridder Newspapers*	3,493,000	34
Newhouse Newspapers*	3,168,000	28
Tribune Co.	2,854,000	8
Dow Jones & Co.	2,339,000	21
Times Mirror Co.*	2,316,000	8
Scripps-Howard Newspapers*	1,515,000	15
Hearst Newspapers	1,321,000	13
Cox Enterprises*	1,195,000	18
New York Times Co.*	1,108,000	12
Thomson Newspapers (U.S.)	1,095,000	71
Cowles Newspapers	971,000	10

*Also owns extensive broadcast properties.

FCC Maximum-ownership Regulations

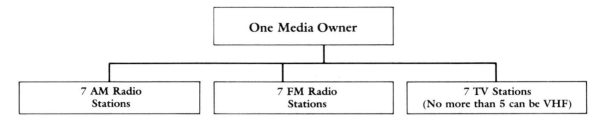

Many reasons are given for the demise of daily newspaper competition: increasing costs of materials and manpower, demand for higher quality, competition from other media (magazines, radio, television), advertiser defection to other media, and so forth. But the fact remains that readers in less than three percent of the 1,500 cities served by daily papers have a choice of two or more newspapers. In fact, only four cities—New York, Los Angeles, Boston, and Washington—had more than two separately owned papers in the early 1980s.

Clearly, this poses a threat even more serious than that of group ownership. In all but our largest American cities, the average citizen has no choice but to accept the editorial content of one newspaper owner. Fortunately, this limited perspective is broadened by the fact that the consumer also has access to TV and radio channels and national magazine subscriptions.

5.3.2 BROADCASTING GROUP OWNERSHIP

Like newspapers (and unlike books, movies, magazines, and records and tapes) broadcast stations cater to a local community. For that reason, the concerns regarding group ownership are similar.

Limitations on Group Ownership

Because broadcasting is a very profitable business, ownership of groups of stations is a very popular corporate enterprise. However, the number of radio and television stations which can use the broadcast spectrum is physically limited (Section 4.1.7), and so government assignment of channels is necessary (Section 9.1.3). The FCC has also determined that group ownership of stations should be controlled. Without government restrictions, it is possible that a few owners (for example, the commercial network and major electronics firms) might have acquired ownership of most of the broadcasting stations very early in the game. Therefore, under authority granted it by the Communications Act of 1934, the FCC has ruled that no one person or corporation (including the networks) may own more than seven AM radio stations, seven FM radio stations, and seven television stations (no more than five of which may be VHF—the other two must be UHF). Thus, the maximum number of stations of all categories which can be held by a single owner is twenty-one.

Networks and Chain Broadcasting

Although in the print realm the term "chain" ownership is virtually synonymous with "group" ownership, the word "chain" is used differently when discussing patterns of broadcast ownership and operation. The term "chain broadcasting" refers to the networking of programs. Rather than compare chain broadcasting—or networking—with group ownership of newspapers, it would be more appropriate to compare chain broadcasting with newspaper press associations (such as AP and UPI) or with features syndicates (which distribute columns and comics).

From a *theoretical communication perspective,* a broadcast network is merely an arrangement whereby a common message (TV or radio program) from one source or sender (network producer) may be sent through different channels (broadcast stations) to reach different receivers (audiences in various communities). In an *economic framework,* the network is a contractual agreement whereby stations affiliated with the network in effect sell their audiences to the network, which then sells the aggregate audience to advertisers.

Even though network-afffiliate relationships are not the same as group ownership, there are some functional similarities. In both cases, a big-media centralized organization

---

The twenty companies listed below were the large group owners of broadcast stations at the end of 1981.[17] Virtually all of these corporations may be considered conglomerates because broadcasting stations account for only a part of their total revenues. Revenues shown are in millions of dollars.

**INSET 5–11
Twenty Largest
Group Owners of
Broadcast Stations**

Group	1980–81 Total Corporate Revenues	Number of Stations Owned		
		AM	FM	TV
General Electric	26,599	3	5	3
Westinghouse	9,336	7	6	5
RCA-NBC	7,985	4	4	5
CBS, Inc.	4,156	7	7	5
General Tire & Rubber	2,524	6	6	4
ABC, Inc.	2,371	6	7	5
Schering-Plough	1,180	7	5	0
Gannett (and Combined)	1,327	6	7	7
Dun & Bradstreet (Corinthian)	1,286	0	0	6
Jefferson-Pilot	867	6	5	2
Washington Post	721	0	0	4
Capital Cities Communications	541	7	6	6
Rollins, Inc.	482	5	1	3
Metromedia	478	6	7	6
Meredith Corp.	420	3	3	5
Cox Broadcasting	376	5	7	5
Taft Broadcasting	339	6	6	7
Harte-Hanks Communications	339	5	6	4
Storer Broadcasting	251	0	1	7
Multimedia	187	4	4	6

produces content material, has certain economic controls, handles distribution of materials, and removes much of the decision-making from local communities. Close to ninety percent of the roughly 775 commerical TV stations on the air in 1982 were affiliated with either ABC, CBS, or NBC. And the networks provide up to two-thirds of the programming for affiliated stations. Therefore, networking—although different from group ownership—has the same effect of reducing the diversity of media viewpoints.

Alarmed at the growing concentration of power in the networks during the 1930s, the FCC issued its "Chain Broadcasting Regulations" in 1941 to reduce network control of the broadcast industry (see Section 4.3.3). NBC was forced to sell one of its two networks; network-affiliate contracts could no longer insist on exclusive ties; affiliates could not be forced to carry unwanted network programming; and networks were forbidden from dictating local advertising rates. These, along with other provisions, generally resulted in lessening the networks' economic dominance of their affiliated stations.

Local Monopolies and the "Duopoly Rule" The FCC also was concerned that one station owner might want to control two or more stations in a given locality. In order to guarantee as much local diversity as possible, the FCC established its "Duopoly Rule"—which simply states that no licensee may own more than one AM station, one FM station, and one TV station in any one market or listening area. Therefore, communities could be assured that each station (of a given broadcast category) would at least be owned by a different broadcaster.

An exception to the "Duopoly Rule" is made for noncommercial stations. Public TV and radio licensees may own more than one station in a given community. For example, one channel can be used for in-school instructional programming while the primary channel is devoted to general audience public TV programming.

Cable TV Ownership Like newspapers and broadcast stations, cable-TV systems are concerned with serving local communities. However, unlike broadcast stations, the cable-TV industry does not have to rely upon scarce radio spectrum allocations. Cable systems, like publishing outfits, can be started wherever there is sufficient economic incentive. And the economic incentive mushroomed during the late 1970s, with the result that there were more than four thousand cable systems in operation by the end of the decade (Inset 5–8).

Without the justification of scarce spectrum resources, the FCC has largely refrained from continued extensive regulation of the cable industry. Therefore, large-group ownership patterns have emerged which are not unlike those of the newspaper business.

5.4   Cross-Media Ownership

While there is cause for concern regarding group ownership of media outlets, many observers feel that cross-media ownership patterns pose even more of a threat to media diversity and to an open media society. For it is cross-media ownership which can establish a virtual media monopoly in a given community—if one entrepreneur owns all of the newspaper, broadcast, and cable outlets for that locality.

5.4.1   EVOLUTION OF CROSS-MEDIA OWNERSHIP

Newspaper ownership of broadcast stations has been a fact of media life from the very start of radio telephony. William E. Scripps, owner of the *Detroit News,* put an experimental station (now WWJ) on the air in the summer of 1920. By the mid-1920s about five percent of all radio stations were owned by newspapers. As more newspapers saw the financial and editorial advantages of owning a radio station, this percentage gradually increased to thirteen percent by 1933 and then peaked at thirty percent around 1940.

FCC Concerns In the early 1940s the FCC began to raise its collective eyebrows at the extent of newspaper control of radio stations, especially in communities where there were no competitive voices. It launched a formal study at about the same time the "Chain Broadcasting Regulations" were being formulated and, although no official ruling came forth, the FCC's concern did have the effect of reversing the trend. By 1952 the percentage of AM radio stations owned by newspaper interests had dropped to around twenty percent. And, with FCC vigilance, it has been dropping ever since, falling to seven percent by the end of the 1970s.

During this period, however, newspapers became interested in the new electronic media. While FM was struggling to get off the ground in 1945 to 1952, the FCC wanted to encourage development of the new radio medium and did nothing to restrain newspaper involvement. Therefore, during this period, newspapers controlled about one-third of the FM stations. FM cross-media ownership has subsequently dropped to about eight percent.

As television grew, so, again did newspaper ownership. For the past two decades the percentage of TV stations owned by newspaper

The fifteen cable-TV system owners listed below all are multiple-system operators (MSOs), some of them operating more than one hundred systems in various localities throughout the country. At the start of 1982 the top ten of these companies controlled more than forty percent of the nation's cable service. And considerably more consolidation is expected in the next few years as early cable pioneers and small cable operators cash in on the impatience of the giant corporations to buy out the smaller companies.[18]

INSET 5–12
Top Fifteen Cable
TV System
Owners

System Owner	Number of Subscribers	Pay-Cable Subscribers
Telecommunications Corp.	2,000,000	1,000,000
American TV and Communications Corp. (Time, Inc.)	1,900,000	1,568,000
Group W Cable	1,700,000	881,000
Cox Cable Communications	1,167,000	1,003,000
Storer Cable Communications	922,000	1,033,000
Warner Amex Cable Communications	907,000	624,000
Times Mirror Cable Television	676,000	427,000
Newhouse Broadcasting	604,000	472,000
Viacom Communications	522,000	360,274
Rogers UA Cable Systems, Inc.	520,000	475,000
Continental Cable Vision, Inc.	475,000	460,000
United Cable TV Corp.	470,000	390,000
Sammons Communications, Inc.	451,000	230,000
TeleCable Corp.	300,000	230,000
Capital Cities Communications, Inc.	297,000	156,000

interests has remained close to thirty percent. And, again, the FCC made warning sounds against the whole concept of cross-media ownership.

The 1975 Divestiture Ruling After formally studying the situation and after several abortive attempts at various kinds of ownership limitations, all aimed at trying to increase the diversity of broadcast station ownership, the FCC came up with its "divestiture ruling" in 1975. This order had the effect of prohibiting an individual or corporation from owning a broadcast station and a newspaper in the same community. In order to avoid undue economic disruption to the existing stations, however, the FCC "grandfathered" all but sixteen existing combinations. These sixteen owners were ordered to divest themselves of either the station or the newspaper. All other owners could continue with the cross-media arrangement until each individual station was sold.

5.4.2 THE ARGUMENTS PRO AND CON

Like most other issues involving media ownership and operation, there is no clear-cut right or wrong answer regarding cross-media ownership. In many instances, cross-owner-

---

One of the most famous, longest, and most bungled cases ever handled by the FCC involved the awarding of the license for Channel 5, Boston. The case ultimately lead to the demise of one of Boston's daily papers.

In 1954, the FCC initiated competitive hearings for the license for Channel 5. After three years of listening to rival claims and mud-slinging, the FCC staff recommended that the license be awarded to an applicant who had no other media interests, thus avoiding any cross-media ownership. The commission, however, overturned the recommendation and awarded the license to a Boston paper, the *Herald Traveler,* citing the paper's greater media experience. This decision was challenged by one of the unsuccessful applicants, who charged that there had been an illicit *ex parte* meeting between the FCC chairman and the newspaper owner. The appeals court ordered the FCC to reconsider its decision.

From 1962 on, the *Herald Traveler* operated the station, WHDH, on a series of four-month temporary licenses. Finally, in 1969, the FCC failed to renew the temporary license and awarded the station to a group of Boston businessmen who had no other media interests. In addition to the *ex parte* issue, this decision was apparently based on the desire to avoid cross-media ownership.

After exhausting its appeals to the appeals court and to the Supreme Court, the *Herald Traveler* gave up the channel in 1972. However, as an unanticipated consequence of the action, the newspaper—which had been relying heavily upon the profits from the television station to stay alive— could no longer publish at a profit. Thus, shortly after giving up the television license, the *Herald Traveler* went out of business also. The attempt to diversify media voices in the Boston area resulted in the permanent silencing of one of these voices.

**INSET 5–13
The Sad Case of
Channel 5, Boston**

---

ship certainly can result in monopoly situations. On the other hand, there are some potential advantages to this variation of big-media ownership.

Dangers of Cross-Media Ownership The obvious drawback of cross-ownership is that fewer media owners have access to the public if one owner controls more than one medium in a given community. The diversity of voices needed in an open society is lost. Nicholas Johnson, a former FCC commissioner and one of the most outspoken critics of concentration of media ownership, writes, "If we are serious about the kind of society we have undertaken, it is clear to me that we simply must not tolerate concentration of media ownership."[19] He continues:

[The] wave of renewed interest in the impact of ownership on the role of media in our society is healthy. . . . For, as the Supreme Court has noted, nothing is more important in a free society than "the widest possible dissemination of information from diverse and antagonistic sources." And if we are unwilling to discuss *this* issue fully today we may find ourselves discussing none that matter very much tomorrow.[20]

The danger of cross-media ownership is especially threatening in small towns and communities, where a local media monopoly is a real possibility. In larger cities where one of several competing newspapers might own one of several competing television stations (for example, the *New York Times* and WPIX, the *Chicago Tribune* and WGN, or the *San Francisco Chronicle* and KRON), there are diverse voices, both in print and on the TV airwaves. But in smaller communities this is not necessarily the case. Only one out of four towns with a population of less than 10,000 has any type of media competition. But eighty percent of communities larger than 200,000 have at least one newspaper and one broadcast station that are not operated by the same owner. Writing in 1976, Sandman et al., go on to state,

And if you believe in media diversity, cross-media ownership *is* dangerous. Fifty-three communities

are now served by only one commercial radio station and one daily newspaper, both owned by the same company. . . . Ten cities have just one commercial TV station and one newspaper, both owned by the same company. . . . Diversity is the strength of democracy. And no media monopoly can supply diversity.[21]

Advantages of Cross-Media Ownership
Nonetheless, several potential benefits of cross-media ownership can be listed. Several of these advantages are economic. As illustrated in Boston WHDH case (Inset 5–13), often a profitable radio or TV station can help to support a marginal newspaper. Lynn Gross points out advantages of both group ownership and cross-media ownership:

Some claim that in an attempt to allow for a multitude of broadcast ownership possibilities, regulators are preventing large companies which own multiple stations from growing. These companies are generally the ones that can undertake the most innovative broadcasting because they have capital to back them up and do not need to be overly concerned with the short-term dollar. For example, newspaper owners are especially efficient at owning broadcasting stations because news functions can double up.[22]

Other arguments in favor of cross-media ownership are journalistic. A most persuasive defense was written in 1955 by Paul Block, publisher of two papers in Toledo. Actually, he was defending single ownership of two newspapers in the same community, but his ideas equally support the concept of publishing-broadcasting cross-ownership.

For one thing, a newspaper which isn't competing against a rival can present news in better balance. There is no need to sensationalize. . . .

The unopposed newspaper can give its reader . . . relief from the pressures of time. Deadlines no longer loom like avenging angels just this side of the next edition. . . . There is more freedom from financial pressure on the business side. A single ownership newspaper can better afford to take an unpopular stand. It can better absorb the loss of money in support of a principle.[23]

5.4.3   CABLE OWNERSHIP

Cable systems are the one other major medium—along with newspapers and broadcast stations—concerned with local community outlets. And it is only natural that broadcasting and publishing companies should take an interest in cable ownership; cable is an obvious extension of other media distribution channels. Thus, it was estimated in 1975 that thirty-five percent of all cable systems were tied in with broadcast station owners, about twenty-five percent had ties with TV program producers, and fifteen percent were owned by newspaper interests.

The FCC does not directly regulate cable operations. However, with its increasing concern over cross-media ownership, the commission has gotten involved in some aspects of cable ownership. Specifically, the FCC has laid down ownership rules which prohibit either a telephone company or a broadcast station from having any ownership interest in a cable system serving the same community that is covered by the phone company or broadcast station. The conflict of interest would be obvious in such a community. Also, the FCC initially prohibited the national networks—because of their nationwide scope—from owning any part of *any* cable system. However, the FCC experimentally lifted this last prohibition in 1981, when CBS was allowed to buy into a cable system to test the feasibility of such cross-media ownership.

Because the FCC has no regulatory powers over the newspaper industry, there are no restrictions involving newspaper ownership of cable system short of anti-trust action by the Justice Department.

Many questions about cable-TV ownership remain unresolved. The field is still relatively young and fluid. It is difficult to predict how advancing technologies might alter the capabilities of cable distribution. How will two-way interactive systems evolve? What role will AT&T play? Will open-circuit broadcasting still be a viable alternative ten years from now? As the cable industry grows, and as other media continue to merge and consolidate, the questions of conglomerate ownership will loom larger and larger.

5.5   Conglomerate Ownership

Did you know that: The *New York Times* also publishes *Family Circle* and owns fifty-five cable TV systems in New Jersey? The parent company of Occidental Life Insurance owned United Artists? American Express is half-owner of the country's fourth largest cable empire? Beautyrest mattresses, No Nonsense pantyhose, the book publishing firm of Simon & Schuster, and Paramount Pictures are all owned by the same company? CBS is one of the nation's largest toy manufacturers as well as the owner of four publishing firms? *Newsweek* is owned and published by the *Washington Post*? General Tire & Rubber Company may lose all sixteen of its radio and TV stations?

Such are the diversifications and potential conflicts of interest within the wonderful world of the media conglomerates.

5.5.1   THE RISE OF THE CONGLOMERATES

The economic incentives which encourage the proliferation of conglomerates in the business world (Section 5.1) were amplified in the 1950s and 1960s. Several of the major Hollywood movie studios, for example, were taken over during this period. RKO Pictures was one of the first to be assimilated when Howard Hughes sold out to General Tire & Rubber Company in 1955. MCA, the talent agency and music publishing firm, purchased Universal in 1962. Three mammoth diversified corporations—Gulf + Western, Transamerica, and Kinney Services—picked up, respectively, Paramount, United Artists, and

Various Methods of Conglomerate Formation

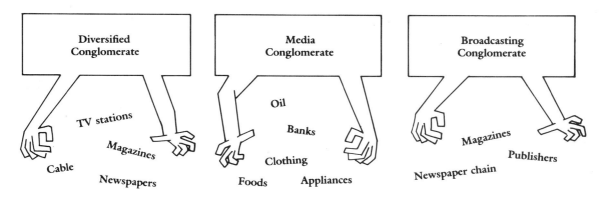

Warner Brothers in 1966, 1967, and 1969. And in 1968 the giant Avco corporation took over Joseph E. Levine's Embassy Pictures. Later, in 1981, Coca-Cola bought Columbia and Transamerica sold United Artists to M-G-M.

As the trend to big-media ownership accelerated, diversified conglomerates were formed in one of two ways. Either a giant holding company involved in many fields (such as Transamerica, Gulf+Western, or the Charter Company) would pick up some media outlets, or a giant media corporation (such as RCA, CBS, or MCA) might buy some non-media businesses as subsidiaries. A third pattern, and a common one, is for an established media operation, as it becomes larger, to spread out into other media fields. A publishing company (Time, Inc., or the Times Mirror Company) might get into broadcasting or a broadcast outfit (NBC, CBS) might move into publishing. This third variation is somewhat of a hybrid between a cross-media ownership and a true conglomerate. The Unit II Appendix lists examples of all three patterns.

5.5.2 MERGERS AND MARRIAGES

Much of the consolidation within the media industries has come about through the purchase of smaller outlets by larger diversified corporations. But a large percentage of big-media growth has been the result of mergers—companies coming together to combine resources into one company. Of the five largest newspaper chains, three have been formed by mergers or large-group assimilations. Knight-Ridder and Scripps-Howard, as their hyphenated corporate names indicate, were both formed when large groups fused. When the Samuel Newhouse chain (the largest media conglomerate that is still privately owned) purchased the eight Booth papers in 1976, it became the second largest newspaper group in terms of circulation.

Many media conglomerates started out with an interest in one medium and subsequently have had to diversify into other media fields in order to maintain their corporate profits. Capital Cities Communications—which started out as Capital Cities Broadcasting—has been expanding in both the newspaper and industrial periodicals areas; in 1981, sixty-four percent of its revenues came from publishing. On the other hand, Harte-Hanks Communications—which started out as Harte-Hanks Newspapers—has been expanding aggressively in media areas other than daily papers; in 1979 it acquired its eleventh radio station, its fourth TV station,

National Telecommunications Services (cable-TV systems), one weekly newspaper, one trade journal, and companies involved in advertising, distribution, and computer information systems.

The biggest merger consummated in broadcasting-newspaper circles up to 1980 was the $370-million takeover of Combined Communications Corporation by the Gannett Newspapers chain in 1979. Many other smaller mergers and acquisitions occur annually throughout the industry. In fact, about fifty or sixty independent newspapers are swallowed up by the larger chains and conglomerates every year.

The Urge to Diversify   Because tax laws and capitalistic incentives encourage plowing profits back into the business venture, the media owner has two choices—*intensification and specialization* (buying more media outlets or channels in one specific medium, which leads to group ownership) or *diversification* (spreading out into other media or non-

---

INSET 5–14
The Gannett-
Combined Merger

When Allen Neuharth took over as president of Gannett Newspapers in 1971, the chain already had about thirty daily papers on its corporate roster. During the 1970s Gannett provoked mounting criticism as it added more and more papers to its fast-growing empire. Critics charged, first, that Neuharth and his company were interested only in making money—not in quality journalism—and, second, that the Gannett chain represented potential nationwide control of editorial policy.

To the first charge Neuharth replied that, yes, he was a businessman; you have to make money before you can be a successful journalist (echoing Adam Smith's sentiments). To the charge that Gannett was building a nationwide editorial position, Neuharth replied, "It would be bad journalism and bad business. We believe completely in the concept of local autonomy—letting our individual editors and publishers decide their own news play and endorsements and everything else."[24] In the 1976 presidential election, for example, sixty percent of the Gannett papers endorsed Ford and forty percent went for Carter, with no apparent pressure from corporate headquarters in any direction.

In 1979, Neuharth, by then chairman of the corporation, engineered what was the largest merger ever in broadcasting conglomerate circles. In a $370-million deal, Gannett took over Combined Communications Corporation, which included—among other holdings—seven TV stations and thirteen radio stations. By 1981 the Gannett domain encompassed eighty-five daily papers, twenty-two weekly newspapers, seven TV and thirteen radio stations, a far-flung billboard chain, Canadian newsprint interests, the Gannett Satellite Information Network, the Gannet News Service, Gateway Productions, Filmpower (a post-production house), the Lou Harris & Associates polling firm, and a silk-screening operation. And Allen Neuharth set for himself "a fairly modest goal—to become the biggest and best total communications company in the country."[25]

---

media fields, resulting in cross-media or conglomerate ownership.)

Whether one starts out in publishing or in broadcasting, the attraction of diversification is strong. Broadcasters tend to diversify because the FCC puts a limit on the number of broadcast stations they can own; they must reinvest in other media outlets. And publishers are attracted to broadcast diversification because of the generally higher profit return on broadcasting enterprises. Also, as a hedge against the future, forward-looking print companies want to make sure they are represented in the emerging electronic technologies as well as in basic resources. For example, three of the larger and more successful publishers—Time, Inc., the New York Times Company, and the Times-Mirror Company—have turned to diversification in order to avoid having all their investments in one limited sphere. All three have interest in paper/newsprint holdings, broadcast stations, and cable-TV systems.

Pay-Cable Program Suppliers　In addition to the actual ownership of cable-TV systems, another major new field has developed around the program producers and packagers which furnish programming to pay-cable systems. *Home Box Office*—the Time, Inc., subsidiary—pioneered the cable packaging business in the mid-1970s and remains the largest pay-cable supplier. *Showtime,* the second largest cable production company, is owned jointly by Group W/Teleprompter, one of the nation's largest multiple-system operators or MSOs, and Viacom International, another top-ten MSO which was formed from CBS holdings when the FCC ordered networks to divest themselves of cable systems.

Networks were not prohibited, however, from entering the pay-cable programming arena. For example, as of mid-1982, ABC television was involved in the following cable operations: ARTS (Alpha Repertory Television Service), a cultural cable network which is a joint venture with the Hearst Corporation; "Daytime," another ABC-Hearst project aimed at women cable viewers; the Satellite "NewsChannel" (see Section 11.3.1), an all-news cable service operated jointly with Group W (Westinghouse); a pay-cable sports venture with ESPN (Entertainment and Sports Programming Network), which is owned by the Getty Oil Company; and Home View Network to supply movies and other materials specifically for at-home recording off-the-air. ABC was also working with Cox Cable Communications to develop two-way interactive services such as at-home shopping and banking.

The profit potential is enormous. The possibilities for intra-industry intrigue are boundless. And the legal entanglements are enough to make corporate lawyers drool for years to come.

Public Broadcasting Ventures　During the early 1980s the nation's noncommercial public TV and radio stations also were becoming involved in various cross-media intricacies. While proposals for a videocassette club and a public TV record label were being studied on the national level, a few cooperative cable-TV trials were being started on the local level—some with cooperation from Home Box Office and Showtime.

5.5.3　CONFLICTS OF INTEREST

There are several potential dangers in conglomerate ownership of various media channels: the possibility of local and even national monopolies; the continuing decrease in the number of independent voices which can be heard throughout the land; and the threat of questionable corporate activities by non-media businesses within the company, as in the RKO General case.

The most prominent danger of conglomerate involvement in the media business is, however, the potential for conflict of interest. To what extent can the media arms of the corporation remain objective where other business interests of the conglomerate are concerned?

Several potential cases come to mind: RCA, CBS, and General Electric, for example, are all major contractors with the government. Their various subsidiary research and manufacturing companies have lucrative ties with defense and space exploration projects (radar, laser devices, guidance systems, computer services, and many other sophisticated electronic lines). To what extent can their station or network operations remain entirely unaware of such ties when involved in journalistic

research for documentaries or background reporting on national defense, government budgets, space exploration, and the like?

Foreign connections pose another potential problem area. The Thomson newspaper chain, which owns about seventy newspapers in the United States, is also a partner in oil explorations with Getty Oil and with Occidental Oil and has extensive magazine holdings in South Africa. To what extent can the Thomson chain editors remain oblivious of these connections? In an even more direct example, the Atlantic Richfield Company owns ninety percent of the *London Observer*. And the influential *Observer*'s news service, in turn, is distributed by the *New York Times*

The entire broadcasting world was stunned when, on January 24, 1980, the FCC, "in one off its harshest rulings ever, . . . judged RKO General, Inc., unfit to own a broadcast license. The 4–3 ruling, unprecedented in its scope, could mean that RKO may have to give up all of its 16 radio and television stations."[26]

The ruling was the result of an eleven-year-old case involving RKO's Boston station, WNAC-TV. However, the decision also applied to WOR-TV, New York, and KHJ-TV, Los Angeles. It could also strip RKO of its thirteen radio station licenses. Essentially, the decision was aimed at questionable business practices by RKO's conglomerate parent, General Tire & Rubber Company.

The charges against General Tire included illegal domestic political contributions, improper overseas payoffs, the filing of misleading reports, defrauding affiliate companies, and pressuring General Tire customers into placing advertising with the RKO stations.

In reacting to the FCC decision, an editorial in *TV Guide* stated,

The sweeping disciplinary move by the Commission—the most severe in its history—seems a harsh judgment against an organization that has provided what one commissioner called "over 25 years of meritorious broadcast service to the public." . . .

More importantly, the FCC's action carries a chilling implication—an insinuation of Governmental control over broadcast editorial power and its resulting access to the public mind.[27]

**INSET 5–15
The RKO General
Case**

news service to about fifteen other U.S. newspapers. Bagdikian wryly observes: "Mobil only buys ads. Arco bought the paper."[28]

One explicit example involving the *New York Times* centered on some of its subsidiary magazines. Among the many periodicals owned by the *Times* were *Modern Medicine* and other specialized medical journals. When the *Times* ran a series on medical incompetence in 1976, medicine-related businesses threatened to drop about $500,000 worth of advertising from the magazines. At that point, the *Times* decided to sell the magazines to Harcourt Brace Jovanovich, the book publisher. The immediate problem was solved, but how many similar situations exist?

The most obvious case in recent years may have been the planned merger of ITT and ABC in 1967. Even while the merger proposal was being evaluated by the FCC and the Justice Department, high-ranking ITT officials made several telephone calls to the *New York Times* and to AP and UPI reporters trying to get more favorable coverage of the ITT position. Nicholas Johnson, one of the three FCC commissioners to vote against the merger, relates:

To me, this conduct, in which at least three ITT officials, including a senior vice president, were involved, was a deeply unsettling experience. It demonstrated an abrasive self-righteousness in dealing with the press, insensitivity to its independence and integrity, a willingness to spread false stories in furtherance of self-interest, [and] contempt for government officials as well as the press . . . .

. . . I ponder what the consequences might have been if ITT's apparent cynicism toward journalistic integrity had actually been able to harness the enormous social and propaganda power of a national television network to the service of a politically sensitive corporate conglomerate.[29]

SUMMARY

In this chapter we have been examining some of the issues involved in big-media ownership patterns—group or chain ownership, cross- media ownership, and conglomerate ownership. Big-media ownership arrangements are here to stay. They are an inevitable part of doing business in twentieth-century America, and they are indispensible to the profit and tax structure of the country.

Given that inevitability, two basic conclusions can be stated. First, *the various big-media owners are not working in collusion to establish a national media editorial position or political policy.* Even as Nicholas Johnson admits, "I do not believe there is a small group of men who gather for breakfast every morning and decide what they will make the American people believe that day."[30] Media corporations are simply out to make lots of money, and the way to make lots of money is to own and operate lots of media channels. The researcher Jon Udell underscores this point:

Considerable evidence supports the claim of group owners that their primary concern and control centers on efficient *business* management of their media enterprises, not on group editorial control. For example, it is not unusual for individual dailies within a newspaper group to have very diverse editorial philosophies ranging from liberal to conservative and from Republican to Democratic. . . . On the other hand, management functions, such as the purchasing of newsprint, may be centrally managed without infringing on the freedom of editors.[31]

Second, however, with the increasing concentration of media ownership in fewer hands, *the diversity of voices is reduced; the range of opinions that can be heard in the open marketplace of ideas becomes restricted.* Even if this restrained range of editorial opinion is not intentional, even if the editorial conformity is basically a result of establishment media intuitively supporting the big-business perspective of middle-class economics, we must still be continually alert to this unintentional narrowness of viewpoint.

The final summation will be left to Sandman et al.:

Any form of media combination reduces, at least in theory, the total number of independent voices that can be heard. It therefore runs contrary to the fundamental premise of the First Amendment, that if the people hear all sides they can make the right decision. . . .

Whatever priority you choose, one conclusion is clear: Diversity of viewpoint is vital to freedom of the press. And media monopoly—*every* form of media monopoly—is antithetical to diversity.[32]

Notes to Chapter 5

1. Ray Eldon Hiebert, Donald F. Ungurait, and Thomas W. Bohn, *Mass Media II: An Introduction to Modern Communication,* 2nd ed. (New York: Longman, 1979), p. 56.

2. Data were compiled from *Standard and Poor's Industry Surveys: Communication,* 24 September 1981, p. C53; and from *Standard and Poor's Industry Surveys: Leisure Time,* 10 September 1981, p. L32, and 15 October 1981, p. L1.

3. Data were compiled from U.S. Bureau of the Census, *Statistical Abstract of the United States: 1979,* 100th ed. (Washington, D.C.: U.S. Government Printing Office, 1979), p. 593; and from U.S. Bureau of the Census, *Statistical Abstract of the United States: 1980,* 101st ed. (1980), p. 595.

4. Frederick C. Whitney, *Mass Media and Mass Communications in Society* (Dubuque, Iowa: Wm. C. Brown, 1975), p. 178.

5. Data from *The Folio: 400,* presented in *Standard and Poor's Industry Surveys: Communication,* 21 September 1981, p. C71.

6. Robert H. Stanley, *The Celluloid Empire: A History of the American Movie Industry* (New York: Hastings House, 1978), p. vii.

7. Data for 1970 to 1976 were from U.S. Bureau of the Census, *Statistical Astract: 1979,* p. 585. 1978 figures were from "1978: Radio's Star Keeps Rising," *Broadcasting,* 10 December 1979, p. 40.

8. *Forbes* Magazine, "Records: The Gorillas Are Coming," in *Readings in Mass Communication: Concepts and Issues in the Mass Media,* 4th ed., ed. Michael C. Emery and Ted Curtis Smythe (Dubuque, Iowa: Wm. C. Brown, 1980), p. 323.

9. Data were taken from U.S. Bureau of the Census, *Statistical Abstract: 1979,* p. 586.

10. John G. Watson, "When Kagan Speaks, TV Listens," *Los Angeles Times,* 17 September 1979, Pt IV, p. 14.

11. Ben H. Bagdikian, "Newspaper Mergers—the Final Phase," in *Mass Media and Society,* 3rd ed., ed. Alan Wells (Palo Alto, Calif.: Mayfield 1979), p. 49.

12. Peter M. Sandman, David M. Rubin, and David B. Sachsman, *Media: An Introductory Analysis of American Mass Communications,* 2nd ed. (Englewood Cliffs, New Jersey: Prentice-Hall, 1976), p. 110.

13. Edwin Newman, "The Power of the Media," *The American Annual, 1979* (New York: Grolier, 1979), p. 41.

14. Wilbur Schramm, *Responsibility in Mass Communication* (New York: Harper & Row, 1957), p. 5.

15. Bagdikian, "Newspaper Mergers," p. 53.

16. Circulation figures and the number of newspapers owned are taken from John Morton Newspaper Research as presented in *Standard and Poor's Industry Survey: Communication,* 24 September 1981, p. C70.

17. Data were taken from "The Top 100 Companies in Electronic Communications," *Broadcasting,* 4 January 1982, pp. 39–73. These figures indicate gross revenues from October 1980 to September 1981. The companies represented include only those with substantial broadcast holdings, e.g., at least four television stations or a total of nine radio and television stations.

18. Data for this table were from "Ranking of Top 100 Cable System Operators," *Cable Business* (published by *Television Digest*), 22 March 1982, p. 27.

19. Nicholas Johnson, *How to Talk Back to Your Television Set* (Boston: Little, Brown, 1967), p. 68.

20. Ibid., p. 76.

21. Sandman et al., *Media,* pp. 113, 119.

22. Lynn S. Gross, *See/Hear: An Introduction to Broadcasting* (Dubuque, Iowa: Wm. C. Brown, 1979), p. 189.

23. Paul Block Jr., "Facing Up to the 'Monopoly' Charge," *Nieman Reports,* July 1955, p. 4.

24. David Shaw, "Newspaper Chains—the Growth Trend," *Los Angeles Times*, 7 September 1978, Pt I, p. 1.

25. "Profile: Gannett's Allen Neuharth: A Joker But No Joke," *Broadcasting,* 23 July 1979, p. 73.

26. Caroline E. Mayer, "FCC Rules RKO General Unfit to Own a Broadcast License," *The Washington Star,* 25 January 1980, Pt C, p. 8.

27. "An Exercise in 'Bureaucratic Overkill'," *TV Guide,* 2 February 1980, p. A-2.

28. Bagdikian, "Newspaper Mergers," p. 56.

29. Johnson, *How to Talk Back to Your Television Set,* pp. 56–57.

30. Ibid., pp. 57–58.

31. Jon G. Udell, *The Economics of the American Newspaper* (New York: Hastings House, 1978), p. 77.

32. Sandman et al., *Media,* pp. 116, 123.

6

Advertising and Audience Patterns

Like the average American consumer, you probably do not stop to think about the amount of advertising you are exposed to every day while you are listening to the radio, reading your daily paper, viewing your favorite TV programs, thumbing through magazines, watching a skywriter plane spell out the name of a suntan lotion, sorting through your "junk mail," and glancing at billboards, store posters, transit ads, telephone-pole campaign flyers, and neon signs. Estimates and research studies vary, but you are probably subjected to between three hundred and a thousand advertising messages every day.[1]

In fact, advertising messages so completely pervade every aspect of our commercial media that this becomes the theme for Chapter 6:

• *Media advertising thoroughly dominates all other considerations of commercial media operation—including the content of nonadvertising messages.*

Before examining the nature of commercial advertising, however, we should recall that not all media systems are supported by advertising revenues.

6.1 Media Support Patterns

If asked "How are the various mass media supported?" the typical media consumer might reply that there are two basic methods—advertising support and outright purchase. True, these are the two most prominent ways of financing the media. But closer inspection will reveal that there are several different support patterns, both direct and indirect.

6.1.1 DIRECT AUDIENCE SUPPORT

This category includes all types of support in which the consumer pays directly for media service or makes a voluntary contribution to any of the media.

Purchase   There are essentially two ways of purchasing media products. One might be called the *occasional* or *nonscheduled* purchase. This includes newsstand purchases of magazines or newspapers, book purchases, and purchases of movie tickets and audio recordings. Each transaction is a specific, separate decision or contract.

The second type of purchase is the *scheduled* or *subscription* agreement. This involves a commitment whereby the media consumer promises to buy a given media product on a regular, continuing basis. Examples include newspaper subscriptions, magazine subscriptions, book- or record-of-the-month clubs, and cable-TV and pay-TV contracts. This type of contractual commitment obviously offers much more security to the media producer.

These two types of purchase arrangements account for the more than $7 billion worth of books sold in 1980, almost $3 billion worth of movie tickets, $3.5 billion worth of audio recordings, and more than $2 billion worth of cable-TV payments (see Inset 5–1).

Voluntary Support   Compared to contractual purchases, direct voluntary support accounts for a relatively small amount. However, for the individual media involved, it can be a significant means of support. Many religious publications, for example, receive sizable voluntary contributions from parishioners as well as from solicitations of various kinds.

The most dramatic type of voluntary media support, however, is that received by public broadcasting stations. With their membership drives, on-the-air pleas for money, and splashy auctions, noncommercial television and radio have long relied heavily upon voluntary contributions from listeners and viewers. In 1977–78, more than three million people coughed up a total of about $75 million (approximately 14 percent of the two services' total budgets) to keep public TV and public radio on the air.

6.1.2 INDIRECT MEDIA SUPPORT

Most of the revenues generated to keep media operations functioning come, however, from indirect sources.

Government Subsidization   Public broadcasting is probably the biggest domestic, civilian recipient of tax dollars for media support. In fiscal 1977–78, municipal governments (including boards of education) contributed more than $44 million (8 percent of public broadcasting's total income); state governments (including state colleges and universities) came up with $174 million (31.5 percent); and the federal government, on a matching grant basis, furnished $161 million (29 percent).

Directly and indirectly, tax dollars are also involved in supporting other media channels. Public libraries, from the local community to the Library of Congress, are largely supported by public funds, as are government printing operations like the U.S. Government Printing Office. Among other forms of support are indirect subsidization through lowered postage rates and government grants to aspiring artists, writers, and filmmakers.

Special-Interest Group Underwriting
Many of the same kinds of groups discussed in Chapter 5 as owners of various media channels also are involved as supporters of various media endeavors, even when they are not directly involved as owners of specific channels. Philanthropic foundations have played a major role. The Ford Foundation, for example, has given more than $300 million to noncommercial broadcasting—most of it during the medium's formative years in the 1950s and early 1960s. Corporate underwriters and private businesses continue to be a major source of support for public broadcasting. Educators, also, contribute to the support of many different kinds of print and electric media channels. One of the most

significant types of special-interest group sub-sidies has come from political and social activists. Anyone who has a cause will sup-port the channels that are willing to help spread the word.

The crucial factor to keep in mind is that whenever some special-interest group is sub-sidizing a media channel, it generally has some purpose or message to promote. For one reason or another such underwriters are interested in reaching us—the media consumers—with some specific information or propaganda.

Advertising Support   By far the largest form of indirect support is advertising income—the very foundation of all commer-cial media. In 1980, total advertising reve-nues received by all advertising media and schemes (including billboards, direct mail, transit ads, matchbook covers, balloons, sky-writing, posters, campaign buttons, etc.) came to almost $55 billion. The importance and indispensability of advertising to our free-enterprise marketing system is empha-sized by Sydney Head:

Advertising plays an essential role in the mecha-nism of mass distribution, as well as a more argu-able role in creating appetites for consumer goods. When the housewife stopped making her own soap and buying shoes from the local crafts-man, she lost direct contact with the sources of supply. Advertising bridges the gap. In self-service stores, instead of interrogating a human salesman, the shopper consults an index of advertising lore in her head and responds to the stimuli of point-of-sale displays and eye-catching packages. Thus advertising, along with packaging, has to a large degree replaced expensive person-to-person sales-manship.[2]

The Ultimate Source   It would be well to remember that eventually all media services are paid for from one source. The money all comes out of one pocket—whether directly or indirectly. Ultimately, the source of all

Billboards comprise a ubiquitous advertising medium in both urban and rural settings.

media support is *you*. You are the media pur-chaser or ticket buyer. You are the taxpayer. You contribute indirectly to various founda-tions and special-interest groups. And, most importantly, you purchase advertised goods and services. Eventually, indirectly, everything comes out of your wallet. There is no other source!

The Purchaser-Advertiser Mix   Books, movies, and audio recordings are supported almost entirely by *direct purchase* (although the consumer may be exposed to some occa-sional theater commercials and promotional advertising on book jackets). At the other extreme, commercial radio and television are supported almost entirely by *advertising reve-nues*. In between are newspapers and maga-zines, which are supported by a *mix of direct purchase and advertising*.

Not all specific media channels fit into these patterns, of course. As mentioned above, open-circuit pay TV, cable TV, and pay cable are television delivery systems which rely upon direct purchase (subscription) rather than advertising.[3] However, advertising may have a future role in these systems.

A very few magazines are supported entirely by direct consumer purchase, carry-ing no advertising at all. *Consumer Reports* and *Mad* magazine are two prime examples. *Reader's Digest* thrived for thirty-three years without advertising, but in 1955 rising costs forced it to poll its readers to see if they would prefer to pay a higher direct price for the magazine or have it turn to advertising support. The readers voted in favor of advertising.

Most newspapers and magazines, therefore, are supported by a mixture of ads and purchases. And the ratio of support roughly reflects the content ratio. Newspapers typically consist of about sixty-five percent advertising and thirty-five percent editorial content; and the average newspaper receives sixty-five to seventy-five percent of its income from advertising. Magazines similarly have a high ratio of advertising to editorial content, although the ratio varies more in magazines than in typical metropolitan newspapers. *Sunset* magazine, for example, may have 112 to 115 pages of advertising in its total of 190 to 200 pages. And for general magazines, advertising dollars furnish an average of about sixty percent of its general revenues.

6.1.3 TOTAL ADVERTISING REVENUES

In 1980, the total advertising income from all sources was $54.5 billion. Of this amount, about sixty percent was received by the major communication mass media (newspapers, magazines, television, and radio) as opposed to specific advertising media (billboards, direct mail, transit flyers, and so forth).

While there have been some slight shifts of emphasis in advertising expenditures (television's share has increased slightly while magazines have slipped), it should be noted that the total advertising market has been increasing by an average of fourteen to fifteen percent per year during the last few years. Thus, even magazines have seen a slight overall increase in advertising revenue. All in all, it would be safe to conclude that the advertising business will remain hale and healthy—even while bumping over the potholes of the national economy's fluctuations.

This table lists the advertising revenues for each of the major mass media in selected years from 1965 to 1980.[4] The figures in parentheses indicate the percentage of the total advertising market captured by each medium every year. (All numbers are given in millions of dollars.)

INSET 6–1
Advertising Expenditures, by Medium, 1965–1980

Year	1965	1970	1974	1976	1978	1980
Newspapers	4,426 (29.0%)	5,704 (29.2%)	8,001 (29.8%)	9,910 (29.4%)	12,690 (29.0%)	15,541 (28.5%)
Magazines	1,232 (8.1%)	1,354 (6.9%)	1,576 (5.9%)	1,875 (5.6%)	2,700 (6.2%)	3,149 (5.8%)
Television	2,515 (16.5%)	3,596 (18.4%)	4,854 (18.1%)	6,721 (19.9%)	8,850 (20.2%)	11,366 (20.9%)
Radio	917 (6.0%)	1,308 (6.7%)	1,837 (6.8%)	2,330 (6.9%)	2,955 (6.8%)	3,702 (6.8%)
Direct Mail	2,324 (15.2%)	2,766 (14.1%)	4,054 (15.1%)	4,813 (14.3%)	6,030 (13.8%)	7,596 (13.9%)
All Other Media*	3,836 (25.2%)	4,822 (24.7%)	6,498 (24.2%)	8,071 (23.9%)	10,515 (24.0%)	13,126 (24.1%)
TOTALS	15,250	19,550	26,820	33,720	43,740	54,480

*"All other media" includes billboards, business papers, transit posters, matchbooks, skywriting, campaign notices, store posters, bumper stickers, handbills, and the like.

6.2 Audience Measurement and Composition

Any media outlet or channel supported by direct consumer purchase has an immediate and tangible method of determining its income—the number of tickets, subscriptions, or copies actually sold. However, advertising support introduces a complicating factor, especially in the case of "free" media such as radio or television whose audiences cannot be directly counted. Any medium which relies heavily (or entirely) upon advertising revenue is, in effect, in *the business of selling audience members to the advertisers*.

6.2.1 CIRCULATION AND RATINGS: THE HEADCOUNTING FUNCTIONS

Any channel supported by advertising must be able to demonstrate to its potential advertisers that it can actually deliver audience members—readers, listeners, or viewers who will receive the advertising messages. This relatively simple "headcounting" job—verifying the size of the audience—has a long history of deception, gimmicks, and fierce competition.

The Audit Bureau of Circulation   From that fateful day in September 1833 when Benjamin Day brought out the first issue of the *New York Sun,* it was apparent that the penny press was to be an advertising medium. During the first few decades of newspaper competition for advertising revenues, readership figures were easily manipulated. Newsstand sales were exaggerated, subscription lists were blatantly padded, and gross gimmicks were used to boost sales. One enterprising publisher randomly inserted dollar bills into a number of copies of his paper, advertised the promotion on the front page, and watched sales soar as customers bought dozens of copies apiece to seek the buried treasure. Some publishers customarily inflated circulation figures to ten times the actual numbers. These mythological numbers were obviously of no use to potential advertisers.

Succumbing to pressure from advertisers, responsible publishers joined with advertisers and advertising agencies to support the establishment of the Audit Bureau of Circulation (ABC) in 1914. This autonomous agency conducts independent audits of newspaper and magazine circulation figures and also serves to monitor procurement of circulation data by the various publications. Today, ABC figures are accepted as the most reliable guide to total circulation numbers (subscriptions plus street sales) in the publishing fields.

Broadcast Ratings   The headcounting function for radio and television is a more delicate operation than for the print media. With newspapers and magazines, the number of copies sold and/or distributed can be physically counted. The broadcast media, however, deal with an ephemeral media experience which cannot be accurately tabulated. There simply is no economically feasible way to determine the precise number of radio or TV sets tuned into a given program at any moment. The only practical solution is to survey a portion of the broadcast audience and then to project a total audience figure from the sample.

The first such listener survey was inaugurated in 1929 when Archibald Crossley formed the Cooperative Analysis of Broadcasting (CAB). Crossley's researchers used a "telephone recall" method, telephoning households in the morning to ask "who had listened to what" the previous evening. This sample became the basis of a *rating*—the percentage of radio sets tuned into a specific program—for major network shows.

Clark-Hooper, Inc., an audience research firm dealing with both magazines and radio, split off its radio operation in 1938. As C. E. Hooper, Inc., the new company became Crossley's main competitor. Based on "telephone coincidental" method (telephoning households and asking "who is listening to what" right now), the monthly "Hooperratings" were generally considered to be more accurate. They were also considerably more expensive.

INSET 6–2 Television Audience Research

Although television audience research can become very complicated and very sophisticated when it is used to examine various demographic distinctions and marketing patterns, the essence of the ratings system can be understood in terms of three concepts:

Households-Using-Television (H.U.T.): The percentage of homes—out of the total number of TV-equipped homes—which actually have the TV set turned on.

Rating: The percentage of the total possible audience (the total number of TV homes) tuned in to a given program.

Share of Audience: The percentage of households which are watching TV (the total Households-Using-Television) that is tuned to a given program.

Thus, the share of the audience will always be higher than the actual rating. (If the households-using-television or H.U.T. were 100 percent, then the rating and the share would be the same.) In other words, the higher the H.U.T., the higher the rating. Even if the share is high, the rating will be low if the H.U.T. is low. Thus, programs shown during prime time (when a large number of sets are turned on in the evening, making for a high H.U.T.) will have much higher ratings than programs shown early on Sunday morning. But the "shares" of all programs on at given time will always total 100 percent.

In the example below, the total circle equals 1,000 TV households. Out of the potential 1,000 viewing homes, only 800 have a TV set turned on. Thus, we have an H.U.T of 80 (percent).

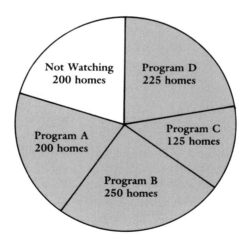

Number of households turned to four different programs. The shaded area represents TV sets turned on (H.U.T. = 800).

Program	Rating*	Share**
A	20.0	25.0
B	25.0	31.3
C	12.5	15.6
D	22.5	28.1

*The number of homes tuned to a given program divided by the total number of TV households (1,000 in this example).

**The number of homes tuned to given program divided by the number of households with the TV set tuned on (800 in this example).

By 1942 the A. C. Nielsen Company, an established market research firm, had introduced its "audimeter." This was an automatic device which could be attached to a receiving set and which would provide a continuous record of when the set was turned on and to what station. It was by far the most accurate manner of surveying receiver usage, but it could not verify who, if anyone, was actually listening. The audimeter and its concomitant "Nielsen rating" became much more important for television than it was for radio. With approximately 1,200 scientifically selected "Nielsen families" across the country, A. C. Nielsen provides its highly publicized weekly projections of TV ratings.

The American Research Bureau (ARB) and its "arbitron" ratings provide the other major nationwide TV ratings service. ARB uses a diary method for gathering national data and a mechanical set-metering device for collecting overnight ratings in major cities. Many other smaller and specialized research firms use methods similar to those described above in collecting listening and viewing data for individual stations and for local programming.

6.2.2 AUDIENCE SIZES AND TRENDS

Taken collectively, Americans are spending increasing amounts of time with the mass media. About 62 million copies of newspapers are distributed throughout the country every day, and most adults (about ninety percent of the population) spend more than half an hour going through the paper. About seventy percent of the population devotes twenty minutes or more scanning the 40 million magazines and other periodicals sold each day. About twenty-five percent of the adult population reads one book a month; total book output for the nation is 3 million copies daily.

More than a thousand television stations, commercial and noncommercial, broadcast to about 156 million TV sets which are turned on more than six and three-quarters hours daily; this is a total of more than one billion reception-hours a day. The average adult viewer watches television three and a half hours every day. And the country's more than nine thousand radio stations transmit to more than 400 million radio sets (close to two receivers per person). The average radio listener reports spending nearly three hours a day with radio, but if all "background" uses

---

The Television Bureau of Advertising compiled data comparing the amount of time that the average American adult spent attending to the four major mass media supported by advertising. Its figures indicate that the total amount of time spent with the media increased by almost an hour a day from 1970 to 1975.[5]

**INSET 6–3
Time Spent
Consuming
Advertising Media**

Time Spent with Each Medium Daily

	1970	1975
Television	139 minutes	179 minutes
Radio	93 minutes	109 minutes
Newspapers	36 minutes	32 minutes
Magazines	21 minutes	21 minutes
TOTAL	289 minutes	341 minutes

were counted the figures would be much higher.

Among the major mass media, only motion picture attendance has shown a substantial decline in recent years. Rising costs, fewer productions, and increased competition from other media (especially television) have all combined to cut down on movie-going habits. In 1914, for example, about 49 million Americans (exactly half of the national population) went to the movies weekly. This number rose to a high of 90 million in 1946 (about sixty-three percent of the population). But by 1977, movie attendance was down to 20 million weekly (less than ten percent of the total population).

Looking at the four major advertising mass media (newspapers, magazines, television, and radio), the Television Bureau of Advertising reported that the American adult in 1975 spent an average of five and two-thirds hours with these media daily.

Fragmentation of the Mass Audience
During the first half of this century, it was customary to speak of the "mass" audience. Advertisers, media practitioners, and the public alike thought in terms of the massive, undifferentiated, homogeneous public which attended *en masse* the popular outpourings of the various media. Half of the population went to the movies every week; the entire nation was captivated by popular network radio programs; the largest metropolitan newspapers approached circulation figures close to a million apiece; best-selling books were read by "everybody"; and magazines such as *Life* and *Look* chronicled America's culture.

However, this view of the monolithic mass began to fall apart shortly after the end of World War II. More sophisticated social-science techniques—psychological studies, market research, audience analysis—began to unveil a new picture of numerous fragmented audiences and interest groups which mingled and merged, disintegrated and dispersed, to form different types of audiences for different media events. Don Pember, writing in the early 1970s, summed up this emerging viewpoint of the shifting audience:

[T]he mass audience is beginning to disintegrate, fall apart, and crumble. The readers of our newspapers, books, and magazines, television and movie viewers, and radio listeners exist today in a state of disarray that could not be found just thirty years ago. No more is the audience being perceived as one big lumpenproletariat. The mass is beginning to fragment into hundreds of smaller parts. . . . Today there are those who question whether the mass audience really exists—or ever existed. Today the key to success is not the number of people who are listening or watching or reading—but in getting the right people to listen or read or watch. The mass has begun to fall apart.[6]

6.2.3 THREE PERSPECTIVES ON MASS COMMUNICATION AUDIENCES

In his penetrating analyses of mass communication theories, Melvin DeFleur has elaborated on three distinct explanations of how individual audience members interact with the mass media and their messages.[7] Each of these "perspectives" helps to explain how the audience responds to content and advertising messages. The three perspectives are not necessarily contradictory or exclusive theories; all three explanations work together.

The Individual Differences Perspective
Behavioral psychologists of the early twentieth century gave us a new understanding of how individuals react to various things in their environments, including messages of the mass media. The older, simpler stimulus-response (S-R) model of communication held that a given stimulus (media message) would trigger an identical response (behavior or feedback) among all audience members. Common sense and direct observation indicated, however, that this simple response pattern was not always forthcoming; different people reacted in different ways to the same

media message. There were intervening variables related to a person's psychological composition or personality which determined the way a given individual would react to a specific communication stimulus.

"Psychographics," the study of these personality variables, led to the concepts of *selective attention* (each person will attend to those media messages that appeal to his or her specific personality) and *selective perception* (each person will interpret a common stimulus differently, in accordance with his or her personality and outlook). Thus, some people will pay attention to *Newsweek* for news while others will rely upon CBS (selective attention); of those who turn to CBS some will see Dan Rather as a liberal and others will view him as a conservative depending upon their individual perspectives (selective perception). This is how stereotypes, prejudices, and self-fulfilling prophecies are perpetuated. *We tend to see what we look for,* what we want to see; *we confirm what we think we know.*

The Social Relationships Perspective
Another explanation of audience reaction to persuasive messages emerged in the early 1940s. A landmark study by Lazarsfeld, Ber-

elson, and Gaudet (examining how mass media influence presidential campaigns) yielded an unexpected and significant finding—that a receiver's personal relationships with family members and associates greatly influence the way he or she will react to a given mass communication stimulus.[8] The receiver of any mass media message is routinely affected by friends, close relatives, and fellow workers who interpret and emphasize certain aspects of the communication process. You are influenced to some extent by these "opinion leaders" in your choice of books, the TV programs you watch, the papers you buy, and the advertising messages you pay attention to.

The discovery of this phenomenon led to the concept of the "two-step flow of communication," which explained how mass media information was filtered through these opinion leaders (first step) and then interpreted and passed on to the secondary or ultimate receivers (second step).

Subsequent research into the diffusion of ideas and technological change has tended to refute and modify many aspects of the origi-

---

The *individual differences perspective* of mass communication explains that there are always a number of variables which are interposed between the stimulus (message) and response (receiver's reaction). These intervening variables constitute the receiver's personality and psychological structure.

**INSET 6–4
The Individual
Differences
Perspective**

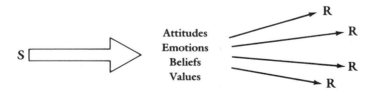

The media stimulus or message (S) is filtered through the attitudes, emotions, beliefs, and values of each individual receiver (R). Thus, each receiver will respond in a different way to a given communication stimulus.

---

nal two-step theory. It was a little too simplistic. Nevertheless, this theory helps to explain some aspects of the mass communication process. It helps to explain why we may or may not be successful when we try, for example, to sell detergent to a housewife, sell the concept of crop rotation to a Third-World farmer, or sell a new clothing fashion to a teenager. We *are* influenced by the opinions of our peers.

The Social Categories Perspective A third way of looking at mass communication and the way individual audience members perceive a given message is by examining group membership or social categories. Audience members who have certain similar characteristics—age, income, sex, occupation, race, and so forth—will tend to behave in a similar fashion when exposed to a given media stimulus or message. This perspective "assumes

that there are broad collectives, aggregates, or social categories in urban-industrial societies whose behavior in the face of a given set of stimuli is more or less uniform."[9]

Many obvious advertising guidelines are derived from this basic perspective. One does not use the *Wall Street Journal* to reach truck drivers, nor does one advertise pantyhose in *Field and Stream*. Neither does an acne medication sponsor the *Lawrence Welk* show.

Whereas the individual differences perspective is based upon psychological principles, DeFleur explains that the "basic assumption of the social categories theory is a sociological one—namely, that in spite of the heterogeneity of modern society, people who have a number of similar characteristics will have similar folkways."[10]

The *social relationships perspective* of the mass communication process recognizes the significance of the "opinion leader" who serves as an informal interpreter of the mass communication message.

INSET 6–5
The Social Relationships Perspective

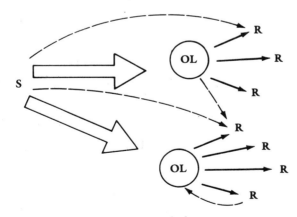

The media message or stimulus (S) is picked up first by the opinion leader (OL), interpreted, and then relayed to the ultimate receiver (R). Of course, the process may be complicated by secondary lines of communication and feedback (dotted lines).

The Combined Effect None of these three perspectives is intended to serve by itself as a comprehensive explanation of how audience members behave. When they are taken together—superimposed on each other—the combined confused effect begins to shed some light on the complicated patterns of our responses to mass communication.

6.2.4 THE STUDY OF DEMOGRAPHICS

Of the three perspectives discussed above, the social categories concept has been of most value to advertisers and market researchers because it deals in readily classifiable categories and therefore lends itself to feasible research techniques. It is fairly easy to determine a person's sex, age, income level, and years of education (social categories). It is not so simple to determine a person's personality characteristics—submissiveness, extroversion, self-image, leadership potential, moral character, optimism, and so forth (individual differences). These are rather subtle and elusive qualities; considerable psychological probing is involved in profiling a person's personality makeup. Similarly, it is much easier to deal in social categories than it is to try to define meaningful social relationships—to determine who are the opinion leaders and media facilitators in various situations. For these reasons, the concept of social categories has emerged as the most useful tool in marketing and advertising research.

The *social categories perspective* groups audience members by easily definable characteristics—age, sex, education, race, and so forth—on the assumption that individuals with such similar traits will react in similar ways when exposed to the same mass media message.

**INSET 6–6
The Social
Categories
Perspective**

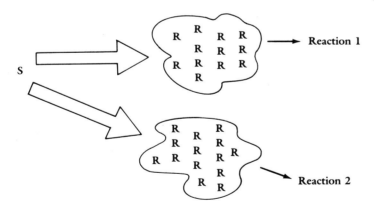

The media stimulus or message (S) is received by groups of individual receivers (R) who are bound together in a group by some common social characteristics. The individual audience members in the same group are likely to respond in a similar fashion.

Demographic Categories The term "demographics" is derived from *demography,* the science of vital and social statistics of populations, and has come to encompass the study of social categories. Once certain demographic characteristics have been determined—a relatively simple task involving a short questionnaire—any individual can be placed into appropriate pigeonholes, classified, sorted, bunched, and bombarded with the most effective communication techniques for specific marketing and advertising campaigns.

The most frequently used demographic breakdowns are those that are the easiest to obtain: *age, sex, income category, marital status, education level, race, and religious affiliation.* Other demographic indices include items like *occupational description, geographical region, ethnic or national origin, and urban-rural residence.* Occasionally a survey also calls for items that are more difficult to ascertain, such as leisure pursuits, eating preferences, buying patterns, and so forth.

Media Demographic Characteristics

Many circulation and ratings services, along with other readership and audience studies, have given advertisers and market researchers a demographic picture of how audience members—including you—tend to use the media.

Newspaper readership increases, for example, with *age* (senior citizens spend more time with the newspaper than young adults), *education,* and *income.* The general inference is that newspaper readers tend to be more concerned about current issues; they tend to be community leaders; they tend to have more at stake in society.

The same is true for *magazines and books.* The better educated and more affluent tend to read more. One study credits continued magazine prosperity to "population increase, more particularly to rising income levels and the expansion of the middle class, to the spread of popular education, and to the increase in leisure time."[11] Another study indicates that in 1979, for example, magazine readership among men earning $20,000 or more was thirty percent above the average.[12]

Magazines are a medium of tremendous diversity, however, and readership obviously varies widely. There is little demographic similarity between the readers of *Cycle World* and the readers of *Family Circle.* The slick and sophisticated city magazines (Section 3.4.5) typify the way that a narrowed demographic target can be pinpointed—eight out of ten readers of city magazines own their own homes, two-thirds have college degrees, seven out of ten households own two or more cars, three out of four are stockholders, and almost eight out of ten heads of households are employed in professional, managerial, official, or proprietorial occupations.[13]

Radio and television consumers, as might be expected, have the opposite demographic characteristics from print consumers. Television viewers tend to represent a relatively lower socioeconomic status (lower incomes, more blue-collar occupations). As far as age categories are concerned, the heaviest television viewers are the very young and the elderly. The lightest TV viewing is among teenagers. Radio, on the other hand, is most popular among teenagers and young adults. Sex is a determining criterion during weekday daytime TV viewing periods, when women tend to control the tube. However, during "equal opportunity time" (weekends and weekday evenings), when more men have access to the set, TV viewing between the sexes tends to balance out. In fact, most studies confirm that, given an equal opportunity for viewing, virtually everyone will spend some time watching television. It comes closer to being the universal mass medium than any of the other communication media.

The audience for the *movies* tends to be younger and better educated than in the past.

The "personal portable" radios and cassette players have further personalized the youth-oriented mediums.

lowing generalizations: young children watch television a lot; teenagers and young adults listen to the radio, go to the movies, and buy records; older adults read more; and retired people turn back to the TV set. Women watch more TV than men (although when household roles are reversed it appears that "house-husbands" watch more than wage-earning wives). People with higher incomes and better educations read more newspapers, magazines, and books, although tastes vary tremendously. Nearly everyone watches television.

One must be cautious in making or using such generalizations, of course. There are numerous exceptions and anomalies which undermine these sweeping statements. Even more important may be the personality characteristics discussed above under the individual differences perspective. Being able to classify and reach media consumers in terms of their leadership potential, submissiveness, extroversion, and other traits would add immeasurably to audience analysis and market research. But, as the author Robert Murphy points out,

The [psychological] questions are not nearly so well answered in terms of the more personal attributes of the men and women in the audience. Do lonely people watch certain kinds of programs? Do aggressive people watch more adventure shows? What are the personality characteristics of people who read editorials or personal advice columns? Some interesting studies have been done, but, by and large, media people and advertisers know little about the psychological characteristics of their audiences.[14]

In the absence of concrete data about the viewing and reading habits of people with specific personality types, the advertising industry falls back upon the obvious and easy-to-obtain demographic distinctions. It tries to sell you a Cadillac by placing ads in prestigious magazines. It pushes a new detergent by advertising on daytime soap operas. And it tries to sell you stereo equipment through commercials placed on FM stations with popular-music formats.

Of those Americans who have at least a year of college education, sixty-five percent attend the movies "frequently or occasionally," while only half of those who have not completed high school go to the movies regularly. On the other hand, forty percent of the population—primarily older people—never go to the movies at all.

One of the more encouraging signs for the *record industry* is that the record-buying public is growing older. Most records today are purchased by consumers aged twenty-five to forty-nine. The post-World War II baby-boom youngsters who came into record-buying prominence with the Beatles in the sixties are still buying records two decades later.

Demographic Outlines Summarizing demographic breakdowns of mass media consumption, one could come up with the fol-

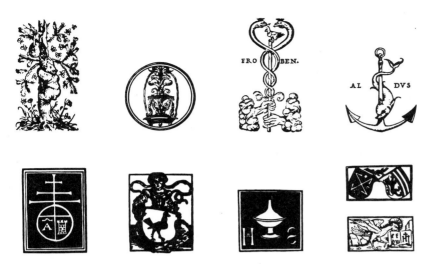

Renaissance printers' marks are an outgrowth of the earlier guild marks and hall marks which served to identify specific craftsmen or manufacturers.

6.3 Evolution of Advertising Structures

Advertising can track its heritage back possibly to early Greek and Roman artisans, and to medieval halls and guilds which certainly identified their products with particular symbols or marks. The guild marks or "hallmarks" were originally a device used to trace inferior workmanship. (The closest example we have today is the slip of paper you sometimes find in the pocket of a new shirt, "Inspected by Number 14.") These hallmarks eventually evolved into symbols of pride in workmanship, becoming precursors of modern advertising.

Early newsletters and papers were carrying commercial announcements and paid advertising by the early 1700s. However, it was not until Benjamin Day conceived of the advertiser-supported newspaper in 1833 (Section 3.3.2) that the modern role of advertising was established. By selling the *New York Sun* for one penny a copy, he could reach enough readers to make it worthwhile for the advertisers collectively to pay a large portion of the cost of the paper.

6.3.1 EMERGENCE OF THE ADVERTISING AGENCY

In the early 1840s, an entrepreneur named Volney Palmer came up with the idea of buying large blocks of space in several newspapers and magazines and then reselling the space—at a slight markup in price—to various advertisers. Palmer was, in essence, a *space broker*. He earned his profit by handling the management of advertising space for the newspapers. He contacted potential buyers and received a small fee from the publishers for each ad he sold.

The Modern Advertising Agency The early advertising agencies were, in essence, representing the publishers. But this provided little help for the potential advertisers, who frequently did not know how to draw up an ad or in which newspapers to place their ads.

The N. W. Ayer & Son Agency, which had been founded in 1869, analyzed the situation and in the mid-1870s turned the basic publisher-agency-advertiser relationship around. Instead of working for the publisher, the Ayer firm started representing the advertiser—offering advertising counsel, making the best media buys, helping to design advertising campaigns, doing whatever it could to help the advertiser get the most for each advertising dollar. Other agencies followed suit, and this basic agency-advertiser structure has remained the backbone of the advertising world for the last century.

Broadcast Advertising   Early radio advertising was clouded by legal and ethical questions about the practice of selling air time. Just as the space broker bought space in wholesale quantities from newspapers and magazines, so, too, the concept of the *time broker* emerged in the early days of radio advertising. Middlemen would purchase large blocks of radio time and then sell it in smaller chunks to individual advertisers. A few stations regarded this as irresponsible and crass commercialism and refused to sell broadcast time to time brokers. Others questioned the practice but participated furtively. Ben Gross relates one such story about a Newark, New Jersey, station: "The station owner was so doubtful of the legality of the procedure that he insisted on receiving payment in cash rather than by check and arranged to meet the broker clandestinely in a hotel, where the money could change hands secretly."[15]

The Contemporary Ad Agency   In about 1925, after fifty years of experience in the serious representation of clients, advertising agencies began to employ more sophisticated social-science techniques in order to take some of the guesswork out of their activities. They began to use market research to test what the audience really wanted, liked, and would buy; sampling procedures to determine audience size; methods of measuring the effect of specific messages on sales in order to devise specific marketing strategies; and cost-effectiveness studies to determine the best media buys (Section 6.4).

6.3.2 MEDIA ADVERTISING PATTERNS

Print and broadcast media are vehicles for both national and local advertising. However, there are certain differences in the specific ways they are used.

Newspaper Advertising Patterns   As you flip through your daily paper, you are broadly aware of two types of advertising content. The *classified ads* are generally set aside in a separate section, with few or no illustrations. They contain notices, personal ads, real estate and "help wanted" ads, and many miscellaneous items for sale—all "classified" into convenient categories. *Display ads* are scattered throughout the paper and often contain artwork or photographs. They frequently occupy large blocks of space and are placed by major retailers and manufacturers.

Display ads are divided into two distinct types of advertising. *Retail advertising* is placed by merchants and other local business concerns. Retail ads are designed to sell goods and services at particular stores or other points-of-sale, and they are frequently sought out by the consumer who is looking for specific information regarding prices and product availability. Retail display advertising accounts for almost sixty percent of the total advertising space.

The other type of display advertising is *national advertising*. Generally sold at higher rates than local ads, national advertisements are placed by nationwide manufacturers, distributors, and suppliers of services. They are usually more persuasive than local ads, which tend to be informative in nature. Co-op advertising is a common hybrid of the two types. In co-op advertising, the national advertiser pays most of the bill to promote the product, but the ad is placed by the local retailer and (unlike most national ads) tells the consumer where to buy the product. Co-op ads are sold at the lower local rate.

Classified ads, which did not become big business until after World War II, are placed by buyers ("help wanted" or items wanted to buy) as well as by sellers. Although some readers peruse the classified and want ads out of general interest or idle curiosity, most readers use the ads to look for specific items or information. "Whereas display seeks the buyer, the buyer seeks the classifieds."[17]

Broadcast Advertising Patterns Radio and television advertising revenues also can be divided into national and local sources. However, the "national" grouping is really made up of two distinct categories: *network* advertising, which encompasses all commercials purchased and aired over a complete radio or television network, and *national spot* advertising, which allows nationwide advertisers to buy time on selected stations in different parts of the country without having to purchase time on the entire network.

Comparing radio and television advertising patterns, one can see that the ratio of local to national advertising is just about reversed. Radio obtains roughly seventy-five percent of its revenue from local sources; television gets more than three-quarters of its income from national sources (national spot and network advertising combined). Traditionally, this is how radio and television have been perceived: radio is a local advertiser's medium; television is a national advertiser's medium.

Newspaper advertising can be categorized as either display (including both retail and national) or classified. It can also be divided into the two categories of local (encompassing both retail and classified) and national. In either case, we have the three divisions diagrammed below. The dollar figures, given in millions, are for 1978.[16]

INSET 6–7
Newspaper Ads:
Classified, Retail,
and National

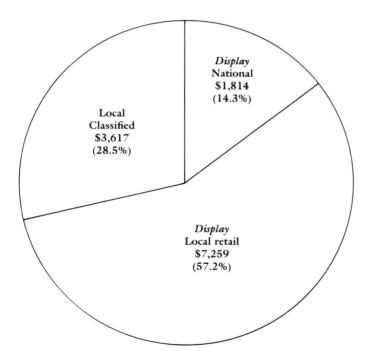

Display
National
$1,814
(14.3%)

Local
Classified
$3,617
(28.5%)

Display
Local retail
$7,259
(57.2%)

Magazine Advertising Patterns

Magazines, even more than television, represent a national advertising medium. Most magazines are intended for a coast-to-coast audience.

There are many exceptions, of course. Regional and city magazines (Section 3.4.5) cater to readers and advertisers of a less than national character. A more dynamic example of localized magazine advertising is the "regional breakout" of a national magazine. Following the lead of the *Wall Street Journal,* which started printing four regional editions back in the 1950s, many large-circulation magazines introduced regional editions. Editorial content remained unchanged in each edition; they were all national publications. However, local and regional advertisers could have their ads placed in one specific edition. Thus, a bank in Atlanta or a classical-music radio station in Los Angeles could afford to run a full-page ad in *Time* or one of its competitors.

As pointed out previously (Inset 3–11), the demise of the large-circulation general-inter-

The regional breakout allows magazines to sell both national ads (as this one for the Aiwa personal portable) and local ads (nearby resorts) side by side in the same issue.

est weekly magazines (*Life, Look, Saturday Evening Post,* and *Colliers*) was caused by television's ability to reach the mass audience with national advertising more efficiently on a cost basis. In an attempt to counter this TV advantage, *Life* and *Look,* for example, went to the regional breakout to attract advertisers who would be less likely to turn to television—local financial institutions, distributors

---

Local radio and TV advertisers are usually local merchants or companies who buy air time on a single station.

National spot advertisers buy air time on a number of selected stations to sell a regional or national product in specific localities.

Network advertisers purchase air time on a complete lineup of stations affiliated with a given radio or television network.

The figures below (all given in millions of dollars) represent the advertising income, for the three advertising categories, in five selected years.[18]

**INSET 6–8
Broadcast
Advertising
Revenues,
1960–1980**

	1960	1965	1970	1975	1980
Radio Totals	654	868	1,257	1,890	3,530
Local	401	553	853	1,401	2,600
National Spot	208	261	355	416	765
Network	45	54	49	73	167
Television Totals	1,456	2,266	3,243	4,722	10,300
Local	240	328	589	1,116	2,500
National Spot	469	796	1,103	1,449	2,900
Network	747	1,142	1,551	2,157	4,800

---

of regional products, auto retailers, and so forth. In 1969 *Life* was publishing 133 regional editions, and *Look* was selling advertising in 75 separate breakouts. The regional breakout, in effect, was the magazine's answer to national spot advertising in radio and television—it gave the advertiser a choice of markets.

The backbone of the magazine industry is, of course, the special-interest magazine. No other medium can reach such a clearly defined audience. Today special-interest magazines cover just about everything from accident prevention to zookeeping techniques. Although many of these audiences are small in number, they tend to be scattered from coast to coast and thus represent targets for national advertisers whose products or services are likely to appeal to the special interests concerned.

The Overall Picture Although there are many exceptions and variations on the national level, general advertising remains spread among the various mass media. Newspapers and radio represent the best outlets for local retailers, small businesses, and regional products. Television and magazines are the most efficient media for reaching a nationwide audience, either a general mass audience or a select target group.

6.4 The Advertising Campaign

Given this overall picture of the advertising environment, exactly how is a nationwide campaign handled? Where do you start? How do you lay out the campaign? How do you select specific media to buy? How do you know what type of presentation has the best chance of working? How will the public react?

6.4.1 AGENCY FUNCTIONS

At the heart of the advertising structure is, of course, the advertising agency, which serves as the essential middleman between the advertiser and the media channels. The "full-service agency" provides a complete range of advertising and marketing services for its advertising client: audience analysis and research, creative plans and strategies, advertisement design and copywriting, media selection and buying, and advertising evaluation and market research. For additional fees,

---

This chart diagrams the relationship between the advertiser (client), advertising agency, and medium/channel in a typical advertising situation. Assuming a rate-card charge of $10,000 for a given advertisement, the monies would be apportioned as indicated.

INSET 6–9 Advertiser/ Agency/ Medium Relationship

	Advertiser/Client	*Ad Agency*	*Medium/Channel*
Functional Relationship	Manufacturers the product Handles distribution	Handles market research, campaign strategy, advertising design, and media placement	Provides space or time for advertising message
Financial Relationship	Pays the full amount of rate care (e.g., $10,000)	Receives a 15% commission (e.g., $1,500)	Receives 85% of the established rate (e.g., $8,500)

the agency will also subcontract for other specific services: advertisement production, publicity and public relations, promotional campaigns, and sales operations.

For these services, the agency typically is paid a commission—usually fifteen percent of the rate charged by the medium carrying the advertisement. The agency's fee comes from the money turned over to the medium; therefore, the advertiser/client pays the full amount of the rate-card charge, the agency gets fifteen percent of that amount, and the medium actually collects eighty-five percent of the rate-card charge. Each medium publishes a "rate card," a list of standard charges for ads of various kinds. A magazine, for example, varies its charges according to its circulation, the size of the ad, the number of colors in which it is to be printed, and, sometimes, its position within the magazine.

Consumer Analysis   At the beginning of a campaign, the agency must find out precisely who buys (or who might buy) the product. Under what conditions? Where? When? What are the needs of the potential consumer? How can the product be presented so that it appeals to those needs? Or, how can new needs be generated? Consumer analysis must include the study of several major distribution characteristics. Analyzing *geographic distribution* includes distinguishing among urban, suburban, and rural markets as well as identifying regional factors. In analyzing *consumption distribution,* the researcher strives to identify precisely who the predominant buyers are for a given product. Who are the heavy cigarette smokers? Who buys the most insurance? Who does the grocery shopping? *Demographic distribution* is closely related to "consumption distribution." Age, income, sex, education, occupation, and marital status are among the prime social categories to be determined. *Psychographic distribution* is an extension of the "individual differences" perspective discussed in Section 6.2.3. The psychological profile of a potential customer—

while more elusive and expensive to obtain—may be a more reliable indicator of successful advertising strategies than any other factor. The authors Heighton and Cunningham point out that psychographic analysis

searches out common characteristics among product purchasers and employs modern psychological testing to obtain the information. The consumer profile for a particular product may show vast differences in demographics, but a fairly consistent pattern in such traits as aggression, compliance, dominance, autonomy, adaptability, and the like.[19]

Advertising Objectives   Advertising is a communication process. And, like any communication task, precise objectives need to be established in order to ensure the chances of a successful communication experience. This is not merely an academic exercise. It is an absolute necessity if a common goal is to be defined, an effective campaign is to be designed, and results are to be measured.

It is essential for the client and advertising agency to have a clear understanding of the advertising objectives, but it is also important for the *consumer* to understand the process—to comprehend what the advertiser hopes to get you to do. In order to be a more discriminating and deliberate message receiver, you must be able to dissect the advertising process. Although the advertisement is essentially a *sender-oriented* message (propaganda), the intelligent reader/viewer/listener should regard it as a *receiver-oriented* communication act, as a message which may or may not be accepted after a critical analysis of its value as information.

6.4.2   CAMPAIGN STRATEGY

The essence of the advertising agency's work is to map out a comprehensive campaign strategy encompassing advertising themes, creative planning, message design, budgeting and account management, media selection and purchase, positioning, production, and evaluation. Frederick Whitney sums up a typical major campaign:

Outline of a National Advertising Campaign

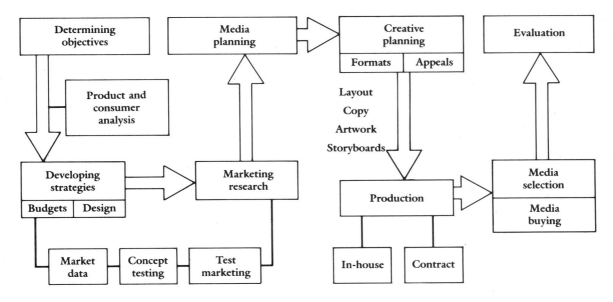

An integrated national campaign involves network television, supplemented by local television in certain markets. It involves major spreads in a dozen or so carefully chosen magazines. Also included is national newspaper coverage and supplementary radio, both in the major markets and in the very minor ones reached effectively only by radio. Billboards on highways across the country and a direct mail campaign to certain selected demographic audiences are utilized. The problems of the traffic department are mind-boggling: those of coordination and scheduling, involving tying the media presentation together into a single theme, determining presentation priorities, coordinating with point-of-sale displays, tying in with public relations and promotional activities, and harnessing the energies of distributors and dealers and subsidiary agencies in fifty states and a number of foreign countries with language differences.[20]

The magnitude of the advertising industry becomes evident when one considers that about ten thousand new goods and services are introduced annually—new food products, cosmetics, clothing lines, electronic innovations, automobile models, household gadgets,

medical products, travel bargains, sporting goods, insurance plans, toys and games, soft drinks, computer advances, and so forth— each one of which involves a scenario similar to the one outlined above.

Message Design   Several aspects of message intent and construction have to be considered at this point. Is the message to be *institutional* (promoting the image of the advertiser), or is it intended to produce *direct sales* for an immediate market impact? How about the approach or *tone* of the ad campaign? Will the advertisements concentrate on a direct, *hard-sell* approach ("Buy now!" "Move fast!")? Or will a *soft-sell* approach be more appropriate—a calmer, lighter, or more humorous tone?

"Positioning"   In the earlier and less sophisticated advertising milieu, advertisers would crudely compete for the entire market, each one trying to appeal to a broad mass

This ad by the national Tobacco Institute is typical of institutional advertising placed by many industries and individual corporations.

who might purchase a given commodity. Increasingly, however, ad agencies and market researchers realized that a given product would have a better chance to gain a solid share of the market if its advertising campaign were "positioned" to appeal to a specific segment of the buying public. "The goal of positioning is to suggest an alternative to the consumer. The advertiser and the agency seek to position the product in a 'market vacuum'—if they can find one!"[21]

The cigarette market is a prime example of positioning. Marlboro is positioned for the "macho" man, along with Winston and others. Virginia Slims was positioned in the early 1960s for the liberated woman. Salem pioneered the romantic image of the young couple in an idyllic woodsy setting, while Belair is positioned for the lovers in an oceanside setting. Kool created the "un-hot" taste position. And numerous low-tar brands (Merit, True, Triumph, Carlton, Pall Mall Lights, for example) are positioned for the analytical thinker who likes to compare statistics.

6.4.3 CREATIVE SERVICES

Once the basic campaign strategy has been mapped out, the design and implementation of the campaign is turned over to the agency's creative team. The size of the creative team will vary with the size of the agency, but ordinarily it will encompass the skills of many specialists: an art director, artists, copywriters, layout people, graphics specialists, and so on. They are concerned with actually writing the copy for both print and broadcast advertisements, laying out the art work, deciding on color applications, and creating the storyboards for TV commercials (static sketches and a script which outline the finished video product).

The Commercial Format One of the crucial responsiblities of the creative team is to develop the most appropriate format for a particular advertising campaign. Heighton and Cunningham list eight specific broadcast formats, most of which can be adapted to print media. The *dramatic format* consists of exposition, conflict, rising action, climax, and resolution. The *problem-solution format* is a specialized cliché of the dramatic form. The *demonstration format* consists of carefully staged presentations showing the product in action. The *interview format* may include humorous, satirical, or "man-on-the-street" interviews. The *testimonial format* features endorsements by common consumers, famous celebrities, or experts. The *spokesperson format* utilizes either a staff announcer or a well-known star as a direct salesperson rather than as an endorser. In the *symbolism format* "the possibilities are endless to the advertiser with a little imagination." And, finally, the *special effects format* uses computer-assisted techniques, flash editing, animation, electronic gimmicks, space-age visuals, and so forth.[22]

Advertising Appeals The creative team must then decide what specific kind of appeal should be used in the advertising campaign. *Rational appeals* are those aimed at the intellect—they make heavy use of facts, testimonials, comparisons, demonstrations, and logical reasoning. Most advertisements rely heavily upon *emotional appeals*—they are designed to touch the receiver's feelings about security, sex, fear, adventure, conformity, loyalty, humor, pride, individuality, curiosity, hero worship, and so on. (See Section 11.8.2.)

As a discriminating media consumer, you should be just as aware of these various appeals as the advertisers are. Does the alluring and seductive model really mean that the car is superior to others? Will the cigarette taste more romantic in the woods? Does the celebrity endorsement mean that a particular bank has better services? Does a mystery ingredient "recommended by doctors" really guarantee that the pain reliever is more effective than others?

6.4.4 PRODUCTION AND EVALUATION

Once the advertising campaign has been laid out and the ads themselves designed—with storyboards for TV commercials—the actual production of the advertisements is started.

Most print ads can be produced "in house" by the agency staff of copywriters and artists, although some unique art and special effects photography may be contracted out to specialized firms. Because radio is primarily a local advertising medium, most radio commercials are designed for simplified production, often utilizing the talent of the announcer or disc jockey of the radio station airing the commercial.

Television commercial production is a much more costly and time-consuming affair. Although some minimal TV production work may be handled by some agencies, most TV commercial production is contracted out to production studios. Hundreds of such independent studios are located in New York, Los Angeles, and other major metropolitan centers. In many instances, local TV stations can handle the production of the TV commercials.

Although there are close to four thousand advertising agencies in the United States, the ten largest agencies control slightly over thirty percent of the total advertising money expended on TV commercials. Hundreds of smaller firms share the advertising revenues for print media. The 1981 billings, listed below, are in millions of dollars.[23]

**INSET 6–10
Ten Largest
Advertising
Agencies, 1981**

Agency	Worldwide Billings
Young & Rubicam	2,355
J. Walter Thompson	2,213
Ogilvy & Mather	1,934
McCann-Erickson	1,849
Ted Bates	1,578
Batten, Barton, Durstine & Osborn (BBDO)	1,400
Leo Burnett	1,336
SSC & B/Lintas	1,168
Foote, Cone & Belding	1,153
Doyle Dane Bernbach	1,150

Market Research and Evaluation   Many aspects of market and product testing are conducted throughout various phases of the advertising campaign development—audience analysis, concept testing, commercial evaluation, test marketing, and so forth. Specialized research firms which use sophisticated sociological testing techniques are hired by most agencies to conduct these evaluations. No major advertising campaign is complete today without an exploration of the market for a new product, an evaluation of the product's design and packaging, an examination of potential consumer reaction and the effectiveness of different advertising appeals, post-production evaluation of the advertisement itself, test marketing in selected communities, and similar research efforts.

6.4.5   MEDIA SELECTION

Inherent throughout the development of the complete campaign strategy is the question of which media to buy and which specific channels to use for the actual advertising messages. The decisions to buy specific media are usually handled by the agency's "media services" team. Detailed demographic study and advertising research will help determine to what extent the client should advertise in the electric media (radio, television) or the various print media (magazines, newspapers, billboards, transit ads, and direct mail).

Electric Versus Print Impact   One of the first considerations is the physical difference between print and electric media. The broadcast signal exists in time; it is ephemeral, fleeting; it is here and then gone. Print messages, on the other hand, exist in a tangible form; they can be reviewed and studied. Print advertisements are better suited for the presentation of detailed information which requires lengthy consideration. Electric messages may have more impact because they cannot be as easily skipped over or tuned out.

Print messages, however, can be more easily avoided; the eye can quickly skip over even a full-page ad.

There are also psychological and physiological differences in that television messages have the impact of moving images and sound while the print media must rely more on abstract verbal symbolization—although attractive color photographic and art layouts play an important eye-catching role. Radio and TV commercials present a "low-effort" message; magazine and newspaper ads present a "high-effort" message (Section 1.6.4).

The media also differ in that broadcast media cannot be expanded; only a certain amount of time exists for the presentation of advertising messages. In print media, on the other hand, space can be expanded; more pages can be added to the newspaper or magazine to carry additional advertising content.

Geographic Selectivity   Many advertisers, of course, want to hit certain selected geographical areas—a city, a state, a particular merchandising region. Certain products—fishing equipment or farming implements, for instance—may have strong regional appeal. A manufacturer may want to concentrate the campaign in one locality at a time. Or an advertiser may want to test market a new product in one specific area. In any of these cases, the advertising campaign would probably include a mix of spot radio and TV commercials and ads in local newspapers, city and/or regional magazines, and "regional breakouts" of national magazines (Section 6.3.2).

Many magazines also have demographic breakouts according to zip codes. Because neighborhoods tend to be homogeneous, the zip code often gives a fairly accurate picture of the income level, racial concentration, age group, educational level, and other demographic characteristics of its residents. Such a breakout is admittedly only a rough distinction; it is far from 100 percent accurate. But it does help the magazine advertiser reach a slightly more specific audience than would otherwise be possible. A magazine can offer an advertiser a demographic breakout, for example, which will deliver a certain edition of the magazine to zip codes where the median income is over $50,000, or to zip codes which contain predominantly Hispanic populations, or to zip codes for small towns and rural areas.

Specialized Selectivity Magazines are especially valuable when an advertiser wants to reach a very select audience—antique collectors, gourmet cooks, motorcycle enthusiasts, and so forth. There is virtually no other medium that can deliver such a specialized audience as the special-interest magazine designed for and purchased by a particular group. Even broader nationwide demographic categories—housewives, Blacks, businessmen—can be reached best by magazines such as *Good Housekeeping, Ebony,* and *Fortune.* Few newspapers or radio or TV stations offer the same degree of selectivity. The author Don Pember gives some extended illustrations:

For example, an airline that sought to sell the advantages of flying to Hawaii for the holidays could put an ad in *Reader's Digest* and reach many potential customers among the thirty million or so readers of the magazine. But for less than one-quarter of the cost the same ad could appear in *Holiday* magazine and reach nearly four million people, most of whom by virtue of their purchase of the magazine have a strong interest in traveling. An advertisement for an expensive after-shave lotion might reach twenty million men if it were carried in *TV Guide*. But for far less money, the advertiser could place his ad in *Playboy,* and while he might not reach as many men, the millions of readers of that expensive and pseudo-sophisticated magazine would be far better prospects for the purchase of costly toiletry items than the general audience of *TV Guide*.[24]

6.4.6 COST-EFFECTIVENESS

One crucial factor in determining advertising campaign strategy is the cost-effectiveness of various media channels. If one medium or channel can reach a given number of people more cheaply than another advertising vehicle, then the one that costs the least would *generally* be considered the more effective channel—with exceptions as noted below.

Cost-Per-Thousand The traditional measure of cost-effectiveness has been the cost-per-thousand, or CPM ("cost-per-mil," metric for "thousandth"). This is a simple arithmetical measure of the dollars it takes to reach a thousand audience units. For television the unit is the household; for newspapers and magazines it is based on circulation; and for radio the CPM measures individual listeners. Although the figures for the different media are actually measuring slightly different audience factors, they do permit broad comparisons that can be revealing. For example, in the late 1970s, the CPM for television and magazines (anywhere from $4 to $8) was considerably higher than that for radio and newspapers (generally below $2).

This difference in CPMs helps to explain the demise of *Life* and the other weekly general-interest magazines. They failed as *advertising* media—not because their *audiences* deserted them. In 1971, the year before *Life* quit publishing as a weekly, it cost an advertiser $7.71 to reach a thousand persons through the magazine. At that time it would have cost an advertiser about $3.60 to reach a thousand TV viewers. Television's lower CPM sealed the fate of the large-circulation general-interest magazines.

One must be careful in using the CPM as a final determination of advertising effectiveness, however. For one thing, the CPM does not take into consideration the particular characteristics of individual media. The moving, colorful, dramatic impact of a television commercial may make its generally higher CPM worth the extra cost. On the other hand, a newspaper or magazine ad may be an especially good buy because of the detailed sales information it can pack into an instructive layout for the consumer who is really interested in doing some serious analysis before making a purchase.

This table compares the extent to which selected major product categories use various editorial media for national advertising campaigns. Dollars spent on billboards, direct mail, transit ads, and so forth are not included. The figure in parentheses indicates the percentage of the national advertising budget for each product category (the percentage of dollars spent in all four mass media) that was allocated to each medium.[25]

For example, network television attracted 65 percent of the national media advertising budget for nonprescription drugs and medical products and 59 percent of the advertising dollars for toiletries and cosmetics, although network TV captured only 38 percent of the overall budget devoted to the products included below. Magazines, on the other hand, while obtaining 22 percent of the total national advertising budget, got 46 percent of the tobacco business and 33 percent of the beer and liquor advertising. Newspapers attracted 16 percent of the overall media dollars spent nationally, but they accounted for 52 percent of the tobacco advertising and 46 percent of the travel and airlines business.

Advertising Dollars (in Millions) Spent in Each Medium
(Parentheses = Portion of the Total for each Medium

	TV Network	TV Spot	Magazines	Newspapers
Total Sales	4,105 (38%)	2,593 (24%)	2,374 (22%)	1,672 (16%)
Product Category				
Automotive, including accessories	416 (36%)	237 (21%)	228 (20%)	269 (23%)
Beer, wine, and liquor	200 (35%)	113 (20%)	193 (33%)	72 (12%)
Clothing and wearing apparel	115 (40%)	58 (20%)	86 (30%)	28 (10%)
Drugs and medical products	346 (65%)	103 (20%)	57 (11%)	22 (04%)
Food and food products	669 (44%)	543 (35%)	174 (11%)	154 (10%)
Household equipment, supplies, appliances, furnishings	203 (33%)	161 (27%)	148 (24%)	95 (16%)
Insurance	67 (38%)	36 (20%)	45 (25%)	30 (17%)
Tobacco products and supplies	9 (02%)		205 (46%)	229 (52%)
Toiletries and toilet goods	589 (59%)	217 (22%)	163 (16%)	25 (03%)
Travel, hotels, resorts, and transportation	42 (11%)	68 (18%)	98 (25%)	179 (46%)

Also, the geographic spread of a given local medium must be considered. It would not make much sense for an appliance dealer at the northern end of the Bronx to advertise over New York City TV—even with a favorable CPM—because few potential customers in Brooklyn and Queens (whom the dealer is paying to reach) would drive that far.

Additionally, a higher CPM is often justified if the advertiser is reasonably assured of reaching a better demographic target. The examples given above by Pember—using *Holiday* or *Playboy,* which would have higher CPMs than *Reader's Digest* or *TV Guide,* in order to reach a more receptive audience—illustrate the value of applying criteria other than the simple CPM comparison.

However, the cost-per-thousand comparison—along with other media selection considerations—is a factor that must be taken into account in the overall advertising campaign strategy.

6.5 Advertising Ethics and Responsibilities

From its inception, advertising has been at the center of a continuing controversy—or series of controversies—about ethics and standards. Do the benefits of advertising outweigh its negative effects? How much should we be concerned about the potential and actual abuses of advertising? How, and to what extent, should advertising be regulated?

6.5.1 BENEFITS OF ADVERTISING

Traditionally, the obvious economic benefits of advertising have been strong enough to outweigh the potential drawbacks. The libertarian arguments in favor of a relatively unfettered advertising marketplace have, for the most part, been accepted in the United States.

Indirect Support of the Mass Media
From the standpoint of most media consumers, one of the most obvious benefits of advertising is that it helps to support the mass

media with less *direct* cost to the individual receiver. Commercial radio and television are supported almost entirely by advertising, and advertising pays up to three-quarters of the costs of magazines and newspapers. Some would argue that the consumer pays for the advertising in the long run; you get stuck with the bill because the prices of the products have to be increased to pay for the advertising. However, for most products, the price markup that is required to pay for advertising is minimal compared to the mark-up that would be required to pay for any other method of mass marketing.

Lowering the Costs of Goods and Services Advertising, in fact, helps to lower the prices that we pay for the advertised products. By creating a larger market, advertising increases the volume of sales and thus contributes to lower retail prices. Murphy points out that "advertising is essential to the volume sales that make possible mass production that in turn allows for low unit price. Volume sales not only allow for low production costs, but allow for a low markup on each item, thereby keeping prices down."[26]

Keeping the Media Independent A third argument in favor of advertising support is that the diversity of advertisers helps to guarantee the independence of the media. The more sponsors or advertisers there are for each program or page, the less chance there is that any single advertiser will exercise much control over the editorial content of the medium. Support either by special-interest groups or by the government would be more likely to result in control of the media messages.

Also, support by advertisers assumes that people will be attending to the media. Therefore, advertisers will gladly provide popular nonadvertising media content (entertainment or news) so that the audience will be exposed to the advertisements. It follows that the more popular the nonadvertising content is, the larger the audience will become, which in turn attracts more advertisers, which in turn helps to guarantee the strength and independence of the medium.

Value of Advertising Information

Another strong argument is that advertising *does* provide useful information for the consumer. You turn to newspaper ads for specific details about store sales. You watch television commercials to compare product claims. You use the classified ads at one time or another. You watch and listen to political commercials before voting.

A good example of this is the neighborhood "shopper" newspaper. Such papers contain more than seventy-five percent ads. They are paid for entirely by advertisers and are circulated free to residents of specific communities. Close to a thousand of these papers are distributed to suburban areas and local neighborhoods throughout the nation, and they are read by consumers primarily for the shopping news and bargains they contain.

Stimulus to the Economy   A final powerful argument for advertising is that—in the best libertarian tradition—advertising is necessary to create the *needs* for new products and services that maintain an expanding economy of abundance. Without advertising, consumers would not realize that they needed luxury automobiles, fur coats and diamonds, cosmetics, electric appliances, computer services, travel bargains, toys and games, microwave ovens, fashionable clothing, and myriad other items. It is the consumption of these goods and services that supports a viable economic pattern in a competitive society.

David Potter points out that "advertising is not badly needed in an economy of scarcity, because total demand is usually equal to or in excess of total supply, and every producer can normally sell as much as he produces. It is when potential supply outstrips demand—

that is, when abundance prevails—that advertising begins to fulfill a really essential economic function. In this situation the producer knows that . . . it is selling capacity which controls his growth."[27] And selling capacity is dependent upon advertising.

Another aspect of the economic role played by advertising is the number of jobs created by the advertising industry. Although exact figures are difficult to obtain, reasonable estimates put the total number of persons directly employed in the advertising field somewhere over 200,000. If we were to count all of the peripheral and advertising-support positions, the total number of individuals would easily approach a quarter of a million wage earners. This is no small segment of the total economic picture.

6.5.2   NEGATIVE EFFECTS OF ADVERTISING

Although many valid arguments can be given to justify the structure of our advertising-support mass media, there is also an impressive number of arguments which can be marshalled against our present advertising practices. Not all of these arguments necessarily contend that we should do away with our present advertising-based economy; rather, these drawbacks can be considered as potential dangers, limitations, or abuses that you should be aware of. The analytical viewer/listener/reader will want to study and consider these arguments—and then decide what personal course of action he or she should pursue.

Creating False Needs and Materialistic Standards   Most advertising is designed to make us *want* things that we really do not *need*. In order to keep the wheels of the economic bandwagon rolling, we are manipulated and seduced into setting ever-higher materialistic goals and then buying those "things" that can fulfill our artificially induced desires—luxury automobiles, fur coats and diamonds, cosmetics, electric knives, fashion jeans, color-coordinated trash compactors, silver ice buckets, electronic games, and so forth. What happens to our humanistic and spiritual values as we strive so desperately to meet these materialistic standards?

The noted historian Arnold Toynbee is one of the most eloquent of the critics arguing against advertising-promoted affluence:

. . . [T]here is a limit, and a narrow one, to the quantity of goods that can be effectively possessed, in the sense of being genuinely enjoyed, by a single human being in a single lifetime. . . . The true end of Man is not to possess the maximum amount of consumer goods per head. When we are considering the demand for consumer goods, we have to distinguish between three things: our needs, our wants, and the unwanted demand, in excess of our genuine wants, that we allow the advertising trade to bully us into demanding if we are both rich enough and foolish enough to let ourselves be influenced by advertising.[28]

Dehumanization of the Consumer A related problem is that the consumer is dehumanized by the whole concept of advertising. Brown et al. point out that "the product of commercial television stations is not programs but audiences. They try to make as much profit as possible by selling audiences to advertisers at prices that are listed in dollars per thousand viewers per mintue of commercial time."[29] The individual receiver is viewed only as a commodity, not as a human being.

This view of the media receiver as nothing more than a consumer is especially disturbing when applied to children. Many public pressure groups and government agencies have become increasingly concerned about the potential ease with which children can be exploited, especially by television commercials. This concern is explored further in Section 11.8.

The Big-Business Syndrome A third negative aspect of advertising is the fact that the objectives of big business, advertising, and the mass media are inexorably intertwined. The commercial media *are* big business. The best interests of big media are the same as the interests of big business, big labor, or big government—mainly to preserve the status

quo, to keep from rocking the profit-making boat, to protect the "Establishment." Media channels, to be sure, may expose blatant governmental corruption or crusade against unfair labor practices, but this is only to bring errant members of the Establishment back into line with the best interests of society as viewed from the big media/business/labor/government perspective. Advertisers do not have to dictate editorial policy. Their needs *are part of* the editorial policy!

One major danger in this system is that there is little opportunity for the extremist's position to be considered. What channels shall we devote to those with unpopular ideas? Where do we guarantee a soapbox from which John Stuart Mill's "minority of one" may be heard (Section 2.2.2)? Or shall we provide media outlets only for those whose viewpoints coincide with the Establishment? Writing in 1957, Paul Lazarsfeld and Robert Merton underscored this problem:

Since the mass media are supported by great business concerns geared into the current social and economic system, the media contribute to the maintenance of that system. . . .

Since our commercially sponsored mass media promote a largely unthinking allegiance to our social structure, they cannot be relied upon to work for changes, even minor changes, in that structure. . . . Social objectives are consistently surrendered by the commercialized media when they clash with economic gains.[30]

Advertising Influence on Content The potential for more direct influence on content also exists. This can take any one of several different forms. It may be as innocuous as a television sponsor's insisting that all cars prominently used in a TV drama be of the advertised brand, or that the hero always be seen drinking the sponsor's beer.

Of more concern is the practice of allowing advertisers to influence news items in either broadcast journalism or newspaper coverage.

This happens, for example, when a major airline which sponsors a network news program threatens to withdraw its sponsorship if the newscast plays up a recent plane crash, or when a new shopping center agrees to buy advertising space in a newspaper if it also gets a certain amount of guaranteed "news" coverage.

Another common practice is for newspapers to create special "news" sections which—although ostensibly designed to give readers information in some legitimate news area—actually are used to generate specialized advertising space. Sandman et al. comment:

Nearly every newspaper has a department or two whose main purpose is to keep advertisers happy by giving them something "appropriate" to appear next to. Frequent offenders include the real estate section, entertainment page, church page, and travel and dining pages.[31]

In a typical Sunday edition of the *Los Angeles Times,* for example, a reader will find about seventy-five pages of movies and home entertainment ads (in the entertainment "Calendar" section), forty pages of ads for home furnishings ("Home" section), at least thirty pages of ads placed by developers ("Real Estate"), and more than ten pages of advertising each for banks and financial services ("Business"), travel ("Travel"), and new books ("Book Review"). The ethical question arises when one asks whether these special "news" sections are really printed to report legitimate news items or are just so much "pap and puffery" used as filler between the ads.

Another form of advertiser influence is actual control of the production of entertainment content, especially in broadcasting. During the Golden Age of radio, for instance, many popular programs were entirely packaged and produced by advertising agencies for their clients. The stars of these programs were indelibly identified with their sponsors, often giving the commercials personally and (in variety and comedy shows) plugging the sponsor's product throughout the content of the program. Among the best-known of these pairings were Jack Benny and Jello, Bob Hope and Pepsodent, Ma Perkins and Oxydol, Jack Armstrong and Wheaties. Daytime serials acquired the name "soap operas," of course, because so many of them were sponsored by soaps, detergents, and household cleansers. Today, on television, the soap manufacturers have gone one step further—Procter & Gamble, the largest *advertiser* in television, is also the *producer* of almost half of the daytime soap operas.[32]

Lower Content Standards Newspapers frequently have engaged in questionable editorial practices in order to increase their circulation and thus attract more advertisers. So, too, have radio and TV broadcasters sacrificed program quality in order to attract the largest possible audience. The media are repeatedly accused of deliberately setting low artistic standards in order to reach as much of the mass audience as they can, of aiming for the "lowest common denominator" with sensationalistic and exploitative programming. The larger the numbers, the greater the advertising rates and the higher the profits.

Potter emphasizes the *instrumental* nature of the content of radio and TV programs, newspaper and magazine articles intended for the mass audience. The messages exist only as instruments to ensure that the audience will be there to pay attention to the advertising. The programs and stories "do not attain the dignity of being ends in themselves; they are rather means to an end; that end, of course, is to catch the reader's attention so that he will then read the advertisement or hear the commercial, and to hold his interest until these essential messages have been delivered."[33]

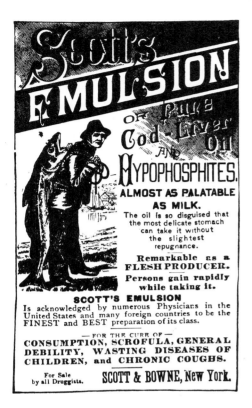

Many turn-of-the-century products used wildly exaggerated claims in their advertising.

Deceitful and Fraudulent Advertising A final argument directed against advertising is that ads are often deliberately misleading or untruthful. During the nineteenth century advertising claims for "snake-oil" elixirs and patent-medicine potions created an image of hucksterism and misrepresentation that the advertising industry is still trying to shake. The wildly exaggerated claims may have been toned down somewhat as audiences have become more sophisticated and discerning, but the extravagant claims and hyperbole still are with us in ads for the magic anti-baldness lotion, the never-burn suntan oil, the omnipotent pain reliever, and the sure-fire get-rich-quick scheme.

Although many of the most blatantly dishonest advertisements have been banned by industry self-regulation and government

agencies, there still exists—at best—a bewildering array of conflicting claims that the overwhelmed consumer has to wade through and decipher. Which car really gets the best mileage under what conditions? Which cigarette has the least tar? Which headache remedy contains what ingredients? Which washing machine will last longer? Which stereo system has the best frequency response? Which insurance policy pays what kind of claims?

SUMMARY

Although there are several other forms of financial support for media systems (direct audience purchase, government tax support, and support by special-interest groups), the overwhelming reality of advertising and the profit motive dominates all other mass communication considerations. This has been the theme of this chapter.

The need to attract large audiences has led to sophisticated research techniques to determine audience size (print circulation and broadcast ratings) and composition (demographics). Various theoretical perspectives help to explain why audience members react in certain ways to media messages—the Individual Differences Perspective, the Social Relationships Perspective, and the Social Categories Perspective.

In order to handle efficiently the growing advertising phenomenon, the advertising agency emerged near the end of the last century. Representing the advertiser as its client, the ad agency serves as the middleman between the advertiser and the media channels. The agency handles a variety of services for its client, either "in house" or by contracting with outside specialized firms: laying out the advertising orientation (including consumer analysis and advertising objectives), mapping out the overall campaign strategy (advertising themes, message design, and positioning), budgeting and account management, creative services (format, emotional appeals, art work, copywriting), production, media selection and purchase (national, spot or regional, and local), cost-effectiveness studies (cost-per-thousand), and evaluation (including market and product testing and research).

Finally, despite the many arguments for and against it, advertising is the predominant form of media support and is likely to remain

so for a considerable period of time. Consumers—receivers of the advertising messages—must learn how to be critical and analytical readers and viewers. Despite the numerous governmental and self-regulatory bodies which attempt to oversee the advertising industry, the only sure defense against advertising abuses is the cautious and discerning consumer.

Notes to Chapter 6

1. A 1970 study by the advertising agency Batten, Barton, Durstine, and Osborne indicated that women are exposed to 305 advertising messages daily while men are subjected to 285. See "A Mere 305 Advertisements Hit Mom Every Day, Not 1,500 BBDO Reports," *Advertising Age,* 19 October 1970, pp. 1, 86.

2. Sydney W. Head, *Broadcasting in America: A Survey of Television and Radio,* 2nd ed. (Boston: Houghton Mifflin, 1972), p. 247.

3. These terms are often confused. Open-circuit *pay TV* refers to a broadcast station which encodes or scrambles its signal so that it can be picked up only with a special decoder. Most pay-TV systems, such as National Subscription Television's ON-TV (which labels itself "America's Private Television Network"), charge a flat fee per month which enables viewers to watch all the movies, sports events, and special programming they wish. *Cable TV,* which started out as "community antenna TV," is essentially just a "super antenna" which pulls in hard-to-receive regular open-circuit stations and pipes the signals to subscribers for a monthly fee (Section 4.4.4). The term *pay cable* refers to those program packagers (such as Time, Inc.'s Home Box Office, or Showtime, or Theta Cable's "Z" channel) which supply special programming services—movies, sporting events, concerts—which are not available over commercial TV. Pay-cable programming is typically delivered by satellite to participating cable-TV systems which, in turn, charge an extra monthly fee to their subscribers.

4. Data were compiled by McCann-Erickson, Inc., New York, N.Y., reprinted in *Standard and Poor's Industry Surveys: Communication,* 29 November 1979, p. C62; and in *Standard and Poor's Industry Surveys: Communication,* 15 April 1982, p. C77.

5. Reported in Charlene J. Brown, Trevor R. Brown, and William L. Rivers, *The Media and the People* (New York: Holt, Rinehart and Winston, 1978), p. 64.

6. Don R. Pember, *Mass Media in America* (Chicago: Science Research Associates, 1974), pp. 331–332.

7. Melvin L. DeFleur, *Theories of Mass Communication,* 2nd ed. (New York: David McKay, 1970), pp. 118–129.

8. Paul F. Lazarsfeld, Bernard Berelson, and Helen Gaudet, *The People's Choice* (New York: Duell, Sloan and Pearce, 1944).

9. DeFleur, *Theories of Mass Communication,* pp. 122–123.

10. Ibid., p. 123.

11. Brown et al., *The Media and the People,* p. 85.

12. *Standard and Poor's Industry Surveys: Communication,* 29 November 1979, p. C71.

13. Ben L. Moon, "City Magazines, Past and Present," in *Readings in Mass Communication: Concepts and Issues in the Mass Media,* ed. Michael C. Emery and Ted Curtis Smythe (Dubuque, Iowa: Wm. C. Brown, 1972), p. 207.

14. Robert D. Murphy, *Mass Communication and Human Interaction* (Boston: Houghton Mifflin, 1977, p. 317.

15. Head, *Broadcasting in America,* p. 287. The story is taken from Ben Gross, *I Looked and I Listened* (New York: Random House, 1954), pp. 66–67.

16. Data compiled from tables in U.S. Bureau of the Census, *Statistical Abstract of the United States: 1979,* 100th ed. (Washington, D.C.: U.S. Government Printing Office, 1979), pp. 595, 596; and from Jon G. Udell, *The Economics of the American Newspaper* (New York: Hastings House, 1978), p. 112.

17. Frederick C. Whitney, *Mass Media and Mass Communications in Society* (Dubuque, Iowa: Wm. C. Brown, 1975), p. 171.

18. Data compiled from FCC reports, presented in U.S. Bureau of the Census, *Statistical Abstract: 1979,* p. 586; and from *Standard and Poor's Industry Surveys: Communication,* 24 September 1981, p. C53.

19. Elizabeth J. Heighton and Don R. Cunningham, *Advertising in the Broadcast Media* (Belmont, Calif.: Wadsworth, 1976), p. 67.

20. Whitney, *Mass Media and Mass Communications,* pp. 323–324.

21. Heighton and Cunningham, *Advertising in the Broadcast Media,* p. 68.

22. Ibid., pp. 98–106.

23. Source was *Advertising Age,* reprinted in *Standard and Poor's Industry Surveys: Communication* 15 April 1982, p. C78.

24. Pember, *Mass Media in America,* p. 333.

25. Sources for data were Television Bureau of Advertising, Media Records, Inc., and Magazine Publishers Association, Inc., reprinted in U.S. Bureau of the Census, *Statistical Abstract: 1979,* pp. 596, 597.

26. Murphy, *Mass Communication and Human Interaction,* p. 198.

27. David M. Potter, *People of Plenty: Economic Abundance and the American Character* (Chicago: University of Chicago Press, 1968), pp. 172–173.

28. Arnold Toynbee, *America and the World Revolution and Other Lectures* (New York: Oxford University Press, 1962), pp. 131, 144.

29. Brown et al., *The Media and the People,* p. 117.

30. Paul Lazarsfeld and Robert Merton, "Mass Communication, Popular Taste and Organized Social Action," in *Mass Culture: The Popular Arts in America,* ed. Bernard Rosenberg and David Manning White (New York: The Free Press, 1957), pp. 465–466.

31. Peter M. Sandman, David M. Rubin, and David B. Sachsman, *Media: An Introductory Analysis of American Mass Communications,* 2nd. ed. (Englewood Cliffs, N.J.: Prentice-Hall, 1976), p. 129.

32. Of the thirteen major daytime soap operas being aired by the three commercial TV networks in 1982, six were produced by Procter & Gamble Productions.

33. Potter, *People of Plenty,* pp. 181–182.

7

Professional and Institutional Patterns

If you ever held a part-time job delivering newspapers, you belonged to a large group of news media employees on the periphery of the mass communication field. You cannot examine the total scope and range of the mass communication industries without considering the great numbers of individuals working in these various support positions for the media—for the telephone companies, for the pulp and paper industries, and in advertising, education, and training. If you consider all the occupations that are concerned somehow with communication and knowledge processing, you come to the theme of Chapter 7:

• *More people are employed in the communications and information fields than in any other industry or occupation in the United States.*

The Communications Revolution The earliest human beings were hunters and gatherers of seeds and nuts. Then they became tillers of the soil, and agriculture became the dominant means of subsistence. Next, people turned to the factories and built the mill towns and industrial cities. Then, sometime during the last two decades, another vocational upheaval took place. As factories became increasingly automated, it took fewer people to run them—and more people to give instructions to the automated assembly lines.

Whether you call this the Electronic Age, the Atomic Age, the Computer Age, or the Space Age, it is the age when men and women are increasingly concerned with *communications*. Scientific formulas, control systems, education, economic institutions, computer languages, social welfare systems, political bureaucracies, data processing—these are all knowledge sharing in one form or another. Add to them increased mass communication and you discover that, for the first time in history, more people in developed countries are now employed in *communicating* things than in *growing* things or *making* things.

Consider the major professions and occupations with which you have daily contact that are, in one way or another, involved with communications and knowledge processing—salespersons, teachers, physicians, secretaries and typists, lawyers, clerks, financial officers, clergy, insurance representatives, computer operators, government officials, social and welfare workers, office managers, supervisors, bureaucrats, real estate brokers, mail carriers, and on and on. Then add in all of the mass media communicators. And you can begin to get some idea for the basis of Wilbur Schramm's statement in 1973:

. . . [I]t is rather clearly evident that we are entering an age of information, in which knowledge rather than natural resources may become the chief resource of mankind and the prime requisite of power and well-being. . . . [W]orkers engaged in providing knowledge to the public now outnumber farmers and industrial workers in the United States.[1]

7.1 Scope of the Communications Professions

The total number of people employed directly by the mass media industries may be estimated from many different sets of figures—from professional associations, government records (U.S. Department of Labor, U.S. Department of Commerce), and various other reporters and publishers.[2]

7.1.1 TOTAL EMPLOYMENT NUMBERS

Averaging the most dependable data available, we could conservatively estimate that well *over two million people are directly or indirectly employed in the mass media and related fields*. This total includes, of course, everyone working for media operations in custodial, clerical, technical, and other support positions.

The print media account for the largest block of employees—almost 900,000—with the nation's 1,800 newspapers having close to 415,000 workers in 1980. All of the radio and television fields account for about as many employees as do newspapers. There are more than a quarter of a million people working in various motion picture fields. The recording industry accounts for another 50,000 employees—including performing artists, producers, engineers, and management categories.

Approximately 200,000 persons are directly employed in the country's 4,400 advertising firms and in other advertising positions. Related media professions include almost another quarter of a million individuals: public relations practitioners, media researchers, marketing workers, station representatives, and numerous other designations.

According to Department of Labor figures, close to 1,300,000 persons are employed as "writers, artists, and entertainers" in the United States. Most of these are counted in the categories listed above—editors, reporters, writers for technical journals, public relations specialists, and so forth. The "entertainers" category includes about 140,000 professional musicians, 25,000 singers, 14,000 actors, and 9,000 dancers.

Related Fields The above figures, which add up to more than two million persons, do not include the millions of people involved indirectly with the media and support industries—equipment manufacturers, retailers, and so forth. The nation's interrelated telephone companies, for example, employ about one million persons. The U.S. Postal Service employs another half-million solely as postal clerks and mail carriers. Backing up the publishing fields are more than 200,000 paper and pulp mill employees who supply the nation's newsprint. On the broadcast side, there are 125,000 workers manufacturing television and radio equipment and another 135,000 repairing the same equipment.

If we could accurately total up all of the occupations that are in any way connected to mass communications, we would probably find that at least five million individuals work directly or indirectly in the mass media.

The Broader "Information" Field   If we enlarge our view to include all persons employed in any way in the processing and communicating of "information"—verbal and mathematical—we could easily include about half of the work force of the United States. One source estimates that 50 million Americans are working full time handling information.[3] Just for starters, at least 1.5 million employees of the federal government work directly with information processing.

The following table shows the estimated employment figures for the several media fields specified. These are averaged and estimated data for 1980. As explained in Footnote 2, sources for these data include many varying and sometimes conflicting references.

INSET 7–1 Number of Persons Employed in Mass Media Industries

Field	Number of Employees
Printing and Publishing	**868,000**
Magazines	83,000
Books	105,000
Booksellers and vendors	50,000
Librarians	215,000
Broadcasting and Telecommunications	**425,000**
Stations and networks	195,000
Cable TV	30,000
Industry and training	200,000
Motion Pictures	**275,000**
Production	225,000
Distribution and exhibition	50,000
Recording Industry	**50,000**
Advertising	**200,000**
Related Media Professions	**215,000**
Public relations	116,000
Media research	30,000
Other industries	50,000
Miscellaneous Performers, Writers, and Entertainers (not included above)	100,000
TOTAL ESTIMATE	2,133,000

7.1.2 PROFESSIONAL AND TRADE ASSOCIATIONS

Another way to measure the total scope of the mass communication industries is to examine the number of professional and trade associations that have been formed. For a variety of reasons—self-regulation, lobbying, public concern, setting professional standards, research, education and training—individuals and companies have come together to form a multitude of varying groups, associations, societies, organizations, guilds, unions, commissions, bureaus, federations, councils, leagues, agencies, committees, institutes, and the like.

The magnitude of America's preoccupation with forming groups is reflected in the *Encyclopedia of Associations,* which lists and describes thousands of associations of every sort.[4] The 1980 edition of this mammoth directory includes 42 active organizations with the word "television" in their titles (in addition to others listed under "broadcasting," "radio," "cable TV," and similar labels); there are at least 60 active associations dealing with motion pictures; and there are 17 societies concerned specifically with journalism education.

The 1980 *Broadcasting Yearbook* lists 177 media-related organizations and professional associations. But even this compilation is not complete. Many print-oriented groups, specialized filmmaking concerns, and industrial or educational organizations are not listed.

Unions and Guilds Akin to the professional associations and societies are the various employee unions, guilds, and federations—groups dedicated to improving the working conditions and paychecks of specific occupational classifications. The authors Hiebert, Ungurait, and Bohn, point out:

The mass communication industry is one of the most heavily unionized in this country. Almost all the various crafts and skills used in the mass communication process are unionized. While in general this is beneficial to both labor and management, union policies regarding wages, work performed, and hiring practices have caused problems . . . .[5]

The newspaper industry is strapped with perhaps the most archaic and fractionalized unionization, some major papers having as many as fourteen or fifteen different unions to deal with. The largest newspaper craft union is the International Typographical Union (ITU), representing composing-room employees.

In the broadcasting, film, and recording industries, there are more than forty different unions and labor organizations; these are broadly divided between the technical and creative occupations. Crafts-workers and engineers are largely represented by the International Brotherhood of Electrical Workers (IBEW), the National Association of Broadcast Employees and Technicians (NABET), and the International Alliance of Theatrical Stage Employees and Moving Picture Operators (IASTE).

In addition to internal struggles for representation, and the omnipresent threat of major work stoppage due to a strike by one union, a major problem is that outsiders have great difficulty in breaking into the crafts fields because the unions have such tight control over their memberships.

On the creative side, the Newspaper Guild was originally a union for professional journalists—reporters and copy editors. It has since expanded to include photographers and clerical, sales, and circulation employees. In the broadcast and film studios, writers are represented by the Writers Guild of America. In television and film, the Directors Guild of America is another creative union which plays a key role in the business.

Performers and actors also have powerful unions. The American Federation of Television and Radio Artists (AFTRA), the Screen Actors Guild (SAG), the Screen Extras Guild (SEG), and the American Federation of Musicians (AFM) all have the power to bring segments of the industry to their knees.

One indication of the scope of the communication professions is the variety of scholarly and research journals (left) and the professional and trade magazines (right), of which only a small selection is illustrated here.

Composers, lyricists, music publishers, and other creative artists are also represented by the two giant copyright associations which protect their royalties and payments—the American Society of Composers, Authors, and Publishers (ASCAP) and Broadcast Music, Incorporated (BMI). Every time a record is played or a song is sung, a fee is paid to either ASCAP or BMI in order to guarantee payment to the author and/or artist. A typical small-market popular-music radio station, for example, may pay about five percent of its gross income in music fees to ASCAP and BMI.

Educational Societies and Associations

Additional evidence of professional concern with standards is found in associations that are involved with media education and professional preparation. The Association for Education in Journalism (AEJ) was established in 1912 and continues to be the primary "umbrella" society for scholars in all fields of journalism and mass communication studies. The AEJ's scholarly periodicals

include *Journalism Quarterly, Journalism Monographs,* and *Journalism Abstracts*.

The Broadcast Education Association (BEA) is the counterpart society for educators specifically involved with television and radio curricular programs in American colleges and universities. Other organizations concerned with media education include the Speech Communication Association, which also publishes several scholarly periodicals in the field, the International Communication Association, the American Academy of Advertising, and the Popular Culture Association.

Professional and honorary societies for individuals also play a crucial role in maintaining academic quality and promoting educational standards in the related communication fields. The largest of these is the society of professional journalists, Sigma Delta Chi, which has both campus chapters in conjunction with university journalism programs and professional chapters for the working press. The comparable broadcasting honorary fraternity is Alpha Epsilon Rho, which is active on many university campuses.

Summing up the importance of all of these varied professional and industrial organizations, Hiebert et al. stress the necessity of trying to keep abreast of such a fluid and rapidly changing field:

The mass media, as institutions in our society, are composed of an intricate fabric of people, products, institutions, production units, service units, and associations, all of which are based on a form of technology. At the root of all mass media is a technical process that must be understood and respected if efficient and successful communication is to take place. No doubt, media institutions are among the most complex in society, and this makes their study intriguing, their operation demanding, their role vital, and their impact difficult to determine.[6]

7.2 Structure of the Publishing Industries

Lasswell's model (Inset 1–4) gave us the five fundamental elements of the communication process: **who, what, channel, audience**

(whom), and **feedback (effects).** In looking at the actual mass mediums, we shall be primarily concerned with the first three of these elements. Although *audience* and *feedback* must be considered as pivotal, indispensable elements in the total communication process, in examining the specific structure of the actual mediums we will be concerned with **who** (origination), **what** (message production), and **channel** (transmission).

Four Components of Media Structure As we look at the way in which mass media are actually organized and structured, the numerous individuals involved could very broadly be divided into four major categories of media occupations. In such a generalized breakdown, Lasswell's **who** designation would have to be separated into two separate categories, as outlined in Inset 7–2.

INSET 7–2 Media Structure Categories

Using fundamental theoretical distinctions, most mass media organizational structures could classify their job descriptions into the following broad categories.

WHO: *Finances and Control*	**WHO:** *Editorial and Creative*	**WHAT:** *Encoding and Production*	**CHANNEL:** *Distribution and Delivery*
Owners	Writers	Directors	Transmitter engineers
Publishers	Authors	Actors	Cable-TV operators
Advertisers	Reporters	Musicians	Film distributors
Sponsors	Editors	Singers	Theater owners
Foundations	Ad copywriters	Set designers	Projectionists
Underwriters	Scriptwriters	Staging directors	Delivery people
Sales representatives	Photographers	Lighting directors	Newspaper carriers
Media buyers	Composers	Stagehands	Mail carriers
Producers	Lyricists	Studio engineers	Booksellers
Fund-raisers	Disc jockeys	Camera operators	Other retailers
	Talk-show hosts	Typesetters	Librarians
		Press operators	
		Photoengravers	
		Compositors	

Stressing the relationship to these four theoretical categories—financing, creative/editorial, production, and distribution—the rest of this chapter will outline the structure of the major mass media fields.

7.2.1 THE NEWSPAPER INDUSTRY

The newspaper field is by far the largest employer in the mass media business, having about twice as many employees as any other single medium. In 1977 the total newspaper annual payroll was about $4.3 billion.[7]

Almost half the total number of newspaper workers have been employed in the production and maintenance areas. These positions—typesetting, photocomposition, press operations—have traditionally demanded

heavy labor concentrations. However, with the move to faster, computer-based composition and streamlined printing techniques (see below), the labor requirements in these areas are being gradually reduced.

Creative: News and Editorial Departments The heart of the newspaper is, of course, the editorial function—reporting news, expressing opinions through columns and editorials, and providing feature material like comics, crossword puzzles, and advice columns.

Although straight reporting—"hard news"—has been giving way to soft features, human interest material, syndicated staples, and similar matters, the news story remains

---

INSET 7–3   Structure of a Typical Newspaper

This simplified organizational chart reflects the typical management structure of a large daily newspaper. With the advertising department corresponding roughly to the "Finances" element in our basic theoretical model (Inset 7–2), the parallel between this chart and the model can be readily seen.

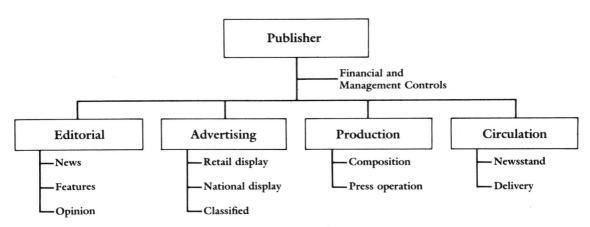

Although details vary from paper to paper, these four functions regularly stand out as discrete operational units.

the core of the editorial function. And the reporter remains the essential soul of the news story, despite the phalanx of assignment editors, copy editors, city editors, and others who supervise, edit, rewrite, and proofread the reporter's every word. The idealism of the young reporter remains strong in American folklore: the adventure of the cub reporter getting his or her first big scoop; the mystique of the investigative reporter who topples a corrupt government official; the crusading zeal of a "new journalism" writer who would wipe out all social injustice; the echoes of Horace Greeley, Joseph Pulitzer, or even Woodward and Bernstein.

The seasoned reporter, of course, adopts a more realistic and balanced appreciation of his or her position. The political reporter Richard Reeves comments:

I am a reporter. . . .

I love it, even if I know it's a kind of prolonged adolescence. That doesn't mean I don't take it seriously—I do, I think it's very, very important, but I'm glad it's fun. . . .

I just wanted to cover good stories, write them well, give the people kind enough to read them a sense of what's going on. I want to be accurate, fair, perceptive and, when I'm lucky, incisive.[8]

Financing: Advertising and Sales Promotion If reporting is the heart of the newspaper, then advertising is the sustenance that makes it all possible. The advertising departments certainly are the financial hub of the entire operation, with display advertising (both retail and national) and classified ads occupying up to two-thirds of the total space in the newspaper (Section 6.3.2). So vital are advertising revenues that in newspaper parlance the editorial space is referred to as "news holes"—space to be filled in around the advertising content.

Distribution: Circulation and Marketing Although circulation revenues may account for only twenty-five to thirty percent of the newspaper's total income (just about enough to pay for the newsprint that it is printed on), circulation is crucial because it

Working at his video-display terminal (VDT), the modern reporter still remains the old-fashioned soul of the newspaper.

represents the volume of readership that can be sold to potential advertisers (Section 6.2.1). The circulation department must be concerned both with home-delivery subscriptions and with newsstand sales. Home-delivery service is more costly to the paper; it involves considerable bookkeeping and promotional costs in soliciting and maintaining subscriptions plus the hefty expense of either a private newspaper deliverer or the U.S. Postal Service. Newsstands and vending machines are much less expensive means of distribution, but such sales are subject to the hazards of weather, traffic, uneventful news days, and the whims of the impulse buyer. The subscription represents a firm circulation base which can be sold to advertisers.

Production: Newspaper Printing Although news gathering, advertising, and circulation methods have changed ony slightly during the twentieth century, production systems have changed drastically during the last two or three decades. Mechanical typesetting equipment such as the Mergenthaler Linotype and giant rotary presses (Section 3.2.3) were the marvels of the Industrial Age, but the turn-of-the-century machines

Rows of VDTs have replaced the typewriters as the predominant keyboarding tool of the contemporary newsroom.

were painfully anachronistic by the 1950s. One of the first changes was the gradual improvement of the offset lithography process (Inset 3–4), which was adopted first by the weeklies and smaller suburban papers. This technique facilitated much higher-quality photo reproduction than the older letterpress systems.

The biggest advance, however, has been in the use of the optical character reader (OCR) and video display terminal (VDT) electric keyboard. With the electronic memory system, once the reporter has typed in the story, editors and proofreaders can read the copy on their own VDT monitors (which are like high-resolution television monitors) and can type in any corrections from their own keyboards. (See Section 12.1.1.) Electronic information is then used to instruct the computer to set up the finished story in "cold type" on a photocomposing machine. No "re-keyboarding" is needed; no molten metal slugs have to be produced.

Many other advances are being developed or are already in operation somewhere; high-speed computer-controlled ink jets to "spray" ink onto newsprint (Inset 12–3); laser plate-engravers; computer assembling of advertising layouts; lightweight metal and plastic

press plates; laser and microwave connections to tie together composing-room operations and printing presses in distant neighborhoods; and satellite systems to tie together regional editions of nationwide newspapers.

7.2.2 THE MAGAZINE INDUSTRY

With more than 80,000 employees and an annual payroll of well over one billion dollars, the magazine field represents a sizable chunk of the mass media picture. However, because of its tremendous specialization and diversity, there is no one generalized organizational pattern that typifies the magazine structure. Although the four basic functions—editorial, advertising, production, and circulation—can be clearly discerned, they are handled differently by different magazine publishers. The size of the staff of a magazine may vary from one or two full-time jacks-of-all-trades (on a small, limited circulation, special-interest periodical) to dozens or even hundreds of specialists.

On the *editorial* staff, many magazines get by with relatively few—if any—full-time writers. Although the major news magazines such as *Time* and *Newsweek* carry a large number of reporters and editors with specific assignments, not unlike a newspaper, most magazines contract out their writing to freelance writers. There is no need to keep a full-time writer on your staff if you are going to ask him or her for only one article a month.

Advertising and *circulation* considerations are often similar to those of a newspaper, with magazines receiving their income from a mix of advertising and sales. Many specialized magazines rely almost entirely upon subscriptions for their sales, while most of the popular consumer mass magazines split their sales income evenly between subscriptions and newsstand purchases. The importance of attracting the impulse buyer at the newsstand or checkout counter leads to intense competition for handsome cover designs and tantalizing titles.

Magazine *production* differs from newspaper production in that few magazines operate their own printing plants. Almost all magazine printing jobs are contracted out to

The layout room of a small magazine reflects the use of graphic media by the modern publisher.

commercial presses. This is partly because a magazine's production people have more time to edit and lay out articles; they are not rushed by last-minute deadlines that necessitate access to their own presses on a twenty-four hour basis. Secondly, and more impor-

tantly, with only a weekly, monthly, or quarterly schedule, a single magazine could not justify the cost of purchasing and maintaining its own press.

7.2.3 THE BOOK INDUSTRY

Although more than a hundred thousand persons are employed in the book industry, most of them are in production and printing occupations. A few are in editorial areas; the rest are in management and distribution (sales). There is, of course, no one involved in obtaining advertising revenue *per se* because that is not a source of income for book publishing.

In the *editorial* or creative segment of the book industry, authors typically line up contracts with publishers by one of three means. First, an author may submit a manuscript directly to the publisher without any agent or prior negotiation; few of these unsolicited manuscripts ever get published. Second, an

---

Although most magazines rely heavily upon outside, nonstaff, free-lance writers, magazine writing is not a field that is easily cracked by the aspiring journalist. Most magazines initiate writing assignments by turning to outside writers that they have used in the past—experienced authors and reporters whose names and styles are well known.

Few neophyte writers get very far by submitting unsolicited manuscripts to popular magazines. Some major mass circulation magazines receive upwards of a hundred thousand unsolicited articles and manuscripts a year! Few will ever see the wet side of a printing press. There are probably between one and two hundred free-lance writers who are able to earn a decent living strictly by their writing. (The beginning writer will often have more luck with specialized magazines that cater to limited audiences or with true-confessions-type magazines—which pay at the rate of something like four to six cents per word.)

If you are a serious beginning writer, however, there are specialized journals that will help you find the right market. *Writer's Digest* and *The Writer* are both monthly magazines that will keep you abreast of the opportunities and pitfalls of free-lance writing. One library resource is *Writer's Market,* an annual publication which summarizes the specifications for some five thousand different markets.

INSET 7–4
The Free-Lance Writer

The interior of a contemporary bookstore indicates the breadth of the bookselling business.

author may work through a literary agent who is experienced in placing manuscripts with publishers and in negotiating contracts. Third, the publishing house may commission a book from a particular author.

Production starts with careful attention to design. From the richly ornamented manuscripts of the medieval codices (Section 3.2.1) to handsomely illustrated and colorful contemporary tomes, the book has always asked to be considered as a work of art. The steps of composition, typesetting, proofreading, page makeup, platemaking, printing, gathering, and binding are similar to the production processes used in newspaper and magazine printing, although they are considerably more complex in most instances.

The final component of the book industry, *distribution,* encompasses two broad categories—bookselling and libraries. With more than fifteen thousand bookstores in the United States (not including mass-market retail establishments such as supermarkets and drugstores) and various mail-order and book-club enterprises, there are perhaps fifty thousand persons employed in the selling of

books. However, for every bookstore in America there are two libraries—excluding elementary and secondary school libraries. And for every person who sells books for a living, there are four engaged in circulating books to the public through community, academic, and specialized libraries.

7.3 Structure of the Broadcast Industries

Following the structural outline developed above, the organization of the radio and television industries—commercial and noncommercial—can be divided roughly into the same four categories: **who** (financial); **who** (creative); **what** (production of the message); and **channel** (transmission).

7.3.1 STATION STRUCTURE

There are approximately 9,000 radio stations (more than 1,000 of them noncommercial) and more than 1,000 television stations (about 270 noncommercial) in the United States (Inset 4–10). Of the almost 200,000 individuals who work directly in the broadcast media, about 170,000 are employed in these ten thousand stations, the rest being employed in various commercial and non-commercial network capacities.

Sales Departments   The financial side of the broadcast station can be represented by the sales department. Here is where all the advertising revenue is generated, clients are wined and dined, accounts are initiated, local commercials are written, and major advertising campaigns are finalized. Knowledge and

proven expertise in the financial aspects of the media enterprise are usually considered such a priority requisite that most of the top broadcast management personnel (general managers and station managers) come up through the sales departments.

In virtually all public TV and radio stations, there is a corresponding department—a fund-raising or "development" office—that is structured to obtain grants from private foundations, encourage corporate "underwriting" (not sponsorship) of programs, hold

INSET 7–5   Structure of a Typical Broadcast Station

Although there are many varations on this basic theme, the organizational structure of a typical radio or television station would resemble that diagrammed below. In a noncommercial (public broadcasting) station, the sales department would be replaced by the corresponding revenue-generating division—"fund-raising" or "development."

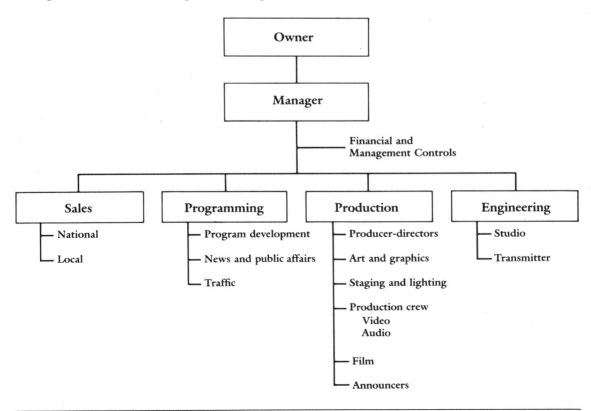

The evening newsshow is one of the most ambitious local productions in many TV stations.

auctions, organize membership drives, solicit other forms of individual donations, and apply for local, state, and federal grants.

Program Departments The creative or editorial function of the broadcast station is encompassed in the program department. Here is where all local programming (other than commercials) is originated, and here is where all syndicated and network programming is funneled. As decisions are made about when all programs are to be aired, the actual broadcast schedule is put together in the programming department.

For network-affiliated stations, network programming may account for up to sixty-five percent of a station's total schedule. Another twenty-five to thirty percent may come from syndicated sources: feature films, old network series, and material produced specifically for syndication—talk shows (*Phil Donahue*), variety programs (*Hee Haw*), game shows (*Family Feud*), nature programs, travelogues, and the like. Independent or nonnetwork-affiliated stations, of course, will rely much more heavily upon syndicated programming. "The local station's role, then, is as primarily an exhibitor of programs created by someone else. . . . In effect, the stations

have little control over much of the programming they telecast."[9]

In most station operations, the news department (which may be a one-person office in a small radio station) will be either a semiautonomous unit of the program department or a completely independent division functioning separately from the program department. In either case, there is an attempt to isolate the news and public affairs functions from the entertainment programming. The idealistic goal of a completely independent and untainted news service is seldom attained, however. The realistic concerns of local competition, ratings, handsome faces, and the need to provide a strong lead-in to the evening's entertainment programming all have an impact upon the output of the news department.

Production Areas In smaller station operations, the production function may be a unit of the programming department; in larger stations—especially in television—the production department itself will often be the largest staff in the station. In this area fall all of the details of message preparation implied in the **what** segment of Lasswell's model; but the production process also encompasses many creative aspects which border on the function of message design and encoding (**who**).

Although terminology and job descriptions may vary slightly from station to station, the following positions are basic to production operations and may be found in most large television studios.

Producer or Executive Producer. The top person in charge of all aspects of a production—conception, scripting, budgeting, casting, production, and possibly scheduling and marketing.

Director. The person in charge of actual production and editing operations in the studio or on a remote location. Directs all picture and sound elements.

Technical Director (or "Switcher"). The top technical position. Performs a crucial production job—controlling the buttons and levers (at the instructions of the program director) to get the right camera pictures, electronic transitions, and special effects on the air.

Associate Director ("Assistant Director" in filmmaking). The director's right-hand person in all aspects of the production. Especially concerned with program timing, performance and technical notes, and commands to the crew. Also known as the "Script Secretary" or "Production Secretary."

Stage Manager. The director's right-hand person on the studio floor. Coordinates all production elements, supervises all crew positions, and gives signals to the talent (performers). Also known as the "Floor Manager" or "Floor Director."

Grips or Stagehands. Floor assistants or crew members responsible for setting up scenery, organizing props, pulling camera cables, manipulating easel graphics, and handling other production details.

Staging Director. The person in charge of all scenery and set elements. May be responsible for scenery design as well as construction and handling of scenic units, cycloramas, props, and so forth.

Lighting Director. This person combines both artistic and technical (engineering) considerations in lighting the set and making sure that the cameras have enough illumination to function properly.

Camera Operators. Those who handle the video cameras in the studio or on remote locations. Usually considered an engineering position, although considerable artistic and creative talent is needed.

Audio Engineer. The person in charge of all microphone usage and placement. Also supervises sound-mixing operations in the audio control room. Basically an engineering job with artistic requisites.

Graphics Artists. A key part of all TV production. Concerned with producing all types of visual aids or "graphics"—title cards, weather maps, informational charts, production credits, sketches and cartoons, stock market charts, animated diagrams, "super cards" (to be superimposed over other picture information), and a hundred other visual items.

Projectionists. The persons in the telecine or master control room who are concerned with playing back videotaped segments, films, and slides for insertion into program productions.

The production of a program starts with the producer or executive producer, who is generally in charge of the entire program budget and production operation—from the script concept and hiring of writers and actors to the final packaging and selling of the finished program. Most of the production details are delegated to the director, who supervises the various artistic and practical aspects of putting a program together—the staging, graphics, acting, music, costumes, script changes, blocking of movement, rehearsals, and finally "calling" the camera shots on the air. The director is also in charge of all post-production editing. In many stations a person who combines both functions, the producer-director, is in charge of all aspects of program design and execution.

Although some staff announcers and performers are used in many of the station's programs, major productions usually draw upon outside, free-lance actors and performers. The same is true for writing assignments. Staff writers and continuity writers may handle many routine station announcements, commercials, and programs, but major productions—especially dramas—are likely to come from outside, free-lance scriptwriters.

Increasingly, the functions of the film unit and the large video remote unit have been growing closer and closer together. Advanced video technologies have resulted in smaller, higher-quality, more rugged electronic cameras and portable video recorders which enable a small team to go on location to cover live events with hand-held cameras and "backpack" recorders—combining the immediacy and economical operation of videotape with the ease and flexibility of film. (See Section 12.2.1)

Engineering   The final organizational unit of any station structure is the all-important engineering staff. In terms of our theoretical model (Inset 7–2), these highly trained technicians actually are employed in two distinct phases of the communication process—*production* and *transmission*.

The most crucial engineering production positions have been outlined in Inset 7–6—the technical director or switcher, the camera operators, and audio engineers. The lighting director also may be an engineer. Studio maintenance engineers, who keep all of the production equipment functioning, should be included in this category, too.

Engineers occupied in the distribution process at the station level are concerned with operating all of the equipment which is involved in getting the television signal (once it is produced in the studio or the editing room) delivered to your individual television set. Starting in the master control room, the signal must be amplified, routed to the transmitter site—often a remote hilltop located miles from the studio and connected by a microwave link—and finally broadcast from the transmitter tower.

It is quite a convoluted and marvelous process that must be completed before any television communication can take place. Consider a simple program, a feature on the wife of a local politician, for example. The news director or executive producer comes up with the idea, perhaps at the suggestion of the sales department or general manager. A writer must then be assigned, and a firm budget must be estblished. A film crew or ENG unit starts to record material. A program slot in the schedule must be found, and the program (if not part of an ongoing news show) must find a sponsor. Several revisions of the script must be approved by layers of bureaucracy; research teams must dig out original material and archival pictures; arrangements must be made for interviews; and legal release forms must be signed. The studio must be scheduled for a dramatic segment; set designers, lighting engineers, graphic artists, and dozens of other production and engineering positions must be assigned and scheduled. After the studio portion of the production has been recorded, a host or announcer must record his or her material. Then, when the film or ENG footage has been edited, the director compiles the entire program using the computerized post-production editing facilities. The program

Single-camera productions are playing an increasingly important role at most TV stations: the one-person ENG operation (left) and the two-person EFP setup (right).

INSET 7–7
The Trend toward EFP and Post-Production Editing

In the past, most television production took place in cavernous TV studios with dozens of production staffers and engineers following the action on four or five cameras and numerous microphones simultaneously; in the control room the TV director watched the studio activity on a bank of television monitors and, following the shooting script, commanded which camera picture should actually be recorded (or transmitted live) at every instant. The entire production was recorded (or transmitted) in "real time"—that is, as the action took place on the studio floor, instantaneous editing decisions were made and the production was wrapped up.

In recent years, however, the trend has been away from such real-time productions. With the development of ENG (electronic news gathering) and EFP (electronic field production) lightweight gear, more production is taking place outside the studio walls; more sophisticated and light-sensitive cameras have made it possible to record pictures under a variety of natural conditions.

Moving away from multiple-camera production, video directors have been adopting more of the single-camera filmic techniques perfected by movie directors over the years. Television programming—news programs, variety shows, interview segments, dramatic productions—can now be recorded in small bits and pieces and assembled later with the aid of sophisticated computer-assisted editing equipment. Much of the TV action has moved from the big recording studio to the post-production editing room.

department schedules the production, and the traffic coordinator handles all related announcements and promotional material. Finally, at the appointed hour, the billions of electronic bits and pieces of the recorded signal are picked up from the videotape, sent through recorder heads, switching apparatus, amplifiers, a microwave transmitter link, and more amplifiers, modulated onto a carrier wave, and broadcast through the transmitter out into open space to be picked up by your television receiver.

And yet the communication process is not complete until you—the individual receiver—turn on your set, tune to the correct channel at the right time, give the program your attention (without dozing off or thumbing through a magazine), assimilate the information, and then form some opinion or change your attitude (the **whom** and **effect** of Lasswell's model).

7.3.2 NETWORK STRUCTURE

The three nationwide commercial television networks—American Broadcasting Company (ABC), Columbia Broadcasting System (CBS), and National Broadcasting Company (NBC)—dominate the commercial television programming. A less prominent role is played by the national commercial radio networks—CBS, NBC, Mutual Broadcasting System (MBS), and four specialized networks run by ABC. Noncommercial broadcasting has two services funded largely by the Corporation for Public Broadcasting (CPB)—the radio network, National Public Radio (NPR), and its television counterpart, Public Broadcasting Service (PBS), which emphasizes that it is a decentralized "interconnection service," not a network.

Additionally, there are dozens of regional, state (in the case of public broadcasting), and special-interest networks for religious programming, sports, and so forth. These national and regional networks collectively employ upwards of twenty thousand to thirty thousand persons.

All networks provide similar kinds of services for their affiliated stations. First, they provide programming; it would be prohibitively expensive for local stations to try to produce enough programming to fill their broadcast days. Second, the networks provide interconnection services—microwave, cable, or satellite—to distribute the programs to the individual stations. Third, in the case of commercial chains, the networks in effect sell the stations' time in the national market.

7.3.3 CABLE, SATELLITE, AND OTHER TECHNOLOGIES

At least another fifty thousand persons are employed in cable TV, satellites, independent production, cassettes and videodiscs, and related technologies which are peripherally connected to the broadcasting industry.

Cable TV This burgeoning field started out basically as a distribution service—delivering broadcast television signals to isolated and valley areas where they otherwise could not be received. Therefore, most of its roughly thirty thousand employees could still be classified as managerial/clerical or technical—concerned with finances or distribution. Few have been involved in the creation of messages.

However, with the rapid growth of pay cable and satellites, many new programming services have been developed to create various programs in order to furnish the cable systems with original material. These programming-oriented enterprises have opened up thousands of new production jobs.

The cable industry may be seen as evolving into a two-bodied structure: (1) the original concept of a "community antenna" distribution system, franchised by a local municipality to relay broadcast signals and provide a delivery service to subscribers in a given area; and (2) the pay-cable production services (Home Box Office, Showtime, and dozens more) which sell their original programming packages to cable systems to augment the programming picked up from local broadcast stations and from distant "superstations."

Satellites Like the original cable-TV systems, satellites are basically just distribution devices. Orbiting more than twenty-two thousand miles above the surface of the earth, a satellite can pick up a signal from anywhere in the United States, for example, and relay it instantaneously to the entire country. Today there are about a dozen communications satellites servicing the television, radio, telephone, and computer industries. RCA (with its Satcom satellites) and Western Union (with its Westar "birds") dominate the market. Each individual satellite is capable of carrying up to twenty-four TV channels.

Although the satellite industry offers relatively limited occupational opportunities—just a few thousand managers and engineers who sell time on the "birds" and run the interconnection facilities—the impact of the satellite on all aspects of telecommunication production has been tremendous. Dozens of specialized networks and cable programming operations have leaped on the satellite bandwagon. PBS leases four Westar channels, and all commercial networks use the orbiting relay stations for routine feeds. Foreign-language networks, sports hookups (about sixty

---

INSET 7–8 Structure of Simplified Cable-TV System

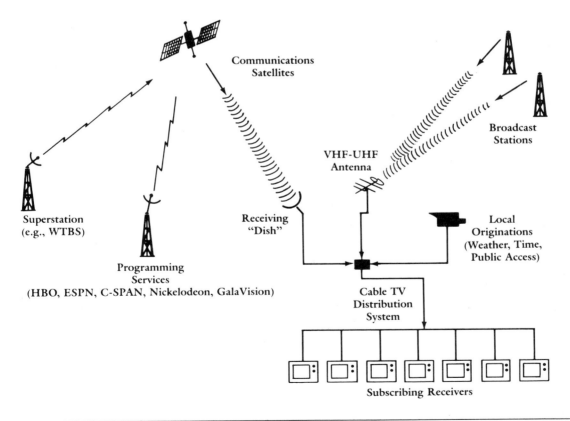

percent of baseball games televised in 1980 used satellites), ethnic chains, superstations, religious networks (at least four nation-wide) also use satellites.

Independent Producers A major segment of the telecommunications industry is made up of independent producers—roughly comparable to free-lance writers in publishing—individuals or corporations who are concerned primarily and immediately with the production of program material. The independent producer may range from the lone cameraman shooting his nature documentary in the wilds of New Guinea to the complex bureaucracy of a major Hollywood operation such as Universal Studios or Columbia Pictures.

Directories list about a thousand production companies and studios which are in the business of producing commercials, educational films, training programs, syndicated materials, television series, and feature films. In fact, the major networks produce little more than their regularly scheduled news programs, documentaries, live "events" coverage (elections, inaugurations, and funerals), and sports coverage. The ongoing entertainment/dramatic series come almost exclusively from the independents.

Videocassettes and Videodiscs How the videocassette (VCR) and videodisc technologies will ultimately affect broadcasting and cable industries remains to be seen. The impact may be supplemental rather than subtractive; that is, consumers may simply add

---

The concept of the "superstation" was launched in 1977 when Ted Turner, an Atlanta-based businessman and communications prophet, decided to give his independent Atlanta station, WTBS, nationwide exposure. Leasing a satellite channel, Turner beamed his station's signals up to the "bird" and then sold its programming to cable companies across the country. Eager to grab another source of relatively inexpensive programming, cable systems from coast to coast began to carry all of Turner's local productions and advertising.

Among other programming, WTBS carried live all of the baseball games of the Atlanta Braves (also owned by Turner), making them the first team with a nationwide audience able to view every game of the season. Viewers were happy with the expanded programming. Cable systems were happy to be able to offer more. Advertisers were happy with the extended audience. Turner was ecstatic. And other broadcasters were worried. As a *Panorama* article expressed it,

Superstations have generated excitement, anger, discord, confusion, trepidation and general consternation in the industry. At the moment, they're kind of like rambunctious teen-agers not yet sure of their place in the world—they can be fun to have around, but they're rough on the furniture.[10]

By the end of 1980, there were five superstations beaming their programming up to satellites and through cable systems across the country: WTBS, Atlanta; WGN-TV, Chicago; KTVU, Oakland; KTTV, Los Angeles; and WOR, New York.

**INSET 7–9
The Superstation**

The lone filmmaker, working miles from the nearest electrical outlet, still represents the spirit of the independent producer.

the existing hardware to their telecommunications diet without dropping any other video consumption. In any case, the independent producers will, at the very least, have one additional potential source of distribution for their wares. For example, in the marketing activity following the introduction of

VCRs, the initial winners appeared to be pornographic flicks; the VRC opened up a totally new—and relatively respectable—avenue of private distribution which had never before been available to them.

INSET 7–10
The Geostationary Communications Satellite

The first satellites used for communication—in the early 1960s—were launched into a low orbit with a resulting path that caused the satellite to appear to move across the sky, dropping over the horizon at regular intervals. Such a disappearing satellite was unsatisfactory for continuous, scheduled communication. What was needed was a satellite which, when viewed from a given point on the earth, would appear to stand still in a stationary point in the sky.

Such a "geostationary" orbit was achieved by positioning the satellite approximately 22,300 miles above the equator. At this height the speed of the satellite matches the rotation of the earth, so that the satellite appears to be hanging in a static position. In this orbit, which has been used for all communications "birds" since the mid-1960s, the satellite has a coverage pattern or "footprint" which includes about one-third of the earth's surface.

The geostationary orbit allows receiving antennas or "dishes" on earth to pick up the satellite's signals without any of the expensive tracking and steering equipment which would be needed to follow a "moving" satellite.

7.4 Structure of the Movie and Recording Industries

Unlike the radio and television fields, the filmmaking and audio recording business gather no revenue from advertisers. Like book publishers, movie and record companies must make their money from direct retail sales. Their structures therefore reflect a different type of organization, consisting of three distinct corporate entities: production centers (message creation); middlemen or distributors (delivery/channel); and retailers and exhibitors (sales and message reception).

7.4.1 THE MOVIE BUSINESS

During the 1920s through the 1940s, the major studios produced the films, distributed them, and owned the theaters in which they played.

The Producers Along with the "Paramount" Decision (Section 4.2.3), several other adversities beset Hollywood during the late 1940s and early 1950s—challenges from postwar European filmmakers, union demands and soaring production and overhead costs, the witch-hunting/blacklisting period (Inset 10–2), and competition from the new medium of television (Section 4.2.4). One significant result of this upheaval was the emergence of the independent producer.

Prior to 1950, the major studios turned out more than ninety percent of all feature films in the United States. Today, the majors account for less than one-quarter of the annual output. The independent filmmakers do not have to support heavy studio "back-lot" maintenance and overhead costs, can often work with smaller crews, usually shoot on location (frequently abroad where they can escape high American labor costs), and work with a degree of autonomy and flexibility that was unknown during the reign of the majors. Actor-stars such as Paul Newman,

Robert Redford, Warren Beatty, and many others have formed their own production companies to bring out their own vehicles or to produce films starring others.

The production aspects of making a film are not unlike those of making a major television dramatic production. Most of the same job functions are involved—actors, directors, assistant directors, set designers, lighting and sound crews, grips and stagehands, musicians, makeup and costume specialists. The cinematographer replaces the electronic camera operator, and the film editor replaces the videotape editor. The processes are *basically* similar, but the production budget may be five to ten times higher for a theatrical film than for a TV film of the same length.

It is in the funding of these major Hollywood independent epics that creative approaches to modern film financing must be learned. And every film must be financed from scratch; each venture requires a new start. "The business of raising such large sums of money is largely one of contacts, finding them, using them, holding them. It is a people business."[11]

The Distributors Not counting pornographic and exploitation films, fewer than two hundred major feature films were produced and released to theaters in 1980. The bulk of these films were distributed by the majors which also once dominated the production scene: Paramount (Gulf + Western), M-G-M/United Artists, Warner Brothers, Universal (MCA), Columbia (Coca-Cola), and Twentieth Century–Fox. Several minor studios were also involved in the distribution of independent and low-budget films: Allied Artists, American-International, Avco-Embassy, and National General. Both the majors and the minors were also, of course, heavily involved in the financing of independent productions.

Film distribution is not the neat, clear-cut operation it once was. Emerging technologies have clouded the silver screen considerably. Theatrical films now obtain much of their eventual revenue from commercial TV showings. Many TV movies are made for domestic television release to be followed by major overseas theatrical distribution. Some major theatrical movies are released simultaneously on pay TV, pay cable, videocassettes, and discs. Some productions are planned for cassette and disc distribution first, to be followed by commercial TV scheduling. And, most important to keep in mind, foreign distribution accounts for over fifty percent of the total annual income of most American theatrical films. (It is little wonder that domestic theater owners are increasingly nervous about their eventual role in the shape of things to come.)

Distribution consists, of course, of much more than just acquiring prints of the film and sending them around to contracted theaters. Gregory sums up the scope of the concept:

Distributors not only function as "designers of the product" but as the merchandisers, creating the "selling strategy," the materials, the budget, the media placement and advertisements, the promotion, and publicity methods, the pricing terms.

But distributors are fond of reminding producers that they (distributors) are not in control of their own destinies, since they are prohibited by law from franchising or having partly or wholly owned subsidiaries at the retail (theater) level.[12]

In a typical year, for example, Hollywood will spend between $600 and $800 million on promotion and advertising of films.

The Exhibitors There are some sixteen thousand movie houses in the United States, including close to four thousand drive-ins. These cinemas account for the final link in the producer-distributor-exhibitor chain of the movie business. And it is the box office receipts at these theaters that determine the eventual monetary returns to the theater owners, the distributor, the producer, and the financial backers.

The legal and financial entanglements among these various parties are extremely complex and convoluted. Hiebert et al. comment:

Before the producer earns any sizable sum, the film must earn roughly 2.5 times its production costs. . . . In effect, interest and distribution costs

---

One creative way to raise the funds for a major motion picture is to contract with various backers, giving them certain rights once the film is producing income. In her analysis of the film business, Mollie Gregory makes an analogy using a pie to represent eventual profits.

Financing a feature film today is like cutting up pieces of the pie and selling off the wedges. For instance, to get enough money to finance the picture, an independent producer might pre-sell the U.S. television rights to a network, sell another wedge to one or more foreign distributors for advance money, sell off the novelization rights and the merchandising rights (if it appeared the film might generate T-shirts or toys), then auction off the music rights to a recording company. Having distributed those wedges, each for a price, the producer now has some leverage with a bank for the remaining budget amount (if the entire film's budget has not already been financed). Of course there are other wedges and combinations, but the idea here is that when the filmmaker sees the picture as "a bundle of rights," not a single entity, the picture's budget (or more) can be raised in the United States and abroad before a foot of film is shot.[13]

**INSET 7–11
Financing the
Feature Film**

In most movie theaters, the popcorn stand is a major source of clear profit.

of a film run about 150 percent of the production costs. Marketing costs in film are among the highest—if not *the* highest—for any major consumer product.[14]

The entire complicated financial setup breeds considerable suspicion and antagonism among the several parties concerned. Gregory sums up the problem:

The issue that sows so much distrust is that no one—not even the theater owners—ever know what the box office gross really is. The producer never knows whether all the distributor's costs registered against the gross are true, any more than the distributor knows if the house nut [a fixed theater overhead figure], deducted by the exhibitor from the box office gross, is true or inflated, or whether the stated weekly gross is true or half of what was actually taken in.[15]

One practical result of this internecine financial squabbling is that the theater owners fall back upon the profits of the concession counter. It is more profitable for the theater owner to charge a lower admission—thus attracting more people to the theater—and then to rely on the patrons' spending more at the popcorn stand, which is profit that does not have to be shared with the distributor, producer, or banks.

Which brings us back to the underlying perspective for this entire unit (Chapters 5, 6, and 7): commercial mass media are, first and foremost, a business!

7.4.2 THE AUDIO RECORDING BUSINESS

Pulling in more retail money than the movies (record sales topped the $3.7 billion mark in 1980), the audio recording industry is both the oldest and the newest of the electric media. Dating back to Edison's crude acoustical tinfoil cylinder in 1877, the record predates radio and the movies. But the modern industry took on its contemporary structure—one of mammoth proportions—only with the advent or rock 'n' roll in the 1950s. Today, tens of thousands of singers and musicians, A & R (artists and repetoire) personnel, agents, managers, producers, engineers, advertising and public relations people, distributors, and retailers work with more than 1,500 record companies which sell discs on at least 2,500 different labels. A total of about 4,000 LP (long-playing) albums and 6,500 45-rpm singles are produced each year.

Production Like the filmmaking field, the record business was dominated up to the late 1940s by several major studios which controlled all aspects of production and distribution. The four majors—RCA Victor, Columbia (CBS), Decca, and Capitol—and three emerging companies—M-G-M, Mercury, and London—controlled most of the record business. These companies owned the major studios, pressed and distributed the records, and had under their employ most of the key personnel involved—artists, producers, A & R staffers, engineers.

But with the technological innovations of the late 1940s, notably audiotape recording and LP records (Section 4.3.4), a new industry evolved, one which saw the rise of countless independent record companies. Several changes also occurred in the marketing and promotion of records. The emergence of television drastically altered the content of radio. Hiebert et al. point out what happened to radio, and to the record.

The music, news, talk, and sports format evolved as the program policy of most U.S. radio stations. *Music* was the dominant element in the mix. Since the recording industry *is* popular music, the phonograph record became the content of radio. This provided free exposure of the record industry's products to a huge, affluent young audience of potential buyers, and the boom was on.[16]

As the teenagers adopted the record industry as their personal medium (and supported it handsomely), younger entrepreneurs and more flexible corporate structures emerged. New companies sprang up overnight, like A & M (swept into financial stability by a series of successes by co-founder Herb Alpert) and Motown (the first Black label to penetrate heavily into the white market).

In the past, the company A & R person was concerned with matching the right musical piece with the right artist in the company's stable of contract performers. Today the artists are independent, and the A & R man or woman is more involved as a talent scout for the record label. The same is true of the producer, who functions largely as an independent intermediary, putting together deals between the performing artists and recording company. The story is identical for the recording engineer. Formerly a company staff technician, today the engineer is an independent craftsman, free to offer his or her skills to any producer setting up a recording session.

As might be expected, then, the record companies have lost their control over the actual production of the recordings. Freelance artists contract with an independent producer, hire an outside engineer, and lease an independent recording studio for the record session. *Forbes* magazine estimates that "there are at least 1,000 recording studios around the country capable of producing a commercial quality record."[17] This free-lancing arrangement has even given rise to a new entrepreneur, the studio broker, who arranges contacts between performers and independent studios which meet the criteria for given recording sessions.[18]

Distribution   Although the major record companies may no longer exercise complete control over the production process, they—like the movie majors—still control much of the distribution process. For example, record labels owned by three of the larger conglomerates—Warner Communications, CBS, and Polygram—control about sixty percent of the market. These giant companies handle the details of record pressing, warehousing, distribution, promotion, and advertising.

Promotion, of course, is a major part of the distribution effort. And radio is the principal instrument in record promotion. As the writer David DeVoss points out, "A record can never be a financial success if it lies outside a radio format."[19]

The emphasis on radio promotion resulted in an industry low in 1959–60, when the "payola" scandals revealed that record companies were regularly paying disc jockeys under the table for plugging selected records on the air (Inset 11–11).

Retailing   Several new retailing trends were initiated in the post-1950 evolution of the new recording industry. New marketing outlets were opened up: *discount dealers* who offered substantially reduced prices for popular records; *record clubs* started by several of the major labels; and *rack-jobbers* who rented space in drug stores and supermarkets and short-circuited some of the traditional distribution. All of these retailing avenues originally helped to open the door for the new generation of youthful patrons. Although eight out of every ten singles have traditionally been bought by persons under twenty-five, in the 1980s almost one-half of all albums are purchased by those between twenty and thirty-four years of age.

New technologies in the playback media also helped to stimulate sales. Audio cartridges (introduced in 1958) and cassettes (brought out in 1964), along with the conventional reel-to-reel audio tapes, account for

The large record supermarket is but one of the several types of record retailing.

about thirty percent of the sound recording market. And finally, as in the movie industry, it should be noted that the overseas market plays an important role in the record business. About one-third of all record sales come from foreign retailing.

7.5 Media-Related Industries

In addition to the several media discussed above, the commercial mass communication milieu has also spawned many related industries that support the media operations. These fields must be considered as part of the total mass media picture.

7.5.1 ADVERTISING

With some 4,400 advertising agencies in the United States employing more than 200,000 persons, advertising is perhaps the largest of the peripheral media fields. A $50 billion-a-year industry, its size underscores the commercial underpinnings of the entire mass media framework.

Structure of the Ad Agency   From the viewpoint of the agency's client—the advertiser—the key person in the agency structure is the *account executive,* the true "middleman" who is the agency's liaison between the advertiser and all of the agency staff specialists. It is the account executive who meets regularly with the client, plans out every facet of the advertising program, follows through on all details, and generally holds the advertiser's hand throughout the whole process. (See Section 6.4.)

The account executive pulls together a planning team or group which functions as a unit to handle that particular advertiser's account. This account group has representatives from research, copywriting, art, layout, production, and media services as needed.

Summing up the importance of advertising in our mass market society, the former president of the American Association of Advertising Agencies (AAAA), Frederick Gamble, states:

Advertising is the counterpart in distribution of the machine in production. By the use of machines, our production of goods and services has been multiplied. By the use of the mass media, advertising multiplies the selling effort. . . . Reaching many people rapidly at low cost, advertising speeds up sales, turns prospects into cus-

Functional Organization of a Typical Advertising Agency

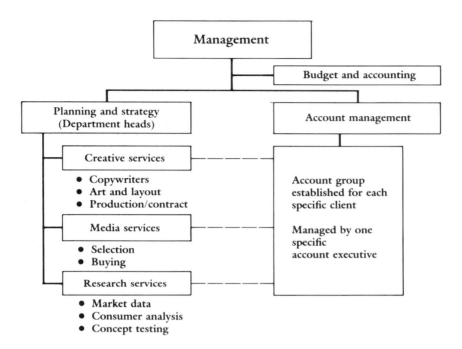

tomers in large numbers and at high speed. Hence, in a mass-production and high-consumption economy, advertising has the greatest opportunity and the greatest responsibility for finding customers.[20]

7.5.2 PUBLIC RELATIONS

Most observers would readily discern a superficial similarity between advertising and public relations. The main distinction is not of purpose, but of method. Advertising is open and direct; public relations—although an established and respected profession—is covert and indirect, usually more manipulative. Martin Mayer, author of *Madison Avenue, U.S.A.*, sums up the difference:

Advertising, whatever its faults, is a relatively open business; its messages appear in paid space or on bought time, and everybody can recognize it as special pleading. Public relations works behind the scenes; . . . usually the public relations practitioner stands at the other end of a long rope which winds around several pulleys before it reaches the object of his invisible tugging. . . . The advertising

man must know how many people he can reach *with* the media, the public relations man must know how many people he can reach *within* the media.[21]

Public relations is actually the much broader concept. It has been with us as long as there have been politicians, manufactured products, churches, and circuses (P. T. Barnum was one of the greatest formative PR practitioners). Today public relations includes the press agent, the presidential press conference, the business luncheon, a university "public information" office, the political image-maker, the housewife who sends out a press release for her garden club, the agent or promoter of a rock band, the celebrity golf tournament for charity, the publicist for a high school band concert, and a thousand other examples of publicity and press manipulation.

Ironically, press relations personnel never have enjoyed good press relations.

Today journalists, from whose ranks many public relations specialists are recruited, tend to look down on them—perhaps a little in envy of their higher salaries, perhaps much more in disdain of their "selling out to the special interests." Intellectuals scorn them as insincere hired manipulators, sometimes sinister, sometimes no more than offensive.[22]

7.5.3 MARKETING RESEARCH

The concept of "marketing research" includes many varied components. *Market data* is gathered to determine exactly what the potential marketplace is, to define the advertising client's position in the market, and to compare competitive data with other firms. *Product information* encompasses the product's design, color, and packaging, its place in the marketplace, and its special features and specific appeals—as well as its problems and shortcomings. *Consumer research* uses census data, sophisticated surveys, and motivational research to try to answer the basic question, "What makes people buy?" *Audience analysis,* like consumer research, uses both demographic and psychographic methods to try to find out who really is reading and listening and viewing what—and why. *Concept testing* helps to determine exactly what kind of campaign strategy and specific appeals should be used to tailor a given product to a particular market. *Test marketing* involves a controlled

---

As an example of a successful public relations campaign, consider the case of the glasphalt parking lot. Playing up environmental awareness, Lucky Breweries had already achieved some good PR value from its recycling program by 1970. Then in mid-1971, Lucky undertook another major environmental PR step—paving its San Francisco parking lot with "glasphalt," a mixture of asphalt and glass chips which holds promise as an environmentally sound pavement.

Lucky's PR chief, Bert Casey, went all out on the event. "The story was a natural. It tied the growing public interest in recycling to the novel idea of paving a parking lot with broken glass."[23] Sending out a hundred and twenty invitations to the media and phoning dozens of editors, Casey managed to get about forty journalists there for the occasion. They witnessed the whole event, attended a press conference, received a press kit, and left with Casey's story.

Casey then sent out two photographs and press releases overnight to more than two thousand media outlets (radio and TV stations and newspapers). Additionally, a two-minute film clip was sent to thirty-five key western television stations.

The results were a PR agent's dream. Both the AP and UPI wire services picked up the press release. More than a hundred newspapers carried the story—which received especially thorough coverage in the San Francisco area—and twenty TV stations aired Casey's glasphalt film clip. The total cost of the campaign was $4,000, a mere pittance compared to the amount of positive publicity generated.

**INSET 7–12
Lucky Breweries:
Successful PR
Campaign**

experimental approach in which products are advertised and sold—following different campaigns and appeals—in various limited markets. *Post-campaign evaluations* attempt to find out exactly what worked and what did not work, and what needs to be revised in the next campaign.[24]

Although most large ad agencies have extensive research staffs, much of this specialized research must be contracted out to research firms. There are close to a hundred such media/advertising-related research houses spread across the nation.

7.5.4 REPRESENTATIVES AND AGENTS

Several other categories of media-related professions could be grouped under the general heading of representatives and agents— those ubiquitous intermediaries whose negotiation and management skills oil the machinery of numerous media "deals" while they grease their own palms with commissions of ten to fifteen percent.

Personal Agents   Anyone who has attained "star" status or who has substantial income, specialized needs, not enough time to attend to business details, or frequent contact with the press may turn to an agent of one description or another. The author uses a literary agent to guarantee solid and professional contact with publishers. The politician uses a press secretary to handle all news-related (PR) functions. The rock star needs both a press agent and a business manager to handle publicity as well as financial details of million-dollar record deals and numerous concert tours.

Talent Agencies   The corporate nature of talent agencies was established in 1898 when the William Morris Agency was formed to represent actors and performers in the legitimate theatre and vaudeville. International Creative Management (ICM), second in size only to William Morris, grew by mergers and acquisitions of smaller talent agencies. As an example of its profit potential, ICM represented the producers, the director, and the

screenwriter of the movie *Jaws,* and the company's earnings from that one film alone have already exceeded $4 million.

Station Reps   Another major middleman in broadcasting is the station representative or "station rep," who is concerned with selling radio and TV station time for national spot advertising (Section 6.3.2). Obviously, it would be impossible for every radio or TV station to have its own salespersons established in every major center of advertising, trying to keep in contact with numerous major nationwide advertisers. So the station rep evolved, starting in 1937, as the go-between linking the individual station with the ad agency/sponsor. In essence, the station rep serves as an extension of the station sales staff, with no rep firm serving more than one station in a given broadcast area. There are more than two hundred sales rep firms in the country, employing some three thousand persons. As the writer John Tebbel observes, however, "There are few, if any, industries where so few companies, employing such a small number of people, account for so many dollars of revenue." [25]

Other Managers and Consultants   Many other media-related representatives of various descriptions exist, in quantities too numerous to detail in this text. More than a hundred *media brokerage* firms specialize in the sale of newspapers, radio and TV stations, and other media properties. Thousands of *communications lawyers,* concentrated in Washington, D.C., specialize in media-related legal questions ranging from slander and libel suits to First Amendment entanglements to contract negotiations. *Media consultants* offer advice on everything from installing a new computerized data retrieval system to improving newspaper management efficiency to upgrading the "look" of local TV news program. Opportunities abound for literally hundreds of classifications of different media-related jobs in the mass communication industries.

7.5.5 PRESS ASSOCIATIONS AND SYNDICATES

Conceived in 1848 when the New York Harbor News Association (precursor to today's Associated Press) was formed, the press association—"wire service" or "news service"—is a large and integral part of any major media operation (Section 3.3.3). There are well over a hundred such services in the United States today, most of which are relatively small and specialized. The two giants are the Associated Press (AP) and United Press International (UPI).

The AP is theoretically a membership cooperative, with member newspapers and broadcast stations having a vote in determining how the organization is run. The UPI was formed in 1958 when the older United Press (founded in 1907 by E. W. Scripps) merged with the International News Service (formed in 1909 by William Randolph Hearst).

Both services supply their clients/members with a full range of print and broadcast news stories, audio and television reports, cable-TV news, news photos, stock market data, weather, sports, and other features. Using telephone, cable, microwave relays, satellites, laser beams, VDT terminals, and computer-based storage and retrieval systems, the two press associations employ thousands of reporters and editors in "bureaus" which reach every corner of the globe.

Syndication   As a counterpart to the wire services, hundreds of specialized syndicates also play a major role in furnishing nonlocal materials to newspapers (Section 3.3.3). Supplying non-news features, syndicates concentrate on columnists, comics, editorial cartoons, puzzles, and similar matter.

In broadcasting—especially television—syndication companies may furnish upwards of twenty-five to thirty percent of the station's schedule (for non-network-affiliated stations it may go as high as eighty to ninety percent). Companies such as Viacom, Film-ways, MCA TV, and Tandem offer scores of movie packages, off-network series, and newly produced materials for sale to stations.

7.5.6 NONCOMMERCIAL EDUCATIONAL AND INDUSTRIAL MEDIA

Before leaving the structure of the media industries, you should glance also at the expanding areas of noncommercial media. At least one billion dollars a year is spent, for example, on some thirteen thousand non-theatrical films for industry, schools, government, and religious groups (compared to fewer than two hundred dramatic films from Hollywood). It is in these loosely related fields that we find the greatest growth, especially in video and computer-related technologies.

Corporate Video   This broad category of telecommunications includes many business and industrial applications: employee training, corporate PR, sales messages and consumer relations, industrial supervision, management and administrative communications, meetings and "teleconferencing," data handling, and myriad other uses. Judith Brush, one of the top researchers in this area, comments:

Many organizations are now engaged in crash-planning projects for the "office-of-the-future," involving integrated data and word processing systems, voice, data, facsimile, teleconferencing, and machine-to-machine telecommunications systems, and video, videographics, and information display systems. Yet no one seems to know exactly how all these new pieces will fit together eventually.[26]

Budgets and personnel demands are growing in this field at the rate of thirty to forty percent each year.

Medical and Health Services   This is another area where the telecommunications field is expanding rapidly. One researcher estimates that of the seven thousand hospitals in the country, more than eighty percent are involved in video to some extent, and three-quarters of them are producing their own programming.[27] Most hospitals are using

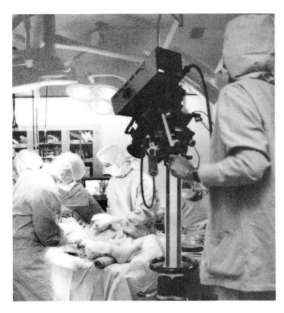

Utilization of television has penetrated into every fold of the American fabric—including most hospital operating rooms.

television and related media for one or more of three basic functions: patient education, in-service training or staff development, and public and community relations.

Government Media   Local, state, and federal governments are involved in media in many ways. It has been said that the federal government is probably the world's largest filmmaker, far outstripping Hollywood's entertainment production. The U.S. Government Printing Office, the *Congressional Record,* the Library of Congress, and some twenty-five thousand public libraries would have to be included in this category. The State Department operates the Voice of America radio network. The federal government gives some support to public broadcasting through the CPB. State and local governments (including boards of education) own about three-quarters of the public television stations in the nation.

Military   The Armed Forces constitute another major media field. Both the Army and the Navy have pioneered in the use of film and television for training purposes. The

Stars and Stripes has a journalistic record that many other newspapers would be jealous of. The Armed Forces Service Radio and Television is one of the largest operations in the world.

Churches and Religious Programming
Religious groups have long made use of free "public service" time on commercial radio and television stations to spread their word. Some of the established denominational church bodies have media organizations that rival the largest station operations. Many of the newer evangelical and charismatic churches have moved aggressively into station ownership, and there currently exist at least four religious networks tied together nationwide by satellite transmissions.

Schools and Universities   There are more than fifteen thousand school districts in the United States, almost all of which have some sort of audiovisual or media program. A couple of dozen schools own their own television stations; hundreds have Instructional Television Fixed Service (ITFS) stations (a special low-power, multiple-channel service in the upper UHF band); and thousands have closed-circuit TV installations. Also, let us not overlook school libraries as one of the nation's largest media investments or the schools themselves as sources of textbooks and other educational materials. And virtually every major college and university has some kind of instructional telecommunications projects; several, in fact, have a dozen or more separate closed-circuit TV installations.

Media education also could be viewed as one of the growing media fields. School curriculum programs at all levels are becoming increasingly concerned with educating students in communication and media fundamentals. Programs in visual literacy have been started at the lower elementary grades; and, at the other end of the educational ladder, more than twenty colleges and universities have established doctoral programs in communications since World War II.

SUMMARY

The media and communications fields are expanding at a dizzying pace. More than half of the working population in the United States is employed in communications and information-handling occupations. There are well over two million people engaged directly or indirectly in the mass media industries.

One indication of the scope of media activity is the hundreds of professional and trade associations and unions designed to promote different segments of the industries, provide services for individual members, undertake lobbying activities, facilitate self-regulation, and protect job security.

The organization and structure of the media industries can be broadly interpreted in a theoretical perspective by comparing them to Lasswell's communication model. **Who** encompasses two aspects: *financial control* (ownership, management, sales, advertisers, publishers, and producers) and *editorial and creative* (writers, reporters, photographers, editors, artists). **What** includes *message producers* (program directors, staging and lighting, camera and audio operators, performers, typesetters, press operators, engineers, and other craftsmen). **Channel** covers *distribution* (newsstand sales, home subscriptions, retail stores, libraries, broadcast station transmitters, network lines, theatrical exhibitions, and so forth).

The corporate structure of those media that are supported substantially by advertising (*newspapers, magazines, television, radio*) generally have organizational patterns that correspond to these four divisions. *Financial control* is represented by advertising or sales departments. The *creative* function is the editorial or programming department. *Production* tasks in broadcasting usually represent more of a creative effort than print production (typesetting and press operations). The *distribution* function includes newspaper and magazine circulation (delivery and sales) and broadcast transmission. Emerging technologies in the telecommunications fields—cable TV, satellites, videocassettes and discs—are largely concerned with distribution developments.

Those media not supported by advertising revenue (*books, movies,* and *audio recordings*) have similar corporate structures in that there is no sales/advertising department. Consequently, their organizational patterns can be divided into three main functions: *production* (encompassing the programming or editorial tasks and covering both the **who** and **what**), *distribution,* and *retailing* (two aspects of the **channel**). In both the movie and recording industries, the last thirty years have seen a decline of the once-powerful major studios and a corresponding rise in the role of the independent producers.

In addition to these specific mass media structures, the mass communication fields are supported by a plethora of related professions and ancillary industries: advertising, public relations, marketing research, agents, station reps, brokers, lawyers, consultants, and so forth. Press associations and syndication services play an important role in the editorial and programming functions.

Finally, in considering the total media picture, noncommercial and educational media represent the fastest-growing segment of the field—industrial telecommunications, medical and health services, government channels, military media, churches and religious programming, and school uses of the media.

Notes to Chapter 7

1. Wilbur Schramm, *Men, Messages, and Media: A Look at Human Communication* (New York: Harper & Row, 1973), p. 17.

2. Due to conflicting and contradictory data furnished by many different agencies and associations, several different sources have been utilized for employment figures. The numbers used throughout this chapter—in the text and in the insets—have been averaged, projected, estimated,

extrapolated, and compromised from the following sources: U.S. Department of Labor, Bureau of Labor Statistics, *Handbook of Labor Statistics 1978,* Bulletin 2000 (Washington, D.C.: U.S. Government Printing Office, 1979), Table 19; U.S. Department of Labor, Bureau of Labor Statistics, *Occupational Projections and Training Data,* Bulletin 2020 (Washington, D.C.: U.S. Government Printing Office, 1979), Table B-1; *Broadcasting Yearbook 1980* (Washington, D.C.: Broadcasting Publications, 1980), Section F; U.S. Bureau of the Census, *Statistical Abstract of the United States: 1979,* 100th ed. (Washington, D.C.: U.S. Government Printing Office, 1979), Tables 687, 681, and 988. Additional data were supplied by the International Television Association, National Association of Broadcasters, National Cable Television Association, Public Relations Society of America, and the Recording Industry Association of America.

3. Marc Porat, producer of the television program "The Information Society" (a film of the Aspen Institute for Humanistic Studies), distributed by the Public Broadcasting Service, October 1980.

4. Nancy Yakes and Denise Akey, eds., *Encyclopedia of Associations,* 14th ed. (Detroit: Gale Research Company, 1980).

5. Ray Eldon Hiebert, Donald F. Ungurait, and Thomas W. Bohn, *Mass Media II: An Introduction to Modern Communication,* 2nd ed. (New York: Longman, 1979), p. 137.

6. Ibid., pp. 138–139.

7. *Statistical Abstract of the United States: 1980,* 101st ed. (Washington D.C.: U.S. Government Printing Office, 1980), p. 590.

8. Richard Reeves, "A Media Monster—Who, Me?" *New York,* 26 November 1973, pp. 37–38.

9. Hiebert et al., *Mass Media II,* p. 310.

10. Frank Donegan and Gary Arlen, "Heavenly Hardware," *Panorama,* May 1980, p. 84.

11. Mollie Gregory, *Making Films Your Business* (New York: Schocken Books, 1979), p. 136.

12. Ibid., p. 164.

13. Ibid., p. 137.

14. Hiebert et al., *Mass Media II,* p. 274.

15. Gregory, *Making Films Your Business,* p. 167

16. Hiebert et al., *Mass Media II,* p. 320.

17. *Forbes* Magazine, "Records: The Gorillas Are Coming," in *Readings in Mass Communication: Concepts and Issues in the Mass Media,* 4th ed., ed. Michael C. Emery and Ted Curtis Smythe (Dubuque, Iowa: Wm. C. Brown, 1980), p. 327.

18. The first such studio broker in the United States, Studio Referral Service, was established by Ellis Sorkin, a former engineer with A & M Records, in Los Angeles in 1980 to help performing groups locate the best studio bargains for their specific recording needs.

19. David DeVoss, "Don't Lay No Boogie Woogie on the King of Rock and Roll," in *Mass Media and Society,* 3rd ed., ed. Alan Wells (Palo Alto, Calif.: Mayfield, 1979), p. 107.

20. Quoted in William L. Rivers, Theodore Peterson, and Jay W. Jensen, *The Mass Media and Modern Society,* 2nd ed. (New York: Holt, Rinehart and Winston, 1971), p. 236.

21. Quoted in ibid.

22. Charlene J. Brown, Trevor R. Brown, and William L. Rivers, *The Media and the People* (New York: Holt, Rinehart and Winston, 1978), pp. 383–384.

23. Peter M. Sandman, David M. Rubin, and David B. Sachsman, *Media: An Introductory Analysis of American Mass Communications,* 2nd ed. (Englewood Cliffs, N.J.: Prentice-Hall, 1976), p. 366.

24. This summary of research approaches is condensed from Elizabeth J. Heighton and Don R. Cunningham, *Advertising in the Broadcast Media* (Belmont, Calif.: Wadsworth, 1976), pp. 76–81.

25. John Tebbel, "Broadcasting's Hidden Power: The TV-Radio Reps," in *Readings in Mass Communication: Concepts and Issues in the Mass Media,* ed. Michael C. Emery and Ted Curtis Smythe (Dubuque, Iowa: Wm. C. Brown, 1972), p. 249.

26. Judith M. Brush, "Where Is Private Video Headed?—A New Study," *Educational and Industrial Television,* October 1980, p. 68.

27. Steve R. Cartwright, "Health Care, a Growing Video Field," *Educational and Industrial Television,* August 1979, p. 33.

UNIT II APPENDIX
Conglomerates and the
Diversification of Media Corporations

Some media corporations are known as such by their names, e.g., Columbia Broadcasting System, Inc., whereas others, like the General Tire & Rubber Company, offer the reader no clues to their media involvement by their names. Therefore, to better understand how the businesses of media work, it is useful to know a little about some of the larger and more interesting media-involved conglomerates. Among those listed here are large diversified conglomerates with some media holdings as well as media corporations that have limited nonmedia operations. For the most part, these brief sketches reflect corporate holdings for the period of 1980 to 1981.

General Electric: Three TV and eight radio stations, thirteen cable-TV systems, consumer electronics products, numerous other consumer and heavy industrial products and services. Largest of all media-involved conglomerates with over $26 billion in gross revenue in 1981.

Westinghouse Electric Corporation: Five TV and thirteen radio stations, the top-ranking Group W with its numerous cable-TV systems (recently acquired from Teleprompter Cable), Group W Satellite Communications, and Group W Productions, consumer and industrial products from nuclear power plants to Longines-Wittnauer watches. The conglomerate's earnings for 1981 topped $9 billion.

RCA Corporation: Five TV and eight radio stations, the NBC radio and TV networks, communication satellite services, Random House, Alfred A. Knopf, Pantheon Books (all publishers), Hertz auto rentals, CIT

Financial Corporation, RCA Victor records, the RCA Selectavision videodisc systems, and numerous other consumer and industrial products and services.

Gulf + Western Industries: Paramount Pictures and Paramount Television, Simon & Schuster publishers, cable services, No Nonsense pantyhose, amusement parks, mining, steel, masonry cement, and many other diversified products.

CBS, Inc.: Five TV and fourteen radio stations, radio and television networks, CBS Cable programming service, CBS Records Group (with several different labels, the world's largest record company), limited local cable systems, Holt, Rinehart and Winston, Fawcett Publications, W. B. Saunders (medical publishers), BFA Educational Media, at least six magazines (including *Family Weekly*), two toy companies, Steinway pianos, X-Acto tools, and businesses in some thirty countries.

Time, Inc.: Six major magazines, book publishing, American TV & Communications Corporation (one of the nation's largest cable-TV system operators), Home Box Office (pay-cable program producer), one TV station, a videocassette club, and forest/paper products.

Warner Communications, Inc.: Warner Brothers films, book publishing, DC Comics (*Superman*), and *Mad* magazine, Panavision film equipment, record companies, Warner-Amex cable systems (half-owned by American Express) the developers of QUBE, Warner Home Video, Atari electronic games, music publishing, Malibu Grand Prix racing, the Franklin Mint, etc.

General Tire & Rubber Company: Tires, chemicals, tennis balls, four TV and twelve radio stations—some of which have been denied renewal of licenses due to questionable business practices while others are being contested.

American Broadcasting Companies, Inc.: Five TV and twelve radio stations, several radio and television networks, heavily involved with numerous cable TV programming systems, motion picture production, four publishing companies (Chilton, Miller, Hitchcock, and Word, Inc.), numerous specialty magazines, amusement parks, and other interests. In 1978–79 ABC sold its 277 movie theaters and ABC Records.

Times-Mirror Company: Los Angeles Times, six other daily papers, specialized book publishing firms (including the New American Library), seven TV stations, cable-TV systems, and extensive paper, newsprint, and forest products holdings.

MCA, Inc.: Universal Pictures, Universal TV Productions, MCA Records (and other labels), music publishing, a period of involvement with videodisc production, G. P. Putnam's Sons book publishers, involvement with cable-TV networks, *The Runner* magazine, banking, and park concessions.

Gannett Company: Seven TV and thirteen radio stations, eighty five daily newspapers, twenty-two weeklies, billboard services, a news service and a satellite network, Canadian newsprint operations, the Lou Harris polling firm. Gannett has launched *USA Today,* a nationwide daily newspaper.

Knight-Ridder Company: Detroit *Free Press,* Philadelphia *Inquirer,* thirty-three other newspapers, four TV stations, and Viewdata Corporation (a telephone-based interactive home videotex system), Knight-Ridder is becoming progressively more involved with cable-TV systems.

McGraw-Hill, Inc.: Extensive trade and text-book publishers, four TV stations, information systems, a corporate training development firm, financial services, and Standard and Poor's Corporation.

New York Times Company: Fifteen newspapers, Cowles magazines (including *Family Circle* and others), three TV and two radio stations, numerous cable-TV systems, book publishing, educational materials, paper mills.

Washington Post Company: The *Washington Post* newspaper, *Newsweek* and *Inside Sports* magazines, and four TV stations.

Capital Cities Communications, Inc.: Six TV and thirteen radio stations, six daily newspapers, Cablecom-General Inc. cable-TV systems, Capital Cities Television Productions, and Fairchild Publications (industry periodicals).

Newhouse Newspapers and Broadcasting: Thirty newspapers, five magazines, seven radio stations, and twenty cable-TV systems.

Scripps-Howard Broadcasting Company: Twenty daily papers, twenty weekly papers, six TV and eight radio stations, and cable-TV systems.

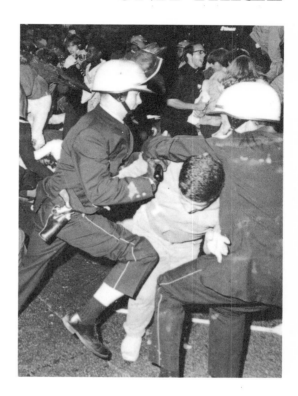

UNIT THREE

As important as it is for you to understand American mass media as *business enterprises* (Unit II), it may be even more essential to understand the mass media as *social phenomena*. Television, newspapers, movies, magazines, books, radio, and recordings have penetrated the social fabric of our daily lives to such an extent that the average American spends more time attending to these media than to any other waking activity except holding down a job. The mass media reflect and modify every aspect of late twentieth-century civilization—all of its wonders and all of its shame. Mass media *are* modern society.

Thus, Unit III will focus on those questions which concern the relationship between mass media and society—*and the individual*. How do the media affect your daily life? What are the major effects of the media upon society? How are your perceptions of your environment shaped by the media? How is your environment itself—from your own household to global conditions—shaped by the media? And, conversely, how do you affect the media? What role should the government play in regulating media channels? How about industry self-regulation? Public pressure groups? What can the individual do to control his or her own media experiences? What about special effects on children? The aged? Racial minorities? The poor? And women? These are some of the crucial issues we will be examining in Chapters 8, 9, and 10.

Mass Media
in a Social Framework

The impact of the mass media upon your life cannot be minimized. Their effects are considerable. In examining the influence of mass communication, you need to look at two parallel concerns. First, there are the effects of the media upon *society*—the way institutions (the family, schools, businesses, churches, government) are affected, the shaping of cultural tastes and moral standards, the determining of our political and economic patterns, and so forth. Second, and perhaps more importantly, there are the effects of mass media upon the *individual*—how you spend your time, how you determine your life-style, how you perceive your self-image, and related personal matters.

The theme of Chapter 8 reflects these two concerns:

• *The effects of mass media on our society as a whole are subtle, deeply ingrained, and occasionally overexaggerated; however, the media have a more profound impact on the daily lives of individual members of our society.*

Critics, scholars, and media professionals have long disagreed about the extent of the mass media's influence. Many would argue that the effects are minimal; however, others would agree with McLuhan, who summed up the all-encompassing impact of the media:

All media work us over completely. They are so pervasive in their personal, political, economic, aesthetic, psychological, moral, ethical, and social consequences that they leave no part of us untouched, unaffected, unaltered. The medium is the message. Any understanding of social and cultural change is impossible without a knowledge of the way media work as environments.[1]

8

Media and the Public: Social and Individual Effects

8.1 The Continuing Debate

Ever since the innovation of the popular press, critics have been blaming most of society's ills on corrupt media—cheap pulp fiction and dime novels, tabloid newspapers, scandalous films, comic books, girlie magazines, radio propaganda, and today's decadent TV programming (Section 1.1.2). Others view mass communication as an opportunity to provide widespread education, democratize political systems, promote higher cultural standards, furnish low-cost entertainment for the masses, and stimulate economic growth. Neither viewpoint is entirely wrong.

8.1.1 THE NEGATIVE-EFFECTS ARGUMENT

Among the various media, television—the "boob tube"—stands out as the target of most critical abuse. William Henry satirically mimics the critics: "Television causes illiteracy, night blindness, drug addiction, sterility and charisma politics, the scholars tell us. It makes our children stupid, our elderly parents fearful, our dogs cross-eyed and neurotic."[2]

Parental groups, psychologists, and the medical profession all have been in the forefront of the critical attack on television. They have been especially concerned about its effects on children. At a 1979 medical convention, for example, pediatricians pointed out "the

---

Jerry Mander, a TV critic, has written extensively about the negative effects of watching television. These excerpts are taken from his article, "Television: The Evil Eye."[3]

**INSET 8–1
Television:
The Evil Eye**

Television is not *only* an environmental pollutant; to a greater extent than ever before, it *is* our environment. TV has become such a huge part of our lives as to be dangerously invisible. As the old saying says, the fish is the last creature to understand the effects of water. . . .

Television *is* a form of hypnosis. When you "tune in" the heart rate slows, the limbs stop moving, brain wave patterns flatten out and the eyes move less than they do during any other living experience—including sleep. [See Inset 1–10.] . . .

Television makes us doubt the validity of our own experience. Things are not "real" anymore unless we see them on TV. . . . It distances us from our own experience of the world. It implants its images inside us. Television has drastically altered the content of people's shared experiences. More and more of what we share are the images placed in our minds by TV. . . . It is a form of brainwashing with four very specific messages: first, keep watching; second, carry the images around in your head; third, buy something; fourth, tune in tomorrow. . . .

For me, the ultimate point of all is that television is inherently antidemocratic, intrinsically autocratic. It cuts us off from our own world, our environment and each other and substitutes a steady stream of mesmerizing images placed in our heads by the people who control the medium. It occupies our minds like an invading army and screens out the realities of our life. And it redefines happiness away from the creative and toward the consumptive.

Television programs, at their most basic level, are no more than the wrapping around commercials. The sole purpose of [commercial] TV is to sell the advertised products, most of which we don't need. The underlying message—and it's a convincing message—is that we cannot create our own happiness, that we need their *things* to make us happy, that we need their images to convince us we're alive. I'd call that the *worst* kind of pollution.

---

problems of violence on television, the danger of children imitating antisocial behavior they observe, the lack of positive role models for minority youngsters and the persuasive tactics of commercials aimed at kids."[4]

Charges against the Media The following list summarizes the major charges that have been made against the mass media:

1. *Passivity* is encouraged as we become a nation of spectators rather than participants.
2. *Lower cultural tastes* result as "art" is popularized to appeal to the masses.
3. *Violence and delinquency* are stimulated by the glut of violent dramatic entertainment to be found in all media, especially on television.
4. *Moral deterioration* is accelerated by the frank portrayal of sexual material.
5. *Political superficiality* is encouraged as we accept political candidates and issues wrapped in brief commercial packages.

6. *Less creativity* occurs because we allow economic considerations and committee decisions to dominate artistic endeavors.
7. *Illiteracy* is on the increase as the popular media detract from the instructional mission of the educational system.
8. *Disintegration of the family* and other social institutions (churches, schools, the free-enterprise system, patriotism) occurs as individuals withdraw from social relationships and responsibilities into a media fantasy world and a "me-first" mentality.

8.1.2 THE POSITIVE-EFFECTS ARGUMENT

Those writers, practitioners, and media theorists who defend the various media point out that the mass media really are necessary and positive segments of contemporary civilization. Our society, they maintain, could not exist without modern mass communication. All of the idealistic goals of the libertarian philosophy (Section 2.2.5) are dependent upon the operation of a free and vital mass

---

In one of his essays for *Newsweek*, the syndicated columnist George F. Will played down the influence of television, pointing out that it "is more mirror than lever."[5]

To represent situation-comedy shows as shapers of the nation's consciousness is to portray the public as more passive and plastic than it is. To represent television journalism as a fundamentally transforming force is to make the nation's politics seem less purposeful, more mindless, more a matter of random causes than is the case. The contours of history are not determined by communications technology. . . . To see the rise of blacks, or the fall of [President Johnson], as primarily a consequence of television is to hollow out history. It discounts the noble and ignoble ideas and passions, heroes and villains and common people who make history.

. . . Modern man, proudly sovereign beneath a blank heaven, is prone to believe that "they" (evil persons, irresistible impulses, impersonal forces) control the world. Astrology, vulgar Marxism and Freudianism, and other doctrines nourish this need. So does the exaggeration of media influence. Journalists and perhaps even serious scholars . . . who study television, are prone to believe that it turns the world. But the world is not that easy to turn.

**INSET 8–2
The
Not-So-Mighty
Tube**

press. Other defenders of mass communication argue that the media really have very little influence on society; therefore, the public can enjoy the harmless diversion of inexpensive entertainment without having to worry about the alleged negative effects.

Arguments for the Media The following list summarizes the arguments in favor of the media:

1. *Inexpensive entertainment* is provided for the majority of the population.
2. *Free speech* is protected by a vigilant press.
3. *Cleaner government* results as corrupt politics are exposed by investigative journalism.
4. *Higher cultural tastes* result as works of art are presented to the masses.
5. *Important and useful information* is made available to all media consumers.
6. *Participatory democracy* is fostered as people become more involved in all political issues.
7. *Higher standards of living* ensue from consumer advertising and mass production.

As with the various charges against the media, there is some truth and a comparable bit of exaggeration in most of the claims outlined above.

The chart in Inset 8–3 offers an expanded list of claims and allegations for and against the media, outlining positive and negative effects on a variety of specific individual and societal issues. These various arguments are explored in some detail in Section 8.4 and in succeeding chapters.

8.2 Research on Mass Communication Effects

When asked what they think mass media are doing to society, many citizens will gladly sound off about its effects: "All the violence on TV is causing too many people to commit crazy acts." "Reading scores in school are falling because of kids watching too much TV." "All the women feel they have to look like fashion models." "Our family doesn't do as much together as we should." "Most of the drug abuse problem is caused by popularizing various drugs through record lyrics." "A lot of kids listen to all the sex-oriented rock and think they have to start fooling around a lot younger."

The fact is, however, that we do not know as much as we think we know about the various effects of mass media exposure. Despite all the charges, claims, accusations, and arguments—the wringing of hands and the pointing of fingers—no one really *knows* anything about the effects of mass communication upon our lives except as uncovered by valid research. DeFleur and Dennis make the point that

it is from research that knowledge about the effects of mass media will come. Such understanding will not result from the pronouncements of preachers, the opinions of politicians, the claims of the PTA, the untested views of critics, or any other form of debate. Like it or not, we are stuck with research—with all its problems and limitations—as our best source for understanding the effects of the media.[6]

What we do know about the effects of mass media consumption is scattered and fragmentary, often contradictory and confusing. Two prominent researchers, Bernard Berelson and Morris Janowitz, have observed:

The effects of communication are many and diverse. They may be short-range or long-run. They may be manifest or latent. They may be strong or weak. They may derive from any number of aspects of the communication content. They may be considered as psychological or political or economic or sociological. They may operate upon opinions, values, information levels, skills, taste, or overt behavior.[7]

Before we examine specific media effects, it will be helpful to look at the various ways in which communication research can be organized and carried out.

Individual Areas	*Positive Effects*	*Negative Effects*	**INSET 8–3**
Escapism	Provides harmless entertainment.	Wastes time.	**Informal Catalog of Conflicting Media Effects**
Recreation	Encourages new interests. Stimulates participation.	Encourages passivity.	
Physiology	Relaxes the viewer/reader.	Hypnotic. Damages eyesight.	
Companionship	Furnishes therapeutic surrogate.	Alienates the individual. Encourages withdrawal.	
Aggressiveness	Provides a needed catharsis, a harmless outlet.	Can stimulate antisocial behavior and violence.	
Consumption	Gives useful information on new products.	Creates false wants, materialistic standards.	
Information	Extends education, knowledge of the world.	Distorts reality. Oversimplifies situations.	

Societal Areas

Social stability	Reinforces social norms. Facilitates gradual social evolution.	Excludes anti-Establishment viewpoints.
Family relations	Draws the family together with common experiences.	Encourages withdrawal and individual interests.
Moral standards	Presents an honest reflection of society.	Emphasizes deviant behavior. Accelerates deterioration.
Culture and art	Promotes widespread dissemination of "culture for the masses."	Lowers artistic standards. Homogenizes art experiences.
Creativity	Provides new avenues for artistic expression.	Stifles creativity. Produces "art by formula."
Cultural and racial relations	Facilitates knowledge of other peoples, races. Promotes understanding.	Perpetuates stereotypes. Increases tensions.
Free speech	Protects freedom of expression.	Accommodates pornography. Threatens national security.
Economy and advertising	Encourages productivity, higher standards of living.	Manipulates the consumer. Allows untruthful advertising.
Education (The "Teacher" Function)	Transmits social heritage. Raises educational levels.	Contributes to illiteracy. Promotes superficiality.
Election politics (The "Forum" Function)	Informs citizens about candidates and issues.	Merchandizes personalities. Oversimplifies issues.
Governance (The "Watchdog" Function)	Exposes political corruption.	Facilitates manipulation by those in power.

8.2.1 TYPES OF RESEARCH

Traditionally, all formal research has been divided into three categories: *historical, descriptive or survey,* and *experimental.* Each has its particular set of disciplines and formats—and its unique problems.

Historical Research This area of research often is used to try to determine causal relationships. What were the causes of this particular event? Why did this effect take place? If this is continued, what will be the result?

Historical research might focus, for example, on the reaction to Orson Welles' 1938 broadcast, *War of the Worlds* (see Inset 4–9). Exactly what happened? How did people perceive the broadcast? How many panicked? To what extent? What factors in the radio show precipitated the effect? What role did the threat of war in Europe play in the panic reaction to the *War of the Worlds?*

Descriptive Research Also referred to as *normative* research, descriptive research is used to find out what really is going on right now. What is the actual standard or "norm"? How many people are reading this or watching that? How are people reacting to an actual media event? Surveys are often used to try to assess the audience's degree of involvement, participation, and reaction.

Descriptive research is heavily used in marketing and advertising research and in audience studies. For example, what is the "pass-on" readership of *Reader's Digest* compared to that of *Playboy*? (A single copy of the average magazine is read by 3.9 adults.) At what rate is the circulation of afternoon newspapers declining? Will consumers be more likely to buy a new detergent if it is packaged in a red carton or in a green and yellow box?

Experimental Research This broad category of research is aimed at uncovering new laws or principles by trying out different factors in a "laboratory" situation. If a given variable is changed, will the end result be changed? By comparing the effects of altering different factors, can we determine what really causes various events? In a given series of comparisons, can we find any universal principles or laws that add to our understanding of a phenomenon?

Experimental research can take many forms: determining which style of printing type results in greater comprehension; ascertaining to what extent flashing a subliminal message on a movie screen will increase popcorn sales (Inset 11–12); or discovering what kind of violent programming stimulus will result in aggressive behavior among young television viewers (Inset 8–10).

8.2.2 AREAS OF RESEARCH

There are many different ways to categorize mass media research. One distinction might be based on the various parts of the communication process. Using Lasswell's model, for example (Inset 1–4), communication research could be divided into five areas: *source analysis* ("**who**"), content or *message analysis* ("says **what**"), *media analysis* ("in which **channel**"), receiver or *audience analysis* ("to **whom**"), and behavioral or *effects analysis* ("with what **effect**").

Source Analysis Apparently a relatively simple question on the surface ("Who is sending out the message?"), this can become a very elusive and complex question when applied to the mass media. To what extent is the owner of a media channel the source? The publisher or station manager? The head of the syndicate or network that furnished the material? What about those more directly involved in the production of the message—the producer, writer, director, cast members, and camera operators? In the case of reality content, would not the source be the person truly making the news, affecting reality—the politician, terrorist, Nobel Prize winner, or sports figure? How is such a news message affected by the reporter or the editor?

Thousands of researchers have investigated the effects of television on young viewers.

On the other hand, shouldn't we consider as the source those persons who actually pay for the channel usage—the advertisers and sponsors? Is this not where the message is really controlled?

Robert Murphy underscores the danger of unrecognized propaganda when the true source is not readily apparent:

One of the common distinctions used to separate propaganda from other kinds of information is whether the true source of information is disclosed. It is one thing to read of the virtues of a new automobile in an advertisement signed by the company that makes it, and quite another to get the same information in a story about new cars in a newspaper or magazine.[8]

Content Analysis Analysis of the actual message can be complex, but it is a revealing indication of how the media achieve their effects. For example, are the facts in a news story presented in a straightforward, objective, unbiased manner? Or are they written in a colorful, subjective manner, with a little interpretation and opinion woven in? Is the content presented in an emotional or a rational tone? How often is a given social act (for example, cigarette smoking) depicted

dramatically in different historical periods? What terms are used to refer to certain people or events: "Black" or "Negro"? "Capitalists" or "business executives"?

Media Analysis This area of communication research is designed to determine what types of effects result from the use of different media. Channel or media analysis must also take into consideration the factors outlined in Section 1.6: the impact of the various media themselves as messages; the distinction between linear (or logical, symbolic) media and nonsequential (or analog) media thinking; differences in the physiological impact of visual and aural channels; the related concepts of low-effort and high-effort media; and possibly even the difference between McLuhan's hot and cool media.

Receiver Analysis Audience analysis has been discussed above (Section 6.2) as one of the key advertising and marketing research tools. Several important aspects of receiver analysis have been theorized but have yet to

Sociologists and media critics have long debated the impact of mass media in changing our moral standards.

be thoroughly researched. Among them are *individual differences* (What special kinds of psychological filters does each of us wear that result in selective attention and selective perception?); *social relationships* (To what extent are we influenced by opinion leaders in Lazarsfeld's "two-step" flow of information?); and *social categories* (How important are the demographic groupings so prized by commercial trend analysts?).

Effects Analysis   The crucial element that concerns us is, of course, the actual effect or result of the communication process. This is the focus of "feedback analysis" or behavioral analysis. What actually *happens* as a result of our exposure to the media? Just one of the many considerations, for example, might be the distinction between *individual effects* and *societal effects*—as reflected in the theme of this chapter.

While the overall impact of the media upon society may—in the long run—be of utmost importance, in the immediate future the most important questions for the reader pertain to the *effects of the media upon the individual— you!* How are your attitudes and behaviors affected? How are you a different person than you would be without mass communication? How is your life-style altered? How much of your time do you turn over to the mass media? How are your relations with your family and friends influenced by the media?

On the other hand, our lives and fortunes are ultimately determined by the kind of society we live in. It is therefore of critical importance that we understand the *relationships between the media and societal changes and behaviors.* How have social values changed? How have our political and governmental structures been altered? How have social institutions like the schools and the churches been affected? Are the media responsible for the spread of violence and sexual deviation?

These questions and related research findings are examined in the sections below.

One way of researching the effects of mass communication is to explore the directness of reactions. A few effects can be traced directly to one specific media event; others result from the cumulative impact of repeated content exposure; and still others are the indirect result of the existence of a medium.

Single Message Segment   Only occasionally does a single media message have a substantial impact upon society. Harriet Beecher Stowe's *Uncle Tom's Cabin* (1852) was a major catalyst in the abolitionist movement. Orson Welles' *War of the Worlds* (1938) triggered a widespread panic (Inset 4–9). One could list a few other isolated examples, but generally only a few single media messages have had such widespread impact. Effects upon individuals, of course, are much more frequent. Almost all of us can recall the impact that a single book, movie, record, or television program has had upon us.

Repeated Message Exposure   Many media effects occur as a result of repeated exposure to a series of related message segments. A series of political cartoons by Thomas Nast in *Harper's Weekly* (1870) helped to pull down the New York political kingpin William Marcy ("Boss") Tweed (Section 3.4.3). The *Amos 'n' Andy* radio series, which started in 1929, helped to create a stereotype of blacks which persisted for decades. Adolph Hitler and Franklin D. Roosevelt both used series of radio broadcasts for effective propaganda purposes. The resignation of President Nixon was the result of a continuing series of revelations during the Watergate period. Today's images of blacks, Latinos, American Indians, Arabs, women, truck drivers, and many other racial, ethnic, and social groups are largely the result of repeated media portrayals.

Concern over the extent to which television may be responsible for an increase in violence throughout society is based largely on the cumulative impact of violence depicted on the video tube. Similarly, declining moral standards can be traced, many critics feel, to the increasing openness with which sexual material is depicted on the TV set and, especially, on the movie screen.

Existence of the Medium   The most indirect and subtle effects of all—especially on the individual—may simply be the existence of a particular medium. Regardless of the content, the fact that you spend time with a given medium is the most powerful personal effect of all. The average American adult devotes close to four hours a day attending to the TV tube; this is a fantastic impact upon one's life! Millions of people center their morning activities around the newspaper. Try to imagine American teenage culture without the record player and transistor radio. The scope of this impact cannot be overlooked in any discussion of the effects of the mass media.

8.3 How Do the Media Achieve Their Effects?

Specifically, how *do* the media achieve their effects—intentionally or incidentally? Social scientists and mass communication researchers have been wrestling with this question for several decades. And from their research findings and speculations has come a body of guesses and theories which broadly indicates that most mass media effects apparently are caused by various kinds of information that the media send out—although some effects are caused simply by exposure to the media, regardless of content. Therefore, these various theories can be divided into four groupings: *receiver-initiated information, persuader-initiated information, incidental information,* and *non-content-oriented exposure.*

8.3.1 RECEIVER-INITIATED INFORMATION

To a greater extent than ordinarily realized, media effects are self-induced. You pick and choose what media experiences you will have; you select the content you want to read or view or listen to. Thus, most of your mass communication contacts are under your own control—either conscious or unconscious.

Individual Variables Personality factors certainly are one major determinant in the way you organize your media relationships. This is the key to the *individual differences* theory (Inset 6–4); your attitudes, beliefs, emotions, and values will always play a crucial role in shaping the way that a given media message will affect you. Individual variables include personality constituents such as self-image, need for security, sense of adventure, cognitive need for information, emotional disposition, aggressiveness, creativity, and other characteristics. These factors affect not only what media messages you expose yourself to (selective attention), but also how you react to those messages (selective perception).

Many media effects are caused by receiver-initiated information.

Individual receiving patterns also play an important role in determining effect. Do you read or view media on a *regular schedule?* Or do you pick and choose according to the content available? How deep is your *media intensity?* Do you concentrate on the message? Or do you use the medium for background while focusing on some other task? What type of *reward* do you expect? Are you after some immediate gratification—the instant reward typical of escapist content? Or are you after a delayed reward of the kind usually associated with reality content?

Group Relationships A second aspect of receiver-initiated effects is related to group relationships. Wilbur Schramm explains:

By group relationships, I mean the groups of persons we work with, play with, and live with, the standards and customs and opinions we share with them, and how much we value the privilege of belonging to the groups and are therefore willing to defend the group standards, customs, and opinions. Man lives in groups. These groups may be as small as a family or as large as a whole society. But much that he does he learns to do from group association and does because of some group reason. . . . Opinions are more stable if they are shared in the groups.[9]

One result of the study of group relationships is the *social relationships* theory (Inset 6–5); the "two-step" flow of communication theorizes that information passes from the media to an "opinion leader" (a respected peer leader at home, work, or play) and on to the eventual receiver.

The *social categories* theory (Inset 6–6) is another aspect of the concern with group relationships. This demographic approach points out that each of us tends to share the same media interests as others of the same gender, age, education, race, occupational group, and so forth. People who are older, better educated, and have higher incomes tend to pay more attention to newspapers while younger people are more likely to be influenced by records and movies.

Medium/Message Selection Theories   In addition to individual-oriented theories and group-relationships theories, there are other explanations that contribute to several specific "selection theories" which help to interpret how you interact with the media.

The *low effort/high reward theory,* which is outlined in Section 1.6.4, states that—other factors being balanced—media consumers will tend to use "low-effort" media. In explaining the concept of *least effort,* Schramm explains that a number of factors may tend to make one medium easier to use than another.[10]

Availability is a major concern; if information or entertainment is available in the living room, you may be tempted to use that channel rather than go out to a theater or to the library. *Expense* may be a factor; you may decide to go to the library rather than to a bookstore to get a specific volume. *Time* could be a consideration; you probably would turn to whatever channel promised to meet your particular needs as quickly as possible. *Role, habit, and custom* are other important factors; we tend to use whatever mediums we have gotten into the habit of using in the past. Another consideration we could add would be *symbol manipulation;* it requires less effort to use audio-pictorial media, which require less symbol interpretation, than to use print media, which involve more symbol sophistication.

The one factor which offsets the principle of least effort is the *promise of reward*. You will select a medium/message which requires more effort if you feel it is worth the effort—that is, if you expect to obtain a greater reward. You may decide that the effort (time, symbol manipulation) involved in doing some extra research in a theoretical journal is worthwhile if you believe that the reward (a higher grade on an academic paper) would be of value.

Uses and gratifications theory   Another approach to a selection theory comes from the body of research based upon examination of "needs" and "gratifications" met by the media (Section 11.2.1). Researchers in this area point out that individuals approach any media experience with specific needs—either consciously expressed or subjectively felt—and they *use* the media channels to fulfill those particular needs whether they know it or not.

In summing up the results of research in this area, DeFleur and Dennis state:

The study of uses and gratifications is difficult. It seeks to understand not only what people attend to but why. Usually, gratifications research tries to see media content as providing the fulfillment of needs, satisfaction of wants, or realization of wishes, in one form or another. It studies how such factors as content, type of medium, circumstances of exposure, and social context can influence the kinds of satisfactions and rewards obtained.[11]

8.3.2   PERSUADER-INITIATED INFORMATION

The above section has been concerned with what were identified in Section 1.5.3 as *receiver-oriented* functions and effects (see Inset 1–9)—entertainment and information

Some media effects are achieved by persuader-initiated information.

deliberately sought out by the communication receiver. This accounts for many of the media effects that can be ascertained. You also must be concerned, however, with *sender-oriented* functions—specifically, persuasion and propaganda.

The Hypodermic Theory Pre–World War I mass communication theory held that the mass press could affect its receivers simply by exposing them to a common stimulus. It was, in this view, like sticking a hypodermic needle of news and entertainment and propaganda directly into the veins of the awaiting public. Also labeled the "magic bullet" theory, this hypothesis stated that all members of the public thus exposed would react in a similar way; the effects would be universal and predictable. However, Schramm explains, it did not always work that simply:

The audience, when observed closely, usually refused to fall over and play dead. It even refused to play target. Sometimes the bullet bounced off,

and at other times the audience actually seemed to be trying to catch the bullet in its hands and eat it like chocolate. . . .

In other words, by the late 1950s the bullet theory was, so to speak, shot full of holes. Mass communication was not like a shooting gallery. . . . The audience was not a passive target; rather, it was extraordinarily active.[12]

"Propaganda for Social Objectives" As the hypodermic theory fell from general acceptance, it became apparent that media persuasion was a much more complicated process than previously thought. In a 1948 essay on the subject, Paul Lazarsfeld and Robert Merton provided a valuable analysis of how mass media persuasion works. Discussing "propaganda for social objectives"— that is, propaganda concerned largely with positive social goals such as improved race relations or educational reforms—they pointed out:

Research indicates that, at least, one or more of three conditions must be satisfied if this propaganda is to prove effective. These conditions may be briefly designated as (1) monopolization (2) canalization rather than change of basic values and (3) supplementary face to face contact.[13]

Monopolization This concept explains that the mass media will have their most profound effects when all media channels are promoting similar messages, when there is no effective counterpropaganda. The promotion of the sale of U.S. war bonds during World War II by the popular singer Kate Smith is often given as an example. With all radio channels open to her emotional appeals on behalf of the war effort, there was a large increase in the sale of war bonds; there was no countermessage. Similarly, Adolph Hitler monopolized all of Germany's mass media for his astounding propaganda successes.

On the other hand, careful researchers tell us that when there are conflicting persuasive messages for competing products—automobiles, political candidates, or savings banks— there is much less impact. The countermessages tend to cancel each other out.

Canalization Most advertising is concerned, nonetheless, with "canalizing" or the *channelling* of pre-existing behavioral inclinations into specific courses of action. If you are convinced that brushing your teeth is a good idea, then media advertising may canalize that belief into your buying a specific brand of toothpaste. If you are inclined to buy a new car, then media advertising may canalize that inclination into your preferring a particular make and model.

Media persuasion is less effective in instilling completely new values and attitudes or in creating substantially different behavior patterns. A racial bigot is not likely to change his or her mind because of a few "brotherhood" public-service announcements on the radio. An atheist is not going to be converted to religion simply by a televised Sunday morning sermon.

Supplementation Most media propaganda is much more successful when it is augmented by ancillary materials, follow-up meetings, and face-to-face contacts. Father Charles E. Coughlin was a notorious "radio priest" of the 1930s who made a large social impact

---

Paul Lazarsfeld and Robert Merton made a lasting contribution to the understanding of mass media effects with their 1948 chapter entitled "Mass Communication, Popular Taste and Organized Social Action." Investigating the social impact of the mass media and the social role of the machinery of the mass media, they pinpointed three areas for particular attention.

First, the authors examined some **social functions of the media,** focusing on three effects: *status conferral,* which results when the media bestow attention on "public issues, persons, organizations and social movement"; *enforcement of social norms,* which occurs as the media publicly expose conditions that are at variance with public moralities; and *narcotizing dysfunction,* which may happen when the media overwhelm the receiver with such a flood of information that it serves "to narcotize rather than to energize the average reader or listener." Each of these effects is explained further in Section 8.4.

Second, Lazarsfeld and Merton examined the effects of mass media which are caused simply by the **structure of ownership and operation of the media,** as examined in Unit II. They were particularly concerned with the underlying *enforcement of social conformism,* pointing out that due to big-business ownership the media "not only continue to affirm the *status quo* but, in the same measure, they fail to raise essential questions about the structure of society" (see Section 5.3). They also considered the impact upon popular taste, concluding that "the effective audience for the arts has become historically transformed" (see Section 11.1.3).

Finally, the authors looked at **propaganda for social objectives,** explaining the need for *monopolization, canalization,* and *supplementation.* "Thus," they concluded in their pre-television essay, "the very conditions which make for the maximum effectiveness of the mass media of communication operate toward the maintenance of the going social and cultural structure rather than toward its change."[14]

**INSET 8–5
Lazarsfeld and
Merton:
A Landmark
Essay**

---

with his anti-Semitic and pro-Nazi broadcasts (Section 11.6.2); however, much of his influence was due to his widespread organization of face-to-face discussion groups and supplemental distribution of newspapers and pamphlets. Hitler did not rely on radio alone; the Nazi party used widespread organized violence, rewards for conformity, and a highly structured network of local indoctrination centers. And hundreds of research studies have shown that the use of television for instructional purposes is much more effective when combined with classroom education and followed up by a live teacher.

Summarizing the impact of mass media for propaganda purposes, Lazarsfeld and Merton conclude:

But these three conditions [monopolization, canalization, and supplementation] are rarely satisfied conjointly in propaganda for social objectives. To the degree that monopolization of attention is rare, opposing propagandas have free play in a democracy. And, by and large, basic social issues involve more than a mere canalizing of preexistent basic attitudes; they call, rather, for substantial changes in attitude and behavior. Finally, . . . the close collaboration of mass media and locally organized centers for face to face contact has seldom been achieved by groups striving for planned social change. . . .

As a result of this threefold situation, the present role of mass media is largely confined to peripheral social concerns and the media do not exhibit the degree of social power commonly attributed to them.[15]

8.3.3 INCIDENTAL INFORMATION

In addition to the way mass media effects are achieved through receiver-initiated information and through persuader-initiated information, you also should examine the indirect or unplanned effects caused by incidental information. These effects may be the most insidious of all, because they are unplanned and hard to detect.

Numerous media effects are triggered by incidental information.

Modeling Theory Derived from the broader principle of "social learning theory," the modeling concept is an attempt to explain the acquisition of particular behavioral patterns from many types of social sources. DeFleur and Dennis define it more precisely:

In its application to mass communication, its main idea is that specific patterns of behavior portrayed by actors can serve as models for those who view them. More specifically, under certain conditions people will imitate these models and adopt their patterns of behavior.[16]

This is all part of the process of *socialization,* the procedure by which people—especially children—learn what society is, what their role is in the human family, and how they can interact effectively with other elements of society (family, friends, church, school, the workplace). The media help us to learn how to treat a younger sibling, what to do when lost, how to cope with a bully, whether to cheat on a school test, how to approach the opposite sex, how to behave on a coffee break, and myriad other examples of social maturation.

Meaning Theory Another type of important indirect influence of the media has come tobe knownas"meaning"theory.Thisholdsthat the mass media play a crucial role in helping us to make sense of the world around us, in giving *meaning* to our physical environment.

Most of us will never know firsthand what it is to pilot a jet aircraft, live in ancient Rome, get beat up in a barroom brawl, live in a slum, scuba dive in a coral reef, be a priest, own a Southern plantation, coach a baseball team, serve time in prison, or float down the Mississippi River on a raft. Yet most of us have opinions and feelings about these realities because we have experienced them vicariously through media portrayals.

Cultural Norms Theory Closely related to meaning theory is what has been termed the "cultural norms" theory. This body of research indicates that the media tend to establish the standards or norms which define acceptable behavior in society. The media present us with a *definition of the situation.*

INSET 8–6
Bandura and the Bobo-Doll Modeling Experiment

Much of the pioneering research in modeling theory has been conducted by Albert Bandura and his associates. One of his classic studies, conducted in the early 1960s, was concerned with the effect of aggressiveness modeling on children.

Bandura set up a laboratory situation in which groups of children watched either a filmed or live model performing aggressive acts against a large, inflated Bobo doll (which is weighted so that it rights itself when knocked over). One group of children witnessed the model being rewarded for this aggressive action; another group saw the model receive neither reward nor punishment; and a third group observed the model being punished for the aggressive behavior.

When left in a room full of toys—including a similar Bobo doll—children in groups one and two tended to exhibit a great deal of imitative, aggressive behavior towards the doll. Members of the third group, who had seen the model punished, were much less likely to show any violence towards the doll.[17]

This and similar experiments are often cited to show that children do follow media models; that they will pick up behavior by *observational learning;* and that when shown a violent model on television they will tend to react in a more aggressive manner. Undoubtedly, imitation and modeling do play an important role in the learning experiences of young children. However, many questions have been raised about this type of psychological research. Can such laboratory results be applied to the real-world environment? How would children differentiate in their behavior toward a doll (which was obviously designed to be knocked over and spring back up) and a human? How did peer pressures influence individual children as they reacted to the doll in front of the group? What do young children perceive the consequences of violence and aggression to be?

Several other questions are raised about research into media and violence in Section 8.4.6.

The media portrayals, in effect, tell us, "This is what everybody is doing. This is how normal people behave in our society. This is the norm for our culture." Whatever the dramatic content—hospital practices, sexual activities, racial portraits, police procedures—we accept the portrayals as reflections of reality.

A point to remember about the *cultural norms* interpretation of "meaning theory" is that dramatic content depends upon conflict, upon the unusual, upon the atypical incident and the unusual reaction. The romantic novel does not reflect the life of an ordinary housewife; few adults will ever find themselves in the circumstances depicted in an Alfred Hitchcock plot; few cowboys ever experienced the action of a typical TV western. In order to be exciting, drama must exaggerate reality—not merely mirror mundane daily existence. Thus, the "definition of the situation" must, of necessity, be exaggerated. Sexual exploits must be writ large; violence must be exceptional. Therefore, the interpretation of reality becomes distorted. And our behavioral patterns would presumably be altered accordingly.

It must be emphasized that *all* of the above explanations and theories have to be interpreted in a social context. The media do not work in a vacuum. Behavioral effects must be viewed as complex patterns which are shaped by many different media and human relationships—parents, friends, teachers, neighbors, relatives, fellow workers, and so forth.

8.3.4 NON-CONTENT-ORIENTED EXPOSURE

One major category of behavioral effects is related to *medium* usage—regardless of any specific content. For this perspective, we return to McLuhan's observation: the medium itself is the message (Section 1.6.1). For many people the mere act of attending to

Many media effects are the result of non-content-oriented exposure.

the medium *is* a behavioral effect of vast significance.

When you have nothing else to do at night, you spend the evening "watching television" (regardless of what programs are on). Often you go out on Saturday night "to the movies" (any film will do). Maybe you "read the paper" (whatever is on the front page) with breakfast. Sometimes you curl up in bed "with a good book" (whichever one it happens to be is inconsequential). You like to study "with the radio" (regardless of specific content). In every instance, it is the mere act of using the medium that forms the behavioral pattern. The specific messages are secondary. The *media* are the messages.

The media cause behavioral effects simply because they exist. Writing about television in 1957, Rolf Meyersohn said,

The entertainment that is television is not simply an accretion of entertainment programs; it is the television set and the watching experience that entertains. Viewers seem to be entertained by the glow and the flow. . . . Television succeeds "because it is there."[18]

So this, then, is the final method by which media achieve their effects. They influence behavior simply because "they are there."

8.4 What Are the Effects of Mass Media?

You now know that the causes of media effects are many and diverse. And you know that the media achieve their effects by convoluted and complex methods. But what exactly can you say about the actual effects themselves? What *are* the effects of mass communication? What is known about the behavioral effects of mass media—gleaned from thousands of research studies—can be classified probably into six broad areas.

8.4.1 MASS MEDIA OCCUPY OUR ATTENTION

The most apparent—and perhaps the most significant—behavioral effect is simply that the media consume tremendous amounts of time: watching television; reading newspapers, magazines, books; listening to the radio and records; going to the movies. Those actions are behaviors of the first magnitude! *This is how you behave in twentieth-century America: you consume the mass media.*

The average adult in the United States spends between four and five hours a day attending to the various mass media! In terms of individual effects—as opposed to social effects—there is no greater impact. Aside from going to school or earning a livelihood, the most common behavior you exhibit is attending to the media!

Passive Diversion   For many people—especially the elderly and the lonely—the presence of the media is a solid and reassuring constant in their lives, a positive and harmless source of companionship and diversion. In his study of television audiences, Gary Steiner relates perceptions such as this:

I'm an old man and all alone, and the TV brings people and music and talk into my life. Maybe without TV I would be ready to die; but this TV gives me life. It gives me what to look forward to—that tomorrow, if I live, I'll watch this and that program.[19]

On the other hand, critics point out, too many individuals settle for media experiences in place of reality. You read about politics instead of getting involved. You watch a travelogue instead of visiting a nearby park. You watch a game show instead of enrolling in an extension class. You listen to the radio instead of learning to play the guitar.

"We are becoming a nation of spectators rather than participants" is probably the most familiar complaint. Your muscles atrophy and your brain waves flatten out as you sit entranced by the printed page, the flickering screen, or the stereo speakers, passively letting others imprint their escapist fare and versions of reality upon your numbed cranium. That, at least, is how many critics would describe the media's effect on you.

Narcotizing Dysfunction   This behavioral effect is closely tied in with Lazarsfeld and Merton's description of narcotizing dysfunction (Inset 8–5)—the bombardment of the media receiver with such an overwhelming mass of social and political information that he or she is numbed into inaction:

In short, he [the reader/listener/viewer] takes his secondary contact with the world of political reality, his reading and listening and thinking, as a vicarious performance. He comes to mistake *knowing* about problems of the day for *doing* something about them. His social conscience remains spotlessly clean. He *is* concerned. He *is* informed. And he has all sorts of ideas as to what should be done. But, after he has gotten through his dinner and after he has listened to his favored radio programs and after he has read his second newspaper of the day, it is really time for bed.[20]

Related to this *political/social* narcotizing effect is a personal ennui generated by a sensory overstimulation of *escapist* content. Spending hours a day enmeshed in the dramatic tribulations of the characters in romantic novels or soap operas, the media consumer can become psychologically paralyzed—unable to cope with his or her own personal problems and responsibilities.

In both cases, the one irrefutable effect of this media exposure is that you spend a tremendous amount of time attending to the media instead of doing something else.

8.4.2 MASS MEDIA INCREASE INFORMATION SHARING

Fulfilling the first of Lasswell's three social functions, *surveillance of the environment* (Section 1.5.1), the media keep you overwhelmingly informed about what is going on in society. The United States is undoubtedly the best-informed nation on the globe—in terms of sheer quantity of information. No political system operates under closer journalistic scrutiny. You are immediately informed of the latest details of every political action, economic move, and social occurrence of any importance. And you are also informed in every area of human interest and concern—you learn about scientific developments, artistic happenings, medical advances, legal decisions, architectural accomplishments, social trends, cultural deviations, environmental deterioration, and so forth. No generation has ever had more information available at its fingertips.

Not only are the media used in formal schooling—textbooks, AV films, instructional television—but they are also an integral part of our general informal educational background. Young children today are much more sophisticated in their understanding of the world and their immediate environment. You learn readily through the media how the political system works, how to fit into the economic structure, what different ethnic groups are like, how to handle the language, how to relate to other people, what your historical heritage is, something about art and

culture, what technology is doing, and a dozen other curricular subjects. As former FCC chairman Newton Minow stated, "I would say that the most important educational institution in this country is not Harvard or Yale or the University of California, but television."[21]

The Trivial, the Misleading, and the Irrelevant   Much of the mass media information with which you are deluged is, of course, trivial and irrelevant—even misleading and distorted. We learn about the birth of quintuplets in a remote village in Peru as quickly as we learn about the shooting of the pope in Vatican City. We know as much about the fashion tastes of the First Lady as we do about the inner workings of the President's Cabinet. We spend as much time with a water-skiing squirrel as we do with water-rescue training techniques.

A more serious problem than the irrelevant and trivial items which clutter our newspaper columns and TV channels is the media's presentation of misleading and distorted pictures of reality. Every mediated picture of reality is somebody else's version of reality. Much of the distortion is unintentional, of course; it occurs quite naturally as reporters, photographers, and editors interpret reality from their own perspectives.

The net effect is that we are a very well-informed society; you have access to increasingly numerous and diverse items of information. But you also have increasing difficulty in sorting out the significant from the trivial, the reality from the distortion.

8.4.3 MASS MEDIA DETERMINE WHAT IS IMPORTANT IN SOCIETY

Virtually all communication researchers and writers seem to agree on one universal effect of the mass media: they possess the power and prestige to determine for you what is important. There are at least three distinct ways in which this is routinely done: *status conferral, agenda setting,* and *establishing materialistic goals.*

Status Conferral Lazarsfeld and Merton in 1948 were among the first to recognize and define the phenomenon of "status conferral"—the ability of the media to confer status on any person, organization, issue, or social movement simply by turning the spotlight on it:

The mass media bestow prestige and enhance the authority of individuals and groups by *legitimizing their status*. Recognition by the press or radio or magazines or newsreels testifies that one has

arrived, that one is important enough to have been singled out from the large anonymous masses, that one's behavior and opinions are significant enough to require public notice.[22]

The status-conferral phenomenon is a self-perpetuating cycle. Once an individual receives any media attention, that person becomes newsworthy; once a person is newsworthy, he or she will receive media attention. Famous people give interviews which make them more famous because they give interviews because they are famous. As the

---

There are many different ways to examine the effects of mass communication. This section attempts to group behavioral effects into six categories, which—although they are intermingled in real life, as they affect each individual media consumer—can be studied as distinct entities.

**INSET 8–7
Categories of
Media Effects**

Category	Behavioral Effects
Passive Diverson Narcotizing Dysfunction	Mass media demand a tremendous amount of time. We spend time (4–5 hours per day) passively instead of participating in life.
Information Sharing	We know much more about what is going on in the world—the important and the trivial.
Status Conferral Agenda Setting Materialistic Goals	The media tell us what is important—what we should be thinking about, what our values and standards should be.
Social Conformity	The media tend to reinforce the status quo due to their big-business orientation. The media promote social regularity, socialization, and cultural and artistic homogenization.
Modification of Social Values	Less through direct manipulation than through "definition of the situation," the media accelerate changes in our cultural norms.
Stimulation of Antisocial Behavior	Under certain conditions, the media *may* trigger antisocial behavior in some individuals—usually violent, rarely sexual.

historian Daniel Boorstin phrased it, "The celebrity is a person who is known for his well-knownness."[23]

Agenda Setting   Closely related to status conferral, the concept of "agenda setting" recognizes the fact that the public has to rely on the mass media to decide what is important—what is newsworthy, what we should be concerned with. What is it we should put on our agenda for discussion? This certainly is a manifestation of Lasswell's second social function, *"the correlation of the parts of society in responding to the environment"* (Section 1.5.1). The media may serve as a forum for public discussion, but it is also the media that decide what goes on the agenda for that public discussion. McCombs and Shaw point out:

Here may lie the most important effect of mass communication, its ability to mentally order and organize our world for us. In short, the mass media may not be successful in telling us what to think, but they are stunningly successful in telling us what to think *about*.[24]

Those things we do not know about—the items that are not placed on our agenda by the media—tend to get resolved in the back rooms by the bureaucrats and lobbyists who are directly involved (and glad to be out of the spotlight).

Materialistic Goals   The media "determine what is important in society" not only through informational programming but also, less directly, through advertising and dramatic portrayals. By these two means, the media constantly parade before us a picture of the good life. In ad after ad they show us the material goods that we should buy (new cars, modern appliances, latest fashions, sporting equipment) and in drama after drama they depict the upper-middle-class life-style that we should emulate (a plush house, travel, meals out).

For those of us who have the resources, the media thereby determine tastes and standards that influence our purchases and our perceptions of ourselves and others: what we should look like, what we should drive, what we should wear, where we should live, and how we should behave.

For those who do not have the resources— the "have-nots"—such advertising and dramatic portrayals can result in increasing frustrations. Sydney Head relates this specifically to television:

The sentimental stereotype of the hungry street urchin pressing his nose against the bakeshop window to get a glimpse of the forbidden goodies within has been replaced by a vision of the deprived and depressed multitudes of the world gazing through the window of television. They look not only hungrily, but angrily. . . . Thence the "revolution of rising expectations."[25]

No social scientist has yet been able to measure precisely the role of television in increasing the resentment of many Third World cultures or in precipitating the riots of American Blacks in the 1960s. But it has undoubtedly been a factor.

Through at least these three methods, then—status conferral, agenda setting, and establishing materialistic goals—the mass media do have the effect of helping to determine what is significant in life: who and what is important, what we should be thinking about, and what life-style we should aspire to.

8.4.4   MASS MEDIA PROMOTE SOCIAL CONFORMITY

In several different ways, the various media are continually at work—generally unintentionally—homogenizing and blending the population into one amorphous mass.

Reinforcing the Status Quo   As discussed in Section 5.3, the mass media—simply because they are big business—tend to promote the same middle-of-the-road, pro-business, pro-Establishment perspectives. In order to reap maximum profits, the media must attract large audiences either to sell their media productions directly or to sell time and space to advertisers who depend upon the large audiences to sell *their* products. Therefore, each channel has to present content that is essentially noncontroversial, bland, and unexceptionable. Stray too far to the political left or right, and one cuts down on one's potential revenues considerably.

Social Regularity The media also contribute more directly to the maintenance of conformity by what has been termed "social regularity." This refers to the inclination of the media—especially in reality content—to remind us of the rewards for social conformity and the punishments for deviant behavior. Murphy illustrates:

The media, too, provide reinforcement for socially accepted conduct. They tell us about boys and girls and impecunious old ladies, who, upon finding large sums of money, turn them over to the police for return to their rightful owners. By their accounts of arrests for selling drugs they constantly remind us of the fate of transgressors. They help us to stay sober by recounting the punishment of those arrested for drunk driving or public intoxication. . . . all in all, they promote social regularity by reminding us, day in and day out, of the rewards of regularity and the penalties for its lack.[26]

Socialization As mentioned in connection with the "modeling theory," the media do have a substantial effect—especially on young viewers and readers—as socializing agents. The media explain and dramatize for children how they should behave as they grow up. The media provide models for father roles and mother roles; they demonstrate how to behave toward the opposite sex; they show how to adjust to other races and ethnic groups. In each instance the model can be positive or negative, beneficial or destructive.

For many groups—racial minorities, the impoverished, immigrants—the picture that is painted is often a discouraging one: constant contact with criminal elements, social

rejection, political alienation, personal militancy. Therefore, it is easy for younger members of these groups to develop a self-deprecating image. They learn early what kind of role they are to assume. The media portrayal contributes to a self-fulfilling prophecy.

Cultural Homogenization Another effect of the media's tendency to promote conformity is the homogenizing of cultural and artistic tastes and standards. We all watch the same network television dramas and variety shows. We buy the same popular records and tapes, whether it is country from Nashville or punk from London. Our dramatic standards, our musical tastes, our artistic likes and dislikes all tend to blend together in one nationwide cultural melting-pot. Many critics, typified by Dwight MacDonald, decry this tendency:

Mass culture is a dynamic, revolutionary force, breaking down the old barriers of class, tradition, taste, and dissolving all cultural distinctions. It mixes and scrambles everything together, producing what might be called homogenized culture. . . . It thus destroys all values, since value judgments imply discrimination.[27]

These four related effects—big-business support of the status quo, reinforcement of social regularity, socialization, and cultural homogenization—all contribute to the same overall effects, the creation of a society whose members tend to share the same cultural experiences, hold similar economic beliefs, support middle-of-the-road politics, and aspire to the same materialistic goals.

8.4.5 MASS MEDIA FACILITATE MODIFICATION OF VALUES

At the same time that the mass media tend to homogenize and solidify our individual values and standards, they also tend to modify and alter our mass values and standards. Subtly and imperceptibly our social mores and cultural patterns are shifted beneath our feet even while we all walk the same path. We cling to a middle-of-the-road position even while the direction of the road is gradually changing.

Direct Manipulation   Little of this modification of values is due to direct and purposeful manipulation by the media. As discussed in Section 8.3, there is little successful manipulation of the mass public opinion. The conditions of monopolization, canalization, and supplementation are seldom coordinated effectively in a mass propaganda movement. When they are, intentionally or unintentionally, the results can be dramatic—Franklin Roosevelt's fireside chats, World War II bond sales, the *War of the Worlds* broadcast, media coverage of the civil rights movement, fashions and fads, the anticigarette campaign, and so forth.

Definition of the Situation   The more pervasive form of modification of our standards, values, and behavior is the indirect and subtle—and usually unintentional—shifting of our social norms. Often this occurs through "definition of the situation" depictions, in which the media present certain repeated dramatic portrayals. The repeated depictions, although exaggerated for dramatic purposes and stereotyped for easy recognition, eventually come to represent reality to the media receiver.

The media's power to define our values and standards is a phenomenon that has long been recognized. The film critic Arthur Knight writes of Hollywood in the 1920s:

Sophisticated sex had suddenly become big box office, whether in comedies or played straight. Drinking scenes abounded in pictures. . . . Divorce, seduction, the use of drugs were presented in film after film as symbols of the fashionable life. America was launched upon an era of high living, and Hollywood was pointing the way.[28]

Even before the movies, the novel had contributed to the same phenomenon: Victorian romantic novels and cheap pulp westerns had both helped to define their respective cultures. The romance of cigarette smoking in the 1930s, the patriotism of the 1940s, the rise of teenage rebellion in the 1950s, the liberalization of sexual mores in the 1960s, the environmentalist movement of the 1970s— each of these changes in fashion, values, or behavior was augmented to some extent by mass media dramatic portrayals which help to define the situation.

Media observers point to sexual standards as one area in which cultural norms are continually shaped by mass communication. In order to attract readers and viewers and moviegoers and record buyers, sexual activity is portrayed grandly, gloriously, unendingly, and—frequently—superhumanly. Sexual intimacy is depicted, for example, as the normal culmination of a first encounter: boy meets girl, girl kisses boy, boy and girl jump into bed. This is presented repeatedly as the cultural norm, the definition of the situation. If this image of the sexual standard is not counteracted by other sources (the family, the church), *monopolization* occurs, and mass media consumers adopt this (depicted) cultural standard as their own standard; their personal behavioral patterns are altered. And thus, the media representation of the social standard *does* become the actual social standard. We become what we read and see and hear because we perceive that is what we should become.

Other observers point out that it is not quite that simple. Hugh Hefner and *Playboy* did not, for example, create the sexual revolution (Section 3.4.5). Victorian standards were loosening up as part of a natural cycle, and *Playboy* just happened to be there when it could serve as a chronicler of our changing mores.

The most conservative position would be to conclude that *mass media do serve to accelerate social changes* that may be taking place anyway. The mass media cannot afford to get too far ahead of their audiences in defining new standards and values because the masses will not be able to identify with what is being defined. On the other hand, the media must be far enough ahead of their audiences to maintain interest and a sense of excitement. In this way, and in other complex ways, the mass media do have the effect of facilitating and speeding up modification of our social values and standards and behavioral patterns.

8.4.6 MASS MEDIA MAY STIMULATE ANTISOCIAL BEHAVIOR

One final category of mass media effects is the center of the loudest controversy surrounding the media. This controversy involves the charge that the media *can,* under some conditions, contribute to undesirable antisocial behavior. Few critics would claim that the media always produce negative effects; but most observers accept the statement that, *in some circumstances,* certain media stimuli *may*

trigger antisocial behavior. The two areas where most concern has been centered have been sex and violence.

Sex in the Mass Media   As discussed above, the media undoubtedly help to accelerate the definition of new sexual standards. The last quarter of a century has witnessed an amazing liberalization of our sexual behavior, and this liberalization has been aided and abetted by ample media exposure: the portrayal of nudity, the use of sexually oriented four-letter words, the depiction of cohabitation as an alternative life-style, the publicizing of extramarital sexual intimacy, the exploration of homosexual values, and so forth.

To the extent, however, that these trends are accepted by mainstream society, they cannot be considered antisocial behavior. Therefore, what we are concerned with is deviant

---

Authorized by Congress and established by President Lyndon Johnson in 1967, the Commission on Obscenity and Pornography was charged with the job of reviewing all existing research on sex and the media, conducting new research as needed, and holding public hearings on the subject. Specifically, the commission was to try to determine if explicit treatment of sex in the media results in antisocial behavior.

In a report published in 1970, the commission—with three members dissenting—recommended that federal, state, and local laws forbidding the sale of pornographic materials to consenting adults be removed from the books for four reasons:

a. There is no empirical evidence that obscene materials cause antisocial attitudes or deviant behavior, even though the material is sexually arousing.
b. Increasingly, large numbers of persons (most frequently middle-aged, middle-income, college-educated males) use pornography for entertainment and information, and these materials even appear to serve a positive function in healthy sexual relationships.
c. Public opinion studies indicate that the majority of Americans do not support legal restriction of adult uses of pornography, and legal attempts to control the distribution of obscene material have failed.
d. Obscenity laws are an infringement of Americans' constitutionally guaranteed right to freedom of speech.[29]

**INSET 8–8
Commission on Obscenity and Pornography**

behavior beyond the limits tolerated by social approval: rape, child molestation, homosexual solicitation, incest, pandering, public exposure. Over the years hundreds of historical, descriptive, and experimental research projects have been undertaken in an attempt to find a causal relationship between explicit sexual material in the media and an increase in antisocial sexual activity.

Three broad generalizations can be drawn from the results of these varied studies. First, erotic material generally succeeds in arousing sexual feelings in both males and females. In normal adults, this aroused sexual excitement frequently leads to increased sexual activity of a socially approved nature (masturbation, intercourse between consenting partners).

Second, little causal relationship has been found to link sexually explicit material with antisocial behavior. The results are generally inconclusive, although there are some indications that there *may* be a connection.

Third, regardless of the behavioral effects of sexual material (whether presented in the movies, in books, on records, in magazines, or, increasingly, on cable TV and videocassettes), arguments against erotica and pornography can be raised on *moral* grounds. For many persons, to quote DeFleur and Dennis,

The explicit portrayal of sex itself [is] seen as a moral transgression, even if it has no effect on other behaviors. It is at this point, where the ultimate resolution is decided by values, that the usefulness of scientific evidence reaches its limits. Scientific findings can show what situation *does* exist, but they cannot show what situation *should* exist.[30]

Violence in the Mass Media Whatever debate has been stirred up over the issue of sex and the media has been far overshadowed by the arguments concerning violence and the media, specifically the medium of television. The controversy is concerned with both *reality* and *escapist* content—the effects of too much news coverage of real-world violence and the results of too much fictionalized violence in dramatic programming.

Between the ages of five and fifteen a child will witness more than thirteen thousand murders on the video tube. The typical youngster will witness countless hours of other violent and aggressive acts—beatings, fist-fights, car chases, domestic quarrels, muggings, kidnappings, knifings, animated cartoon violence, actual news coverage of guerrilla wars, natural catastrophes, terrorist activities, bank robberies, and the like. The catalog is endless. What effect does all this have on the child? How does a constant parade of violence affect the impressionable adult?

Hundreds of individual research studies have been conducted in this area, with widely varying results. Jesse Steinfeld, the former surgeon general of the United States, comments on the results of the landmark study, published as *Television and Social Behavior,* that was compiled by his Scientific Advisory Committee (Inset 8–9):

These studies—and scores of similar ones—make it clear to me that the relationship between televised violence and antisocial behavior is sufficiently proved to warrant immediate remedial action. Indeed, the time has come to be blunt: We can no longer tolerate the present high level of televised violence that is put before children in American homes.[31]

In his comprehensive summary of research studies dealing with television and human behavior, George Comstock makes the point in more measured and qualified tones:

The viewing of television violence appears to increase the likelihood of subsequent aggressiveness. This conclusion derives from the pattern of results of dozens of laboratory experiments, field experiments, and surveys. It also hides many complexities. The relationship of television violence to aggression and antisocial behavior is a topic that reveals the strengths and weaknesses of social and behavioral science, and illustrates many of the problems in drawing generalizations applicable to future events from the limited circumstances of specific studies.

The evidence is that television may increase aggression by teaching viewers previously unfamiliar hostile acts, by generally encouraging in various ways the use of aggression, and by triggering aggressive behavior both imitative and different in kind from what has been viewed.[32]

These conclusions were underscored by a report prepared by the National Institute of Mental Health in 1982. The study, *Television and Behavior: Ten Years of Scientific Progress and Implications for the Eighties,* concluded that there was "overwhelming" evidence that dramatized violence on television leads to aggressive behavior by children and teenagers. Designed as a follow-up to the 1971 surgeon general's report, the investigation was a review of hundreds of laboratory and field-study research efforts.

In our brief look at the effects of media violence, we will focus on four related aspects of the problem: *modeling, catharsis,* the *"mean world" syndrome,* and *desensitization.*

Modeling and Imitative Behavior The primary theory that is offered to explain the manner in which television and other media may stimulate violent or aggressive acts is the modeling theory—the "monkey see, monkey do" analysis (see Inset 8–6).

This theory was given renewed impetus during the 1970s by several highly publicized examples of obvious TV modeling. The most famous real-life instance was probably the D. B. Cooper caper. Cooper, an airline skyjacker, apparently succeeded in his crime by parachuting from the ransomed airliner with his extorted loot. Inspired by his boldness and the extensive media coverage given to the incident, some fifteen imitators tried the same stunt in the next few months. Several fictional incidents in TV dramas shown

---

With strong prodding from Senator John Pastore, then chairman of the Senate subcommittee on communications, and with more than one million dollars in congressional funding, the surgeon general of the United States supervised the amassing of a comprehensive review of all that was known about the effects of television violence. Under the title *Television and Social Behavior,* the five-volume (plus summary) report was published in 1971. It encompassed dozens of new studies and reviewed hundreds of prior research projects.

The massive work was riddled with qualifications, limitations, and disclaimers. It repeatedly pointed out the difficulties of conducting valid research in this complex area. Findings were labeled "tentative" and "conditional." Many were "inconclusive." It is remarkable that the report came up with as firm a conclusion as it did:

Thus the two sets of findings (laboratory and survey) converge in three respects: a preliminary and tentative indication of a causal relation between viewing violence on television and aggressive behavior; an indication that any such causal relation operates only on some children (who are predisposed to be aggressive); and an indication that it operates only in *some* environmental contexts.[33]

This conclusion is all the more remarkable when one considers that five of the twelve researchers in charge of the project were directly or indirectly connected with TV networks.

**INSET 8–9
Surgeon General's
Report on
Television
Violence**

during the early 1970s also inspired gruesome real-life imitations: a stabbing similar to that portrayed in the TV movie *The Marcus-Nelson Murders,* a senseless murder-by-burning like one featured in the telecast of the film *Fuzz,* and a broom-handle rape as depicted in the TV movie *Born Innocent.*

Each of the actual crimes was apparently triggered by the antecedent TV drama. But the question that is difficult to answer is, What would the perpetrators of these crimes have done without television as a model? Would they have remained law-abiding citizens? Most of the research seems to indicate that a media event can trigger such imitative behavior only if the conditions are right and if the imitator is otherwise disposed to such an action. Head comments:

. . . [S]pecific research on the influence of violence in the media suggested that the media at most accentuate tendencies already present. A violent episode in a program might "trigger" a person already prone to violence or crime, but would not be likely to precipitate such acts by individuals not already inclined toward antisocial behavior as the results of influences other than the media.[34]

Catharsis   An opposing viewpoint is the "catharsis" hypothesis. Following the lead of Professor Seymour Feshbach, a few researchers are investigating the theory that when viewing a violent scene, the viewer releases his or her own aggressive feelings and thus is less inclined to act out any pent-up antisocial behavior. In other words, watching a little violence each day will help guarantee that you will not have to act out any aggressive behavior directly.

Comstock points out the difficulty, again, of separating one cause from another in the complex pattern of human behavior: "Television violence under certain circumstances is capable of reducing subsequent aggressiveness, but the cause appears to be inhibition following upon anxiety over aggression rather than catharsis."[35] The difficulty is in trying to unravel the intertwined threads of a person's behavioral responses to determine what specific factors were at work in causing a particular behavior.

Fear and the "Mean World" Syndrome
One of the less dramatic but potentially more meaningful effects of media violence has been called the "mean world" syndrome. People who are exposed to a large dose of violence—dramatized TV and film violence as well as newspaper and magazine accounts of real-life violence—tend to view the world as a hostile and threatening environment.

Professor George Gerbner, one of the foremost researchers of media violence, has demonstrated, for example, that heavy TV viewers are more likely to exaggerate the amount of violence in the real world, that they have greater fear of being personally assaulted, and that they are much less likely to trust other people. Gerbner also points out the danger of this situation—a frightened society would welcome increased protection even at the cost of freedom.

Fearful people want—demand—protection and will accept, if not actually welcome, oppression in the name of safety. Our research shows that heavy viewing of television cultivates a sense of risk and danger in real life. Fear invites aggression that provokes still more fear and repression. The pattern of violence on TV may thus bolster a structure of social controls even as it appears to threaten it.[36]

Desensitization   The final potential result of media violence is just the opposite of fear—a callousness or desensitization. This perspective offers the view that continual doses of media violence make us not aggressive, not fearful, but simply passive and less caring. TV viewers may become so overwhelmed with violence that they tend not to react when confronted with real violence.

This viewpoint, which is upheld by some research, is closely related to the *narcotizing dysfunction* described by Lazarsfeld and Merton. You can become so saturated with an environment of violence that you do not distinguish and react to the real thing. You

One of the problems with research in an area such as media violence is the interrelationship of a great number of variable factors. Aside from the problems of relating laboratory research to real-life situations, and the difficulty of generalizing from small experimental groups to larger numbers of normal and abnormal individuals, there are numerous factors involved simply in the definition of "violence."

For example, after hundreds of research studies, there has been little definitive work done on the importance and relationships of these following factors:

- *Human vs. nonhuman violence.* How are we affected by scenes of tornado destruction? A documentary on a slaughter house?
- *Real (actual news) vs. dramatized violence.* How were Americans affected by actual footage from the Vietnam War compared to dramatized World War II battle scenes?
- *Realistic vs. fantasy violence.* How different is the animated violence of a cartoon in its effect?
- *Live vs. recorded violence.* In the case of actual news events, what difference does it make if we are witnessing an actual live report (an "eyewitness" remote coverage from the scene of a police shootout) or a recorded version of the same event three hours later?
- *Primary vs. incidental violence.* Does it matter whether the dramatized violence is an integral part of the plot or merely an incidental attention-grabber?
- *Depicted vs. implied violence.* What difference does it make if the violence is shown in gory detail or merely described as it happened off-screen?
- *Condoned vs. condemned violence.* Even if the violence is cast in a disapproving manner, does it matter if the act goes unpunished or not?
- *Consequential vs. nonconsequential violence.* Is the audience shown the lasting and disabling results of a violent act or is the act glossed over with little depiction of the painful after-effects?

There are many important unanswered questions listed above. And there are thousands upon thousands of combinations and permutations of the above factors. For example, it may be that a very gory and realistic portrayal of a victim being stabbed may have a somewhat cathartic effect while a more sanitized version of the scene would have a completely different impact. Off-screen, implied violence which is clearly approved may have a more negative effect than on-screen violence which is clearly disapproved. A news report from the scene of a murder may leave us with more of a heightened "mean world" syndrome than a ficitonalized setting involving a bloody gangland massacre.

Clearly there needs to be considerably more research on these variables before we can pinpoint exactly what the effects of media violence are.

become less easily shocked by real violence. Head comments:

Even the apparent growth of indifference to violence—the standers-by and the passers-by who witness violent crimes without lifting a hand to help the victims—seemed attributable to the surfeit of media violence. Perhaps people had become "desensitized" because of constant exposure to meaningless, consequence-free violence in the media.[37]

SUMMARY

The mass media play an extraordinary role in our lives, dominating a great part of our daily existence. Both individual and societal effects have been extensively researched by behavioral scientists. Some observers point out the positive effects of mass communication. The media, they claim, provide inexpensive entertainment, protect First Amendment rights, help to guarantee honest government, spread art and culture, provide widespread information, facilitate participatory democracy, and raise our standard of living. Others point out the negative effects. In their view, the media encourage passivity, lower cultural values, stimulate violence and delinquency, contribute to moral deterioration, cultivate political superficiality, discourage individual creativity, lower educational standards, and further the disintegration of the family.

Research in mass communication—historical, descriptive, and experimental—can be centered on any one of five aspects of the communication process: source, message, media, audience, and results. The latter category—effects or behavioral analysis—is in many ways the most crucial and intriguing area of study.

Complex behavioral reactions are undoubtedly caused by a combination of several factors. *Receiver-initiated information* causes many different effects, depending upon individual variables, group relationships, and the interplay of various selection theories (low effort/high reward, uses and gratifications).

Persuader-initiated information (exemplified by the hypodermic theory and the monopolization/canalization/supplementation explanation) probably accounts for fewer effects than it is generally given credit for. On the other hand, *incidental information* probably results in greater behavioral effects than ordinarily realized—through the processes explained by the modeling theory and meaning (cultural norms) theory. Finally, *non-content-oriented exposure*—the mere act of attending to the media regardless of content—is perhaps the most pervasive effect of all.

We could probably group the actual behavioral effects of mass media into six categories: (1) The media occupy our attention, which may result in narcotizing dysfunction. (2) The media create a well-informed citizenry, although the important information may be hard to distinguish from the trivial and the misleading. (3) The media determine what is important for us through status conferral, agenda setting, and the establishment of materialistic goals. (4) The media contribute to social conformity by reinforcing the status quo and promoting social regularity, socialization, and cultural homogenization. (5) The media facilitate the modification of values, although they do so less by direct manipulation than by defining the cultural norms. (6) Sometimes the media stimulate antisocial behavior, occasionally of a sexual nature but more often of a violent nature.

Behavioral effects are such a complex and interrelated bundle of responses that it may never be possible to understand fully what makes different people react in various ways to media stimuli. The frustrations and complications of research in this area were summed up more than a third of a century ago by Bernard Berelson: "Some kinds of *communication* of some kinds of *issues,* brought to the attention of some kinds of *people* under some kinds of *conditions,* have some kinds of effects."[38]

While this chapter has been concerned with how the media affect or control the public, Chapter 9 turns to the ways in which the public—through government regulation—controls the media.

Notes to Chapter 8

1. Marshall McLuhan and Quentin Fiore, *The Medium Is the Massage: An Inventory of Effects* (New York: Bantam Books, 1967), p. 26.

2. William A. Henry III, "Commentary," *The Boston Globe,* reprinted in *Los Angeles Times,* "Television Times," 6 July 1980, p. 3.

3. Jerry Mander, "Television: The Evil Eye," *Medical Self-Care,* Spring 1980, pp. 30–32.

4. Lee Margulies, "MDs Ticked Off at Video for Kids," *Los Angeles Times,* "Calendar," 7 June 1979.

5. George F. Will, "The Not-So-Mighty Tube," *Newsweek,* 8 August 1977, p. 84.

6. Melvin L. DeFleur and Everette E. Dennis, *Understanding Mass Communication* (Boston: Houghton Mifflin, 1981), p. 273.

7. Bernard Berelson and Morris Janowitz, eds., *Reader in Public Opinion and Communication,* 2nd ed. (New York: Free Press, 1966), p. 379.

8. Robert D. Murphy, *Mass Communication and Human Interaction* (Boston: Houghton Mifflin, 1977), p. 345.

9. Wilbur Schramm, *Responsibility in Mass Communication* (New York: Harper & Row, 1957), p. 54.

10. See Wilbur Schramm, *Men, Messages, and Media: A Look at Human Communication* (New York: Harper & Row, 1973), pp. 105–109.

11. DeFleur and Dennis, *Understanding Mass Communication,* p. 403.

12. Schramm, *Men, Messages, and Media,* pp. 244–245.

13. Paul F. Lazarsfeld and Robert K. Merton, "Mass Communication, Popular Taste and Organized Social Action," in *The Communication of Ideas,* ed. Lyman Bryson (New York: Harper & Brothers, 1948), p. 113.

14. Ibid., pp. 101, 105, 107, 109, 118.

15. Ibid., p. 117.

16. DeFleur and Dennis, *Understanding Mass Communication,* p. 358.

17. A. Bandura and S. A. Ross, "Transmission of Aggression through Imitation of Aggressive Models," *Journal of Abnormal and Social Psychology,* 63 (1961): 575–582.

18. Rolf B. Meyersohn, "Social Research in Television," in *Mass Culture: The Popular Arts in America,* ed. Bernard Rosenberg and David M. White (Glencoe, Ill.: Free Press, 1957), p. 347.

19. Quoted in Gary A. Steiner, *The People Look at Television: A Study of Audience Attitudes* (New York: Alfred A. Knopf, 1963), p. 26.

20. Lazarsfeld and Merton, "Mass Communication," p. 106.

21. Quoted in Clifford Terry, "Vast Wasteland Revisited," *TV Guide,* 16 October 1976, p. 6.

22. Lazarsfeld and Merton, "Mass Communication," p. 101.

23. Daniel J. Boorstin, "From Hero to Celebrity: The Human Pseudo-Event," in *Inter/Media: Interpersonal Communication in a Media World,* ed. Gary Gumpert and Robert Cathcart (New York: Oxford University Press, 1979), p. 25.

24. Maxwell E. McCombs and Donald L. Shaw, "The Agenda-Setting Function of the Press," in *Enduring Issues in Mass Communication,* ed. Everette E. Dennis, Arnold H. Ismach, and Donald M. Gillmor (St. Paul: West, 1978), p. 97.

25. Sydney W. Head, *Broadcasting in America,* 2nd ed. (Boston: Houghton Mifflin, 1972), pp. 513–514.

26. Murphy, *Mass Communication and Human Interaction,* pp. 350–351.

27. Dwight MacDonald, "Theory of Mass Culture," *Diogenes* III (Summer, 1953), pp. 5, 13–14.

28. Arthur Knight, *The Liveliest Art: A Panoramic History of the Movies* (New York: New American Library, 1957), p. 111.

29. *Report of the Commission on Obscenity and Pornography* (Washington, D.C.: Government Printing Office, 1970).

30. DeFleur and Dennis, *Understanding Mass Communication,* p. 404.

31. Jesse L. Steinfeld, "TV Violence Is Harmful," in *Mass Media and Society,* 3rd ed., ed. Alan Wells (Palo Alto, Calif.: Mayfield, 1979), p. 341.

32. George Comstock, Steven Chaffee, Natan Katzman, Maxwell McCombs, and Donald Roberts, *Television and Human Behavior* (New York: Columbia University Press, 1978), p. 13.

33. The five volumes of the surgeon general's report were concerned with media content and control, social learning, adolescent aggression, patterns of use, and television's effects. The report was published by the Government Printing Office, Washington, D.C., in 1971. The quotation is from the summary volume, *Television and Growing Up,* p. 11.

34. Head, *Broadcasting in America,* p. 510.

35. Comstock et al., *Television and Human Behavior,* p. 14.

36. George Gerbner, "Scenario for Violence," in Wells, *Mass Media and Society,* p. 352.

37. Head, *Broadcasting in America,* p. 510.

38. Bernard Berelson, "Communications and Public Opinion," in *Mass Communications,* ed. Wilbur Schramm (Urbana: University of Illinois Press, 1949), p. 500.

Information is power. Those who control what information we receive, what news and knowledge we have access to, can control out thoughts and our actions. In all cultures, the struggle for control has centered around the institutions and agencies that control information—the government, the news media, schools, churches and temples, tribal councils, the home. Ever since the first American colonists waded ashore, the confrontation between the press and the government has been a classic battle.

Virtually everyone could agree that there needs to be some sort of balance between the power of the media and the authority of the government. The theme of Chapter 9 concerns the importance of finding and maintaining such a balance:

• *The vitality and success of a free society depend upon its ability to determine and nourish the delicate balance between freedom of the media and authority of the government.*

The government and the press are in continual conflict, maintaining a dynamic tension that is essential for the health of a free people. Both claim to represent the people—and they both do. Citizens lose if either side assumes unchecked control.

If the government succeeds in suppressing the press, society slips into a totalitarian state in which there is little hope of personal freedom. As Schramm reminds us,

Obviously, the basic responsibility of the mass media is to remain free. Their freedom must be defended against challenge from whatever source—whether from government, from opposing political philosophies, from business and class allegiances, from power and pressure groups, and from special-interest forces within the media themselves.[1]

On the other hand, the media cannot remain completely unchecked outside of a theoretically pure libertarian state. In today's complex and fragile society, most observers would concede the need for *some* restraints on

9

Media and the Government: Regulation and Controls

the media. The power of the press is considerable. From the fiery writings of Thomas Paine and Samuel Adams to the investigative journalism of Watergate reporters, the mass media (even when operating under considerable governmental constraints) have demonstrated the power to shatter monarchies and topple presidencies. What protection does society need against the potential abuses of an unregulated press? What about national security? Protection from unwanted obscene materials? An individual's right to privacy? A fair trial? Protection against slander and libel? Religious respect? These are all guarantees or privileges which most of us want to defend and protect, yet which could be threatened by an unregulated and irresponsible press.

Our concern, then, is to find the appropriate balance of freedom and control, to determine the optimum amount of regulation necessary to maintain the media as a healthy organ within the body of our society.

9.1 Structure of Government Controls

Much of our discussion will be focused at the federal level—at Congress, the presidential staff, Supreme Court decisions, and regulatory agencies. However, a tremendous amount of media control occurs at the state and local levels—through community censorship boards, local cable franchises, state public utilities regulations, and so forth.

9.1.1 OWNERSHIP CONTROLS AND CONTENT REGULATION

As we look at the various kinds of control that government can exercise over media channels, two primary distinctions can be made. On the one hand we have matters of *ownership and business practices*—determining who shall own and operate various media enterprises and under what conditions. On the other hand, we then have controls over *content and*

programming—determining what materials can be printed, transmitted, and otherwise distributed through established channels.

Ownership and Business Controls One of the main areas of government control has grown out of the nation's traditional distrust of monopolies—the stifling of competition—and the controlling of prices by large trusts. The Sherman Anti-Trust Act of 1890, which forbids "every contract . . . in restraint of trade or commerce among the several states," has been the basis for numerous governmental actions intended to keep the media channels from being dominated by a small handful of news and entertainment moguls. Chapter 5 traced the antitrust conflicts over many different kinds of media ownership and control—*group ownership, cross-media ownership,* and *conglomerate ownership.*

Government controls over ownership and operation are probably most evident in the telecommunications areas. Since 1934 the Federal Communication Commission (FCC) has held the ultimate authority over radio and television stations as well as telegraph, telephone, cable, and satellite operations. The rationale for this control is simply that telecommunications channels—assigned spaces in the electromagnetic spectrum—are a limited natural resource (Inset 4–4). There is only enough "air space" to allow a finite number of broadcasting stations. These few radio and television channels have always been considered "public airwaves"—they cannot be owned exclusively by a given media entrepreneur. Therefore, it is necessary for some governmental agency, at the federal level, to be responsible for determining how these public channels should be used. Enter the FCC.

At the *state and local* levels many ownership questions are settled by various boards, commissions, and other agencies. State public utility commissions, for example, control the rates and types of services of many telecommunications media. Much legislative and executive action centers at the state level. One of the most important areas of control is the awarding of local cable-TV franchises by

As an indication of local authority over media coverage, Chicago police clamp down on antiwar protesters and press representatives alike at the 1968 Democratic Convention.

One of the strongest examples of stringent media restrictions on local news coverage occurred at the 1968 Democratic convention in Chicago. Mayor Richard Daley, anticipating trouble from antiwar demonstrators, clamped down on press coverage of both the convention and the anti-Vietnam rallies in nearby parks.

In the convention itself, press representation on the floor of the arena was severely limited. Only 45 floor passes were allocated among about 1,100 reporters who were trying to cover the proceedings. Each network was limited to one mobile camera on the convention floor. The CBS reporter Mike Wallace was arrested and forcibly hustled out of the convention hall; many other reporters complained of repeated harassment by security and police forces. The president of CBS News, Richard Salant, called the Chicago controls "the most flagrant and comprehensive efforts at news manipulation that we've ever met."[2]

Outside the convention hall, at Grant Park and Lincoln Park, police clamped down even harder on press coverage of the antiwar demonstrations. News crews were kept from the scenes of clashes between the police and the demonstrators. Many newspeople were roughed up by the police; about twenty-five received substantial injuries. Mayor Daley blamed the media representatives for the confrontation: "They're in the crowd and many of them are hippies themselves in television and radio and everything else. They are a part of the movement and some of them are revolutionaries and they want these things to happen."[3]

municipal governments; this regulation of ownership and rates represents substantial authority over the burgeoning cable industry.

Programming and Content Controls

Arguments are most heated when regulation over content and programming is discussed. Here is where broadcasters, moviemakers, and print publishers alike decry any attempts to regulate news coverage and entertainment content. Here is where First Amendment considerations are debated. Here is where cries of "censorship" are hurled at the regulators. Here is where advertising controls are imposed.

The issue is debated most heatedly at the national level and centers on regulatory agencies such as the FCC and the Federal Trade Commission (FTC). However, considerable control is also wielded at the local level. City and county law enforcement agencies, for example, can exercise tremendous control over local news coverage.

Most issues of content regulation or censorship can be divided into three areas: *national security*, which includes questions of sedition, treason, and military secrecy; *morals and taste*, in which questions of obscenity, pornography, and religious blasphemy arise; and *individual rights*, which includes questions of defamation, copyright protections, privacy, free trial, equal access, honesty in advertising, and related issues. These three categories of content regulation are discussed below in Sections 9.2, 9.3, and 9.4, respectively.

9.1.2 PRINT MEDIA AND THE FREEDOM OF THE PRESS

From the earliest hieroglyphics, the writing/ printing media have been subject to severe authoritarian controls. After Gutenberg's press and the ensuing Reformation, control of printing operations was shifted from the religious authorities to the political authorities. From the fifteenth century on, English

printers were subjected to strict government controls.

Printers and publishers, spurred on by libertarian thinking and writings such as Milton's *Areopagitica* (Section 2.2.2), persisted in their efforts to print freely. In the American colonies, there soon were so many printers that the government simply could not enforce any realistic licensing restrictions. By the early 1700s, publishers had *essentially* won the "right to print," (Section 2.2.4).

The Continuing Struggle With the acquittal of John Peter Zenger in 1735 (Inset 2–2) and with the expiration of the 1798 Alien and Sedition Acts, the press had gained some ground in its battle to speak out critically. The right to criticize, however—like the right to print—is a fragile freedom.

In times of national peril or international unrest, the delicate balance of governmental authority and media freedoms is easily threatened. During the Civil War, a few Northern newspapers were silenced. (But, considering the intense antagonism exhibited by some antiwar editors, Lincoln and his generals acted with considerable restraint.) During World War I, the Espionage Act of 1917 and the Sedition Act of 1918 led to the elimination of many German-language publications and socialist newspapers and magazines. Editors espousing unpopular positions must remain ever vigilant in exercising their precious freedom to criticize.

Even the editors of mainstream news journals find themselves looking over their shoulders and choosing their words carefully during periods of political excess and domestic upheaval. Examples of such periods in our recent history include the McCarthy Era of the early 1950s (Inset 3–8); the Vietnam Era, when antiwar protestations drew government reprisals; and the Watergate debacle, when press reports of wrongdoing in high places were initially surpressed (Inset 11–6). The threat of military control of the press is a chilling possibility. As recently as 1982, retired General William Westmoreland, former commander of U.S. forces in Vietnam, stated: "The military cannot win wars

In the middle of 1971 the U.S. government succeeded, for the first time in the history of the republic, in imposing prior restraint upon the American press—temporarily at least.

Daniel Ellsberg, a foreign policy specialist working for the Rand Corporation on a study commissioned by the government, became increasingly disenchanted with America's role in the Vietnam War as he read through some seven thousand pages that had been classified as secret information. Angered at the manner in which the American people had been deceived by their leaders and entangled in Vietnam, Ellsberg "leaked" the Pentagon Papers—which chronicled the way that America had become increasingly involved in Southeast Asia—to Neil Sheehan of the *New York Times*.

The *Times* labored over both the ethical and the editorial problems of the material for three months before releasing the first of a planned ten-day series on Sunday, June 13, 1971. Within two days, the Nixon administration had obtained a temporary restraining order from a federal district court which, in effect, was the first instance of prior restraint ever invoked by the federal government. Underscoring the urgency of the situation, the Supreme Court, by a five-to-four vote, upheld the temporary prior restraint order until it could hear the full arguments in the case.

Court arguments centered on the question of national security: Did the published information (and the remainder of the planned sixty-page series) really threaten the security of the country? Ellsberg had not released any actual defense secrets to the *Times*, and the *Times* editors had deleted much sensitive material. The papers were more an embarrassment to the Kennedy, Johnson, and Nixon administrations than they were a national threat.

An eloquent summary of the real issues involved was made by District Court Judge Murray L. Gurfein before the case reached the Supreme Court:

If there be some embarrassment to the Government in security aspects as remote as the general embarrassment that flows from any security breach, we must learn to live with it. The security of the Nation is not at the ramparts alone. Security also lies in the value of our free institutions. A cantankerous press, an obstinate press, a ubiquitous press must be suffered by those in authority in order to preserve the even greater values of freedom of expression and the right of the people to know.[4]

On June 30, 1971, the Supreme Court handed down a six-to-three decision which lifted the temporary injunction and allowed the *Times* to continue publishing its historical analysis of our involvement in the Vietnam War. The Supreme Court ruling, which involved nine separate opinions from the nine justices, was certainly interpreted as a defeat for the Nixon administration. However, it was less than a complete victory for the press. The Court's decision was rendered on the narrow question of whether or not the Pentagon Papers—as they were being published—represented a threat to national security (they did not). The Court did not rule on the larger issue of freedom of the press and the question of the constitutionality of prior restraint.

The *New York Times'* publication of the "Pentagon Papers" (originally entitled "Vietnam Archive") raised a serious constitutional conflict between issues of national security and freedom of the press.

without public support and therefore should control the news media during wartime."[5]

The Right of Access to Information Of the three rights of the press discussed in Section 2.2.4, none is more precarious than the right of access to information. The press is accorded no special privileges to dig out information from court sessions, legislative bodies, or executive offices. The Pentagon Papers case was a victory for the right to print (and criticize); it was *not* a victory for the right to obtain information from the government.

The media's right of access to the courts is largely based on tradition and historical precedent. Reporters, along with other members of the public, are occasionally excluded from court sessions by the presiding judge when it is deemed that other rights may be jeopardized—the right of the defendant to a fair trial, the right of privacy for a juvenile.

Newspaper photographers and radio and TV reporters have had an especially difficult time trying to penetrate courtrooms. Recent technological developments have so reduced the need for bulky equipment or special lighting, however, that several states have begun to allow film and televised coverage of trials. The results to date seem to indicate that electronic coverage of courtroom activities hampers neither the dignity nor the justice of the proceedings.

Problems of access to information are more prevalent at the state and local levels than at the federal level. Local city councils, county boards, water districts, boards of education, and power commissions all seem to prefer to conduct their business with as little public attention as possible. However, under constant pressure from the press and public, most states have enacted versions of "open meeting" laws which require the public business (that is, the business of government) to be conducted in public.

At the national level, some degree of access was guaranteed with the 1966 Freedom of Information Act, which is primarily concerned with granting public access to public records. Aimed at the executive branch and the regulatory agencies (such as the FCC, FTC, Securities and Exchange Commission, Federal Aviation Administration, Interstate Commerce Comission, and so forth), the act requires that most public records be made more accessible.

However, Congress spelled out nine specific exemptions to the act, official reasons why public authorities could—if they wished—withhold information. These include considerations such as national security, intraagency rules and regulations, trade secrets, invasions of personal privacy, specialized financial documents, sensitive law-enforcement materials, and the like. Using these exclusions, the entrenched bureaucrat or paranoid public official can still find many ways to thwart the intention of the act. Also, Congress has periodically considered amendments which would water down the act; and the Reagan administration has repeatedly attempted to weaken provisions of the act on the grounds that this would strengthen law enforcement.

Likewise, the "Government in the Sunshine Act" (Section 2.2.4) contains a number of exemptions, roughly paralleling the exclusions of the Freedom of Information Act, which allow for needed executive sessions and special closed sessions. However, the net result of both acts is that the public and the media are being allowed to monitor more executive and regulatory meetings than before.

The evolution of these three freedoms of the press—to print, to criticize, to gain access to information—has been a continuing story of modest gains won only through repeated pressure and diligence in the face of constant threats of repressive governmental actions.

9.1.3 BROADCASTING AND THE FEDERAL COMMUNICATIONS COMMISSION

After KDKA, Pittsburgh, went on the air in 1920 and WEAF, New York City, started selling commercial air time in 1922, hundreds of enterprising radio station operators fired up their transmitters. By the mid-1920s close

to seven hundred major stations and more than a thousand smaller radio operations were clogging the airwaves. They broadcast haphazardly and illegally on whatever channels they chose and used any frequencies that were convenient, often at unauthorized transmitter power. (See Section 4.3.2.)

The consequence was the Radio Act of 1927, which created the Federal Radio Commission (FRC). Under the act, the commission would license stations in the *public interest, convenience and/or necessity* for three-year periods. Any station which did not meet this "public interest" criterion would not have its license renewed. Also, any station which blatantly violated FRC rules and regulations could have its license revoked at any time. Such decisions by the commission were not absolute but could be appealed to the U.S. Court of Appeals and finally to the Supreme Court, where ultimately most decisions regarding governmental control of broadcasting have been made.

In 1934 Congress decided to consolidate several regulatory functions which had been spread among various bodies. The media concerned were the telephone, the Atlantic cable, the telegraph, and radio. To handle all these communication-related fields, it created the Federal Communications Commission. The FRC was subsumed within the new body. The seven FCC commissioners and their 2,500-person staff today exercise regulatory control over many aspects of the telecommunications field—radio, television, cable TV, microwave, satellites, telephone, telegraph, and the like.

Up to 1981, radio and TV stations continued to be licensed for three-year periods. However, the Reagan administration intensified the trend toward deregulation, and extended license periods were adopted. TV stations are now licensed for five years, and radio stations enjoy a seven-year license term.

Ownership Controls In order to qualify as a station licensee, an applicant must meet certain basic criteria. He or she must be an American citizen, have a good character record, demonstrate adequate financial resources, and have access to sound technical expertise. Because many applicants may meet these criteria in a typical competitive license hearing, the FCC turns to its ubiquitous and unspecified criterion of "public interest" to determine who will get the license. In considering what would be in the best public interest of the community involved, the FCC has looked at such things as proposed programming policies, access to programming sources, media experience, and *ownership of other media channels.*

If a broadcast station applicant owns other media channels—whether publishing interests, cable or related telecommunications operations, or other stations—this represents a broader media background, more related experience, and additional resources (especially when it comes to gathering news). On

---

As more and more radio stations crowded the airwaves in the early 1920s, Secretary of Commerce Herbert Hoover found himself faced with a dilemma. He was charged under the Radio Act of 1912 with issuing licenses to all broadcast applicants. Following that mandate, he assigned wavelengths, hours of operation, and broadcasting power for a flood of stations in an attempt to avoid interference among the numerous transmitters. However, court decisions in 1923 and again in 1925 made it clear that he had no authority to enforce such regulations; the Radio Act of 1912 simply did not provide for any enforcement powers.

Therefore, Hoover called a series of National Radio Conferences—one a year from 1922 to 1925—to bring together government officials, radio broadcasters, and engineering advisors to wrestle with the problems of spectrum utilization. Out of these conferences a growing consensus was reached on several issues: (1) "In technical matters, broadcasting clearly needed a governmental traffic cop."[6] (2) Because the airwaves were not private property, radio stations should be licensed to serve the public interest. (3) There should be no government regulation or interference in matters of program content, advertising, or network arrangements. (The capitalistic motives of the broadcasters generally matched the free-enterprise philosophy of the Coolidge-Hoover administration.)

Finally, after several earlier attempts, Congress passed the Radio Act of 1927. This created the Federal Radio Commission (FRC), whose five appointed members were to regulate the radio industry. The FRC would have the authority to define the nature of services to be provided, allocate frequencies, classify stations according to power assigned, determine transmitter locations, and make other regulations to prevent interference. But the FRC would have no power to censor or control programming.

However, the commission would have to use some criterion in determining who should receive the station licenses. There would be numerous applicants for the limited channels available, and the FRC would have to select from among the contenders. Congress determined that this criterion would be the "public interest, convenience and/or necessity"—a deliberately vague and idealistic goal.

**INSET 9–3
The Creation of
the Federal Radio
Commission**

the other hand, it also means one less media owner—one less diverse viewpoint—in the community. The commission has issued two major rules limiting ownership patterns: the limitation on group ownership to seven stations in each broadcast category and the duopoly rule limiting ownership in a given community (Section 5.3.2).

Cable and Deregulation   However, starting in the mid-1970s, Washington has swung increasingly toward less regulation in telecommunications. Beginning with the Ford administration and continuing through the Carter and Reagan presidencies, the FCC has been talking more and more about reregulation, deregulation, or unregulation. Cable technologies have been a principal concern.

In the 1960s the FCC had decided to initiate cable regulations for two reasons. First, cable companies were not paying copyright fees for the signals that they delivered to new customers. Second, when cable systems started importing distant signals (brought in from TV stations beyond the normal coverage pattern of local stations), they threatened the concept of localism and community service.

The FCC issued several rules regarding the payment of copyright fees to program suppliers, imposed certain restrictions on the importation of distant signals, stressed the necessity of supplying "access channels" (allowing community voices access to cable channels for local input), and required two-way transmission capabilities for larger systems. The net result was that the FCC had committed itself to the concept of over-the-air broadcasting stations and was regulating cable TV in ways that stifled cable's growth.

Subsequently—in the late 1970s and early 1980s— several of these cable regulations were rescinded by the FCC or overturned by the Supreme Court. With the recent political trend calling for a reduction of federal regulation in virtually all areas (airlines, natural gas prices, and so forth), it is likely that cable and other telecommunications technologies will be further deregulated. Such deregulation will facilitate the libertarian ideal of letting the marketplace determine how much the consumer pays for what kind of services.

Programming Controls   In addition to ownership considerations, the FCC has always been involved peripherally with programming concerns. This is in spite of the specific provision (Section 326) of the Communications Act which prohibits the commission from exercising any form of censorship of programming content.

In keeping with the spirit of libertarianism, the ideals of the founding fathers of the nation, the Constitution, and the political dangers of meddling too much with the concept of freedom of speech, the Communications Act of 1934 expressly forbids the FCC from getting involved in any manner of programming censorship. Section 326 of the act is as follows (note that the term "radio" is interpreted throughout the act as referring to television and all other forms of telecommunications):

Nothing in this Act shall be understood or construed to give the Commission the power of censorship over the radio communications or signals transmitted by any radio station, and no regulation or condition shall be promulgated or fixed by the Commission which shall interfere with the right of free speech by means of radio communication.

**INSET 9–4
Censorship and
Section 326**

Nevertheless, the FCC cannot help but get involved with programming. The commission is charged with making sure that the stations are operated in the public interest, and programming is virtually the only guide that can be used to determine whether or not the public interest is being served. There have been several ways that this programming oversight has been accomplished in the past. With the current emphasis on deregulation, these traditional methods have been considerably curtailed or cut out altogether.

Before an applicant could obtain a broadcast license, he or she had to undertake a formal *"ascertainment process."* This involved a detailed system of community surveys, interviews with local leaders, and other provisions for public input—all following a prescribed FCC format. The object was to determine as reliably as possible exactly what the community concerns and problems were. Then, supposedly, these community concerns would be considered as the station's programming philosophy was formulated and carried out. By 1982 the ascertainment process was all but completely scrapped by the FCC.

Guidelines Without telling stations exactly what to program, the FCC has also become involved from time to time in issuing what have been interpreted as more or less formal *guidelines* for stations to follow. For instance, in 1946 the FCC came out with an eighty-page document entitled *Public Service Responsibility of Broadcast Licensees,* which was promptly dubbed the "Blue Book." It encouraged stations to carry sustaining (non-sponsored) programs, local live materials, programs devoted to public issues, and a "reasonable number" of offerings dealing with news, education, agriculture, religion, and other minority interests. Even though the guidelines were nonquantitative, and were offered as an essay on good programming practices rather than as a firm set of regulations, broadcasters were understandably concerned about potential infringement on their freedom of programming.

In 1960 the FCC again issued a broad document outlining programming guidelines. Its *Programming Policy Statement* reaffirmed the broadcasters' obligation to meet local community needs and then listed fourteen program elements "usually necessary to meet the public interest." These included local programs, children's material, news, weather, sports, religion, education, public affairs, agriculture, editorializing, minority interests, and entertainment. This second statement did not stir up as much anxiety as the earlier document.

Jawboning Another significant approach to programming controls is through informal negotiating or "jawboning." Although there are no provisions for such activity in the Communications Act, there are occasions when commission members simply sit down and informally discuss problems with broadcasters. The result is often an informal consensus among FCC members, network officials, station managers, and/or other involved parties about the course of action to be pursued. Even though no offical action is taken, considerable pressure can be applied in this manner.

9.1.4 CENSORSHIP OF MOVIES AND RECORDS

Most of the concern over regulation of movies and recordings has been in the area of *content*—as opposed to *ownership.* The only significant instance of government involvement in ownership questions was the 1940s "Paramount" case (Section 4.2.3), in which the Supreme Court—after more than ten years of antitrust investigations, hearings, litigation, and appeals—finally ruled that the major studios had engaged in illegal monopolistic practices and must break up their production-distribution-exhibition chains.

However, in late 1981, the Justice Department announced that it was going to review the Paramount case. The implication from the antiregulatory, pro-business Reagan administration is that major studios may be allowed to reenter the exhibition business.

Film Censorship For many decades motion pictures did not enjoy the same kinds of First Amendment protections that the press and broadcast media were gradually winning. The federal government never was directly involved in any national film censorship, but for many decades the Supreme Court upheld the rights of states and municipalities to censor films exhibited locally—a ringing endorsement of prior restraint. As

---

INSET 9–5
Family
Viewing
Time

In the early 1970s considerable public criticism was being directed at the commercial networks and individual stations for what was perceived as excessive sex and violence in TV programming. Much of this criticism followed in the wake of the surgeon general's 1971 report on television violence (Inset 8–9).

Because they could not legislate programming standards without violating Section 326, the FCC commissioners met privately with network leaders and representatives from the National Association of Broadcasters (NAB) in the fall of 1974. Shortly thereafter each network announced plans to reduce violence by voluntarily instituting some version of a "family viewing period" during which only programs suitable for viewing by the entire family would be broadcast. The NAB then incorporated the concept of Family Viewing Time into its code (see Section 10.2.1). This voluntary arrangement barred nonfamily programming from the first hour of network prime-time entertainment programming each evening (generally eight to nine o'clock) and from the hour immediately preceding the prime-time slot.

The new code provision was brought to court when the writers', directors', and actors' guilds and organizations filed a suit charging the networks, the FCC, and the NAB with abridgment of freedom of speech. And, ironically, the writers, directors, and actors were joined by citizens' groups (the National Citizens' Committee for Broadcasting and Action for Children's Television) who charged that the process of public input had been shortcircuited because of the private meetings held between the FCC and the broadcasters. It was a strange alignment, indeed, with the broadcasters and FCC (normally antagonists) lined up on one side while the public pressure groups (normally aligned with the FCC) stood behind the producers of the objectionable programming.

In 1976 the U.S. District Court ruled against the FCC and the networks. Eugene Foster sums up the reason for the decision:

The meetings between Wiley [chairman of the FCC] and industry leaders constituted a "jawboning" which resulted in a change in programming desired by government but which government could not constitutionally accomplish through regulation or legislation. In this particular instance, the pressure by the FCC had been so great that the judge ruled it an unconstitutional infringement on free speech.[7]

However, the U.S. Court of Appeals overruled the District Court, thus refusing to outlaw the jawboning process.

early as 1915, the Supreme Court, unanimously upholding an Ohio censorship law, ruled "that the exhibition of moving pictures is a business pure and simple, originated and conducted for profit, like other spectacles, not to be regarded . . . as part of the press of the country or as organs of public opinion."[8] By 1950 some ninety cities (including most of the nation's largest) and six states (Pennsylvania, Ohio, Kansas, Massachusetts, Maryland, and Virginia) had active censorship boards whose influence was felt nationwide.

Then, in 1952, the Supreme Court reversed its earlier position. Roberto Rosselini's film *The Miracle* had been banned in many areas on the grounds of sacrilege. (The plot revolved around a simple girl who believed she had been raped by St. Joseph.) Declaring that "motion pictures are a significant medium for the communication of ideas," the Court endowed the film industry with limited First Amendment protections.[9]

Local censorship now had to be justified in each instance, and First Amendment rights had to be considered. In essence, the issue of prior restraint was cast in an ambiguous perspective—neither completely condoned nor completely outlawed—which left the film industry and the courts to haggle over specific censorship questions for decades to come.

Controlling the Record Industry Of all the popular mass media, none has enjoyed more freedom from censorship than the record industry. Neither press restraints, nor censorship boards, nor spectrum limitations have hampered its freedom of expression. And only peripherally have the record companies been involved in antitrust actions.

Although the recording business is subject to the same federal obscenity laws that govern the airwaves, these regulations have seldom been employed to halt the distribution of records and tapes. Radio waves penetrate the home uninvited, and therefore government regulators feel more of an obligation to oversee what is sent out on those airwaves. Records enter the home, on the other hand,

as a result of deliberate purchases and with the specific approval of the media consumer. Therefore, there is less need to be concerned about protecting the record buyer from content that might be morally or socially objectionable. The record industry, in effect, has been allowed to change and modify its standards as America's standards of taste and language and moral behavior have evolved.

The only instances in which record censorship of some kind has been attempted have been in conjunction with the broadcasting of records. As pointed out in Section 4.3.4, a symbiotic relationship between the two popular aural media has evolved. To a large extent, records have become the content of radio. And, to that extent, the use of records can be regulated by the FCC.

One notable example occurred in 1970 when the FCC—alarmed by the increasing number of complaints received from people who objected to drug-oriented recorded music's being played on the radio—issued a statement to all radio stations reminding them that they were responsible for the lyrics of the music they played. The FCC could not order an outright ban on drug rock, but it did implicitly let the licensees know that such content could be considered when the station's performance in the "public interest" was evaluated at license-renewal time.

9.2 Censorship and National Security

As outlined above, most areas of programming regulation or censorship can be divided into three categories: national security, morals and taste, and individual rights.

9.2.1 SECURITY AND SECRECY

Most Americans champion the cause of "freedom of speech" and the "freedom of the press." On the other hand, most Americans also would agree that there certainly are some kinds of information that the government—especially the military—should be allowed to keep secret from the public (and from our potential foreign enemies). Who needs to know exactly where our nuclear submarines are deployed at this instant? Or precisely where our intercontinental ballistic missiles are targeted? Should all of the intelligence-gathering activities of the Central Intelligence Agency be made public?

Military Secrets   In most instances, you probably would accept the argument that it is in your own best interests (that is, the public interest) that such military and espionage information not be made public. But where does a country draw the line? Who is to determine what information should be kept from the public and what should be open to citizens for inspection? In the case of the H-bomb article, for example (Inset 9–7), would

the public interest have been served if the government had succeeded in keeping the material from ever being made public?

To a great extent, the press has enjoyed a large measure of freedom from governmental attempts at prior restraint because it has shown considerable self-restraint in numerous sensitive areas. The H-bomb article incident was only the second time the federal government had succeeded in obtaining a temporary restraint—and it has never managed to permanently halt any publication with prior restraint orders. On quite a few occasions, on the other hand, various news organs have

---

The comedian George Carlin recorded a comedy monologue entitled "Filthy Words" during a live nightclub performance in the early 1970s. In the satirical routine, Carlin repeatedly used "seven dirty words" that "you couldn't say on the public airwaves." However, New York radio station WBAI(FM)—owned by the liberal Pacifica Foundation and known for its controversial programming—decided to air the record during an afternoon program dealing with contemporary society and changing language patterns.

John R. Douglas, a private citizen who happened to be on the planning board of Morality in Media, was driving in his car listening to the station with his fifteen-year-old son when the program was aired. Indignant at the public airing of such language, Douglas filed a formal complaint against the station with the FCC. It was the only complaint the FCC received. But one letter is sufficient for the FCC to act upon.

The commission described the program as "patently offensive as measured by contemporary community standards for the broadcast medium" in describing "sexual or excretory activities and organs, at times of the day when there is a reasonable risk that children may be in the audience."[10] The FCC then issued a declaratory ruling asserting that it had the authority to take action against the station. However, rather than impose any immediate sanction, the commission announced that it would place the incident in the station's file for review at license-renewal time.

Ultimately, the Supreme Court ruled against the station on a five-to-four vote, upholding the right of the FCC to analyze programming after it has been broadcast in order to determine the "public interest" performance of the licensee. In effect, the court declared that although Section 326 prohibits prior censorship, it does not prohibit postbroadcast review.

**INSET 9–6
WBAI
and the
"Seven Dirty
Words"**

Early in 1979, a free-lance writer named Howard Morland prepared a detailed story, ostensibly using only publicly available information, which described how a hydrogen bomb is constructed. Morland's declared purpose in writing the article was to give the public enough information to make intelligent decisions about military policies.

The article was prepared for the *Progressive* magazine, a liberal journal published in Madison, Wisconsin. Prior to publication, the editor of the magazine forwarded a copy of the article to the government to verify its accuracy. The Justice Department responded by obtaining a temporary restraining order against publication; this was followed by a preliminary injunction.

The article was held up in the courts for months while the magazine's lawyers contended that all of the material was, indeed, in the public domain. The magazine also argued strongly for its First Amendment guarantees against prior restraint.

Government attorneys arguing for a permanent injunction pointed out that this incident was much more serious than the Pentagon Papers, the only other case where the federal government had obtained (if only for a few days) a court order authorizing prior restraint. The Pentagon Papers had merely been historically embarrassing; the H-bomb article contained real information that could prove genuinely harmful to the national security.

The whole question was rendered moot in late 1979 when Charles Hansen, a computer programmer and amateur bomb hobbyist, drew up an eighteen-page letter which substantially revealed the construction details of an H-bomb. Hansen sent his letter to Senator Charles Percy to support the *Progressive's* claim that the basic design of the bomb could be obtained from public sources. Simultaneously, Hansen sent his letter to several independent newspapers. The Justice Department managed to get a preliminary injunction in time to stop the *Daily Californian* from printing the letter, but another small paper, the *Madison* (Wisconsin) *Press Connection*, printed Hansen's H-bomb details before the government could stop it. At that point—with the information already in print—the Justice Department dropped its injunction against the *Progressive* and the original Morland article.

The issue was therefore pragmatically, if unsatisfactorily, resolved without any final legal decision from the Supreme Court. Two essential questions remain unanswered. Were the *Progressive's* First Amendment rights violated by the five-month injunction? Did not the *Progressive* show a breach of journalistic professionalism and self-restraint by publishing material which potentially could have endangered the nation's military security?

voluntarily withheld the publication of sensitive material because such publication would have posed a potential threat to national security (see Section 10.2).

During wartime, especially, the military is greatly concerned with the issue of national secrets. And the press has generally behaved responsibly. Nevertheless, the question remains: Would the exceptional conditions of wartime ever justify exceptionally repressive measures against the media? The Supreme Court has never ruled definitively on that question.

9.2.2 FIRST AMENDMENT CONFLICTS

Virtually every great legal battle comes down to opposing rights: your right to host a loud party versus your neighbor's right to peace and quiet; your right to breathe clean air versus your friend's right to enjoy an occasional cigar. Thus, First Amendment considerations come down to the citizen's right to communicate a message to the American people versus the government's (or another citizen's) right to suppress that message. This debate has continued throughout our constitutional history.

There has never been a majority of justices sitting on the Supreme Court who would hold that freedom of the press is absolute, that the First Amendment freedoms should be considered so sacrosanct that they could never be suspended. Chief Justice Fred Vinson, in a 1950 opinion dealing with political strikes, reminded the nation that First Amendment freedoms are themselves "dependent upon the power of constitutional government to survive."[11] If the government should fall (whether or not due in part to the unabridged exercise of freedoms guaranteed under the Constitution), then all constitutionally granted rights would disappear anyway. Therefore, all governments can be expected to act first to guarantee their own survival by suspending whatever rights might be necessary in the name of national security and survival of the political order. But how do you determine when to suspend individual rights for the greater public good? Where do you draw the line?

"A Clear and Present Danger"   Every nation, including the United States, must have laws protecting the country from treason and subversion. Some, such as the 1798 Alien and Sedition Acts (Section 2.1.3), are much more restrictive than others. The Alien and Registration Act of 1940 (commonly known as the Smith Act), for instance, states that it is "unlawful for any person . . . to knowingly . . . advocate . . . or teach . . . the desirability . . . of overthrowing . . . any government in the United States by force or violence." This would appear to be a reasonable and prudent safeguard. The difficulty arises, however, in trying to determine the rights of dissenters.

In a 1919 decision, Supreme Court Justice Oliver Wendell Holmes originated a phrase that has long provided one informal guideline for interpreting such possibly treasonable utterances against the government:

The question in every case is whether the words used are used in such circumstances and are of such a nature as to create a clear and present danger that they will bring about the substantive evils that Congress has a right to prevent. It is a question of proximity and degree.[12]

The implication of this "clear and present danger" criterion is that if there is time for rational discussion and debate, there is no need to restrict First Amendment rights. The freedoms of speech, press, and assembly should be revoked only when danger is imminent and there is no time to turn to reasonable discourse.

9.2.3 EXTENSION OF EXECUTIVE AUTHORITY

There are numerous ways that the executive office of the president can apply various forms of pressure on the media in an attempt to control unfavorable news and press coverage.

Abuse of the "National Security" Label

One of the most common tactics of politicians in power is to use the "national security" label in order to prevent material from reaching the public. The more a bureaucrat or an elected official can withhold from public scrutiny, the more secure and comfortable his or her job is.

Many governmental officials at all levels have the authority to classify material—to label it "secret" or "top secret" and thus conceal it from public view and media scrutiny. In truth, much of this is done simply as a matter of convenience (to avoid taking the time to explain it to the public) or as outright political manipulation (to cover up embarrassing materials like the Pentagon Papers). Much of what is stamped "secret" should more honestly be marked simply "censored." The political scientist Bernard Rubin sums up the abuse of the label:

That one phrase, *national security*, has been used so often to conceal official plans, policies, and actions that we no longer know its meaning. With so much evidence of inanity and corruption heavily censored before the public was informed by the press, no citizen can be certain that national security is in his best interest.[13]

Pressure from the White House

The office of the President of the United States, one of the most public positions in the world, has an array of antipress tactics to be used when political fortunes dictate. And the presidency of Richard M. Nixon offers one of the most incisive studies of modern press-President relationships.

From the early years of the ill-fated Nixon administration, it was evident that the government was pursuing a deliberate program of intimidation of the press. Less than a year after the inauguration, Vice-President Spiro T. Agnew launched a campaign to discredit the media. He was generally perceived to be the chief antimedia spokesman for "an administration which considered itself surrounded by enemies."[14] He continued his antipress tirades for four years—almost until the day he resigned in disgrace.

Agnew was not alone in attacking the media from a perch in the White House. Nixon also created the Office of Telecommunications Policy (OTP), an amalgamation of several lesser offices and advisory bodies, which became the major White House agency in the attack on the media. OTP staffers lobbied Congress, "advised" the FCC on policy matters, and brought direct pressure to bear on networks. They were especially effective in attacking the Corporation for Public Broadcasting (CPB) and the entire public television structure, which had displeased Nixon because of its Eastern "elitist" and "liberal" programming bias. Exercising his ultimate control over the CPB, Nixon vetoed its funds for the 1972–73 fiscal year.

Nixon's final presidential confrontation with the media was the two-year Watergate cover-up and the ensuing theater of the absurd (Inset 11–6). Much of the suspense and conflict centered around the endless hours of confidential audio tapes that Nixon had recorded in the Oval Office. Consistently declaring his rights of "executive privilege" and invoking "national security," Nixon refused to release the tapes until ordered to do so by a unanimous ruling of the Supreme Court. His resignation followed in two weeks.

Informal Regulation

There are many other ways that the executive branch of the federal government can exercise informal controls over the various media. Direct congressional lobbying and pressure on regulatory agencies are but two of the more obvious methods. The way in which the presidential press secretary conducts business is a key factor. Certain newspeople find that they will have more access to the White House if their coverage is compatible with the administration's views. "News leaks" manage to fall into a few favored channels. The manner in which a press conference is structured can have a major impact on the control of news.

9.2.4 PROTECTION OF SOURCES

One other consideration in news gathering and reporting is also related to national security and law enforcement in general. This is the protection and anonymity that reporters can offer to their confidential sources and tipsters. Much investigative journalism relies heavily upon anonymous tips and news breaks from undisclosed sources, either within government agencies or within underworld circles. Such sources obviously have to have assurances from the reporters that their identities will not be disclosed; otherwise they might lose their livelihoods of even their lives.

In order to assist reporters in protecting such sources, some twenty states have passed "shield laws" designed to guarantee reporters the right to remain silent when questioned about their sources. However, many of these shield laws have not held up in the courts, and many reporters have been found in contempt of court, fined, and even jailed. Two of the most celebrated cases in the 1970s involved William Farr of the *Los Angeles Times*, who refused to reveal his source for inside information concerning the Charles Manson murder trial, and Myron Farber of the *New York Times*, who refused to turn over confidential notes made in his investigation of the murder charges against Dr. Mario Jascalevich. Both Farr and Farber spent weeks in jail as the price of protecting their sources.

In 1972 the Supreme Court heard appeals in three separate cases involving a reporter's attempt to shield anonymous sources of information. The Court heard the three cases as one (*Branzburg* v. *Hayes*) and handed down a mixed decision which failed to protect news sources but did not completely strike down some form of First Amendment protection.

Paul Branzburg, a reporter for the *Louisville Courier-Journal*, had used inside sources in investigating the availability and use of illegal drugs in Kentucky. Earl Caldwell, a black reporter for the *New York Times*, had won the confidence of leaders of the Black Panther Party and had covered their activities for the *Times*. Paul Pappas, a television reporter-photographer for WTEV in New Bedford, Massachusetts, had been allowed inside a local Black Panther headquarters in anticipation of a police raid which he was going to cover. (No raid took place, and Pappas filmed no story.) All three newsmen had been subpoenaed by federal grand juries or other investigative bodies and ordered to divulge sources of information and notes and tape recordings of interviews. All three refused and appealed their way to the Supreme Court.

The Court ruled five-to-four against the three reporters, arguing that news reporters could not be excused from the normal citizen's duty to cooperate with grand jury investigations. The press could not be granted special First Amendment privileges which did not apply to the rest of the public.

The Court did provide some hope of relief, however. It stated that under some conditions (which did not apply in these cases), news gathering could be protected by First Amendment interpretations; and it paved the way for limited shield laws both at the state and federal levels.

**INSET 9–8
Branzburg,
Caldwell,
and Pappas**

The fact that law enforcement agencies and the courts can legally force reporters to divulge their confidential sources is a form of indirect regulation in that it tends to "dry up" substantial avenues of news gathering. Following the *Branzburg* decision, many states passed new shield laws or reinforced older ones. And two years after the *Stanford Daily* case (Section 11.3.4), Congress passed the Privacy Protection Act, which prohibited police agencies from searching newsrooms for unpublished notes or visual materials except under carefully limited conditions. However, the fact remains that reporters and their sources can never be completely sure of the amount of protection they have.

9.3   Morality and Public Taste

The second large category of content/programming regulation concerns material that is offensive to significant segments of the audience—profanity, nudity, blatant sexual material, attacks on religion, excessive violence, and so forth. Although few people will ever be able to agree on exactly what they mean by "obscene," these vaguely defined sins are all connected with standards of morality. And, insofar as we all have individual standards and definitions of what is right and wrong, guardians of society will always be debating what should and should not be printed and shown and projected for the rest of society to be exposed to.

9.3.1   BLASPHEMY AND HERESY

Concern with censorship in these areas started with the church. Through the Middle Ages, the pope exercised virtual totalitarian authority over the channels of communication. Any voice raised against God was *blasphemy*. And any voice raised against the church—in criticism, challenge, irreverence, or sarcasm—was deemed *heresy*, with punishment ranging from excommunication to

burning at the stake. In effect, blasphemy and heresy are to the church what sedition is to the government.

Even after the Reformation and separation of church and state, many religious taboos were written into the laws of the land—in the New World as well as the Old. Religion, including religious dissent, was to be encouraged; but attacks on religion and disrespect for the church were not to be tolerated. There are still blasphemy laws and "blue laws" on the books of many states. These holdovers from puritanical New England prohibitions outlaw profanity (taking the Lord's name in vain), dancing, the use of contraceptives, drinking and/or working on Sundays, and similar activities. Today, however, most of our concerns about the regulation of public morality are centered on secular obscenity laws.

9.3.2   OBSCENITY AND PUBLIC MORALITY

Most adults would probably tend to accept minimal regulation which would prevent persons from unwanted exposure to obscene and pornographic materials. The problem is in determining where to draw the line. How are you to decide when your right to enjoy "adult humor" over the radio or your right to peruse the ads for adult theaters conflicts with your aunt's right not to be exposed to such materials? When does a person's freedom of speech (including the right to utter profanities in a restaurant) interfere with your right to enjoy your chocolate mousse in peace and reverence?

The Supreme Court and Obscenity Decisions   The highest court in the land has repeatedly held that obscenity which has no purpose beyond being obscene is not protected by the First Amendment. In order to qualify for protection, material must have serious literary, political, or social value. (This viewpoint is not unlike the 1915 decision of the Supreme Court, discussed in Section 9.1.4, which held that motion pictures could not enjoy First Amendment protection because they were articles of commerce, not

The inability of courts to define and outlaw "obscenity" has given rise to profitable adult theaters and "porno" districts in most major cities across the nation.

We do not accede to appellee's suggestion that the constitutional protection for a free press applies only to the exposition of ideas. The line between the informing and the entertaining is too elusive for the protection of the basic right. Everyone is familiar with instances of propaganda through fiction. What is one man's amusement, teaches another man's doctrine.[16]

This paved the way for the *Miracle* decision, which extended First Amendment rights to the movies four years later (Section 9.1.4).

In 1957, in the landmark case of *Roth* v. *United States,* the Supreme Court issued its most definitive ruling to that point. While upholding the validity of federal and state obscenity laws, the Court issued the following guideline in an attempt to define or determine obscenity:

Whether to the average person, applying contemporary community standards, the dominant theme of the material taken as a whole appeals to prurient interest.[17]

Incorporating the "dominant effect" theme of the *Ulysses* decision, this criterion, worded by Justice William Brennan, also stressed the concepts of contemporary standards and community values.

Throughout the 1960s the Supreme Court found itself resolving an increasing number of obscenity cases, trying to define and judge numerous specific instances of profanity, nudity, sexual activity, and amoral themes. As it became more and more engulfed in hairsplitting distinctions, the Court tended to interpret its own guidelines with increasing liberality. Just about any story or film with a plot or a few moralistic utterances was determined to have "redeeming social value" and therefore could not be censored.

Much of the confusion lay in the attempt to define exactly what is meant by "obscenity." Applying the *Roth* guideline of "prurient interest" limits the obscene to those materials which are clearly designed to arouse lascivious or lustful thoughts or behavior. Such a definition excludes consideration of material that

speech.) The main problem that the Supreme Court has had to wrestle with over the decades, then, is how to define obscenity so as to exclude it from constitutional protection.

A British judge in 1868 first set down the "Hicklin rule," which asked "whether the tendency of the matter charged as obscene is to deprave and corrupt those whose minds are open to such immoral influences and into whose hands a publication of this sort might fall."[15] This definition stood in American courts until 1934, when an appeals court overruled the banning of James Joyce's *Ulysses.* The banning was improper, said the court, because the "dominant effect" of the entire work had not been taken into consideration. A work could not be declared obscene just because of a few lustful or profane passages. Literary and social values also had to be considered.

The Supreme Court took a major step in extending First Amendment protection to entertainment content (although not to obscenities) in 1948 with the *Winters* decision:

is violent or grotesque—regardless of how repulsive or lacking in redeeming social value it may be. The narrow definition also excludes the use of vulgar language *per se*. The use of sexual or scatalogical terms in expressing social or political convictions is protected. In 1971 the Supreme Court ruled, for example, that the phrase "Fuck the draft" lettered on a person's clothing was a political statement, not a sexual obscenity, and therefore was protected under the First Amendment.[18]

With the conservative *Miller* ruling of 1973, the Supreme Court accomplished several objectives. First, it placed obscenity cases under the jurisdiction of the state and local governments, not only ridding the high court of a burdensome case load but establishing the principle that it really must be the local community which decides what it wants and does not want. Second, the decision was intended to make criminal convictions simpler to obtain. Finally, it tried to set down

the most precise guidelines yet in defining obscenity. However, this proves to be such an individual judgment, such a fluctuating matter of taste, that an explicit definition still remains one of the judiciary's most elusive goals.

The FCC and Obscenity Actions   In the broadcasting arena the FCC has always walked a thin line, trying to hand out station licenses on the basis of programming that is in the "public interest, convenience and necessity" without violating Section 326's prohibition against censorship.

The FCC is also hampered by the fact that it has no direct regulatory powers over the networks themselves; only the stations have licenses. Therefore, when a network engages in a questionable programming practice, the FCC responds by warning stations that are affiliated with that network. For example, in

---

In the sixteen years following the *Roth* decision, the Supreme Court found itself involved in hundreds of obscenity cases. These often involved making minor decisions and trivial distinctions that the Court felt could be better made at the local level. The Court also had developed a pattern of making more and more liberal decisions under Chief Justice Earl Warren during the 1960s.

By the early 1970s, the Court contained four of President Nixon's appointees, and its political tone had been reversed. The Court, now under Chief Justice Warren Burger, took a decidedly conservative approach. In 1973 three obscenity cases came before the Court: *Miller* v. *California, Paris Adult Theater* v. *Slaton,* and *Kaplan* v. *California.* Treating them as one issue, the justices handed down a five-to-four ruling which became known as the *Miller* Decision.

Writing for the conservative majority, Burger set down these guidelines, which are a more restrictive return to the *Roth* criteria:

The basic guidelines for the trier of fact must be: (a) whether "the average person, applying contemporary community standards" would find that the work, taken as a whole, appeals to the prurient interest, (b) whether the work depicts or describes, in a patently offensive way, sexual conduct specifically defined by the applicable state law, and (c) whether the work, taken as a whole, lacks serious literary, artistic, political, or scientific value.[19]

**INSET 9–9
The *Miller*
Decision**

1937 Mae West took part in a sketch about Adam and Eve on the *Edgar Bergen/Charlie McCarthy Show*. During the live broadcast she improvised quite a few "oohs" and grunts and sexy innuendos that had not been in the script or in the rehearsal. Thousands of indignant letters flowed to the stations, the network, and the FCC, and some even found their way into the *Congressional Record*. In response, the FCC sent a letter to each of the NBC affiliates reminding them that they were responsible for whatever they broadcast (whether or not they could control unanticipated live material from the network) and that their programming would be reviewed at license-renewal time.

The commission has had to deal with explicit profanities and obscene programming at times, of course. In 1962, a full decade before the "Seven Dirty Words" case (Inset 9–6), the FCC took action against a South Carolina station for obscene programming. Charlie Walker was a popular if somewhat off-color disc jockey for WDKD in Kingstree. When warned by the FCC that Walker's suggestive material was not in the public interest, the station management responded by pointing out that Walker was not actually guilty of violating the federal obscenity act. Besides, they argued, he was extremely popular and therefore was not defying community standards. However, the FCC took a dim view of such reasoning and failed to renew the station's license at the end of its three-year license period.

9.4 Protection of Individual Rights

This final category of content control is concerned with the protection of a variety of individual rights that have been recognized in connection with mass communication.

9.4.1 DEFAMATION: PROTECTING THE REPUTATION

This is a classic example of the confrontation of opposing rights: the right of the press to print/broadcast without censorship versus the right of the individual not to have his or her

reputation unfairly damaged. *Defamation* is usually defined as any communication or expression which exposes an individual to contempt, ridicule, or hatred, or which causes the individual to be shunned or avoided, or which injures the individual in his or her business. *Slander* is spoken defamation, any oral remark that is not written down. *Libel*, usually considered the more serious civil offense, is any defamatory statement that is reproduced in print.

Defenses against Defamation   Because it would be virtually impossible to report anything about an accused criminal, a dishonest politician, or an untalented performer without damaging the reputation of the individuals involved, some sort of antidefamation protection is needed for the media. Three traditional defenses have guarded the press against unwarranted libel and slander suits, and a fourth defense appears to be evolving.

Truth   Ever since the trial of John Peter Zenger (Inset 2–2), truth has generally—in most states—been accepted as an adequate defense against libel suits. A truthful statement may still, technically, be a defamation; but as long as the reporter can prove that a story was true and accurate in all its essential aspects, he or she is fairly well protected against any libel action.

Qualified Privilege   In order for government to function, many officeholders are granted protection from libel suits. This protection is known as *qualified privilege*. A public prosecutor could not accuse an arrested person of a crime in the courtroom without such protection. Legislators would be severely limited in what they could say during debates. What is privileged—that is, exempt from defamation charges—can vary from state to state, and the distinctions sometimes

Senators Howard Baker, Lowell Weicker, and Sam Ervin (right) confer with committee counsels during the Watergate hearings. Like all legislators, they enjoy "qualified privilege" which protects them from defamation suits.

can get quite involved. "A police arrest record, a trial, and a Senate speech are all privileged, but an unofficial interview with the police chief, the judge, or the senator is not."[20]

The courts have extended this privilege to members of the media in reporting such privileged matter. If the police arrest record, the proceedings of the courtroom, and the debate on the Senate floor could not be reported accurately in the press, then such government activities would be, for all practical purposes, carried on in private. Therefore, the media have been given the right to report drunken driving arrests, prosecutors' accusations, and bombast from the Senate chambers.

Fair Comment   No book reviewer or film critic could give an honest opinion in print if not protected against libel suits. Therefore, courts have ruled that criticism of public persons, institutions, and works offered for public approval are protected if the opinions are based on fact and are not delivered with malice. That is, a film reviewer can state that a new film directed by so-and-so is a rotten film; but if the reviewer says that the director was drunk on the set half the time (an allegation of fact) or if the reviewer never even bothered to see the movie (an indication of malice), then the reviewer may be sued for libel.

Lack of Malice or Recklessness   A final defense against libel charges revolves around the intent and manner in which a published item is presented. If there is an absence of malice or recklessness in the statement made, the item will probably be protected. Some court decisions have given the press additional protection by stating that a defamed *public official* has to prove "actual malice" on the part of the media channel distributing a story. Subsequent decisions, however, have tended to give more protection to the private individual than to the press. And the Supreme Court has seemed inclined to throw much of the responsibility for libel decisions back to the state level.

9.4.2 COPYRIGHT: PROTECTING THE WRITER/ARTIST/PERFORMER

If you wrote a song and performed it for some of your friends and then found out a couple of years later that a local recording group had included your song (without your permission) on a new album, how would you feel? Cheated. This is what the copyright concept is all about: making sure that the writer/author/composer/publisher/performer/artist—anyone involved as a "creator" of any work—gets his or her fair share of the income from the sale of that work. If artists and songwriters and novelists were not adequately compensated and given credit whenever their work was reproduced, then there would be virtually no incentive or reward for creative or scholarly pursuits.

The General Revision of 1976   When the Copyright Act of 1909 was enacted, of course, Congress had no precognition of the effects of broadcasting, the record industry, photocopying, cable TV, satellites, or computers, and the act was therefore hopelessly antiquated by the mid-twentith century. After years of haggling, Congress passed the Act for the General Revision of the Copyright Law, which went into effect on January 1, 1978. The new act protects the copyright of any creative work for the lifetime of the author/creator plus fifty years. The law sets forth seven categories of protected works: literary works; music (including lyrics); dramatic works (including accompanying music); dance and pantomimes; photographs, paintings, and sculpture; film, video, and other audiovisual works; and sound recordings.

The Doctrine of "Fair Use"   Such a law is necessary to protect the rights of the individual creator, but it presents formidable obstacles to the publisher or broadcaster who may want to use a picture, a quotation, a musical theme, a character, or any other creation from someone else's work. Over the years the courts have established the doctrine of *"fair use"* which enables publishers and broadcasters to make limited use of copyrighted works if certain criteria are met. In the 1976 revision, an attempt was made to codify this judicial doctrine by spelling out four criteria which would be considered in the determination of a "fair use" of any work: the purpose and character of the use (including consideration for nonprofit uses); the nature of the copyrighted work; the amount of the work reproduced; and the effect of the use upon the potential market for the work. This "fair use" provision is intended to strike a balance between the right of the individual copyright holder to legitimate compensation for his or her work and the right of the publisher/broadcaster to freedom of the press.

9.4.3 FAIR TRIAL AND THE RIGHT OF PRIVACY

Another classic case of conflicting rights involves the public's right to know versus the individual's right to conceal, the freedom of the press to probe versus your right to protect your privacy. Supreme Court Justice Louis Brandeis once called the right of privacy "the most comprehensive of rights and the right most valued by civilized men."[21] But there obviously are situations in which this valued right of privacy becomes sacrificed upon the altar of mass communication. The problem lies in defining the point at which information about a person's private affairs becomes a legitimate matter of public interest.

There are three types of situations in which an individual's private actions have traditionally been regarded as valid areas of public concern. One is *when someone's private actions have a potential impact upon the rest of the community*. A man's drinking habits may be his personal affair; but if he is arrested for driving while intoxicated, then his actions become a matter for public concern. A rich neighbor may indulge his personal eccentricities in private; but if his estate becomes the center of a religious cult, it may be a legitimate item of community interest.

An obvious situation in which an individual's right of privacy has been sacrificed occurs *when an act is conducted in public*. Any act in a public place is, by its nature, a public act. If a business executive is having an affair with his or her secretary and they go to a baseball game where the TV camera picks up a shot of them in the crowd, they cannot claim invasion of privacy.

A third situation in which private affairs can be considered public occurs *when the individual involved has attained sufficient prominence to be considered a public figure*. Once a person pushes himself or herself into the public spotlight, he or she implicitly surrenders the right to be left alone. Entertainers, politicians, sports figures, and the wealthy have all, to some extent, asked for public recognition or acclaim—and they must live with it. Senator Wilbur Mills could expect to make headlines when his car was stopped late at night and he was found in an intoxicated condition with a local stripper (1974). Senator Thomas Eagleton could expect to have his psychiatric record mentioned when he was nominated for the vice-presidency (1972). When tennis stars Billie Jean King and Martina Navratilova revealed their past lesbian experiences, they could expect public reaction (1981).

The Right to a Fair Trial　A specialized aspect of the right to privacy concerns the right of an accused person to a trial without undue publicity or distortion. The Sixth Amendment of the Constitution does not explicitly guarantee a "fair" trial; what it states is that "the accused shall enjoy the right to a speedy and public trial, by an impartial jury. . . ." The traditional interpretation of the amendment is that the right to a *public*

The line between legitimate media coverage of a public personage and unwarranted intrusion often has to be defined by the courts. A single-minded and aggressive free-lance photographer named Ronald Galella had earned his living for years through his unrelenting pursuit of the widow of President Kennedy, Jacqueline Onassis, and her children, photographically recording their every public and semipublic move. Court records indicate that he followed Ms. Onassis mercilessly everywhere she went—to church, funeral services, the theater, schools, restaurants, on board yachts. He forced his way into revolving doors with her. He pursued her in a power boat while she was swimming.

Ironically, Galella sued Ms. Onassis because she and the secret service agents assigned to her tried to prevent him from earning his living—for example, she donned sunglasses every time she spotted him, thereby making his pictures less salable.

She, in turn, countersued for damages and asked the court to enjoin Galella from harassing her and the children. In ruling in her favor, the federal district court established firm restrictions on the type of contact the photographer could make with Ms. Onassis and her family. For example, he could not come within 150 feet of Ms. Onassis or within 225 feet of her children. Both the district court and the appeals court concurred that the First Amendment could not be used as a shield to justify such aggressive behavior on his part.[22]

**INSET 9–10
Jacqueline Kennedy Onassis and Intrusion**

As part of the price for becoming a public figure, special Watergate prosecutor Leon Jaworski had to sacrifice personal privacy and take his turn in the media spotlight.

trial is granted in order to guarantee *fairness*.

In practice, however, the concern has often been that too much pre-trial publicity, too much public access to the courtroom, and/or too much media coverage of the proceedings might impair the fairness of the verdict. In 1954, for example, Dr. Sam Sheppard was found guilty in the brutal murder of his wife. The pre-trial publicity had generated so much nationwide attention that the trial itself was turned into a media circus. Media representatives filled almost the entire courtroom; photographers constantly hounded everyone connected with the proceedings. In 1966 the Supreme Court ruled that the trial was conducted in such a bizarre environment that Sheppard must receive a new trial. This time he was acquitted—after spending more than ten years in prison. Clearly, the cause of justice was not served by admitting the press to the trial.

Among the results of the Sheppard case was a series of judicial decisions and actions that were designed to prevent unfair trials— at the expense of freedom of the press. Courts have ruled, for example, that certain kinds of material which are not admissable as evidence should not be released by the media prior to a trial: the criminal record of the accused, nonvoluntary confessions made prior

to the trial, and results of any unlawful search. Pre-trial release of such prejudicial material would make selection of an impartial jury extremely difficult.

Another common tool of trial judges which became increasingly popular in the 1960s and 1970s (but may be declining in the 1980s) is the use of "restrictive orders," or *gag orders* as they are popularly known. Such orders prohibit the press from reporting specific information that may be revealed during a pre-trial or preliminary hearing. The journalist Dan Rottenberg observes,

The effect of these rulings is that the public's professional sources of information—police and prosecutors on one hand, the media on the other—are shut off, but amateur communicators— defendants, relatives, witnesses, rumormongers— are free to spread their versions, however inaccurate.[23]

A third, and most alarming, restriction on the freedom of the press is the practice of actually closing the pre-trial hearing and the trial itself to the public and the media. During 1979 and 1980 alone, more than four hundred judicial attempts were made throughout the United States to close criminal proceedings to the public; more than half of these succeeded and were upheld in appeals courts.

9.4.4 EQUAL TIME AND THE FAIRNESS DOCTRINE

Because of their unique position—that is, because they occupy space on the limited electromagnetic spectrum—radio and TV stations have never been able to enjoy the freedoms of speech extended to the print media. Two separate and distinct restrictions have been placed on broadcasters.

Section 315 When Congress drew up the Communications Act of 1934, creating the FCC, it incorporated one section to make sure that broadcast stations would not discriminate against political candidates of any party. Section 315 of the communications Act reads in part:

If any licensee shall permit any person who is a legally qualified candidate for any public office to use a broadcasting station, he shall afford equal opportunities to all other such candidates for that office in the use of such broadcasting station: *Provided*, That such licensee shall have no power of censorship over the material broadcast under the provisions of this section.

This is the "equal time" provision which requires that if a station sells time to a Republican candidate for dogcatcher, for example, it must also offer to sell time at the same rate to the Democratic, American Independent, Peace and Freedom, Libertarian, Citizens Party, Socialist, and Vegetarian candidates, as well as to aspiring dogcatchers from all other legally qualified parties.

In 1959 Congress amended the section to exempt from its equal-time requirements all bona fide news programming—newscasts, news interviews, documentaries (in which a candidate's appearance is incidental), and on-the-spot coverage of live events. Without

such an exemption, a station could hardly function to cover daily news. If a local dedication ceremony, for instance, included a twelve-second shot of the mayor cutting a ribbon, then the station would be obligated to offer twelve seconds of free time to all other candidates running for mayor.

In order to facilitate televised debates between the presidential candidates of the major parties, Congress merely temporarily suspended Section 315 in 1960, allowing the Kennedy-Nixon debates. In 1976 and 1980 the presidential debates (Carter-Ford and Reagan-Carter, respectively) were bona fide news events staged and controlled by the League of Women Voters: theoretically, the TV networks were merely covering the live events.

The Fairness Doctrine Although it is often confused with the "equal time" provision of Section 315, the FCC's Fairness Doctrine is more of a policy statement than a quantifiable regulation. It is concerned with "fairness," not with "access." It is concerned with issues, not necessarily candidates, and it stipulates simply that issues must be treated with fairness, not necessarily with equal time.

The FCC said, in effect, that broadcasters should get involved in controversial issues; they should even editorialize; but they had the responsibility to see that the audience was presented with a fair and balanced picture of all points of view. The Fairness Doctrine has been the basis for all the "responses to broadcast editorials" that are frequently aired on most stations, as well as the basis for major actions such as John Banzhaf's successful crusade against cigarette advertising (Inset 1–8).

Modification of Section 315 For years there has been discussion of modifying or even eliminating the "equal time" provision of Section 315 and the Fairness Doctrine (which was incorporated into Section 315 in

1959). The argument is that with the increasing number of cable-TV channels, satellite services, and other video distribution technologies, there is no longer any need to require every broadcast station to present all sides of every issue. There are enough radio and TV outlets to ensure that every viewpoint will be heard.

With the inauguration of the Reagan administration, the FCC has pushed forward in this area of deregulation. Congress was considering legislation to eliminate Section 315 in 1981–82; however, the push to eliminate Section 315 is balanced by the self-interests of incumbent senators and representatives who enjoy the access to the media guaranteed them by the "equal time" provision.

9.4.5 HONESTY: PROTECTING THE CONSUMER

Our final area of inquiry into media regulation is the category of consumer protection, specifically as it relates to deceptive advertising. There was little concern for consumer protection up to the turn of the century. This was the era of unbridled and unregulated mass media in the best libertarian spirit, the era of "snake-oil" salesmen, bloated newspaper circulation figures, traveling medicine shows, yellow journalism, and *Caveat emptor* ("Let the buyer beware"). As we approached World War I with an increasing sense of sobriety and responsibility, the industry and government alike began to review advertising practices. The same year that the Audit Bureau of Circulation was created, 1914 (Section 6.2.1), saw the establishment of the Federal Trade Commission (FTC). Originally the concern of the federal regulators was that fraudulent advertising gave an unfair advantage to the frauds, thereby penalizing the honest businessman. Concern for the hapless consumer did not take shape until 1938, when the Wheeler-Lee amendments were added to the Federal Trade Commission Act.

Today more than twenty different federal agencies and bodies are concerned with regulation of advertising to some extent or

---

On June 1, 1949, the FCC issued a lengthy statement, "In the Matter of Editorializing by Broadcast Licensees." In this policy document the commission reversed its earlier anti-editorial position and spelled out the manner in which stations should editorialize but treat controversial issues with fairness. This excerpt is from the summary of the statement.

[Programming decisions] must be exercised in a manner consistent with the basic policy of the Congress that radio be maintained as a medium of free speech for the general public as a whole rather than as an outlet for the purely personal or private interests of the licensee. This requires that licensees devote a reasonable percentage of their broadcasting time to the discussion of public issues of interest in the community served by their stations and that such programs be designed so that the public has a reasonable opportunity to hear different opposing positions on the public issues. . . . Such presentation may include the identified expression of the licensee's personal viewpoint as part of the more general presentation of views or comments on the various issues, but the opportunity of licensees to present such views as they may have on matters of controversy may not be utilized to achieve a partisan or one-sided presentation of issues.[24]

**INSET 9–11
The Fairness
Doctrine**

another. They include the FCC, the U.S. Postal Service, the Food and Drug Administration, the Securities and Exchange Commission, the Patent Office, and the Alcohol and Tobacco Tax Division of the Internal Revenue Service. But it is the FTC which wields the greatest influence of all.

In the early 1970s, the FTC began taking a more aggressive stance on behalf of the consumer, adding more armaments to its war on deception. The FTC began insisting that all advertisements be not just literally true, but *true in all of their implications*. This "truth in implication" concept was used, for instance, in 1970 against Firestone Tire & Rubber Company, which was advertising its "safe tire." The FTC made Firestone back down because it could not be asserted that every tire was absolutely safe under all conditions. About the same time, the commission also began to demand that advertisers in certain industries, such as the auto industry, back up their claims with *adequate substantiation*. The FTC was not accusing individual advertisers of fraudulent claims; it was just putting the burden of proof on the advertisers, asking them to supply technical data and evidence to demonstrate that their comparisons and testing methods were valid. The commission also now requires some advertisers, such as cigarette and insecticide manufacturers, to include clear messages warning of the hazards and dangers associated with their products.

The First Amendment and the Regulation Pendulum   In order to protect individual rights by providing the consumer with honest information, the FTC has intruded heavily into the arena of the First Amendment. Under a pure libertarian system, the government would not be concerned with misleading advertising or even outright lies. Advertisers would be free to parade any and all false declarations before the wary public, and you would be responsible for determining the truth of conflicting claims. But in today's complex and technological society,

this would be a virtual impossibility. There is no way that you, the average consumer—no matter how intelligent and diligent you may be—could decipher the elaborate claims with which you are bombarded in advertising concerning chemicals, mileage claims, comparison tests, food additives and preservatives, environmental dangers, synthetic fabrics, miracle drugs, and so on.

So the government responded—through the Federal Trade Commission—to our call for increased protection. The pendulum swung toward consumer safeguards. In the conflict between the freedom of the media to print or broadcast whatever they wish versus the right of the individual not to be deceived, we have accepted this abridgment of the First Amendment.

However, in the current Washington climate of deregulation, the pendulum of federal intervention has been swinging away from the FTC, reducing its power in some areas and returning other regulation authority to the states.

SUMMARY

An underlying tenet of our country—and a basic theme for this book (Chapter 2)—is that a free democratic society is absolutely dependent upon a free and vigorous mass media system. Under a modified libertarian (or "social responsibility") political system, the mass media channels must be left as open as possible and should be restricted only when necessary for other overriding concerns. But how are you to determine what these other necessary overriding concerns are? When do you shut down the open media channels? When is free inquiry of the press to be halted? Who is to make these decisions? Schramm sums up the dilemma we face in a free democratic nation:

The mass media must be free in order to represent the public's right to know. But what are the limits on that right? For example, what happens when the right to know conflicts with other old and honored rights: the right of an individual to privacy, the right of an individual to fair trial, the right of government to withhold information when it feels the public interest requires it, or the media's right to serve their own interest in withholding information? These are questions of conflicting responsibilities, which cannot be answered simply by saying that the public's right to know is overriding, and the right of free press is bounded only by law. In all these cases the boundaries of responsible performance need to be adjudicated and redrawn.[25]

In examining areas of legitimate government controls or regulation, we have looked at both *ownership controls* (especially broadcast licensing) and *content regulation*. We have examined the *FCC regulation of broadcast programming*, and we have noted the relative lack of controls on the *cable-TV*, *movie*, and *record* industries.

Most content controls can be divided into three areas. First are concerns over *national security*—questions about military secrets, First Amendment conflicts, the abuse of executive authority, and the protection of sources. Second, we as a people are concerned about *morality and public taste*—originally heresy and blasphemy, but today primarily obscenity—and the attempts of the Supreme Court and the FCC to determine what to censor and

what to leave untouched. Third, there are several areas where freedom of the press conflicts with *rights of the individual*: *defamation* (protecting one's reputation); *copyright* (protecting one's creative works); *privacy* and the *right to a fair trial*; *equal time* and the *Fairness Doctrine*; and *honesty in advertising* (protecting the consumer).

In every one of these situations, the questions always come down to this: How much freedom of the media should society give up in order to protect other freedoms and rights? We are forever faced with the dilemma of conflicting rights: your right to know versus my right to keep something concealed; your freedom of speech versus my right to protect myself. As long as society is able to continue the debate on each of these conflicting rights, it ought to be able to maintain a healthy dynamic equilibrium between the media and the government.

Chapter 10 turns from government regulation to other forms of societal control of the media—industry self-regulation and public pressure.

Notes to Chapter 9

1. Wilbur Schramm, *Responsibility in Mass Communication* (New York: Harper & Row, 1957), p. 6.

2. Quoted in "The First 50 Years of Broadcasting: 1968," *Broadcasting*, 6 July 1981, p. 72

3. Ibid., p. 73.

4. Quoted in "The Need for Cantankerous Press," in *Readings in Mass Communication: Concepts and Issues in the Mass Media*, ed. Michael C. Emery and Ted Curtis Smythe (Dubuque, Iowa: Wm. C. Brown, 1972), p. 355.

5. "Wartime Control of Media Proposed," *Los Angeles Times*, 19 March 1982, Part II, p. 3.

6. Christopher H. Sterling and John M. Kittross, *Stay Tuned: A Concise History of American Broadcasting* (Belmont, Calif.: Wadsworth, 1978), p. 88.

7. Eugene S. Foster, *Understanding Broadcasting* (Reading, Mass.: Addison-Wesley, 1978), p. 153.

8. *Mutual Film Corporation* v. *Industrial Commission of Ohio*, 236 U.S. 230 (1915).

9. *Burstyn* v. *Wilson*, 343 U.S. 495 (1952).

10. "WBAI Ruling: Supreme Court Saves the Worst for the Last," *Broadcasting*, 10 July 1978, p. 20.

11. *American Communications Association* v. *Douds*, 339 U.S. 382 (1950).

12. *Schenck* v. *U.S.*, 249 U.S. 47 (1919).

13. Bernard Rubin, *Media, Politics, and Democracy* (New York: Oxford University Press, 1977), p. 65.

14. Ibid., p. 77.

15. Quoted in Peter M. Sandman, David M. Rubin, and David B. Sachsman, *Media: An Introductory Analysis of American Mass Communications*, 2nd ed. (Englewood Cliffs, N.J.: Prentice-Hall, 1976), p. 174.

16. *Winters* v. *New York*, 333 U.S. 507 (1948).

17. *Roth* v. *U.S.*, 354 U.S. 476 (1957).

18. *Cohen* v. *California*, 403 U.S. 15 (1971).

19. *Miller* v. *California*, 413 U.S. 15 (1973).

20. Sandman et al., *Media*, p. 177.

21. *Olmstead* v. *United States*, 277 U.S. 438 (1928).

22. *Galella* v. *Onassis*, 353 F. Supp. 196. Decision of the U.S. Court of Appeals, Second Circuit, can be found at 487 F.2d 986 (1973).

23. Dan Rottenberg, "Do News Reports Bias Juries?" in *Mass Media and Society*, 3rd ed., ed. Alan Wells (Palo Alto, Calif.: Mayfield, 1979), p. 296.

24. "In the Matter of Editorializing by Broadcast Licensees," 13 FCC 1246, 1 June 1949, reprinted in Frank J. Kahn, ed., *Documents of American Broadcasting* (New York: Appleton-Century-Crofts, 1968), pp. 373–374.

25. Schramm, *Responsibility in Mass Communication*, p. 7.

Citizens' groups publicize their opposition to certain editorial content. Consumers boycott the products of advertisers who support objectionable programming. Important social leaders meet privately with top media decision makers. The result of all this pressuring, posturing, and publicizing is a complex matrix of compromises and concessions that leads to a substantial amount of media self-regulation.

The media industries regulate their own output—or engage in self-censorship—for three main reasons: (1) Media leaders are genuinely concerned about the impact of their messages, and they feel a sincere social responsibility to be a positive force in the national community. (2) The media industries want to enhance their credibility and social acceptance and, incidentally, their profitability by appearing to be socially responsible. (3) By policing their own content, the communication industries can hope to forestall governmental regulation. This last reason is the most common, and it becomes the theme of this chapter.

• *Most mass media self-regulation is forced upon the communication industries by public pressures and is adopted in an attempt to preclude further government regulation.*

Schramm points out that it is the first of these explanations, however—the sense of social responsibility and "gradual professionalization of the industry"—that offers the most hope for the future of mass communication:

But we have more hope for the slower method, the gradual growth of the industry in responsibility and professional spirit . . . the increasing amount of professional education in the field, the activities of professional and trade associations in mass communication, the beginnings of self-criticism in the media, and the effects of awards and prizes for excellent performance in mass communication.[1]

10
Media and Self-Regulation: Pressure Groups and Critics

10.1 Newspapers and the Press

The beginning of the twentieth century witnessed the newspaper industry at the height of its prosperity and the depth of its credibility. It was then a flamboyant industry, characterized by yellow journalism and sensationalistic excesses, outrageous circulation claims, and the warmongering diatribes of William Randolph Hearst and others. However, goaded by voices from the nineteenth century such as Horace Greeley of the *New York Tribune*, Henry Raymond of the *New York Times*, and Joseph Pulitzer of the *New York World*, newspaper editors started to exercise self-restraint and accept some responsibility for promoting the common good.

10.1.1 AMERICAN SOCIETY OF NEWSPAPER EDITORS

The Roaring Twenties was a decade of riotous celebration of the end of the Great War, flagrant violation of Prohibition, unrestrained merrymaking and unrepressed wantonness, boom and prosperity, bathtub gin and the Charleston. Set against this boisterous background, the mass media frequently reflected the excesses of the period (for example, in "jazz journalism," Inset 3–7), but they also countered those trends with moves toward restraint and responsibility. Each of the major divisions of the popular media—newspapers, radio, and the movies—formed its own professional association during the 1920s, and each one first established its code of self-regulation.

In 1922 a responsible group of newspaper editors formed the American Society of Newspaper Editors (ASNE) and thereby established a precedent for similar groups to follow. The next year saw the ASNE setting forth its *Code of Ethics or Canons of Journalism*. The ASNE code combined traditional libertarian principles—calling for the recognition of freedom of the press as a "vital right of

mankind"—with a dedication to social responsibility—stressing sincerity, truthfulness, accuracy, impartiality, fair play, and decency, as well as responsibility. (See Unit III Appendix.)

In 1973 the Society of Professional Journalists, *Sigma Delta Chi*—an association of individual members of the journalistic profession—adopted its code of ethics. Stressing the newsperson's responsibility to serve the truth, this code also placed the journalist's function in a constitutional context:

> We believe in public enlightenment as the forerunner of justice, and in our Constitutional role to seek the truth as part of the public's right to know the truth. . . . The public's right to know of events of public importance and interest is the overriding mission of the mass media.

Other print-oriented groups—the American Newspaper Publishers Association (ANPA), the Associated Press Managing Editors (APME), the Investigative Reporters and Editors (IRE), the Magazine Publishers Association (MPA), and the American Library Association (ALA), among many others—have also adopted lofty codes of ethics or uplifting statements of purpose. Such codes and goals may be helpful in articulating basic principles, but, like the Ten Commandments, they are only as valuable as the intentions of the men and women who must live by them and enforce their policies.

10.1.2 INTERNAL REGULATION

In addition to the formal codes and goals adopted by industrywide groups, involved checks and guidelines within each publishing outlet—each newspaper and magazine—regulate standards and practices.

Gatekeeping Functions Throughout the communication industries there are innumerable information specialists and media managers whose jobs are concerned with deciding what news and information gets passed on to the public. These persons (reporters, photographers, copy editors, feature editors, city editors, managing editors, publishers, owners, and their counterparts in the broadcast-

Typical Gatekeeping Functions In a Newspaper

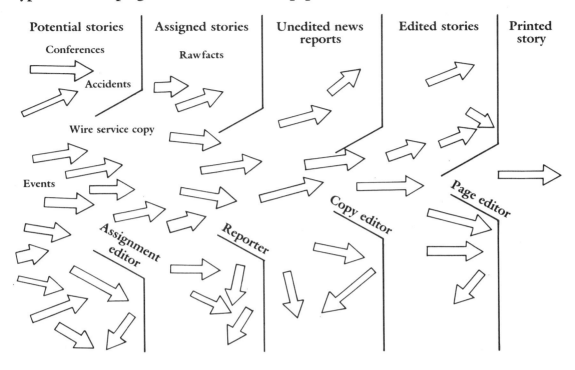

ing and film industries) all have a hand in determining what selected bits of data and knowledge can pass through the limited "gates" of the media channels. Actually, only about ten percent of the material available to the editor of a newspaper (local reporters' stories, PR releases, wire service copy, and so forth) ever gets published; that is all there is room for.

In describing these gatekeeping functions, Schramm writes:

Instead of referring to them as filters, let us use the term *gatekeeper*. . . . They include the reporter deciding what facts to put down about a court trial or an accident or a political demonstration, the editor deciding what to print and what to discard from the wire news, the author deciding what kinds of people and events to write about and what view of life to present, the publisher's editor deciding what authors to publish and what to cut out of their manuscripts, the television or film producer deciding where to point his camera, the film editor deciding what to edit out and leave on

the cutting-room floor, the librarian deciding what books to purchase, the teacher deciding what textbooks or teaching films to use. . . .[2]

Self-Restraint and National Security   Self-imposed censorship is most obvious during wartime, but even during "peacetime" crises there are numerous examples of such self-restraint. In the Pentagon Papers case (Inset 9–2), the source of the news leak (Daniel Ellsberg), the reporter (Neil Sheehan), and the *Times* editors all withheld and edited information before passing their material on to the next gatekeeping level. James Reston of the *New York Times* had knowledge of the U.S. high-altitude spy plane flights over Russia for more than a year before one of our U-2 planes was shot down in 1960; but he had not written about the reconnaissance missions because of his own sense of national security. The *New York Times* had advance information about the Russian missile build-up in Cuba in 1962, and they also knew that President Kennedy was going to make a dramatic stand; but they held off printing anything until after Kennedy had announced the naval blockade, which turned out to be a significant diplomatic triumph for the United States. In late 1979 several news reporters, both American and Canadian, had ferreted out the fact that six Americans were secretly hiding in the Canadian embassy during the early part of the Iranian hostage confrontation; but they all withheld this information until the six were safely returned and the Canadian staffers were securely out of Iran in early 1980.

On the other hand, there is the case of the *Progressive* magazine and the H-bomb article (Inset 9–7). In this instance, the question could be asked: Did not the press channel show a lack of professional self-restraint by attempting to print an article which was potentially damaging to the nation's military security? Many segments of the press rallied to the First Amendment defense of the *Progressive*; others decried the lack of responsibility on the magazine's part.

This is the constant question facing every newsperson: When should one back off and voluntarily agree not to print something which may or may not endanger the national security? And when should one defy authority and proclaim one's First Amendment rights by printing something against government orders?

Questions of self-restraint do not apply solely to problems of national security, of course. The issues of public morality and individual rights (as discussed in Chapter 9) also represent many thorny and sensitive dilemmas. In every case, responsible members of the press must continually raise similar questions about the appropriateness of self-regulation. When to restrain oneself and

when to exercise one's freedom of speech? As long as these questions continue to be asked, we can maintain the dynamic tension between a free press and a healthy public.

10.2 Broadcasting and the NAB

Broadcasters became involved with self-regulation through the back door. Initially it was a matter of self-interest—possibly even survival—that caused radio stations to band together in an industry association.

10.2.1 THE NATIONAL ASSOCIATION OF BROADCASTERS

In the struggle to preserve individual rights to the ownership of creative works, composers and authors had formed a performing rights and copyright-licensing agency in 1914—the American Society of Composers, Authors, and Publishers (ASCAP). Concerned with declining revenues from the sale of sheet music, ASCAP was convinced that record sales and radio broadcasts of recorded phonograph music were cutting into sheet music sales.

In order to present a unified front in negotiations with ASCAP, the fledgling radio broadcasters managed to convene a small group of stations in 1923 and formally organize themselves into a loose coalition grandiosely called the National Association of Broadcasters (NAB). The NAB soon broadened its scope to include many other vital concerns—promotion of the radio medium in general, the need for technical cooperation, the question of politicians broadcasting on the air, efforts to get favorable legislation passed in Congress, and worry about malpractice within the industry.

The Radio Codes   It was concern over this last area—malpractice activities among some of the radio stations—that led the NAB to establish its first code of ethics in 1929. Throughout the decades, the NAB radio codes have undergone many revisions. In general, the codes have been divided into two main sections. The section on *program standards* has been divided into subsections devoted to news, controversial public issues, community responsibility, political broadcasts, advancement of education and culture, religion, dramatic programs, responsibility toward children, and "general" (encompassing everything from the portrayal of handicapped persons to gambling on sports programs).

The *advertising standards* section has dealt with general advertising standards, presentation of advertising, acceptability of advertisers and products (including a ban on hard liquor), advertising of medical products, time standards (the amount of broadcast time to be used for advertising), contests, and premiums and offers.

The Television Codes   The NAB television code, like the radio code, has been mainly a list of restrictive "do's" and "don'ts," running on for page after page of specific prohibitions. Following the spirit of the 1929 code of ethics, both broadcasting codes have been basically self-censorship documents, concerned with the picayune details of a *social-responsibility* commitment. There has been little concern with the *libertarian* ideals voiced, for instance, in the ASNE canons—no clarion calls for freedom of speech.

The whole idea of industry self-regulation was clouded late in 1981 when the U.S. District Court in Washington ruled that the NAB television code was to be terminated

---

This original NAB code of ethics, adopted on March 25, 1929, reflects a strong social-responsibility philosophy:

First. Recognizing that the Radio audience includes persons of all ages and all types of political, social and religious belief, every broadcaster will endeavor to prevent the broadcasting of any matter which would commonly be regarded as offensive.

Second. When the facilities of a broadcaster are used by others than the owner, the broadcaster shall ascertain the financial responsibility and character of such client, that no dishonest, fraudulent or dangerous person, firm or organization may gain access to the Radio audience.

Third. Matter which is barred from the mails as fraudulent, deceptive or obscene shall not be broadcast.

Fourth. Every broadcaster shall exercise great caution in accepting any advertising matter regarding products or services which may be injurious to health.

Fifth. No broadcaster shall permit the broadcasting of advertising statements or claims which he knows or believes to be false, deceptive or grossly exaggerated.

Sixth. Every broadcaster shall strictly follow the provisions of the Radio Act of 1927 regarding the clear identification of sponsored or paid-for material.

Seventh. Care shall be taken to prevent the broadcasting of statements derogatory to other stations, to individuals, or to competing products or services, except where the law specifically provides that the station has no right of censorship.

Eighth. Where charges of violation of any article of the Code of Ethics of The National Association of Broadcasters are filed in writing with the Managing Director, the Board of Directors shall investigate such charges and notify the station of its findings.[3]

INSET 10–1
**NAB
Code of Ethics**

---

until further notice. Even though it was voluntary in nature, it still constituted a monopolistic concept; the code restrictions on commercial advertisements violated antitrust laws by prohibiting certain advertising practices. (The prohibitions pertained to the number and length of commercials.) Therefore, the NAB television code, for all practical purposes, has ceased to serve as an operational document. The spirit of the industry code is still continued, however, by the restrictions and self-censorship standards followed by individual stations (Section 10.2.4).

10.2.2 THE RTNDA CODE

The *Code of Broadcast News Ethics,* unlike the NAB codes, voices some basic libertarian ideals and expresses its concern for freedom of the broadcast press. This code, adopted originally in 1966 by the Radio-Television News Directors Association (RTNDA), is more reminiscent of the spirit of the ASNE canons. The bulk of the RTNDA code does, of course, emphasize the responsibilities and ethics of the broadcast journalist, stressing such things as accuracy, comprehensiveness, lack of sensationalism, absence of bias, respect for a person's privacy and right to a fair trial, and overall sense of professionalism.

But the code goes on to defend the First Amendment rights of the news broadcaster much more forcefully than the NAB codes. Article Six, for example, is concerned with the right of access to information. And Article Seven defends the right of broadcast journalism to engage in analysis and editorializing: "Broadcast journalists recognize the responsibility borne by broadcasting for informed analysis, comment and editorial opinion on public events and issues."[4]

In essence, the NAB codes were primarily concerned with *self-censorship;* the RTNDA Code, while stressing the need for social responsibility, also is concerned with libertarian *freedom of the press.*

10.2.3 ENFORCEMENT PROBLEMS

The major problem with the NAB and RTNDA codes is that they have no teeth— no real means of enforcement. The whole concept of *self*-regulation means simply that there is no agency, except one*self,* to see that one's self-imposed standards are followed. Any station which failed to comply with the NAB code lost the right to hang the NAB "Seal of Good Practice" in its reception lobby and could not display the seal when signing on or off the air in the wee small hours of the morning. This was hardly a strong incentive for compliance with the code.

Therefore, it is not surprising that individual radio and television stations were not strongly committed to the NAB codes. Only about one-third of all radio stations and a little over half of all TV stations subscribed to their respective NAB codes. (Most nonmembers objected to the limitations on the amount of commercial time allowed.) For this reason, the broadcast industry's claim of self-regulation is regarded by some as little more than a publicity gimmick. "It is an ideal which is more theoretical than practical, an exercise in self control for those who have agreed to be controlled."[5]

10.2.4 NETWORK AND STATION STANDARDS

In addition to the national codes of the NAB and RTNDA, the major commercial networks and most individual radio and TV stations have their own written or unwritten codes as well as the employees responsible for enforcing the code provisions. Known as "broadcast standards" or "continuity acceptance" or "broadcast practices," these station and network operations often will provide quite rigorous self-censorship.

A major commercial network may have thirty or more persons working in the broadcast standards division. Typically, the division head reports directly to top management and is independent of the production, programming, and sales departments. Broadcast standards representatives will be ever ready to suggest plot changes, tone down stereotypes, request script changes, modify rough dialogue, eliminate violence, approve costumes, frown at suggestive movements, cover up cleavages, and edit camera shots. The broadcast standards department is concerned not only with public taste and morals, but also with protection of individual rights—checking copyright clearances, questions of defamation, invasions of privacy, and honesty of advertising claims.

10.3 Motion Pictures and the Hollywood Codes

Meanwhile, back in the Roaring Twenties, the motion picture business was being pushed closer and closer to self-regulation. Not only were the movies popularizing the lush and loose life, but the real-life escapades of Hollywood moguls and instant millionaires also seemed to focus on drugs, bootleg booze,

---

The late 1940s witnessed one of the most depressing incidents of self-censorship that the broadcasting and motion picture industries have ever experienced. After the end of World War II, America was launched into an anticommunist campaign spearheaded by the House Un-American Activities Committee (which included a freshman congressman from California, Richard M. Nixon). The committee (HUAC) soon directed its spotlight on Hollywood, where the prospect of uncovering communist activity in the heart of the nation's entertainment capital promised substantial publicity dividends.

Starting in 1947, the committee heard from a host of "friendly" witnesses (including Ronald Reagan, who had just been elected president of the Screen Actors Guild) and from a number of "unfriendly" witnesses (including the infamous "Hollywood Ten," all of whom eventually spent some time in prison on contempt charges for refusing to cooperate with the HUAC investigation). Although a number of prominent film and broadcasting people resisted the HUAC's guilt-by-association innuendos and witch-hunting tactics, most of the entertainment industry caved in to the committee's pressures.

The repugnant aspect of this whole period was the cowardly and secretive manner in which people were denied employment. *Blacklisting* was the practice of secretly circulating lists of individuals—usually in creative positions—who were accused of any kind of left-wing activity, membership, former membership, or interest, or who were thought to have friends or relatives involved in left-wing groups. These names were seldom made public; the lists were circulated in private—from producers to network officials to agencies to, most importantly, advertisers. Actors, directors, and writers suddenly found themselves out of work but unable to find anyone who would openly confront them with specific charges.

This three-year stretch of panicky self-censorship was summed up by Sterling and Kittross: "The period of the communist scare and blacklisting—in which the industry, through fear and cowardice, let others control it—was a grim era in broadcasting and film and the arts generally."[6]

**INSET 10–2
The
Red Scare and
Blacklisting**

high-speed cars, and fast women. The film historian Arthur Knight notes, "By 1922 Hollywood had gained the reputation of being not only the most glamorous but also the most corrupt city in the United States."[7]

10.3.1 WILL HAYS AND THE MPPDA

Amid increasing public cries for some sort of national censorship, the film industry responded by establishing the Motion Picture Producers and Distributors of America (MPPDA) in 1922. To head up the new organization, the MPPDA selected Will H. Hays as its first "czar." As postmaster general in the Harding administration, chairman of the Republican National Committee, and an elder in the Presbyterian church, Hays gave the office the kind of political and moral stature that was needed.

To forestall the pressure for federal censorship, the "Hays Office" (as the MPPDA came to be known) set up a regulatory system which did little more than codify the elements commonly snipped by local censorship boards around the country. This listing of objectionable material became formalized as the *Code of the Motion Picture Industry* in 1927.

Public criticism continued to mount, however, especially from the Catholic church. In 1930 the MPPDA strengthened its production code, "which went about as far as it could toward expressing the Catholic bishops' viewpoint without converting the movies from entertainment to popular theology."[8] The code, like the broadcast codes, was largely proscriptive, spelling out what could not be done. But what evolved was a theory of "compensating values." Lustful scenes of nudity and debauchery could be presented as long as it was pointed out that these things were not nice, that such sinful happenings were to be punished. Knight sums up the approach: "The studios . . . could present six reels of ticket-selling sinfulness if, in the seventh reel, all the sinners came to a bad end,

. . . they could go through all the motions of vice if, at the last moment, virtue triumphed."[9]

The Legion of Decency   Such an approach failed to silence the strongest public pressure for long, however. In 1933 the Catholic church established the Legion of Decency, which promoted boycotts of movies that the church considered indecent. With strong support from Protestants and Jews, the Legion of Decency proved to be a formidable reformer of Hollywood's product—the first really successful public pressure group on a national scale.

In reaction to this substantial pressure, the MPPDA earnestly revamped its self-regulation. In 1934 the Hays Office released its new *Code to Govern the Making of Motion and Talking Pictures,* and, for the first time, Hollywood took the business of self-regulation seriously. Shots of legs, lingerie, and horizontal lovemaking were replaced by scenes of fully-clad actors and actresses portraying husbands and wives who slept in different beds. These fairly stringent self-imposed standards were to dominate the industry for close to two decades.

10.3.2 ERIC JOHNSON AND THE MPAA

Will Hays finally stepped down and was followed in 1945 by Eric A. Johnson, a politically active industrialist and president of the nationwide Chamber of Commerce of the United States. Just as the prestige and background of Hays had helped to quell criticism from religious and moralist quarters in the 1920s and 1930s, so it was hoped that Johnson's position and prestige would help to silence Hollywood's new critics—the postwar communist hunters. For it was the Chamber of Commerce which issued the 1945 report, *Communist Infiltration in the United States,* that indirectly led to the HUAC investigations (Inset 10–2).

Johnson changed the MPPDA's title to the Motion Picture Association of America (MPAA), and he moved the MPAA headquarters from New York to Washington. His

INSET 10–3 The MPAA Ratings and Shifting Standards

The definitions of the four MPAA rating classifications have not changed over the years:

G —All ages admitted. General audiences.

PG — All ages admitted. Parental guidance suggested. Some material may not be suitable for children.

R — Restricted. Persons under seventeen must be accompanied by a parent or adult guardian.

X — No one under seventeen (eighteen in some areas) admitted.

However, the movies which fall into these various categories have changed significantly in little over a decade. The following chart indicates that fewer films are being produced in the "G" category, while "R" is attracting many more releases.

	Percentage of films rated in each category	
	1969 *(325 films rated)*	*1979* *(366 films rated)*
G	25%	6%
PG	43%	42%
R	25%	45%
X	7%	7%

At the same time, the guidelines for each category are becoming more lenient. *Midnight Cowboy*, released as an "X" in 1969, was rerated as "R" the following year and would probably be a "PG" today. Up until 1976, any film which used the word "fuck" received an automatic "R" rating. In that year *All the President's Men* was released—with all of its salty language intact—with a "PG" rating. Many other changes in standards have followed. Bare breasts and naked rear ends (of both genders) are frequently displayed today in "PG" films which certainly would have rated an "R" a decade ago. In other words, if the standards of ten years ago were still being applied to the ratings today, the trends indicated in the above chart would be even more dramatic.

Partly due to these fluctuating standards, many critics have called for modifications in the MPAA ratings system. Most would like to see additional categories included. Some would include a new category between "PG" and "R"; others call for inserting a new distinction between "R" and "X." Others would like to see a more descriptive labeling of movies in the broad "R" category: "RL" for strong language; "RS" for sexually explicit material; and "RV" for heavy violence.

business and political connections, however, were not enough to stem the spread of the Red Scare, and he found himself presiding over an industry increasingly torn by internal dissension and decimated by the lingering effects of the blacklisting purge.

In an effort to hold on to the dwindling movie audience, Hollywoood returned to bolder films—movies with powerful social themes, more explicit sex, and bloodier violence. By the mid-1950s, as television became the family entertainment medium, the public apparently was ready for more mature morality on the movie theater screen.

10.3.3 JACK VALENTI AND THE MPAA RATINGS

After Eric Johnson's death, Jack Valenti—a presidential assistant to Lyndon Johnson—was tapped for the MPAA post in 1966. Valenti's major contribution to Hollywood's self-regulation has been the MPAA ratings system that was introduced in 1968. Based upon European models, the familiar "G," "PG," "R," and "X" ratings are simply descriptive labels which give the moviegoer some idea of what to expect in a film. The MPAA ratings do not reflect self-censorship so much as they represent an information service for the public. Sandman et al. comment: "In effect, the rating system took the film industry off the self-censorship hook. Henceforth, the industry would simply announce which movies were 'clean' and which were 'dirty.'" The rest was up to the public."[10]

Ultimate implementation of the ratings system is carried out by the theaters—specifically by the ticket sellers and ticket takers, who can look the other way when underage patrons purchase tickets. But it is a voluntary system that has taken much of the heat off the motion picture industry.

10.4 Advertising and Other Industries

Shortly after the turn of the century, the advertising community also began to see the need for self-regulation. The first local Better Business Bureau (BBB) was established in 1913, one year before both the Audit Bureau of Circulations and the Federal Trade Commission. Local BBBs are now operating in some 130 communities throughout the United States and Canada. These business-supported agencies are the primary self-regulatory mechanism in the advertising field.

Advertising Associations   Several industry organizations may be found in the advertising world. The American Association of Advertising Agencies (AAAA) is primarily concerned with the welfare of the advertising agency. The Association of National Advertisers (ANA) is comprised of more than four hundred corporate members (manufacturers, retailers, and service businesses) who are the major buyers of advertising space and time. The final agency which has become involved with self-regulation is the American Advertising Federation (AAF), the only advertising organization that represents the entire field—advertisers, media, agencies, and related business.

10.4.1 NATIONAL ADVERTISING REVIEW BOARD

The three advertising groups mentioned above (AAAA, ANA, AAF) got together with the national Council of Better Business Bureaus (CBBB) and drew up plans for a complex new self-regulation agency—the National Advertising Review Board (NARB). Established in 1971, the NARB is an industrywide agency which exists solely to investigate and act upon complaints of false or misleading advertising. The NARB consists of fifty unpaid members who are appointed by a council (consisting of the AAAA, ANA, AAF, and CBBB presidents) to serve two-year terms.

These fifty members represent advertisers, ad agencies, and "public" interests, and they are available to serve on ad hoc panels as needed to review specific advertising complaints. Before being heard by an NARB panel, each complaint goes through a preliminary screening and negotiating process conducted by the National Advertising Division

(NAD) of the CBBB. Only if the complaint is not resolved at the NAD level is the case assigned to an NARB panel.

The NAD and NARB actions and findings, of course, do not have any legal weight. The whole process is entirely voluntary. However, the findings of each NARB panel are virtually always accepted by the offending advertisers. If any advertiser were to refuse to

---

Any complaint about fraudulent or deceitful advertising submitted to the National Advertising Division (NAD) of the Council of Better Business Bureaus (CBBB) is processed by the National Advertising Review Board (NARB) through the following steps:

INSET 10–4
The
NAD/NARB
Review Process

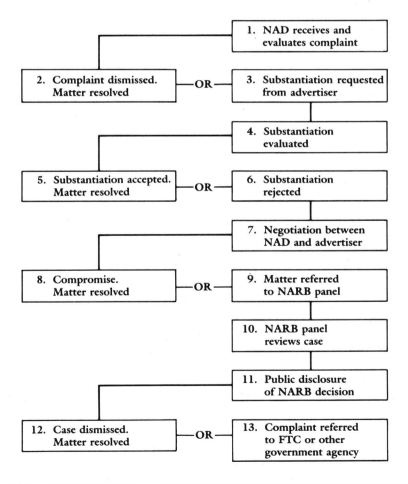

abide by a finding of an NARB panel, the NARB would then turn the complaint over to the FTC or other appropriate government agency. In the first ten years of its operation, the NARB never turned any case over to the federal regulators.

10.4.2 SELF-REGULATION IN OTHER MEDIA INDUSTRIES

In addition to the print media, the broadcasting industry, motion pictures, and the advertising field in general, other segments of the mass media have their own self-regulatory mechanisms.

The Recording Industry Association of America (RIAA) In many ways the audio recording field has less need for internal self-regulation than other mass media; there is less concern about freedom of the press and libertarian rights; there is no involvement with "right to know" issues. And as a fairly specialized entertainment industry, aiming at self-selected audiences, there is relatively little public outcry about morality and obscenity—except when radio broadcasting raises public consciousness and concern over profanity or drug-related lyrics (Section 9.1.4). Nevertheless, the RIAA does fulfill certain minimal self-regulation responsibilities, serving "as a public-relations arm as well as arbiter of production standards and controls."[11]

The Comics Magazine Association of America (CMAA) Founded originally in 1947, the CMAA later reorganized and adopted its thirty-nine-point *Code of the CMAA,* which is designed to protect children from undesirable content—torture, kidnapping, excessive bloodshed, narcotics, profanity, nudity, sex perversion, and so forth. The code also promotes positive social values—crime does not pay, marriage and religion are to be respected—and establishes advertising standards. As a self-regulatory device, the code has succeeded to the extent that ninety percent of the comics industry voluntarily submits its publications for CMAA approval and prior self-censorship.

The Public Relations Society of America (PRSA) Concerned with the public image of its field, the PRSA has long been involved with upgrading the professionalism of the industry. Its first *Code of Professional Standards for the Practice of Public Relations* was written in 1954 and has been periodically updated. The code consists of a "Declaration of Principles," which combines the best of libertarian ideals with acknowledgment of social responsibility, and fourteen "Articles of the Code," which spell out specific industry principles and practices.

10.5 Media Criticism and Awards

The health, vitality, and honesty of a medium can be gauged by the ways in which it responds to internal and external criticism; this becomes another avenue of self-regulation. Does it listen openly and honestly to criticism? Or is the medium defensive and self-protective, trying to blame its errors and misjudgments on outside forces? On the other hand, how does the medium handle praise and applause? Do prestigious awards help to inspire better preformance? Or are various media awards merely self-congratulatory, backslapping PR affairs?

10.5.1 SELF-EVALUATION AND MUTUAL CRITICISM

Newspaper columnists and critics regularly carry judgmental reviews of movies, TV and radio, theater, records, books, and other media. Television reviewers have gotten into the act with regular evaluations of film and other arts. Magazines have a lengthy history of critiquing the output of other media channels. And books, of course, have long zeroed in on the excesses of other media.

The first sustained criticism of the media, however, was probably a series of articles by Will Irwin in *Collier's* magazine in 1911

The *Columbia Journalism Review* and the *Washington Journalism Review* are two of the country's respected journals of media criticism.

attacking newspapers in general. Irwin pointed out that editorial opinions were creeping into the news coverage, that the press had become an integral part of the big-business syndrome, and that "the commercial nature of the paper was responsible for many of its shortcomings."[12] Several books over the next few years savagely attacked the newspaper industry with muckraking fury. There was Upton Sinclair's *The Brass Check* in 1919, which denounced the newspaper's subservience to big business, George Seldes's *Freedom of the Press* in 1935 and his *Lords of the Press* in 1938, and others. Magazine columns, such as A. J. Liebling's "The Wayward Press" in *The New Yorker* (1944 to 1963), added to the literature of media criticism.

Journals of Criticism   In 1961, with a $35,000 advance from Columbia University, the *Columbia Journalism Review (CJR)* was launched. Now a bimonthly publication, this is the oldest and most prestigious of the regular journals dedicated to media criticism. Its statement of policy, carried in every issue, sets forth its purpose of journalistic self-criticism:

. . . to assess the performance of journalism in all its forms, to call attention to its shortcomings and strengths, and to help define—or redefine—standards of honest, responsible service,

. . . [Also] to help stimulate continuing improvement in the profession and to speak out for what is right, fair, and decent.

The *CJR* continues to be the professional leader in media criticism, containing contributions from outstanding leaders and critics both inside and outside of the field of journalism and publishing articles defending as well as attacking the media.

Other journalism reviews have been started since the inauguration of the *CJR*. One of the most dynamic was the *Chicago Journalism Review*. Founded in 1968 as a response to the media involvement in the Democratic convention/antiwar riots (Inset 9–1), the review "aggressively criticized the city's press and offered a forum for general media criticism and self-improvement until its demise in 1975."[13] The *Washington Journalism Review (WJR)*, founded in 1979, continues as a strong critical voice in the media field. Wide-ranging in scope—considering everything from political to sports coverage—*WJR* encompasses all media, including TV, books, and magazines.

Self-criticism and the Ombudsman   One of the more interesting innovations at the local level is the ombudsman. *Ombudsman* is a Scandinavian term for an official who is in charge of public grievances and who has the authority to do something about them. A. H. Raskin of the editorial board of the *New York Times* proposed in a 1966 article that newspapers establish their own "Departments of Internal Criticism." Such an office would have to be headed by an experienced and dedicated newspaper professional who had the determination, independence, responsibility, and authority to become, in effect, an "in-house" critic assigned to find fault with and correct errors in his or her own newspaper.

One of the first major newspapers to set up an ombudsman was the *Washington Post* which tapped the noted media critic Ben Bagdikian for the position. Bagdikian gives the *Post* credit for "being the first paper to put a man to work not just to correct errors but to comment publicly and critically on his own paper in his own paper."[14]

Today, probably about ten percent of all daily papers have an ombudsman or some comparable position. (Many news channels undoubtedly feel it is unnecessary to pay someone to criticize one's work when there are so many competitors and public critics who are glad to do it for free.) Altogether, though, about three-quarters of all the papers in the country have some regularized process for correcting and retracting errors, from press councils (see below) to regular daily features to reader-feedback coupons.

10.5.2 THE COMMISSION ON FREEDOM OF THE PRESS

As noted in Section 2.4.3, when the Commission on Freedom of the Press released its report, *A Free and Responsible Press,* in 1947, most members of the Establishment press were lukewarm to openly hostile in their reactions (Inset 2–9). Publishers and journalists were upset because the liberally oriented report issued a firm call for moral responsibility on the part of the press, asking for a much stronger commitment to self-criticism and social responsibility than the conservatively oriented press was ready to consider at the time.

Bernard Rubin notes that the president of the ASNE was especially outspoken in his condemnation of the report, denouncing the members of the commission as "left-wing" professors without any newspaper experience. Rubin then asks of the ASNE head:

Was that gentleman especially angered by the Commission's proposal that the "members of the press engage in vigorous mutual criticism" or by the proposal that an independent agency be created to "appraise and report annually upon the performance of the press"? . . . Perhaps what was disturbing was the Commission's recommendation that lying by the press be investigated, with particular attention to "persistent misrepresentation of the data required for judging public issues."[15]

Rubin concludes that, "The recommendations of [Robert Hutchins'] Commission in 1947 have weathered well and are obviously pertinent to current affairs. . . . The impact of its conclusions has been subtle but steadily growing in importance to many opinion leaders."[16]

10.5.3 PRESS AND MEDIA COUNCILS

One follow-up to the commission's report has been the introduction of a few press and media councils throughout the nation. Usually consisting of both representatives of the public and delegates from the media, the press councils (also known as news councils or media councils) are "voluntary, private, nongovernmental, lay citizen groups meeting in unfettered, uninhibited, objective and responsible criticism of the press with a view to forcing upon the proprietors of the media a measure of self-discipline."[17]

In 1966 a small series of grants from the Mellett Fund for a Free and Responsible Press, administered by the American Newspaper Guild, was used to start experimental councils in California, Oregon, and Illinois. Today, about a dozen local press councils—generally in smaller communities—are functioning in the United States. Unfortunately, the concept has also failed in numerous localities.

Because the press councils function like citizens' advisory committees they really have no legal standing and no powers of enforcement. As with all forms of self-regulation, their main tools are publicity and persuasion. However, this extralegal status often can be a plus factor in resolving media grievances. Donald Gillmor points out:

Press councils are an admission that many problems of press freedom and responsibility cannot satisfactorily be resolved in the courts. . . .

Mediation is the key function of a press council. A hearing before it can be an intermediate step between a purely informal resolution of a grievance between a reader and an editor and a court action, which in fact is a form of governmental intervention. Often the intermediate step is well worth taking.[18]

The National News Council Established in 1973, initially by the Twentieth Century Fund, the National News Council consists of eighteen members—ten from the public and eight representing the media. Its success rests solely upon its effectiveness as a voluntary mediation service and upon its powers of persuasion and publicity. The *Columbia Journalism Review,* for example, publishes the findings and recommendations of all council investigations.

The council has received generally good support and endorsement from the media involved. Proponents of the council point out that the extralegal body enhances media credibility, promotes social responsibility, and takes the heat off demands for further governmental controls. Opponents of the council (most notably the *New York Times*) argue that the media are already sufficiently criticized by public and professional sources, that a national agency like the council could conceivably be the forerunner of increased governmental surveillance, and that most media

channels are already doing an adequate job of self-regulation.

During its first four years, the National News Council handled almost 500 specific complaints about the media. (The TV networks drew most of the wrath of the public, with newspapers coming in second.) The full council investigated 125 of those complaints, upholding (totally or partially) 25 of the charges, finding that 73 of the objections were unwarranted, and dismissing 27 other criticisms (one of which was withdrawn).

Despite its general acceptance by the media and its modest success with cases handled to date, the National News Council suffers from a serious drawback. For an organization that relies upon publicity for effectiveness, it has had very low public visibility. It simply has not received enough attention from the public and the media (the same media it seeks to regulate) to have the sustained impact it would like to have.

**INSET 10–5
The
Minnesota
Press
Council**

Although there are other regional and state press councils, the most successful and visible has been the Minnesota Press Council. Established in 1971, the Minnesota body has served as a model for other groups interested in setting up larger-than-local press councils. Its twenty-four members are equally divided between lay citizens and press representatives. The council's votes are seldom, if ever, split into solid public versus press blocs that deadlock issues.

All complaints are screened first by a grievance hearing panel which has to decide (a) whether the complainant has tried in good faith to settle the issue with the newspaper or broadcast station, and (b) whether the issue is a legitimate concern for adjudication by the full council. If the case is accepted by the body, then an eight-member committee gathers evidence and listens to testimony from both sides, presenting its findings and recommendations to the entire council.

The full body will then either accept the committee's report (with any dissenting opinions) or reverse the recommendation. In either case, the council (whose meetings have all been open to the public) will then issue its findings with as much publicity as possible to all media in the state. In the first few years of its existence, the Minnesota Press Council has ruled against the media at least as frequently as it has found in their favor.

10.5.4 OUTSIDE CRITICISM

As indicated above, criticism of the media by professional media critics and reviewers—book reviewers, theater critics, record columnists, radio and television reviewers, and so forth—has long been a part of the self-regulation environment. Fortunately, as each medium matures, so does the level of criticism of that medium.

Criticism of the Medium as a Whole
Every new medium, when it enters the mainstream of popularity in the elitist-popular-specialized curve (Section 3.1), is initially criticized simply as a medium. Content is ignored as critics and social commentators look at the new medium-as-message. So it was with the emergence of the Kinetoscope parlors, the press of the yellow journalism era, the early comic books, and so forth. And the audiences initially endorse each new medium in a similar undiscriminating, all-encompassing embrace of the new technology. During the nickelodeon era, the public flocked to the movies with the same kind of uncritical acceptance that still characterizes much TV viewing today.

Sydney Head makes the point about television criticism:

. . . critics condemn broadcasting as a whole, rather than selecting for appraisal those items of content which merit critical attention. Book reviewers never make such sweeping judgments about "print" or art critics about "paint." "The new art is carelessly judged as a whole; the old arts are carefully judged by only parts of their performance good enough to demand judgment."[19]

During this period of the adolescence of each medium, there is also the irresistible tendency to judge the medium by its least important products—the daily outpouring of mediocrity which is needed financially to sustain a few works of merit. Hollywood of the 1930s was characterized by its overwhelming number of "B" gangster films and westerns; motion pictures such as *Gone with the Wind* and *The Wizard of Oz* were looked on as exceptions from the Hollywood film factory. The turn-of-the-century press was characterized as the period of "yellow journalism," and the significant contributions of investigative reporting during the period were largely downplayed. And television, today, is still largely judged by the level of regularly scheduled weekly series, game shows, and soap operas rather than by the occasional artistic TV movie or significant documentary, or the continuing news coverage.

Public Reaction to Criticism   If the reviewers' analyses and recommendations are ignored by the media consumer, then such critical efforts are largely in vain. Television seems especially prone to this problem. Whereas members of the public may be swayed by a movie or book review (or a review pertaining to any medium in which individual productions are purchased separately), the home TV viewer will pretty much watch whatever comes up next. This occurs even though the level of television criticism is being uplifted. *TV Guide* points out:

But the increased integrity and independence of the critic—like his increased skill and skepticism—do not seem to translate into increased influence with the ultimate audience: the television viewer. . . .

If someone is going to see a movie or a play or an opera . . . he or she may pay some attention to what the critics say, if only because admission, parking and, perhaps, dinner and/or a baby sitter now represent a substantial investment. But with television, the only investment is the time and the effort required to switch on the channel. Why should they take a critic's word for something when they can find out for themselves with three strides and a flip of the wrist?[20]

This phenomenon of ignoring the critic of the accessible medium is directly related to Schramm's "low effort/high reward" theory (Section 1.6.4). The easier it is to use a medium—and the smaller the anticipated reward—the less reason there is for seeking or heeding a critical review.

Ironically, the most significant source of media criticism, from a *mass communication point of view,* may well be the source of the above quotation, *TV Guide.* With its weekly circulation of close to 20 million (Inset 3–12), it can exert far more influence on the TV-viewing public than such scholarly and professional periodicals as the *Columbia Journalism Review* and the numerous trade journals, or such literate and erudite magazines as *The New Yorker,* or even such papers as the *New York Times,* which has a circulation of less than a million.

In addition to its program listings, feature articles on buxom starlets, and often superficial program reviews, *TV Guide* does include significant (albeit somewhat abbreviated) essays and analyses of serious merit. These lead articles, which appear in almost every issue, do give the popular television audience some insight into the major issues facing the mass media today.

10.5.5 PROFESSIONAL AND POPULAR AWARDS

A final aspect of media criticism and professional development is the number of various awards and prizes annually handed out to media practitioners in recognition of work well done. Supposedly such recognition encourages the other, nonwinning members of the several media to strive toward higher standards of performance in the hope of ultimately gaining similar critical and popular acclaim.

Possibly the most sought-after prize of all is the Nobel Prize for literature, which—like its companion prizes for peace, economics, medicine, chemistry, and physics—carries a cash grant of close to $200,000. The numerous Pulitzer prizes also carry a high degree of public esteem. The Pulitzer journalism categories include international, national, and local reporting; editorial and commentary writing; criticism; photography; and several other areas. Other major journalism trophies include the Sidney Hillman Awards, the Overseas Press Club Awards, and the George Polk Memorial Awards (all of which include both print and broadcast journalism). Other

literature accolades include the National Book Awards, the National Book Critics Circle prizes, and specialized honors such as the John Newbery Medals for children's literature.

The motion picture industry is dominated by the popular Oscar awards. Given out by the Academy of Motion Picture Arts and Sciences since 1928, the Oscars have been tainted by charges that the awards can be greatly influenced (if not purchased outright) by expensive Hollywood advertising campaigns designed to influence members of the academy. More prestigious critical film honors include awards presented by the New York Film Critics Circle, the National Society of Film Critics, the Hollywood Foreign Press Association (Golden Globe Awards), and international competitions such as the Cannes Film Festival.

The Academy of Television Arts and Sciences uses its Emmy awards to try to capture the excitement and prestige of the motion picture presentations. However, it generally falls short—partially because the Emmy honors are split up into a baffling array of categories and subcategories so that the awards become almost meaningless. In 1978, for instance, "best actor" honors went to Carroll O'Connor (comedy series), Edward Asner (drama series), Fred Astaire (drama or comedy special), Michael Moriarty (limited series), and Barnard Hughes (single performance in a drama or comedy series). More meaningful and highly acclaimed broadcast honors are represented by the George Foster Peabody Broadcasting Awards (which are to broadcast journalism what the Pulitzer prizes are to the press), the Writers Guild TV Awards, and the Golden Globe TV Awards (of the Hollywood Foreign Press Association).

Carrying through the tradition of the "named" awards, the theater has its Antoinette Perry or Tony Awards, which are sponsored by the American Theatre Wing and the League of New York Theatres. Other dramatic citations are the New York Drama Critics Circle Awards and the Obie Awards (for off-Broadway plays and performances). The recording industry has its Grammy honors, which are presented by the National Academy of Recording Arts and Sciences, as well as the American Music Awards, the Academy of Country Music Awards, and other assorted specialized categories.

Although most of these awards and prizes represent a substantial amount of industry backslapping and PR puffery, to some extent they also represent the media's attempts to reward and encourage higher standards of performance. This is especially true in the fields of journalism and literature, where the Nobel, Pulitzer, and Peabody prizes are recognized as true indications of outstanding achievement.

10.6 Pressure Groups and the Public

Public pressure groups are nothing new to the American press. They have existed for well over a hundred years. The first prominent self-appointed public censorship group was probably the New York Society for the Suppression of Vice, organized in 1873 by Anthony Comstock. For forty years, Comstock led this zealous group of conscientious citizens in their crusade against smut and obscenities in print. Many other local,

---

The prestige of the Pulitzer Prize and the reputation of the *Washington Post* were both dealt a serious blow in April 1981 when it was revealed that a *Post* reporter, who had won the coveted Pulitzer prize for feature writing, had fabricated most of her story. Janet Cooke, who had been with the *Post* for about a year, had written a sensitive and emotional feature story about an eight-year-old heroin addict named Jimmy, his mother, and her drug-dealing live-in lover.

The Washington police had launched a major citywide search for the youth, whose plight had stirred up the emotions of thousands of readers. And the *Post* even editorially criticized the police and the capitol's mayor for not being able to find the boy. Months later, after being awarded the Pulitzer prize for her moving story, Cooke admitted that major parts of the story were a fabrication; "Jimmy" did not exist.

Cooke issued a statement saying, "The [article] was a serious misrepresentation which I deeply regret. I apologize to my newspaper, my profession, the Pulitzer board and all seekers of the truth." After her Pulitzer award was announced it was also discovered that substantial portions of Cooke's professional résumé had been falsified as well; both her academic background and her reporting experience had been misrepresented. Cooke resigned. The *Post* apologized to the mayor, the police department, its readers, and the Pulitzer board. One of the members of the Pulitzer board observed, "The press is a fragile institution, and this could happen to anyone. In any kind of institution you have to depend on the integrity of your people. Every institution, including the press, is vulnerable to someone who does not tell the truth. This is a saddening moment for everyone. . . ."[21]

**INSET 10—6
The
Pulitzer
Fraud**

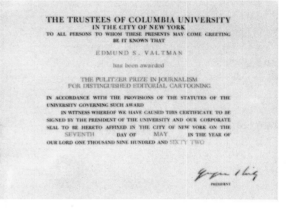

Four of the media fields' popular and prestigious awards include (clockwise, from top left) the Oscar, the Emmy, the Peabody, and the Pulitzer prize.

regional and national groups have been formed, most of them primarily concerned with cleaning up a given medium. Prominent among these groups was the Legion of Decency (Section 10.3.1), whose functions have largely been taken over by the National Catholic Office for Film.

Groups which have long existed for purposes other than media regulation have increasingly been turning their attention to questions of media abuses, particularly abuses by television. And these groups have been especially concerned with children's fare. Professional associations, service clubs, parents' organizations, labor unions, citizens' advisory bodies—these have all raised their voices against media practices of which they disapprove. In mid-1976 the American Medical Association (AMA) attacked TV violence as both a medical and an environmental hazard, declaring that such bloodletting posed a very real health danger to young viewers.

And in the fall of 1976 the National PTA (Parent-Teacher Association) initiated its strong anti-TV violence campaign. Its tactics included those traditional approaches available to such public pressure groups: monitoring and cataloguing TV programs; letter-writing campaigns; visits to stations, networks, and sponsors; contacting legislators; local and national boycotts of programming and, more importantly, of advertisers who sponsored offensive programming; support of research programs; and seminars and public hearings.

10.6.1 PUBLIC PRESSURE GROUPS AND CITIZEN CENSORSHIP

In the spirit of the Society for the Suppression of Vice and the Legion of Decency, many other contemporary groups have been formed to mold the media to meet certain standards. As most contemporary concern is

---

One form of citizen censorship has been public pressure to remove "offensive" works from the community and school libraries. Although Hitler-inspired Nazi book burnings seem completely inconsistent with the American experience, similar suppression has repeatedly surfaced in our nation's media history.

Many instances have occurred in which local communities—often led by religious fundamentalists—have forced school libraries to get rid of books that contained impure language, suggestive sexual material, or disputed scientific themes such as the theory of evolution. In 1953 U.S. libraries around the world banned more than one hundred books and pamphlets that had been identified by Senator Joseph McCarthy as containing subversive and pro-communist material. Several public book-burning ceremonies were conducted.

As recently as 1981, a nationwide survey revealed that one out of five U.S. schools was under pressure to ban one or more books from the school library and/or classrooms. The survey—conducted by the Association of American Publishers, American Library Association, and Association for Supervision and Curriculum Development—involved almost 1,900 questionnaires sent out to librarians, principals, and superintendents.

Among the books found under attack were Mark Twain's *Huckleberry Finn,* Shakespeare's *The Merchant of Venice,* Hawthorne's *The Scarlet Letter,* Hemingway's *A Farewell to Arms,* Aldous Huxley's *Brave New World,* George Orwell's *1984,* Alexander Solzhenitsyn's *One Day in the Life of Ivan Denisovich,* the American Heritage Dictionary (for defining "to bed" as a verb), and assorted works by John Steinbeck, Maurice Sendak, Rod McKuen, E. B. White, and many others. As a *Los Angeles Times* editorial observed, "It strikes us that one could assemble a stimulating library just from that selection."[22]

INSET 10–7 Book Burning and Banning

A small group of citizens from Warsaw, Indiana, participate in a local "bookburning" to rid the community of offensive material found in the public schools.

focused on television, these broadcasting-oriented groups have become most prominent in recent years.

National Citizens' Committee for Broadcasting (NCCB) Headed by a prestigious board of directors which includes consumer advocate Ralph Nader and former FCC commissioner/citizen activist Nicholas Johnson, the NCCB plays a prominent role at the national level. The NCCB works through national publications, putting out a biweekly magazine, *Access,* which reports on media activities around the country, and also a quarterly newsletter, *Media Watch,* which has become an effective forum for public regulation efforts. The NCCB also works with local community groups and public service law firms, helps to raise financial support for citizen movements, takes part in legal actions (see Inset 9–5), and disseminates other information.

Action for Children's Television (ACT) Under Peggy Charren's leadership, a group of Boston mothers who were upset over the quality of children's programming and the caliber and quantity of advertising aimed at their offspring formed ACT in the late 1960s, and it soon snowballed into a national organization with considerable consumer clout. Using its national magazine, *re:act,* the group has organized other grassroots campaigns, launched successful lobbying movements aimed at both Congress and the FCC, joined several legal battles (Inset 9–5), and helped to support research projects. As a result of this activity, ACT has been directly or indirectly reponsible for several positive changes in the areas of children's programming and advertising.

National Coalition on TV Violence (NCTV) Emerging in the early 1980s, the NCTV has established itself as a prestigious professional group focused on the one issue of violence in the broadcast media. Composed largely of physicians, psychiatrists, and psychologists, the coalition relies heavily upon a strong scholarly and scientific research base. Its primary tools are publicity and lobbying at the national level.

The Coalition for Better Television (CBTV) This is an umbrella association which represents a coming together of up to 1,800 local and national groups—largely conservative political and fundamentalist church organizations. Spearheaded by the Reverend Donald Wildmon from Tupelo, Mississippi, the coalition's original single-minded purpose was to rid the video tube of sex and immorality. The CBTV claims to have some 4,500 "trained monitors" (drawn from its constituent groups) to rate network programming for its sex and sin content.

ry Falwell's Moral Majority was originally a member of Wildmon's coalition, but it
has subsequently pulled out to pursue its
own course of public pressure. With some
$500,000 budgeted for its TV campaign (and
an estimated 21 million sympathizers), the
Moral Majority by itself plans to have a significant impact on network programming.

10.6.2 BOYCOTTING PROGRAMMING AND THE ADVERTISERS

One of the most controversial tactics of any
pressure group is the attempt to hit the
broadcaster and advertiser where it hurts—in
the wallet. Organizing a consumer boycott of
specific programming and products is one
of the most widely discussed weapons of consumer activists, and one of the most difficult
to pull off successfully. This is precisely the
technique proposed by Wildmon's coalition,
however: Identify the TV programming that
is most offensive; urge people not to watch
these programs; publicize the names of the
sponsors of those shows among the millions
of coalition supporters; and then refuse to
buy any products from the offending companies, thus forcing potential advertisers to
refuse to sponsor the targeted programs.

In 1969 Action for Children's Television (ACT) began urging the FCC
to take a closer look at what was going on in children's programming and
advertising. Among other requests, ACT wanted the FCC to ban advertising altogether on programs aimed specifically at youngsters. Over the
next four years, the commission held occasional hearings on the subject.
It was apparent that the FCC hesitated to issue any firm rules because of
the restrictions of Section 326 of the Federal Communications Act, which
forbid the commission to exercise any act of censorship or direct control
of content. However, both the Senate and the House of Representatives,
faced with increasing public pressure, made it clear that they wanted some
sort of action from the FCC.

In 1974 the commission succeeded in obtaining general consensus
through two forms of friendly persuasion or implied coercion. First, it
held a series of "jawboning" sessions with the broadcast industry to let
TV leaders know how the FCC felt about children's programming and
advertising. Second, it issued a "policy statement" which, although it does
not have the legal standing of a formal ruling, does spell out what the
commission expects of its broadcast licensees.

These actions, which also stimulated modifications in the NAB Code,
resulted in four changes in children's advertising (along with other alter-
ations in programming practices): (1) the amount of time devoted to
children's commercials was reduced by about forty percent; (2) commercial
material was to be clearly separated from program content; (3) "host
selling" (sales pitches given by the program emcee) would be abolished;
and (4) deceptive or misleading implications would be eliminated (for
example, failing to disclose that batteries were not included in the advertised product).

INSET 10–8
ACT **And
Children's
Advertising**

John Hurt, head of the "Clean Up TV" campaign (part of the CBTV), defends the use of the boycott:

We're not trying to take any shows off the air. And we're not trying to force our moral judgments on anybody else. What we're really trying to do is get 'em to clean up the act some—I mean explicit scenes, adultery, sexual perversion, incest. We are asking every morally decent person to speak up and let his position be known.[23]

On the other hand, the author Isaac Asimov provides an entertaining counterpoint to the concept of the boycott—or any form of citizen censorship:

The New Puritans will reckon up the sex-points, watching narrowly for every hint of cleavage, for every parting of kissing lips, and will then lower the boom on all advertisers who fail the test. By striking at the pocket-nerve, the Puritans hope to produce a new kind of television that will be as clean, as pink, as smooth and as plump as eunuchs

usually are. . . . If you set up a standard of purity and right-thinking and begin to demand that this be the standard for all; if you take to watching your neighbor lest he disagree with your conception of right, and punish him if he does so; if you make certain we all think alike or, if necessary, don't think at all; then there surely will be a general crushing of intellectual liveliness and growth.

In a healthy society, dissent is free and can be endured. If you think that a sex-ridden society, or a permissive society, or a think-as-you-please society is *not* healthy, you have but to try the kind of society in which unbridled repression sees to it that you think, write, say and do only what some dominating force says you may, and you will then find out what an unhealthy society really is.[24]

Actually, there have already been some limited examples of advertisers being pressured not to sponsor certain programs. In 1977 General Motors backed down from sponsoring the TV movie *Jesus of Nazareth* when it proved to be too controversial for some fundamentalist religious groups.

In early 1982, the Coalition for Better Television (CBTV) announced a boycott of NBC programming and RCA products. The coalition apparently chose to focus on NBC and its parent corporation for three reasons: (1) NBC had broadcast a 1981 Christmas special featuring a *Playboy* "playmate," a sacrilegious move that was especially repugnant to the CBTV leadership; (2) NBC appeared to be potentially more vulnerable to boycott pressure than the other networks because of its generally lower audience ratings; and (3) RCA markets a wide line of consumer items (including Hertz car rentals) which would be susceptible to a sustained boycott.

Ironically, however, other public pressure groups do not necessarily approve of the use of the boycott. Action for Children's Television, for instance, circulated a petition urging opposition to the boycott even though it supported many of the same goals. ACT claimed that "the censorship tactics of the Coalition for Better Television limit options and threaten the free exchange of ideas in a free society." At the time of publication of this book, it was too early to assess the effectiveness of the CBTV boycott.

What critics such as Asimov are concerned about is that consumers and censors could band together to force the cancellation of any programming which did not meet with the approval of a majority of a given public. If media can be coerced into banning sex today, how about unpopular social ideas tomorrow? How about eliminating unorthodox political philosophies? A compelling case could even be made for a corollary to John Stuart Mill's argument about the rights of a minority of one (Section 2.2.2). If but one person desires to have access to pornography or programs which feature violence or bad taste or poor acting or unpopular ideas, does the majority have the right to deny that person such access?

10.7 Minorities and Special-Interest Groups

There can be no argument about the fact that many minorities and special-interest groups do have legitimate complaints about the content of much of the mass media. Racial minorities, ethnic groups, the elderly, children, women, homosexuals, the poor, blue-collar workers, teenagers, certain professions—each of these groups has valid complaints about the way they are depicted in the media, both in drama and in news reporting.

Fictional Misrepresentation   The problems of accurate media portrayal are compounded by two factors, economic and dramatic. Fictional misrepresentation is encouraged economically by the demographic realities of the purchasing audiences. Most media consumers are white, middle-class, young adults. Thus, the financial necessities of the mass media—which are largely commercially supported—dictate that this is the predominant audience that the media must reach. And one reaches this audience with stories about white, middle-class, young adults. Therefore, the elderly,

the very young, blacks, Hispanics, Asian-Americans, and the poor are not as likely to be featured in a proportional number of media stories.

Fictional misrepresentation is also encouraged by dramatic necessities. As pointed out in Section 8.3.3 in the discussion of the *definition of the situation,* dramatic incidents must focus on conflict, the unusual, and the exaggerated situation. Comstock et al., observe: "Television, like Elizabethan drama, Broadway plays, the modern (or any) novel, movies, and any medium of fiction, presents a created world that cannot be expected to contain a probability sample of real life."[25] Thus, we are exposed to many more dramas about doctors, lawyers, and police officers than we are about accountants, dressmakers, and welders even though the latter occupations far outnumber the former.

10.7.1   RACIAL AND ETHNIC MINORITIES

Mass media treatment and depiction of racial minorities generally evolves through three stages: nonrecognition, ridicule/stereotyping, and regulation/realism.[26]

The Black Experience   In the broadcast media, blacks moved from the nonrecognition stage to the ridicule stage when *Amos 'n' Andy* joined the NBC Blue network in 1929. While the program's broad racial stereotypes and verbal slapstick would appear insulting today, they were generally accepted half a century ago. It was, after all, a step above nonrecognition. And ridicule, it must be acknowledged, is a basic ingredient of all situation comedy. Much humor is based upon the stereotype, the caricature, the clown—whether done in whiteface or blackface (Amos and Andy were played by whites). Amos and Andy, it could be argued, were no more insulting to Blacks than Dagwood Bumstead or Archie Bunker have been to whites.

Although there were a few early attempts at Black comedy and variety TV series during the 1950s (including a two-year revival of *Amos 'n' Andy*), the first successful dramatic black star (or co-star) of a regularly scheduled series was a youthful Bill Cosby in *I Spy*, which debuted in 1965. In the 1970s and early 1980s a number of Black situation comedies found their way to the television screen—*Sanford and Son, Good Times, That's My Mama, What's Happening? The Jeffersons, Diff'rent Strokes,* and *Benson,* to name the most popular. Taken individually, each series presented a caricature which might be slapstick or sophisticated but which had a comedic appeal that could attract white audiences as well as Black, thereby making the series a commercial success. Taken collectively, these series helped to give the mass audience a broad picture of Black experiences that added up to a more realistic image than any single series could hope to achieve.

In the more specialized media of radio, movies, audio recording, magazines, and newspaper publishing, Blacks have won more recognition and parity—to a great extent because of the opportunities for ownership of Black media outlets and individual productions.

Other Ethnic Groups Most observers would agree that other groups—Hispanics, American Indians, Asian-Americans, and various ethnic groups such as Jews, Italian-Americans, Polish-Americans, and Arabs, for example—fare not much better than Blacks. Hispanics, for example, comprise about 10 percent of the American population. Yet a study of prime-time and Saturday morning

---

It is inevitable that pressure groups will collide. What one group wants, another group finds abhorrent. While the Gay Activists Alliance calls for fair and sensitive portrayal of homosexuals, for example, other groups want them banned altogether as sinful aberrations of a sick society. Interestingly, the National Citizens' Committee for Broadcasting (NCCB) is one of the most active groups arguing against the narrow pressuring of special-interest groups.

When a number of CBS affiliates surrendered to pressure from religious groups and refused to carry two abortion-related episodes of the situation comedy *Maude,* the NCCB asked the FCC to investigate whether or not the stations' capitulation was in the public interest. The NCCB has opposed other narrow-interest groups also, generally pushing for as much "openness" as possible in TV programming.

The *Maude* incident revealed an important tactic followed by many pressure groups. It is often easier to put local pressure on individual stations than it is to influence decisions at the network level. When CBS announced that its 1974 rerun schedule would include the two programs which dealt with middle-aged Maude's decision to seek an abortion, the network was sharply attacked by the U.S. Catholic Conference. Network officials staunchly defended the decision and refused to budge. At that point, the conference applied pressure—through every Catholic diocese and parish in the country—at the station level. Every CBS affiliate was deluged with angry phone calls and indignant mail, and ultimately forty-one of the network's two hundred affiliates chose not to broadcast the two programs.

**INSET 10–10
Maude and the NCCB as a Counterpressure Group**

The wide variety of Black images portrayed in a diversity
of situation comedies helps to guard against the creation
of a stereotype based upon a single character. Pictured
above are scenes from *Sanford and Son*, *The Jeffersons*,
Diff'rent Strokes, and *Benson*.

entertainment television programming from 1975 to 1978 found that only 1.5 percent of the dramatic speaking roles were Hispanics.[27] Chicanos, Puerto Ricans, Cubans, and other Latin Americans still find themselves at the ridicule stage—most often stereotyped as lazy clowns, busboys, bandits, or members of street gangs.

One of the most recent and most persistent stereotypes is probably that of the modern Arab. One pressure group, Americans for Middle East Understanding, writes, "In recent years the mass media have exploited to an excessive degree the stereotype of the Arab, in spite of the known detrimental effects of such exploitation. Stereotyping is not only a crime against Arabs and Arab nations, but also against the human spirit."[28]

A major victory for minority forces was won by the American Indians in their apparently successful effort to halt the production of the TV miniseries *Hanta Yo*. Based upon the best-selling novel by Ruth Bebee, the ten-hour mini-series was contracted by ABC. However, various scholars and pressure groups from the Sioux tribes claimed that the work was not an accurate portrayal and succeeded in halting work on the controversial project while it was in the script development stage. The critic Howard Rosenberg comments on the significance of the Indian victory:

In fact, if it goes down, it will be first major casualty in ever-widening clashes between the TV establishment and protest groups. That would be the upset of upsets, a powerful network brought to its shaking knees by an undetermined number of Sioux who sometimes have been unable to agree even among themselves on all they found objectionable about "Hanta Yo."[29]

The "Frito Bandito" commercial for Frito-Lay's tortilla chips illustrates one way pressure groups can eventually achieve their goals. The ad campaign featured a cartoon character, the Frito Bandito, a caricature of a Mexican bandit who stole Frito chips from honest customers. Several Mexican-American groups filed protests with the three commercial TV networks, asking that they not run the offensive commercials. After listening politely, the networks announced that they would not back down immediately but that they would talk to the ad agency. *TV Guide* points out that the networks operate slowly and unobtrusively:

Despite the networks' public display of stubbornness, the fact is that they do listen quietly to what pressure groups are saying. . . . In effect, the broadcaster publicly stands his ground while, in the privacy of story conferences and film-editing sessions, he may yield inch by inch.[30]

The Los Angeles NBC station, KNBC—sensitive to its large Hispanic audience—then announced that it would no longer accept the Frito-Lay commercials. After a longer period of study, NBC finally decided that it would also refuse the commercials. ABC and CBS continued to air the sales messages, but Frito-Lay and its ad agency eventually chose to drop the commercials. The entire process took about three years, but the continual pressure by the several Hispanic groups ultimately won out.

**INSET 10–11
The
"Frito Bandito"
Commercial**

10.7.2 · THE YOUNG, THE BAD, AND THE UGLY

While many pressure groups are concerned with the impact of various mass media on racial and ethnic minorities, others are equally concerned about the media's effects on various age groups—specifically, on young children, on teenagers, and on the elderly.

Children and the Media   As discussed in Chapter 8, social critics, psychologists, parents, religious leaders, sociologists, and educators have all become increasingly alarmed about the impact of mass media—especially television—on young children. Although some observers point out that the potential negative effects have always been with us in all of the media and that such impact has always been exaggerated, most social analysts do agree that there is cause for concern, if not alarm.

Among other charges leveled at television—with some amount of research backing—are the following: TV suffocates creativity and imagination. Television viewing develops an attitude of spectatorship—a passivity—rather than active participation. Excessive viewing tends to weaken family relationships. The fun-and-circus TV environment, coupled with the message that all problems can be resolved in thirty minutes, has fostered a low tolerance for the frustrations of learning and working out social relationships. Television has become a primary socializing agent for young viewers, reinforcing sex-role stereotypes and emphasizing materialistic success factors—"The lesson of most TV series is that the rich, the powerful and the conniving are the most successful."[31]

Violence has been an uppermost concern for critics of children's video fare. The generalized effects described in Section 8.4.6 all are intensified with youngsters—including desensitization, causing children to "tolerate violence in others because they have been conditioned to think of it as an everyday thing."[32]

Another primary target of "kidvid" critics has been the heavy commercialization of the Saturday morning and late afternoon kiddie "ghettos." By the time the average teenager has graduated from high school, he or she has been bombarded with some 350,000 commercials. Using a combination of hard-sell and misleading (for the young mind) sophisticated advertising techniques, these commercials push questionable toys, fads, and junk foods with a terrifying efficiency. Critics have probably been most alarmed about sugar-coated breakfast cereals and fast foods (washed down with soft drinks) as the main ingredients of many childhood diets.

As a result, many of the public pressure groups mentioned above (Section 10.6.1) have reacted with varying degrees of success. The PTA, AMA, various labor unions, and—especially—ACT have all had an impact at the national level. The ultimate goal of ACT is to convince networks that they should get rid of children's commercials altogether. All children's programming, ACT maintains, should be carried on a sustaining or public service basis. At the local level, groups such as the Michigan-based Lansing Committee for Children's Television have been successful in getting local stations to delete the more violent children's programming from their late afternoon schedules.

The Teenage Image   The teenage years have become somewhat sullied and distorted following the squeaky-clean innocence of early TV situation comedies such as *Father Knows Best, Leave It to Beaver,* and the *Adventures of Ozzie and Harriet.* Just as the teenage motion picture image evolved from the soda-fountain environment of Mickey Rooney and Judy Garland in the *Andy Hardy* series of the late 1930s to the defiant stance of James Dean in *East of Eden* and *Rebel without a Cause* during the mid-1950s, so has the television version of the teenager been transformed into a troubled picture of sex, rebellion, confusion, and drugs. Of the fifteen TV movies dealing with adolescent themes in 1980–81, about half of them were involved with sexual themes such as seduction, rape, teacher-student affairs, and teenage prostitution.

Soap operas, too, have been turning to teenage problems in an attempt to lure more young viewers as adult women leave the daytime audience for outside occupations. Teenage pregnancies, runaways, drug addicts, and dangerously confused youths fill the screen in distorted *definition of the situation* scripts. This, of course, is where the drama is, where the conflicts and crises can lure the most viewers.

Many groups, including religious organizations and social agencies like ACT, are concerned with the deteriorating teenage image. They fear the socializing and modeling influences if these negative images are the predominant roles that young people have to identify with.

Senior Citizens' Pressure Groups Unlike teenagers, older people watch a lot of television—and they are more concerned about their image. Their image, they point out, is all too faint. During a typical seven-day period the average TV viewer will watch about three hundred speaking parts during prime-time viewing. Of these, only seven will be over age sixty-five. And you will view an older man in a leading role only once a week, and older woman starring in a program only once every three weeks.

The reason for this is a combination of *consumer demographics* (older people do not spend their money as exuberantly as younger consumers, so therefore advertisers are less concerned about reaching them) and *perceived unattractiveness.* Network programmers simply believe that most TV viewers want to watch pretty fresh faces and youthful bodies. One network official bluntly states, "People just don't like to see old people. People are afraid of seeing older performers on TV."[33]

But, also unlike teenagers, older citizens are quite vocal and active—and unwilling to accept their fading image. The Gray Panthers, America's leading senior activist group, are especially forceful in this area. Lydia Bragger, head of the Panthers' Media Watch monitoring committee, has been active in the fight and is convinced that the elder media consumers are gradually getting a better image. For one thing, evolving demographics are on their side. In 1900 less than ten percent of the U.S. population was fifty-five or older; by 1980 that percentage had risen to more than twenty percent; and by the year 2030 it will be close to thirty percent.

10.7.3 GENDER DISCRIMINATION AND SEXUAL LIFE-STYLES

In addition to racial discrimination and age-based prejudices, there are other omissions and misrepresentations in the media.

The Female Majority In late 1979, George Gerbner and Nancy Signorielli of the Annenberg School of Communications at the University of Pennsylvania, released the results of a massive ten-year study which monitored some 1,365 individual programs and analyzed almost 17,000 dramatic characters. The study, *Women and Minorities in Television Drama* (which also indicated that blacks, Hispanics, the elderly, and the young are all underrepresented), revealed that men have outnumbered women about three to one in speaking parts over the last decade. And the ratio has not changed much through the years, although women have increased their number of starring roles in recent years.

The most discouraging part of the picture is that female characters appear generally as part of the bland background—"benign" and "powerless"—while males dominate the leadership and decision-making roles. The overall result is that television tends to perpetuate the traditional stereotype of the female as generally helpless and dependent, unfit to handle many chores outside the home.

Combatting this image, associations such as the National Organization for Women (NOW) have been applying pressure through conventional channels in an attempt to attain a fairer representation. In addition to protesting the bland and diminished image in television drama, NOW also has been fighting to strengthen the female image in commercials. Too often, the women in commercials have been depicted simply as sex objects or as helpless creatures to be rescued by some masculine guardian angel.

The Homosexual Task Forces Rising from nonrecognition to occasional ridicule (Milton Berle in drag in the late 1940s), homosexuals generally remained in the closet until the 1970s, when several serious dramas attempted to deal with "the homosexual problem." But these productions (the TV movie *That Certain Summer,* two episodes of *Marcus Welby, M.D.,* and one show on *Police Woman*) generally portrayed homosexuals as sick, dangerous, or remorseful.

As a result of these dramatizations, the New York-based National Gay Task Force staged several sit-ins and eventually got the NAB Television Code Review Board to issue a directive which recommends that homosexuals be treated in a more sympathetic manner. Today, the Gay Activists Alliance and the Los Angeles–based Gay Media Task Force are both working with producers in reviewing scripts. To help attain a more positive image of the homosexual in today's TV drama, they are gradually eradicating the lisping, limp-wristed image of yesterday's caricature. Like many other protest groups, the homosexual community has found the right places to apply pressure to the corporate media body.

SUMMARY

Often to forestall additional government controls, the mass media industries have developed a mixture of professional self-regulation and public-pressure responsiveness. The press has a long history of industry regulation built around documents such as the ASNE Code of Ethics and the Sigma Delta Chi Code of Ethics. Other internal gatekeeping checkpoints promote self-restraint in areas of national security, public morality, and individual rights. The broadcast media rely on the NAB Codes of Radio and Television as generally proscriptive lists of "do's" and "don'ts." The RTNDA Code of Broadcast News Ethics, like the various press canons, represents more of a balance between libertarian and social-responsibility concerns.

Self-regulation in the motion picture field has evolved through a series of production codes to the present MPAA ratings system. The advertising business has several associations involved in self-regulation; their efforts are coordinated through the NARB system of appeals. The recording industry, the comic book publishers, and the public relations field all have their own self-regulatory mechanisms, too.

Considerable media regulation is achieved through mutual media criticism and public self-evaluation (such as the ombudsman concept). The 1947 Commission on Freedom of the Press was responsible for furthering the concept of press and media councils—including the National News Council. Outside professional media criticism has matured with the increasing sophistication of the media. Professional and popular awards help to define higher standards of performance—especially prestigious prizes such as the Pulitzer and Peabody awards.

Public pressure is brought to bear on the media through a variety of sources. Existing national groups—like the PTA and AMA—can be mobilized to fight particular media problems. On the other hand, specialized organizations—such as the NCCB, NCTV, and ACT—can be formed to work for reform within a given medium. Other groups—such as the Coalition for Better Television—work for citizen control with tactics such as boycotts. Many minority groups (racial and ethnic communities, age groupings, women, homosexuals, and others) have legitimate concerns with their specific portrayals in the media—nonrecognition, ridicule, and stereotyping. They use similar pressure tactics and approaches to achieve needed reforms and improved media images.

Schramm asks several penetrating closing questions:

Finally, to what extent can the great audience be expected to take full partnership in the task of keeping mass communication responsible? Is the mass communication audience doomed to relative passivity or inarticulateness, to be represented only by a few organized minority groups and articulate critics? . . . Or is it possible that an articulate, critical audience may develop to provide the check on mass communication which everyone feels is needed, but which nobody feels should be provided by government? . . . And if indeed there are strong feelings within the public as to what kind of performance is wanted from mass communication, through what machinery can and should those feelings be expressed?[34]

Notes to Chapter 10

1. Wilbur Schramm, *Responsibility in Mass Communication* (New York: Harper & Row, 1957), p. 9.

2. Wilbur Schramm, *Men, Messages, and Media: A Look at Human Communication* (New York: Harper & Row, 1973), pp. 138–139.

3. Reprinted in Frank J. Kahn, ed., *Documents of American Broadcasting* (New York: Appleton-Century-Crofts, 1968), pp. 308–309.

4. *Code of Broadcast News Ethics,* reprinted in Mary B. Cassata and Molefi K. Asante, *Mass Communication: Principles and Practices* (New York: Macmillan, 1979), p. 293.

5. Joel Persky, "Self-Regulation of Broadcasting—Does It Exist?" in *Mass Media and Society,* 3rd ed., ed. Alan Wells (Palo Alto, Calif.: Mayfield, 1979), p. 369.

6. Christopher H. Sterling and John M. Kittross, *Stay Tuned: A Concise History of American Broadcasting* (Belmont, Calif.: Wadsworth, 1978), p. 307.

7. Arthur Knight, *The Liveliest Art: A Panoramic History of the Movies* (New York: New American Library, 1957), p. 111.

8. Robert Sklar, *Movie-Made America: A Cultural History of American Movies* (New York: Random House, Vintage Books, 1975), p. 173.

9. Knight, *The Liveliest Art,* pp. 112–113.

10. Peter M. Sandman, David M. Rubin, and David B. Sachsman, *Media: An Introductory Analysis of American Mass Communications,* 2nd ed. (Englewood Cliffs, N.J.: Prentice-Hall, 1976), p. 346.

11. Ray Eldon Hiebert, Donald F. Ungurait, and Thomas W. Bohn, *Mass Media II: An Introduction to Modern Communication,* 2nd ed. (New York: Longman, 1979), p. 138.

12. Schramm, *Responsibility in Mass Communication,* p. 87.

13. Warren K. Agee, Phillip H. Ault, and Edwin Emery, *Introduction to Mass Communications,* 6th ed. (New York: Harper & Row, 1979), p. 69.

14. Ben Bagdikian, "The Saga of a Newspaper Ombudsman," in *Readings in Mass Communication: Concepts and Issues in the Mass Media,* 2nd ed., ed. Michael C. Emery and Ted Curtis Smythe (Dubuque, Iowa: Wm. C. Brown, 1974), p. 74.

15. Bernard Rubin, *Media, Politics, and Democracy* (New York: Oxford University Press, 1977), p. 67.

16. Ibid., pp. 68, 69.

17. Donald G. Brignolo, "How Community Press Councils Work," in *Readings in Mass Communication: Concepts and Issues in the Mass Media,* ed. Michael C. Emery and Ted Curtis Smythe (Dubuque, Iowa: Wm. C. Brown, 1972), p. 65.

18. Donald M. Gillmor, "Press Councils in America," in *Enduring Issues in Mass Communication,* ed.. Everette E. Dennis, Arnold H. Ismach, and Donald M. Gillmor (St. Paul: West, 1978), p. 341.

19. Sydney W. Head, *Broadcasting in America,* 2nd ed. (Boston: Houghton Mifflin, 1972), p. 497. The quotation is from Lyman Bryson, *The Next America: Prophecy and Faith* (New York: Harper & Brothers, 1952), p. 135.

20. David Shaw, "The Rise of Healthy Skeptics," *TV Guide,* 19 March 1977, p. 7.

21. "Washington Post Reporter Admits Hoax Won Pulitzer," *Los Angeles Times,* 16 April 1981, Pt I, pp. 1, 10.

22. "Bookworms," *Los Angeles Times,* 3 August 1981, Pt II, p. 4

23. Ron Powers, "The New 'Holy War' against Sex and Violence," *TV Guide,* 18 April 1981, p. 8.

24. Isaac Asimov, "Censorship: It's 'A Choking Grip,'" *TV Guide,* 18 July 1981, p. 13.

25. George Comstock, Steven Chaffee, Natan Katzman, Maxwell McCombs, and Donald Roberts, *Television and Human Behavior* (New York: Columbia University Press, 1978), p. 33.

26. For a full discussion of the nonrecognition–ridicule–regulation hypothesis, see C. C. Clark, "Television and Social Controls: Some Observations on the Portrayal of Ethnic Minorities," in *Television Quarterly,* 8 (1969): 18–22.

27. The study was conducted by Bradley Greenberg of Michigan State University.

28. Jack G. Shaheen, "The Arab Stereotype on Television," *The Link* (New York: Americans for Middle East Understandings), April/May 1980, p. 1.

29. Howard Rosenberg, "Proposed 'Hanta Yo' Miniseries a No Go?" *Los Angeles Times,* 27 February 1981, Pt VI, p. 1.

30. Max Gunther, "Life in a Pressure Cooker," *TV Guide,* 9 February 1974, p. 7.

31. Robert Liebert, quoted in "What TV Does to Kids," *Newsweek,* 21 February 1977, p. 65.

32. Ronald Drabman, quoted in ibid.

33. Don Kowet, "Is TV Stuck on Youth?" *TV Guide,* 27 September 1980, p. 5.

34. Schramm, *Responsibility in Mass Communication,* p. 9.

UNIT III APPENDIX
The Statement of Principles of the
American Society of Newspaper Editors (ASNE)

Reproduced below is A Statement of Principles of the American Society of Newspaper Editors. It sets forth the responsibilities and obligations of the journalist. In 1975, it replaced the Canons of Journalism mentioned in the text.

PREAMBLE

The First Amendment, protecting freedom of expression from abridgment by an law, guarantees to the people through their press a constitutional right, and thereby places on newspaper people a particular responsibility.

Thus journalism demands of its practitioners not only industry and knowledge but also the pursuit of a standard of integrity proportionate to the journalist's singular obligation.

To this end the American Society of Newspaper Editors sets forth this Statement of Principles as a standard encouraging the highest ethical and professional performance.

ARTICLE I—Responsibility

The primary purpose of gathering and distributing news and opinion is to serve the general welfare by informing the people and enabling them to make judgments on the issues of time. Newspapermen and women who abuse the power of their professional role for selfish motives or unworthy purposes are faithless to that public trust.

The American press was made free not just to inform or just to serve as a forum for debate but also to bring an independent scrutiny to bear on the forces of power in the society, including the conduct of official power at all levels of government.

ARTICLE II—Freedom of the Press

Freedom of the press belongs to the people. It must be defended against encroachment or assault from any quarter, public or private.

Journalists must be constantly alert to see that the public's business is conducted in public. They must be vigilant against all who would exploit the press for selfish purposes.

ARTICLE III—Independence

Journalists must avoid impropriety and the appearance of impropriety as well as any conflict of interest or the appearance of conflict. They should neither accept anything nor pursue any activity that might compromise or seem to compromise their integrity.

ARTICLE IV—Truth and Accuracy

Good faith with the reader is the foundation of good journalism. Every effort must be made to assure that the news content is accurate, free from bias and in context, and that all sides are presented fairly. Editorials, analytical articles and commentary should be held to the same standards of accuracy with respect to facts as news reports.

Significant errors of fact, as well as errors of omission, should be corrected promptly and prominently.

ARTICLE V—Impartiality

To be impartial does not require the press to be unquestioning or to refrain from editorial expression. Sound practice, however, demands a clear distinction for the reader between news reports and opinion. Articles that contain opinion or personal interpretation should be clearly identified.

ARTICLE VI—Fair Play

Journalists should respect the rights of people involved in the news, observe the common standards of decency and stand accountable to the public for the fairness and accuracy of their news reports.

Persons publicly accused should be given the earliest opportunity to respond.

Pledges of confidentiality to news sources must be honored at all costs, and therefore should not be given lightly. Unless there is clear and pressing need to maintain confidences, sources of information should be identified.

These principles are intended to preserve, protect and strengthen the bond of trust and respect between American journalists and the American people, a bond that is essential to sustain the grant of freedom entrusted to both by the nation's founders.

—adopted by the ASNE board of directors, Oct. 23, 1975.

UNIT FOUR

In previous units, you have looked at the mass media in a theoretical framework (Unit I), as business structures (Unit II), and from a societal perspective (Unit III). In this final unit, you will be examining the future of the media. Where are they going? And what will be your future involvement with mass communication?

Chapter 11 will deal with the future of the content of the mass media. Building on an understanding of past and present message patterns, you will better be able to speculate about future entertainment, news, and propaganda content.

Chapter 12 is concerned with the emerging technologies of print and electronic communication. In the light of the glittering array of fantastic new tools of production, distribution, storage, and reception of information, the old distinctions among publication, broadcast, and film technologies begin to break down.

Finally, Chapter 13 challenges you to think about your future relationships with the media. What will be the role of the future media consumer? What impact will the media have upon you? How will you interact with the exploding channels? What responsibilities will you assume?

Mass Media in a Future Framework

In Section 1.5 we pointed out three basic divisions of media messages or functions— *escapism* or entertainment (both diversion and art), *reality* or news (information and instruction), and *propaganda* (editorial, advertising, and political persuasion). Each of these three categories of mass communication raises different types of issues pertaining to future audience needs, uses, effects, and behavior.

Entertainment messages stimulate questions about your future use of leisure time and the relationships of art and culture. News content is involved with numerous specific issues and problems—most of them relating to the objectivity of the media and the resulting picture of reality that will be presented to you. And persuasive messages, of course, raise many concerns about the ways in which you will continue to be manipulated by the media—especially for political and commercial purposes. These are the kinds of topics that lead to the theme of Chapter 11:

• *Each communication category of media content—escapism (entertainment), reality (news), and propaganda (persuasion)—poses specific problems and questions relating to its future social relationships with audiences.*

11

The Future of Media Content: Entertainment, News, and Persuasion

11.1 Entertainment: Popular Culture and Fine Art

In discussions of the popular mass media, the question of "art" is almost always a consideration. Can a popular work—one which reaches hundreds of thousands, or even millions, of persons—ever be considered a genuine work of art?

11.1.1 DIVERSION AND ART

When you speak of "escapism" or entertainment, there are two different concepts you could have in mind. On the one hand, there is pure *diversion*—recreation, distraction, something to do when there is nothing better to do. And then, on the other hand, there is *artistic satisfaction*—the response to aesthetic achievement, the discriminating pleasure of appreciating a skillful and inspirational performance.

To a great extent, your future use of a particular media message, whether for diversion or artistic purposes, will depend upon your perception of the function of the medium. Use of a medium purely for the sake of attending to the medium—using the *medium as the message* by skimming through the morning paper, for example, or reading a book at bedtime, or turning on the radio for company—is almost always associated with diversion behavior. You are not seeking out satisfying works of art when you routinely turn to a given medium, regardless of specific content, just because the medium is there.

Artistic satisfaction implies more, of course, than elitist cultural performances of ballet, opera, and Shakespeare. Any form of entertainment which lifts us above routine boredom-killing escapism might qualify as meeting the criterion of aesthetic fulfillment. A classic Charlie Chaplin two-reeler, a well-staged and well-executed rock concert, a satirical column by a newspaper humorist, an awe-inspiring magician, or even a talk-show appearance by a witty and imaginative conversationalist—these can all be considered artistic performances.

11.1.2 FOUR FORMATS OF ENTERTAINMENT COMMUNICATION

Essentially, all entertainment can be reduced to four basic formats—*drama, performance, contests,* and *conversation.* That is all there is.

Each of the four entertainment formats discussed in this section—drama, performance, contests, and conversation—have historical roots which can be traced back to the beginnings of human development. *Conversation* was the dominant form of entertainment from the earliest campfire on. When characters were portrayed to add dimension to the art of storytelling, the *drama* was born. The earliest religious ceremonies featured *performance* with the chant, the song, and dance. And athletic *contests* and competitions have always been a basic form of entertainment.

Each of these primitive entertainment formats evolved into the popular media of various historical periods—the Greek drama, the Roman circus, medieval jugglers and troubadours. Modern print and electric technologies have but facilitated a refinement and expansion of these basic diversions. Future entertainment content will be but an extension of these formats.

Anne Roiphe relates television to the earliest use of these formats:

An age or so away, primitive man danced wild steps around night fires to scare away evil spirits and to comfort himself that he was not helpless against the demonic, destructive forces in the universe. Man has always invented stories, gods and heroes to give him a sense of understanding and control of the lightning, the thunder, accident and death. I think we use our television set in many of the same ways. We huddle about its blue light looking for relief, control and understanding, magic to be worked on all those confusing forces that push us about.[1]

INSET 11–1
Historical Foundations of Entertainment Formats

CHAPTER FORTY-ONE

Moby Dick

I, ISHMAEL, was one of that crew; my shouts had gone up with the rest; my oath had been welded with theirs; and stronger I shouted, and more did I hammer and clinch my oath, because of the dread in my soul. A wild, mystical, sympathetical feeling was in me; Ahab's quenchless feud seemed mine. With greedy ears I learned the history of that murderous monster against whom I and all the others had taken our oaths of violence and revenge.

For some time past, though at intervals only, the unaccom-

Four categories of mass media entertainment: *drama* (the novel); *performance* (TV musicians); *contests* (crossword puzzle); and *conversation* (TV talk show)

And future specific efforts in each of these areas may occasionally be elevated to works of art.

Drama One of the broadest forms of entertainment is the drama, the craft of storytelling. Drama can be defined as any format which takes characters, real or fictional, and weaves them into a plot with a story line: a novel, a stage play, a theatrical movie, a TV soap opera, a magazine short story, a comic strip, or an animated cartoon. The dramatic entertainment may focus on any of numerous themes or *genre:* the western, the historical romance, cops and robbers, fantasy, melodrama, situation comedy, classical tragedy, science fiction, biography, and so forth.

Of the various dramatic formats in television, for example, most artistic concern is focused on single works of art—the *self-contained drama* and its near relatives, the *anthology* series (single presentations within a continuing framework), and the *mini-series* (the extended presentation of a single work of art). The *episodic drama* (the situation comedy and the noncontinuous dramatic series) and the *serialized soap opera* both tend to exploit the dramatic form for the sake of building a continuing audience loyalty based more upon familiar and popular characters than upon artistic dramatic treatment.

Performance The word "performance" is used in a limited sense to mean an exhibition or presentation of some specific nonacting appearance by an entertainer. The performer presents himself or herself, without assuming any dramatic characterization, simply to display a given talent—as a singer, for example, or a tap dancer, a guitarist, a magician, a dare-devil stunt person, an orchestra leader, a juggler, a ballerina, a stand-up comedian, or an acrobat. In print media, the same performer function might be fulfilled by a humor columnist, a photographer, a cartoonist, or a poet.

Performers in these categories ask that they also be judged as artists. They ask that their talents be evaluated and appreciated by standards comparable to those established for playwrights, actors, and directors. And, indeed, the world's great singers, musicians, humorists, mimes, and other performers certainly deserve to have their offerings judged as works of art.

Contests A third category of media entertainment could be considered under the broad heading of "contests"—any kind of media event or content that involves either audience participation or coverage of competition between opposing contestants. The primary example, of course, would be sports coverage, from the heights of the Olympics to the depths of the *Battle of the Network Stars*. Newspaper and magazine treatment of sports activities also fall into this category.

Other types of contest entertainment include all manner of games and competition programs in the broadcast media—quiz contests, game shows, celebrity matches, and audience participation stunts. The underlying criteria which identify the media event as contest entertainment are that (1) there is an element of competition, which may or may not involve the viewer, and (2) the outcome is not scripted. In print media, contest entertainment includes crossword puzzles, word games, bridge and chess columns, circulation-building contests, and the like.

In the debate over whether or not the mass media can be thought of as vehicles for true art, the contest formats are seldom considered. Although some sports competition (gymnastics, figure skating, diving) involve a grace and beauty that demand artistic appreciation, most examples of sports and games competition seldom reach truly aesthetic plateaus.

Conversation A final format of entertainment communication is simply talk, conversation among two or more people, which may take either of two forms: *one-way presentations,* as in a radio show with a disc jockey, a newspaper gossip column, a humorous essay, or any other format in which a mass media personality is talking directly to the audience; and *eavesdropping* formats in which the audience is invited to drop in and witness a conversation among other parties, such as TV talk shows, panel discussions, interviews, a newspaper advice column, and so forth.

With NBC's introduction of the *Today* program (1952) and the *Tonight Show* (1954), television launched what is probably its most original format. By the early 1980s, a video addict in one of the nation's larger cities could watch more than fourteen hours of broadcast talk shows every day (with the aid of a videocassette recorder to delay programs telecast at the same time).[2] The phenomenon of the talk show had become one of the medium's prime entertainment formats.

11.1.3 THE DEBATE OVER POPULAR ENTERTAINMENT AND ART

Although some of the formats discussed above (drama, performance) more often deserve to be judged by artistic criteria than others (contests, conversation), the question of *what is art* remains unanswered. If a creative work is appreciated by a large number of individuals—if it is "popular"—then can it be considered something artistic? The elitist definition of art would say "no." To be true art, a work must be something that cannot be appreciated by the common individual. If the masses can admire a given work of art, then

Three definitions of art: *fine art* (serious sculpture); *folk art* (Mexican cups); and *popular art* (paper weight).

what is left for the truly discriminating critic to appreciate?

The Elitist Views Critics have always lamented the fact that large numbers of the masses have turned to popular media. The early nineteenth-century poet and critic Samuel Taylor Coleridge, for example, warned against undiscriminating and excessive reading of novels:

I will run the risk of asserting, that where the reading of novels prevails as a habit, it occasions in time the entire destruction of the powers of the mind: it is such an utter loss to the reader, that it is not so much to be called pass-time as kill-time. It conveys no trustworthy information as to facts; it produces no improvement of the intellect, but fills the mind with a mawkish and morbid sensibility, which is directly hostile to the cultivation, invigoration, and enlargement of the nobler faculties of the understanding.[3]

And a little later, the distinguished French observer Alexis de Tocqueville commented derisively on the state of American art: "In aristocracies a few great pictures are produced; in democratic countries a vast number of insignificant ones. In the former, statues are raised of bronze: in the latter, they are modeled in plaster."[4] He argued eloquently that a democracy simply could not produce a culture of high artistic quality and lofty standards.

Fine Art, Folk Art, and Popular Art In a famous 1948 essay, Lyman Bryson discussed three categories of art: *fine art,* works created by artists for their own aesthetic satisfaction with little thought given to either popular appeal or commercial success; *folk art,* the common art forms developed by an entire culture for ritualistic, social, or utilitarian purposes; and *popular art,* creative works which measure their success by the size of their audiences and the volume of their profits.

Sociologically speaking, popular art is a product of the machine age. It was not possible until we had cheap print and the cinema and broadcasting. . . . They made it possible for millions upon millions to enjoy vicarious living. They cost so much and were produced on such a scale that they had to appeal to huge audiences which meant that they found low common denominators of interest and taste.[5]

Lowest Common Denominator   Economic realities dictate that the mass media lessen the quality of their content in an attempt to reach as many people as possible—by appealing to the "lowest common denominator." This trend can be traced back to Benjamin Day and the penny press (Section 3.3.2) when he, and other editors, determined that

the new (lower) class of readers wanted popular and sensational news items rather than strong editorial content and in-depth news of significance.

Thus, it is argued by the elitist critics, television and other popular arts debase all culture. The people are exposed to a massive dose of muck and mediocrity that passes for literature. They no longer can discriminate between fine art and popular art.

Defending Popular Art   On the other hand, many critics through the years have provided strong arguments in defense of mass or popular culture. Lazarsfeld and Merton, for example, try to put the impact of mass media and popular art into an historical perspective:

If esthetic tastes are to be considered in their social setting, we must recognize that the effective audience for the arts has become historically transformed. Some centuries back, this audience was largely confined to a selected aristocratic elite.

One of the astounding realities of the mass media is the insatiable rate at which they utilize popular art. The publishing industry turns out more than one hundred new books or revisions every day, many of which are intended to be works of art. Hollywood releases about five new entertainment films each week. But the most massive of all the media, of course, is television. The average TV station, programming about twenty hours a day, has to schedule more than seven thousand hours of video content a year. The three commercial networks must grind out over sixteen hundred hours of new prime-time evening programming each year (excluding reruns, daytime soap operas, and so forth). James Brown compares television's demand with that of the live theater:

We should reflect on more than 2,000 years of staged drama, and consider how many theatrical plays of those centuries we even know, much less care about or read or stage in our own time. We can recall that of 8,000 plays copyrighted each year and recorded in the Library of Congress, only 80 plays are produced (for highly selective audiences) annually on or near Broadway, of which 15 to 20 may be moderately successful. . . . The fact that the [television] medium produces several outstanding multi-hour presentations a month deserves more praise than the meager annual productivity of Broadway.[6]

INSET 11–2
The Quantities of Popular Mass Art

Relatively few were literate. And very few possessed the means to buy books, attend theaters and travel to the urban centers of the arts. Not more than a slight fraction, possibly not more than one or two per cent, of the population composed the effective audience for the arts. These happy few cultivated their esthetic tastes, and their selective demand left its mark in the form of relatively high artistic standards.[7]

At the other end of the socioeconomic spectrum, the masses throughout history have had to amuse themselves with baser entertainments—card games, cockfighting, drinking contests, folk dancing, gambling, and chasing wenches. The masses never have been in a position to appreciate fine art.

Thus, the argument goes, the media have tended to raise the general level of artistic consciousness by bringing to the masses *some* cultural events, no matter how popularized or predigested they may be. Television viewers are exposed to ballet sequences, popular operas, occasional fine motion picture dramas, outstanding serious musical performances, condensations of classic novels, and so forth. Exposing the masses to *some* fine art through the mass media is better than offering no glimpses of the finer arts at all.

And besides, argue the defenders of mass culture, what is wrong with popular art anyway? More than a century ago, America's acclaimed "poet of the people," Walt Whitman, wrote a stirring appeal for a popular, democratic art that would break with the aristocratic standards of elitist cultures:

I should demand a program of culture, drawn out, not for a single class alone, or for the parlors or lecture rooms, but with an eye to the practical life, the west, the workingman, the facts of farms and jack-planes and engineers. . . . I should demand of this program or theory a scope generous enough to include the widest human area . . . and not restricted by conditions ineligible to the masses. The best culture will always be that of the manly courageous instincts, and loving perceptions, and of self-respect—aiming to form, over this continent, an ideocracy of universalism.[8]

11.2 Entertainment: Popular Art and Leisure

Even as you debate the relative merits of fine art, folk art, and popular art, another related question emerges: Is popular art all that bad for you? Does popular art have any redeeming virtues—other than being successful commercially? Can we define in the future a socially constructive role for mass culture, or must it be conceded that popular art has no positive cultural effect?

11.2.1 THE POSITIVE ARGUMENT: USES AND GRATIFICATIONS

Individuals come to the mass media with a variety of personal needs—the need to escape boredom, a curiosity about one's environment, a lack of specific information, a yearning for aesthetic pleasure, a need for companionship, the necessity to reinforce one's value system, a desire to heighten one's emotional state, and so forth (Section 8.3.1). A selected medium and message must satisfy that specific need or the individual receiver will turn to some other mass communication experience. Thus, the argument goes, any escapist/diversion medium usage is justified because it meets the particular individual's need for escapism at that moment.

Is it fair to ask a popular medium to fulfill a specific artistic need by supplying fine art or high culture if the receiver/audience is not asking for that need to be gratified? Should not the audiences (rather than some self-appointed critics) be able to determine what manner of content—art or diversion—they expect from a medium? If readers, viewers, and listeners ask only for gossip, crossword puzzles, disc jockeys, comic books, and situation comedies, do the critics have the right to demand more from a medium?

The Katzenjammer Kids

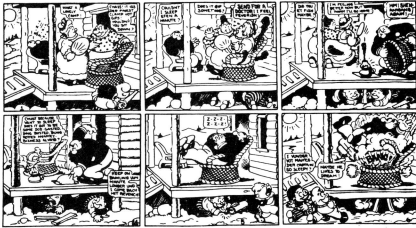

A 1920 version of
The Katzenjammer Kids

Escapism/diversion through popular art has been an integral part of each mass medium from its earliest days. As every medium developed, it quickly recognized the mass appeal of popular art forms that are still utilized today.

• *1897*. The comic strip "The Katzenjammer Kids" first appeared. Still running today, it is the most durable comic strip of all time.
• *1903*. Directed by Edwin S. Porter, *The Great Train Robbery* was the prototype of the narrative movie. This nine-minute western (the first) was the earliest film to use modern camera and editing devices.
• *1913*. Utilizing thirty-two clues, the world's first crossword puzzle was published in the *New York World*.
• *1929*. *Amos 'n' Andy*, a blackface ethnic comedy carried over from minstrel shows, made its debut on the NBC Blue network. It probably did more to sell radio sets than any other early broadcast series.
• *1937*. Although there were some earlier attempts, *Detective Comics* was the first comic book in the format we would recognize today.
• *1948*. Featuring Milton Berle, the *Texaco Star Theater* was the TV reincarnation of the vaudeville show, and it did for the new video medium what Amos 'n' Andy had done for radio two decades earlier. With his zany slapstick routines and his female impersonations, "Uncle Milty" became known as Mr. Television for the medium's first decade.

11.2.2 THE NEGATIVE ARGUMENT: DANGERS OF DIVERSION

Other critics point out the negative effects and dangers inherent in escapist/diversion entertainment (see Section 8.4). Such entertainment, they claim, tends to promote individual and group *apathy* (including "narcotizing dysfunction"); diminish conversational, creative, and physical skills as we become more *passive*; stimulate certain types of *antisocial behavior* (deviant sex and violence); and offer *misleading or inappropriate advice* and guidance on talk shows and in advice columns and soap operas. Most of all, from an artistic point of view, mass entertainment tends to *lower cultural standards* and popular tastes (Section 11.1.3).

The argument emerges that mass media entertainment—unless it qualifies as art—is not only time-wasting, but is actually hazardous to one's psychological and cultural health. Audiences should be discouraged in the future from enjoying mass communication solely as a popular diversion. Ernest van den Haag, in a summary of the elitist critical viewpoint, emphasizes the problem of uncritical exposure to the massive doses of diluted diversion that passes for entertainment.

We have already stressed that mass media must offer homogenized fare to meet an average of tastes. Further, whatever the quality of the offerings, the very fact that one after the other is absorbed continuously, indiscriminately and casually, trivializes all. . . . The impact of each of the offerings of mass media is thus weakened by the next one. But the impact of the stream of all mass-media offerings is cumulative and strong. It lessens people's capacity to experience life itself.[9]

Such a constant diet of tasteless confections—full of preservatives and artificial sweeteners, but with no real nutrition—will eventually lead to cultural starvation. This synthetic gratification can only detract from the real experiences of life and art itself. You can never be truly fulfilled if you exist only for the substitute diversion of popular art. By using the mass media to escape from reality—by using your leisure time for diversionary, mediated pursuits—you are, indeed, escaping from life itself.

Your future relationships with entertainment media depend to a great extent upon your definition of art, your perception of the value of popular culture, your adherence to the Puritan work ethic (which frowns upon pure diversion unless it can be justified as "art appreciation"), and your own needs that you bring to the media experience.

11.3 News: Sufficiency of Information

Several questions can be raised about the future of news coverage in the mass media. (1) *Will news coverage be adequate?* Is there enough news? Are the right stories being covered? Are the important events of our times given abundant coverage? Are we given sufficient in-depth information to paint a realistic picture of our environment? (2) *Will news coverage be accurate and objective?* Are facts presented accurately? Are all sides of an issue treated fairly? Are reporters and editors objective in their approach? (3) *What role can be played by alternate news channels?* Can other forms of news dissemination help to alleviate the problems of adequacy and objectivity discussed above? What is the future role of minority media? The underground press? Public broadcasting?

These questions are examined in the next three sections.

11.3.1 MAKING ROOM FOR MORE NEWS

The primary problem in dealing with news coverage is simply the sheer magnitude of the job. There is no way that *all* of the news can

In addition to covering the daily sessions of the House of Representatives, C-SPAN also provides public affairs interviews and features. Above, Vice President George Bush responds to a viewer question on a "live" nationwide call-in program.

be delivered to everyone who is interested in all things interesting. And this cannot change drastically in the near future. Nevertheless, there are proposals and potentials for the expansion of news coverage in some of the media, especially in the telecommunications areas.

In mid-1980, a group of about thirty independent (non-network) TV stations launched the Independent Network News (INN), a nightly nationwide news program offered during prime-time viewing hours. Also in 1980, ABC initiated its 11:30 P.M. *Nightline* to examine the major news story of the day. Late in 1982, each of the commercial TV networks instituted late-night and early-morning (between midnight and 7:00 A.M.) extended news shows. All three commercial TV networks have long wanted to expand their evening news programs to one hour, but pressure from affiliate stations (who would lose millions of dollars in local advertising revenues) has been the main stumbling block.

The most promising area for possible expansion of electronic news coverage, however, probably lies with the cable-TV systems—which theoretically could devote dozens of channels to news and public affairs. The Atlanta entrepreneur Ted Turner (Inset 7–9) inaugurated the twenty-four-hour Cable News Network (CNN) in mid-1980. Within a year, ABC and Westinghouse announced plans to start a joint venture to operate two twenty-four-hour cable-TV news services to be labeled Satellite NewsChannels. And eight days later, Turner came back with an announcement of plans for his second twenty-four-hour cable news network, CNN-2.

Other specialized news and public affairs cable coverages have been put into operation. One of the more interesting is the Cable-Satellite Public Affairs Network (C-SPAN), a nonprofit cooperative set up by the cable-TV industry in 1979, which provides daily, live, gavel-to-gavel coverage of the proceedings of the U.S. House of Representatives.

Although it is likely that additional news channels will be opened up in the future, the crucial question is: What will you—and other media consumers—do with those channels?

11.3.2 FOCUSING ON THE INSIGNIFICANT AND SENSATIONAL

Another problem is that of emphasizing news items that are basically insignificant and/or sensational—giving the people what they *want* rather than what is important, what they are willing to pay for because it caters to their sense of morbid curiosity, scandal, and gossip. How can this change in the future? More than a century and a quarter ago, Thoreau commented on the trivial content of the popular penny press:

And I am sure that I never read any memorable news in a newspaper. If we read of one man robbed, or murdered, or killed by accident, or one house burned, or one vessel wrecked, or one steamboat blown up, or one cow run over on the Western Railroad, or one mad dog killed, or one lot of grasshoppers in the winter—we never need read of another. One is enough. If you are acquainted with the principle, what do you care for myriad instances and applications? To a philosopher all *news*, as it is called, is gossip, and they who edit and read it are old women over their tea.[10]

Indeed, it may be appropriate to ask if we are not now—and potentially even more so in the future—in danger of consuming too much news. Perhaps we are entering a period of "communication inflation," in which news messages diminish in value as we are exposed to more and more of them.

Although there have always been elements of entertainment and pandering in the presentation of news, the trend toward popularizing and sugarcoating the news took a noticeable leap forward (or backward) in the 1970s with the spread of the "happy news" format on television. In this format, show-business elements are injected into local TV newscasts in an attempt to liven the program and increase the ratings by making the news-*show* more fun to watch. Handsome new faces and attractive personalities, joined by

---

With its roots planted firmly in the "yellow journalism" of the 1890s and the "jazz journalism" of the 1920s (Inset 3–7), the *New York Post* reigns today as the undisputed king of daily sensationalism (sharing the overall honors with weekly publications such as the *National Enquirer, Star,* and *Globe*). Purchased by the flamboyant Australian publisher Rupert Murdoch in 1976, the *Post* has substantially increased its circulation (although it still loses millions of dollars a year) with its torrid photo-journalism and screaming half-page headlines—such as "NIXON AIDES WERE DRUGGED," "BARE PLOT TO STEAL ELVIS' BODY," "NUDE MAN LEAPS 85 FLOORS," "SEX TAPES STUN D.C.," and so on.

Combining these features with its tabloid format (half the size of a standard newspaper) and its short and punchy articles, which mix hard news with trivia and gossip, the *Post* has managed to attract a large audience who, as one critic sarcastically puts it, "are the kind of people who move their lips while they read—and probably while they think."[11]

Staffers at the *Post* and other defenders call such critics "elitist eggheads," pointing out, "It's snobbish to tell us this is what you ought to be telling your readers." And the executive editor adds, in the best free-enterprise libertarian fashion, "We've got the circulation. That answers all the criticism."[12]

INSET 11–4
The *New York Post*: Sensationalism Lives On

eccentric weathercasters and other featured players, chat and joke their way through the evening's quota of mayhem and turmoil.

One crucial question concerning the future of mass media news has to center on the extent to which popular news will continue to be trivialized.

The Disaster Syndrome Another problem is that of trying to maintain a healthy news mix between normality and calamity. When society is functioning normally, there is no news. But when things get fouled up, then we have something newsworthy. Five hundred airplanes may take off and land every day at a major airport without incident; but if one plane overshoots the runway and slides ten feet off the pavement, then we have *news*.

The difficulty lies in covering aberrant news events (crime, natural disasters, violence, governmental corruption, warfare, accidents, financial catastrophes, terrorism) on a daily basis without creating a fatalistic gloom-and-doom impression that the planet is coming apart at the seams. How do you report daily that thousands of airplanes took off and landed safely, that millions of government workers carried out their routine jobs responsibly, and that crops are growing peaceably in Iowa and Indiana? Such items do not constitute "hard news" and do not attract very large audiences. How can the news media maintain an appropriate balance in the future?

11.3.3 ADEQUATE BACKGROUND COVERAGE AND IN-DEPTH TREATMENT

The media, especially radio and television, do a good job of covering *events*, those happenings (either scheduled or unanticipated) which result in high drama, conflict, or colorful ceremony. They do a poorer job in reporting on *situations*, the underlying conditions which (if left unnoticed) often erupt into ugly events.

It was much easier to report on the 1971 prison riots at Attica, New York—the event—than it would have been to devote the resources to do an adequate job of examining the need for prison reform—the situation which led to the event in which forty-three men were killed. Media reacted slowly and generally responsibly in covering the twelve-day *event* at the Three-Mile Island nuclear power plant in 1979; but they could have rendered a much more valuable public service if they had devoted adequate time in the years preceding the accident to examining the total *situation* and the arguments surrounding nuclear energy.

The problem, of course, is that there is no way of knowing ahead of time which situations need priority investigation because they are more likely to lead to earthshaking events. Also, the total resources of all news media could never be enough to produce background reports on every possible situation of significance. How can this balance be improved in the future?

The Documentary While newspapers and—to an even greater extent—magazines have been able to devote considerable energy and space to background and feature reporting to examine situations, the film and broadcast media have developed the genre of the "documentary." The classic form of the silent film documentary was established with Robert Flaherty's realistic documentation of Eskimo life in *Nanook of the North* (1922) and his beautiful South Seas study *Moana* (1926). The American film documentary reached maturity with the Depression-era works of Pare Lorentz for the Roosevelt administration—*The Plow That Broke the Plains* (1936) and *The River* (1937).

Cutting across media lines, *Time* magazine launched its successful radio documentary series, *The March of Time,* in 1931. The weekly newsmagazine-of-the-air combined news and dramatic techniques to document three or four of the more significant events of the preceding week. And in 1935 *Time* began its series of film documentaries, also entitled *The March of Time.*

Television embraced the documentary format with occasional in-depth studies which appeared on *CBS Reports,* NBC's *White Paper* series, and ABC's *Close-Up* series, among many other programs. Although news and public affairs documentaries on the commercial networks have always had to fight the second-class scheduling status awarded to them by the network's entertainment-oriented executives, they nevertheless—with some sixty to eighty programs a year—have managed periodically to shake the tranquility of a nation with presentations such as Edward R. Murrow's 1960 classic for CBS, *Harvest of Shame,* ABC's *Crucial Summer: The 1963 Civil Rights Crisis,* and NBC's 1973 *Pensions: The Broken Promise.*

How will the conventional sixty-minute documentary format be modified in the future? At one end of the spectrum, there has emerged a trend toward flashier and shorter "mini-documentary" segments; these are often integrated into ongoing news programs (for example, a five-part series of five-minute inserts probing local law enforcement practices may be incorporated into the six o'clock news). There also has evolved the "instant news documentary," a hurriedly assembled thirty- or sixty-minute in-depth news program, which is often scheduled late in the evening of the day on which a major news event has occurred.

At the other end of the spectrum, there is the block buster multipart documentary. In June 1981, CBS broadcast on five consecutive weeknights a five-hour in-depth probing of our military preparedness, *The Defense of the United States.* Nine months in the making, this unprecedented work involved more than eighty CBS news staffers, fourteen separate camera crews (roaming from Moscow to the Egyptian desert), and a million-dollar budget. The macro-documentary fared well

---

**INSET 11–5
Telling on the
Pentagon**

In 1971 CBS triggered what was perhaps the strongest government attack on any broadcast news department up to that point. The network aired a controversial documentary, *The Selling of the Pentagon,* which examined the large public relations budget expended by the Pentagon in its attempt to sell the defense program to the public. Angered by the tone of the program, conservative congressional representatives turned the spotlight on CBS in a full-scale hearing before a congressional subcommittee which was set up specifically to examine the methods used by CBS in editing the documentary.

Disturbed by the editing of interviews with several Pentagon officials, the committee members felt that segments were taken out of context and that opinions had been distorted. Therefore, the committee asked to view the "out-takes," the portions of the filmed interviews that were not incorporated into the final program.

Dr. Frank Stanton, then president of CBS, eloquently denied the right of Congress to examine such unedited material. The editing process of any news establishment must remain protected by the First Amendment, he argued. Unimpressed by such a line of reasoning, the committee voted to cite Stanton and CBS for contempt of Congress. However, the full House—perhaps anticipating the public reaction to the jailing of a respected network president—refused to go along with the contempt citation.

---

with viewers, two of the five parts attracting better than a thirty percent share of the audience. Will there be a future for such extended documentaries in prime time?

11.3.4 GATHERING THE NEWS

Although limited time and space prohibit the mass media from disseminating as much news as might be desired, you must also look at the obstructions that restrict the gathering of news.

Protection of Sources   One continuing problem facing investigative reporters is that of being able to protect their contacts and confidential sources of inside information. Undoubtedly, the most significant sustained investigative journalism of the twentieth century was the Watergate story. The entire two-year episode, which culminated in the resignation of the U.S. president, often hinged upon the confidential information supplied to reporters Woodward and Bernstein by the mysterious, and still undisclosed, anonymous source known as "Deep Throat."

However, the cases of Branzburg, Caldwell, and Pappas (Inset 9–8) served to warn the press that the "shield laws" of individual states could not be counted on to protect reporters from having to divulge their sources of confidential information to the courts.

One significant court battle concerning the protection of sources involved a university paper, *The Stanford Daily.* In 1971 local police—armed with a search warrant—went through the newsroom of the campus paper looking for unpublished photographs taken at a recent demonstration. Maintaining that the surprise search was illegal, the newspaper filed suit; but seven years later the Supreme Court declared that law enforcement agencies could engage in unannounced searches— when possessing a valid search warrant—if they had reasonable belief that the news organization had information relevant to a criminal investigation. In order to soften the impact of this police authority, Congress

The "ambush interview" is designed to catch private individuals or public figures off guard.

passed the Privacy Protection Act of 1980 which prohibits search-warrant seizure of unpublished news materials except in certain carefully delineated situations.

What about the future? Are reporters and news operations likely to find it easier or more difficult to keep their sources confidential?

Ethics of News-Gathering Techniques
Other problems often arise when assertive journalists get deeply involved in investigative reporting. Should reporters try to trick sources with loaded or deceptive questions? Should news agencies pay informants for exclusive information or interviews? Are there situations in which a news organization may legitimately use threats or blackmail in order to get information from a source?

The CBS news magazine *60 Minutes* set a precedent in September 1981 when it turned the cameras on its internal operations and spent an hour publicly questioning its own muckraking techniques—walking into an office unannounced with cameras rolling (the "ambush interview"), surprising a person during an interview with previously undisclosed information, planting a reporter to act as a naive customer in order to entrap a shady business operator, and other controversial procedures. Such practices, if used indiscriminately and aggressively, can result in dramatic but often misleading investigative news reporting.

On June 17, 1972, *Fiddler on the Roof* staged its 3,225th performance, thus setting a record as Broadway's longest-running show. That same day five men carrying electronic "bugging" equipment were caught breaking into Democratic National Headquarters in the Watergate office building in Washington, D.C. This event marked the debut of a twenty-six-month media drama that was to set records for longest-running political debacle.

The *Washington Post* assigned two metropolitan reporters, Bob Woodward and Carl Bernstein, to cover the relatively minor event. The national election was hardly affected by the incident as President Nixon overwhelmed Senator George McGovern in a landslide. However, Woodward and Bernstein—with the encouragement of editor Ben Bradlee and publisher Katherine Graham—continued with the Watergate story, sensing a much larger involvement of key government officials. With weeks of painstaking research, checking out innumerable leads, and relying heavily upon a secret and still unidentified inside source known only as "Deep Throat," the two reporters managed to keep the story before the public into early 1973.

In May, as top White House officials resigned, the Senate Select Committee on Presidential Campaign Activities began televised hearings. America remained glued to the video tube throughout the Senate hearings, which eventually elicited the revelation that Nixon had been secretly making audiotapes of all White House meetings "for historical purposes." Standing behind a cloak of national security and "executive privilege," Nixon repeatedly refused to cooperate with the courts and turn over the subpoenaed tapes.

By early 1974, the television focus had turned to the House Judiciary Committee, which had already started an inquiry into impeachment proceedings. Nixon lost his court battles when the Supreme Court ruled unanimously in July 1974, that he must turn over the subpoenaed tapes. And the tapes, when finally surrendered, demonstrated that Nixon was involved in the cover-up attempt as early as a week after the Watergate breakin. On August 8, 1974, Richard Nixon became the first American president to resign from office.

Despite all of the pressure that the administration could bring to bear, the White House could not snuff out the media event of the century. Two tenacious reporters managed to keep their inside sources confidential; courageous newspaper editorial leadership kept the investigation alive when official channels were unable or unwilling to probe deeper; and television brought it into everyone's living rooms with live Senate and House proceedings.

All of these problems—limitations on channel space, the emphasis on the trivial and the sensational, the lack of in-depth coverage, and the difficulties in gathering news—complicate the job of delivering sufficient information today and tomorrow; and they also raise serious questions about the accuracy and objectivity of news.

11.4 News: Accurate and Objective Information

When you examine our basic communication model (Inset 1–6), you can readily see that the news, our mediated picture of reality, can be distorted or misinterpreted at every stage of the communication process—by the *source,* by the sender of the *message,* by the nature of the *media* or channels involved, and by the perspectives and activities of the *receiver.* Even *feedback* plays a role.

11.4.1 SOURCE DISTORTIONS

News may be twisted by the newsmaker either on purpose or by accident. *Unintentional distortion* occurs, for example, when reporters rely on the same familiar sources for interviews and reactions to world events—prominent politicians, ranking bureaucrats, popular entertainment stars. This tendency of the media to return to the same newsmakers over and over again illustrates the "status conferral" phenomenon. Accidental factors such as the location of an event—its proximity to a news reporter—and its timing in relation to channel deadlines also result in inadvertent distortion.

Intentional Distortion   The greater problem, however, is intentional manipulation of the news media by the source or newsmaker. Politicians, business leaders, entertainment stars, terrorists, consumer advocates, racial leaders,

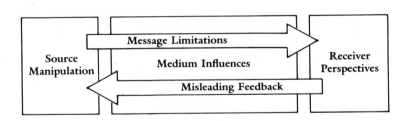

INSET 11–7
Distortion in the Communication Process

Objectivity in the mass communication of news and reality is an elusive goal which is seldom, if ever, achieved. Distortion of information and news items occurs throughout all phases of the communication process. *Source manipulation* includes deliberate falsehoods, creation of pseudo-events, press relations, and so forth. *Message limitations* encompass both sender problems in the construction of messages (reporter and editor biases, advocacy journalism) and gatekeeping judgments. *Medium influences* include such factors as visual emphases, commercial realities of mass news dissemination, and media competition. *Receiver perspectives*—media selection and message perception—affect the way a news message is received. *Misleading feedback,* which can be based upon uninformed opinions, misuse of feedback channels, or ignored responses, also contributes to the problem of distortion.

educators, military commanders, philanthropists, church authorities, environmentalists, welfare recipients—every group of citizens/activists has a story to get before the public, a reason to manipulate the news media.

During the early years of the Vietnam War, for example, most journalists had to rely heavily upon information and reports from the Pentagon; the story of the war was pretty much the story that Washington officialdom wanted the American public to have. But after the Tet offensive, early in 1968, the press realized that it could no longer rely on the distorted view from the Pentagon.

Among the many tools employed to control the news is the use of the *pseudo-event*—an occurrence or event which is staged specifically for the sake of making news and attracting the media. These include press conferences, ribbon-cutting dedications, press briefings, ceremonial speeches and banquets, demonstrations, stunts to raise money for a charity (the origin of the March of Dimes), and desperate acts of political activists (such as skyjacking an airliner) to call attention to a perceived injustice. Minority groups, environmentalists, and other activists who are often denied the traditional channels of access open to big business and government have refined the use of the pseudo-event. Examples include Martin Luther King's 250,000-strong March on Washington in 1963 and the week-long blockade of the Diablo Canyon nuclear power plant in California by the Abalone Alliance in 1981.

11.4.2 MESSAGE DISTORTIONS

As the news story is being compiled by the news media's message-makers (editors, producers, reporters), distortion can occur in several different ways.

Gatekeeping Viewpoints At each gatekeeping layer, individual views of reality cannot help but affect the way the news message is structured. Owners and advertisers, for example, are closer to the big-business establishment and typically will represent a

Politicians and public officials routinely hold press conferences and stage other pseudo-events in order to keep their images in the media.

conservative point of view, while the reporters and photographers often identify more closely with the working class and reflect a more liberal attitude. Decisions made at each of these levels distort what news eventually reaches the public.

Shaping Reality The media also, however, actually help to shape the real world. The fact that the press is covering an event helps to shape that event. "Spontaneous demonstrations" are planned for the media; happenings are staged for the cameras; sporting events are scheduled and controlled by media coverage. The 1968 National Advisory Commission on Civil Disorders reported:

Most newsmen appear to be aware and concerned that their very physical presence can exacerbate a small disturbance, but some have conducted themselves with a startling lack of common sense. . . . Reports have come to the Commission's office of individual newsmen staging events, coaxing youths to throw rocks and interrupt traffic, and otherwise acting irresponsibly at the incipient stages of a disturbance.[13]

11.4.3 MEDIUM DISTORTIONS

There are several other ways in which the media themselves distort the news-reporting process. These distortions occur merely because of the distinct characteristics of the media channels and the ways they relate to each other.

Visual Emphasis To see the media's reliance upon visual appeal, you need only to look at the front page of the daily paper, the pictorial content in tabloid papers and the *National Enquirer,* the photojournalism of weekly newsmagazines, the photo essays of *Life,* and the daily coverage of television news. That which can be photographed—the dramatic, the physical action—is exciting news; nonphotogenic items are less newsworthy.

As the noted British journalist and scholar Sir William Haley has observed, "Visual news values are almost in inverse ratio to real news values. What is most exciting to see is generally the least important to know about."[14] But then, how does one photograph a trillion-dollar national debt or the deteriorating ozone layer?

Commercial Realities and Competition Other problems emerge from the economic and competitive facts of life. News must be seen as a complement to the *advertising function.* When the Sunday edition of a major metropolitan newspaper carries numerous specialized sections devoted to "news" about real estate, travel, books, business, home entertainment, and so forth, can the editorial content really be considered substantial news information when the whole section exists primarily as an advertising vehicle for real estate developers, airlines, publishers, banks, and stereo retailers? Also, how must the early evening TV news be designed in order to serve as an effective lead-in to the prime-time *entertainment programming?* In both instances, the function of the news content is to bring media consumers to the place or time in which the advertising dollars have been spent.

11.4.4 RECEIVER DISTORTIONS

Several of the difficulties outlined previously also can be related to the way news messages are selected and perceived by individual media consumers.

Medium and Message Selection Schramm's explanation of "low-effort" media (Section 1.6.4) is borne out by research. Annual polls by the Roper Organization continually confirm the fact that more people turn to television for "news about what's going on in the world" than to newspapers. In 1980, some sixty-four percent of the population—up from fifty-one percent in 1959—indicated that they relied mostly on television for their news.

Message Perception Other factors influence in the way media consumers actually perceive the news. The individual differences perspective (Section 6.2.3) helps to explain how people will inevitably distort media messages to fit their own attitudes and preconceived pictures of reality.

11.4.5 FEEDBACK DISTORTION

Finally, we should note that the accuracy and objectivity of news reporting also can be affected by the way feedback is handled. Much of this is due simply to uninformed opinions and misleading feedback. People are often put in a situation in which feedback is expected or demanded even though they are not ready to provide any intelligent opinions. For example, the Gallup and Lou Harris organizations will poll voters prior to an election and make some statistically valid predictions about how people are inclined to vote *at that point,* which may be weeks before the election. But many voters do not actually make up their minds until immediately before they vote; thus, the earlier predictions are distorted by premature and uninformed feedback—which is disseminated by the media.

Misuse of Feedback Channels   Other feedback distortions occur which can substantially affect the way that the media perceive the public attitude, and thus can alter (to use Lasswell's phrase, Section 1.5.1) "the correlation of the parts of society in responding to the environment." Examples of this include the fact that the articulate and literate are more likely to provide receiver feedback than the illiterate and downtrodden. In many cases, also, a well-organized nationwide campaign by a given lobbying group can significantly distort the feedback process by creating the impression that there is much more reaction than really exists; note the successes of the National Rifle Association or the early impact of the Catholic Legion of Decency (Section 10.3.1).

A final form of feedback distortion may simply be the *ignored responses*—the tendency of some media or message-makers to ignore public feedback when the response is light. The best way to guard against such a possibility, or against any form of feedback distortion, in fact, is more feedback; the more there is, the more difficult it becomes to ignore, and the greater the possiblity that all sides will be represented fairly.

11.5   News: Alternate Channels

The problems in news coverage discussed above derive largely from the fact that the *mass* media are under pressure to reach the largest possible audiences. One response to such problems is to develop and utilize alternate channels of information, channels that are not so heavily dependent upon mass audiences and large advertisers. Three such possible alternatives have evolved over the years—minority media, the underground press, and public broadcasting. What is the future of each of these alternative channels?

11.5.1   MINORITY MEDIA

The newspapers, magazines, and broadcast stations that are owned and operated by Blacks, Hispanics, Asian Americans, and American Indians play an important role in disseminating ethnic entertainment and news to large segments of the American public that otherwise would be limited to middle-class white culture.

The Black Press and Broadcasters   By the mid-1970s there were some 325 Black newspapers in the United States, with a combined circulation of about seven million. Virtually all of the Black newspapers are local, and most are basically conservative in their political outlook—covering Black society, business, church news, and so forth. They are, after all, commercial enterprises and are rooted firmly in the Black establishment.

Blacks have fared well in the more specialized media, particularly in radio and magazines, where an individual or a group can own and operate a media outlet aimed at a smaller target audience. Blacks own about one hundred radio stations across the country, and several hundred more program exclusively for Blacks even though they are owned by non-Blacks. Special federal programs designed to encourage minority ownership of media outlets through financial incentives and tax advantages helped to crack the television barrier in 1979, when two TV stations were purchased by Black groups.

Hispanic Media   With roughly 25 million Hispanic citizens, the United States is the fourth-largest Spanish-speaking country in the world. There are numerous Chicano,

Essence, Black Enterprise, Jet, and *Ebony* are four of the most successful Black magazines.

The *Colored American Magazine* folded in 1909 because its publisher could not find adequate financial backing. And most of today's approximately 250 magazines aimed at the Black American are still struggling to convince establishment retailers that middle-class Black readers are good advertising targets. As one Black publisher lamented, "We can get the record companies to advertise in our magazine. But we can't get Pioneer, Sony or other stereo companies to place ads. What do they think Black people play those records on?"[15]

Although many Black magazines are making it as marginal successes, four stand out as solid triumphs in terms of significant advertising volume. *Ebony* is the most successful, with 1980 advertising revenues of almost $18 million and a circulation of 1.3 million. In second place is *Jet,* a weekly news magazine, with close to $8 million in advertising revenue and a circulation of more than 700,000. Both *Ebony* and *Jet* are published by the John H. Johnson Publishing Company of Chicago, the largest Black publishing force in the country. Johnson also puts out *Tan, Ebony, Jr.,* and other specialized Black magazines.

The other two dominant Black magazines are *Essence: The Magazine for Today's Black Woman,* published by Essence Communications, Inc., and *Black Enterprise,* a business magazine put out by Earl G. Graves Publishing. These magazines rank only slightly behind *Jet* in advertising revenue and circulation.

Puerto Rican, and Cuban activist papers and periodicals throughout the country (concentrated more heavily in cities such as Los Angeles, New York, and Miami), but there were only nine Spanish-language dailies being published in 1979.

In the broadcast area, more than six hundred radio stations aim some of their programming at the Spanish-speaking audience, roughly one hundred of them on a full-time basis. And there are about twenty Hispanic TV stations. Although the majority of these stations, both radio and TV, are owned by Anglos and are operated strictly for commercial profit, they do nevertheless function as Latino cultural outlets. Looking to the future, Hispanic scholar Félix Gutiérrez has observed, "Given the current and projected growth of Latinos in the United States, it is clear that Latinos will continue to have a growing impact on existing and developing media systems."[16]

Other Minority Channels   Other racial and ethnic groups also have specialized media channels available to them. Although Asian Americans, for example, owned no radio or television outlets as of 1980, they were involved in a number of programming services. In many large cities, one can find some programming (often a few hours a week on an otherwise English-language station) in Chinese, Japanese, or Korean.

Even though there is a small handful of radio stations owned by Native Americans, their access to the media is complicated by financial, legal, and cultural problems. Despite the problems in these areas, the ethnic and racial media outlets—Black, Hispanic, Asian American, Native American, and others—do represent an alternate voice for millions of media consumers.

11.5.2   THE UNDERGROUND PRESS

Another alternative channel for the expression of unorthodox, anti-Establishment viewpoints emerged in the 1960s. (See Section 3.3.5.) A forum was needed to debate the Vietnam War, to defend the environment against the onslaught of big business, to express anti-Establishment views on sexual life-styles, obscenities, and drugs, to fight for an end to racial inequities, to protest the draft, and to present other views and values that seldom were editorially supported in the conventional press.

The movement that was born out of this sense of rebellion was characterized by the underground press, guerrilla television, cinema verité filmmakers, subjective magazines, and other forms of "alternative journalism." The writing and reporting styles were personal, subjective, crusading—seldom concerned with objectivity and balance.

Video groups such as Raindance and Alternate Media Center (New York City), April Video Cooperative (Washington, D.C.), and Media Access (Menlo Park, California) sprang up around the country. Most used newer "small format" video technologies (lightweight cameras and portable video recorders). At least a hundred such outfits were in evidence during the late 1960s and early 1970s.

Transition to the Traditional   Despite all of the furor and intensity of the underground press, the first big surge of such iconoclastic journalism has ebbed. It has been estimated that at its peak, in the early 1970s, there were about three thousand underground papers. Today, many—if not the vast majority—have either folded or drastically changed their images. One reason for the demise of these papers was that they succeeded in their respective causes—we got out of Vietnam, Establishment politics were dealt a severe blow in Watergate, the draft was ended, alternate life-styles (cohabitation, homosexuality) have to some extent been acknowledged, and obscenities and nudity are no longer a novelty. Also, many causes championed by the underground press were picked up by the Establishment press—environmental protection, racial equality, consumer awareness, and similar issues. In both instances, the *raison d'être* for the adversary paper was undermined, and the underground channels went out of business.

A number of underground papers have survived. However, their very success has transformed the character of the endeavor. Any radical movement or institution—once it becomes successful and established—becomes, by definition, part of the new conventional Establishment. Once papers such as the *Village Voice* and *Los Angeles Free Press* became established and started to build large circulations, they evolved into successful capitalistic enterprises; they attracted larger and more traditional advertisers. So the character of the underground press has evolved considerably.

11.5.3 PUBLIC BROADCASTING

Starting in 1953, universities, school systems, state boards, and nonprofit community groups began to activate channels reserved by the FCC for noncommercial, educational TV. Circulating film and, later, videotapes of programs, these stations structured a loosely organized "National Educational TV" network. By 1967 there were close to 150 ETV stations on the air, most of them transmitting in-school instructional classes, university tele-courses, adult education series, fine arts and cultural materials, and public affairs documentaries.

A major turning point was reached in 1967, when Congress passed the Public Broadcasting Act. The Corporation for Public Broadcasting (CPB) was then established. This was followed shortly by the creation of the Public Broadcasting Service (PBS) and National Public Radio (NPR). For the first time, noncommercial TV and radio had live, interconnected network services.

Programming and Financing Changes The older label of "educational TV" was dropped as being too stodgy and pedagogical and replaced with the fresh designation "public

TV." Programming practices also were subtly altered. Basic education series (for example, fifteen weeks on child psychology or twenty weeks of American Indian history) were gradually replaced with more fine arts and cultural programs—especially British imports. Drama replaced basic instruction in literacy; opera replaced guitar lessons.

An interesting dilemma was intensified as public broadcasting (radio and television) began to attract more financial support from a variety of sources—the federal government (although its share was cut back by the Reagan administration), corporate underwriting, state agencies, philanthropic foundations, individual viewer contributions, and, starting in 1982, an experiment with limited advertising. Whoever furnishes the money for public broadcasting potentially can exercise some indirect control, if not outright censorship, over programming priorities and content. Programming pressure from these various sources have led to charges that public TV and radio have become increasingly pro-establishment and elitist during the last decade or so. Ideally, where should funding for public broadcasting come from in the future?

To some degree, then, public radio and TV, like the minority media and underground press, could encompass viewpoints and news stories that might be overlooked by the mass press and commercial broadcasting. But, in practice, each of these less-than-mass mediums must also face economic realities in its future. No alternate channel can exist very long with nothing to support it but energy and idealism. To a very real extent, the futures of minority media, the underground press, and public broadcasting are dependent upon outside economic and political factors.

11.6 Persuasion: Editorializing and Manipulation

In a free society, we willingly agree to submit ourselves to persuasion and propaganda. You know that every time you turn on the TV set or open the newspaper, you are going to be bombarded with advertising, political, and editorial messages. It is part of the price you pay for a viable, economically independent mass communication system. Nevertheless, many questions can be raised about the ways in which you are influenced, manipulated, deceived, and seduced beyond your conscious awareness. How are propaganda techniques likely to change in the future?

11.6.1 THE DEMISE OF EDITORIALIZING

One recognizable trend has been the diminution of the editorial voice. During the nineteenth century, the publisher and editor reigned supreme—Horace Greeley of the *New York Tribune* (Section 3.3.2); William Cullen Bryant, the voice of the *New York Evening Post;* and crusaders like Joseph Medill, Joseph Pulitzer, and William Randolph Hearst.

Several factors have contributed to the muffling of the thundering editors of the last century: major media corporations are concerned more with the marketplace of advertising revenue than with the marketplace of ideas; many more specialized media outlets are available to advocate voices (magazines, broadcast stations); the Fairness Doctrine, while applying specifically to radio and TV, probably exerted a mollifying influence on all media; society has become so complex that there are few clear-cut issues which lend themselves to easy answers and strong editorial stands; and there is probably less political abuse than a century ago. For all these reasons, the clarion call of the crusading editor has been significantly muted.

11.6.2 PERSUASION AND MANIPULATION IN ENTERTAINMENT AND RELIGIOUS PROGRAMMING

Aside from direct editorializing, there are many other subtle—and not-so-subtle—areas where editorial persuasion is practiced.

Entertainment Content Entertainment has been used as a means of persuasion since humankind's earliest chants and dramas. There are many examples of the persuasive impact of entertainment formats—the popular novel *(Uncle Tom's Cabin),* the cartoon (Thomas Nast's attack on Tammany Hall, Inset 8–4), the motion picture *(Dr. Strangelove),* the situation comedy *(Amos 'n' Andy),* the comic strip ("Doonesbury"), the record (any Beatles album), the TV mini-series *(Roots),* and so forth.

American entertainment media—especially the electric media (broadcasting and film)—are most effective as persuaders as they help to establish the cultural norms, to "define the situation" (Section 8.3.3). They influence us by telling us what everybody else is doing and how we should therefore behave. Thus, the entertainment media exercise persuasion both *intentionally* (through deliberate dramatic portrayals, for example) and *unintentionally* (by defining the cultural norms for us).

Religious Broadcasting Broadcast religion has been a mainstay of radio and television since early stations started carrying remote broadcasts of church services during the 1920s. Traditional religious sects—Catholics, Jews, and various Protestant denominations—have long made use of "public service" air time donated by radio and TV stations and networks. Discussions, moralistic dramas, and variety formats have attracted devout listeners and viewers for decades to programs such as *Lamp unto My feet, The Lutheran Hour, The Christophers, It Is Written,* the *American Jewish Hour,* and *This Is the Life.*

One continuing feature of the broadcast pulpit has been the electronic evangelist. From the televised coverage of the major crusades of Billy Graham and Oral Roberts, the format has expanded to encompass regular weekly programming by revivalists such as Robert Schuller, Jimmy Swaggart, Jerry Falwell, Rex Humbard, and numerous others—all preaching various forms of salvation and political conservatism. Close to sixty different syndicated religious series reach an estimated 30 million viewers each week.

A further step was taken when religious broadcasters began to buy and operate their own stations—and even networks. In 1961 Rev. M. G. "Pat" Robertson purchased an unprofitable UHF station in Virginia Beach, Virginia, and he has since parlayed that humble start into a $22-million production and administrative facility which is the heart of his Christian Broadcast Network (CBN)— now the second largest satellite-cable network in the country.

Religious broadcasters currently own a total of about 1,400 radio and TV stations.

Many of these—especially born-again Christian outlets—rely upon programming formats that are adapted from entertainment programs. Such talk-variety shows can be lucrative in terms of revenue generated. The *PTL Club* ("Praise the Lord"), for example, brings in over $50 million in donations annually. As video delivery systems multiply in the coming decades (Section 12.3), it is certain that the electronic pulpit will continue to expand its influence.

**INSET 11–9
Foreign Lobbyists
and the
American Media**

Foreign governments which are lobbying for more foreign aid or arms sales, which want to improve their images on human rights, or which hope to stimulate U.S. tourism and investment are all spending millions of dollars in an effort to woo American newspaper readers and TV viewers.

Several different techniques are used. Official government information services provide news releases and film footage; ambassadors and high-ranking state visitors stage American tours, holding press conferences and appearing on TV interview programs; "travelogues" (actually produced by government agencies) are supplied to American travel editors and TV travel shows. American PR firms are hired. Lavish parties are held for the local and national press. Paid junkets to the foreign countries are offered.

Such blatant manipulation efforts involve substantial finances. The British Information Service budgets $1.6 million annually for its U.S. activities, and it succeeds, among other things, in pushing the official British position on the fighting in Northern Ireland. According to estimates, the oil-producing Arab states are paying in excess of $15 million a year for American public affairs consultants and PR firms to promote their images. South Africa has probably spent over $10 million in recent years to influence U.S. public opinion. (Both South Africa and Korea have been the targets of congressional probes into their lobbying activities.) For example, in one year alone (1977), South Africa was able to place twelve of its government-made films on TV stations and cable-TV systems that reached more than 30 million Americans. These "travelogues" obviously made no mention of any of South Africa's racial policies or political problems.

Many other countries of Europe, the Middle East, Africa, and Asia have similar propaganda campaigns aimed at the American public through legitimate news outlets, print and broadcast interviews, travel features and TV travelogues, and any other channel available to manipulation by skilled PR practitioners.

11.7 Persuasion: Politics and Politicians

In a free society, few topics are as vital, as compelling, or as fascinating, as the study of the multifaceted ways in which the individual citizens interact with their governmental representatives through the convoluted channels of the mass media.

11.7.1 CHOOSING OUR ELECTED PUBLIC OFFICIALS

The election process is one area where the media will continue in the future to play an increasingly important role—in several different ways. The media provide a vast canvas for *political advertising*. The major Democratic and Republican candidates spent over $16 million apiece in the 1980 campaign *before* the nominating conventions were held.

In addition to the obvious advertising function, the mass media play a crucial role in *agenda setting* and *status conferral*. The media determine, for example, which candidates will get what kinds of serious coverage early in the campaign. Those who are ignored at the starting gate have a hard time trying to make up for that early deficit. The media also set the agenda as far as issues are concerned—deciding whether to focus on domestic or foreign affairs, the environment or energy, missiles or inflation.

Many critics point out, however, that the media—especially television—hardly focus on issues at all; they are too busy concentrating on personalities and superficial impressions. The slick advertising and public relations techniques which are so effective in selling soap or automobiles are also used effectively to sell politicians to the public in thirty-second and sixty-second campaign commercials. Newsman Robert MacNeil eloquently describes the extent to which television has become synonymous with politics in the United States:

Television *is* American politics in the way that television *is* American sports. The whole of American life is suffused with it. We have television in

our pores, in our psyches; perhaps even, God forbid, in our genes. There is no once-only, static effect. It is continuous.

As television evolves, so does the democracy, because television helps to shape the institutions of the democracy. Like the human digestive system, television alters what it consumes—comedy, sports, news, drama, education, religion. It is doing that to politics.[17]

The Primaries and Caucuses   Media involvement with the election process can be examined in three distinct phases—the primaries and caucuses, the national conventions, and the general election campaign. The February New Hampshire primary, which draws the attention of the news media at the beginning of the long drawn-out political process, plays a role far out of proportion to the size of its delegations to the nominating conventions. At a 1980 debate between Ronald Reagan and George Bush in a high school in Nashua, there were forty-one television cameras covering the momentous event.

However, the January precinct caucuses in Iowa have managed to upstage even New Hampshire. In 1976 Jimmy Carter emerged with a surprise victory in that state and was no longer known as "Jimmy Who?" Therefore, in January 1980, the networks descended upon Iowa with almost three hundred newspeople and technicians to probe, predict, and project the early—and otherwise insignificant—results. As Ron Nessen, the former press secretary to President Ford, points out,

[T]elevision acts like a giant megaphone in the election campaign, greatly amplifying and magnifying the significance of events, and thereby affecting future events.

. . . [T]elevision's massive coverage and premature judgments do influence the nominating process by exaggerating the importance of early races.[18]

The National Nominating Conventions

In the old days, national nominating conventions were important institutions. There the political delegates from all states actually got together, fought among themselves, and eventually agreed on one person as the party nominee. However, it has not been like that for more than three decades. Nationwide TV coverage, which started in 1952, has resulted in political conventions that are designed as spectacles and media events rather than as working conventions.

As the functional aspects of the convention waned in favor of the video extravaganza, the major networks began to ask whether it was worth the expense. In 1980, ABC, CBS, and NBC lost a total of close to $20 million in air time while they shelled out an estimated $40 million collectively to send about two thousand journalists, technicians, back-

---

The importance of media momentum and the necessity of getting a strong start in the primary/caucus process was amply demonstrated in the 1980 elections. Ronald Reagan was one out of seven candidates fighting to gain the Republican nomination for president (the others being John Anderson, Howard Baker, George Bush, Philip Crane, John Connally, and Robert Dole). Bush, with his New England background, was considered by the polls to be the frontrunner in the New Hampshire primary. However, through a combination of effective media coverage and heavy campaign spending, Reagan managed to beat Bush in this first primary.

Under the federal campaigning laws, candidates who accepted government matching funds in 1980 were allowed to spend no more than $17.6 million before the summer conventions. Eager to maintain his early momentum, Reagan had spent eighty-seven percent of his allotment by the end of April. And his strategy worked. Four months before the convention, Reagan had eliminated virtually all of his Republican competition.

On the other hand, Senator Edward Kennedy stumbled in the starting gate and never was able to regain his early popularity. Pre-campaign polls showed Kennedy a large favorite to beat the incumbent President Carter and outsider Jerry Brown. However, in an exclusive CBS interview calculated to be televised just before he would announce his candidacy, Kennedy was interviewed by correspondent Roger Mudd. Mudd questioned Kennedy about—among other issues—the Chappaquiddick tragedy, his deteriorating marriage, and his reasons for wanting to become president.[19] Inarticulate and evasive, Kennedy failed miserably in his first major media event of the election season. As Robert MacNeil reported,

In that painful interview, timed to be seen just before the official campaign kickoff, Kennedy could not satisfactorily answer questions about Chappaquiddick, or even why he was running for President. His incoherence colored everything thereafter written or said about him. It became something to recover from, like an accident.[20]

But Kennedy never did recover. He was never able to mount an effective challenge to Carter, who had the nomination sewed up well before the convention.

The 1976 debates between presidential candidates Jimmy Carter and incumbent Gerald Ford gave the voters an opportunity to view something other than slickly packaged political commercials.

up personnel, and tons of equipment and facilities to cover the two conventions. Many observers have predicted that the networks will refuse in the future to give the Democrats and Republicans each four nights of free prime-time publicity to stage their political pageantry when there is so little real news involved.

The General Election   After the conventions have confirmed the nominees, national attention shifts to follow the fortunes of the two major (and perhaps several independent or minor-party) candidates. Here is where media critics are most vocal about the influence of slick political ads packaged by PR and advertising firms, in which the candidates are merchandized like canned hams or patent medicines.

One positive alternative to the thirty-second commercial and the occasional longer political speech or partisan film is the *debate*— the formal opportunity for the candidates to come together in a head-on confrontation.

The researcher George Comstock and his colleagues offer this conservative summary:

The trend toward reduced party allegiance over the past 15 years and the presence of unusual numbers of undecided or wavering voters (such as in the 1976 presidential election), increase the opportunity for television to have an effect. . . . Evidence from 1976 suggests that in this close election, where voter indecision was high and the Ford-Carter debates were an electoral media event, television played a particularly significant role in facilitating the reaching of a decision by individual voters about which of the major candidates to vote for.[21]

11.7.2   GOVERNMENT USE OF THE MEDIA

The next issue concerns the way in which government leaders and bureaucrats—once they are installed in office—use the media for propaganda and manipulation of the public.

What are the legitimate uses of the media for information and persuasive purposes? How are government uses of persuasive media likely to change in the future?

Every government on the planet, in both open and closed societies, must use the media to inform and lead the populace. Government bodies at all levels allow access to certain government sources while closing other doors; they use press conferences, news releases, official briefings, and unauthorized news "leaks" to favored members of the media.

Television and the Presidency

Manipulation of the media is concentrated mainly at the executive levels. Fred Friendly, the former president of CBS news, put it eloquently:

No mighty king, no ambitious emperor, no pope, or prophet ever dreamt of such an awesome pulpit, so potent a magic wand. In the American experiment with its delicate checks and balances, this device [television] permits the First Amendment and the very heart of the Constitution to be breached, as it bestows on one politician a weapon denied to all others.[22]

On the other hand, it can be argued that no modern post-TV president—neither Eisenhower, Kennedy, Johnson, Nixon, Ford, Carter nor Reagan—has been able to exploit fully the personal potential of the medium. The media themselves contain the checks and balances—the commentators and columnists, the editors and muckrakers— to provide a needed constraint on too ambitious a president. In fact, the four presidents preceding Reagan all left the Oval Office with their images tarnished by the media.

Presidential manipulation of the mass media did not start with Richard Nixon or Jimmy Carter. During the colonial period, favored publishers were often given positions as postmasters. Alexander Hamilton and Thomas Jefferson began the tradition of the partisan press (Section 3.3.1). Andrew Jackson at one time had fifty-seven journalists on the government payroll. Abraham Lincoln carefully cultivated relations with the most influential editors during his administration (Inset 3–5).

After the turn of the century, Teddy Roosevelt was credited with managing the news more skillfully than any of his predecessors in the White House, using news leaks and trial balloons to test public opinion. Woodrow Wilson initiated the formal press conference; he also set up the Committee on Public Information as a wartime propaganda agency.

Franklin Roosevelt was perhaps the most successful manipulator of all media presidents. During his fifteen years as president, he held almost a thousand press conferences. But he may best be remembered for his famous radio "fireside chats," which were remarkably effective in rallying the people and inspiring confidence in his policies during the Depression.

Dwight Eisenhower's administration marked the beginning of the era of the political image makers—the advertising and PR specialists. By 1957, the Civil Service Commission listed almost seven thousand "informational and editorial" positions in the executive departments of the government. John F. Kennedy initiated the live television press conference, whereas Lyndon Johnson preferred small, intimate, informal gatherings of the few full-time White House correspondents.

Of all the presidents of the United States, none has been a more fascinating media study than Richard Nixon. He was a skilled orator and extemporaneous speaker, an outstanding debater. At times he used the broadcast media especially effectively in his rise to power. And in the end, it was the media that brought him down. But, as columnist James Reston expressed it, "he has never really understood the function of a free press or the meaning of the First Amendment."[23] Especially distrustful of the working press, Nixon held fewer press conferences than any of his modern predecessors, averaging one about every two months. He preferred instead to reach the public directly over television; he addressed the nation thirty-two times (using all three networks each time) in his five and a half years in office.

The presidents following Nixon have been more cautious and self-conscious in their press relationships. Although he was well liked by the press, Gerald Ford always remained something of an unknown, an outsider who slipped into the White House by accident. Similarly, Jimmy Carter was an enigma, a hazily defined amateur who carefully utilized the media symbols of the common man—he was shown, for example, walking down Pennsylvania Avenue after his inauguration, playing softball with the media, and wearing a sweater while delivering a televised fireside chat reminiscent of FDR's.

With his film and broadcast background, Ronald Reagan began his presidential career with perhaps the biggest media advantage of any recent president. He enjoyed widespread editorial support from the conservative, capitalistic press and yet retained enough of the common-man image to maintain good relationships with the working press. The future association of the presidency and the media will remain one of the most intriguing areas of mass communication study.

11.7.3 THE MEDIA-GOVERNMENT BALANCE

In an examination of the relationships between government and the media, it becomes apparent that the press exerts tremendous influence over the political process. The media serve as an effective check on governmental excesses—through editorial opinions, gatekeeping decisions, agenda setting, feedback channels, and investigative reporting. The people would appear to have some confirmation of Lasswell's "watchdog" and "forum" functions (Section 1.5.1).

This results in a natural and continually wavering antagonism between the media and the government. Neither side completely trusts the other; they are contending sources of information and power. And the balance constantly shifts like a pendulum swinging back and forth, supporting the government in one phase and then swinging back to give the media more credibility and power a few years later.

Fortunately, both the government and the media recognize the need for such a balance. As indicated by constitutional restraints on the government, and by self-censorship and regulatory restraints on the press, both sides accept the need for this permanent, but fluctuating, standoff. And as long as the pendulum continues to swing in the future, the people have some reassurance that the system is still working; the security of the government will remain intact, and the vitality of the media will still be protected.

11.8 Persuasion: Advertising Ethics and Methods

Fifty to sixty percent of the space in the typical daily newspaper or popular magazine is devoted to advertising messages. When you watch television, fifteen to twenty-five percent of the time (depending on the time of day) is devoted to commercials—up to thirty or more different products may be pitched at you in a single broadcast hour. The average American will be exposed to at least three hundred advertising messages in a given day (Chapter 6). This is a tremendous amount of propaganda that you voluntarily expose yourself to—roughly one hour per day of reading, viewing, and listening to persuasive messages that are designed to influence what you do, buy, and think.

11.8.1 ISSUES REGARDING ADVERTISING'S ROLE

How might the future role of advertising be changed? How will you modify your relationship with advertising content?

Children's Advertising For decades, many groups—parents, educators, psychologists, consumer and activist organizations—have been concerned about the ethics of advertising aimed at young children. (See Inset 10–8.) Comic books, magazines, radio, and especially television have all been the target of efforts to control the amount and content of advertising aimed at impressionable young minds.

Most objections are centered on the types of products that are advertised—sugar-laden breakfast foods, expensive toys, candy-coated medicines, dangerous playthings. Not only are most of these products and gimmicks unnecessary, but some can also be decidedly harmful. Children's advertising helps to set up attitudes and perceptions that are carried into adult years. Such attitudes and perceptions can lead to unrealistic demands in adulthood, intolerance of the ambiguities of life, inflated materialistic standards, an obsession with instant gratification (through sex, chemicals, financial acquisitions), and frustration in dealing with normal problems. Comstock et al. emphasize that more research needs to be done in the areas of "influences on health-related practices, such as dietary preferences, and on basic values, such as materialism or acquisitiveness."[24]

Advertiser Control of Content Other questions concerning the propriety of advertising (outlined in Section 6.5.2) are centered on the ways in which advertising—in print as well as broadcasting—affects the editorial content of noncommercial messages: the "big-business" establishment syndrome, direct influence on content, and lowering of content standards by appealing to the "lowest common denominator."

Several examples of *advertiser control of nonadvertising content* were discussed previously. These include exhibiting the sponsor's product in TV drama, advertiser influence in editing news content, newspaper sections devoted to "content" which promotes a particular industry, and actual sponsor production of the nonadvertising content.

Another problem is the *desire to avoid making the advertiser look bad*. This may lead to sensitive handling of news stories which involve a sponsor's product—for example, an airlines crash, a bank embezzlement, an accident at a department store, a lawsuit involving the family of a major advertiser, environmental violations by an oil company, and so forth.

11.8.2 ISSUES RAISED BY ADVERTISING METHODS

While many questions are raised about the ethics involved in the very existence of advertising as a source of financial revenue and editorial control, many other issues center on the ways in which advertising tactics are employed. How are media consumers influenced and manipulated—increasingly without their realizing it—to do, buy, and think as the advertisers wish? What can you do to protect yourself in the future?

Advertising Appeals Advertisers have always tried to appeal to various emotions and basic drives when trying to sell you particular products.

Some of these basic human needs and drives (and their accompanying emotional appeals) are the following: *physical survival* and self-preservation, including the needs for food, water, shelter, warmth, and security (appealing to the emotional states of fear, hate, anger, competition, acquisition); *reverence* and worship (security, patriotism, loyalty, love, submission); *physical comfort* (relaxation, pleasant sensations such as tastes and smells, physical well-being); *sexual satisfaction* (sensual pleasures, biological urges, and ego gratification); *ego fulfillment* (pride, power, authority, appeals to logic); *freedom* (adventure, challenge, curiosity, competition, individuality, and independence); *acceptance* (conformity, companionship, friendship, trust, loyalty, and imitation); *altruism,* the desire to help others (sympathy, love, pity, shame, and guilt); and *aesthetic pleasure* (orderliness, creativity, color, sounds, visual enjoyment).

These appeals have led to dozens of specific advertising approaches and campaigns through the decades. For example, acceptance/conformity is translated into the *bandwagon* ("join the crowd," "everybody's doing it," buy America's "most popular car"); reverence leads to the *testimonial* ("if Bob Hope says so . . ."); the desire for physical survival lends itself to *scare tactics* ("invest for the future," buy now "before it's too late"). Most of these approaches are fairly obvious and easy to spot. What advertisers wanted, however, was a more sophisticated means of manipulating consumers' subconscious emotional drives without arousing their intellectual awareness.

The biggest scandal ever to hit commercial television was the result of sponsor control and packaging. In 1955, the cosmetics firm of Revlon, Inc., inaugurated *The $64,000 Question* on CBS. The series was produced, packaged, and controlled by Revlon, its ad agency, and a few independent producers; CBS had very little say in how the program was put together. NBC countered with *Twenty-One,* which was similarly packaged. Within a year there were numerous big-money quiz shows on the air, all controlled by sponsors and ad agencies. At one point Revlon was producing and sponsoring the top *two* shows in the popularity ratings, *The $64,000 Question* and its sequel, *The $64,000 Challenge.*

In 1958 the first rumors began to circulate that many of the shows were being rigged, that certain popular contestants were being supplied with answers to the tough questions. Within days some twenty quiz shows were hurriedly withdrawn as television's first major programming scandal unfolded.

A New York grand jury investigation was followed by congressional probing in a special House subcommittee. The nation was stunned as popular *Twenty-One* winner Charles Van Doren, a faculty member at Columbia University, admitted his involvement and detailed the process by which he was coached in giving winning answers. Many other winners suffered similar public disgrace. Although none of them was found guilty of criminal activities which resulted in any jail term, they did paint blunt pictures of the commercial pressures which led to such unethical public deception.

At the same time the quiz scandals hit the headlines, the radio industry was facing a similar crisis with revelations of the widespread practice of "payola." Record companies were supplying lavish gifts (cars, trips, women, drugs) to disc jockeys in return for on-the-air promotion of certain records. Sterling and Kittross point out the repercussions of these two concurrent transgressions:

The shock waves that went through the industry as a result of the quiz show and payola scandals made many persons wonder about the merits of the high pressure and stakes of broadcasting and especially of the demand for high ratings to please advertisers.[25]

**INSET 11–11
Advertiser Control
and the TV Quiz
Scandals**

Motivational Research   Shortly after World War II, psychologists and behavioral researchers began probing the hidden depth of consumers' subconscious layers. One early practitioner of this motivational analysis was Louis Cheskin, who defined his new science this way:

Motivation research is the type of research that seeks to learn what motivates people in making choices. It employs techniques designed to reach the unconscious or subconscious mind because preferences generally are determined by factors of which the individual is not conscious. . . . Actually in the buying situation the consumer generally acts emotionally and compulsively, unconsciously reacting to the images and designs which in the subconscious are associated with the product.[26]

Vance Packard, in his classic book, *The Hidden Persuaders,* explains how consumers are viewed by such psychological manipulators: "Typically they see us as bundles of daydreams, misty hidden yearnings, guilt complexes, irrational emotional blockages. We are image lovers given to impulsive and compulsive acts."[27] Much of this basic work on motivational manipulation can be traced back to fundamental Freudian explanations and other theories of the subconscious, which hold that much of our behavior is determined by repressed sexual drives, latent hostilities, childhood fantasies, and associations with color and other symbology. Thus, automobiles are sold as sex objects and status symbols; vacation trips are designed as means of getting back at our parents; detergents are merchandised as colors, shapes, and designs; and deodorants become phallic symbols.

Dishonesty in Advertising   Finally, you might look at the potential for outright deceit—blatant lies and deception in advertising messages. Despite the fact that the vast majority of advertisers are essentially honest (they would rather persuade and manipulate than cheat), despite the attempts at industry self-regulation (through the NARB and its constituent groups, Section 10.4.1), and despite the policing actions of the FTC (Section 9.4.5), there are still numerous examples of dishonest and fraudulent advertising schemes.

Heighton and Cunningham list several specific types of misleading advertising techniques. There is the *bait and switch operation,* advertising a specific item at a very low "come-on" price and then enticing the consumer to buy a much higher-priced item. *Pseudoscientific claims* encompass questionable testing procedures, unethical dramatizations, partial claims, and qualifying "weasel words" (such as "virtually," "can be," and "tests indicate"). *Manipulated statistics* use small and biased samples, inaccurate "averages," and misleading comparative data. Some ads claim that *secret and unique ingredients and additives* have been added to cosmetics, soaps and detergents, patent medicines, gasoline, toothpaste, and so forth (Anacin's "painkiller most recommended by doctors" is simple aspirin). *Phony demonstrations,* although not as prevalent as they used to be, still do appear on TV occasionally. *False analogies and unspecified comparisons* are based on sneaky semantic deceptions and implications which cleverly say nothing of substance but appear to be making a point. The authors conclude:

Truth in advertising escapes definition. The problems it poses are like a changing kaleidoscope, and so are the solutions. One thing is clear, however: the responsibility for establishing and maintaining truth in advertising must be shared. Government regulation, self-regulation, and consumer education must work in harmony to achieve high standards.[28]

SUMMARY

As we examine mass media in a social framework, quite a few questions and issues are raised concerning the way we will interact in the future with specific entertainment, news, and persuasion content.

Probing one step deeper into our subconscious than motivational research is the controversial theory of *subliminal perception*. According to this theory, it is possible to encode and project a message in such a fashion that it is received and decoded below the threshold of conscious perception. The media consumer is not aware that he or she is actually perceiving the message. Wilson Bryan Key defines the process as

sensory inputs into the human nervous system that circumvent or are repressed from conscious awareness—or, more simply, inputs that communicate with the unconscious. The term has, of course, popular implications which suggest brainwashing, manipulation, and other unsavory—though romantic—practices.[29]

One of the first practical advertising demonstrations occurred in the early 1960s when a special projector (capable of projecting a message for as short a duration as 1/3000th of a second) was used in a movie theater to superimpose on the screen the messages "Hungry? Eat Popcorn" and "Drink Coca-Cola" during the motion picture. Although movie patrons never consciously "saw" the messages, popcorn and Coca-Cola sales both increased spectacularly when the respective messages were subliminally projected.

Audio subliminal projection occurs when verbal messages are superimposed over musical selections, for example, at a volume or frequency which is just barely out of conscious range—but still subliminally perceptible. Tests have indicated that when antishoplifting messages ("Shoplifting is a crime" or "Shoplifters go to jail") have been subliminally blended into background music at a department store, the shoplifting rate has dropped.

Probably the most common form of subliminal message manipulation is airbrushing sexual symbols or words into an otherwise innocuous-looking ad layout. Ice cubes in liquor advertisements seem to be the favorite target. Professor Key illustrates numerous examples in which only with studied conscious effort—but with an instantaneous subthreshold perception—various words, genitalia, and suggestive poses can be discerned.

Many other examples can be studied—the cigarette as a phallic symbol (in various stages of erection), the use of suggestive words ("come" is a predominate favorite), a half-peeled orange as a symbolic undressing of a woman. Not all subliminal messages are sexual—the dog is often used as a surrogate symbol for friendship or loyalty, for example. Dying flowers, a suggestion of a cross, many other hidden symbols can be projected and analyzed.

Although Key's observations are not universally embraced, there are undoubtedly many aspects of subliminal communication that do deserve considerably more attention, analysis, and research.

Entertainment   Generally, entertainment content—films, TV programs, novels—may be considered either for *diversion* or for *aesthetic satisfaction.* Can something designed to reach millions of persons—primarily for commercial purposes—ever meet artistic criteria? These questions apply to all four of the essential entertainment formats—*drama, performance, contests* (including sports), and *conversation.*

The elitist viewpoint would claim that spreading "art" to the masses only debases the whole concept of art. In defining *fine art, folk art,* and *popular art,* however, defenders of popular art point out that a given artistic effort should not be condemned simply because it is liked by a large number of people. Also, they argue that the mass media— by exposing large numbers of people to some works of art—can gradually elevate the artistic standards of the common man and woman.

A related issue concerns the merit of entertainment content that is designed purely for diversion, without any artistic pretensions at all. If an audience member asks for nothing more than simplistic *escapism,* should we expect a medium to provide *art?*

News   With news and reality content, we face questions dealing with both the adequacy and the objectivity of the news. Is there sufficient news coverage? Due greatly to popular pressures, mass media news channels tend to focus on the *sensational* and *trivial,* contrasting "happy news" formats with the *disaster syndrome.* Although in-depth articles in magazines and broadcast documentaries help to fill the gap, there is still too much emphasis on *events* and not enough investigation of background *situations.* There are also many problems connected with gathering the news—access to data, protection of sources, and questionable news-gathering techniques.

Many questions of news accuracy and objectivity can be studied in the context of

various distortions of the communication model: source distortions, message distortions, medium distortions, receiver distortions, and even feedback distortions.

As a partial answer to these problems of sufficient and objective news coverage, several types of alternative media have evolved. *Minority media* (such as the black and Hispanic press and broadcast stations) serve specific ethnic groups. The *underground press* (including guerrilla television and independent filmmakers) provides an anti-Establishment voice. And *public broadcasting* (noncommercial radio and television) serves selected cultural tastes.

Persuasion   Many questions need to be asked about propaganda and manipulation of the public. In addition to formal editorializing, advocacy mass communication is present in *entertainment* content (drama, cartoons) and *religious broadcasting.*

Persuasion is of special concern in political relationships. The media have a major influence on *how we elect our government officials* through the coverage of primaries and caucuses, national conventions, and general elections. A second major area of concern is *how the government uses the media*—especially the executive branch and specifically the White House, whose power has increased greatly in recent years. The vitality of both our political and our media systems depends on our recognizing the natural and healthy antagonism and competition between the media and the government and maintaining a *balance of power* between the two mass institutions of information and influence.

Finally, we are concerned with several issues involved in direct commercial advertising, especially with *children's advertising* and various forms of *advertiser control of content.* Media receivers need to be especially aware of how the advertisers are trying to manipulate us constantly—through emotional *advertising appeals,* by the use of sophisticated *motivational research,* with occasional *dishonest advertising,* and especially through *subliminal perception.* Over a quarter of a century ago, Vance Packard stated, "We still have a strong defense available against such persuaders: we can choose not to be persuaded. In virtually all situations we still have the choice, and we cannot be too seriously manipulated if we know what is going on."[30] Unfortunately, when we get into the areas of subliminal communication and outright dishonest advertising, we cannot always know what is going on; we are then engaged in a fraudulent form of persuasive communication which frustrates the libertarian ideal of the search for truth.

In all areas of mass communication, however—entertainment, news, and persuasion—we will find that in the future the individual will have to assume much more responsibility for the selection and interpretation of all media content. You will be increasingly in charge of your own media experiences. Much of this will be due to the emergence of the new technologies discussed in Chapter 12.

Notes to Chapter 11

1. Anne Roiphe, "Ma and Pa and John-Boy in Mythic America: The Waltons," in *Television: The Critical View*, 2nd ed., ed. Horace Newcomb (New York: Oxford University Press, 1979), p. 9.

2. This compilation of the total number of hours of daily TV talk shows included local productions, syndicated shows (*John Davidson, Phil Donahue, Mike Douglas,* and *Merv Griffin*), and network offerings (*Today, Good Morning America, Dick Cavett, Tonight,* and *Tomorrow*). Although some of these programs offered a substantial portion of news and variety/performance elements, the underlying format was that of conversation. This compilation did not include programs that were devoted entirely to news (for example, CBS's *Morning* with Charles Kuralt), educational talk, public affairs discussions (*Meet the Press, Face the Nation, Issues* and *Answers*), religion, health and exercise, financial discussions, "magazine" formats, and programs aimed at specific age groups (*Over Easy, Mister Rogers*). It was concerned only with popular, broadly based, entertainment-oriented conversation/interview shows.

3. Quoted in Charlene J. Brown, Trevor R. Brown, and William L. Rivers, *The Media and the People* (New York: Holt, Rinehart and Winston, 1978), p. 410.

4. Alexis de Tocqueville, "In What Spirit the Americans Cultivate the Arts," in *Mass Culture: The Popular Arts in America*, ed. Bernard Rosenberg and David Manning White (New York: Free Press, 1957), pp. 29–30.

5. Lyman Bryson, "Popular Art," in *The Communication of Ideas*, ed. Lyman Bryson (New York: Harper & Brothers, 1948), p. 278.

6. James A. Brown, "The Professor's View," in *Broadcast Management: Radio and Television*, ed. James A. Brown and Ward L. Quall (New York: Hastings House, 1975), pp. 439–440.

7. Paul F. Lazarsfeld and Robert K. Merton, "Mass Communication, Popular Taste and Organized Social Action," in *The Communication of Ideas*, ed. Bryson, p. 109.

8. Walt Whitman, "From Democratic Vistas," in *Mass Culture*, ed. Rosenberg and White, p. 38.

9. Ernest van den Haag, "Of Happiness and of Despair We Have No Measure," in *Enduring Issues in Mass Communication*, ed. Everette E. Dennis, Arnold H. Ismach, and Donald M. Gillmor (St. Paul: West, 1978), p. 47.

10. Henry David Thoreau, *Walden: Or, Life in the Woods* (New York: New American Library, Signet Books, 1963), p. 68.

11. Doyle McManus, "Sensational News!—N.Y. Post Formula Works," *Los Angeles Times*, 28 August 1981, Pt I, p. 10.

12. Ibid., p. 10.

13. National Advisory Commission on Civil Disorders, *Report* (New York: Bantam Books, 1968), p. 377.

14. Sir William Haley, "Where TV News Fails," *Columbia Journalism Review*, 9, no. 1 (Spring, 1970), p. 7.

15. Pamela Moreland, "Black Magazines: Publishing Field's 'Invisible' Giant Flexes Its Muscles," *Los Angeles Times*, 4 October 1981, Pt VI, p. 1.

16. Félix Gutiérrez, "Latinos and the Media," in *Readings in Mass Communication: Concepts and Issues in the Mass Media,* 4th ed., ed. Michael Emery and Ted Curtis Smythe (Dubuque, Iowa: Wm. C. Brown, 1980), p. 373.

17. Robert MacNeil, "Politics and Television," *TV Guide,* 28 June 1980, pp. 5–6.

18. Ron Nessen, "Now Television's the King-maker," *TV Guide,* 10 May 1980, pp. 7–8.

19. The "Chappaquiddick tragedy" refers to a 1969 incident which many observers say clouded Senator Kennedy's political career permanently. Driving home from a late-night party on Chappaquiddick Island, Kennedy drove off a darkened unmarked bridge. His companion in the car, Mary Jo Kopechne, was drowned. Although Kennedy was never held responsible for her death, many questions were raised about his alleged panic and an abortive cover-up attempt; and he did plead guilty to the charge of leaving the scene of an accident.

20. MacNeil, "Politics and Television," p. 5.

21. George Comstock, Steven Chaffee, Natan Katzman, Maxwell McCombs, and Donald Roberts, *Television and Human Behavior* (New York: Columbia University Press, 1978), pp. 15–16.

22. Fred Friendly, "Foreword," in Newton N. Minow, John Bartlow, and Lee M. Mitchell, *Presidential Television* (New York: Basic Books, 1973), pp. vii–viii.

23. Quoted in William L. Rivers, Theodore Peterson, and Jay W. Jensen, *The Mass Media and Modern Society,* 2nd ed. (New York: Holt, Rinehart and Winston, 1971), p. 137.

24. Comstock et al., *Television and Human Behavior,* p. 12.

25. Christopher H. Sterling and John M. Kittross, *Stay Tuned: A Concise History of American Broadcasting* (Belmont, Calif.: Wadsworth, 1978), p. 348.

26. Quoted in Vance Packard, *The Hidden Persuaders* (New York: David McKay, 1957), pp. 7–8.

27. Ibid., p. 7

28. Elizabeth J. Heighton and Don R. Cunningham, *Advertising in the Broadcast Media* (Belmont, Calif.: Wadsworth, 1976), p. 255.

29. Wilson Bryan Key, *Subliminal Seduction: Ad Media's Manipulation of a Not So Innocent America* (Englewood Cliffs, N.J.: Prentice-Hall, 1973), p. 18.

30. Packard, *The Hidden Persuaders,* p. 265.

Chapter 11 was essentially concerned with questions about the *content* of mass communication in the future. In this chapter, you will be considering the *technologies* of both emerging and future communications—the newer developments in use today and the systems still on the drawing board. Some fairly cataclysmic changes in the way we rely on communication and how we use it are predicted by one of the more popular futurists of our time.

Alvin Toffler, in *The Third Wave*, tells us that the mass production of highly standardized goods may soon be replaced by a far more individualized approach to production. This, in effect, will mark the end of the industrial age (the period of the "Second Wave") during which we reached our current technological level and which we in the "industrialized West" first arrived at about the time of the American Revolution—concurrent with the emergence of the mass media.

Throughout the Second Wave era the mass media grew more and more powerful. Today a startling change is taking place. As the Third Wave thunders in, the mass media, far from expanding their influence, are suddenly being forced to share it. They are being beaten back on many fronts at once by what I call the "de-massified media."

. . . Each of today's mass circulation dailies now faces increasing competition from a burgeoning flock of mini-circulation weeklies, biweeklies, and so-called "shoppers." . . . Having reached saturation, the big-city mass-circulation daily is in deep trouble. De-massified media are snapping at its heels.[1]

During this coming era we will rely ever more on communications; but perhaps, as Toffler predicts, a lessening of reliance on mass production will result in some reduction in our reliance on mass communication. And we will have more opportunities for individual selection among the popular entertainment, news/information, and propaganda/persuasion messages available to us at any time. In effect, the new age will be the age of the media consumer—in which each of us will have increasing responsibility for our own mass communication as well as a multitude of varying specialized communication experiences. What the technological developments outlined in this chapter all point to is this theme:

• *As consumers, we must become aware of the increasing flexibility and sophistication of the emerging media technologies so as to use them intelligently.*

12.1 New Print Technologies

In considering almost any technology, you will find electronics playing the primary role, although developments in optics, chemistry, and mechanical engineering also perform indispensable functions. Thus, if you are going to examine innovations in printing technology—taking into account all the various technologies—your primary focus will be on electronics. Even firms that only recently were identified solely with electronics, such as IBM, have now assumed major roles in printing and publishing.

12.1.1 PUBLISHING AND THE VIDEO-DISPLAY TERMINAL

As anyone who has watched the *Lou Grant* television series knows, the video-display terminal (VDT) has encroached upon newspaper city rooms, large and small. The system has had its opponents. Some users tend to feel uncomfortable with it; and when it fails,

---

Word processors originally started as typewriters with some capability of storing the information on a medium other than the typed page. Usually this was in the form of magnetic tape or, later, magnetic storage cards and discs.

The need for an efficient way to edit text helped to provide the stimulus for the development of the word processor with *video-display* output. A page of existing text that needed some revision could be brought more or less in its entirety from the magnetic medium on which it was stored onto the television screen of the device and then manipulated (with insertions, deletions, and changes) as rapidly as the operator could work the typewriter keys. No mechanical hammers or paper transports had to be moved. Thus, a convert toward processors, the author William Brashler exclaims, "It takes the drudgery out of writing. I correct a mistake on the screen in a second, and the printer retypes the page in three seconds. No more retyping the whole page by hand."[2]

Soon these devices made it feasible to identify large sections of previously typed material on the screen and move them about electronically to reformat the "page" glowing on the tube. After the page is constructed in the form that satisfies the operator/editor, commands can be given to the device to restore the material in the magnetic medium. From there, another electronic command from the operator sends the recorded "page" to some automated device—like an electric typewriter—there to be printed as text on a sheet of paper.

**INSET 12–1
Word Processors
and Video-
Display Output**

Many publishing firms now rely on word-processing systems with multiple video display terminals (VDTs) linked together to channel efficiently the production of documents and publications.

all hell breaks loose! Yet, nearly every publishing firm that can afford such a system is getting one. Why?

The answer lies in the fact that moving pieces of paper from place to place is far more cumbersome than moving information—no matter how complex—back and forth on wires. In essence, the video-display terminal systems were developed concurrently with *word processors*.

The Wired Publishing Office The obvious implication of this technology is that there is no need for the users to limit themselves to free-standing machines and then carry the magnetically recorded pages around for editing; a publisher who is working against tight deadlines could tie all of the VDT devices together so that the pages could be electronically transferred form originator to editor to the final typesetter. This is the stage at which many publishing houses find themselves in the mid-1980s. Firms (not only newspapers) which produce a lot of documents are now discovering that word processors can be used to save money by eliminating unneeded "rekeyboarding" of text (Section 7.2.1).

Electronic Compositors and Typesetting at a Distance As indicated above, the step between final text editing and submission of the copy to a typesetter tended still to be handled more or less "manually" in the early 1980s. However, the essentially mechanical typesetting devices were by then almost extinct.

It was the IBM Corporation which—once it had introduced the Selectric or "bouncing ball" typewriter—came out with an affordable composing (or typesetting) device, the Selectric Composer, which the firm soon upgraded to the Selectric Memory Composer. Meanwhile, other firms were applying electronic and computer-based techniques to slightly more expensive and complex photographic typesetting equipment, and, during the 1970s, typesetting devices that espoused many of the characteristics of video-based word processors were being commonly used by publishing firms, both small and large.

With the current increase in the acceptance of word-processing *networks*—sometimes referred to as *distributed systems*—all tied into

Although the typewriter was invented long after Gutenberg developed the first movable type for typesetting, it is a simpler system and easier to understand. Ordinary typewriters work on a "unitary spacing" principle, whereby every letter—be it "i" or "W"—is allocated the same amount of space on the paper, whereas in set type letters are allocated "proportional spacing" according to their relative size. Thus a capital "W" would be allowed four or five times as much space as the lower case "i," depending on the type style.

Variable spacing on a composer   `Text typed on a typewriter`

Similarly, conventional typewriters only offer single, double, or triple spaces between lines (some offer half spaces), whereas in typesetting the spacing (referred to as "leading" because the spaces were filled in with lead in early typesetting schemes) is variable in terms of small increments called "points." The point value is also used to indicate the height of the letters being typeset. In essence, typesetting allows for great variety, whereas typewriting is limited to a few variables.

Typewriters, until recently, all worked on the principle of *impact printing*, whereby a metallic device bearing the physical shape of the letter struck an inked ribbon which left the impression of the letter on the sheet of paper. The device could be hammerlike, as in older typewriters, or the spherelike typing element of IBM's Selectric typewriter. Recently, typewriters with spinning "daisy wheels" and "thimbles" bearing the letter shapes have become available. All these rely on the device's impact on a ribbon to make the impression.

Typesetting, as originally conceived, produced material to be used for making the printing "plates" to be installed into the press itself (Inset 3–3). Hence, no image on paper was needed during the setting of the type. The modern techniques involving photography and IBM's Selectric Composer, however, produced paper copy which was then converted, using photochemical processes, into the printing plate. The important difference is that the IBM device works like a typewriter, using the impact-printing technique, whereas the photographic composers use light to project letters onto photosensitive paper which is then processed to yield visible text. This results in the finest quality print.

The modern phototypesetting machine is a complex device that can either be operated directly from a keyboard which allows the operator to view the resulting printing instructions on a video display, or can be controlled through telephone lines by computer commands generated at remote terminals providing all the needed printing information. Many machines will instantly select from a variety of typestyles and project these characters in any selection of needed type sizes onto the photographic paper in the machine. Some versions can even "set" entire completed pages, rather than columns to be later pasted by hand into made-up pages.

Some phototypesetting bypasses the manual keying in of text by optically reading clean typewritten manuscript pages using optical character recognition (OCR) equipment. This leaves only the typestyle, size, and layout decisions for the operator.

small or mid-sized computers, the next step in typesetting technology had arrived. Instead of physically carrying the typed text copy to the compositors for typesetting, that task also is being assumed by electronic communications channels.

When such remote composing systems were also able to display on their video screens the actual appearance of the expected final product, they were ready for incorporation into the fully automated publishing house. Here the writers are able to participate in the visualization of the actual final page as it would be printed and facilitate the process by making decisions as to final length, subheads, location on the page, and so forth, while writing. Similarly, authors working at home on their word processors can send to their printers their electronically composed and formatted material over telephone lines. We have thus arrived at a stage in communications sophistication in which creative workers can begin to produce books remotely.

When it comes to the production of large quantities of print (even as few as hundreds of copies), the older printing technologies (Section 3.2.3) still more or less prevail. However, the popularity of "instant printing" does tell us something of the increased involvement of the public in what almost amounts to "mini-publishing" by individual consumers. Even twenty years ago, few people or community groups would have seriously considered "publishing" a newsletter or flier on their own; doing so now is routine.

12.1.2 INNOVATIVE PRINT TECHNOLOGIES

In addition to typewriting and the traditional modern techniques for typesetting (Inset 3-4), there have arisen several novel technologies for forming text on paper. These may further revolutionize printing.

The High-Speed Printers For years, large computers had rapidly produced enormous quantities of data, and a technology had to be invented for "printing out" these voluminous quantities of information. This led to the development of printing devices which could work at incredible speeds. These specialized high-speed printers have existed for decades, spewing forth tons of paper per hour. Most of the image-forming techniques used by these printers produced the familiar "computer printout look" designed for speed of printing, not appearance. One of these "ugly ducklings" is the print output of the *dot-matrix* printer. In the last several years this has promised to evolve into something of an elegant swan, and two of its cousins, the evolving *ink-jet* printer and *laser* printer, both promise to initiate an equally startling revolution in printing technology.

The Programmable Text Imager Until recently, the printers described above were essentially hardware-based. This meant that the manufacturers built the printers so as to produce a letter or character of a particular size and shape and that was all the machine could provide. However, it is in the very nature of these newer types of printers that the printing device, or "head," *creates* the characters rather than relying on sets of stamplike imprinting hammers stored in the machine. Consequently, the *matrix imager*—which is controlled by the microprocessor "chips"—can create any character one could desire.

This allows the keyboard operator or copywriter to indicate, while "typing in" the original text on the word processor, in what size the style of type font the material should be printed out and which words should appear in **boldface** or in *italics* for emphasis. These printing commands can be intermixed throughout the document and are actually executed by the printer when "typing out" the text the first time—in a continous uninterrupted process. This is a radical improvement over recent technology in which every time one wanted to change type style or size, the operator stopped typing, removed the typing element, located the next one to be used, inserted it into the machine, and resumed typing.

Once the quality of the characters and figures formed by the new generation of programmable dot-matrix and ink-jet printers has reached a level acceptable to book publishers, a form of truly "remote publishing" will have become feasible. Those that can afford the new laser typesetters, have already attained that status.

12.1.3 NEWSPAPER PUBLISHING AT A DISTANCE

The *New York Times* publishes a national edition by electronically sending all of the required information to regional locations where the newspaper is printed and delivered to local readers. The *Wall Street Journal* has also relied for years on satellite distribution of copy content to regional publishing centers where the actual newspapers are then produced.

The *dot-matrix* system works usually as a modified impact printer (insofar as a ribbon is used in most varieties of dot-matrix printing), whereas the *ink-jet* approach needs no ribbon because the printing head actually squirts the ink that makes up the letters directly onto the sheet of paper. Both the dot-matrix and the ink-jet rely on a scanning principle, roughly similar to that used to produce the television image. Like the Selectric typing element that moves across the paper—instead of the paper's being carried by a platen moving back and forth past the printing station (as in the conventional hammer typewriter)—so too do these "printing heads" scan across each sheet.

The dot-matrix head consists of a bar enclosing a "string" of rods that are moved in and out of it by electronically controlled electromagnets. It is this bar with its little rods that forms the letters as it moves across the paper. Thus, one single "element" is used to form every character on the sheet, and there is no need to rely on a number of individual character-shaped elements to imprint the characters themselves.

The ink-jet head consists of a tiny jet (0.0015 in. in diameter) that squirts out a closely spaced string of electrically charged ink droplets which are attracted to the oppositely charged sheet of paper. The jet has a "valve" that can be electromagnetically turned on and off to control the passage of single drops. Furthermore, the jet can be swept up and down within its narrow limits to, in effect, "paint" the letters onto the sheet of paper. Typically, such a printer can generate 64 characters per second. If image quality is not important, that speed can be doubled.

Programmable text imagers are designed to print out directly a varied stream of different text sizes and styles (as illustrated below) without stopping the machinery to change typing/printing elements.

The standard printer will HAVE UP TO 11 TYPEFACES WHICH CAN BE COMBINED WITHIN THE SAME DOCUMENT AND EVEN WITHIN THE SAME LINE. THE "4 PASS" QUALITY IS PRODUCED BY FOUR HORIZONTAL PASSES OF A 7 PIN PRINT HEAD WITH SLIGHT VERTICAL MOTION OF THE PAPER BETWEEN PASSES. The characters are formed with 12 mil dots placed to 1 mil accuracy *horizontally* and *3.5 mils* vertically. **Most knowledgable observers**

INSET 12–3 The Dot-Matrix and Ink-Jet Printers

Using sophisticated optical character recognition (OCR) systems to read pages of typed manuscripts, some book publishers can input text for final composition without the need for a human typesetter.

These techniques foreshadowed the initiation of Gannett company's nationwide daily newspaper, *USA Today*. Introduced in the fall of 1982, the general-interest paper (which focuses on national and international politics, financial news, sports, and life-style features) is produced in Virginia, outside Washington, D.C., and then transmitted by satellite to plants around the country for printing and delivery to many of the nation's largest markets.

Again, this underscores the principle that it is cheaper to transport information in electronic form (satellite transmission of typeset copy) than it is to move the same information printed on paper (sending hundreds of thousands of copies of newspaper across the country by air transport).[3]

12.1.4 VIDEO STILL PICTURES AND COMPUTER IMAGING

In 1981 video technology penetrated the still photography realm with Sony's introduction of MAVICA, or magnetic video camera. Although the potential value of the camera in the art and amateur photography markets will probably be debated for some time, its utility in news photography is quite apparent.

Newspaper publishers, because of the quality of newsprint and the use of high-speed presses, have never been able to achieve very high-image quality in the photographs presented on the pages of newspapers. The main criterion has always been impact and newsworthiness. Newspapers settled for coarser halftone engraving and wirephoto transmission of grainy images. Consequently, the limited-quality image definition attainable with the MAVICA—with its TV-like scanning-line still picture—could be acceptable for news prints. The big value inherent in the MAVICA is that, just as with facsimile transmission technology (Inset 12–7), the image may be readily transmitted over any electronic channel.

Thus, a news photographer who has just taken the "picture of the week" does not have to waste valuable hours driving to the newspaper office, developing the film, and making prints from it. The image captured by the magnetic camera could be telephoned in,

The Sony MAVICA is a non-film still-picture camera that uses video technology to record color still images on magnetic discs called MAVIPAKS.

evaluated on the spot as to its newsworthiness, shunted through a number of editors and gatekeepers, and then materialize on the computer-imaged page "galleys" in a matter of minutes.

Image Creation Systems   Whereas the magnetic video camera is used to *record* images from the environment, electronic technology is equally suited for the *creation* or generation of images in the way that painters and graphic artists create visuals. The electronic devices will still require of their operators the sensibilities of an artist, just as the author using a word processor must be as creative a writer as one who writes everything out longhand.

Unlike the still-picture video camera, the image-generation systems offer extremely high resolution. These provide as their end product two different entities. One is a recording of the image on a magnetic disc, which can be easily "read back" into the system for revisions or for making further copies. The other is a photographic copy, usually a 35-mm slide.

Computer Simulators   The next level of electronic sophistication is computer creation of *moving images*. The computing power needed is substantially greater, and the complexity of working with these devices also exceeds that posed by systems designed for the generation of still pictures. Synthesized moving visuals have been developed for

---

A prototype of the MAgnetic VIdeo CAmera, or MAVICA, was introduced to the public by the Sony Corporation in the fall of 1981. Externally, the MAVICA is shaped like a conventional 35-mm still camera and utilizes the same kinds of lenses. However, instead of using film, the camera is loaded with a reusable *magnetic* disc. Therefore, instead of photochemically forming the image on film, the MAVICA "captures" the image using a charge-coupled device (CCD)—a sensor originally invented at Bell Laboratories in 1969—which then reproduces a television-like signal representing the still image. Up to fifty such "image signals" may be recorded onto the tiny magnetic disc that Sony has called the MAVIPAK. In this sense the camera acts like a small video camera/recorder combination that can record fifty still images.

Like the video camera, the MAVICA is intended to "play back" its images immediately on a television set. In order to obtain "hard copies"— that is, color prints on photographic paper—a special printing device will be marketed, but some users would probably send their discs to a service bureau to get prints in the same way that slides are typically taken to a lab to have prints made.

INSET 12–4
The MAVICA

Using sophisticated computing techniques, Dr. James Blinn at the Jet Propulsion Laboratory has made several scientific films that create realistic colored images moving in three dimensions. This still, from a film produced for PBS's *Cosmos* series, illustrates a computer-generated representation of the formation of the DNA molecule.

numerous television commercials, artistic creations, and for training purposes; and more and more of the entertainment programming of the future can be expected to emanate from the computer-graphics artists.

Some of the most unusual visual simulations have emerged in three categories. One is the creation of the fantastic, frequently abstract animations often seen in TV commercials and in visually striking films some of which are created to visualize music. The 1982 feature film *Tron* relied heavily upon computer-generated moving images of this type. The second category is the creation of simplified representations of the real world that change directly in response to an operator's actions; an example is the constantly changing view from an airplane cockpit recreated by flight simulation trainers. The last category is scientific simulations of the kind seen in the PBS-TV series *Cosmos*. Much of that work was done by a scientist working at the Jet Propulsion Laboratory in California, Dr. James F. Blinn. His realistic simulations of submicroscopic processes were both visu-

ally striking as well as scientifically accurate simulations of real-world processes. Says Blinn, "We call it 'artificial reality'—the result of using computer graphics to produce objects that exist only as numbers in computer memory."[4] Other examples of this approach are found in architectural simulations in which viewers are able to inspect three-dimensional electronic "blueprints" of proposed structures from any vantage point of their choosing. At this time, all of these techniques are quite expensive.

12.2 Video and Electronic Production

Emerging video technologies can best be discussed in several major categories—roughly corresponding to the basic communication model (Inset 1–6). First, this section will be concerned with some of the changes in the ways video programs are *produced*. Second, there follows a discussion of what is happening with *distribution* systems (Section 12.3), a topic closest to the category of "communication." Third, related to distribution, is a look at some points regarding the new information *storage* systems (Section 12.4). And finally, it is necessary to understand some of the implications of what will be available to consumers in the way of *reception* technologies (Section 12.5).

Advances in the way video communications are produced or put together are evident in several categories: miniaturization of cameras and recorders, replacing camera tubes with charge-coupled devices (CCDs), high-definition video, digital recording, videodisc production, and implications for filmmaking techniques.

12.2.1 MINIATURIZATION

Although the techniques of electronic news gathering (ENG) and electronic field production (EFP) are becoming commonplace, it is nonetheless necessary to understand what these technologies imply for television producers and what, in a sense, the new technologies are almost forcing them to undertake.

Burrows and Wood discuss the extent to which the ENG and EFP capabilities have transformed broadcast and nonbroadcast journalism and entertainment:

With computer-based editing facilities, it was now possible to put together a very polished studio or location production using only a single electronic television camera. . . .

Thus, for both dramatic programs and journalistic purposes, the concept of single-camera video production came into its own in the mid-1970s. . . .

And as the equipment became even lighter and less expensive, other nonbroadcast video programming turned to ENG/EFP techniques; corporate

---

The "lightweight" portable equipment of the electronic newsperson of last year is already becoming obsolete with what appears to be almost a quantum leap in further miniaturization of equipment. Thus in 1981, the industry saw the separate videorecorder further miniaturized and integrated *into* the camera. The introduction of several "camcorders" truly made it feasible for a single newsperson to gather video information of a quality acceptable for network dissemination. The camcorder operator can singlehandedly document an event, recording action visuals and synchronized sound onto videocassettes, while carrying only one piece of equipment that can weigh less than twenty pounds.

Developments such as this again facilitate access to information insofar as it is easier and cheaper to dispatch a single person to an event; a news-gathering agency can more readily afford to "blanket" its coverage area with information gatherers. Also, the more compact equipment facilitates access to locales where obtrusive equipment might be excluded and offers the newspeople some slight anonymity. Where the appearance of a television crew often becomes "news" in itself, or spurs those present to "create something newsworthy" (Section 11.4.2), the arrival of a single video reporter may be a lesser incentive to action and therefore not distort the news as much as a larger crew.

**INSET 12–5
The
Camcorder**

The RCA Hawkeye is one of several video camera-and-recorder combinations on the market. The single unit is more compact, easier to transport, and more convenient for a single operator to use such a "recam" than a separated camera and recorder system.

The Hitachi VKC-1000 was the first commercially distributed video camera that did not use a picture tube to produce the television picture. A small electronic chip, using the CCD principle, senses the image formed by the lens and generates the video picture.

video, medical uses, training materials, government productions, schooling applications, and cable TV were all moving out of the studio and into the field.[5]

A new era of portability and immediacy was introduced. The ubiquitous combination of the lightweight television camera and the portable videorecorder could go anywhere, could get there fast, and could even broadcast live back to the studio (with a direct microwave link to the studio and transmitter). Audiences came to expect, and broadcasters learned to deliver, immediate "live and direct" coverage from anywhere at any time—political conventions, zany stunts, fighting in Ireland, flooding in Asia, and assassinations in Egypt.

12.2.2 THE CCD CAMERAS

Along with the professional camcorders have come similar, although far lower-priced and more compact, analogs intended for the consumer market of the mid-1980s. Most of these devices are based on yet another inno-

vation in video technology. Like the MAVICA, the consumer-oriented camcorders use a type of charge-coupled device (CCD) to create the electronic images, thereby doing away with the bulkier and more fragile video camera tubes.

The CCD is a tiny, flat, light-sensing, "chiplike" device which—along with so many other innovations—is a direct outgrowth of the computer revolution. The CCDs are extremely lightweight, less fragile, and supposedly can be expected eventually to deliver image sharpness equivalent to that attainable with the high quality vacuum-tube-based camera sensors of today (Section 4.1.6). At the beginning of the 1980s, the CCD has emerged as a serious contender in the video field.

12.2.3 HIGH-DEFINITION VIDEO

The American television image is built up of a "raster" made up of 525 parallel scanning lines, each of which, depending on the quality of the system, has from some 250 to 500 individually discernible fluctuations in color and brightness (Inset 4–2). Most home TV sets offer us far less resolution than this.

This image is generally acceptable on a nine-teen-inch TV set, but it becomes a bit grainy on larger sets and is downright granular and "fuzzy" on the large-projection television systems—which presently provide a satisfactory picture only if viewed from a distance. Yet, several technologies exist to make large-screen, high-definition theatrical projection of televised images a reality, and the commercial interests for exploiting these technologies are on the rise. Thus, an editorial laments:

One of the problems is that we have not yet defined the ballpark for high definition. Is this the 2,000 or so horizontal lines of resolution suggested by one engineer; is it the 1,125 lines demonstrated by the Japanese NHK broadcasting service and Sony Corporation, or is it the 655 lines shown by Compact Video to the attendees at the annual conference of the Society of Motion Picture and Television Engineers in Los Angeles recently?[6]

High-definition television necessitates recording and transmitting about two to six times as much information per TV channel as is done currently. This multifold increase lies beyond the current capacities of the methods *presently* used to transmit and record television images. The assigned broadcast channels (Inset 4–4) cannot carry such a detailed signal; and the current video recorders would be overloaded. Consequently, different and wider broadcasting frequencies must be allocated; and fundamentally different recorders must be designed.

12.2.4 DIGITAL RECORDING

Another technological innovation in both video and audio manipulation is in the shift from analog to digital signals.[7] Presently, much of what is done with television picturization is in the form of an analog signal created by the camera, recorded as an analog on videotape, and transmitted, received, and depicted on the receiver tube as an analog signal. This conventional technique is relatively simple and inexpensive to produce, but

leaves the signal vulnerable to various forms of degradation (audio static and video "snow," for example).

Most of this degradation or "noise" can be eliminated if the analog signal is converted to a digital one. One of the other immediate benefits is that a digitized video signal can undergo numerous repeated duplications without any substantial degradation of copies further removed from the original. This feature greatly facilitates repeated editing and duplicating of video material.

Also, once the video signal is transformed to a digital code, it is then possible—with the use of the *digital video manipulator*—to subject the signal (and resulting picture) to an amazing array of special electronic effects: continuous image compression, image expansion and stretching, the video split (which pulls the picture apart in the center), the "squeeze zoom" (which can reduce a picture to a pinpoint while replacing it with another image), the push-off (which shoves a frame off the screen sideways), and the rotating cube, among many others.

12.2.5 VIDEODISCS

Prototype videodisc systems were introduced by the Germans in the early 1970s and were being test marketed for years before their nationwide release in America at the beginning of the 1980s. As a storage technology, the alternative videodisc systems will be discussed later (Section 12.4.2). However, the disc also presents new challenges to production technologies. What differentiates the production of videodiscs is that for the first time there exists a way to present the users of video materials with the opportunity to receive still images in the same way that pictures in a book or album may be viewed—one at a time, and in any random order.

With laser videodisc systems, you can precisely locate and "freeze" any one of 54,000 specific single images or frames. You can display that single frame on the television screen without wearing out the disc, even if the image were to be kept "frozen" for hours. Thus, it is easy to mix large numbers of both stills and motion sequences— and to allow

A digital video manipulator is a special-effects generator that can manipulate a video signal (once it is converted to a digital format) in numerous creative ways not otherwise possible. Starting with the original images, top left and right, some special effects include the rotating cube image push-off, center left, the movable framed insert, center right, the disappearing zoomed insert, bottom left, and the matted squeezed images, bottom right.

 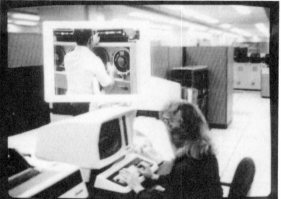

the viewer to select from among them as is needed. This opens up the opportunity to develop enyclopedias of still and motion visual information for active viewing. The process is referred to as the "interactive" use of video; the viewer/user interacts with the video information.

However, the design and production of such materials present the producers with unique and complex problems. Keeping track of, and properly allocating, tens of thousands of images tends to overload ordinary editing methods; this requires an alternative approach. The problem is further complicated by the fact that because the videodisc player can equally rapidly locate and access (play back) a consecutively numbered sequence of images as it could images somewhat removed from each other (say frames numbered 13,288, 44,005, 32,881), the program producer must develop complex yet error-free schedules for allocating all the content onto a disc. This, again, calls for the involvement of the computer. Indeed, the computer is integral to sophisticated use of videodisc technology.

Professor Nicholas Negroponte of MIT, one of the innovators in videodisc use, puts it succinctly:

An optical videodisc without access to a computer is like an airplane without wings: it's not a meaningful machine. . . . A wonderful and often used example is a kind of electronic encyclopedia. We have so much information out there that there is no reason to expect anybody to look at even ten percent of it. When you read an encyclopedia, you have a very limited amount of information on a topic. With an electronic encyclopedia you have the opportunity to read it as a ten-year-old or as a professional. You can read it as somebody who has a very cursory interest or someone who has a very in-depth requirement. And this can't be done with an encyclopedia. So what I'm trying to illustrate with this example is that you're storing, if you will, a network of information that will be explored by different people in different ways. And that's going to be the new opportunity.[8]

12.2.6 VIDEO INCURSIONS INTO FILMMAKING

Not only is it likely that high-definition video will eventually compete directly with film technology in theatrical presentations, but video techniques are already being incorporated into filmmaking. For example, the Hollywood firm of Image Transform has introduced a technology for making film copies of videotaped material which are free of the scanning lines and other distracting effects associated with the video image. These techniques rely on some elaborate computer processing to modify the electronic information as it is being transferred to film.

What this implies is that many of the economies available through electronic program production—exemplified by the ability of daytime soap opera production companies to routinely produce an hour of programming in one day of studio time—can be made available to motion picture producers, should they choose to work that way.

Furthermore, some major film production giants, such as Zoetrope Studios and Lucasfilm, are experimenting with the use of television as a technology to be used as an intermediate process enroute to the production of the final film itself. Electronic techniques are used in scriptwriting, storyboard manipulation, and in various aids to visualizing the final program before motion picture cinematography is begun.[9]

What this indicates is that television techniques can be used to make filmmaking a lot more efficient by eliminating many of the costly procedures for which large amounts of expensive film are literally wasted with conventional production techniques.

12.3 Video Distribution Technologies

It appears that in the world of the Third Wave the old reliance on the movement of physical *things* (for example, paper and film) to convey information is past. In a sense we are back to our preliterate oral tradition (Section 1.7.1), wherein also only the information moved—in those times by word of mouth

Motion picture studios increasingly rely on everpresent video equipment to control and manage the filmmaking process.

rather than via recorded message—without the need to haul about clay tablets, letters, microfiche, or reels of tape. The differences between these ages lie in the speed with which the information can be moved, the quantities that can be moved, and, of course, the virtually unlimited distances the information can span (for example, our communication with probes passing Saturn).

Even with the relatively expensive medium of television, we find that we are on the dawn of a new era of consumer control; we are entering the specialization phase of the "elitist-popular-specialist" pattern (Section 3.1). In America we have the population size, the relative affluence, the education, and the leisure to support a pluralistic system of television distribution technologies.

Scientists are now maintaining communication with probes that far outreach our ability to transport humans. This JPL artist's rendition shows the *Voyager 2* satellite looking back upon Neptune after its scheduled 1989 rendezvous.

12.3.1 CABLE SYSTEMS

Although born of humble beginnings (Section 4.4.4), cable systems such as Warner Amex's QUBE, for one, have now been active for years and have aptly demonstrated the feasibility of two-way communication as well as the proliferation of channels with programming content beyond the retransmission of regular broadcast fare.

Cable systems offer channels that are devoted exclusively to first-run movies, all sports, children's programming, superstations, ethnic programming, twenty-four-hour news, high culture, pornography, coverage of the proceedings of the House of Representatives, and other specialized interests. Indeed, there may be numerous movie channels on a single cable system.

However, will most viewers actually make use of this bounty the cable purveyors are serving forth? Consider, for example, these entertaining—if cynical—comments of a potential new cable customer.

But on that great day when the cable installer came and draped his line through my trees, I began to wonder if I had made a terrible mistake. If cable television meant that at any time of the day or night there would be something worth watching—British dramas, Big Apple documentaries, Bogart classics, wildlife adventures, concerts, debates, uncut first-run movies—what would become of my life? . . .

Well, I needn't have worried. Cable television, I quickly learned, is still television. . . . Three of the 24 channels are devoted to teletyped weather, news and stock reports, respectively. . . . So, as a practical matter, cable has added only 11 new stations to my range of choices, and none of them is worth writing home about. One is entirely devoted to sports; another shows nothing but children's programming . . . and a third is a Spanish channel boasting a quiz show that seems to involve passing various vegetables under contestants' noses and having them guess what they are. . . .

We also get two New York stations specializing in old movies and "Odd Couple" reruns; and Home Box Office, the crown jewel of cable, which costs $8 a month.[10]

How Cable Systems Work A cable system is somewhat analogous to a telephone system in that it consists of a network of wires which connects a central distribution point to the subscribers' homes. However, cable systems differ in that the information flows out from the center, with almost no information flowing back, and no information flows *between* different subscribers. With current technology, this type of cable system can carry some eighty to one hundred different television transmissions simultaneously.

The cable system originates from a sophisticated distribution center or "head-end." This could exceed in complexity what is to be found in a local broadcast station. The cable system head-ends that will be set up in the 1980s will most likely involve several types of functions. As always, the system must have antennas for receiving local or nearby programming from available television broadcasters because that is the minimum users will expect. Also, cable systems may carry radio programming, especially if serving areas with typically poor radio reception. However, the modern head-end will also purchase programming from other sources, many designed specifically to feed cable systems. Much of this programming is received from satellite transmissions by way of an earth station or satellite receiving "dish" and its associated paraphernalia, such as videorecorders to enable delayed retransmissions.

In addition to acquired programming, a cable company will typically generate some offerings of its own—ranging from simple material such as the time, weather, and stock quotes to shopping information, film and book reviews (perhaps sponsored by local cinemas and bookstores), to some full-fledged coverage of local events, often produced with volunteer production teams.

Most large cable systems also provide some kind of "public access" programming opportunity whereby individuals from the community may submit their homemade videorecordings for transmission; often the cable system actually maintains a minimal production studio where individuals coming in "off the street" may produce programming for distribution to the community.

Interactive Systems Many cable companies that have made the provisions for two-way transmission are offering interactive services. Several QUBE systems have been installed, and these mushrooming systems offer viewers opportunities to interact with program producers and personalities by "voting" with

INSET 12–6 The Cable/Satellite Service Networks

In order to serve the growing publics that the cable networks have as subscribers, a number of supply services have been organized. These all disseminate their programming over various satellite systems. Some of the more prominent ones are shown in this list published by *Video*. This gives only a partial indication of material typically found on some cable networks in 1981.[11]

How They Do It in Cincinnati

Warner-Amex is offering 36 channels to Cincinnati citizens. Basic cable costs $6.95, with an additional $3 to be connected to the QUBE interactive system. Viewers must also pay extra for four of the channels: The Movie Channel ($6.75), Home Box Office ($7.50), Showtime ($9.95), and Front Row ($3.95); total cost—$34.15 per month.

Program Guide Your key to the world of QUBE. Complete channel listings and program information, 24 hours a day.

Time/Weather/Community Bulletin Board Up-to-the-minute time/weather reports. What's happening in and around Greater Cincinnati. Plus programs preempted on the networks.

WTBS Atlanta superstation. See the Hawks and the Braves live. Plus original programming and TV and movie classics 24 hours a day.

Educational Access Exclusive programming produced and broadcast from Greater Cincinnati high schools.

News Amex/AP News Wire Up-to-the-minute news from the AP news wire. Plus the American Stock Exchange.

Telecampus ACSN You can take college courses at home for credit. Career development, cultural awareness classes, plus more from the Appalachian Community Service Network.

Front Row G & PG movies only, commercial-free.

The Movie Channel 24-hour movie service. G-, PG-, and R-rated movies, commercial-free, unedited.

Color Bars This display can be used to adjust the color balance on your television set 24 hours a day.

QUBE Interact Participate in game shows, make purchases, take part in community polling from your living room.

Home Box Office Movies, Las Vegas shows, sports specials at a variety of times throughout the month. G, PG, & R, commercial-free, unedited.

MSN TV, movie, and cowboy classics. Consumer inquiry and special children's programming.

WGN Chicago superstation. The Cubs and the White Sox live. Plus TV classics.

BET Black Entertainment Television. Movies, specials, sports, and gospel programming.

CNN 24-hour world-wide news channel. Covering sports, business, finance, and science.

Nickelodeon/Arts Children's programs throughout the day. Commercial-free and non-violent. In the evening, Arts brings you music, dance, and drama.

Shopping Guide Comparison shopping in area supermarkets. Weekly update, grocery and area gasoline prices.

NYSE New York Stock Exchange. Up-to-the-minute stock reports and financial news all day.

QUBE Update New program information and what you might want to know about QUBE services.

Movie Guide About the movies on QUBE Cable: where they're playing, when they're playing, and how they're rated, 24 hours a day.

Horizons Science, sports, travel, crafts: a variety of family entertainment and information.

Greater Cincinnati Original programming from the QUBE studios and around the Greater Cincinnati area.

USA Network National and international sports. Special events live from Madison Square Garden. Plus Calliope, children's programming in the early weekday mornings.

Showtime Broadway shows, live concerts, films, foreign films, and late-night programs. Commercial-free and unedited.

SPN TV and movie classics for the family. Plus Telefrance, USA, and The English Channel.

WOR New York independent channel bringing you the Mets and the Knicks live. Plus TV and movie classics.

Color Radar 24-hour home weather radar channel.

QUBE Cinema 1 Movies. Push the red "authorize" button, and for a set price see a film on a pay-for-view basis.

Religious Inspirational religious programming, 24 hours a day.

QUBE Cinema 2 Pay-for-view movies.

QUBE Cinema 3 Pay-for-view movies.

ESPN 24-hour sports channel.

QUBE Cinema Plus Pay-for-view movies and entertainment specials.

Public Access Local programming by people in the Greater Cincinnati area.

Live & Learn Participate in college or non-credit courses. Pay-for-view.

C-Span The United States House of Representatives in session live via satellite from Washington, D.C. Plus local government access, community council meetings, and programs of special concern.

The control handset for the QUBE system not only facilitates ready access to some thirty channels of programming, but also offers a "message" readout and five "response" buttons for interacting with the system.

their feedback devices. Viewers may also participate as individuals, since they may indicate purchase requests (as on book review shows) which will be filled and billed to their service. In addition to shopping services, another major individualized convenience that is expected to grow is extended banking operations.

Going along with the two-way potentialities are services such as wiring the subscribers' homes with fire alarms and burglar alarms and even, for the elderly and the infirm, with "life sign" indicators—buttons to be pushed daily (or more frequently) to notify some central service agency that all is well. When no daily signal is sent, someone is dispatched to the residence to investigate.

The implications of this type of individualized identification have raised the specter of a "Big Brother" who may benignly or malevolently keep tabs on the activities and attitudes of subscribers, therefore potentially severely affecting their rights to anonymity and privacy. This is certainly one area where society—and the individual consumer—will have to determine priorities and safeguards.

Fiber-Optic Cable   To meet the demand for the hundreds of cable channels that might be needed for interactive uses, some alternative to coaxial cable was needed. This is being found in the fiber-optic conduit. The technology for passing light down a flexible narrow rod of glass has existed for several decades, but problems of manufacturing the "rod" to appropriate tolerances, developing coatings for the glass cylinder, and obtaining appropriate light sources all took some time to resolve.

The laser (an acronym for "Light Amplification by Stimulated Emission of Radiation") provides a source of light in which the light emitted is of one frequency and the wavefronts are aligned. This means that the *coherent* laser light can be focused into a virtually parallel fine beam that does not tend to spread and diffuse rapidly the way that "incoherent," or normal, light does. Thus, the laser provides an ideal source for generating light to be sent down an optical filament. Also, the light source is of such incredibly high frequency (Inset 4—4) that it is possible to impose numerous broadcast signals on top of the "carrier beam," that is, to *modulate* the light. Fiber-optic laser systems have been put into use in a variety of short-range applications in numerous commercial systems, but, according to the experts, problems still remain to be overcome.

Attaining the ability to carry more than fifty channels per filament, as is now routinely done by one coaxial cable, is thought to be decades away. However, because the price of optical fibers is constantly dropping, it is thought that bundles of fibers may soon replace the coaxial cable for many uses. And the optical fiber provides a better signal quality, requires less amplification in the line, and is relatively impervious to any radio frequency interference (either in "leaking out" interference or in picking up static from the environment). The biggest problem in using fiber optics to replace coaxial cable at this time appears in the complexity associated with "tapping" off the trunk line into users' facilities (that is, taking "leads" into homes from the main cable bundle on the street).[12]

12.3.2 NARROWBAND TRANSMISSION

As introduced in Sections 4.1.6 and 4.1.7, transmitting a moving image requires scanning it frequently and then sending out the "string" of information about the image—approximately 7.5 million bits of data every second. A very wide channel must be used in order to transmit all the information needed. Channels that wide demand a carrying capacity that is too great to be simply sent through regular wire, like that used for the telephone, but need the more expensive broadband coaxial cable.

One way to minimize the need for broadband cable is simply to avoid sending moving images and to settle instead for still images. This is called *facsimile transmission*. After all, the luxury of moving images is something we need only occasionally in order to communicate ideas. In most instances, a few well-selected still images typically convey all the information one needs.

Means for sending such still images over "the wire" have existed for decades; the first wirephotos were transmitted by news services in the 1920s. However, recently the cost of the devices for doing so have dropped to the point where an average office can afford to own a facsimile receiver/transmitter and transmit images (maps, charts, blueprints) routinely by telephone. The image is scanned in much the same way that the TV image is scanned, and over a period of minutes—instead of a small fraction of a second—the information is transmitted and then recreated by a parallel scanning device at the receiving end.

To save transmission channel capacity, this scheme of sending still images along with an audiotrack was demonstrated as part of an early educational satellite project (ATS-6), launched by NASA in 1974. Numerous simultaneous audio/still-image broadcasts could be sent in place of a single television transmission. This allowed the remote teaching of many simultaneous lessons that used

---

INSET 12–7
Facsimile Transmission

The principle behind narrowband transmission is simply that the narrower the bandwidth of the channel is, the longer it takes to send a given amount of picture information. A conventional video picture has something like 250,000 separate elements of picture information (525 scanning lines multiplied by close to 500 points of illumination on each scanning line). And thirty images or frames containing that much information can be sent over a 6 megaHertz TV channel every second (utilizing 4.3 megaHertz for actual video data)—hence our figure of 7.5 million pieces of television information every second.

If, however, you have a narrowband channel available (part of a radio carrier or a telephone line) that can send only a fraction of that information per second, it just takes a lot longer to send the data required to build up one picture. A television channel is approximately 600 times wider (or broader) than an AM radio channel, for example. Therefore, it would take 600 times longer to send a television-quality picture over an AM channel; instead of one TV picture every thirtieth of a second, it would take twenty seconds for one picture.

Depending upon the specific narrowband used—anything from a sideband or subcarrier of an FM radio channel to a long-distance telephone hookup—it may take from a few seconds to several minutes to send one still facsimile of a scanned picture.

still visuals, whereas only one motion visual lesson could have been taught using the conventional television channel.

12.3.3 COMMUNICATION SATELLITES

Although cable systems came into being long before the first communication satellites went into orbit, the current growth of cable networks is directly dependent upon what the satellite systems make feasible—reasonably inexpensive distribution of large amounts of programming. With pre-satellite technology, only the major networks could afford to operate such nationwide programming services. Today, however, many programmers can offer substantial packages to cable systems.

The Geosynchronous Satellite When it became possible to launch satellites into earth orbit, one of their most valuable uses was to be for communication. Such satellites are all located in geosynchronous, or "fixed," orbits precisely about the Equator. (See Inset 7–10.)

The first satellites were no more than reflectors of radio frequencies, and the signals returning from them were incredibly faint. Communication satellites were next equipped with a device containing perhaps only one signal receiver, an amplifier, and a retransmitter which sent the information back on a different frequency. This device is called a *transponder*. The signals are received and transmitted using directional antennas that resemble small copies of the large "dishes" of the earth stations. The satellite itself is covered with solar photovoltaic cells which generate electricity from sunlight to power the satellite transmissions. Modern communication satellites typically carry twenty-four transponders for video material and numerous other channels for voice and data transmission.

Direct-to-Home Satellite Transmissions
In the early 1980s the home satellite "earth station" was beginning to be a routine toy

Although many communications satellites have been relatively compact, this Hughes-built *Intelsat IV-A* dwarfs the technicians working on it.

for the well-to-do videophile. Complete satellite reception systems—consisting of a microwave reflecting antenna "dish" of about ten feet in diameter, a signal collector at the focal point of the dish, a low-noise amplifier, coaxial cabling, a microwave-frequency receiver/tuner, and a downconverter for feeding the resulting signals into a regular television set—could be purchased for around $5,000. However, the satellite programming that such users receive was never intended for home consumption, and the legality of using such setups for home use had not yet been settled in the courts by late 1982.

During this period, a number of projects were instituted to demonstrate the feasibility of far simpler and more convenient direct broadcasting satellite (DBS) reception systems. These all depended on the use of broadcast spectrum frequencies higher than those currently assigned to video channels for communication satellites. The use of higher frequencies makes it possible to use smaller reception antennas, a change that was imperative if the dish cost and manipulability were to be brought into line with consumer budgets. Dishes about one meter in diameter were demonstrated; and all the receiving paraphernalia listed above was designed into the television set itself. The proposed costs were slightly more than a tenth of the larger system.

However, the adoption of such a DBS system also would require worldwide standardization—just as international agreements are

---

INSET 12–8 Communications Satellites

As communications satellites are launched, they are each positioned into internationally agreed-upon "parking" orbits above the Equator. Presently these positions are five degrees apart to facilitate locating them from earth. The available spaces are rapidly filling up and further expansion may well require replacement instead of addition; that is, unless a new spacing that crowds the satellites closer together is agreed upon.

At the beginning of the 1980s these satellites were extended like a string of pearls all along the Equator over the information-hungry Western Hemisphere. The list of Comsats and Satcoms, Westars and Aniks appeared to be growing almost monthly.

The approximate composition of the satellite string as it existed in 1982 is shown below:

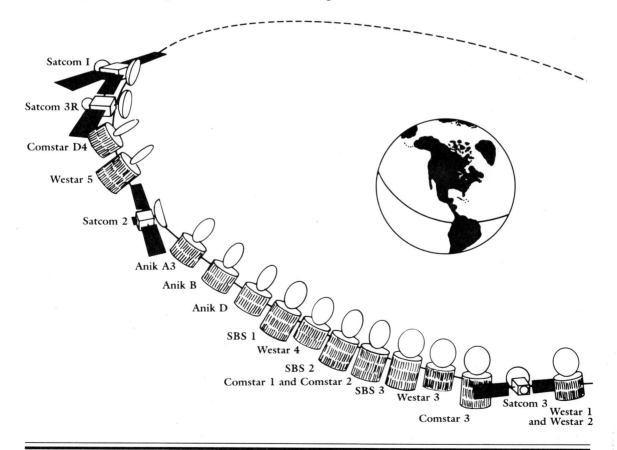

With satellite reception of TV programming, even the camper ostensibly trying to "get away from it all" can continue to satisfy a television appetite in the forest campground.

necessary to make the transition to high-definition video or to digital video. Indeed, it is being suggested that the ideal move is to tie all three of these together into one totally new system, which would not be replacing any existing service but would be in effect introducing something completely different.

12.3.4 TELETEXT

The labels "teletext" and "videotex" (without the final *t*) are used to describe the several methods of transmitting nonmotion images for eventual display on a television tube. These signals may be sent in addition to the picture on a regular broadcast transmission, or they may occupy a full channel on a coaxial cable network, or they may even be sent by way of the telephone line, which then is electrically connected to a television set for eventual display of the information. That information is typically text but may also be graphs, maps, or even stylized pictures.

The teletext still picture may—at the viewer's discretion—either be superimposed over the regular moving image or made to replace the image on the screen. Each teletext "page" can typically carry from about fifty to one hundred words of text, much less than the printed page. A high-definition TV system could transmit teletext pages of considerably more detail, however.[13] The best-known form of teletext is *closed captioning* for hearing-impaired viewers.

In the case of captioning, the viewer can only choose to view the caption that accompanies a given picture or to receive an uncaptioned transmission. With a full teletext service, the viewer is provided access to what amounts to a video-magazine made up of a series of pages, typically anywhere from about fifty to one hundred pages. Any one page in such a format may be accessed or called up in a number of seconds.

Teletext Transmission Alternatives
The most conventional way to send teletext information is along with a regular television program transmission—in a sense the information rides "piggyback" in some of the

Although some teletext pages are produced with elegant graphic layout and even multi-stage revelation of information, the bulk of non-broadcast cable teletext conveys simple and straightforward messages.

unused blank video signal. In this format two sources of information—one moving and one still frame—are transmitted together. With a decoder the viewer can elect to view either one or both.

Another method is to use the entire television channel for the teletext signal. For broadcast television that is presently out of the question because the few available channels are too much in demand to be "wasted" on strictly teletext use. However, that problem does not arise with cable channels because theoretically a single cable channel could be used to transmit numerous pages of teletext information.

The third alternative is the transmission of graphic information by way of the telephone.

A number of different teletext systems have been developed in different countries. Perhaps the most familiar is the British version, CEEFAX. It has the longest track record, having been in regular use since the mid-1970s. It is also the simplest, insofar as the technology used is relatively straightforward and inexpensive.

A more sophisticated system, which is also more expensive to encode and to decode at the receiver, is a French system—with the catchy name of a mythical Greek personage, ANTIOPE. (In order to come up with a cute acronym the French made "ANTIOPE" stand for "Acquisition Numerique et Transmission d'Information Organiseé en Pages d'Ecriture!" Roughly translated, this means, "numerical acquisition and transmission of information organized into written pages.")

The third prominent teletext system is the Canadian one, called TELIDON. The type of encoding used in TELIDON makes it possible to generate subtly colored high-definition graphics and text in *any* style, be it Greek, Cyrillic (the Russian alphabet), or Arabic. Along with the quality goes the highest price tag of all, although it is expected that with mass production the unit cost for the decoder for a home set can be brought to well under $500.

One other extensively used videotex system is the British PRESTEL, operated by the British Postal Service. Its signals are sent over the telephone rather than included in broadcast television. PRESTEL is an interactive access system permitting users to request specific information from a central facility. The television set is still the display medium and therefore has to be electronically connected to the telephone.

INSET 12–9
The Various
Teletext **and**
Videotex **Systems**

(The term "videotex" is more commonly used for wired systems—either cable or telephone—which have a two-way or interactive capability.) This type of interactive format has been in use in Great Britain for some time as the PRESTEL system. (See Inset 12–9.) Systems somewhat similar in concept—using home computers as medium-priced interface devices—are available in the United States in a variety of systems. The best known of these in the early 1980s were subscription services such as The Source, a subsidiary of *Reader's Digest*, and CompuServe, which offers electronic delivery of major U.S. newspapers.[14]

12.3.5 LOW-POWER TELEVISION

In addition to regular open-circuit, full-power television broadcasting stations that reach mass audiences and are required to provide the public with a balanced and complete programming package, three types of alternative low-power, limited-range systems have been authorized. These have operated at frequencies higher than UHF television and have now been authorized for operation at the frequencies that a regular television set can receive.

1. *Instructional Television Fixed Service (ITFS)*. This form of television transmission was introduced in 1963 to permit a school system to broadcast up to four different programs to remote classrooms. ITFS systems operate in the microwave frequencies and have a range limitation of about twenty-five miles. ITFS has made school television a success in many communities.

2. *Multipoint Distribution Service (MDS)*. In 1970 the ITFS concept was extended to commercial users who were licensed to distribute either commercial communications or entertainment programming to subscribers within a restricted range. Since 1975 MDS has been heavily used by some pay-TV companies (such as Home Box Office) to transmit

programming to apartment complexes and homes not connected to a cable system. The economics of such usage has stimulated commercial users to petition the FCC to reallocate most of the ITFS channels for MDS.

3. *Low-Power Television*. The nature of full-power television emphasizes the needs of the majority at the expense of minority audiences and interests. In the early 1980s the FCC approved the concept of "low-power television." This would allow large numbers of new commercial stations to be established in areas where they would not interfere with existing full-power, full-service stations. These new stations would use highly directional antennas to focus their coverage and restrict the power of their signals. License applications that emphasize minority-group needs would be considered preferentially.

12.4 The New Storage Media

Closely related to the distribution function is the problem of storage and retrieval of telecommunications information. Although there are several esoteric and experimental storage systems being developed, we shall primarily be concerned with two major storage formats—recording on *cassettes* and the *videodiscs*.

12.4.1 VIDEORECORDING AND CASSETTES

Compact and inexpensive home videocassette recorders (VCRs) began to have a real market impact around 1980. Although the VCR units themselves are still considerably more expensive than radios or even television sets, the cost of using them has plummeted. Thus, the cost of tape for an hour's recording has now reached two dollars; and because the tape is reusable, recording video material can be considered inexpensive.

The legality of using a home VCR to record copyrighted material off the air is unresolved at the time of the publication of this text. Although court rulings have indicated that such consumer use is a technical violation of the Copyright Act, potential judicial and legislative remedies are being sought. Those in favor of allowing consumers to copy material off the air argue that the videocassette recorder is largely a "time-shift machine." The off-the-air recordings are simply viewed at a time more convenient to the machine's owner.

Progressive Miniaturization   The first successful videocassette recorders appeared about 1970—the ¾-inch format machines. Since then, several other formats have been introduced, aimed initially at the home consumer market. The first step was to reduce tape width to ½-inch and slow the tape's rate of movement through the machine, thereby making a smaller and less expensive cassette

feasible. The first of these was the *Beta* format introduced by Sony in the mid-1970s; it was soon followed by the Video Home System, or *VHS* standard, developed by the Japan Victor Corporation (JVC).

In 1980 an additional, even smaller, standard for videocassettes appeared on the market. The cassette used tape ¼-inch wide and was enclosed in a housing the size of a standard audiocassette.

In late 1982, a compact version of the VHS format, dubbed VHS-C, appeared. The system is compatible with standard VHS equip-

---

Both the Beta and the VHS systems were initially released in only one-speed versions. As it became economical to further miniaturize the recording heads and as recording tape coatings were improved, two progressively slower speeds were added. Thus, most of the new VHS VCRs can record and play back in three speeds. The current Beta format VCRs for home use record in the two slower speeds and play back all three. The fast-speed version of Beta has been reserved by Sony exclusively for their industrial line.

As the videotape material itself is fairly expensive, all these modifications substantially reduced the costs for the users. The costs of the two incompatible systems are quite similar.

What differentiates the two is that the Beta system uses a smaller standard cassette which is limited to a maximum of five hours of recording time. The standard VHS cassette is larger and can record for six hours. The movement of the tape through the two machines differs, as shown in the illustrations below:

**INSET 12–10
The Two Popular
Videocassette
Formats**

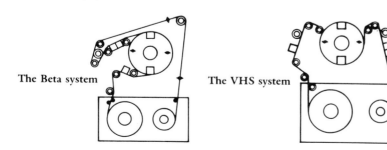

The Beta system   The VHS system

This miniaturized, lightweight VHS videorecorder from JVC (the HR-C3U) uses a small 20-minute cassette that can be inserted into an adapter for playback on standard VHS videorecorders.

ment yet uses a reduced-size twenty-minute cassette. The portable recorder for it weighs about five pounds and is about as large as a medium-sized audiocassette recorder.

At the time that the new consumer camcorders were announced by Sony, Panasonic, and Hitachi in 1980 (Inset 12–5), the manufacturers also demonstrated even more compact video storage media. One entry was a videocassette the size of the miniaturized audiocassette introduced for pocketable dictation equipment in the mid-1970s. With the appearance of the MAVICA, one can expect that disc storage may soon be introduced for lightweight video recorders as well.

12.4.2 VIDEODISC SYSTEMS

Just as there are several incompatible videocassette systems, so too are there several videodisc standards. However, the disc formats differ from one another in far more fundamental ways than do the several cassette recording standards.

Like its audio counterpart—the audiodisc or phonograph record—the videodisc is a mass-produced playback-only medium. The home consumer can no more record video material on a videodisc than you can record sound onto an LP record! And, insofar as phonograph records and audiotape recorders have coexisted on the consumer market for several decades, one may expect similar coexistence for the two video analogs.

The Laser System Developed by the J. V. Philips Company, the "LaserVision" (LV) system was the first format to make it to the market. The video information is recorded in the surface of the disc in the form of microscopic "pits" pressed into the disc surface which are detected, or read, by an extremely narrow and precisely focused beam of laser light which is made to electronically track the microscopic tracks on the spinning disc. This signal is then amplified and converted into a regular composite TV signal which is fed out of the player into the antenna terminals of any home television set.

The chief advantages of the LV system stem from the fact that the laser does not degrade the disc. There is *no physical contact with the disc*; hence, there is no wear. The information in the pits is below a protective surface coating; therefore, the discs are resistant to dirt and damage. The quality of the television image can be substantially better than the best broadcast reception, and the audiotrack may be recorded in high-fidelity stereo. Also, each individual frame is identified by number. Therefore, locating any single frame of the program is easy and can be very rapid because the laser light beam used to read the disc can be moved about with great ease and precision. And, because the light beam does not wear the disc, a single frame may be viewed indefinitely with no harm to the disc or the player—something that is not feasible with videocassettes (or with the capacitively tracked disc formats).

The CED Capacitive System The shortcoming of the laser-based videodisc system is the expense of the laser technology and the sophisticated control mechanisms needed to move the beam to its precise location. RCA, therefore, developed its own less expensive alternative disc format, called the CED ("capacitive electronic disc") system. The player costs substantially less than the laser unit—indeed, its price approximates that of an expensive phonograph record turntable. Also, it appears that producing the discs may be less expensive. The information in this format is located simply by a stylus, analogous to a phonograph stylus (or needle). The stylus physically tracks and reads the capacitance or difference in electrical charges of the video signal in the record surface below the groove.

The quality of the resulting image appears comparable to the LV format, but the rapid access, stereo sound, and freeze-frame features were lacking in the early production models. Also, the CED disc requires protected handling (it is extremely vulnerable to dust and finger oils) and *is* subject to wear. However, for most home users who would use the disc solely for entertainment programming playback, none of these limitations represents a major problem.

The VHD Capacitive System A similar, but again incompatible, capacitively read format is also about to enter the market. It too uses the less expensive stylus principle, but it eliminates the need for tracking grooves; instead, the stylus tracks the embedded video information electronically. JVC's version of this system promises ultimately to offer still-frame capability, and the format already offers stereo sound and slightly more robust discs. However, this system—like the CED— would be unable rapidly and at random to access individual frames on the disc. This format is called the "video high density" or VHD system, and players are planned by a number of electronics firms.

A duality seems to be developing in these systems. For the home film viewer, the capacitive systems seem to be acceptable. For the educational and industrial user, however, the more expensive but more flexible laser-based systems offer obvious advantages. The rapid random-access capability of the laser

systems is what makes these formats truly interactive—an LV system can find and display any one of 54,000 individual frames within seconds.

Digital Disc Recording Because of its enormous data-storing capacity, the videodisc does not need to be only a recording of visual images—whether moving or as still pictures. The video material stored on discs is in the form of *analog* signals. However, the videodisc can equally effectively store *digital* information. With the increased interest in some of the "super high-fidelity" capabilities of digital audio recording technology, it is the videodisc player—in a somewhat modified form—that has become the prime candidate for reproducing digital music. Hybrid systems which store both digital sound and analog images have been demonstrated.

Because videodiscs may be used to reproduce any digital information, they are also an ideal medium for storing large libraries of computer programs—be these for data-processing purposes or for playing video games. It appears that videodiscs could store far more programs than the audiocassettes or even magnetic discs presently used with small computers.

Beyond the Disc Although the videodiscs in their several forms presently represent the most sophisticated type of information storage available, there are other systems in the offing. *Photo-optically recorded videodiscs* are being developed for limited-use purposes and may revolutionize the industrial use of the videodisc. Various *magnetic disc storage* systems are becoming more affordable; these allow rapid entry and reading of material and in a sense offer some of the best features of magnetic tape cassettes and discs. Experimentation with *bubble-memory technology* promises further quantitative breakthroughs in solid-state information storage.

The most compact form of information storage is possibly the *hologram*. These elusive image-storage films are being used with more and more success as the laser systems needed to form holograms are becoming increasingly flexible, sophisticated, and, at the same time, affordable. A hologram can store much more than a seemingly three-dimensional visible image. Holograms can also store tiny data bits which can be "read" and decoded in ways analogous to the decoding of magnetic information on tape.

12.5 Reception and Display Systems

Ultimate utilization of all the technologies outlined above depend, of course, upon the reception and display apparatus that is the final component in the communication chain. Here, too, the home consumer can look forward to eye-boggling advances.

12.5.1 THE TV SET OF THE FUTURE

You can expect the home television set to remain the prime device for the reception of the mass communication message. However, the familiar TV receiver has been undergoing a continuous chain of changes since its inception (for example, all-channel reception which first included UHF, the more or less rectangular tube, color reception, remote controls, and so forth). You can anticipate that this modification process will continue and that the changes will include more versions of the multi-image screen that enables you to monitor more than one channel simultaneously.

Caption and Teletext Decoders   For some years the Sears retail stores have been selling television sets with built-in decoders for closed captions (Section 12.3.4). Whether any one teletext standard will be adopted in the United States in the near future remains to be seen, but sets able to deal with teletext can be expected to be reasonably similar in concept to those with the caption decoders.

Television with Stereo   In 1981 some manufacturers introduced stereo television sets on the market even though transmission of stereo broadcasts in the United States is not expected for some time. The reason behind this anticipatory move is the increasing popularity of VCRs and videodisc players with stereo sound capability, for which no ready-made receivers existed. One of the incidental advantages of stereo sound is the ability to offer bilingual soundtracks—something of definite value to increasing multilingual populations in the metropolitan areas.

Expanded Channel Receivers   At the start of the 1980s, you also saw the introduction of television sets able to receive more channels than the 83 VHF and UHF bands required by the all-channel legislation of 1964. Thus, sets are being offered that can tune 105 (or more) different channels. Again, this is not in response to any change in what is now being broadcast—few communities have more than a dozen channels available—but to the desire to eliminate the cumbersome channel conversion boxes provided by cable services. The new receivers are, as the advertising copy writers like to put it, "cable ready."

High-Definition Video   As indicated above, high-definition video thus far has been seen only experimentally. At present, no means for broadcasting a high-definition video signal by way of the existing VHF and UHF television channels has been suggested. However, such transmission is feasible over new channels that could be created for the microwave frequencies that are used for DBS satellite transmissions and over cable.

Future high-definition video systems are not expected to be compatible with any television receivers now in operation. Thus, if a new standard is introduced, you can also expect that changes will be made in the proportions of the picture tube itself.

Modified Aspect Ratios   The shape of the TV picture tube—its "aspect ratio"—was set at three units high and four units wide when the first standards were agreed upon decades ago. This aspect ratio has dictated the shape of all program materials seen on television and of course has wreaked havoc with attempts at telecasting wide-screen theatrical films—showing only the central part of the picture frequently leaves out much of the action.

Consequently, one can expect that the reformatted television systems of the near future will adopt some rather different aspect ratio, probably closer to that of wide-screen movies than anything else. Indeed, 1981 saw the Sony Corporation demonstrate wide-screen television as a commercially available projection TV technology.

The "Tubeless" Flat-Screen Set   Ever since its invention, the biggest obstacle to a truly convenient television set has been its main component—namely, the bulky picture tube itself. In order to function, the tube has to have a substantial distance between the front screen and the electron gun in the back (similar to the camera tube diagrammed in Inset 4–2). This makes the set cumbersome and uses up floor area. Furthermore, as the manufacturers produce ever larger sets, the weight of the picture tube becomes a limiting factor. The picture tube alone in a thirty-inch color television receiver weighs about two hundred pounds!

Two types of flat-screen alternatives have been suggested over the years. One is the bent-tube approach being developed by the British firm of Sinclair Electronics and by the Sony Corporation. This still utilizes the vacuum tube but uses sophisticated electronic design to fold the path of the electron beam, thereby reducing the effective length of the tube. However, such a tube is still not flat, just stubbier, it still carries the weight penalty of the vacuum tube, and it is still vulnerable to shock damage. Bent-tube sets appeared on the market in 1982.

The other approach is the use of an analog to the display of a pocket calculator, using either liquid-crystal display or some type of light-emitting diode. Indeed, the ideal flat screen set would hang on the wall like a painting, and as such would have a picture

The flat television receiver with a liquid crystal display screen, such as this prototype introduced by Toshiba years ago, might not be commercially marketed in the near future.

equal in size to what the average home projection television sets offer.

The Toshiba Corporation and others have displayed prototype flat black-and-white television sets based on the liquid-crystal display principle. The problem with the sets shown thus far is that they are truly minuscule—the screen size is around two inches. The sets are extremely portable, of course, but they are also very hard to see—especially because liquid-crystal displays do not glow of themselves and must be viewed in reflected light. Much more work is obviously needed.

Projection Television   Any television set with a good-sized lens positioned in front of it will project an image the focal distance of the lens. The problem is that such a device projects only a dimly visible image in a totally darkened room. The engineering problems to be solved have been in designing large lenses which could be sold at affordable prices, making the television image bright enough without overheating, and putting all the components together into a reliable package that does not go out of focus or require a forklift to move.

Most of these problems appear to have been solved in recent years. Projection television systems are currently reasonably bright, quite reliable, and almost affordable to the well-to-do. However, the current technology serves to underscore the fact that low-definition video, when projected to a large size, becomes glaringly poor in resolution. There are certainly appropriate applications for projection television, as in bars and small lecture halls, but its attractiveness to the home user seems restricted to the true videophile until a re-formatted high-definition system is adopted.

Three-Dimensional Television A number of prototypes of 3-D television have been demonstrated. Indeed, German television has had nationwide demonstrations of the technology. Most of the systems rely on the viewers' using special polarized goggles just as has been done with 3-D cinema (Section 4.2.4). However, other more sophisticated high-technology alternatives are being tried out and may eventually surface on the consumer markets.

12.5.2 THE HOME TELECOMMUNICATIONS CENTER

Whereas the media enthusiast of a decade ago would have owned a hi-fi set and a television receiver with perhaps an audio recorder of some type, the paraphernalia that the well-outfitted "media nut" of today would need to own could be barely squeezed into a single room. If you include in all this an earth station for direct satellite reception, outfitting such a center could easily cost as much as what most people paid for homes a decade ago.

The home communication center of the future would probably be centered around a personal computer with its printer and associated pheripheral equipment.

The Entertainment Complex Obviously, you would start by being wired into one or more cable systems and perhaps an over-the-air subscription television (pay-TV) service as well. There would be a stereo television set capable of receiving some 105 (or more) channels. The large-screen projection system could be hooked up either to the videodisc player or the VCR unit—which, of course, would have its own camera and editing equipment for making "home video movies." Naturally, all this mess of equipment would be too complex to plug together and unplug as needed, so the center would be equipped with a computerized switching device for feeding the different incoming signals to different equipment as needed.

The Computer Interface The TV receiver would also serve as the video display terminal for your personal home computer. Integrating this computer into the cable system would open up yet another host of uses for the television set. For example, you could obtain for a fee from the cable system entire "software" libraries of game programs as well as other more utilitarian programs for doing your income taxes or estimating the value of your stock portfolio at any given moment.

The System Accessories The computer facility would certainly have to sport a *printer* and a telephone *modem*. The printer would allow you to use the computer as a word processor and to obtain hard copies of the textual programs coming in over the cable or the telephone by way of the modem interface device. The computer would need to have one or more "floppy disc" drives to permit rapid access to the video game programs or to record incoming programs on one while you were using the other.

And, of course, there would have to be a videogame control center—game paddles, positioners, and firing buttons—so that you could develop more manual dexterity than would be possible if you had to enter all the game commands by keying them in on the computer's keyboard.

The Instructional Function The telecommunications center could also become your tutor. For decades, the TV set has been providing one-way instruction in the form of

---

The development of a large-scale computer-based instructional system first started at the University of Illinois in the summer of 1960 with a system called PLATO—the acronym standing for "Programmed Logic for Automated Teaching Operations." By the 1970s the fourth generation (PLATO IV) was in service, and students had used it for hundreds of thousands of hours of successful learning. Through the Control Data Corporation, the manufacturer of the computer in which PLATO is based, the system is now available nationwide and is being used by thousands of learners. Several similar large-scale systems (such as the MIT–Brigham Young University TICCIT program) also are available nationwide.

The PLATO system was designed primarily as a computer-assisted instruction (CAI) system. As such, it was designed around a nonstandard terminal, quite different from (and incompatible with) a television set. Now, however, a home television interface has been developed, and PLATO is available to cable subscribers.[15]

Instructional developers program into the PLATO computer a body of course content along with instructions on how to "teach" this to the students. The computer can then display this course material on the remote user terminals that are linked by cable or telephone lines to the central computer. This course content is displayed as a short segment (or page) and sent out one page at a time to the video screen of the user's terminal whenever the student calls in the course program.

In conjunction with each piece of instruction that the terminal displays, the computer program also presents some task for the learner to do. This may be a multiple-choice question, a request to point with the finger to some feature on the screen, or an instruction to type an answer on the keyboard. On the basis of the learner's response, the computer's program then decides what type of further action to take.

A typical PLATO course may run for dozens of hours and require a semester of full-time study to complete. The course may incorporate outside reading, field trips, and so on. Most of the testing will be done by the computer, which is also programmed to evaluate the learner's performance and provide corrective feedback.[16]

INSET 12–11
The *PLATO*
Computer-
Assisted
Instruction System

Relying on the PLATO system's audio production features, as well as its touch-sensing display screen (below), children not yet able to read can be taught successfully. At the same time, rooms full of terminals (as seen above at the University of Illinois) make cost-effective use of PLATO's huge data handling capabilities.

courses ranging from the popular *Sunrise Semester* to telecourses on public television. Cassettes and videodiscs also provide instructional programming on every subject from auto repairs to zucchini cookery. Once the home computer is tied into this mini-network, the discs and cassettes can be made *interactive*. This means that the computer program will select an individualized response or instructional segment which is tailored to your specific feedback or input to the program. For example, if you respond to a computer question by selecting answer "A," the program will respond in one way; if you select answer "B," the program will give you an additional hint; if you select "C," the machine will present some other information; and so forth.

The "Smart" Television What all this has been leading to is the development of a home system with considerable "intelligence" or information processing capability of its own. Ideally, if this center is clever enough (that is, if *you* properly program the computer and control/switching equipment, as one does with a programmable videocassette recorder), the center's components could be made to collect only that incoming information (once incoming programs are provided with identifying markers or labels) which you need. The center could then display it for you when you have the time or inclination.

SUMMARY

This chapter has presented a cursory glance at some of the current and impending hardware developments which are drastically altering your communications environment today and in the near future. *Electronic publishing advances* (VDT composing, computer typesetting, remote printing systems, high-speed printers, and computer imaging systems) are revolutionizing the way in which newspapers, magazines, and books are put together and distributed.

Telecommunications marvels include video and electronic *production advances* (miniaturization, CCD cameras, high-definition video, digital recording, videodisc production, and filmmaking applications), *distribution technologies* (cable systems, narrowband transmission, satellites, teletext, and low-power television), *storage media* (videocassettes and videodiscs), and *reception and display systems* (the TV set of the future and the home telecommunications center).

The technological changes outlined above hint at a communication/information upheaval of mind-boggling proportions. The computer scientist Christopher Evans stated in 1978:

. . . [W]hile in chronological space, to coin a phrase, the twenty-first century might be no great distance away, in *event space*, to coin another, it [is] stupendously remote. More changes would occur in the two decades immediately ahead than have taken place in the last century and a half.[17]

As the technology presents itself, you must learn to work with it—or, if necessary—work against it in an informed manner. Some of the human responses to technological change will be discussed in the final chapter.

Notes to Chapter 12

1. Alvin Toffler, *The Third Wave* (New York: Bantam Books, 1980), pp. 158–159.

2. J. D. Reed, "Plugged-in Prose," *Time*, 10 August 1981, p. 68.

3. For more information, see "Gannett Ready to Go with 'USA Today,' " *Broadcasting*, 21 December 1981, pp. 58–59.

4. For a more detailed discussion of many of these electronic processes, see the special "Cosmos" issue of the *American Cinematographer*, specifically the article by James F. Blinn, Pat Cole, and Charles E. Kolhase, "Computer Magic for 'Cosmos,' " *American Cinematographer*, October 1980, p. 1018.

5. Thomas D. Burrows and Donald N. Wood, *Television Production: Principles and Techniques*, 2nd ed. (Dubuque, Iowa: Wm. C. Brown, 1982), pp. 14–15.

6. C. S. Tepfer, "How High a Definition for HDTV?" *Educational and Industrial Television*, December 1981, p. 26.

7. An *analog signal* is an electrical signal which is an actual representation or analog of the original scene being imaged; it consists of infinitesimal fluctuations in the electric current that correspond to light and dark areas in the original picture scene. A *digital signal* takes the analog signal and converts it into a series of binary numbers—the same coding that forms the basis for all computer operations. Each of the 500 points on a single scanning line, for instance, can be expressed as a binary number from 1 to 256, which in turn is represented by a series of off-or-on instructions.

8. David Allen, "Conversation with Nicholas Negroponte," *Videography*, October 1981, pp. 46–47.

9. For more information, see Golda Savage, "Coppola's Electronic Cinema Process," *Millimeter*, October 1981, p. 53ff.

10. Andrew Ward, "Hooked," *TV Guide*, 31 October 1981, p. 35ff.

11. Howard Blumenthal, "100 Cable Channels—Public Excess?" *Video*, November 1981, p. 60.

12. For a fuller discussion, see Brad Metz, "Cost Effectiveness of Fiber Optics Getting Closer Look," *Cable Age*, 5 October 1981, p. 20ff.

13. For more information, see Sammy R. Danna, "FEP—Field's Teletext System," *Educational and Industrial Television*, October 1981, p. 42.

14. For more information, see Christopher Byron, "May the Source Be with You," *Time*, 26 October 1981, p. 63.

15. News item, titled "PLATO Computer System Begins Cable Television Field Test," under "Computer News," *Educational Technology*, November 1981, p. 4.

16. Two good articles about PLATO are D. Alpert and D. L. Bitzer, "Advances in Computer-Based Education," *Science*, 20 March 1970, pp. 1582–1590; and S. G. Smith and B. A. Sherwood, "Educational Uses of the PLATO Computer System," *Science*, 23 April 1976, pp. 344–352.

17. Christopher Evans, *The Micro Millennium* (New York: Viking Press, 1979), p. 201.

In the preceding chapter you looked at what is happening on the frontier of the mass media technologies. You saw what is entering the market and what is still waiting in the corridors. It is now time to take a look at how these technologies can be expected to influence your life and what you as a responsible media user need to do both to control your communication environment and to benefit from what technology affords you.

Many of the "gee whiz" kinds of innovations that were discussed in Chapter 12 are promoted and promised by bands of eager futurists, innovators, inventors, and manufacturers—all of whom have a vested interest in trying to convince you that the very future of the human race (at least its material and social well-being) is contingent upon their products and prognostications. However, just because something *can* be produced (or is available and appears to promise impressive results) does not mean that the innovation will be successful or that it will be deserving of your support or enthusiasm.

For a variety of reasons, many technological innovations have never reached the marketplace. Perhaps manufacturing costs could not be brought to competitive levels, or the public seemed unwilling to accept the products during test marketing, or negative side effects were foreseen, or the products were tentatively introduced and still failed to "make it." It is also wise for us not to get overly enthusiastic about all that the equipment-mongers are heralding as possible solutions to the problems of our society.

Every new medium of communication has been heralded with hope and argument that *this* one will bring about the millenium, will inform and educate with more depth and insight, will entertain with most taste and creativity, will better reflect the diversity of cultures and views of America, so producing wiser, more cultivated citizens and a more perfect democracy. The same hopes attended the advent of film as a mass medium at the turn of

13

The Future Media Consumer

the century, attended radio in the 1920s and television in the 1940s, as now attend the new medium of cable television tied to computer technology.[1]

What is stressed in this chapter is that the technological innovations just introduced all call for more responsibility from the user. This will be the theme of Chapter 13.

• *Due to the increasing flexibility and sophistication of the emerging media technologies, the role of the media receiver/consumer will become increasingly important.*

13.1 The Impact of the New Technologies

The new technologies will most likely exert conflicting pressures on you. You may well find yourself in a tug of war, being alternately offended, captivated, and delighted by what these technologies open up for you. Some of the obvious cautions about the challenges ahead are sounded by Alvin Toffler.

The Blip Culture Evaluating the merits of these new technologies is made more difficult by the very diversity of forms in which this glut of information reaches us. We must consider Toffler's warnings to us—and we in essence still fall into the world of the Second Wave, being used to having our information well organized by its senders—when he refers to the "blip culture":

Instead of receiving long, related "strings" of ideas, organized and synthesized for us, we are increasingly exposed to short modular blips of information—ads, commands, theories, shreds of news, truncated bits and blobs that refuse to fit into our pre-existing mental files. The new imagery resists classification, partly because it falls outside our old conceptual categories, but also because it comes in packages that are too oddly shaped, transient, and disconnected. Assailed by what they perceive as

as the bedlam of blip culture, Second Wave people feel a suppressed rage at the media.[2]

Toffler goes on to indicate a solution to this problem:

Instead of merely receiving our mental model of reality, we are compelled to invent it and continually reinvent it. This places an enormous burden on us. But it also leads toward greater individuality, a de-massification of personality as well as culture.[3]

The Information Society Toffler then ties this in with the way media consumers of the future might react to the overwhelming amounts of information that may soon be available:

Above all this, the de-massification of the civilization, which the media both reflects and intensifies [sic], brings with it an enormous jump in the amount of information we all exchange with one another. And it is this increase that explains why we are becoming an "information society."[4]

However, such an "information society" may not serve to educate and improve the lot of all people equally. Although not extremely expensive, the cost of the information technologies will be sufficiently high to keep large segments of the society from spending their discretionary income to gain information. With time, the less affluent may become even more "information poor" than the well-to-do, thereby broadening the gap between the "haves" and the "have-nots," between the leaders and the followers. People must be educated as to the value of information skills.

These warnings lead us to consider some broad and general changes that the new technologies are likely to bring about: (a) an increased emphasis on the individual consumer, possibly at the expense of some broad societal concerns; (b) substantial shifts in the workplace from the office or the plant to the home; (c) diversification of the varieties of entertainment available to the home; (d) greater reliance on computer technology to provide you with your essential needs; and (e) the need to learn how to deal with the process of change itself.

13.1.1 EMPHASIS ON INDIVIDUALIZATION

It is not just that the new technologies allow information disseminators to inundate the consumers of information with more information, but that mass communicators can now afford to send out increasingly individualized information for smaller and more specialized groups of consumers (Section 3.1). And, of course, these individual consumers will themselves—by their newfound ability to interact with the media—produce and modify the information that is sent out to other receivers.

One of the expected implications of such a multiplication of your information sources may be a tendency to rely increasingly on your individual media environment as a guide to your values and actions. This would tend to negate further Lazarsfeld's "two-step" theory (Inset 6–5). If you need to interact with your fellow employees and friends only infrequently in order to meet your occupational, educational, and entertainment needs, might you not be in danger of slowly alienating yourself from all others in social relationships?

The Citizen's Band Phenomenon An interesting precursor of things to come may be manifest in what has been happening as a result of the popular adoption of citizen's band (CB) radio. By 1977, it was reported that some 25 million CB radios were in use in the United States.

It is revealing to compare the use of CB technology to its logical predecessor, amateur or "ham" radio. The amateur radio operator has to demonstrate a level of technical skill and an understanding of legal and ethical responsibilities in order to pass an examination that is required to obtain a ham license. However, since the citizen's band was opened up for the "man in the street," the CBer simply mails in a form with a check to the FCC for his or her license. No demonstration of competency, and little knowledge of ethical practices or responsibility, is required.

Serious radio amateurs appear to operate as highly social beings. They tend to congregate into groups and clubs, exchanging postcards of call letters internationally and building far-reaching friendships. They routinely volunteer for various social service roles and use assigned communication channels for responsible and socially constructive purposes.

On the other hand, Powell and Ary have observed that CBers tend to take a different tack:

Communication over CB radio offers a disembodied voice without real ownership. Code names (handles) and coded language allow concealment while extending the opportunity for fantasizing an idealized self-image through name choice, i.e., "Super Stud," "Happy Hooker," etc. The personal commitments inherent in face-to-face situations, even telephonic communication, can be safely converted to an impersonal recitation of code words or phrases without loss of a sense of participation.[5]

Powell and Ary go on to discuss the feeling of superficial fellowship projected by CBers in their specialized "slanguage":

A brotherhood exists, but without binding obligations. . . . From this kind of social milieu evolves a few form of communication, another way of adapting to the impersonality of expanding electronic communication, a way of making oneself heard without great risk—communication without commitment.[6]

Because CB radio allows its users anonymity, it *does* tie people together and allows those who otherwise might be too bashful or physically isolated to interact. However— also because of the anonymity that the medium affords—it is perhaps not surprising that CB radio is as often used to help people avoid the law, by prostitutes to arrange solicitations, and by criminals to plot their crimes. A device "for the citizenry" has taken on a somewhat asocial if not even antisocial cast.

The CB radio is not the only likely culprit in the media story. Any new technology which provides entertainment in an isolating manner offers such a potential. Thus, for example, the portable radio, "the transistor," and its current and upcoming manifestations—such as the personal mini-stereo player—all tend to make the mass consumer a loner.

All of the portable entertainment devices have been sources of pleasure to the inherently lonely. The question to be answered is, Can society benefit from turning the gregarious into loners? Once the new folded-screen and bent-tube portable compact television sets start to saturate the market, pity the driver who assumes that pedestrians can spare the attention to glance up to avoid the onrushing traffic!

The tiny personal stereo cassette players let media consumers isolate themselves while still allowing their gregarious instincts draw them into crowds.

The portable, battery-powered, stereo cassette player or radio equipped with a feather-light headset—such as Sony's "Walkman" model—has become one of those ubiquitous popular technologies that inadvertently serves in a dual role. Its intended purpose, to allow its wearer to enjoy high-fidelity programming away from the home, is met admirably. If skiing down a snowy mountain to the strains of Beethoven or the Beatles were not exhilarating, fewer people would be doing it. However, as with so much concerning the media, there appears to be a darker side to this phenomenon as well.

People traditionally have left their houses to walk their dogs, to be on the street or in nature, to rub elbows in a crowd, to listen to the wind or the surf. Many of us tend to be isolated in our homes. Venturing forth is a way for us to be social animals, to mingle with others. By going out to walk your "Walkman," by "plugging yourself in" to whatever medium you choose, you negate this aspect of your humanity. The ultimate expression of such negation may well be the rollerskater—totally immersed in his or her portable disco machine, which is inaudible to everyone else—doing complex pirouettes backwards at full speed down a crowded beachfront boardwalk, oblivious to the young and old in his or her path. Such media consumption tends to isolate the consumer totally.

**INSET 13–1
Walking the
Walkman**

Weighing slightly over a pound, the Sony Watchman features a flattened cathode-ray tube in which the path of the beam is bent on its way to the screen.

Removal from Reality   There is also a process of distancing from *real* sources that the media-committed audiences tend to undergo. As we become increasingly dependent on the electronic or print media—rather than attending live presentations such as nightclubs, church services, or political rallies—we tend slowly to gravitate toward that exaggerated state of alienation from reality so charmingly depicted in Peter Seller's film rendition of Jerzy Kozinski's *Being There,* in which the protagonist, Chauncey, views the whole world as but a weak reflection of the ultimate reality of television. We also get a bit of that same flavor when we consider the football fan who attends a game at the stadium with a portable color television on his or her lap tuned to the broadcast of the same game. (See Inset 8–1.)

These kinds of media uses provide good examples of the potential of the new technologies to become agents for societal alienation.

13.1.2   CHANGES IN THE WORKPLACE

As was indicated in Section 12.1.1 in the discussion of remote publishing made possible through the use of devices such as the word processor, it is feasible for much word-based work to be shifted away from the traditional office context. This would cover not only various creative tasks—as in the example of writers—but also a lot of secretarial, managerial, data-processing, decision-making, and merchandizing tasks. What would be some of the direct advantages of this?

Savings in Energy   The immediate benefit to be realized would be a reduction in the need to move people and equipment around. Fuel would be saved and the environment would be less polluted if fewer people had to commute to and from work. With the new technologies, many needed interactions between workers could be conducted electronically.

The promise of electronic meetings as a substitute for travel is alluring. If business air travel were reduced by only 20 percent, Americans would save 50,000 barrels of jet fuel per day; a 20 percent reduction in business travel by auto would save another 80,000 barrels per day. If half the office work force adopted "telework," savings from reduced commuter traffic could be between 470,000 and 640,000 barrels of gasoline per day by 1985.[7]

The energy necessary to create the electricity to power communication links would be quite small by comparison. We could also reduce the masses of paper that we now consume both for permanent records and for transitory messages. Electronic data transfer and storage could greatly reduce such physical waste if we could only restrain our newly found ability to create mountains of documents—to duplicate photocopies and to generate computer printouts—with the push of a button.

Re-establishing Family Relationships

Although working at home would reduce some of the camaraderie found among co-workers in the workplace, it could help to strengthen certain family relationships. Parents working at home could serve as role models and intellectual foils for their children—offering clear examples of what work and the work ethic are all about and developing with their children the kinds of bonds that were more common in earlier ages.

But there is also a darker side to the home as a potential workplace. Parents who can put up with their children for a brief period each day might be tempted to resort to child abuse when constantly in their presence. Similarly, the stability of many families might be threatened by the increased bickering between family members that could erupt when the safety valve of going off to work had been removed. Clearly, new ways of coping will have to be learned if the social setting is in fact transformed by advances made possible with electronic communication.

Job Flexibility Work at home would also make productivity feasible for people who otherwise would not be available to the world of work—either because they had made commitments to their families, because physical handicaps made getting to work too difficult, or because the individual was unwilling or unable to relocate in order to be acceptably near the workplace.

Also, if the office buildings were emptied out, the hours during which work is accomplished could change. Work could be done when the worker was able and willing to work, and not when the clock dictated work time. Probably homeworkers would earn incomes based on piecework rather than on time invested. Making sure that such people were paid equitably would also call for a re-evaluation of the work output of employees in more conventional work settings.

13.1.3 INCREASED VARIETIES OF HOME ENTERTAINMENT

Obviously, as more and more channels for the dissemination of entertainment programming open up, there comes an increased opportunity for more programming to fill those channels. In the past no outlets of any significance existed for amateur-level recorded productions (except in the case of audio recordings), but this can now be expected to change. The various forms of "narrowcasting" specialization have already paved the way. For example, the public-access channels of the cable networks seldom go begging for programming to be shown on them.

Limited-Edition Entertainment Releases

To be profitable, a videodisc needs to sell at least several tens of thousands of copies. Many paperback books (although less expensive) do enjoy such sales, even though the same titles enjoyed only modest success in hardcover editions or were never published in hardcover at all. In the same way, entertainment programming that would never have been commercially successful on network television (and, perhaps not even on the satellite/cable combinations directed to smaller audiences) may well be profitable in the form of videodiscs.

As for videocassettes, the production of a few dozen copies is easy to amortize (although one could not expect to reap substantial profits with an "edition" of a few dozen cassettes); and if you wish to sell your homemade productions inexpensively, several cooperatives have been formed to help artists distribute such low-budget programming. When the only option available was the 16mm film, the costs of distribution served to inhibit all but the most motivated "underground" artists, and few viewers could afford to acquire experimental programs.

13.1.4 THE IMPACT OF THE COMPUTER

We tend to be impressed by the awesome features of the giant computers, but we cannot afford to overlook what is being accomplished with the microprocessors (or "chips"), which, although they serve as the building blocks of the big computers, have become integrated into a multitude of devices entering common, everyday usage. Inexpensive microprocessors control our conventional still cameras, operate our microwave ovens, control the functioning of videocassette recorders and videodisc players, control numerous feedback functions in our autos, run a multitude of children's toys and videogames, and, of course, are the backbone of our pocket calculators and digital watches. But, above all, it is this ubiquitous microprocessor that makes most of the data manipulation technology discussed above at all feasible.

Without the inexpensive computing power that the cheap microprocessors make possible, our ability to interact with the media electronically would be out of the question. The PLATO system (Inset 12–11), take as an example of a grand-scale interactive program, is conceivable because it offers access to enormous computing power at a quite reasonable cost.

In the future, the main thrusts in computer growth will probably be continuations of long-term trends—namely, prices for a given computing ability will decrease, and the computers (both the super "number crunchers" and the tiny microprocessors seemingly tucked away into everything) will be able to store more information which they can process more easily and at faster rates. Also, you can expect the new machines to perform more and more "intelligently," making their use by untrained operators easier. As time

---

INSET 13–2
Setting Our
Standards by the
"Big Media"

When media sources are diversified, at least two questions of quality standards arise. Might the programming lean to elitism? Might we prematurely reject innovative programs from amateur producers?

Mass programming tends to be a general "leveler" of tastes, and (as indicated in Section 11.1) it at least brings the lowest expectations for art up to the minimal level. However, providing a greater variety of programming may tend to feed further the needs of a cultural elite and allow the tastes of the mass audiences to sink further to levels set by those who purvey entertainment at the lowest common denominator.

One can hope that the emerging avenues of distribution for amateur works will help to short-circuit a problem of criticism that is likely to arise. When you attend a community theater or school play, listen to a local musical group playing at the neighborhood bar, or admire the creative attempts of a neighbor, you tend to have a fairly tolerant and encouraging attitude toward the endeavors of amateurs. However, when you read something in print or see it on the tube, you tend to apply higher standards usually reserved for the big-budget, polished productions of the commercial media. (Instructional television has long suffered from this unintentional comparison; every video teacher is expected to come across like Johnny Carson.) We need to develop a middle ground of critical expectations, the ability to evaluate low-budget amateur offerings on an appropriate scale—even though they may be presented through the same receiving medium as a Bob Hope special.

goes on, the performance of the computers will appear more and more humanlike, because we, as humans, will design them that way. The time will soon come when the seemingly "intelligent computer" will be among us, and a certain eerie feeling may arise when you have to interact directly with inanimate computer-controlled robot equipment that is behaving in disconcertingly humanlike fashion.

You can expect that computers will offer some indispensable services to everyone who lives in the industrialized parts of the world, and as a result you will become increasingly dependent on them. Whether this will strengthen or weaken your intellectual resolve and willingness to think for yourself may well be one of the more important questions for society to answer in the next decade.

13.2   Problems and Challenges

The very process of technological innovation introduces a number of problems, somewhat independently of human response to the technologies. Serious consideration of such concerns is a twentieth-century necessity; and, as the rate of innovation becomes ever more rapid, concern over change may come to dominate our thinking.

13.2.1   SOME PROBLEMS RESULTING FROM CHANGE ITSELF

Technological change tends to build upon itself—to snowball. Thus, we find that the rate of technological change is an ever-increasing factor in itself. New technologies are arriving on the market after ever shorter intervals, and surprisingly many of them imply such profound changes in the way the various professions can carry out their work that ignoring the new devices can be hazardous to survival in business.

Obsolescence   In the business world it is hard to justify the replacement of equipment long before it starts to show signs of wear. Many manufacturers of professional lines of equipment are acknowledging their awareness of this problem, and consequently one finds improved versions of equipment being withheld from the market so that a substantial number of improvements can be incorporated before the new versions are released. This is being done even though the incorporation of only a few improvements might make the new device attractively saleable. This constant pressure to upgrade has led to what has been termed "the danger of discard"—just one of the pitfalls for businesses which enter into fields that encompass high technology.

A parallel situation exists with consumer products. Perhaps you are in the market for a new TV set—maybe one with remote controls. You could buy what you want right now. Or should you wait until you can also get a receiver with capacity for 105 channels, stereo sound, a built-in telephone, internal circuitry for cable, MDS, and satellite reception? How long do you wait? When is the optimum time to make the purchase?

The Need to Facilitate Change   Not only is such a mounting pace of change tending occasionally to overpower industrial decision makers, but it also places a burden on the average person. This type of "future shock," as Alvin Toffler has termed it, encroaches upon everyone, and it is most assuredly a potential occupational hazard for the future media professional. Barring future planetary catastrophes, such as nuclear war or environmental holocaust, technological change is likely to be with us on a permanent basis.

Dealing with it, learning to live with it, calls for what could be called "change facilitation." This can be a psychological as well as a technological concern. Thus, the technological change facilitator would need to be able to predict when are the best times for firms to upgrade their equipment and when to wait, when to adopt a new system and when to stick with the current one, when to embrace a new technology and when to post-pone a major shift. Indeed, it appears that, sooner or later, *change facilitation* will become a topic of serious study in its own right. Consultants in the field have already become a professional reality.

For example, when is the optimum time for the communication industry to propose a *change* to a new 1,100-line high-definition, digitally encoded, two-to-one aspect ratio television system? The technology is ready. How about the regulators? The marketers? The producers? The consumers?

13.2.2 EMERGING TELEPHONE TECHNOLOGY

In order to illustrate the pervasive nature of change, it may be instructive to examine the process by looking at one simple commu-nication device—the telephone. Ever since the introduction of the touch-tone "keypad" to replace the dialing disc some two decades ago, the lowly telephone has been undergoing subtle but important changes, many of them during the latter half of the 1970s. Thus, in

The fully mobile telephone (such as the General Communications Systems, Inc. Mark 1000) allows business people with a budget to stay in constant contact everywhere they go.

many service areas, the keypad can be used to encode automated commands into the system to automatically transfer calls to keyed-in numbers—as well as other convenience features.

One way of making people more aware of technologies and their impact is to introduce them early in their careers to such concerns (which is what this chapter is all about). Frequently such instruction borrows from the concept of "literacy," that is, the ability to read and write or "print literacy."

Thus, there are programs in "visual literacy" and "computer literacy." Now "media literacy" and even "video literacy" are being taught. In order to help educate the public about how television works and how its subtle impact on viewers affects society, several major educational research cen-ters, with the help of government funding, designed four different "Critical TV Viewing Skills" programs. These were produced for preschool-aged children, the elementary grades, teenagers, and adults. The intent was to increase awareness and to make viewers conscious of their viewing habits so that greater self-direction could be exercised. Some typical topics are selective viewing, limited viewing, and teaching children how to learn to discriminate between fantasy and reality.[8]

**INSET 13–3
Alternative Forms
of Literacy**

New Services and Equipment With the entry of competing manufacturers into the telephone-set market, a number of automated and remote telephones have been introduced. The automated telephones can be programmed, using a variety of techniques, to dial specific numbers on the basis of abbreviated commands. If the line is busy, the telephone can be programmed to redial automatically until the line becomes free. Cordless telephones are available that are coupled into miniature, extremely short-range radio transceivers (transmitter and receiver combined) and thus may be used at distances up to a couple of hundred yards from your house.

For longer distances, there have also been significant developments. First, the pocket pagers, which formerly could only "beep" to indicate to the bearer that it was time to telephone the office, now provide the bearer with detailed messages. Second, radio telephone systems like those that were used by taxi or police services—on which typically only abbreviated conversations with a central office were feasible—have now been expanded to offer full-fledged, private-line interparty telephone service. Such systems had always been available for VIPs, but not to the ordinary well-to-do businessman. With sophisticated channel-sharing technology, wherein calls are automatically "handed over" by transmitters from one service area to another service area as the subscriber travels about, thousands of individuals can be simultaneously using fully portable telephones in any given area, yet not crowd the airspace.

Other services are starting to rely on the capabilities of the touch-tone keypad. Thus, once a person has telephoned a location outfitted with the appropriate equipment, the touch-tone pad may be used to key in numerical data into a computer system with no need for human operators at the receiving end. Transmitting bank business over the telephone system (with no human intervention) has become a reality in many locations.

The telephone set itself has become a data entry terminal.[9]

Automated Calling Equipment Everyone is familiar with telephone answering equipment. Businesses are also utilizing the inverse—automated telephone *calling* equipment! Automated systems can be equipped with tape-recorded segments, or they can be tied into a computer-based speech-synthesizing device which is programmed with specific lists of numbers to call. Many such systems are capable of simulating fairly convincing two-way conversations, although none yet are able to analyze and act upon response content.

The French Telematique The French telephone service has gone one step beyond the ordinary voice-only telephone with the large-scale introduction in the early 1980s of the Telematique Programme. In addition to voice communication, this telephone system allows text to be transmitted either with an accessory to the home television set or with a separate device. This device replaces the ordinary telephone with a combination "terminal" which includes the telephone, a video display, and a typewriter keyboard. The Telematique is *not* a "picturephone" (that is, the user cannot connect a camera to it to send images back and forth) but a videotex transmitter and receiver. With it, users can carry out a variety of numerical data and text transactions, going well beyond what can be done with the touch-tone keypad when sending data, say, to a bank. Thus, the Telematique Programme combines some of the services offered by the British PRESTEL system (Section 12.3.4) as well as other proposed cable-television services in the United States such as the cable linkup to PLATO (Inset 12–11). For the French participants in the Telematique Programme, the day when one can earn a living manipulating text and other data from the home has arrived.

Problems with Privacy Engineers working on the frontiers of information science have recently developed ways in which calls made on any type of communication equipment

The French Telematique system is an ambitious interactive operation which enables participants at home to manipulate many forms of data.

could be coded, or encrypted, in such a manner that no one but the intended recipient could unscramble them. This appeared to be a major breakthrough, insofar as the device used fairly inexpensive microprocessor systems and could therefore be marketed for relatively reasonable prices.[10] However, the patent for the system was suppressed by the federal government in a totally unprecedented action.[11] In effect, the federal government has determined that it is not in the nation's best interest to allow individual citizens to engage in totally private telephonic or radio communication! The reason was that public release of such a device would make all future attempts at code breaking pointless, and much of what security agencies (such as the FBI and CIA) tend to do for a living would become meaningless!

The Role of the AT&T   In most of these developments, the American telephone giant has been intimately involved. The American Telephone and Telegraph Company (AT&T), a government-protected monopoly, has always come under close FCC regulation. However, starting with several FCC moves and court decisions in the late 1960s and continuing through various congressional bills in the early 1980s, the trend has been toward increasing deregulation of the communications giant.

The policy has been to ease off on controls on AT&T so that it and its subsidiaries can compete freely within all of the emerging communication technologies—in the fields of data processing, microwave services, satellite

---

A series of articles which ran in the *New York Times* in 1978–1979 described some of the potential applications of telephone communications links:

The phone will automatically put through a wake-up call to you in the morning—using your prerecorded message. . . . Dash off a memo at your desk, and it will be automatically transmitted to receiving devices attached to phones throughout your company. . . . an hour before quitting time, you'll phone the microwave oven to start the roast. . . .

You will vote by phone, and the mail will come by phone. . . .

The phone may be wedded to the TV set, or wall screen. You'll shop at home by calling up mops and looking them over on your screen. Do your banking by phone. You want to read the newspaper? Dial it up on the phone.[12]

**INSET 13–4
What the
Telephone Could
Do for You**

communications, narrowband slow-scan television (Section 12.3), and other residential telecommunications operations.

Corporate Restructuring The 1982 out-of-court settlement between the monolithic AT&T Corporation and the Justice Department ended the eight-year battle by the government to break up the giant monopoly. In the divestiture agreement, AT&T agreed to sell off its twenty-two local telephone companies, in return for which it would be permitted to retain its Western Electric manufacturing arm, its pioneering Bell Laboratories, its Long Lines division, and AT&T International. Additionally, AT&T was given the green light to move more aggressively into cable TV, videotex services, and a variety of other data-processing and computer linkups. In effect, AT&T is getting out of the local phone business and moving to become a stronger competitive factor in long-distance telecommunicaiton technology of all kinds.

13.3 Interaction with the Media

It becomes apparent that many of the "new media" have been developed on the assumption that the user will interact with the media. That is, you are expected to have more *control* over what you select or reject— and over what components *within* each program you consider in an active manner. Beyond direct interaction, there exist other avenues for feedback and control, many of which have been discussed in earlier chapters. (See for example, Sections 1.4, 6.2, and 10.6.) The most dramatic of the media innovations, however, have been those that offer some form of direct interaction with program content.

As an example, let us consider an extreme form of futuristic interaction with the media. Frederik Pohl and Cyril Kornbluth, in *Space Merchants,* a science-fiction novel written some thirty years ago, postulate a future in which society is totally under the control of the merchandisers of goods, with consumers exerting their choices only at the pleasure of the merchants. Pohl and Kornbluth introduce us to a futuristic airplane without windows in which every seat faces a television screen. The TV shows a nonstop series of commercials with no nonadvertising program content at all. However, the media consumer is given one option to "interact." By inserting a coin in the TV slot, the viewer can buy a short period of having the TV turned off![13]

13.3.1 DIRECT INTERACTION WITH THE MEDIA

Not all of the possibilities for interaction are the results of the new technological breakthroughs. Many have been available to us since the days when we acquired the first radio with an on-off switch, and with a power cord we were always *free* to unplug (unlike those future travelers).

Conventional Approaches to Interaction Up to now, much of your interaction with the media has been of this passive nature. You are free to turn off the program or turn to another channel or source of media input. However, you are also able to call in to broadcast stations offering "talk" programs, and you can try to get your opinions published in the "Letters to the Editor" columns. And, of course, the media user may criticize programs by writing or making phone calls to the producers, applying various forms of group pressure, relaying displeasure to sponsors of programs, or even complaining to the regulatory agencies.

Much more direct forms of interaction have been built into the various communication systems that go out of their way to solicit

The inexpensive silicon chip microprocessor will be bringing an ever increasing variety of interactive toys and games into the marketplace.

media consumer participation. Talk-radio producers are obviously asking for feedback and participation in the form of incoming calls to be put on the air, but it is inconceivable that the majority of listeners could or would call at any *one* time. The viewers of the QUBE cable system networks are routinely requested to interact with the program content by indicating their reactions, preferences, or responses by pushing one of the several feedback buttons which are provided with their cable-connected sets. In this instance, all viewers *are* asked to respond, and their statistical aggregate response may be considered.

Such techniques are most suitable for assessing public responses to the varied public issues that such programs are able to present to their viewers. Feedback may thus be obtained and quite carefully tabulated. There remains, however, the problem that decision makers will be tempted to take such data as a reasonable expression of the "will of the public" simply because it is so neatly packaged—*in spite of* the fact that the audience of any typical cable-TV program will not in any sense be representative of a community's overall population. (See "Misuse of Feedback Channels," Section 11.4.5.)

Content Interaction/Participation An ultimate form of entertainment television programming may be presented on other

systems. Experimental dramatic programs have been produced in which a number of alternative courses of action are performed and recorded during the production. This amounts to a "branching program." The presentation of the program is then halted periodically, and the audience is polled as to how it would like to see the events proceed. On the basis of viewer decisions, the various alternative courses of plot development are then transmitted.

Similar interactive programs have been quite successfully executed live on stage with talented groups of improvisational actors. A series of children's books called "Choose Your Own Adventure Books" also allows the reader to choose variations in the adventures that make up the books.[14]

Computer "Games" A popular variety of this type of interactive simulation—executed on a somewhat grander scale—has appeared on the market in the form of various relatively inexpensive chess computers and computer-simulated "adventure games." In these computer contests, players are presented with challenges by the program (usually as text on the screen, occasionally as line drawings with captions) and then are given the opportunity to exercise numerous options in determining their journeys through the simulated "world" of the game. The more sophisticated versions of such games may keep players involved for days or weeks. Obviously the popular TV arcade games also depend on skill at interacting with the program, but the outcomes of one's choices are less radical and are dependent not on careful deliberation but rather on ability to react swiftly.

Although their influence is debated by sociologists and educators, from the point of view of mass communications it seems clear that one of the most significant psychological aspects of the development of all these

The video game arcade has replaced the pool hall as a primary adolescent socializing center.

When the video pong games first surfaced, they appeared in waiting rooms and lounges and hotel lobbies to help customers while away dead time and bring in some profits for the proprietors. Once video games attained their current level of sophistication, they settled into arcades, just as pinball machines had done in earlier years. And, just like pinball machines, they were popular. However, the video games, precisely because of their interactive sophistication, have been far more seductive; and it appears that they are separating youngsters from more of their coins than is deemed acceptable by those who care for the children's welfare.

In the early 1980s (after doing battle with video games featuring various forms of conventional warfare and interstellar shoot-outs), school administrators and civic leaders singled out "Pac-Man"—a voracious computer creation that gobbles up electronic images and player's coins alike—as the epitome of video arcade evil. Video arcades, for all practical purposes, are like all arcades and pool halls—dens of iniquity! More than gaming can take place in these steamy settings, and youths, it is argued, should be kept away. At the other extreme, some educators maintain that it is up to educational developers to make instruction as much "fun" as Pac-Man; also, the video games do help teach hand-eye coordination, quick reflexes, concentration, and an introduction to computer usage. Other sociologists have observed that school kids are spending the quarters provided for their lunch money on video games—and consequently going hungry.

Only one fact stands out as a certainty: educators, psychologists, and ministers will continue to debate the relative evils and merits of the video arcade as America's youth relentlessly pursue "energizer" dots while avoiding the colored monsters.

sophisticated computer/video games is simply the fact that the consumer/viewer is actively participating in the structuring and controlling of images on the face of the screen. For the first time, starting with the introduction of the rudimentary "pong" games in the mid-1970s, the video user was *actually able to exercise control over a television screen*—flipping paddles, firing rockets, maneuvering objects, choosing pathways, answering questions, and so forth. No longer would the TV consumer be at the mercy of distant producers and network officials; now you could actually manipulate video images yourself. The psychological die was cast; the consumer could be in control of this device, which heretofore had been only a receptacle of mass-produced messages!

Future Simulation Uses As the technology evolves and computing costs keep decreasing, it is possible that large-scale simulator systems will eventually become affordable, not perhaps for home use, but for more extended use in education and training—like the cockpit-flight simulators and training simulators now used in the space program. Although

the cost of developing computer programs that can generate an infinitely flexible variety of intricate visual programs are extravagant at the very least, the costs of producing interactive systems by *recording* a large series of photographic images that may be used, and then playing these back, is only "expensive." Thus, for example, what amounts to a visual simulation for an entire city has been developed.

It is quite conceivable that instructional programs as elegant as this can be made available to the public within a decade or so. Heavily interactive instruction is already available on PLATO (Inset 12–11), and the incorporation of videodiscs into the system could greatly expand the extent to which users who have access to cable channels and sophisticated programming can modify their media experiences for themselves.

13.3.2 INDIRECT INTERACTION AND RECEIVER FEEDBACK

Most of the forms of indirect interaction with the media that are presently available to media users will probably remain as effective in the future as they are now.

To demonstrate some of the possibilities of large-scale interactive recorded television material, Andrew Lippman of MIT's Architecture Machine Group developed a system for a simulated trip through the town of Aspen, Colorado. In it an extensive selection of images was recorded on two parallel laser videodiscs, which are played back interactively controlled by a minicomputer. A stranger interested in becoming familiar with the town can use this "experiential map" to request either sequences of moving images or individual pictures stored on the discs. Thus, one can cater to many of the prospective visitor's personal tastes—one can freely "drive" through the streets, look at computer-generated dynamic cartographic overviews, or explore buildings and spaces encountered en route.

The material on the discs was photographed so that the "visitor" could travel at various speeds along a street, stop at will, turn corners, or turn around and see the reverse view of the street. One could also request views of the town in fall or winter, thereby choosing the season for the simulated "visit."[15]

INSET 13–6 The Town of Aspen— on a "Movie Map"

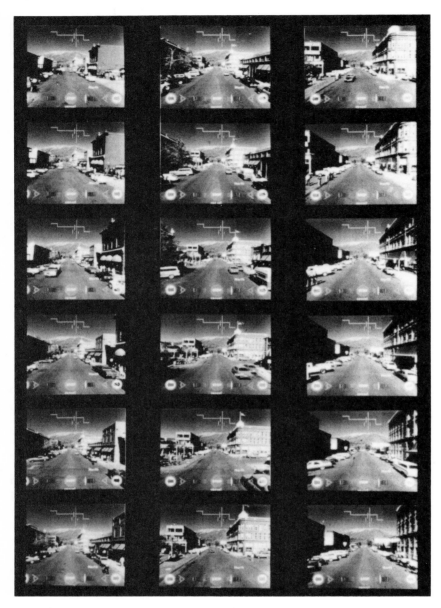

A matrix of images from the videodisc-based "movie map" of Aspen, Colorado, showing scenes along a main street and the side view options at various points. The coded signs on the bottom of each image show user control options.

Receiver Feedback Most mass media channel operators claim to be looking for active feedback from the media consumers. Television stations like to run "man in the street" interviews; they solicit reactions from "quali-fied spokesmen of opposing viewpoints" for any and all issues—including, say, an editorial against child abuse (as if anyone arguing *for* child abuse were ever likely to surface!). All this appears conscientious and public-spirited, but one must remember that *selection* at a great many gatekeeping levels is operating here. Thus, the likelihood of hearing the opinion of any one specific individual is small.

A much more comprehensive form of feedback was an offer made in 1974 by the *Charleston Gazette*. It guaranteed that anyone criticized in the paper would have the opportunity to respond and that the response would be issued in as prominent a location in the newspaper as the original editorial or attack. Of course, this means that the news seeker would have to be attacked by the paper before he or she could gain access to the media. Indeed, this difficulty of access introduces another problem for the media user.

Access to the Media It is one thing to react to the media. It is quite another to try to obtain access with an original idea of your own—an idea which the media (rightly or wrongly) have elected to ignore. If the idea you wish to disseminate is too complicated or undramatic, it will be ignored, and the public will be spared dull (though possibly important) content. If, on the other hand, the idea is radical, heretical, or otherwise extremely controversial, the media will typically opt not to "rock the boat," and again access is likely to be denied. (See Section 11.5.)

One disturbing result of this limited media availability is that frustrated would-be media users may resort to some form of violent protest—knowing that protest itself becomes news. Once the aggressive act has been carried out, the news media—presented with a newsworthy event—will feel obligated to hear out the protester's ideas.

Access and the "Fairness Doctrine" For more than three decades, the Fairness Doctrine (Inset 9–11) and its accompanying Public Attack Rules guaranteed aggrieved individuals and groups a legal shot at obtaining an opportunity to respond to any broadcast matter deemed unfair. Similarly, citizens' groups could protest effectively by challenging broadcast stations' licenses at renewal time, and effective programming compromises could often be worked out.

However, with the Reagan administration's emphasis on deregulation (following the trend started by Ford and continued by Carter), these avenues of consumer control and feedback may be severely curtailed. In effect, Reagan's political philosophy is that of de-emphasizing the *social responsibility* concept and returning to a purer form of *libertarianism* (Sections 2.2 and 2.4)—fewer government controls, let the free marketplace of ideas determine Truth, and let the consumer beware.

13.4 Responsibilities of the Media Consumer

As we grope our way through the 1980s, there are two parallel developments which will dictate how our future relationships with the media will be structured. First, *there is the incredible communications explosion which overwhelms us with its bewildering array of present and future media channels*. The socio-economic factors which have led to the phenomena of the specialized media (Section 3.1) combine with the dazzling wizardry of the emerging technologies to overpower us with an incomprehensible multitude of media conduits—the potential of a hundred different television channels, dozens of radio outlets in every community, over a hundred new books published every day, specialized sections of several newspapers delivered through one's video tube, thousands upon thousands of consumer magazines. All these are yours now—or in the very new future.

Second, *there is the increasing trend toward government deregulation*. Starting in the mid-1970s, each succeeding Washington administration (Ford, Carter, Reagan) has leaned toward decreased control of the communications industries. This may be the result not so much of a continuing conservative political philosophy (although that is an obvious factor) as it is of the pragmatic recognition that the increasing volume of media channels defies regulation. Not only do the multiplying numbers of channels help to guarantee that a variety of voices will be heard in the best libertarian search for Truth, but also the sheer magnitude of the regulating/censoring job to be done recalls Milton's arguments of over three hundred years ago (Section 2.2.2). The job of regulation/licensing is simply too vast to be handled by any combination of government regulatory agencies. The bureaucracy required to license and regulate all broadcast stations, networks, cable systems, subscription services, computer linkups, sidebands, CB operators, and the like would frankly be too massive.

The combination of these two trends—the increasing number of channels and decreasing government regulation—leads to one inescapable conclusion: *more and more in the future, the individual media consumer is going to have to assume increasing responsibility for his or her mass communication experiences.* This ties in with the themes of both the first chapter (the receiver can have an impact upon the mass communication process) and the current chapter (the role of the media consumer/receiver will become increasingly

important). The increased responsibility of the media consumer can be evidenced in at least three ways—media selection, media interpretation, and media feedback.

1. Media Selection Your first and most obvious form of control is your use of the media. What are you going to read? What magazines do you really want to buy? Which section of what newspaper will you glance at? What radio station do you automatically tune to? What movies are you going to see this month? And what will you watch on television? Most important, perhaps, is the question of *how much* media exposure you want. How many hours a day are you going to turn over to the media channels? How much media saturation can the individual receiver tolerate? It does not matter how complete the home video-computer-communication-entertainment-education center becomes; one hopes that individuals will retain a need to occasionally get away from it all. Turn off the electrons and take a walk in the fresh air. Much of what has been written here urges you to consider carefully the implications of unrestricted access to nonstop media.

Regarding the issue of ever-increasing availability of media programming, the information scientist Christopher Evans raises some rather nagging doubts about our future willingness to abandon the security of such an entertainment-based comfort blanket.

INSET 13–7
The Media
Comfort Blanket

. . . No matter how attractive the home environment, perhaps humans will always periodically want to meet up in large social groups to fulfill some instinctive gregarious need. It may be that unceasing and unchallenging comforts of the home will ultimately cloy, and that from time to time humans will deliberately set out to make themselves *un*comfortable by foraging out in spaceships to some inhospitable corner of the universe. Even this may not be enough to prevent a totally introverted society, for the combination of powerful home computers and stunningly effective three-dimensional video might provide totally credible pseudo-challenges, and by so doing completely blunt the edge of human curiosity and dynamism. If so, human exploration of space has already passed its peak and twenty-first-century *homo sapiens* will immerse himself totally in TV, leaving the twin challenges of space and time to the computers.[16]

Another increasingly important question concerns how much you are willing to pay. (The question in this case is asked about direct, out-of-pocket payments. Indirectly you pay for the "free media" through added-on costs that media advertising sponsors pass on to the consumers.) With the proliferation of pay TV and pay-cable services, one could wind up with a mass communications bill of nearly a hundred dollars a month to a single cable firm. If a consumer subscribes to several cable and computer services, that bill can reach several hundred dollars a month. In the most literal sense of the concept, the marketplace will determine eventually how many pay-cable services and which computer networks will make it as commercial successes. And it will depend basically upon how much you—the consumer—are willing to spend.

2. Media Interpretation   Another major area of consumer responsibility is, of course, how you personally accept, interact with, and intrepret the tremendous quantity of mass communication that you ingest daily. What do you accept as true? What points need to be further documented? What sources are biased? Which bits of news are really important? Which are trivial? How do you become a discriminating media consumer? What do you accept as art? What is trash? How do you establish your own individual criteria for entertainment content? How will you keep from being covertly persuaded and influenced by the "hidden persuaders"?

In reviewing the behavioral effects of the mass media (Section 8.4)—consumption of time, information sharing, determining what is important, promoting conformity, modification of values, and possible stimulation of antisocial behavior—ask yourself how *you* are affected. To what extent are you aware of these effects as you read, listen, and watch the media? How are *you* being directly and indirectly influenced? What do you want to do to control your own media-related behavioral patterns?

In effect, you are in control of your media destiny. What are you doing to exercise that control?

3. Media Feedback   As has been stressed repeatedly in this book, there are numerous avenues of feedback and interaction which you can utilize to exert pressure on the message suppliers. As an individual (Section 1.4), as an "opinion leader" (Section 6.2), and as a member of a larger group (Section 10.6), you can influence the media in several ways—through direct financial support, audience membership, advertiser support (and boycotts), direct participation (letters to the editor, press releases, talk radio, public-access cable, interactive channels, and so forth), delayed response (contacting publishers and broadcasters, using both government regulatory and industry self-regulatory channels, the National News Council, ombudsmen, and other citizens' advisory groups), and even professional criticism. This responsibility is not to be taken lightly, as Whetmore forcefully reminds us.

Talking back to your TV set may seem like a revolutionary task, but it is something that every media consumer has the *right* and the *responsibility* to do. The concept that the airwaves belong to everyone is beautiful but often our airwaves, like our beaches, forests, and other natural resources, are misused. Only the "rightful owners" can put a stop to it before the damage is irreparable."[17]

To what extent do *you* take advantage of these channels?

In 1957 Wilbur Schramm wrote a thoughtful analysis of responsibility in mass communication. His concluding thoughts hold true today:

Ultimately, . . . the audience calls the tune. The people hold the trumps. And the only question is whether they will play their cards. . . .

It seems to me clearly possible for the great audience to become a live, responsive, discriminating audience, to make its opinions and wishes known to the media, and in its own quiet way to enforce those opinions and wishes on the media. . . .

The basic responsibility of the public, therefore, is to make itself, as far as possible, an alert, discriminating audience.[18]

Finally, Schramm concludes with this thought: "But I should like to suggest that all of us who enjoy the protections and advantages of a free communication system do indeed have some obligation to justify our existence under it."[19]

No other institution in contemporary American society is as deserving of our attention and study—our criticism and our feedback—as our mass media. They keep us free from political tyranny—while they preach the gospel of Establishment subjugation.

They open unto us a window to the world—while keeping us locked into our living room easy chair. They challenge our minds with the greatest inspirations of humankind—while trying to mold us into a conforming, consumptive mass. They promise hope, enlightenment, escape, and a new tomorrow—while they are accused of stimulating violence, illiteracy, and moral decay.

And, what is most significant: they are *yours*. Your mass media. Your advertisers. Your crusading reporters. Your responsibilities. What are you going to do with them?

Notes to Chapter 13

1. Charlene J. Brown, Trevor R. Brown, and William L. Rivers, *The Media and the People* (New York: Holt, Rinehart and Winston, 1978), p. 22.

2. Alvin Toffler, *The Third Wave* (New York: Bantam Books, 1980), p. 166.

3. Ibid.

4. Ibid., pp. 166–167.

5. Jon T. Powell and Donald Ary, "Communication without Commitment," in *Mass Media and Society*, 3rd ed., ed. Alan Wells (Palo Alto, Calif.: Mayfield, 1979), p. 119.

6. Ibid., p. 123.

7. These statistics are reported by Richard C. Harkness in *Technology Assessment of Telecommunications/Transportation Interactions*, a three-volume report of the National Science Foundation published in 1976 (available from National Technical Information Service, Nos. PB272–694, PB272–695, and PB272–696); and in Robert Johansen, Jacques Vallee, and Kathleen Spangler, *Electronic Meetings* (Reading, Mass.: Addison-Wesley, 1979), pp. 122–123.

8. For more information about the various television literacy programs, contact the program developers at the Far West Laboratory, 1855 Folsom Street, San Francisco, Calif. 94103, or the Division of Learning and Media Research at the Southwest Educational Development Laboratory, 211 E. Seventh Street, Austin, Tex. 78701, or the Boston University School of Public Communication, Boston, Mass.

9. For more information on developments in telephone technology, see John S. Mayo, "Evolution of the Intelligent Telecommunications Network," *Science*, 12 February 1982, pp. 831–837. Indeed, the entire 12 February 1982 issue is devoted to topics applicable to the last section of this text.

10. For further details read "Uncrackable Code?", *Time*, 3 July 1978, p. 55.

11. For a discussion of the nature of the governmental actions, see G. B. Kolata, "Computer Encryption and the National Security Agency Connection," *Science*, 29 July 1977, pp. 438–440; and Gina Kolata, "CIA Director Warns Scientists," *Science*, 22 January 1982, p. 383.

12. As summarized in N. R. Kleinfield, "Hello, It's Ma Bell," *Reader's Digest*, July 1980, p. 113.

13. Frederik Pohl and Cyril M. Kornbluth, *Space Merchants* (New York: Ballantine Books, 1953).

14. An example of such a book would be Edward Packard's *The Cave of Time* (Toronto: Bantam, 1979).

15. Andrew Lippman, "Movie Maps: An Application of the Optical Videodisc to Computer Graphics," published in 1980 by the Association for Computing Machinery (1980 ACM 0-89791-021-4/80/0700-0032).

16. Christopher Evans, *The Micro Millenium* (New York: Viking Press, 1978), p. 229.

17. Edward J. Whetmore, *Mediamerica: Form, Content, and Consequence of Mass Communication* (Belmont, Calif.: Wadsworth, 1979), p. 189.

18. Wilbur Schramm, *Responsibility in Mass Communication* (New York: Harper & Row, 1957), pp. 355–356.

19. Ibid., p. 365.

UNIT IV APPENDIX
Useful Media Organizations for Consumer Action

Following is a list of organizations, agencies, and media firms that the active media consumer should be aware of—both for research purposes and for public action and feedback.

Government

Federal Communications Commission (FCC)
Consumer Assistance Office
1919 M Street, NW
Washington, DC 20554
(202) 632-7000

Broadcasting

American Broadcasting Company (ABC)
7 West 66th Street
New York, NY 10023
(212) 887-7777

Columbia Broadcasting System (CBS)
News Division
524 West 57th Street
New York, NY 10019
(212) 957-4114

Corporation for Public Broadcasting
1111 16th Street, NW
Washington, DC 20036
(202) 293-6160

National Association of Broadcasters
1771 N Street, N.W.
Washington, DC 20036
(202) 293-3500

National Broadcasting Company (NBC)
30 Rockefeller Plaza
New York, NY 10020
(212) 664-4444

National Cable TV Association
918 Sixteenth Street, N.W.
Washington, DC 20006
(202) 775-3550

National Public Radio (NPR)
2025 M Street, NW
Washington, DC 20036
(202) 833-2200

Public Broadcasting Service (PBS)
475 L'Enfant Plaza West, SW
Washington, DC 20024
(202) 488-5000

Film

Academy of Motion Picture Arts and
  Sciences
8949 Wilshire Boulevard
Beverly Hills, CA 90211
(213) 278-8990

American Film Institute
John F. Kennedy Center for the Performing
  Arts
Washington, DC 20655
(202) 828-4040

Motion Picture Association of America
522 Fifth Avenue
New York, NY 10036
(212) 840-6161

Publishing

American Newspaper Publishers Association
11600 Sunrise Valley Drive
Reston, VA 22091
(703) 620-9500

American Society of Newspaper Editors
1350 Sullivan Trail
Easton, PA 18042
(215) 252-5502

Association of American Publishers
One Park Avenue
New York, NY 10016
(212) 689-8920

Comics Magazine Association of America
41 East 42nd Street
New York, NY 10017
(212) 682-8144

Magazine Publishers Association
575 Lexington Avenue
New York, NY 10022
(212) 752-0055

National Newspaper Association
491 National Press Building
Washington, DC 20045
(202) 466-7200

Advertising and Marketing

American Association of Advertising
  Agencies
200 Park Avenue
New York, NY 10017
(212) 682-2500

American Marketing Association
250 S. Wacker Drive
Chicago, IL 60606
(312) 648-0536

Public Relations Society of America
845 Third Avenue
New York, NY 10022
(212) 826-1750

Public Organizations

Action for Children's Television (ACT)
46 Austin Street
Newtonville, MA 02160
(617) 527-7870
Organized to "encourage and support quality
  programming for children; to eliminate
  commercialism from children's programs;
  to require a reasonable amount of
  programming each week designed for
  children of different ages."

American Council for Better Broadcasts
  (ACCB)
120 E. Wilson
Madison, WI 53707
(608) 257-7712
Supports development of "critical viewing
  skills and broadcasting of good radio and
  television programs." Sponsors children's
  education on critical television viewing
  skills.

Cable Television Information Center (CTIC)
2100 M Street, NW
Washington, DC 20037
(202) 872-8888
Provides information concerning government
  regulations, industry trends, current and
  projected technology, etc.

Citizens Communication Center of the
  Institute for Public Representation
  (CCCIPR)
% Georgetown University Law Center
600 New Jersey Avenue, NW
Washington, DC 20001
(202) 624-8390
Represents citizens and community groups
  attempting to remind the broadcast
  industry that it is a trustee for the public.

Clean Up TV Campaign
P.O. Box 218
Joelton, TN 37080
(615) 876-0510
Represents religious and civic groups
  interested in "cleaning up TV."

Coalition for Better Television (CBTV)
P.O. Box 1398
Tupelo, MS 38801
(601) 844-5038
Represents religious groups united to fight
  "excessive and gratuitous violence,
  vulgarity, sex, and profanity" on
  commercial television.

Foundation to Improve Television (FIT)
50 Congress Street, Suite 925
Boston, MA 02109
(617) 523-5520

Represents individuals who wish to "increase and promote the proper utilization of television, particularly for children."

National Association for Better Broadcasting (NABB)
7918 Naylor Ave.
Los Angeles, CA 90045
(213) 474-3283

Conducts studies of children's programs and of consumer interests in broadcasting law and regulations.

National Citizen Communication Lobby (NCCL)
P.O. Box 19101
Washington, DC 20036
(202) 466-8290

Formed for education and representation regarding citizen and audience rights in television and radio.

National Citizens Committee for Broadcasting (NCCB)
P.O. Box 12038
Washington, DC 20005
(202) 462-2520

"A citizen-supported, nonprofit organization whose purpose is to improve the quality of broadcasting through concerted public action."

National Coalition on Television Violence (NCTV)
P.O. Box 647
Decatur, IL 62521
(217) 429-6668

Educational and research organization committed to decreasing the amount of television and film violence.

National Federation for Decency (NFD)
P.O. Box 1398
Tupelo, MS 38801
(601) 844-5036

Organized to promote "the biblical ethic of decency in American Society with a primary emphasis on television."

National News Council
1 Lincoln Plaza
New York, NY 10023
(212) 595-9411

Investigates complaints from the public regarding biased or unbalanced news in all print and broadcast media.

Rexnord Resource Center
200 Executive Drive
Brookfield, WI 53005
(414) 784-5000

Offers a "Media/Citizen Dialogue Program" in conjunction with the "First Amendment Congress," a federation of publishers, journalists, broadcasters, and other concerned groups.

Task Force for Community Broadcasting (TCB)
8456 S. Rhodes
Chicago, IL 60619
(312) 873-8739

INDEX

†